Managerial Accounting

Pearson

At Pearson, we have a simple mission: to help people make more of their lives through learning.

We combine innovative learning technology with trusted content and educational expertise to provide engaging and effective learning experience that serve people wherever and whenever they are learning.

We enable our customers to access a wide and expanding range of market-leading content from world-renowned authors and develop their own tailor-made book. From classroom to boardroom, our curriculum materials, digital learning tools and testing programmes help to educate millions of people worldwide — more than any other private enterprise.

Every day our work helps learning flourish, and wherever learning flourishes, so do people.

To learn more, please visit us at: www.pearson.com/uk

Managerial Accounting

Selected chapters from:

Horngren's Cost Accounting
Sixteenth Edition, Global Edition
Srikant M. Datar and Madhav V. Rajan

Harlow, England • London • New York • Boston • San Francisco • Toronto • Sydney • Dubai • Singapore • Hong Kong
Tokyo • Seoul • Taipei • New Dehli • Cape Town • São Paulo • Mexico City • Madrid • Amsterdam • Munich • Paris • Milan

Pearson
KAO Two
KAO Park
Harlow
Essex CM17 9NA

And associated companies throughout the world

Visit us on the World Wide Web at:
www.pearson.com/uk

© Pearson Education Limited 2019

Compiled from:

Horngren's Cost Accounting
Sixteenth Edition, Global Edition
Srikant M. Datar and Madhav V. Rajan
ISBN 978-1-292-21154-1
© Pearson Education Limited 2018

All rights reserved. No part of this publication may be reproduced, stored in a retrieval system, or transmitted in any form or by any means, electronic, mechanical, photocopying, recording or otherwise, without either the prior written permission of the publisher or a licence permitting restricted copying in the United Kingdom issued by the Copyright Licensing Agency Ltd, Barnard's Inn, 86 Fetter Lane, London, EC4A 1EN.

ISBN 978-1-787-64337-6

Printed and bound in Great Britain by CPI Group.

CONTENTS

Chapter 1   The Manager and Management Accounting   1
Chapter 1 in *Horngren's Cost Accounting*, Sixteenth Edition, Global Edition
Srikant M. Datar and Madhav V. Rajan

Chapter 2   An Introduction to Cost Terms and Purposes   28
Chapter 2 in *Horngren's Cost Accounting*, Sixteenth Edition, Global Edition
Srikant M. Datar and Madhav V. Rajan

Chapter 3   Cost–Volume–Profit Analysis   66
Chapter 3 in *Horngren's Cost Accounting*, Sixteenth Edition, Global Edition
Srikant M. Datar and Madhav V. Rajan

Chapter 4   Job Costing   107
Chapter 4 in *Horngren's Cost Accounting*, Sixteenth Edition, Global Edition
Srikant M. Datar and Madhav V. Rajan

Chapter 5   Activity-Based Costing and Activity-Based Management   152
Chapter 5 in *Horngren's Cost Accounting*, Sixteenth Edition, Global Edition
Srikant M. Datar and Madhav V. Rajan

Chapter 6   Master Budget and Responsibility Accounting   197
Chapter 6 in *Horngren's Cost Accounting*, Sixteenth Edition, Global Edition
Srikant M. Datar and Madhav V. Rajan

Chapter 7   Flexible Budgets, Direct-Cost Variances, and Management Control   249
Chapter 7 in *Horngren's Cost Accounting*, Sixteenth Edition, Global Edition
Srikant M. Datar and Madhav V. Rajan

Chapter 8   Capital Budgeting and Cost Analysis   288
Chapter 21 in *Horngren's Cost Accounting*, Sixteenth Edition, Global Edition
Srikant M. Datar and Madhav V. Rajan

The Manager and Management Accounting

1

All businesses are concerned about revenues and costs.

Managers at companies small and large must understand how revenues and costs behave or risk losing control of the performance of their firms. Managers use cost accounting information to make decisions about research and development, production planning, budgeting, pricing, and the products or services to offer customers. Sometimes these decisions involve tradeoffs. The following article shows how understanding costs and pricing helps companies like Coca-Cola increase profits even as the quantity of products sold decreases.

FOR COCA-COLA, SMALLER SIZES MEAN BIGGER PROFITS

Can selling less of something be more profitable than selling more of it? As consumers become more health conscious, they are buying less soda. "Don't want to drink too much?" Get a smaller can. "Don't want so many calories?" Buy a smaller can. "Don't want so much sugar?" Just drink a smaller can. In 2015, while overall sales of soda in the United States declined in terms of volume, industry revenue was higher. How, you ask? Soda companies are charging more for less!

Coca-Cola has been the market leader in selling smaller sizes of soda to consumers. Sales of smaller packages of Coca-Cola—including 8-packs of 12-ounce bottles and 7.5-ounce cans—rose 15% in 2015. Meanwhile, sales of larger bottles and cans fell. The price per ounce of Coke sold in smaller cans is higher than the price per ounce of Coke sold in bulk. The resulting higher profits from the sales of smaller sizes of soda made up for the decrease in total volume of soda sold. If these trends toward buying smaller cans continue, Coca-Cola will be selling less soda, but making more money, for years to come.

By studying cost accounting, you will learn how successful managers and accountants run their businesses and prepare yourself for leadership roles in the firms you work for. Many large companies, including Nike and the Pittsburgh Steelers, have senior executives with accounting backgrounds.

LEARNING OBJECTIVES

1. Distinguish financial accounting from management accounting

2. Understand how management accountants help firms make strategic decisions

3. Describe the set of business functions in the value chain and identify the dimensions of performance that customers are expecting of companies

4. Explain the five-step decision-making process and its role in management accounting

5. Describe three guidelines management accountants follow in supporting managers

6. Understand how management accounting fits into an organization's structure

7. Understand what professional ethics mean to management accountants

urbanbuzz/Alamy Stock Photo

Sources: Mike Esterl, "Smaller Sizes Add Pop to Soda Sales," *The Wall Street Journal,* January 27, 2016 (http://www.wsj.com/articles/smaller-sizes-add-pop-to-soda-sales-1453890601); Trefis, "How Coke Is Making the Most Out of Falling Soda Volumes," January 5, 2016 (http://www.trefis.com/stock/ko/articles/327882/how-coke-is-making-the-most-out-of-falling-soda-volumes/2016-01-05).

Financial Accounting, Management Accounting, and Cost Accounting

LEARNING OBJECTIVE 1

Distinguish financial accounting

...reporting on past performance to external users

from management accounting

...helping managers make decisions

As many of you have already learned in your financial accounting class, accounting systems are used to record economic events and transactions, such as sales and materials purchases, and process the data into information helpful to managers, sales representatives, production supervisors, and others. Processing any economic transaction means collecting, categorizing, summarizing, and analyzing. For example, costs are collected by category, such as materials, labor, and shipping. These costs are then summarized to determine a firm's total costs by month, quarter, or year. Accountants analyze the results and together with managers evaluate, say, how costs have changed relative to revenues from one period to the next. Accounting systems also provide the information found in a firm's income statement, balance sheet, statement of cash flow, and performance reports, such as the cost of serving customers or running an advertising campaign. Managers use this information to make decisions about the activities, businesses, or functional areas they oversee. For example, a report that shows an increase in sales of laptops and iPads at an Apple store may prompt Apple to hire more salespeople at that location. Understanding accounting information is essential for managers to do their jobs.

Individual managers often require the information in an accounting system to be presented or reported differently. Consider, for example, sales order information. A sales manager at Porsche may be interested in the total dollar amount of sales to determine the commissions paid to salespeople. A distribution manager at Porsche may be interested in the sales order quantities by geographic region and by customer-requested delivery dates to ensure vehicles get delivered to customers on time. A manufacturing manager at Porsche may be interested in the quantities of various products and their desired delivery dates so that he or she can develop an effective production schedule.

To simultaneously serve the needs of all three managers, Porsche creates a database, sometimes called a data warehouse or infobarn, consisting of small, detailed bits of information that can be used for multiple purposes. For instance, the sales order database will contain detailed information about a product, its selling price, quantity ordered, and delivery details (place and date) for each sales order. The database stores information in a way that allows different managers to access the information they need. Many companies are building their own enterprise resource planning (ERP) systems. An ERP system is a single database that collects data and feeds them into applications that support a company's business activities, such as purchasing, production, distribution, and sales.

Financial accounting and management accounting have different goals. As you know, **financial accounting** focuses on reporting financial information to external parties such as investors, government agencies, banks, and suppliers based on Generally Accepted Accounting Principles (GAAP). The most important way financial accounting information affects managers' decisions and actions is through compensation, which is often, in part, based on numbers in financial statements.

Management accounting is the process of measuring, analyzing, and reporting financial and nonfinancial information that helps managers make decisions to fulfill the goals of an organization. Managers use management accounting information to:

1. develop, communicate, and implement strategies,
2. coordinate product design, production, and marketing decisions and evaluate a company's performance.

Management accounting information and reports do not have to follow set principles or rules. The key questions are always (1) how will this information help managers do their jobs better, and (2) do the benefits of producing this information exceed the costs?

Exhibit 1-1 summarizes the major differences between management accounting and financial accounting. Note, however, that reports such as balance sheets, income statements, and statements of cash flows are common to both management accounting and financial accounting.

Cost accounting provides information for both management accounting and financial accounting professionals. **Cost accounting** is the process of measuring, analyzing, and reporting financial and nonfinancial information related to the costs of acquiring or using

EXHIBIT 1-1 Major Differences Between Management and Financial Accounting

	Management Accounting	Financial Accounting
Purpose of information	Help managers make decisions to fulfill an organization's goals	Communicate an organization's financial position to investors, banks, regulators, and other outside parties
Primary users	Managers of the organization	External users such as investors, banks, regulators, and suppliers
Focus and emphasis	Future-oriented (budget for 2017 prepared in 2016)	Past-oriented (reports on 2016 performance prepared in 2017)
Rules of measurement and reporting	Internal measures and reports do not have to follow GAAP but are based on cost-benefit analyses	Financial statements must be prepared in accordance with GAAP and be certified by external, independent auditors
Time span and type of reports	Varies from hourly information to 15 to 20 years, with financial and nonfinancial reports on products, departments, territories, and strategies	Annual and quarterly financial reports, primarily on the company as a whole
Behavioral implications	Designed to influence the behavior of managers and other employees	Primarily reports economic events but also influences behavior because manager's compensation is often based on reported financial results

resources in an organization. For example, calculating the cost of a product is a cost accounting function that meets both the financial accountant's inventory-valuation needs and the management accountant's decision-making needs (such as deciding how to price products and choosing which products to promote). However, today most accounting professionals take the perspective that cost information is part of the management accounting information collected to make management decisions. Thus, the distinction between management accounting and cost accounting is not so clear-cut, and we often use these terms interchangeably in the book.

Businesspeople frequently use the term *cost management*. Unfortunately, the term does not have an exact definition. In this book we use **cost management** to describe the activities managers undertake to use resources in a way that increases a product's value to customers and achieves an organization's goals. In other words, cost management is not only about reducing costs. Cost management also includes making decisions to incur additional costs—for example, to improve customer satisfaction and quality and to develop new products—with the goal of enhancing revenues and profits. Whether or not to enter new markets, implement new organizational processes, and change product designs are also cost management decisions. Information from accounting systems helps managers to manage costs, but the information and the accounting systems themselves are not cost management.

> **DECISION POINT**
> How is financial accounting different from management accounting?

Strategic Decisions and the Management Accountant

A company's **strategy** specifies how the organization matches its own capabilities with the opportunities in the marketplace. In other words, strategy describes how an organization creates value for its customers while distinguishing itself from its competitors. Businesses follow one of two broad strategies. Some companies, such as Southwest

LEARNING OBJECTIVE 2

Understand how management accountants help firms make strategic decisions

...they provide information about the sources of competitive advantage

Airlines and Vanguard (the mutual fund company), follow a cost leadership strategy. They profit and grow by providing quality products or services at low prices and by judiciously managing their costs. Other companies such as Apple and the pharmaceutical giant Johnson & Johnson follow a product differentiation strategy. They generate profits and growth by offering differentiated or unique products or services that appeal to their customers and are often priced higher than the less-popular products or services of their competitors.

Deciding between these strategies is a critical part of what managers do. Management accountants work closely with managers in various departments to formulate strategies by providing information about the sources of competitive advantage, such as (1) the company's cost, productivity, or efficiency advantage relative to competitors or (2) the premium prices a company can charge over its costs from distinctive product or service features. **Strategic cost management** describes cost management that specifically focuses on strategic issues.

Management accounting information helps managers formulate strategy by answering questions such as the following:

- *Who are our most important customers, and what critical capability do we have to be competitive and deliver value to our customers?* After Amazon.com's success selling books online, management accountants at Barnes & Noble outlined the costs and benefits of several alternative approaches for enhancing the company's information technology infrastructure and developing the capability to sell books online. A similar cost–benefit analysis led Toyota to build flexible computer-integrated manufacturing plants that enable it to use the same equipment efficiently to produce a variety of cars in response to changing customer tastes.

- *What is the bargaining power of our customers?* Kellogg Company, for example, uses the reputation of its brand to reduce the bargaining power of its customers and charge higher prices for its cereals.

- *What is the bargaining power of our suppliers?* Management accountants at Dell Computers consider the significant bargaining power of Intel, its supplier of microprocessors, and Microsoft, its supplier of operating system software, when considering how much it must pay to acquire these products.

- *What substitute products exist in the marketplace, and how do they differ from our product in terms of features, price, cost, and quality?* Hewlett-Packard, for example, designs, costs, and prices new printers after comparing the functionality and quality of its printers to other printers available in the marketplace.

- *Will adequate cash be available to fund the strategy, or will additional funds need to be raised?* Procter & Gamble, for example, issued new debt and equity to fund its strategic acquisition of Gillette, a maker of shaving products.

The best-designed strategies and the best-developed capabilities are useless unless they are effectively executed. In the next section, we describe how management accountants help managers take actions that create value for their customers.

DECISION POINT
How do management accountants support strategic decisions?

LEARNING OBJECTIVE 3
Describe the set of business functions in the value chain and identify the dimensions of performance that customers are expecting of companies

…R&D, design, production, marketing, distribution, and customer service supported by administration to achieve cost and efficiency, quality, time, and innovation

Value-Chain and Supply-Chain Analysis and Key Success Factors

Customers demand much more than just a fair price; they expect quality products (goods or services) delivered in a timely way. The entire customer experience determines the value a customer derives from a product. In this section, we explore how a company goes about creating this value.

Value-Chain Analysis

The **value chain** is the sequence of business functions by which a product is made progressively more useful to customers. Exhibit 1-2 shows six primary business functions: research

EXHIBIT 1-2 Different Parts of the Value Chain

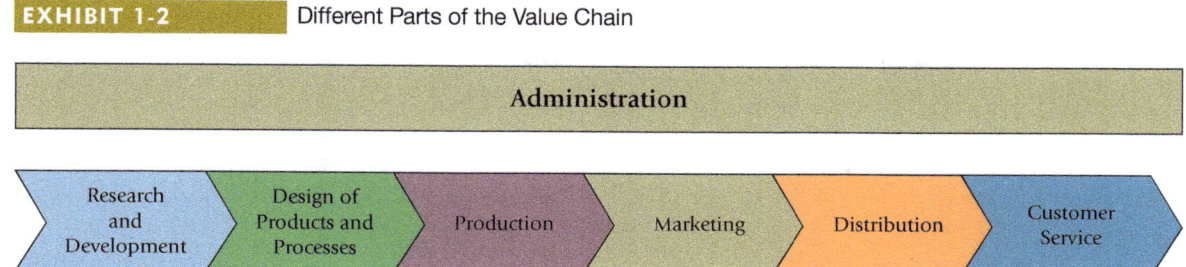

and development (R&D), design of products and processes, production, marketing, distribution, and customer service. We illustrate these business functions with Sony Corporation's television division.

1. **Research and development (R&D)**—generating and experimenting with ideas related to new products, services, or processes. At Sony, this function includes research on alternative television signal transmission and on the picture quality of different shapes and thicknesses of television screens.
2. **Design of products and processes**—detailed planning, engineering, and testing of products and processes. Design at Sony includes deciding on the component parts in a television set and determining the effect alternative product designs will have on the set's quality and manufacturing costs. Some representations of the value chain collectively refer to the first two steps as technology development.[1]
3. **Production**—procuring, transporting, and storing ("inbound logistics") and coordinating and assembling ("operations") resources to produce a product or deliver a service. The production of a Sony television set includes the procurement and assembly of the electronic parts, the screen and the packaging used for shipping.
4. **Marketing (including sales)**—promoting and selling products or services to customers or prospective customers. Sony markets its televisions at tradeshows, via advertisements in newspapers and magazines, on the Internet, and through its sales force.
5. **Distribution**—processing orders and shipping products or services to customers ("outbound logistics"). Distribution for Sony includes shipping to retail outlets, catalog vendors, direct sales via the Internet, and other channels through which customers purchase new televisions.
6. **Customer service**—providing after-sales service to customers. Sony provides customer service on its televisions in the form of customer-help telephone lines, support on the Internet, and warranty repair work.

In addition to the six primary business functions, Exhibit 1-2 shows an administration function, which includes accounting and finance, human resource management, and information technology and supports the six primary business functions. When discussing the value chain in subsequent chapters of the book, we include the administration function within the primary functions. For example, included in the marketing function is the function of analyzing, reporting, and accounting for resources spent in different marketing channels, whereas the production function includes the human resource management function of training frontline workers. Each of these business functions is essential to companies satisfying their customers and keeping them satisfied (and loyal) over time.

To implement their corporate strategies, companies such as Sony and Procter & Gamble use **customer relationship management (CRM)**, a strategy that integrates people and technology in all business functions to deepen relationships with customers, partners, and distributors. CRM initiatives use technology to coordinate all customer-facing activities (such

---
[1] M. Porter, *Competitive Advantage* (New York: Free Press, 1998).

as marketing, sales calls, distribution, and after-sales support) and the design and production activities necessary to get products to customers.

Different companies create value in different ways. Lowe's (the home-improvement retailer) does so by focusing on cost and efficiency. Toyota Motor Company does so by focusing on quality. Fast response times at eBay create quality experiences for the online auction giant's customers, whereas innovation is primarily what creates value for the customers of the biotech company Roche. The Italian apparel company Gucci creates value for its customers through the prestige of its brand. As a result, at different times and in different industries, one or more of the value-chain functions are more critical than others. For example, a company such as Roche emphasizes R&D and the design of products and processes. In contrast, a company such as Gucci focuses on marketing, distribution, and customer service to build its brand.

Exhibit 1-2 depicts the usual order in which different business-function activities physically occur. Do not, however, interpret Exhibit 1-2 to mean that managers should proceed sequentially through the value chain when planning and managing their activities. Companies gain (in terms of cost, quality, and the speed with which new products are developed) if two or more of the individual business functions of the value chain work concurrently as a team. For example, a company's production, marketing, distribution, and customer service personnel can often reduce a company's total costs by providing input for design decisions.

Managers track costs incurred in each value-chain category. Their goal is to reduce costs to improve efficiency or to spend more money to generate even greater revenues. Management accounting information helps managers make cost–benefit tradeoffs. For example, is it cheaper to buy products from a vendor or produce them in-house? How does investing resources in design and manufacturing increase revenues or reduce costs of marketing and customer service?

Supply-Chain Analysis

The parts of the value chain associated with producing and delivering a product or service—production and distribution—are referred to as the *supply chain*. The **supply chain** describes the flow of goods, services, and information from the initial sources of materials and services to the delivery of products to consumers, regardless of whether those activities occur in one organization or in multiple organizations. Consider Coke and Pepsi: Many companies play a role in bringing these products to consumers as the supply chain in Exhibit 1-3 shows. Part of cost management emphasizes integrating and coordinating activities across all companies in the supply chain to improve performance and reduce costs. For example, to reduce materials-handling costs, both the Coca-Cola Company and Pepsi Bottling Group require their suppliers (such as plastic and aluminum companies and sugar refiners) to frequently deliver small quantities of materials directly to their production floors. Similarly, to reduce inventory levels in the supply chain, Walmart requires its suppliers, such as Coca-Cola, to directly manage its inventory of products to ensure the right amount of them are in its stores at all times.

EXHIBIT 1-3 Supply Chain for a Cola Bottling Company

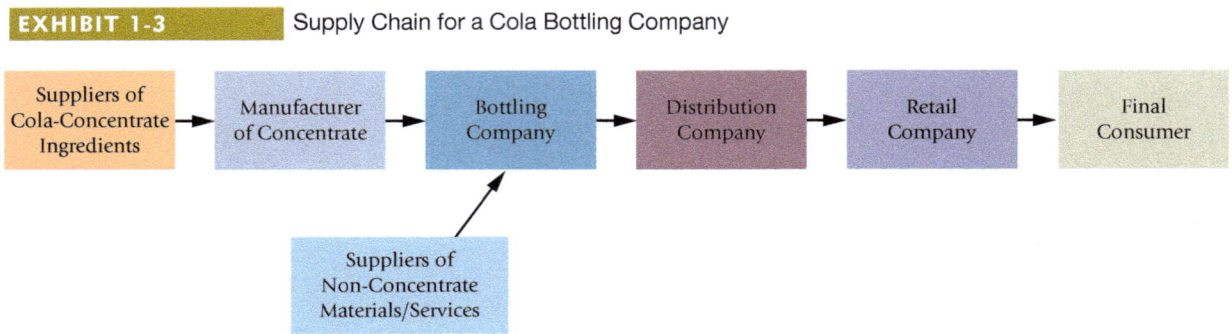

Key Success Factors

Customers want companies to use the value chain and supply chain to deliver ever-improving levels of performance when it comes to several (or even all) of the following:

- **Cost and efficiency**—Companies face continuous pressure to reduce the cost of the products they sell. To calculate and manage the cost of products, managers must first understand the activities (such as setting up machines or distributing products) that cause costs to arise as well as monitor the marketplace to determine the prices customers are willing to pay for the products. Management accounting information helps managers calculate a target cost for a product by subtracting from the "target price" the operating income per unit of product that the company wants to earn. To achieve the target cost, managers eliminate some activities (such as rework) and reduce the costs of performing other activities in all value-chain functions—from initial R&D to customer service (see Concepts in Action: Trader Joe's Recipe for Cost Leadership). Many U.S. companies have cut costs by outsourcing some of their business functions. Nike, for example, has moved its manufacturing operations to China and Mexico, and Microsoft and IBM are increasingly doing their software development in Spain, Eastern Europe, and India.

- **Quality**—Customers expect high levels of quality. **Total quality management (TQM)** is an integrative philosophy of management for continuously improving the quality of products and processes. Managers who implement TQM believe that every person in the value chain is responsible for delivering products and services that exceed customers' expectations. Using TQM, companies design products or services to meet customer needs and wants, to make these products with zero (or very few) defects and waste, and to minimize inventories. Managers use management accounting information to evaluate the costs and revenue benefits of TQM initiatives.

- **Time**—Time has many dimensions. Two of the most important dimensions are new-product development time and customer-response time. New-product development time is the time it takes for companies to create new products and bring them to market. The increasing pace of technological innovation has led to shorter product life cycles and more rapid introduction of new products. To make new-product development decisions, managers need to understand the costs and benefits of a product over its life cycle, including the time and cost of developing new products.

    Customer-response time describes the speed at which an organization responds to customer requests. To increase the satisfaction of their customers, organizations need to meet their promised delivery dates as well as reduce their delivery times. Bottlenecks are the primary cause of delays. For example, a bottleneck can occur when the work to be performed on a machine exceeds its available capacity. To deliver the product on time, managers need to increase the capacity of the machine to produce more output. Management accounting information can help managers quantify the costs and benefits of doing so.

- **Innovation**—A constant flow of innovative products or services is the basis for the ongoing success of a company. Many companies innovate in their strategies, business models, the services they provide, and the way they market, sell, and distribute their products. Managers rely on management accounting information to evaluate alternative R&D and investment decisions and the costs and benefits of implementing innovative business models, services, and marketing plans.

- **Sustainability**—Companies are increasingly applying the key success factors of cost and efficiency, quality, time, and innovation to promote **sustainability**—the development and implementation of strategies to achieve long-term financial, social, and environmental goals. The sustainability efforts of the Japanese copier company Ricoh include energy conservation, resource conservation, product recycling, and pollution prevention. By designing products that can be easily recycled, Ricoh simultaneously improves sustainability and the cost and quality of its products.

CONCEPTS IN ACTION: Trader Joe's Recipe for Cost Leadership

BirchTree/Alamy Stock Photo

Trader Joe's has a special recipe for cost leadership: delivering unique products at reasonable prices. The grocery store chain stocks its shelves with low-cost, high-end staples (cage-free eggs and sustainably harvested seafood) and affordable luxuries (Speculoos cookie butter and Sriracha and roasted garlic BBQ sauce) that are distinct from what traditional supermarkets offer. Trader Joe's can offer these items at everyday low prices by judiciously managing its costs.

At Trader Joe's, customers swap selection for value. The company has relatively small stores with a carefully selected, constantly changing mix of items. While typical grocery stores carry 50,000 items, Trader Joe's sells only about 4,000 items. In recent years, it removed nonsustainable items from its shelves, including genetically modified items. About 80% of the stock bears the Trader Joe's brand, and management seeks to minimize costs of these items. The company purchases directly from manufacturers, which ship their items straight to Trader Joe's warehouses to avoid third-party distribution costs. With small stores and limited storage space, Trader Joe's trucks leave the warehouse centers daily. This encourages precise, just-in-time ordering and a relentless focus on frequent merchandise turnover.

This winning combination of quality products and low prices has turned Trader Joe's into one of the hottest retailers in the United States. Its stores sell an estimated $13 billion annually, or $1,734 in merchandise per square foot, which is nearly double Whole Foods, its top competitor.

Sources: Beth Kowitt, "Inside the Secret World of Trader Joe's," *Fortune*, August 23, 2010 (http://archive.fortune.com/2010/08/20/news/companies/inside_trader_joes_full_version.fortune/index.htm); Christopher Palmeri, "Trader Joe's Recipe for Success," *Bloomberg Businessweek*, February 21, 2008 (http://www.bloomberg.com/bw/stories/2008-02-20/trader-joes-recipe-for-success); Allessandra Ran, "Teach Us, Trader Joe: Demanding Socially Responsible Food," *The Atlantic*, August 7, 2012 (http://www.theatlantic.com/health/archive/2012/08/teach-us-trader-joe-demanding-socially-responsible-food/260786/); Aaron Ahlburn and Keisha McDonnough, "Retail ShopTopic," *Retail Research*, September 2014, Jones Lang LaSalle, Inc. (http://www.us.jll.com/united-states/en-us/Research/JLL-ShopTopic-Grocery-share.pdf); "Trader Joe's Customer Choice Award Winners," Trader Joe's Co. press release, Monrovia, CA: January 4, 2016 (http://www.traderjoes.com/digin/post/trader-joes-customer-choice-award-winners).

The interest in sustainability appears to be intensifying among companies. General Electric, Poland Springs (a bottled-water manufacturer), and Hewlett-Packard are among the many companies incorporating sustainability into their decision making. Sustainability is important to these companies for several reasons:

- More and more investors care about sustainability. These investors make investment decisions based on a company's financial, social, and environmental performance and raise questions about sustainability at shareholder meetings.
- Companies that emphasize sustainability find that sustainability goals attract and inspire employees.
- Customers prefer the products of companies with good sustainability records and boycott companies with poor sustainability records.
- Society and activist nongovernmental organizations, in particular, monitor the sustainability performance of firms and take legal action against those that violate environmental laws. Countries with fast-growing economies, such as China and India, are now either requiring or encouraging companies to develop and report on their sustainability initiatives.

Management accountants help managers track the key success factors of their firms as well as those of their competitors. Competitive information serves as a *benchmark* managers use to continuously improve their operations. Examples of continuous improvement include Southwest Airlines' efforts to increase the number of its flights that arrive on time, eBay's efforts to improve the access its customers have to online auctions, and Lowe's efforts to

DECISION POINT

How do companies add value, and what are the dimensions of performance that customers are expecting of companies?

continuously reduce the cost of its home-improvement products. Sometimes, more fundamental changes and innovations in operations, such as redesigning a manufacturing process to reduce costs, may be necessary. To successfully implement their strategies, firms have to do more than analyze their value chains and supply chains and execute key success factors. They also have to have good decision-making processes.

Decision Making, Planning, and Control: The Five-Step Decision-Making Process

We illustrate a five-step decision-making process using the example of the *Daily News*, a newspaper in Boulder, Colorado. Subsequent chapters of the book describe how managers use this five-step decision-making process to make many different types of decisions.

The *Daily News* differentiates itself from its competitors by using (1) highly respected journalists who write well-researched news articles, (2) color to enhance attractiveness to readers and advertisers, and (3) a Web site that delivers up-to-the-minute news, interviews, and analyses. The newspaper has the following resources to deliver on this strategy: an automated, computer-integrated, state-of-the-art printing facility; a Web-based information technology infrastructure; and a distribution network that is one of the best in the newspaper industry.

To keep up with steadily increasing production costs, Naomi Crawford, manager of the *Daily News*, needs to increase the company's revenues in 2017. As she ponders what she should do in early 2017, Naomi works through the five-step decision-making process.

1. **Identify the problem and uncertainties.** Naomi has two main choices:
   a. increase the selling price of the newspaper or
   b. increase the rate per page charged to advertisers.

   The key uncertainty is the effect any increase in prices or rates will have on demand. A decrease in demand could offset the price or rate increases and lead to lower rather than higher revenues. These decisions would take effect in March 2017.

2. **Obtain information.** Gathering information before making a decision helps managers gain a better understanding of uncertainties. Naomi asks her marketing manager to talk to some representative readers to gauge their reaction to an increase in the newspaper's selling price. She asks her advertising sales manager to talk to current and potential advertisers to assess demand for advertising. She also reviews the effect that past increases in the price of the newspaper had on readership. Ramon Sandoval, management accountant at the *Daily News*, presents information about the effect of past increases or decreases in advertising rates on advertising revenues. He also collects and analyzes information on advertising rates competing newspapers and other media outlets charge.

3. **Make predictions about the future.** Based on this information, Naomi makes predictions about the future. She concludes that increasing prices would upset readers and decrease readership. She has a different view about advertising rates. She expects a marketwide increase in advertising rates and believes that increasing rates will have little effect on the number of advertising pages sold.

   Naomi recognizes that making predictions requires judgment. She looks for biases in her thinking. Has she correctly judged reader sentiment or is the negative publicity of a price increase overly influencing her decision making? How sure is she that competitors will increase their advertising rates? Is her thinking in this respect biased by how competitors have responded in the past? Have circumstances changed? How confident is she that her sales representatives can convince advertisers to pay higher rates? After retesting her assumptions and reviewing her thinking, Naomi feels comfortable with her predictions and judgments.

4. **Make decisions by choosing among alternatives.** When making decisions, a company's strategy serves as a vital guidepost for the many individuals in different parts of the organization making decisions at different times. Consistent strategies provide a common purpose for these disparate decisions. Only if these decisions can be aligned with its strategy will an organization achieve its goals. Without this alignment, the

---

LEARNING OBJECTIVE 4

Explain the five-step decision-making process

...identify the problem and uncertainties; obtain information; make predictions about the future; make decisions by choosing among alternatives; implement the decision, evaluate performance, and learn

and its role in management accounting

...planning and control of operations and activities

company's decisions will be uncoordinated, pull the organization in different directions, and produce inconsistent results.

Consistent with a product differentiation strategy, Naomi decides to increase advertising rates by 4% to $5,200 per page in March 2017, but not increase the selling price of the newspaper. She is confident that the *Daily News*'s distinctive style and Web presence will increase readership, creating value for advertisers. She communicates the new advertising rate schedule to the sales department. Ramon estimates advertising revenues of $4,160,000 ($5,200 per page × 800 pages predicted to be sold in March 2017).

Steps 1 through 4 are collectively referred to as *planning*. **Planning** consists of selecting an organization's goals and strategies, predicting results under various alternative ways of achieving those goals, deciding how to attain the desired goals, and communicating the goals and how to achieve them to the entire organization. Management accountants serve as business partners in these planning activities because they understand the key success factors and what creates value.

The most important planning tool when implementing strategy is a *budget*. A **budget** is the quantitative expression of a proposed plan of action by management and is an aid to coordinating what needs to be done to execute that plan. For March 2017, the budgeted advertising revenue of the *Daily News* equals $4,160,000. The full budget for March 2017 includes budgeted circulation revenue and the production, distribution, and customer-service costs to achieve the company's sales goals; the anticipated cash flows; and the potential financing needs. Because multiple departments help prepare the budget, personnel throughout the organization have to coordinate and communicate with one another as well as with the company's suppliers and customers.

5. **Implement the decision, evaluate performance, and learn.** Managers at the *Daily News* take action to implement and achieve the March 2017 budget. The firm's management accountants then collect information on how the company's actual performance compares to planned or budgeted performance (also referred to as scorekeeping). The information on the actual results is different from the *predecision* planning information Naomi and her staff collected in Step 2, which enabled her to better understand uncertainties, to make predictions, and to make a decision. Allowing managers to compare actual performance to budgeted performance is the *control* or *postdecision* role of information. **Control** comprises taking actions that implement the planning decisions, evaluating past performance, and providing feedback and learning to help future decision making.

Measuring actual performance informs managers how well they and their subunits are doing. Linking rewards to performance helps motivate managers. These rewards are both intrinsic (recognition for a job well done) and extrinsic (salary, bonuses, and promotions linked to performance). We discuss this in more detail in a later chapter (Chapter 23). A budget serves as much as a control tool as a planning tool. Why? Because a budget is a benchmark against which actual performance can be compared.

Consider performance evaluation at the *Daily News*. During March 2017, the newspaper sold advertising, issued invoices, and received payments. The accounting system recorded these invoices and receipts. Exhibit 1-4 shows the *Daily News*'s advertising revenues for March 2017. This performance report indicates that 760 pages of advertising (40 pages fewer than

EXHIBIT 1-4 Performance Report of Advertising Revenues at the *Daily News* for March 2017

	Actual Result (1)	Budgeted Amount (2)	Difference: (Actual Result − Budgeted Amount) (3) = (1) − (2)	Difference as a Percentage of Budgeted Amount (4) = (3) ÷ (2)
Advertising pages sold	760 pages	800 pages	40 pages Unfavorable	5.0% Unfavorable
Average rate per page	$5,080	$5,200	$120 Unfavorable	2.3% Unfavorable
Advertising revenues	$3,860,800	$4,160,000	$299,200 Unfavorable	7.2% Unfavorable

the budgeted 800 pages) were sold. The average rate per page was $5,080, compared with the budgeted $5,200 rate, yielding actual advertising revenues of $3,860,800. The actual advertising revenues were $299,200 less than the budgeted $4,160,000. Observe how managers use both financial and nonfinancial information, such as pages of advertising, to evaluate performance.

The performance report in Exhibit 1-4 spurs investigation and **learning**, which involves examining past performance (the control function) and systematically exploring alternative ways to make better-informed decisions and plans in the future. Learning can lead to changes in goals, strategies, the ways decision alternatives are identified, and the range of information collected when making predictions and sometimes can lead to changes in managers.

The performance report in Exhibit 1-4 would prompt the management accountant to raise several questions directing the attention of managers to problems and opportunities. Is the strategy of differentiating the *Daily News* from other newspapers attracting more readers? Did the marketing and sales department make sufficient efforts to convince advertisers that, even at the higher rate of $5,200 per page, advertising in the *Daily News* was a good buy? Why was the actual average rate per page ($5,080) less than the budgeted rate ($5,200)? Did some sales representatives offer discounted rates? Did economic conditions cause the decline in advertising revenues? Are revenues falling because editorial and production standards have declined? Are more readers getting their news online?

Answers to these questions could prompt the newspaper's publisher to take subsequent actions, including, for example, adding more sales personnel, making changes in editorial policy, putting more resources into expanding its presence online and on mobile devices, getting readers to pay for online content, and selling digital advertising. Good implementation requires the marketing, editorial, and production departments to work together and coordinate their actions.

The management accountant could go further by identifying the specific advertisers that cut back or stopped advertising after the rate increase went into effect. Managers could then decide when and how sales representatives should follow up with these advertisers.

Planning and control activities must be flexible enough so that managers can seize opportunities unforeseen at the time the plan was formulated. In no case should control mean that managers cling to a plan when unfolding events (such as a sensational news story) indicate that actions not encompassed by that plan (such as spending more money to cover the story) would offer better results for the company (from higher newspaper sales).

The left side of Exhibit 1-5 provides an overview of the decision-making processes at the *Daily News*. The right side of the exhibit highlights how the management accounting system aids in decision making.

DECISION POINT

How do managers make decisions to implement strategy?

Planning and control activities get more challenging when monitoring and managing innovation and sustainability. Consider the problem of how the *Daily News* must innovate as more of its readers migrate to the Web to get their news. Now follow the five-step process we described earlier. In Step 1, the uncertainties are much greater. Will there be demand for a newspaper? Will customers look to the *Daily News* to get their information or to other sources? In Step 2, obtaining information is more difficult because there is little history that managers can comfortably rely on. Instead, managers will have to make connections across disparate data, run experiments, engage with diverse experts, and speculate to understand how the world might evolve. In Step 3, making predictions about the future will require developing different scenarios and models. In Step 4, managers will need to make decisions knowing that conditions might change in unanticipated ways that will require them to be flexible and correct course midstream. In Step 5, the learning component is critical. How have the uncertainties evolved and what do managers need to do to respond to these changing circumstances?

Planning and control for sustainability is equally challenging. What should the *Daily News* do about energy consumption in its printing presses, recycling of newsprint, and pollution prevention? Among the uncertainties managers face is whether customers will reward the *Daily News* for these actions by being more loyal and whether investors will react favorably to managers spending resources on sustainability. Information to gauge customer and investor sentiment is not easy to obtain. Predicting how sustainability efforts might pay off in the long run is far from certain. Even as managers make decisions, the sustainability landscape will doubtlessly change with respect to environmental regulations and societal expectations, requiring managers to learn and adapt.

EXHIBIT 1-5

How Accounting Aids Decision Making, Planning, and Control at the *Daily News*

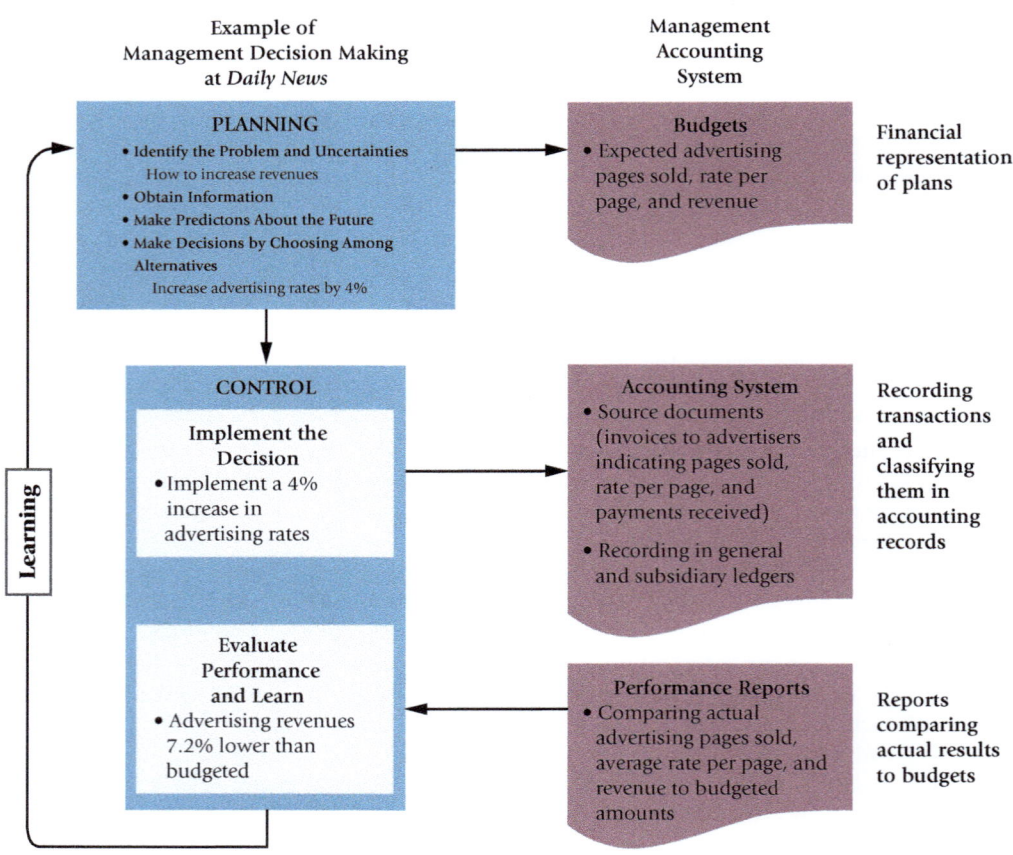

Do these challenges of implementing planning and control systems for innovation and sustainability mean that these systems should not be used for these initiatives? No. Many companies find value in using these systems to manage innovation and sustainability. But, in keeping with the challenges described earlier, companies such as Johnson & Johnson use these systems in a different way to obtain information around key strategic uncertainties, to implement plans while being mindful that circumstances might change, and to evaluate performance in order to learn. We will return to the themes of innovation and sustainability at various points in the book.

Key Management Accounting Guidelines

LEARNING OBJECTIVE 5

Describe three guidelines management accountants follow in supporting managers

...employing a cost–benefit approach, recognizing behavioral as well as technical considerations, and calculating different costs for different purposes

Three guidelines help management accountants provide the most value to the strategic and operational decision making of their companies: (1) employ a cost–benefit approach, (2) give full recognition to behavioral and technical considerations, and (3) use different costs for different purposes.

Cost–Benefit Approach

Managers continually face resource-allocation decisions, such as whether to purchase a new software package or hire a new employee. They use a **cost–benefit approach** when making these decisions. Managers should spend resources if the expected benefits to the company exceed the expected costs. Managers rely on management accounting information to quantify expected benefits and expected costs (although all benefits and costs are not easy to quantify).

Consider the installation of a consulting company's first budgeting system. Previously, the company used historical recordkeeping and little formal planning. A major benefit of installing a budgeting system is that it compels managers to plan ahead, compare actual to budgeted information, learn, and take corrective action. Although the system leads to better decisions and consequently better company performance, the exact benefits are not easy to measure. On the cost side, some costs, such as investments in software and training, are easier to quantify. Others, such as the time spent by managers on the budgeting process, are more difficult to quantify. Regardless, senior managers compare expected benefits and expected costs, exercise judgment, and reach a decision, in this case to install the budgeting system.

Behavioral and Technical Considerations

When utilizing the cost–benefit approach, managers need to keep in mind a number of technical and behavioral considerations. Technical considerations help managers make wise economic decisions by providing desired information (for example, costs in various value-chain categories) in an appropriate format (for example, actual results versus budgeted amounts) and at the preferred frequency (for example, weekly or quarterly). However, management is not confined to technical matters. Management is primarily a human activity that should focus on encouraging individuals to do their jobs better. Budgets have a behavioral effect by motivating and rewarding employees for achieving an organization's goals. So, when workers underperform, for example, behavioral considerations suggest that managers need to discuss ways to improve their performance with them rather than just sending them a report highlighting their underperformance.

Different Costs for Different Purposes

This book emphasizes that managers use alternative ways to compute costs in different decision-making situations because there are different costs for different purposes. A cost concept used for the purposes of external reporting may not be appropriate for internal, routine reporting.

Consider the advertising costs associated with Microsoft Corporation's launch of a product with a useful life of several years. For external reporting to shareholders, Generally Accepted Accounting Principles (GAAP) require television advertising costs for this product to be fully expensed in the income statement in the year they are incurred. However, for internal reporting, the television advertising costs could be capitalized and then amortized or written off as expenses over several years if Microsoft's management team believed that doing so would more accurately and fairly measure the performance of the managers that launched the new product.

We now discuss the relationships and reporting responsibilities among managers and management accountants within a company's organization structure.

DECISION POINT
What guidelines do management accountants use?

Organization Structure and the Management Accountant

We focus first on broad management functions and then look at how the management accounting and finance functions support managers.

LEARNING OBJECTIVE 6

Understand how management accounting fits into an organization's structure

...for example, the responsibilities of the controller

Line and Staff Relationships

Organizations distinguish between line management and staff management. **Line management**, such as production, marketing, and distribution management, is directly responsible for achieving the goals of the organization. For example, managers of manufacturing divisions are responsible for meeting particular levels of budgeted operating income, product quality and safety, and compliance with environmental laws. Similarly, the pediatrics department in a hospital is responsible for quality of service, costs, and patient billings. **Staff management**, such as management accountants and information technology and human-resources management, provides advice, support, and assistance to line management. A plant manager (a line function) may be responsible for investing in new equipment. A management accountant (a staff function) works as a business partner of the plant manager by preparing detailed operating-cost comparisons of alternative pieces of equipment.

Increasingly, organizations such as Honda and Dell are using teams to achieve their objectives. These teams include both line and staff management so that all inputs into a decision are available simultaneously.

The Chief Financial Officer and the Controller

The **chief financial officer (CFO)**—also called the **finance director** in many countries—is the executive responsible for overseeing the financial operations of an organization. The responsibilities of the CFO vary among organizations, but they usually include the following areas:

- **Controllership**—provides financial information for reports to managers and shareholders and oversees the overall operations of the accounting system.
- **Tax**—plans income taxes, sales taxes, and international taxes.
- **Treasury**—oversees banking and short- and long-term financing, investments, and cash management.
- **Risk management**—manages the financial risk of interest-rate and exchange-rate changes and derivatives management.
- **Investor relations**—communicates with, responds to, and interacts with shareholders.
- **Strategic planning**—defines strategy and allocates resources to implement strategy.

An independent internal audit function reviews and analyzes financial and other records to attest to the integrity of the organization's financial reports and to adherence to its policies and procedures.

The **controller** (also called the *chief accounting officer*) is the financial executive primarily responsible for management accounting and financial accounting. This book focuses on the controller as the chief management accounting executive. Modern controllers have no line authority except over their own departments. Yet the controller exercises control over the entire organization in a special way. By reporting and interpreting relevant data, the controller influences the behavior of all employees and helps line managers make better decisions.

Exhibit 1-6 shows an organization chart of the CFO and the corporate controller at Nike, the leading footwear and sports apparel company. The CFO is a staff manager who reports to and supports the chief executive officer (CEO). As in most organizations, the corporate controller at Nike reports to the CFO. Nike also has regional controllers who support regional managers in the major geographic regions in which the company operates, such as the United States, Asia Pacific, Latin America, and Europe. Because they support the activities of the

EXHIBIT 1-6

Nike: Reporting Relationship for the CFO and the Corporate Controller

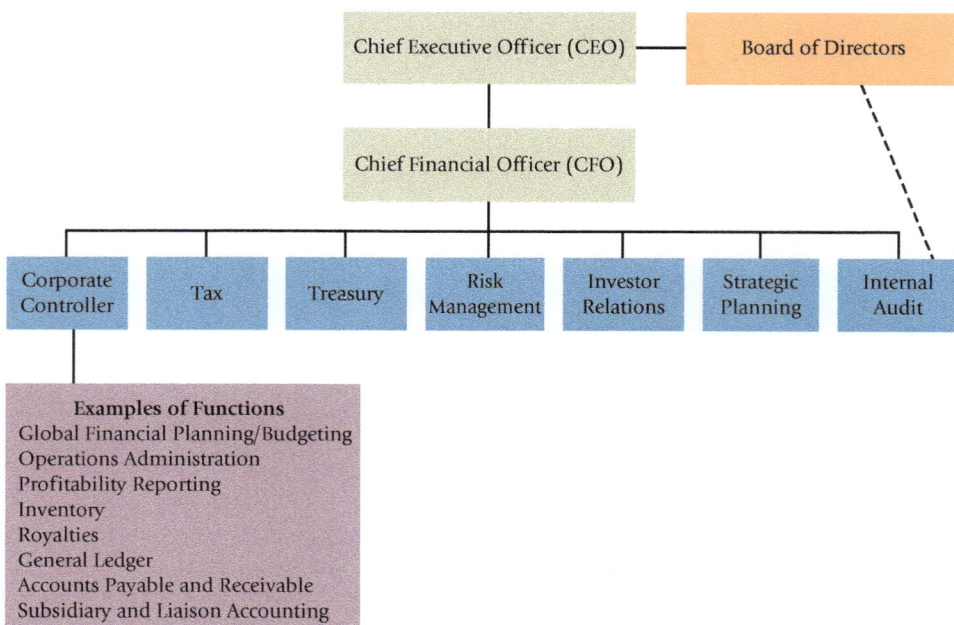

regional manager, for example, by managing budgets and analyzing costs, regional controllers report to the regional manager rather than the corporate controller. At the same time, to align accounting policies and practices for the whole organization, regional controllers have a functional (often called a dotted-line) responsibility to the corporate controller. Individual countries sometimes have a country controller.

Organization charts such as the one in Exhibit 1-6 show formal reporting relationships. In most organizations, there also are informal relationships that must be understood when managers attempt to implement their decisions. Examples of informal relationships are friendships (both professional and personal) among managers and the preferences of top management about the managers they rely on when making decisions.

Think about what managers do to design and implement strategies and the organization structures within which they operate. Then think about the management accountants' and controllers' roles. It should be clear that the successful management accountant must have technical and analytical competence *as well as* behavioral and interpersonal skills.

Management Accounting Beyond the Numbers[2]

To people outside the profession, it may seem like accountants are just "numbers people." It is true that most accountants are adept financial managers, yet their skills do not stop there. The successful management accountant possesses several skills and characteristics that reach well beyond basic analytical abilities.

Management accountants must work well in cross-functional teams and as a business partner. In addition to being technically competent, the best management accountants work well in teams, learn about business issues, understand the motivations of different individuals, respect the views of their colleagues, and show empathy and trust.

Management accountants must promote fact-based analysis and make tough-minded, critical judgments without being adversarial. Management accountants must raise tough questions for managers to consider, especially when preparing budgets. They must do so thoughtfully and with the intent of improving plans and decisions. Before the investment bank JP Morgan lost more than $6 billion on "exotic" financial investments (credit-default swaps) in 2012, controllers should have raised questions about these risky investments and the fact that the firm was essentially betting that improving economic conditions abroad would earn it a large profit.

They must lead and motivate people to change and be innovative. Implementing new ideas, however good they may be, is difficult. When the United States Department of Defense (DoD) began consolidating more than 320 finance and accounting systems into a common platform, the accounting services director and his team of management accountants held meetings to make sure everyone in the agency understood the goal for such a change. Ultimately, the DoD aligned each individual's performance with the transformative change and introduced incentive pay to encourage personnel to adopt the platform and drive innovation within this new framework.

They must communicate clearly, openly, and candidly. Communicating information is a large part of a management accountant's job. When premium car companies such as Rolls Royce and Porsche design new models, management accountants work closely with engineers to ensure that each new car supports a carefully defined balance of commercial, engineering, and financial criteria. These efforts are successful because management accountants clearly communicate the information that multidisciplinary teams need to deliver new innovations profitably.

They must have high integrity. Management accountants must never succumb to pressure from managers to manipulate financial information. They must always remember that their primary commitment is to the organization and its shareholders. In 2015, Toshiba, the

> **DECISION POINT**
> Where does the management accounting function fit into an organization's structure?

---

[2] United States Senate Permanent Subcommittee on Investigations. *JPMorgan Chase Whale Trades: A Case History of Derivatives Risks and Abuses*. Washington, DC: Government Printing Office, March 15, 2013; Wendy Garling, "Winning the Transformation Battle at the Defense Finance and Accounting Service," Balanced Scorecard Report, May–June 2007; Bill Nixon, John Burns, and Mostafa Jazayeri, *The Role of Management Accounting in New Product Design and Development Decisions*, Volume 9, Issue 1. London: Chartered Institute of Management Accountants, November 2011; and Eric Pfanner and Magumi Fujikawa, "Toshiba Slashes Earnings for Past Seven Years," *The Wall Street Journal* (September 7, 2015).

Japanese maker of semiconductors, consumer electronics, and nuclear power plants wrote down $1.9 billion of earnings that had been overstated over the previous seven years. The problems stemmed from managers setting aggressive profit targets that subordinates could not meet without inflating divisional results by understating costs, postponing losses, and overstating revenues.

Professional Ethics

LEARNING OBJECTIVE 7

Understand what professional ethics mean to management accountants

...for example, management accountants must maintain integrity and credibility in every aspect of their job

At no time has the focus on ethical conduct been higher than it is today. Corporate scandals at Arthur Andersen, a public accounting firm; Countrywide Financial, a home mortgage company; Enron, an oil and gas company; Lehman Brothers, an investment bank; Toshiba, a Japanese conglomerate; and Bernie Madoff Investment Securities have seriously eroded the public's confidence in corporations. All employees in a company must comply with the organization's—and more broadly, society's—expectations of ethical standards.

Ethics are the foundation of a well-functioning economy. When ethics are weak, suppliers bribe executives to win supply contracts rather than invest in improving quality or lowering costs. In the absence of ethical conduct, customers have little confidence in the quality of products produced and become reluctant to buy them, causing markets to fail. Prices of products increase because of higher prices paid to suppliers and fewer products being produced and sold. Investors are unsure about the integrity of financial reports, affecting their ability to make investment decisions, resulting in a reluctance to invest and a misallocation of resources. The scandals at Ahold, an international supermarket operator, and Tyco International, a diversified global manufacturing company, and others make clear that value is quickly destroyed by unethical behavior.

Institutional Support

Accountants have special ethical obligations, given that they are responsible for the integrity of the financial information provided to internal and external parties. The Sarbanes–Oxley legislation in the United States was passed in 2002 in response to a series of corporate scandals. The act focuses on improving internal control, corporate governance, monitoring of managers, and disclosure practices of public corporations. These regulations impose tough ethical standards and criminal penalties on managers and accountants who don't meet the standards. The regulations also delineate a process for employees to report violations of illegal and unethical acts (these employees are called whistleblowers).

As part of the Sarbanes–Oxley Act, CEOs and CFOs must certify that the financial statements of their firms fairly represent the results of their operations. In order to increase the independence of auditors, the act empowers the audit committee of a company's board of directors (which is composed exclusively of independent directors) to hire, compensate, and terminate the public accounting firm to audit a company. To reduce their financial dependency on their individual clients and increase their independence, the act limits auditing firms from providing consulting, tax, and other advisory services to the companies they are auditing. The act also authorizes the Public Company Accounting Oversight Board to oversee, review, and investigate the work of the auditors.

Professional accounting organizations, which represent management accountants in many countries, offer certification programs indicating that those who have completed them have management accounting and financial management technical knowledge and expertise. These organizations also advocate high ethical standards. In the United States, the Institute of Management Accountants (IMA) has also issued ethical guidelines. Exhibit 1-7 presents the IMA's guidance on issues relating to competence, confidentiality, integrity, and credibility. To provide support to its members to act ethically at all times, the IMA runs an ethics hotline service. Members can call professional counselors at the IMA's Ethics Counseling Service to discuss their ethical dilemmas. The counselors help identify the key ethical issues and possible alternative ways of resolving them, and confidentiality is guaranteed. The IMA is just one of many institutions that help navigate management accountants through what could be turbulent ethical waters.

> **EXHIBIT 1-7**
>
> Standards of Ethical Behavior for Practitioners of Management Accounting and Financial Management
>
> **STATEMENT OF ETHICAL PROFESSIONAL PRACTICE**
>
> Members of IMA shall behave ethically. A commitment to ethical professional practice includes: overarching principles that express our values, and standards that guide our conduct.
>
> **PRINCIPLES**
>
> IMA's overarching ethical principles include: Honesty, Fairness, Objectivity, and Responsibility. Members shall act in accordance with these principles and shall encourage others within their organizations to adhere to them.
>
> **STANDARDS**
>
> A member's failure to comply with the following standards may result in disciplinary action.
>
> **I. COMPETENCE**
>
> Each member has a responsibility to:
>
> 1. Maintain an appropriate level of professional expertise by continually developing knowledge and skills.
> 2. Perform professional duties in accordance with relevant laws, regulations, and technical standards.
> 3. Provide decision support information and recommendations that are accurate, clear, concise, and timely.
> 4. Recognize and communicate professional limitations or other constraints that would preclude responsible judgment or successful performance of an activity.
>
> **II. CONFIDENTIALITY**
>
> Each member has a responsibility to:
>
> 1. Keep information confidential except when disclosure is authorized or legally required.
> 2. Inform all relevant parties regarding appropriate use of confidential information. Monitor subordinates' activities to ensure compliance.
> 3. Refrain from using confidential information for unethical or illegal advantage.
>
> **III. INTEGRITY**
>
> Each member has a responsibility to:
>
> 1. Mitigate actual conflicts of interest, regularly communicate with business associates to avoid apparent conflicts of interest. Advise all parties of any potential conflicts.
> 2. Refrain from engaging in any conduct that would prejudice carrying out duties ethically.
> 3. Abstain from engaging in or supporting any activity that might discredit the profession.
>
> **IV. CREDIBILITY**
>
> Each member has a responsibility to:
>
> 1. Communicate information fairly and objectively.
> 2. Disclose all relevant information that could reasonably be expected to influence an intended user's understanding of the reports, analyses, or recommendations.
> 3. Disclose delays or deficiencies in information, timeliness, processing, or internal controls in conformance with organization policy and/or applicable law.
>
> *Source: IMA Statement of Ethical Professional Practice*, 2016. Montvale, NJ: Institute of Management Accountants. Reprinted with permission from the Institute of Management Accountants, Montvale, NJ, www.imanet.org.

Typical Ethical Challenges

Ethical issues can confront management accountants in many ways. Here are two examples:

- **Case A:** A management accountant is concerned about the commercial potential of a software product for which development costs are currently being capitalized as an asset rather than being shown as an expense for internal reporting purposes. The firm's division manager, whose bonus is based, in part, on the division's profits, argues that showing development costs as an asset is justified because the new product will generate profits. However, he presents little evidence to support his argument. The last two products from the division have been unsuccessful. The management accountant wants to make the right decision while avoiding a difficult personal confrontation with his boss, the division manager. (This case is similar to the situation at Toshiba where senior managers set aggressive divisional targets and divisional accountants inflated divisional profits to achieve them.)

- **Case B:** A packaging supplier, bidding for a new contract, offers a management accountant of the purchasing company an all-expenses-paid weekend to the Super Bowl. The supplier does not mention the new contract when extending the invitation. The management accountant is not a personal friend of the supplier. He knows cost issues are critical when it comes to approving the new contract and is concerned that the supplier will ask for details about the bids placed by competing packaging companies.

In each case, the management accountant is faced with an ethical dilemma. Ethical issues are not always clear-cut. Case A involves competence, credibility, and integrity. The management accountant should request that the division manager provide credible evidence that the new product is commercially viable. If the manager does not provide such evidence, expensing development costs in the current period is appropriate.

Case B involves confidentiality and integrity. The supplier in Case B may have no intention of asking questions about competitors' bids. However, the appearance of a conflict of interest in Case B is sufficient for many companies to prohibit employees from accepting "favors" from suppliers.

Exhibit 1-8 presents the IMA's guidance on "Resolution of Ethical Conflict." For example, if the divisional management accountant in Case A is not satisfied with the response of the division manager regarding the commercial viability of the product, he or she should discuss the issue with the corporate controller. The accountant in Case B should discuss the invitation with his or her immediate supervisor. If the visit is approved, the accountant should inform the supplier that the invitation has been officially approved subject to following corporate policy (which includes not disclosing confidential company information).

Most professional accounting organizations around the globe issue statements about professional ethics. These statements include many of the same issues discussed by the IMA in Exhibits 1-7 and 1-8. For example, the Chartered Institute of Management Accountants (CIMA) in the United Kingdom advocates five ethical principles similar to those shown in Exhibit 1-7: professional competence and due care, confidentiality, integrity, objectivity, and professional behavior.

> **DECISION POINT**
> What are the ethical responsibilities of management accountants?

EXHIBIT 1-8

Resolution of Ethical Conflict

RESOLUTION OF ETHICAL CONDUCT

In applying the Standards of Ethical Professional Practice, you may encounter problems identifying unethical behavior or resolving an ethical conflict. When faced with ethical issues, you should follow your organization's established policies on the resolution of such conflict. If these policies do not resolve the ethical conflict, you should consider the following courses of action:

1. Discuss the issue with your immediate supervisor except when it appears that the supervisor is involved. In that case, present the issue to the next level. If you cannot achieve a satisfactory resolution, submit the issue to the next management level. If your immediate superior is the chief executive officer or equivalent, the acceptable reviewing authority may be a group such as the audit committee, executive committee, board of directors, board of trustees, or owners. Contact with levels above the immediate superior should be initiated only with your superior's knowledge, assuming he or she is not involved. Communication of such problems to authorities or individuals not employed or engaged by the organization is not considered appropriate, unless you believe there is a clear violation of the law.
2. Clarify relevant ethical issues by initiating a confidential discussion with an IMA Ethics Counselor or other impartial advisor to obtain a better understanding of possible courses of action.
3. Consult your own attorney as to legal obligations and rights concerning the ethical conflict.

Source: IMA Statement of Ethical Professional Practice, 2016. Montvale, NJ: Institute of Management Accountants. Reprinted with permission from the Institute of Management Accountants, Montvale, NJ, www.imanet.org.

PROBLEM FOR SELF-STUDY

Campbell Soup Company incurs the following costs:

a. Purchase of tomatoes by a canning plant for Campbell's tomato soup products
b. Materials purchased for redesigning Pepperidge Farm biscuit containers to make biscuits stay fresh longer
c. Payment to Backer, Spielvogel, & Bates, the advertising agency, for advertising work on the Healthy Request line of soup products
d. Salaries of food technologists researching feasibility of a Prego pizza sauce that has minimal calories
e. Payment to Safeway for redeeming coupons on Campbell's food products
f. Cost of a toll-free telephone line used for customer inquiries about using Campbell's soup products
g. Cost of gloves used by line operators on the Swanson Fiesta breakfast-food production line
h. Cost of handheld computers used by Pepperidge Farm delivery staff serving major supermarket accounts

Classify each cost item (a–h) as one of the business functions in the value chain in Exhibit 1-2 (page 25).

Solution

a. Production
b. Design of products and processes
c. Marketing
d. Research and development
e. Marketing
f. Customer service
g. Production
h. Distribution

DECISION POINTS

The following question-and-answer format summarizes the chapter's learning objectives. Each decision presents a key question related to a learning objective. The guidelines are the answer to that question.

Decision	Guidelines
1. How is financial accounting different from management accounting?	Financial accounting is used to develop reports for external users on past financial performance using GAAP. Management accounting is used to provide future-oriented information to help managers (internal users) make decisions and achieve an organization's goals.
2. How do management accountants support strategic decisions?	Management accountants contribute to strategic decisions by providing information about the sources of competitive advantage.
3. How do companies add value, and what are the dimensions of performance that customers are expecting of companies?	Companies add value through research and development (R&D), design of products and processes, production, marketing, distribution, and customer service. Customers want companies to deliver performance through cost and efficiency, quality, timeliness, and innovation.

Decision	Guidelines
4. How do managers make decisions to implement strategy?	Managers use a five-step decision-making process to implement strategy: (1) identify the problem and uncertainties; (2) obtain information; (3) make predictions about the future; (4) make decisions by choosing among alternatives; and (5) implement the decision, evaluate performance, and learn. The first four steps are planning decisions. They include deciding on an organization's goals, predicting results under various alternative ways of achieving those goals, and deciding how to attain the desired goals. Step 5 is the control decision, which includes taking actions to implement the planning decisions, evaluating past performance, and providing feedback that will help future decision making.
5. What guidelines do management accountants use?	Three guidelines that help management accountants increase their value to managers are (a) employing a cost–benefit approach, (b) recognizing behavioral as well as technical considerations, and (c) identifying different costs for different purposes.
6. Where does the management accounting function fit into an organization's structure?	Management accounting is an integral part of the controller's function. In most organizations, the controller reports to the chief financial officer, who is a key member of the top management team.
7. What are the ethical responsibilities of management accountants?	Management accountants have ethical responsibilities that relate to competence, confidentiality, integrity, and credibility.

TERMS TO LEARN

Each chapter will include this section. Like all technical terms, accounting terms have precise meanings. Learn the definitions of new terms when you initially encounter them. The meaning of each of the following terms is given in this chapter and in the Glossary at the end of this book.

budget
chief financial officer (CFO)
control
controller
cost accounting
cost–benefit approach
cost management
customer relationship management (CRM)
customer service
design of products and processes
distribution
finance director
financial accounting
learning
line management
management accounting
marketing
planning
production
research and development (R&D)
staff management
strategic cost management
strategy
supply chain
sustainability
total quality management (TQM)
value chain

ASSIGNMENT MATERIAL

Pearson MyLab Accounting

Questions

1-1 How does management accounting differ from financial accounting?
1-2 "Management accounting should not fit the straitjacket of financial accounting." Explain and give an example.
1-3 How can management accounting information help managers formulate strategies?
1-4 Define the term "value chain" and state its six primary business functions.

1-5 Explain the term *supply chain* and its importance to cost management.

1-6 "Management accounting deals only with costs." Do you agree? Explain.

1-7 How can management accountants help improve quality and achieve timely product deliveries?

1-8 Describe the five-step decision-making process.

1-9 Distinguish planning decisions from control decisions.

1-10 What three guidelines help management accountants provide the most value to managers?

1-11 "Technical and basic analytical competence are necessary but not sufficient conditions to becoming a successful management accountant." Do you agree? Why?

1-12 As the new controller, reply to the following comment made by your plant manager: "When I employ a proper accounting software, which can process all my daily accounting records and provide me with all necessary reports and analyses, I am not sure what additional value our accountants will bring to the business. I know enough about my business to understand the computer-generated reports."

1-13 Where does the management accounting function fit into an organization's structure?

1-14 What is the role of ethics in a well-functioning economy? List a few groups of stakeholders who may suffer in an economic system governed by weak ethics.

1-15 Provide one example of an ethical issue in relation to suppliers and its possible impact on customers and the market when ethics is weak.

Multiple-Choice Questions

Pearson MyLab Accounting

1-16 Which of the following is not a primary function of the management accountant?
a. Communicates financial results and position to external parties.
b. Uses information to develop and implement business strategy.
c. Aids in the decision making to help an organization meet its goals.
d. Provides input into an entity's production and marketing decisions.

©2016 DeVry/Becker Educational Development Corp. All Rights Reserved.

Exercises

1-17 Value chain and classification of costs, computer company. Compaq Computer incurs the following costs:
a. Electricity costs for the plant assembling the Presario computer line of products
b. Transportation costs for shipping the Presario line of products to a retail chain
c. Payment to David Kelley Designs for design of the Armada Notebook
d. Salary of computer scientist working on the next generation of minicomputers
e. Cost of Compaq employees' visit to a major customer to demonstrate Compaq's ability to interconnect with other computers
f. Purchase of competitors' products for testing against potential Compaq products
g. Payment to television network for running Compaq advertisements
h. Cost of cables purchased from outside supplier to be used with Compaq printers

Classify each of the cost items (**a–h**) into one of the business functions of the value chain shown in Exhibit 1-2 (page 25).

Required

1-18 Value chain and classification of costs, pharmaceutical company. Pfizer, a pharmaceutical company, incurs the following costs:
a. Payment of booth registration fee at a medical conference to promote new products to physicians
b. Cost of redesigning an insulin syringe to make it less painful
c. Cost of a toll-free telephone line used for customer inquiries about drug usage, side effects of drugs, and so on
d. Equipment purchased to conduct experiments on drugs yet to be approved by the government
e. Sponsorship of a professional golfer
f. Labor costs of workers in the packaging area of a production facility
g. Bonus paid to a salesperson for exceeding a monthly sales quota
h. Cost of FedEx courier service to deliver drugs to hospitals

Classify each of the cost items (**a–h**) as one of the business functions of the value chain shown in Exhibit 1-2 (page 25).

Required

1-19 Value chain and classification of costs, fast-food restaurant. Burger King, a hamburger fast-food restaurant, incurs the following costs:

a. Cost of oil for the deep fryer
b. Wages of the counter help who give customers the food they order
c. Cost of the costume for the King on the Burger King television commercials
d. Cost of children's toys given away free with kids' meals
e. Cost of the posters indicating the special "two cheeseburgers for $2.50"
f. Costs of frozen onion rings and French fries
g. Salaries of the food specialists who create new sandwiches for the restaurant chain
h. Cost of "to-go" bags requested by customers who could not finish their meals in the restaurant

Required

Classify each of the cost items (**a–h**) as one of the business functions of the value chain shown in Exhibit 1-2 (page 25).

1-20 Key success factors. Dominion Consulting has issued a report recommending changes for its newest manufacturing client, Gibson Engine Works. Gibson currently manufactures a single product, which is sold and distributed nationally. The report contains the following suggestions for enhancing business performance:

a. Develop a rechargeable electric engine to stay ahead of competitors.
b. Adopt a TQM philosophy to reduce waste and defects to near zero.
c. Reduce lead times (time from customer order of product to customer receipt of product) by 20% in order to increase customer retention.
d. Negotiate faster response times with direct material suppliers to allow for lower material inventory levels.
e. Benchmark the company's gross margin percentages against its major competitors.

Required

Link each of these changes to the key success factors that are important to managers.

1-21 Key success factors. Dalworth Construction Company provides construction services for major projects. Managers at the company believe that construction is a people-management business, and they list the following as factors critical to their success:

a. Hire external consultants to implement six sigma principles in the company for sustainable quality improvement.
b. Take steps to increase employee morale and motivation by applying motivational models so that overall employee productivity increases.
c. Benchmark company's total costs of projects with its major competitors so that errors and wastages are minimized.
d. Carry out a training need analysis of the existing employees and train them accordingly.
e. Use modern tools and machineries so that cost of construction goes down and overall quality improves.

Required

Match each of these factors to the key success factors that are important to managers.

1-22 Planning and control decisions. Gregor Company makes and sells brooms and mops. It takes the following actions, not necessarily in the order given. For each action (**a–e**), state whether it is a planning decision or a control decision.

a. Gregor asks its advertising team to develop fresh advertisements to market its newest product.
b. Gregor calculates customer satisfaction scores after introducing its newest product.
c. Gregor compares costs it actually incurred with costs it expected to incur for the production of the new product.
d. Gregor's design team proposes a new product to compete directly with the Swiffer.
e. Gregor estimates the costs it will incur to distribute 30,000 units of the new product in the first quarter of next fiscal year.

1-23 Planning and control decisions. Fred Harris is the president of United Maintenance Service. He takes the following actions, not necessarily in the order given. For each action (**a–e**) state whether it is a planning decision or a control decision.

a. Fred contemplates procuring a digital lathe machine advised by his chief maintenance engineer.
b. Fred estimates the job cost of providing maintenance service to a local factory.
c. Fred calculates the total cost of materials in an annual maintenance contract to a client.
d. Fred decides to expand service offerings to nearby construction companies.
e. Fred makes a comparative analysis of administrative overheads with budgeted overheads.

1-24 Five-step decision-making process, manufacturing. Real's Bees makes products for personal care and sells through retail outlets and grocery stores. Its product line includes products for facial and body skin care, lip care, baby care, and outdoor remedies. The company wishes to enter into the hair care segment to make its product line stronger. The managers at Real's Bees take the following actions before taking the final decision. The actions are not listed in the order they are performed.

a. Production managers, with the help of cost managers and research wing of the company, prepare an estimate of costs for introducing hair care products.
b. Managers expect to grab a good market quickly by selling hair care products to the existing customers.
c. The company decides to introduce a new hair care product rather than introduce a new variant of any existing product.
d. Sales managers estimate they will sell more hair care products in the middle-age group.
e. The managers feel that introduction of hair care products is necessary to cope with competitors.
f. Incremental revenues by selling the new hair care product are budgeted.
g. Sales managers conduct Internet research to find out the present sales growth in the hair care market.

Required

Classify each of the actions (**a–g**) as a step in the five-step decision-making process (identify the problem and uncertainties; obtain information; make predictions about the future; make decisions by choosing among alternatives; implement the decision, evaluate performance, and learn).

1-25 Five-step decision-making process, service firm. Brook Exteriors is a firm that provides house-painting services. Richard Brook, the owner, is trying to find new ways to increase revenues. Mr. Brook performs the following actions, not in the order listed.

a. Mr. Brook decides to buy the paint sprayers rather than hire additional painters.
b. Mr. Brook discusses with his employees the possibility of using paint sprayers instead of hand painting to increase productivity and thus profits.
c. Mr. Brook learns of a large potential job that is about to go out for bids.
d. Mr. Brook compares the expected cost of buying sprayers to the expected cost of hiring more workers who paint by hand and estimates profits from both alternatives.
e. Mr. Brook estimates that using sprayers will reduce painting time by 20%.
f. Mr. Brook researches the price of paint sprayers online.

Required

Classify each of the actions (**a–f**) according to its step in the five-step decision-making process (identify the problem and uncertainties; obtain information; make predictions about the future; make decisions by choosing among alternatives; implement the decision, evaluate performance, and learn).

1-26 Professional ethics and reporting division performance. Joshua Wilson is the controller of Apex Frame Mouldings, a division of Garman Enterprises. As the division is preparing to count year-end inventory, Wilson is approached by Doug Leonard, the division's president. A selection of inventory previously valued at $150,000 had been identified as flawed earlier that month and as a result was determined to be unfit for sale. Leonard tells Wilson that he has decided to count the selected items as regular inventory and that he will "deal with it when things settle down after the first of the year. After all," and adds, "the auditors don't know good picture frame moulding from bad. We've had a rough year, and things are looking up for next year. Our division needs all the profits we can get this year. It's just a matter of timing the write-off." Leonard is Wilson's direct supervisor.

Required

1. Describe Wilson's ethical dilemma.
2. What should Wilson do if Leonard gives him a direct order to include the inventory?

1-27 Professional ethics and reporting division performance. Hannah Gilpin is the controller of Blakemore Auto Glass, a division of Eastern Glass and Window. Her division has been under pressure to improve its divisional operating income. Currently, divisions of Eastern Glass are allocated corporate overhead based on the cost of goods sold. Jake Myers, the president of the division, has asked Gilpin to reclassify $65,000 of packaging materials, which is included in the cost of goods sold, as production cost, which is not. Doing so will save the division $30,000 in allocated corporate overhead. The packing materials in question are needed to carry the finished goods to retail outlets. Gilpin does not see a reason for the reclassification of costs, other than to avoid overhead allocation costs.

Required

1. Describe Gilpin's ethical dilemma.
2. What should Gilpin do if Myers gives her a direct order to reclassify the costs?

Problems

1-28 Planning and control decisions, Internet company. PostNews.com offers its subscribers several services, such as an annotated TV guide and local-area information on weather, restaurants, and movie theaters. Its main revenue sources are fees for banner advertisements and fees from subscribers. Recent data are as follows:

Month/Year	Advertising Revenues	Actual Number of Subscribers	Monthly Fee per Subscriber
June 2015	$ 415,972	29,745	$15.50
December 2015	867,246	55,223	20.50
June 2016	892,134	59,641	20.50
December 2016	1,517,950	87,674	20.50
June 2017	2,976,538	147,921	20.50

The following decisions were made from June through October 2017:

a. June 2017: Raised subscription fee to $25.50 per month from July 2017 onward. The budgeted number of subscribers for this monthly fee is shown in the following table.
b. June 2017: Informed existing subscribers that from July onward, monthly fee would be $25.50.
c. July 2017: Offered e-mail service to subscribers and upgraded other online services.
d. October 2017: Dismissed the vice president of marketing after significant slowdown in subscribers and subscription revenues, based on July through September 2017 data in the following table.
e. October 2017: Reduced subscription fee to $22.50 per month from November 2017 onward.

Results for July–September 2017 are as follows:

Month/Year	Budgeted Number of Subscribers	Actual Number of Subscribers	Monthly Fee per Subscriber
July 2017	145,000	129,250	$25.50
August 2017	155,000	142,726	25.50
September 2017	165,000	145,643	25.50

Required

1. Classify each of the decisions (a–e) as a planning or a control decision.
2. Give two examples of other planning decisions and two examples of other control decisions that may be made at PostNews.com.

1-29 Strategic decisions and management accounting. Consider the following series of independent situations in which a firm is about to make a strategic decision.

Decisions

a. Stila Cosmetics is considering introducing an anti-aging facial cream with natural ingredients.
b. Kontron Computers is deliberating to produce a special type of microprocessor with an advanced technology which will bring down the cost of production.
c. Pelican Industries wants to install biometric system in its factory to reduce idle labor time and increase productivity.
d. Coral Health Solutions decides to introduce a unique telemedicine facility for its remote patients.

Required

1. For each decision, state whether the company is following a cost leadership or a product differentiation strategy.
2. For each decision, discuss what information the managerial accountant can provide about the source of competitive advantage for these firms.

1-30 Strategic decisions and management accounting. Consider the following series of independent situations in which a firm is about to make a strategic decision.

Decisions

a. Lactalis Foods is planning to come out with a special tetrazzini made with seafood, mushrooms, cream, and cocktail sauce.
b. Vanford Soap has started producing a new bar of soap, eyeing the low-cost segment of the soap market in which the company does not have much presence.
c. Diato Inc., a manufacturer of drill machines, is considering applying to a tender by quoting a very low price to supply 1,000 pieces of drill machines with standard features.
d. Smart Pixel is considering introducing a new tablet model that features a powerful processor with ample RAM to facilitate video calling, which is one of its unique features.

Required

1. For each decision, state whether the company is following a cost leadership or a product differentiation strategy.
2. For each decision, discuss what information the management accountant can provide about the source of competitive advantage for these firms.

1-31 Management accounting guidelines. For each of the following items, identify which of the management accounting guidelines applies: cost–benefit approach, behavioral and technical considerations, or different costs for different purposes.

1. Analyzing whether to keep the billing function within an organization or outsource it.
2. Deciding to give bonuses for superior performance to the employees in a Japanese subsidiary and extra vacation time to the employees in a Swedish subsidiary.
3. Including costs of all the value-chain functions before deciding to launch a new product, but including only its manufacturing costs in determining its inventory valuation.
4. Considering the desirability of hiring an additional salesperson.
5. Giving each salesperson the compensation option of choosing either a low salary and a high-percentage sales commission or a high salary and a low-percentage sales commission.
6. Selecting the costlier computer system after considering two systems.
7. Installing a participatory budgeting system in which managers set their own performance targets, instead of top management imposing performance targets on managers.
8. Recording research costs as an expense for financial reporting purposes (as required by U.S. GAAP) but capitalizing and expensing them over a longer period for management performance-evaluation purposes.
9. Introducing a profit-sharing plan for employees.

1-32 Management accounting guidelines. For each of the following items, identify which of the management accounting guidelines applies: cost–benefit approach, behavioral and technical considerations, or different costs for different purposes.

1. Analyzing whether to avail an export order for which overtime payments are required.
2. Deciding on a short-term shutdown of a factory because of the lack of demand for products due to the seasonal factor. The short-term shutdown may save some overhead costs, but will result in incurring compensations to the retrenched workers.
3. Considering whether to charge the heavy repairs made to the factory premises as an expense for financial reporting purposes or capitalizing and expensing them over a longer period for management performance-evaluation purposes.
4. Deciding to impose supervisory control to limit the wastage of materials.
5. Considering introducing a performance bonus scheme to increase the productivity of employees.
6. Analyzing whether to increase the production capacity to meet the growing demands for products.
7. Contemplating changing the production process to save production time resulting in increased production.

1-33 Role of controller, role of chief financial officer. George Jimenez is the controller at Balkin Electronics, a manufacturer of devices for the computer industry. The company may promote him to chief financial officer.

1. In this table, indicate which executive is *primarily* responsible for each activity.

Activity	Controller	CFO
Managing the company's long-term investments		
Presenting the financial statements to the board of directors		
Strategic review of different lines of businesses		
Budgeting funds for a plant upgrade		
Managing accounts receivable		
Negotiating fees with auditors		
Assessing profitability of various products		
Evaluating the costs and benefits of a new product design		

2. Based on this table and your understanding of the two roles, what types of training or experience will George find most useful for the CFO position?

1-34 Budgeting, ethics, pharmaceutical company. Chris Jackson was recently promoted to Controller of Research and Development (R&D) for BrisCor, a *Fortune* 500 pharmaceutical company that manufactures prescription drugs and nutritional supplements. The company's total R&D cost for 2017 was expected (budgeted) to be $5 billion. During the company's midyear budget review, Chris realized that current R&D expenditures were already at $3.5 billion, nearly 40% above the midyear target. At this current rate of expenditure, the R&D division was on track to exceed its total year-end budget by $2 billion!

In a meeting with CFO Ronald Meece later that day, Jackson delivered the bad news. Meece was both shocked and outraged that the R&D spending had gotten out of control. Meece wasn't any more understanding when Jackson revealed that the excess cost was entirely related to research and development of a new drug, Vyacon, which was expected to go to market next year. The new drug would result in large profits for BrisCor, if the product could be approved by year-end.

Meece had already announced his expectations of third-quarter earnings to Wall Street analysts. If the R&D expenditures weren't reduced by the end of the third quarter, Meece was certain that the targets he had announced publicly would be missed and the company's stock price would tumble. Meece instructed Jackson to make up the budget shortfall by the end of the third quarter using "whatever means necessary."

Jackson was new to the controller's position and wanted to make sure that Meece's orders were followed. Jackson came up with the following ideas for making the third-quarter budgeted targets:

a. Stop all research and development efforts on the drug Vyacon until after year-end. This change would delay the drug going to market by at least 6 months. It is possible that in the meantime a BrisCor competitor could make it to market with a similar drug.
b. Sell off rights to the drug Martek. The company had not planned on doing this because, under current market conditions, it would get less than fair value. It would, however, result in a one-time gain that could offset the budget shortfall. Of course, all future profits from Martek would be lost.
c. Capitalize some of the company's R&D expenditures, reducing R&D expense on the income statement. This transaction would not be in accordance with GAAP, but Jackson thought it was justifiable because the Vyacon drug was going to market early next year. Jackson would argue that capitalizing R&D costs this year and expensing them next year would better match revenues and expenses.

Required

1. Referring to the "Standards of Ethical Behavior for Practitioners of Management Accounting and Financial Management," Exhibit 1-7 (page 37), which of the preceding items (**a–c**) are acceptable to use? Which are unacceptable?
2. What would you recommend Jackson do?

1-35 Professional ethics and end-of-year actions. Phoenix Press produces consumer magazines. The house and home division, which sells home-improvement and home-decorating magazines, has seen a 15% reduction in operating income over the past 15 months, primarily due to an economic recession and a depressed consumer housing market. The division's Controller, Sophie Gellar, has been pressurized by the CFO to improve her division's operating results by the end of the year. Gellar is considering the following options for improving the division's performance by the end of the year:

a. Cancelling three of the division's least profitable magazines, resulting in the layoff of 30 employees.
b. Selling the new printing equipment that was purchased in February and replacing it with discarded equipment from one of the company's other divisions. The previously discarded equipment no longer meets current safety standards.
c. Recognizing unearned subscription revenue (cash received in advance for magazines that will be delivered in the future) as revenue when cash is received in the current month (just before the fiscal year-end), instead of depicting it as a liability.
d. Reducing liability and expenses related to employee pensions. This would increase the division's operating income by 5%.
e. Recognizing advertising revenues that relate to February in December.
f. Delaying maintenance on production equipment until January, although it was originally scheduled for October.

Required

1. What are the motivations for Gellar to improve the division's year-end operating earnings?
2. From the point of view of the "Standards of Ethical Behavior for Practitioners of Management Accounting and Financial Management," Exhibit 1-7 (page 37), which of the preceding items (**a–f**) are acceptable? Which of the aforementioned items are unacceptable?
3. How should Gellar handle the pressure to improve performance?

1-36 Professional ethics and end-of-year actions. Linda Butler is the new division controller of the snack-foods division of Daniel Foods. Daniel Foods has reported a minimum 15% growth in annual earnings for each of the past 5 years. The snack-foods division has reported annual earnings growth of more than 20% each year in this same period. During the current year, the economy went into a recession. The corporate controller estimates a 10% annual earnings growth rate for Daniel Foods this year. One month before the December 31 fiscal year-end of the current year, Butler estimates the snack-foods division will report an annual earnings growth of only 8%. Rex Ray, the snack-foods division president, is not happy, but he notes that the "end-of-year actions" still need to be taken.

Butler makes some inquiries and is able to compile the following list of end-of-year actions that were more or less accepted by the previous division controller:

a. Deferring December's routine monthly maintenance on packaging equipment by an independent contractor until January of next year.
b. Extending the close of the current fiscal year beyond December 31 so that some sales of next year are included in the current year.

c. Altering dates of shipping documents of next January's sales to record them as sales in December of the current year.
d. Giving salespeople a double bonus to exceed December sales targets.
e. Deferring the current period's advertising by reducing the number of television spots run in December and running more than planned in January of next year.
f. Deferring the current period's reported advertising costs by having Daniel Foods' outside advertising agency delay billing December advertisements until January of next year or by having the agency alter invoices to conceal the December date.
g. Persuading carriers to accept merchandise for shipment in December of the current year even though they normally would not have done so.

Required

1. Why might the snack-foods division president want to take these end-of-year actions?
2. Butler is deeply troubled and reads the "Standards of Ethical Behavior for Practitioners of Management Accounting and Financial Management" in Exhibit 1-7 (page 37). Classify each of the end-of-year actions (a–g) as acceptable or unacceptable according to that document.
3. What should Butler do if Ray suggests that these end-of-year actions are taken in every division of Daniel Foods and that she will greatly harm the snack-foods division if she does not cooperate and paint the rosiest picture possible of the division's results?

1-37 Ethical challenges, global company environmental concerns. Contemporary Interiors (CI) manufactures high-quality furniture in factories in North Carolina for sale to top American retailers. In 1995, CI purchased a lumber operation in Indonesia, and shifted from using American hardwoods to Indonesian ramin in its products. The ramin proved to be a cheaper alternative, and it was widely accepted by American consumers. CI management credits the early adoption of Indonesian wood for its ability to keep its North Carolina factories open when so many competitors closed their doors. Recently, however, consumers have become increasingly concerned about the sustainability of tropical woods, including ramin. CI has seen sales begin to fall, and the company was even singled out by an environmental group for boycott. It appears that a shift to more sustainable woods before year-end will be necessary, and more costly.

In response to the looming increase in material costs, CEO Geoff Armstrong calls a meeting of upper management. The group generates the following ideas to address customer concerns and/or salvage company profits for the current year:

a. Pay local officials in Indonesia to "certify" the ramin used by CI as sustainable. It is not certain whether the ramin would be sustainable or not. Put highly visible tags on each piece of furniture to inform consumers of the change.
b. Make deep cuts in pricing through the end of the year to generate additional revenue.
c. Record executive year-end bonus compensation accrued for the current year when it is paid in the next year after the December fiscal year-end.
d. Reject the change in materials. Counter the bad publicity with an aggressive ad campaign showing the consumer products as "made in the USA," since manufacturing takes place in North Carolina.
e. Redesign upholstered furniture to replace ramin contained inside with less expensive recycled plastic. The change in materials would not affect the appearance or durability of the furniture. The company would market the furniture as "sustainable."
f. Pressure current customers to take early delivery of goods before the end of the year so that more revenue can be reported in this year's financial statements.
g. Begin purchasing sustainable North American hardwoods and sell the Indonesian lumber subsidiary. Initiate a "plant a tree" marketing program, by which the company will plant a tree for every piece of furniture sold. Material costs would increase 25%, and prices would be passed along to customers.
h. Sell off production equipment prior to year-end. The sale would result in one-time gains that could offset the company's lagging profits. The owned equipment could be replaced with leased equipment at a lower cost in the current year.
i. Recognize sales revenues on orders received but not shipped as of the end of the year.

Required

1. As the management accountant for Contemporary Interiors, evaluate each of the preceding items (a–i) in the context of the "Standards of Ethical Behavior for Practitioners of Management Accounting and Financial Management," Exhibit 1-7 (page 37). Which of the items are in violation of these ethics standards and which are acceptable?
2. What should the management accountant do with regard to those items that are in violation of the ethical standards for management accountants?

2 An Introduction to Cost Terms and Purposes

LEARNING OBJECTIVES

1. Define and illustrate a cost object
2. Distinguish between direct costs and indirect costs
3. Explain variable costs and fixed costs
4. Interpret unit costs cautiously
5. Distinguish inventoriable costs from period costs
6. Illustrate the flow of inventoriable and period costs
7. Explain why product costs are computed in different ways for different purposes
8. Describe a framework for cost accounting and cost management

What does the word *cost* mean to you?

Is it the price you pay for something of value, like a cell phone? A cash outflow, like monthly rent? Something that affects profitability, like salaries? Organizations, like individuals, deal with different types of costs. They incur costs to generate revenues. Unfortunately, when times are bad and revenues decline, companies may find that they are unable to cut costs fast enough, leading to Chapter 11 bankruptcy. This was the case with surf wear company, Quiksilver.

HIGH FIXED COSTS BANKRUPT QUIKSILVER[1]

In 2015, surf wear company, Quiksilver, announced it had filed for Chapter 11 bankruptcy. Its high fixed costs—costs that did not decrease as the number of boardshorts and hoodies sold declined—crippled the company.

In the 1990s and early 2000s, Quiksilver rode the wave of young shoppers emulating the cool lifestyle and fashions of surfers, skateboarders, and snowboarders to financial success. During this time, the company opened hundreds of retail stores worldwide, many in expensive areas such as Times Square in New York. This expansion saddled the company with a huge amount of debt. In 2015, as sales rapidly declined, the company collapsed under the weight of its high fixed operating costs—like long-term leases and salaries—and crippling debt-servicing payments. After declaring bankruptcy, Quiksilver began rapidly selling off non-core brands and closing many retail stores.

As the story of Quiksilver illustrates, managers must understand their firms' costs and closely manage them. Organizations as varied as the United Way, the Mayo Clinic, and Sony generate reports containing a variety of cost concepts and terms managers need to understand to effectively run their businesses. This chapter discusses cost concepts and terms that are the basis of accounting information used for internal and external reporting.

Richard Naude/Alamy Stock Photo

---

[1] *Sources:* Andrew Khouri, "Wipeout: Quiksilver files for Chapter 11 bankruptcy in U.S.," *Los Angeles Times*, September 9, 2015 (http://www.latimes.com/business/la-fi-quiksilver-bankruptcy-20150909-story.html); Deborah Belgum, "Oaktree Capital Working on Buying Quiksilver," *California Apparel News*, November 3, 2015 (https://www.apparelnews.net/news/2015/nov/03/oaktree-capital-working-buying-quiksilver).

Costs and Cost Terminology

A **cost** is a resource sacrificed or forgone to achieve a specific objective. A cost (such as the cost of labor or advertising) is usually measured as the monetary amount that must be paid to acquire goods or services. An **actual cost** is the cost incurred (a historical or past cost), as distinguished from a **budgeted cost**, which is a predicted, or forecasted, cost (a future cost).

When you think of a cost, you invariably think of it in the context of putting a price on a particular thing. We call this "thing" a **cost object**, which is anything for which a cost measurement is desired. Suppose you're a manager at BMW's automotive manufacturing plant in Spartanburg, South Carolina. Can you identify some of the plant's cost objects? Now look at Exhibit 2-1.

You will see that BMW managers not only want to know the cost of various products, such as the BMW X6 sports activity vehicle, but they also want to know the costs of services, projects, activities, departments, and supporting customers. Managers use their knowledge of these costs to guide decisions about, for example, product innovation, quality, and customer service.

Now think about whether a manager at BMW might want to know the *budgeted cost* or the *actual cost* of a cost object. Managers almost always need to know both types of costs when making decisions. For example, comparing budgeted costs to actual costs helps managers evaluate how well they did controlling costs and learn about how they can do better in the future.

How does a cost system determine the costs of various cost objects? Typically in two stages: accumulation followed by assignment. **Cost accumulation** is the collection of cost data in some organized way by means of an accounting system. For example, at its Spartanburg plant, BMW collects (accumulates) in various categories the costs of different types of materials, different classifications of labor, the costs incurred for supervision, and so on. The accumulated costs are then *assigned* to designated cost objects, such as the different models of cars that BMW manufactures at the plant. BMW managers use this cost information in two main ways: (1) when *making* decisions, for instance, about how to price different models of cars or how much to invest in R&D and marketing and (2) for *implementing* decisions, by influencing and motivating employees to act, for example, by providing bonuses to employees for reducing costs.

Now that we know why it is useful for management accountants to assign costs, we turn our attention to some concepts that will help us do it. Again, think of the different types of costs that we just discussed—materials, labor, and supervision. You are probably thinking that some costs, such as the costs of materials, are easier to assign to a cost object than others, such as the costs of supervision. As you will learn, this is indeed the case.

Direct Costs and Indirect Costs

Cost are classified as direct and indirect costs. Management accountants use a variety of methods to assign these costs to cost objects.

- **Direct costs of a cost object** are related to the particular cost object and can be traced to it in an economically feasible (cost-effective) way. For example, the cost of steel or tires is a direct cost of BMW X6s. The cost of the steel or tires can be easily traced to or

> **LEARNING OBJECTIVE 1**
>
> Define and illustrate a cost object
>
> ...examples of cost objects are products, services, activities, processes, and customers

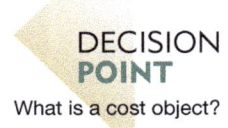

DECISION POINT

What is a cost object?

> **LEARNING OBJECTIVE 2**
>
> Distinguish between direct costs
>
> ...costs that are traced to the cost object
>
> and indirect costs
>
> ...costs that are allocated to the cost object

EXHIBIT 2-1 Examples of Cost Objects at BMW

Cost Object	Illustration
Product	A BMW X6 sports activity vehicle
Service	Telephone hotline providing information and assistance to BMW dealers
Project	R&D project on enhancing the navigation system in BMW cars
Customer	Herb Chambers Motors, the BMW dealer that purchases a broad range of BMW vehicles
Activity	Setting up machines for production or maintaining production equipment
Department	Environmental, health, and safety department

identified with the BMW X6. As workers on the BMW X6 line request materials from the warehouse, the material requisition document identifies the cost of the materials supplied to the X6. Similarly, individual workers record on their time sheets the hours and minutes they spend working on the X6. The cost of this labor can easily be traced to the X6 and is another example of a direct cost. The term **cost tracing** is used to describe the assignment of direct costs to a particular cost object.

- **Indirect costs of a cost object** are related to the particular cost object, but cannot be traced to it in an economically feasible (cost-effective) way. For example, the salaries of plant administrators (including the plant manager) who oversee production of the many different types of cars produced at the Spartanburg plant are an indirect cost of the X6s. Plant administration costs are related to the cost object (X6s) because plant administration is necessary for managing the production of these vehicles. Plant administration costs are indirect costs because plant administrators also oversee the production of other products, such as the Z4 Roadster. Unlike steel or tires, there is no specific request made by supervisors of the X6 production line for plant administration services, and it is virtually impossible to trace plant administration costs to the X6 line. The term **cost allocation** is used to describe the assignment of indirect costs to a particular cost object.

Cost assignment is a general term that encompasses both (1) tracing direct costs to a cost object and (2) allocating indirect costs to a cost object. Exhibit 2-2 depicts direct costs and indirect costs and both forms of cost assignment—cost tracing and cost allocation—using the BMW X6 as an example.

Cost Allocation Challenges

Managers want to assign costs accurately to cost objects because inaccurate product costs will mislead managers about the profitability of different products. This could result, for example, in managers unknowingly promoting less-profitable products instead of more-profitable products.

Managers are much more confident about the accuracy of the direct costs of cost objects, such as the cost of steel and tires of the X6, because these costs can be easily traced to the cost object. Indirect costs are a different story. Some indirect costs can be assigned to cost objects reasonably accurately. Others are more difficult.

Consider the cost to lease the Spartanburg plant. This cost is an indirect cost of the X6—there is no separate lease agreement for the area of the plant where the X6 is made. Nonetheless, BMW *allocates* to the X6 a part of the lease cost of the building—for example, on the basis of an estimate of the percentage of the building's floor space occupied for the production of the X6 relative to the total floor space used to produce all models of cars. This approach measures the building resources used by each car model reasonably and accurately. The more floor space a car model occupies, the greater the lease costs assigned to it. Accurately allocating other indirect costs, such as plant administration, to the X6, however, is more difficult. For example, should these costs be allocated on the basis

EXHIBIT 2-2

Cost Assignment to a Cost Object

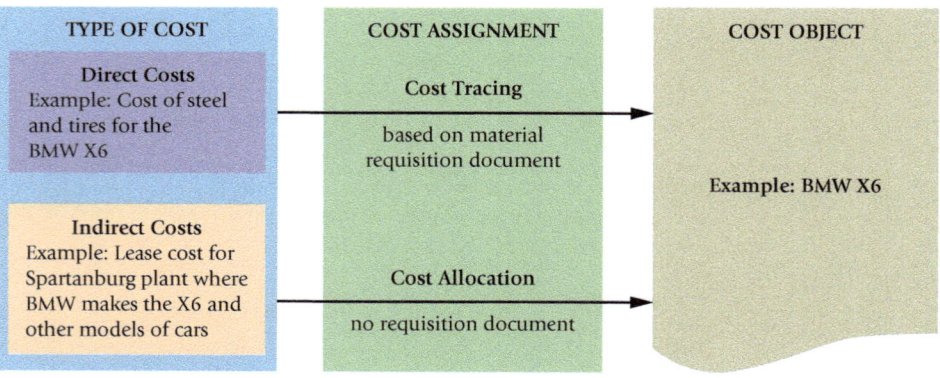

of the number of employees working on each car model or the number of cars produced of each model? Measuring the share of plant administration used by each car model is not clear-cut.

Factors Affecting Direct/Indirect Cost Classifications

Several factors affect whether a cost is classified as direct or indirect:

- **The materiality of the cost in question.** The smaller the amount of a cost—that is, the more immaterial the cost is—the less likely it is economically feasible to trace it to a particular cost object. Consider a mail-order catalog company such as Lands' End. It would be economically feasible to trace the courier charge for delivering a package to an individual customer as a direct cost. In contrast, the cost of the invoice paper included in the package would be classified as an indirect cost. Why? Although the cost of the paper can be traced to each customer, it is not cost-effective to do so. The benefits of knowing that, say, exactly 0.5¢ worth of paper is included in each package do not exceed the data processing and administrative costs of tracing the cost to each package. The time of the sales administrator, who earns a salary of $45,000 a year, is better spent organizing customer information to help with a company's marketing efforts than tracking the cost of paper.

- **Available information-gathering technology.** Improvements in information-gathering technology make it possible to consider more and more costs as direct costs. Bar codes, for example, allow manufacturing plants to treat certain low-cost materials such as clips and screws, which were previously classified as indirect costs, as direct costs of products. At Dell, component parts such as the computer chip and the DVD drive display a bar code that can be scanned at every point in the production process. Bar codes can be read into a manufacturing cost file by waving a "wand" in the same quick and efficient way supermarket checkout clerks enter the cost of each item purchased by a customer.

- **Design of operations.** Classifying a cost as direct is easier if a company's facility (or some part of it) is used exclusively for a specific cost object, such as a specific product or a particular customer. For example, General Chemicals classifies the cost of its facility dedicated to manufacturing soda ash (sodium carbonate) as a direct cost of soda ash.

Be aware that a specific cost may be both a direct cost of one cost object and an indirect cost of another cost object. *That is, the direct/indirect classification depends on the choice of the cost object.* For example, the salary of an assembly department supervisor at BMW is a direct cost if the cost object is the assembly department. However, because the assembly department assembles many different models, the supervisor's salary is an indirect cost if the cost object is a specific product such as the BMW X6 sports activity vehicle. A useful rule to remember is that the broader the cost object definition—the assembly department, rather than the X6—the higher the direct costs portion of total costs and the more confident a manager will be about the accuracy of the resulting cost amounts.

One final point. A company can incur a cost—sacrifice a resource—without the cost being recorded in the accounting system. For example, certain retirement health benefits are only recorded in the accounting system after an employee retires although the cost is incurred while the employee is actually providing the service. Environmental costs are another example. Many companies, for example General Electric, have had to incur significant costs at a later date to clean up the environmental damage that was caused by actions taken several years earlier. To force managers to consider these costs when making decisions, some companies such as Novartis, the Swiss pharmaceutical giant, are imputing a cost in their cost accounting system for every ton of greenhouse gases emitted to surrogate for future environmental costs. These costs can be a direct cost of a product if they can be traced to a specific product. More commonly, these costs are associated with operating a manufacturing facility and cannot be traced to a specific product. In this case, they are indirect costs.

DECISION POINT

How do managers decide whether a cost is a direct or an indirect cost?

Cost-Behavior Patterns: Variable Costs and Fixed Costs

LEARNING OBJECTIVE 3

Explain variable costs and fixed costs

...the two basic ways in which costs behave

Costing systems record the cost of resources acquired, such as materials, labor, and equipment, and track how those resources are used to produce and sell products or services. This allows managers to see how costs behave. Consider two basic types of cost-behavior patterns found in many accounting systems. A **variable cost** changes *in total* in proportion to changes in the related level of total activity or volume of output produced. A **fixed cost** remains unchanged *in total* for a given time period, despite wide changes in the related level of total activity or volume of output produced. Note that costs are defined as variable or fixed for *a specific activity* and for *a given time period*. Identifying a cost as variable or fixed provides valuable information for making many management decisions and is an important input when evaluating performance. To illustrate these two basic types of costs, again consider the costs at BMW's Spartanburg, South Carolina, plant.

1. **Variable costs.** If BMW buys a steering wheel at $600 for each of its BMW X6 vehicles, then the total cost of steering wheels is $600 times the number of vehicles produced, as the following table illustrates.

Number of X6s Produced (1)	Variable Cost per Steering Wheel (2)	Total Variable Cost of Steering Wheels (3) = (1) × (2)
1	$600	$ 600
1,000	600	600,000
3,000	600	1,800,000

The steering wheel cost is an example of a variable cost because *total cost* changes in proportion to changes in the number of vehicles produced. However, the *cost per unit* of a variable cost is constant. For example, the variable cost per steering wheel in column 2 is the same regardless of whether 1,000 or 3,000 X6s are produced. As a result, the total variable cost of steering wheels in column 3 changes proportionately with the number of X6s produced in column 1. So, when considering how variable costs behave, always focus on *total* costs.

Panel A in Exhibit 2-3 shows a graph of the total variable cost of steering wheels. The cost is represented by a straight line that climbs from left to right. The phrases "strictly variable" or "proportionately variable" are sometimes used to describe the variable cost behavior shown in this panel.

Now consider an example of a variable cost for a different activity—the $20 hourly wage paid each worker to set up machines at the Spartanburg plant. The setup labor cost is a variable cost for setup hours because setup cost changes in total in proportion to the number of setup hours used.

2. **Fixed costs.** Suppose BMW incurs a total cost of $2,000,000 per year for supervisors who work exclusively on the X6 line. These costs are unchanged in total over a designated range of vehicles produced during a given time span (see Exhibit 2-3, Panel B). Fixed costs become

EXHIBIT 2-3

Graphs of Variable and Fixed Costs

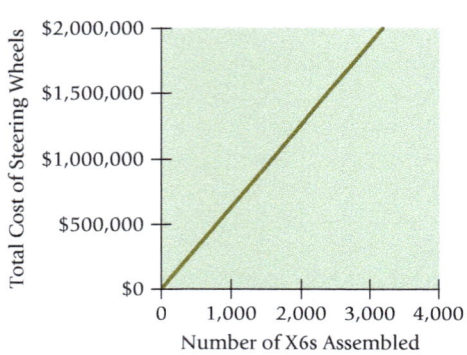

PANEL A: Variable Cost of Steering Wheels at $600 per BMW X6 Assembled

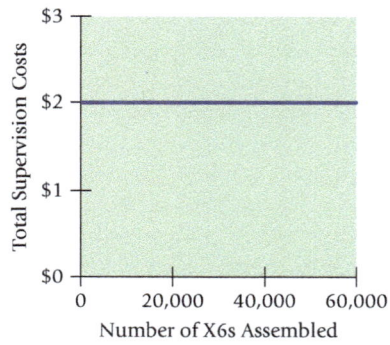

PANEL B: Supervision Costs for the BMW X6 assembly line (in millions)

smaller and smaller on a per-unit basis as the number of vehicles assembled increases, as the following table shows.

Annual Total Fixed Supervision Costs for BMW X6 Assembly Line (1)	Number of X6s Produced (2)	Fixed Supervision Cost per X6 (3) = (1) ÷ (2)
$2,000,000	10,000	$200
$2,000,000	25,000	$ 80
$2,000,000	50,000	$ 40

It is precisely because *total* line supervision costs are fixed at $2,000,000 that the fixed supervision cost per X6 decreases as the number of X6s produced increases; the same fixed cost is spread over a larger number of X6s. Do not be misled by the change in fixed cost per unit. Just as in the case of variable costs, when considering fixed costs, always focus on *total costs*. Costs are fixed when total costs remain unchanged despite significant changes in the level of total activity or volume.

Why are some costs variable and other costs fixed? Recall that a cost is usually measured as the amount of money that must be paid to acquire goods and services. The total cost of steering wheels is a variable cost because BMW buys the steering wheels only when they are needed. As more X6s are produced, proportionately more steering wheels are acquired and proportionately more costs are incurred.

Contrast the plant's variable costs with the $2,000,000 of fixed costs per year incurred for the supervision of the X6 assembly line. This level of supervision is acquired and put in place well before BMW uses it to produce X6s and before BMW even knows how many X6s it will produce. Suppose that BMW puts in place supervisors capable of supervising the production of 60,000 X6s each year. If the demand is for only 55,000 X6s, there will be idle capacity. Supervisors on the X6 line could have supervised the production of 60,000 X6s but will supervise only 55,000 X6s because of the lower demand. However, BMW must pay for the unused line supervision capacity because the cost of supervision cannot be reduced in the short run. If demand is even lower—say only 50,000 X6s are demanded—the plant's line supervision costs will still be $2,000,000, and its idle capacity will increase.

Unlike variable costs, fixed costs of resources (such as for line supervision) cannot be quickly and easily changed to match the resources needed or used. Over time, however, managers can take action to reduce a company's fixed costs. For example, if the X6 line needs to be run for fewer hours because the demand for the vehicles falls, BMW may lay off supervisors or move them to another production line. Unlike variable costs that go away automatically if the resources are not used, reducing fixed costs requires active intervention on the part of managers.

Do not assume that individual cost items are inherently variable or fixed. Consider labor costs. Labor costs can be purely variable for units produced when workers are paid on a piece-unit basis (for each unit they make). For example, some companies pay garment workers on a per-shirt-sewed basis, so the firms' labor costs are variable. That is, total costs depend on how many shirts workers make. In contrast, other companies negotiate labor union agreements with set annual salaries that contain no-layoff clauses for workers. At a company such as this, the salaries would appropriately be classified as fixed. For decades, Japanese companies provided their workers a lifetime guarantee of employment. Although such a guarantee entails higher fixed labor costs, a firm can benefit because workers are more loyal and dedicated, which can improve productivity. However, during an economic downturn, the company risks losing money if revenues decrease while fixed costs remain unchanged. The recent global economic crisis has made companies very reluctant to lock in fixed costs. Concepts in Action: Zipcar Helps Twitter Reduce Fixed Costs describes how a car-sharing service offers companies the opportunity to convert the fixed costs of owning corporate cars into variable costs by renting cars on an as-needed basis.

A particular cost item could be variable for one level of activity and fixed for another. Consider annual registration and license costs for a fleet of planes owned by an airline company. Registration and license costs would be a variable cost that would change with the

CONCEPTS IN ACTION ▸ Zipcar Helps Twitter Reduce Fixed Costs

Mike Kahn/Green Stock Media/Alamy Stock Photo

In many cities worldwide, car sharing is an effective way for companies to reduce spending on gas, insurance, and parking of corporate cars. Zipcar—a car sharing company that provides an "on-demand" option for urban individuals and businesses to rent a car by the week, the day, or even the hour—has rates beginning around $7 per hour and $79 per day (including gas, insurance, and about 180 miles per day).

Let's think about what Zipcar means for companies. Many businesses own company cars for getting to meetings, picking up clients, making deliveries, and running errands. Traditionally, owning these cars has involved high fixed costs, including buying the asset (car), maintenance costs, and insurance for multiple drivers.

Now, however, companies like Twitter, based in downtown San Francisco, can use Zipcar for on-demand mobility while reducing their transportation and overhead costs. From a business perspective, Zipcar allows Twitter and other companies to convert the fixed costs of owning a company car to variable costs. If business slows or a car isn't required to visit a client, Twitter is not saddled with the fixed costs of car ownership. Of course, when business is good, causing Twitter managers to use Zipcar more often, they can end up paying more overall then they would have paid if they purchased and maintained the car themselves. It is also convenient. "We ... avoid the cost of taking taxis everywhere or the time delays of mass transit," said Jack Dorsey, the online social networking service's co-founder. "Zipcar's the fastest, easiest way to get around town."

Along with cutting company spending, car sharing services like Zipcar contribute to environmental sustainability. In 2015, research found that Zipcar's business program eliminated the need for roughly 33,000 cars across North America. Kaye Ceille, the company's president said, "Businesses are increasingly conscious of their environmental footprint, and we're proud that ... Zipcar for business has many significant environmental benefits for companies, including reducing vehicles on the road."

Sources: Elizabeth Olsen, "Car Sharing Reinvents the Company Wheels," *New York Times*, May 7, 2009 (http://www.nytimes.com/2009/05/07/business/businessspecial/07CAR.html); Zipcar, Inc., "Case Studies: Twitter" (http://www.zipcar.com/business/is-it/case-studies); Zipcar, Inc., "San Francisco Bay Area Rates & Plans (http://www.zipcar.com/sf/check-rates); "New Research Finds Business Use of Zipcar Reduces Personal Car Ownership," Zipcar, Inc. press release, Boston, MA, July, 27, 2015 (http://www.zipcar.com/press/releases/z4breducescarownership).

DECISION POINT

How do managers decide whether a cost is a variable or a fixed cost?

number of planes the company owned. But the registration and license costs for a particular plane are fixed regardless of the miles flown by that plane during a year.

Some costs have both fixed and variable elements and are called *mixed* or *semivariable* costs. For example, a company's telephone costs may consist of a fixed monthly cost as well as a cost per phone-minute used. We discuss mixed costs and techniques to separate out their fixed and variable components in Chapter 10.

TRY IT! 2-1 Pepsi Corporation uses trucks to transport bottles from the warehouse to different retail outlets. Gasoline costs are $0.15 per mile driven. Insurance costs are $6,000 per year. Calculate the total costs and the cost per mile for gasoline and insurance if the truck is driven (a) 20,000 miles per year or (b) 30,000 miles per year.

Cost Drivers

A **cost driver** is a variable, such as the level of activity or volume, that causally affects costs over a given time span. An *activity* is an event, task, or unit of work with a specified purpose—for example, designing products, setting up machines, or testing products. The level of activity or volume is a cost driver if there is a cause-and-effect relationship between a change in the level of activity or volume and a change in the level of total costs. For example, if product-design costs change with the number of parts in a product, the number of parts is a cost driver of product-design costs. Similarly, the miles driven by trucks to deliver products are a cost driver of distribution costs.

The cost driver of a variable cost is the level of activity or volume whose change causes proportionate changes in the variable cost. For example, the number of vehicles assembled is the cost driver of the total cost of steering wheels. If setup workers are paid an hourly wage, the number of setup hours is the cost driver of total (variable) setup costs.

Costs that are fixed in the short run have no cost driver in the short run but may have a cost driver in the long run. Consider the costs of testing, say, 0.1% of the color printers produced at a Hewlett-Packard plant. These costs consist of equipment and staff costs of the testing department, which are difficult to change. Consequently, they are fixed in the short run regardless of changes in the volume of production. In this case, volume of production is not a cost driver of testing costs in the short run. In the long run, however, Hewlett-Packard will increase or decrease the testing department's equipment and staff to the levels needed to support future production volumes. In the long run, volume of production is a cost driver of testing costs. Costing systems that identify the cost of each activity such as testing, design, or setup are called *activity-based costing systems*.

Relevant Range

Relevant range is the band or range of normal activity level or volume in which there is a specific relationship between the level of activity or volume and the cost in question. For example, a fixed cost is fixed only in relation to a given wide range of total activity or volume (at which the company is expected to operate) and only for a given time span (usually a particular budget period). Suppose BMW contracts with Thomas Transport Company (TTC) to transport X6s to BMW dealerships. TTC rents two trucks, and each truck has an annual fixed rental cost of $40,000. The maximum annual usage of each truck is 120,000 miles. In the current year (2017), the predicted combined total hauling of the two trucks is 170,000 miles.

Exhibit 2-4 shows how annual fixed costs behave at different levels of miles of hauling. Up to 120,000 miles, TTC can operate with one truck; from 120,001 to 240,000 miles, it operates with two trucks; and from 240,001 to 360,000 miles, it operates with three trucks. This pattern will continue as TTC adds trucks to its fleet to provide more miles of hauling. Given the predicted 170,000-mile usage for 2017, the range from 120,001 to 240,000 miles hauled is the range in which TTC expects to operate, resulting in fixed rental costs of $80,000. Within this relevant range, changes in miles hauled will not affect the annual fixed costs.

Fixed costs may change from one year to the next, though. For example, if the total rental fee of the two trucks increases by $2,000 for 2018, the total level of fixed costs will increase to $82,000 (all else remaining the same). If that increase occurs, total rental costs will be fixed at this new level ($82,000) for 2018 for the miles hauled in the 120,001 to 240,000 range.

The relevant range also applies to variable costs. Outside the relevant range, variable costs, such as direct materials costs, may no longer change proportionately with changes in production volumes. For example, above a certain volume, the cost of direct materials may

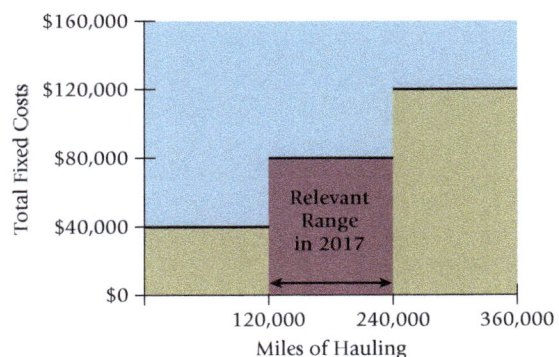

EXHIBIT 2-4

Fixed-Cost Behavior at Thomas Transport Company

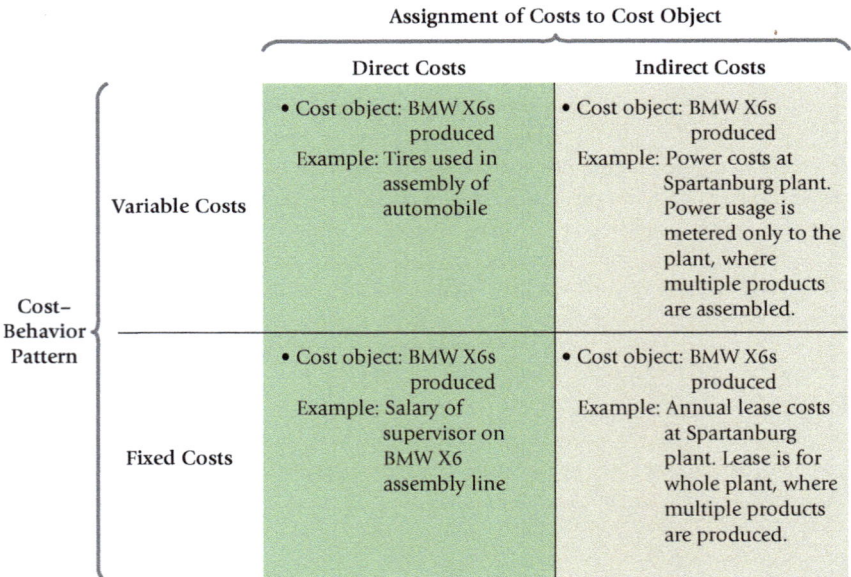

EXHIBIT 2-5

Examples of Costs in Combinations of the Direct/Indirect and Variable/Fixed Cost Classifications for a Car Manufacturer

increase at a lower rate because a firm may be able to negotiate price discounts for purchasing greater amounts of materials from its suppliers.

Relationships Between Types of Costs

We have introduced two major classifications of costs: direct/indirect and variable/fixed. Costs may simultaneously be as follows:

- Direct and variable
- Direct and fixed
- Indirect and variable
- Indirect and fixed

Exhibit 2-5 shows examples of costs in each of these four cost classifications for the BMW X6.

Total Costs and Unit Costs

LEARNING OBJECTIVE 4

Interpret unit costs cautiously

...for many decisions, managers should use total costs, not unit costs

The preceding section concentrated on the behavior patterns of total costs in relation to activity or volume levels. But what about unit costs?

Unit Costs

A **unit cost**, also called an **average cost**, is calculated by dividing the total cost by the related number of units produced. In many decision contexts, calculating a unit cost is essential. Consider the booking agent who has to make the decision to book Paul McCartney to play at Shea Stadium. She estimates the cost of the event to be $4,000,000. This knowledge is helpful for the decision, but it is not enough.

Before reaching a decision, the booking agent also must predict the number of people who will attend. Without knowing the number of attendees, she cannot make an informed decision about the admission price she needs to charge to recover the cost of the event or even on whether to have the event at all. So she computes the unit cost of the event by dividing the total cost ($4,000,000) by the expected number of people who will attend. If 50,000 people attend, the unit cost is $80 (4,000,000 ÷ 50,000) per person; if 20,000 attend, the unit cost increases to $200 ($4,000,000 ÷ 20,000). Unless the total cost is "unitized" (that is, averaged by the level of activity or volume), the $4,000,000 cost is difficult to use to make decisions. The unit cost combines the total cost and the number of people in a simple and understandable way.

Accounting systems typically report both total-cost amounts and average-cost-per-unit amounts. The units might be expressed in various ways. Examples are automobiles assembled, packages delivered, or hours worked. Consider Tennessee Products, a manufacturer of speaker systems with a plant in Memphis. Suppose that, in 2017, its first year of operations, the company incurs $40,000,000 of manufacturing costs to produce 500,000 speaker systems. Then the unit cost is $80:

$$\frac{\text{Total manufacturing costs}}{\text{Number of units manufactured}} = \frac{\$40,000,000}{500,000 \text{ units}} = \$80 \text{ per unit}$$

If 480,000 units are sold and 20,000 units remain in ending inventory, the unit-cost concept helps managers determine total costs in the income statement and balance sheet and, therefore, the financial results Tennessee Products reports to shareholders, banks, and the government.

Cost of goods sold in the income statement, 480,000 units × $80 per unit	$38,400,000
Ending inventory in the balance sheet, 20,000 units × $80 per unit	1,600,000
Total manufacturing costs of 500,000 units	$40,000,000

Unit costs are found in all areas of the value chain—for example, the unit cost of a product design, a sales visit, and a customer-service call. By summing unit costs throughout the value chain, managers calculate the unit cost of the different products or services they deliver and determine the profitability of each product or service. Managers use this information, for example, to decide the products in which they should invest more resources, such as R&D and marketing, and the prices they should charge.

Use Unit Costs Cautiously

Although unit costs are regularly used in financial reports and for making product mix and pricing decisions, *managers should think in terms of total costs rather than unit costs for many decisions*. Consider the manager of the Memphis plant of Tennessee Products. Assume the $40,000,000 in costs in 2017 consist of $10,000,000 of fixed costs and $30,000,000 of variable costs (at $60 variable cost per speaker system produced). Suppose the total fixed costs and the variable cost per speaker system in 2018 are expected to be unchanged from 2017. The budgeted costs for 2018 at different production levels, calculated on the basis of total variable costs, total fixed costs, and total costs, are:

Units Produced (1)	Variable Cost per Unit (2)	Total Variable Costs (3) = (1) × (2)	Total Fixed Costs (4)	Total Costs (5) = (3) + (4)	Unit Cost (6) = (5) ÷ (1)
100,000	$60	$ 6,000,000	$10,000,000	$16,000,000	$160.00
200,000	$60	$12,000,000	$10,000,000	$22,000,000	$110.00
500,000	$60	$30,000,000	$10,000,000	$40,000,000	$ 80.00
800,000	$60	$48,000,000	$10,000,000	$58,000,000	$ 72.50
1,000,000	$60	$60,000,000	$10,000,000	$70,000,000	$ 70.00

A plant manager who uses the 2017 unit cost of $80 per unit will underestimate actual total costs if the plant's 2018 output is below the 2017 level of 500,000 units. If the volume produced falls to 200,000 units due to, say, the presence of a new competitor and less demand, actual costs would be $22,000,000. The unit cost of $80 times 200,000 units equals $16,000,000, which underestimates the actual total costs by $6,000,000 ($22,000,000 − $16,000,000). In other words, *the unit cost of $80 applies only when the company produces 500,000 units*.

DECISION POINT

How should managers estimate and interpret cost information?

An overreliance on the unit cost in this situation could lead to insufficient cash being available to pay the company's costs if volume declines to 200,000 units. As the table indicates, for making this decision, managers should think in terms of total variable costs, total fixed costs, and total costs rather than unit cost. As a general rule, first calculate total costs, then compute the unit cost, if it is needed for a particular decision.

Business Sectors, Types of Inventory, Inventoriable Costs, and Period Costs

> **LEARNING OBJECTIVE 5**
>
> Distinguish inventoriable costs
>
> ...assets when incurred, then cost of goods sold
>
> from period costs
>
> ...expenses of the period when incurred

In this section, we describe the different sectors of the economy, the different types of inventory that companies hold, and how these factors affect commonly used classifications of inventoriable and period costs.

Manufacturing-, Merchandising-, and Service-Sector Companies

We define three sectors of the economy and provide examples of companies in each sector.

1. **Manufacturing-sector companies** purchase materials and components and convert them into various finished goods. Examples are automotive companies such as Jaguar, cellular-phone producers such as Samsung, food-processing companies such as Heinz, and computer companies such as Lenovo.

2. **Merchandising-sector companies** purchase and then sell tangible products without changing their basic form. This sector includes companies engaged in retailing (for example, bookstores such as Barnes & Noble and department stores such as Target); distribution (for example, a supplier of hospital products, such as Owens and Minor); or wholesaling (for example, a supplier of electronic components such as Arrow Electronics).

3. **Service-sector companies** provide services (intangible products)—for example, legal advice or audits—to their customers. Examples are law firms such as Wachtell, Lipton, Rosen & Katz; accounting firms such as Ernst & Young; banks such as Barclays; mutual fund companies such as Fidelity; insurance companies such as Aetna; transportation companies such as Singapore Airlines; advertising agencies such as Saatchi & Saatchi; television stations such as Turner Broadcasting; Internet service providers such as Comcast; travel agencies such as American Express; and brokerage firms such as Merrill Lynch.

Types of Inventory

Manufacturing-sector companies purchase materials and components and convert them into finished goods. These companies typically have one or more of the following three types of inventory:

1. **Direct materials inventory.** Direct materials in stock that will be used in the manufacturing process (for example, computer chips and components needed to manufacture cellular phones).

2. **Work-in-process inventory.** Goods partially worked on but not yet completed (for example, cellular phones at various stages of completion in the manufacturing process). This is also called **work in progress**.

3. **Finished-goods inventory.** Goods (for example, cellular phones) completed, but not yet sold.

Merchandising-sector companies purchase tangible products and then sell them without changing their basic form. These companies hold only one type of inventory, which is products in their original purchased form, called *merchandise inventory*. Service-sector companies provide only services or intangible products and do not hold inventories of tangible products.

Commonly Used Classifications of Manufacturing Costs

Three terms commonly used when describing manufacturing costs are *direct materials costs*, *direct manufacturing labor costs*, and *indirect manufacturing costs*. These terms build on the direct versus indirect cost distinction we described earlier in the context of manufacturing costs.

1. **Direct materials costs** are the acquisition costs of all materials that eventually become part of the cost object (work in process and then finished goods) and can be traced to the cost object in an economically feasible way. The steel and tires used to make the BMW X6 and the computer chips used to make cellular phones are examples of direct material costs. Note that the costs of direct materials include not only the cost of the materials themselves, but the freight-in (inward delivery) charges, sales taxes, and customs duties that must be paid to acquire them.
2. **Direct manufacturing labor costs** include the compensation of all manufacturing labor that can be traced to the cost object (work in process and then finished goods) in an economically feasible way. Examples include wages and fringe benefits paid to machine operators and assembly-line workers who convert direct materials to finished goods.
3. **Indirect manufacturing costs** are all manufacturing costs that are related to the cost object (work in process and then finished goods), but cannot be traced to that cost object in an economically feasible way. Examples include supplies, indirect materials such as lubricants, indirect manufacturing labor such as plant maintenance and cleaning labor, plant rent, plant insurance, property taxes on the plant, plant depreciation, and the compensation of plant managers. This cost category is also referred to as **manufacturing overhead costs** or **factory overhead costs**. We use *indirect manufacturing costs* and *manufacturing overhead costs* interchangeably in this book.

We now describe the distinction between inventoriable costs and period costs.

Inventoriable Costs

Inventoriable costs are all costs of a product that are considered assets in a company's balance sheet when the costs are incurred and that are expensed as cost of goods sold only when the product is sold. For manufacturing-sector companies, all manufacturing costs are inventoriable costs. The costs first accumulate as work-in-process inventory assets (in other words, they are "inventoried") and then as finished goods inventory assets. Consider Cellular Products, a manufacturer of cellular phones. The cost of the company's direct materials, such as computer chips, direct manufacturing labor costs, and manufacturing overhead costs create new assets. They start out as work-in-process inventory and become finished-goods inventory (the cellular phones). When the cellular phones are sold, the costs move from being assets to cost of goods sold expense. This cost is matched against **revenues**, which are inflows of assets (usually cash or accounts receivable) received for products or services customers purchase.

Note that the cost of goods sold includes all manufacturing costs (direct materials, direct manufacturing labor, and manufacturing overhead costs) incurred to produce them. The cellular phones may be sold during a different accounting period than the period in which they were manufactured. Thus, inventorying manufacturing costs in the balance sheet during the accounting period when the phones are manufactured and expensing the manufacturing costs in a later income statement when the phones are sold matches revenues and expenses.

For merchandising-sector companies such as Walmart, inventoriable costs are the costs of purchasing goods that are resold in their same form. These costs are made up of the costs of the goods themselves plus any incoming freight, insurance, and handling costs for those goods. Service-sector companies provide only services or intangible products. The absence of inventories of tangible products for sale means service-sector companies have no inventoriable costs.

Period Costs

Period costs are all costs in the income statement other than cost of goods sold. Period costs, such as design costs, marketing, distribution, and customer service costs, are treated as expenses of the accounting period in which they are incurred because managers expect these

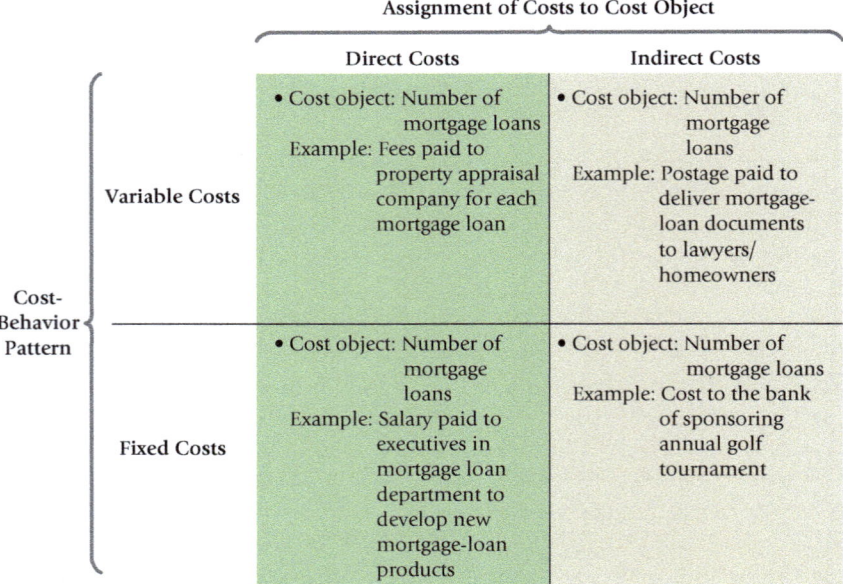

EXHIBIT 2-6

Examples of Period Costs in Combinations of the Direct/Indirect and Variable/Fixed Cost Classifications at a Bank

costs to increase revenues in only that period and not in future periods. For manufacturing-sector companies, all nonmanufacturing costs in the income statement are period costs. For merchandising-sector companies, all costs in the income statement not related to the cost of goods purchased for resale are period costs. Examples of these period costs are labor costs of sales-floor personnel and advertising costs. Because there are no inventoriable costs for service-sector companies, all costs in the income statement are period costs.

An interesting question pertains to the treatment of R & D expenses as period costs.[2] As we saw in Chapter 1, for many companies in industries ranging from machine tools to consumer electronics to telecommunications to pharmaceuticals and biotechnology, innovation is increasingly becoming a key driver of success. The benefits of these innovations and R & D investments will, in most cases, only impact revenues in some future periods. So should R&D expenses still be considered period costs and be matched against revenues of the current period? Yes, because it is highly uncertain whether these innovations will be successful and result in future revenues. Even if the innovations are successful, it is very difficult to determine which future period the innovations will benefit. Some managers believe that treating R & D expenses as period costs dampens innovation because it reduces current period income.

Exhibit 2-5 showed examples of inventoriable costs in direct/indirect and variable/fixed cost classifications for a car manufacturer. Exhibit 2-6 shows examples of period costs in direct/indirect and variable/fixed cost classifications at a bank.

DECISION POINT

What are the differences in the accounting for inventoriable versus period costs?

Illustrating the Flow of Inventoriable Costs and Period Costs

LEARNING OBJECTIVE 6

Illustrate the flow of inventoriable and period costs

...in manufacturing settings, inventoriable costs flow through work-in-process and finished-goods accounts and are expensed when goods are sold; period costs are expensed as incurred

We illustrate the flow of inventoriable costs and period costs through the income statement of a manufacturing company, where the distinction between inventoriable costs and period costs is most detailed.

Manufacturing-Sector Example

Follow the flow of costs for Cellular Products in Exhibits 2-7 and 2-8. Exhibit 2-7 visually highlights the differences in the flow of inventoriable and period costs for a manufacturing-sector company. Note how, as described in the previous section, inventoriable costs go through

---

[2] Under Generally Accepted Accounting Principles (GAAP) in the U.S., all R & D costs are expensed for financial accounting. International Financial Reporting Standards (IFRS) permit the capitalization of some development costs for financial accounting.

EXHIBIT 2-7 Flow of Revenue and Costs for a Manufacturing-Sector Company, Cellular Products (in thousands)

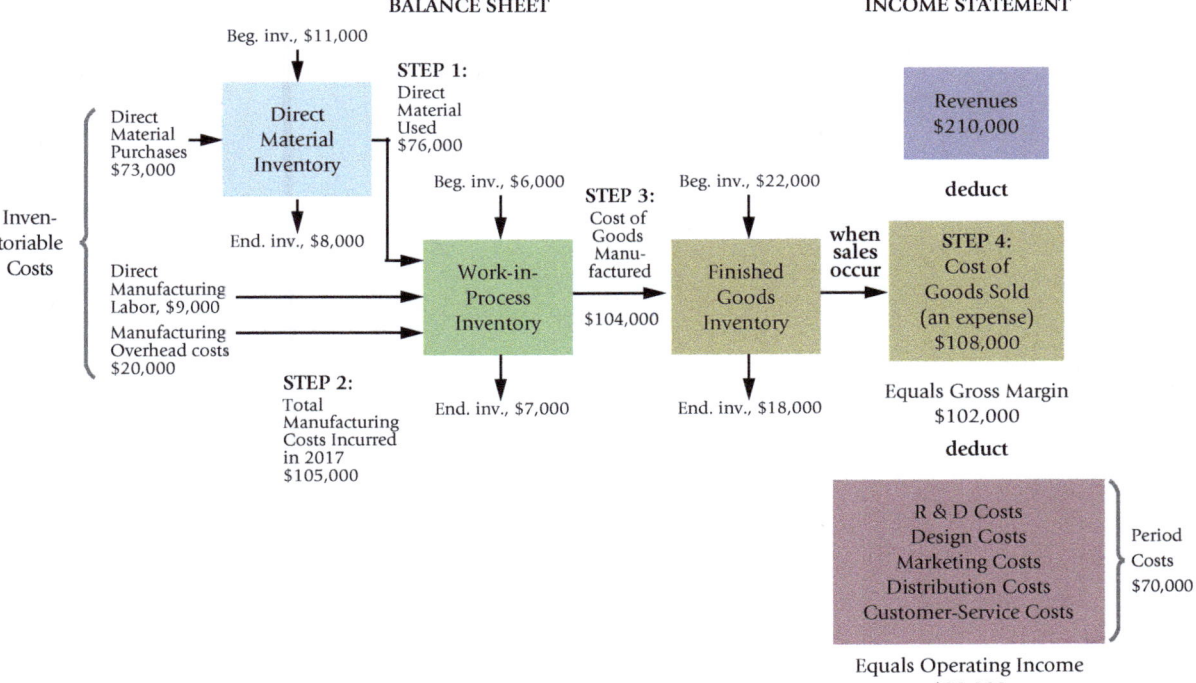

the balance sheet accounts of work-in-process inventory and finished-goods inventory before entering the cost of goods sold in the income statement. Period costs are expensed directly in the income statement. Exhibit 2-8 takes the visual presentation in Exhibit 2-7 and shows how inventoriable costs and period expenses would appear in the income statement and schedule of cost of goods manufactured of a manufacturing company.

We start by tracking the flow of direct materials shown on the left in Exhibit 2-7 and in Panel B in Exhibit 2-8. To keep things simple, all numbers are expressed in thousands, except for the per unit amounts.

Step 1: Cost of direct materials used in 2017. Note how the arrows in Exhibit 2-7 for beginning inventory, $11,000, and direct material purchases, $73,000, "fill up" the direct materials inventory box and how direct materials used, $76,000, "empties out" direct material inventory, leaving an ending inventory of direct materials of $8,000 that becomes the beginning inventory for the next year.

The cost of direct materials used is calculated in Exhibit 2-8, Panel B (light blue–shaded area), as follows:

Beginning inventory of direct materials, January 1, 2017	$11,000
+ Purchases of direct materials in 2017	73,000
− Ending inventory of direct materials, December 31, 2017	8,000
= Direct materials used in 2017	$76,000

Step 2: Total manufacturing costs incurred in 2017. Total manufacturing costs refers to all direct manufacturing costs and manufacturing overhead costs incurred during 2017 for all goods worked on during the year. Cellular Products classifies its manufacturing costs into the three categories described earlier.

(i) Direct materials used in 2017 (shaded light blue in Exhibit 2-8, Panel B)	$ 76,000
(ii) Direct manufacturing labor in 2017 (shaded blue in Exhibit 2-8, Panel B)	9,000
(iii) Manufacturing overhead costs in 2017 (shaded dark blue in Exhibit 2-8, Panel B)	20,000
Total manufacturing costs incurred in 2017	$105,000

Note how in Exhibit 2-7 these costs increase work-in-process inventory.

EXHIBIT 2-8 Income Statement and Schedule of Cost of Goods Manufactured of a Manufacturing-Sector Company, Cellular Products

PANEL A: INCOME STATEMENT

Cellular Products
Income Statement
For the Year Ended December 31, 2017 (in thousands)

	B	C
Revenues		$210,000
Cost of goods sold:		
Beginning finished goods inventory, January 1, 2017	$ 22,000	
Cost of goods manufactured (see Panel B)	104,000	
Cost of goods available for sale	126,000	
Ending finished goods inventory, December 31, 2017	18,000	
Cost of goods sold		108,000
Gross margin (or gross profit)		102,000
Operating (period) costs:		
R&D, design, mktg., dist., and cust.-service cost	70,000	
Total operating costs		70,000
Operating income		$ 32,000

Steps 4 brackets rows: Beginning finished goods inventory through Cost of goods sold.

PANEL B: COST OF GOODS MANUFACTURED

Cellular Products
Schedule of Cost of Goods Manufactured[a]
For the Year Ended December 31, 2017 (in thousands)

	B	C
Direct materials:		
Beginning inventory, January 1, 2017	$ 11,000	
Purchases of direct materials	73,000	
Cost of direct materials available for use	84,000	
Ending inventory, December 31, 2017	8,000	
Direct materials used		$ 76,000
Direct manufacturing labor		9,000
Manufacturing overhead costs:		
Indirect manufacturing labor	$ 7,000	
Supplies	2,000	
Heat, light, and power	5,000	
Depreciation—plant building	2,000	
Depreciation—plant equipment	3,000	
Miscellaneous	1,000	
Total manufacturing overhead costs		20,000
Manufacturing costs incurred during 2017		105,000
Beginning work-in-process inventory, January 1, 2017		6,000
Total manufacturing costs to account for		111,000
Ending work-in-process inventory, December 31, 2017		7,000
Cost of goods manufactured (to income statement)		$104,000

[a] Note that this schedule can become a schedule of cost of goods manufactured and sold simply by including the beginning and ending finished goods inventory figures in the supporting schedule rather than in the body of the income statement.

> Diana Corporation provides the following information for 2017:
>
> | | |
> |---|---|
> | Beginning inventory of direct materials, 1/1/2017 | $12,000 |
> | Purchases of direct materials in 2017 | $85,000 |
> | Ending inventory of direct materials 12/31/2017 | $ 7,000 |
> | Direct manufacturing labor costs in 2017 | $30,000 |
> | Manufacturing overhead costs in 2017 | $40,000 |
>
> Calculate the total manufacturing costs incurred in 2017

Step 3: Cost of goods manufactured in 2017. **Cost of goods manufactured** refers to the cost of goods brought to completion, whether they were started before or during the current accounting period.

Note how the work-in-process inventory box in Exhibit 2-7 has a very similar structure to the direct materials inventory box described in Step 1. Beginning work-in-process inventory of $6,000 and total manufacturing costs incurred in 2017 of $105,000 "fill up" the work-in-process inventory box. Some of the manufacturing costs incurred during 2017 are held back as the cost of the ending work-in-process inventory. The ending work-in-process inventory of $7,000 becomes the beginning inventory for the next year, and the $104,000 cost of goods manufactured during 2017 "empties out" the work-in-process inventory while "filling up" the finished-goods inventory box.

The cost of goods manufactured in 2017 (shaded green) is calculated in Exhibit 2-8, Panel B, as follows:

Beginning work-in-process inventory, January 1, 2017	$ 6,000
+ Total manufacturing costs incurred in 2017	105,000
= Total manufacturing costs to account for	111,000
− Ending work-in-process inventory, December 31, 2017	7,000
= Cost of goods manufactured in 2017	$104,000

Step 4: Cost of goods sold in 2017. The cost of goods sold is the cost of finished-goods inventory sold to customers during the current accounting period. Looking at the finished-goods inventory box in Exhibit 2-7, we see that the beginning inventory of finished goods of $22,000 and cost of goods manufactured in 2017 of $104,000 "fill up" the finished-goods inventory box. The ending inventory of finished goods of $18,000 becomes the beginning inventory for the next year, and the $108,000 cost of goods sold during 2017 "empties out" the finished-goods inventory.

This cost of goods sold is an expense that is matched against revenues. The cost of goods sold for Cellular Products (shaded olive green) is computed in Exhibit 2-8, Panel A, as follows:

Beginning inventory of finished goods, January 1, 2017	$ 22,000
+ Cost of goods manufactured in 2017	104,000
− Ending inventory of finished goods, December 31, 2017	18,000
= Cost of goods sold in 2017	$108,000

Exhibit 2-9 shows related general ledger T-accounts for Cellular Products' manufacturing cost flow. Note how the cost of goods manufactured ($104,000) is the cost of all goods completed during the accounting period. These costs are all inventoriable costs. Goods completed during the period are transferred to finished-goods inventory. These costs become cost of goods sold in the accounting period when the goods are sold. Also note that the direct materials, direct manufacturing labor, and manufacturing overhead costs of the units in work-in-process inventory ($7,000) and finished-goods inventory ($18,000) as of December 31, 2017, will appear as an asset in the balance sheet. These costs will become expenses next year when the work-in-process inventory is converted to finished goods and the finished goods are sold.

EXHIBIT 2-9 General Ledger T-Accounts for Cellular Products' Manufacturing Cost Flow (in thousands)

Work-in-Process Inventory				Finished Goods Inventory				Cost of Goods Sold
Bal. Jan. 1, 2017	6,000	Cost of goods manufactured	104,000 →	Bal. Jan. 1, 2017	22,000	Cost of goods sold	108,000 →	→ 108,000
Direct materials used	76,000				→ 104,000			
Direct manuf. labor	9,000			Bal. Dec. 31, 2017	18,000			
Indirect manuf. costs	20,000							
Bal. Dec. 31, 2017	7,000							

TRY IT! 2-3

Diana Corporation provides the following information for 2017:

Beginning work-in-process inventory, 1/1/2017	$ 9,000
Total manufacturing costs incurred in 2017	$160,000
Ending work-in-process inventory, 12/31/2017	$ 8,000
Beginning inventory of finished goods, 1/1/2017	$ 15,000
Ending inventory of finished goods, 12/31/2017	$ 21,000

Calculate (a) Cost of goods manufactured in 2017 and (b) Cost of goods sold in 2017

We can now prepare Cellular Products' income statement for 2017. The income statement of Cellular Products is shown on the right side in Exhibit 2-7 and in Exhibit 2-8, Panel A. Revenues of Cellular Products are (in thousands) $210,000. Inventoriable costs expensed during 2017 equal cost of goods sold of $108,000.

$$\text{Gross margin} = \text{Revenues} - \text{Cost of goods sold} = \$210,000 - \$108,000 = \$102,000.$$

The $70,000 of operating costs composed of R&D, design, marketing, distribution, and customer-service costs are period costs of Cellular Products. These period costs include, for example, salaries of salespersons, depreciation on computers and other equipment used in marketing, and the cost of leasing warehouse space for distribution. **Operating income** equals total revenues from operations minus cost of goods sold and operating (period) costs (excluding interest expense and income taxes) or, equivalently, gross margin minus period costs. The operating income of Cellular Products is $32,000 (gross margin, $102,000 − period costs, $70,000). If you are familiar with financial accounting, recall that period costs are typically called selling, general, and administrative expenses in the income statement.

Newcomers to cost accounting frequently assume that indirect costs such as rent, telephone, and depreciation are always costs of the period in which they are incurred and are not associated with inventories. When these costs are incurred in marketing or in corporate headquarters, they are period costs. However, when these costs are incurred in manufacturing, they are manufacturing overhead costs and are inventoriable.

Because costs that are inventoried are not expensed until the units associated with them are sold, a manager can produce more units than are expected to be sold in a period without reducing a firm's net income. In fact, building up inventory in this way defers the expensing of the current period's fixed manufacturing costs as manufacturing costs are inventoried and not expensed until the units are sold in a subsequent period. This in turn actually *increases* the firm's gross margin and operating income even though there is no increase in sales, causing outsiders to believe that the company is more profitable than it actually is. We will discuss this risky accounting practice in greater detail in Chapter 9.

Recap of Inventoriable Costs and Period Costs

Exhibit 2-7 highlights the differences between inventoriable costs and period costs for a manufacturing company. The manufacturing costs of finished goods include direct materials, direct manufacturing labor, and manufacturing overhead costs such as supervision, production control, and machine maintenance. All these costs are inventoriable: They are assigned to work-in-process inventory until the goods are completed and then to finished-goods inventory until the goods are sold. All nonmanufacturing costs, such as R&D, design, and distribution costs, are period costs.

Inventoriable costs and period costs flow through the income statement at a merchandising company similar to the way costs flow at a manufacturing company. At a merchandising company, however, the flow of costs is much simpler to understand and track. Exhibit 2-10 shows the inventoriable costs and period costs for a retailer or wholesaler, which buys goods for resale. The only inventoriable cost is the cost of merchandise. (This corresponds to the cost of finished goods manufactured for a manufacturing company.) Purchased goods are held as merchandise inventory, the cost of which is shown as an asset in the balance sheet. As the goods are sold, their costs are shown in the income statement as cost of goods sold. A retailer or wholesaler also has a variety of marketing, distribution, and customer-service costs, which are period costs. In the income statement, period costs are deducted from revenues without ever having been included as part of inventory.

> **DECISION POINT**
> What is the flow of inventoriable and period costs in manufacturing and merchandising settings?

Prime Costs and Conversion Costs

Two terms used to describe cost classifications in manufacturing costing systems are *prime costs* and *conversion costs*. **Prime costs** are all direct manufacturing costs. For Cellular Products,

Prime costs = Direct material costs + Direct manufacturing labor costs = $76,000 + $9,000 = $85,000

As we have already discussed, the greater the proportion of prime costs (or direct costs) to total costs, the more confident managers can be about the accuracy of the costs of products. As information-gathering technology improves, companies can add more and more direct-cost categories. For example, power costs might be metered in specific areas of a plant and identified as a direct cost of specific products. Furthermore, if a production line were dedicated to manufacturing a specific product, the depreciation on the production equipment would be a direct manufacturing cost and would be included in prime costs. Computer software companies often have a "purchased technology" direct manufacturing cost item. This item, which represents payments to suppliers who develop software algorithms for a product, is also included in prime costs. **Conversion costs** are all manufacturing costs other than direct

EXHIBIT 2-10 Flow of Revenues and Costs for a Merchandising Company (Retailer or Wholesaler)

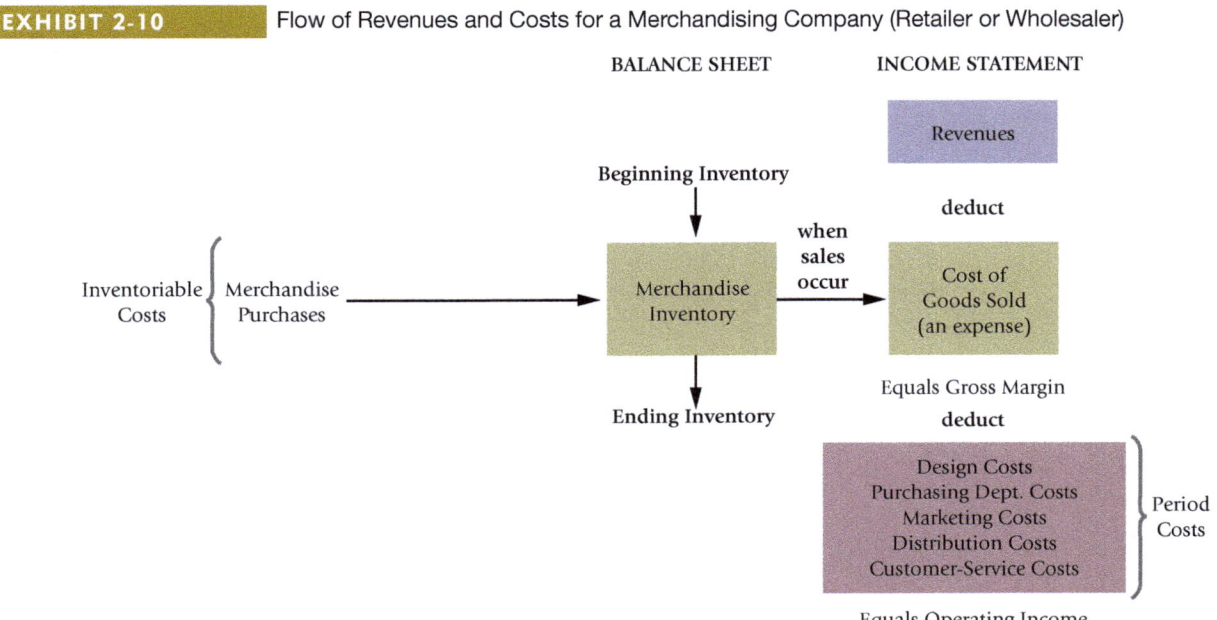

material costs. Conversion costs represent all manufacturing costs incurred to convert direct materials into finished goods. For Cellular Products,

$$\text{Conversion costs} = \begin{array}{c}\text{Direct manufacturing}\\ \text{labor costs}\end{array} + \begin{array}{c}\text{Manufacturing}\\ \text{overhead costs}\end{array} = \$9{,}000 + \$20{,}000 = \$29{,}000$$

Note that direct manufacturing labor costs are a part of both prime costs and conversion costs.

Some manufacturing operations, such as computer-integrated manufacturing (CIM) plants, have very few workers. The workers' roles are to monitor the manufacturing process and to maintain the equipment that produces multiple products. The costing systems in CIM plants do not have a direct manufacturing labor cost category because direct manufacturing labor cost is relatively small and because it is difficult to trace this cost to products. In a CIM plant, the only prime cost is the cost of direct materials. The conversion costs for such a plant are largely manufacturing overhead costs.

Measuring Costs Requires Judgment

LEARNING OBJECTIVE 7

Explain why product costs are computed in different ways for different purposes

...examples are pricing and product-mix decisions, government contracts, and financial statements

Measuring costs requires judgment. That's because there are alternative ways for managers to define and classify costs. Different companies or sometimes even different subunits within the same company may define and classify costs differently. Be careful to define and understand the ways costs are measured in a company or situation. We first illustrate this point for labor costs.

Measuring Labor Costs

Consider labor costs for software programming at companies such as Apple, where programmers work on different software applications for products like the iMac, the iPad, and the iPhone. Although labor cost classifications vary among companies, many companies use multiple labor cost categories:

- Direct programming labor costs that can be traced to individual products
- Overhead costs (labor related)
    - Indirect labor compensation for
        Office staff
        Office security
        Rework labor (time spent by direct laborers correcting software errors)
        Overtime premium paid to software programmers (explained next)
        Idle time (explained next)
    - Salaries for managers, department heads, and supervisors
    - Payroll fringe costs, for example, health care premiums and pension costs (explained later)

To retain information on different categories, *indirect labor costs* are commonly divided into many subclassifications, for example, office staff and idle time costs. Note that managers' salaries usually are not classified as indirect labor costs. Instead, the compensation of supervisors, department heads, and all others who are regarded as management is placed in a separate classification of labor-related overhead.

Overtime Premium and Idle Time

Managers need to pay special attention to two classes of indirect labor—overtime premium and idle time. **Overtime premium** is the wage rate paid to workers (for both direct labor and indirect labor) in *excess* of their straight-time wage rates. Overtime premium is usually considered to be a part of indirect costs or overhead. Consider the example of George Flexner, a junior software programmer who writes software for multiple products. He is paid $40 per hour for straight-time and $60 per hour (time and a half) for overtime. His overtime premium is $20 per overtime hour. If he works 44 hours, including 4 overtime hours, in one week, his gross compensation would be classified as follows:

Direct programming labor: 44 hours × $40 per hour	$1,760
Overtime premium: 4 hours × $20 per hour	80
Total compensation for 44 hours	$1,840

In this example, why is the overtime premium of direct programming labor usually considered an overhead cost rather than a direct cost? After all, the premium can be traced to specific products that George worked on while working overtime. Overtime premium is generally not considered a direct cost because the particular job that George worked on during the overtime hours is a matter of chance. For example, assume that George worked on two products for 5 hours each on a specific workday that lasted 10 hours, including 2 overtime hours. Should the product George worked on during hours 9 and 10 be assigned the overtime premium? Or should the premium be prorated over both products? Prorating the overtime premium does not "penalize"—add to the cost of—a particular product solely because it happened to be worked on during the overtime hours. *Instead, the overtime premium is considered to be attributable to the heavy overall volume of work. Its cost is regarded as part of overhead, which is borne by both products.*

Sometimes, though, overtime can definitely be attributed to a single product. For example, the overtime needed to meet the launch deadline for a new product may clearly be the sole source of overtime. In such instances, the overtime premium is regarded as a direct cost of that product.

Another subclassification of indirect labor is the idle time of both direct and indirect labor. **Idle time** refers to the wages paid for unproductive time caused by lack of orders, machine or computer breakdowns, work delays, poor scheduling, and the like. For example, if George had no work for 3 hours during that week while waiting to receive code from another colleague, George's earnings would be classified as follows:

Direct programming labor: 41 hours × $40/hour	$1,640
Idle time (overhead): 3 hours × $40/hour	120
Overtime premium (overhead): 4 hours × $20/hour	80
Total earnings for 44 hours	$1,840

Clearly, in this case, the idle time is not related to a particular product, nor, as we have already discussed, is the overtime premium. Both the overtime premium and the costs of idle time are considered overhead costs.

Benefits of Defining Accounting Terms

Managers, accountants, suppliers, and others will avoid many problems if they thoroughly understand and agree on the classifications and meanings of the cost terms introduced in this chapter and later in this book. Consider the classification of programming labor *payroll fringe costs*, which include employer payments for employee benefits such as Social Security, life insurance, health insurance, and pensions. Consider, for example, a software programmer who is paid a wage of $40 an hour with fringe benefits totaling, say, $10 per hour. Some companies classify the $40 as a direct programming labor cost of the product for which the software is being written and the $10 as overhead cost. Other companies classify the entire $50 as direct programming labor cost. The latter approach is preferable because the stated wage and the fringe benefit costs together are a fundamental part of acquiring direct software programming labor services.

Caution: In every situation, it is important for managers and management accountants to pinpoint clearly what direct labor includes and what direct labor excludes. This clarity will help prevent disputes regarding cost-reimbursement contracts, income tax payments, and labor union matters, which often can take a substantial amount of time for managers to resolve. Consider that some countries, such as Costa Rica and Mauritius, offer substantial income tax savings to foreign companies that generate employment within their borders. In some cases, to qualify for the tax benefits, the direct labor costs must at least equal a specified percentage of a company's total costs.

When managers do not precisely define direct labor costs, disputes can arise about whether payroll fringe costs should be included as part of direct labor costs when calculating the direct labor percentage for qualifying for such tax benefits. Companies have sought to classify payroll fringe costs as part of direct labor costs to make direct labor costs a higher percentage of total costs. Tax authorities have argued that payroll fringe costs are part of overhead. In addition to payroll fringe costs, other debated items are compensation for training time, idle time, vacations, sick leave, and overtime premium. To prevent disputes, contracts and laws should be as specific as possible about accounting definitions and measurements.

Different Meanings of Product Costs

At a more general level, many cost terms used by organizations have ambiguous meanings. Consider the term *product cost*. A **product cost** is the sum of the costs assigned to a product for a specific purpose. Different purposes can result in different measures of product cost, as the brackets on the value chain in Exhibit 2-11 illustrate:

- **Pricing and product-mix decisions.** For the purposes of making decisions about pricing and promoting products that generate the most profits, managers are interested in the overall (total) profitability of different products and, consequently, assign costs incurred in all business functions of the value chain to the different products.

- **Reimbursement under government contracts.** Government contracts often reimburse contractors on the basis of the "cost of a product" plus a prespecified margin of profit. A contract such as this is referred to as a "cost-plus" agreement. Cost-plus agreements are typically used for services and development contracts when it is not easy to predict the amount of money required to design, fabricate, and test items. Because these contracts transfer the risk of cost overruns to the government, agencies such as the Department of Defense and the Department of Energy provide detailed guidelines on the cost items they will allow (and disallow) when calculating the cost of a product. For example, many government agencies explicitly exclude marketing, distribution, and customer-service costs from product costs that qualify for reimbursement, and they may only partially reimburse R&D costs. These agencies want to reimburse contractors for only those costs most closely related to delivering products under the contract. The second bracket in Exhibit 2-11 shows how the product-cost calculations for a specific contract may allow for all design and production costs but only part of R&D costs.

EXHIBIT 2-11

Different Product Costs for Different Purposes

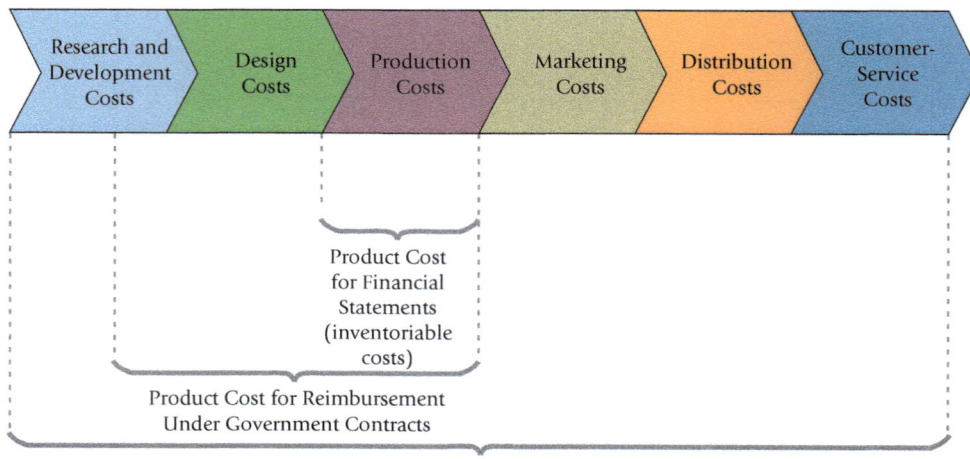

> **EXHIBIT 2-12**
>
> Alternative Classifications of Costs
>
> 1. Business function
>   a. Research and development
>   b. Design of products and processes
>   c. Production
>   d. Marketing
>   e. Distribution
>   f. Customer service
> 2. Assignment to a cost object
>   a. Direct cost
>   b. Indirect cost
> 3. Behavior pattern in relation to the level of activity or volume
>   a. Variable cost
>   b. Fixed cost
> 4. Aggregate or average
>   a. Total cost
>   b. Unit cost
> 5. Assets or expenses
>   a. Inventoriable cost
>   b. Period cost

- **Preparing financial statements for external reporting under Generally Accepted Accounting Principles (GAAP).** Under GAAP, only manufacturing costs can be assigned to inventories in the financial statements. For the purposes of calculating inventory costs, product costs include only inventoriable (production) costs.

As Exhibit 2-11 illustrates, product-cost measures range from a narrow set of costs for financial statements—a set that includes only production costs—to a broader set of costs for reimbursement under government contracts to a still broader set of costs for pricing and product-mix decisions.

This section focused on how different purposes result in the inclusion of different cost items of the value chain of business functions when product costs are calculated. The same caution about the need to be clear and precise about cost concepts and their measurement applies to each cost classification introduced in this chapter. Exhibit 2-12 summarizes the key cost classifications. Using the five-step process described in Chapter 1, think about how these different classifications of costs help managers make decisions and evaluate performance.

> **DECISION POINT**
>
> Why do managers assign different costs to the same cost object?

1. **Identify the problem and uncertainties.** Consider a decision about how much to price a product. This decision often depends on how much it costs to make the product.
2. **Obtain information.** Managers identify the direct and indirect costs of a product in each business function. Managers also gather other information about customers, competitors, and the prices of competing products.
3. **Make predictions about the future.** Managers estimate what it will cost to make the product in the future. This requires managers to predict the quantity of the product they expect the company to sell as well as have an understanding of fixed and variable costs.
4. **Make decisions by choosing among alternatives.** Managers choose a price to charge based on a thorough understanding of costs and other information.
5. **Implement the decision, evaluate performance, and learn.** Managers control costs and learn by comparing the actual total and unit costs against budgeted amounts.

The next section describes how the basic concepts introduced in this chapter lead to a framework for understanding cost accounting and cost management that can then be applied to the study of many topics, such as strategy evaluation, quality, and investment decisions.

A Framework for Cost Accounting and Cost Management

The following three features of cost accounting and cost management can be used for a wide range of applications:

1. Calculating the cost of products, services, and other cost objects
2. Obtaining information for planning and control and performance evaluation
3. Analyzing the relevant information for making decisions

> **LEARNING OBJECTIVE 8**
>
> Describe a framework for cost accounting and cost management
>
> ... three features that help managers make decisions

We develop these ideas in Chapters 3 through 11. The ideas also form the foundation for the study of various topics later in the book.

Calculating the Cost of Products, Services, and Other Cost Objects

You have already learned that costing systems trace direct costs and allocate indirect costs to products. Chapters 4 and 5 describe systems such as job costing and activity-based costing, which are used to calculate total costs and unit costs of products and services. The chapters also discuss how managers use this information to formulate strategies and make pricing, product-mix, and cost-management decisions.

Obtaining Information for Planning and Control and Performance Evaluation

Budgeting is the most commonly used tool for planning and control. A budget forces managers to look ahead, to translate a company's strategy into plans, to coordinate and communicate within the organization, and to provide a benchmark for evaluating the company's performance. Managers strive to meet their budget targets, so budgeting often affects the behavior of a company's personnel and the decisions they make. Chapter 6 describes budgeting systems.

At the end of a reporting period, managers compare the company's actual results to its planned performance. The managers' tasks are to understand why differences (called variances) between actual and planned performance arise and to use the information provided by these variances as feedback to promote learning and future improvement. Managers also use variances as well as nonfinancial measures, such as defect rates and customer satisfaction ratings, to control and evaluate the performance of various departments, divisions, and managers. Chapters 7 and 8 discuss variance analysis. Chapter 9 describes planning, control, and inventory-costing issues relating to capacity. Chapters 6, 7, 8, and 9 focus on the management accountant's role in implementing strategy.

Analyzing the Relevant Information for Making Decisions

When designing strategies and implementing them, managers must understand which revenues and costs to consider and which ones to ignore. Management accountants help managers identify what information is relevant and what information is irrelevant. Consider a decision about whether to buy a product from an outside vendor or make it in-house. The costing system indicates that it costs $25 per unit to make the product in-house. A vendor offers to sell the product for $22 per unit. At first glance, it seems it will cost less for the company to buy the product rather than make it. Suppose, however, that of the $25 to make the product in-house, $5 consists of plant lease costs that the company has already paid under a lease contract. Furthermore, if the product is bought, the plant will remain idle because it is too costly to retool the plant to make another product. That is, there is no opportunity to use the plant in some other profitable way. Under these conditions, it will cost less to make the product than to buy it. That's because making the product costs only an *additional* $20 per unit ($25 − $5), compared with an *additional* $22 per unit if it is bought. The $5 per unit of lease cost is irrelevant to the decision because it is a *past* (or *sunk*) cost that has already been incurred regardless of whether the product is made or bought. Analyzing relevant information is a key aspect of making decisions.

When making strategic decisions about which products and how much to produce, managers must know how revenues and costs vary with changes in output levels. For this purpose, managers need to distinguish fixed costs from variable costs. Chapter 3 analyzes how operating income changes with changes in units sold and how managers use this information to make decisions such as how much to spend on advertising. Chapter 10 describes methods to estimate the fixed and variable components of costs. Chapter 11 applies the concept of relevance to decision making in many different situations and describes methods managers use to maximize income given the resource constraints they face.

Later chapters in the book discuss topics such as strategy evaluation, customer profitability, quality, just-in-time systems, investment decisions, transfer pricing, and performance evaluation. Each of these topics invariably has product costing, planning and control, and decision-making perspectives. A command of the first 11 chapters will help you master these topics. For example, Chapter 12 on strategy describes the balanced scorecard, a set of financial and nonfinancial measures used to implement strategy that builds on the planning and control functions. The section on strategic analysis of operating income builds on ideas of product costing and variance analysis. The section on downsizing and managing capacity builds on ideas of relevant revenues and relevant costs.

DECISION POINT

What are the three key features of cost accounting and cost management?

PROBLEM FOR SELF-STUDY

Foxwood Company is a metal- and woodcutting manufacturer, selling products to the home-construction market. Consider the following data for 2017:

Sandpaper	$ 2,000
Materials-handling costs	70,000
Lubricants and coolants	5,000
Miscellaneous indirect manufacturing labor	40,000
Direct manufacturing labor	300,000
Direct materials inventory, Jan. 1, 2017	40,000
Direct materials inventory, Dec. 31, 2017	50,000
Finished-goods inventory, Jan. 1, 2017	100,000
Finished-goods inventory, Dec. 31, 2017	150,000
Work-in-process inventory, Jan. 1, 2017	10,000
Work-in-process inventory, Dec. 31, 2017	14,000
Plant-leasing costs	54,000
Depreciation—plant equipment	36,000
Property taxes on plant equipment	4,000
Fire insurance on plant equipment	3,000
Direct materials purchased	460,000
Revenues	1,360,000
Marketing promotions	60,000
Marketing salaries	100,000
Distribution costs	70,000
Customer-service costs	100,000

Required

1. Prepare an income statement with a separate supporting schedule of cost of goods manufactured. For all manufacturing items, classify costs as direct costs or indirect costs and indicate by V or F whether each is a variable cost or a fixed cost (when the cost object is a product unit). If in doubt, decide on the basis of whether the total cost will change substantially over a wide range of units produced.
2. Suppose that both the direct material costs and the plant-leasing costs are for the production of 900,000 units. What is the direct material cost of each unit produced? What is the plant-leasing cost per unit? Assume that the plant-leasing cost is a fixed cost.
3. Suppose Foxwood Company manufactures 1,000,000 units next year. Repeat the computation in requirement 2 for direct materials and plant-leasing costs. Assume the implied cost-behavior patterns persist.
4. As a management consultant, explain concisely to the company president why the unit cost for direct materials did not change in requirements 2 and 3 but the unit cost for plant-leasing costs did change.

Solution

1.

Foxwood Company
Income Statement
For the Year Ended December 31, 2017

Revenues		$1,360,000
Cost of goods sold		
Beginning finished-goods inventory, January 1, 2017	$ 100,000	
Cost of goods manufactured (see the following schedule)	960,000	
Cost of goods available for sale	1,060,000	
Deduct ending finished-goods inventory, December 31, 2017	150,000	910,000
Gross margin (or gross profit)		450,000
Operating costs		
Marketing promotions	60,000	
Marketing salaries	100,000	
Distribution costs	70,000	
Customer-service costs	100,000	330,000
Operating income		$ 120,000

Foxwood Company
Schedule of Cost of Goods Manufactured
For the Year Ended December 31, 2017

Direct materials		
Beginning inventory, January 1, 2017		$ 40,000
Purchases of direct materials		460,000
Cost of direct materials available for use		500,000
Ending inventory, December 31, 2017		50,000
Direct materials used		450,000 (V)
Direct manufacturing labor		300,000 (V)
Indirect manufacturing costs		
Sandpaper	$ 2,000 (V)	
Materials-handling costs	70,000 (V)	
Lubricants and coolants	5,000 (V)	
Miscellaneous indirect manufacturing labor	40,000 (V)	
Plant-leasing costs	54,000 (F)	
Depreciation—plant equipment	36,000 (F)	
Property taxes on plant equipment	4,000 (F)	
Fire insurance on plant equipment	3,000 (F)	214,000
Manufacturing costs incurred during 2017		964,000
Beginning work-in-process inventory, January 1, 2017		10,000
Total manufacturing costs to account for		974,000
Ending work-in-process inventory, December 31, 2017		14,000
Cost of goods manufactured (to income statement)		$ 960,000

2. Direct material unit cost = Direct materials used ÷ Units produced
    = $450,000 ÷ 900,000 units = $0.50 per unit
   Plant-leasing unit cost = Plant-leasing costs ÷ Units produced
    = $54,000 ÷ 900,000 units = $0.06 per unit
3. The direct material costs are variable, so they would increase in total from $450,000 to $500,000 (1,000,000 units × $0.50 per unit). However, their unit cost would be unaffected: $500,000 ÷ 1,000,000 units = $0.50 per unit.
    In contrast, the plant-leasing costs of $54,000 are fixed, so they would not increase in total. However, the plant-leasing cost per unit would decline from $0.060 to $0.054: $54,000 ÷ 1,000,000 units = $0.054 per unit.
4. The explanation would begin with the answer to requirement 3. As a consultant, you should stress that the unitizing (averaging) of costs that have different behavior patterns can be misleading. A common error is to assume that a total unit cost, which is often a sum of variable unit cost and fixed unit cost, is an indicator that total costs change in proportion to changes in production levels. The next chapter demonstrates the necessity for distinguishing between cost-behavior patterns. You must be wary, especially about average fixed cost per unit. Too often, unit fixed cost is erroneously regarded as being indistinguishable from unit variable cost.

DECISION POINTS

The following question-and-answer format summarizes the chapter's learning objectives. Each decision presents a key question related to a learning objective. The guidelines are the answer to that question.

Decision	Guidelines
1. What is a cost object?	A cost object is anything for which a manager needs a separate measurement of cost. Examples include a product, a service, a project, a customer, a brand category, an activity, and a department.
2. How do managers decide whether a cost is a direct or an indirect cost?	A direct cost is any cost that is related to a particular cost object and can be traced to that cost object in an economically feasible way. Indirect costs are related to a particular cost object but cannot be traced to it in an economically feasible way. The same cost can be direct for one cost object and indirect for another cost object. This book uses *cost tracing* to describe the assignment of direct costs to a cost object and *cost allocation* to describe the assignment of indirect costs to a cost object.
3. How do managers decide whether a cost is a variable or a fixed cost?	A variable cost changes *in total* in proportion to changes in the related level of total activity or volume of output produced. A fixed cost remains unchanged *in total* for a given time period despite wide changes in the related level of total activity or volume of output produced.
4. How should managers estimate and interpret cost information?	In general, focus on total costs, not unit costs. When making total cost estimates think of variable costs as an amount per unit and fixed costs as a total amount. Interpret the unit cost of a cost object cautiously when it includes a fixed-cost component.
5. What are the differences in the accounting for inventoriable versus period costs?	Inventoriable costs are all costs of a product that a company regards as an asset in the accounting period in which they are incurred and which become cost of goods sold in the accounting period in which the product is sold. Period costs are expensed in the accounting period in which they are incurred and are all of the costs in an income statement other than cost of goods sold.

Decision	Guidelines
6. What is the flow of inventoriable and period costs in manufacturing and merchandising settings?	In manufacturing settings, inventoriable costs flow through work-in-process and finished-goods accounts, and are expensed as cost of goods sold. Period costs are expensed as they are incurred. In merchandising settings, only the cost of merchandise is treated as inventoriable.
7. Why do managers assign different costs to the same cost objects?	Managers can assign different costs to the same cost object depending on the purpose. For example, for the external reporting purpose in a manufacturing company, the inventoriable cost of a product includes only manufacturing costs. In contrast, costs from all business functions of the value chain often are assigned to a product for pricing and product-mix decisions.
8. What are the three key features of cost accounting and cost management?	Three features of cost accounting and cost management are (1) calculating the cost of products, services, and other cost objects; (2) obtaining information for planning and control and performance evaluation; and (3) analyzing relevant information for making decisions.

TERMS TO LEARN

This chapter contains more basic terms than any other in this book. Do not proceed before you check your understanding of the following terms. The chapter and the Glossary at the end of the book contain definitions of the following important terms:

- actual cost
- average cost
- budgeted cost
- conversion costs
- cost
- cost accumulation
- cost allocation
- cost assignment
- cost driver
- cost object
- cost of goods manufactured
- cost tracing
- direct costs of a cost object
- direct manufacturing labor costs
- direct materials costs
- direct materials inventory
- factory overhead costs
- finished-goods inventory
- fixed cost
- idle time
- indirect costs of a cost object
- indirect manufacturing costs
- inventoriable costs
- manufacturing overhead costs
- manufacturing-sector companies
- merchandising-sector companies
- operating income
- overtime premium
- period costs
- prime costs
- product cost
- relevant range
- revenues
- service-sector companies
- unit cost
- variable cost
- work-in-process inventory
- work in progress

ASSIGNMENT MATERIAL

Questions

2-1 Define cost object and give three examples.
2-2 What is the main difference between direct costs and indirect costs?
2-3 Why do managers consider direct costs to be more accurate than indirect costs?
2-4 Name three factors that will affect the classification of a cost as direct or indirect.
2-5 Explain whether a business department can be a cost object.
2-6 What is a cost driver? Give one example.
2-7 What is the relevant range? What role does the relevant-range concept play in explaining how costs behave?

2-8 Why and when is it essential to calculate a unit cost?

2-9 Describe how manufacturing-, merchandising-, and service-sector companies differ from one another.

2-10 What are three different types of inventory that manufacturing companies hold?

2-11 Distinguish between inventoriable costs and period costs.

2-12 Define the following: direct material costs, direct manufacturing-labor costs, manufacturing overhead costs, prime costs, and conversion costs.

2-13 Why are overtime premium and idle time considered as indirect costs?

2-14 Define product cost. Describe three different purposes for computing product costs.

2-15 What are three common features of cost accounting and cost management?

Multiple-Choice Questions

Pearson MyLab Accounting

2-16 Applewhite Corporation, a manufacturing company, is analyzing its cost structure in a project to achieve some cost savings. Which of the following statements is/are correct?

I. The cost of the direct materials in Applewhite's products is considered a variable cost.
II. The cost of the depreciation of Applewhite's plant machinery is considered a variable cost because Applewhite uses an accelerated depreciation method for both book and income tax purposes.
III. The cost of electricity for Applewhite's manufacturing facility is considered a fixed cost, even if the cost of the electricity has both variable and fixed components.

1. I, II, and III are correct.
2. I only is correct.
3. II and III only are correct.
4. None of the listed choices is correct.

2-17 Comprehensive Care Nursing Home is required by statute and regulation to maintain a minimum 3 to 1 ratio of direct service staff to residents to maintain the licensure associated with the Nursing Home beds. The salary expense associated with direct service staff for the Comprehensive Care Nursing Home would most likely be classified as:

1. Variable cost.
2. Fixed cost.
3. Overhead costs.
4. Inventoriable costs.

2-18 Frisco Corporation is analyzing its fixed and variable costs within its current relevant range. As its cost driver activity changes within the relevant range, which of the following statements is/are correct?

I. As the cost driver level increases, total fixed cost remains unchanged.
II. As the cost driver level increases, unit fixed cost increases.
III. As the cost driver level decreases, unit variable cost decreases.

1. I, II, and III are correct.
2. I and II only are correct.
3. I only is correct.
4. II and III only are correct.

2-19 Year 1 financial data for the ABC Company is as follows:

Sales	$5,000,000
Direct materials	850,000
Direct manufacturing labor	1,700,000
Variable manufacturing overhead	400,000
Fixed manufacturing overhead	750,000
Variable SG&A	150,000
Fixed SG&A	250,000

Under the absorption method, Year 1 Cost of Goods sold will be:

a. $2,550,000
b. $2,950,000
c. $3,100,000
d. $3,700,000

2-20 The following information was extracted from the accounting records of Roosevelt Manufacturing Company:

Direct materials purchased	80,000
Direct materials used	76,000
Direct manufacturing labor costs	10,000
Indirect manufacturing labor costs	12,000
Sales salaries	14,000
Other plant expenses	22,000
Selling and administrative expenses	20,000

What was the cost of goods manufactured?

1. $124,000
2. $120,000
3. $154,000
4. $170,000

©2016 DeVry/Becker Educational Development Corp. All Rights Reserved.

Exercises

2-21 Computing and interpreting manufacturing unit costs. Minnesota Office Products (MOP) produces three different paper products at its Vaasa lumber plant: Supreme, Deluxe, and Regular. Each product has its own dedicated production line at the plant. It currently uses the following three-part classification for its manufacturing costs: direct materials, direct manufacturing labor, and manufacturing overhead costs. Total manufacturing overhead costs of the plant in July 2017 are $150 million ($15 million of which are fixed). This total amount is allocated to each product line on the basis of the direct manufacturing labor costs of each line. Summary data (in millions) for July 2017 are as follows:

	Supreme	Deluxe	Regular
Direct material costs	$ 89	$ 57	$ 60
Direct manufacturing labor costs	$ 16	$ 26	$ 8
Manufacturing overhead costs	$ 48	$ 78	$ 24
Units produced	125	150	140

Required

1. Compute the manufacturing cost per unit for each product produced in July 2017.
2. Suppose that, in August 2017, production was 150 million units of Supreme, 190 million units of Deluxe, and 220 million units of Regular. Why might the July 2017 information on manufacturing cost per unit be misleading when predicting total manufacturing costs in August 2017?

2-22 Direct, indirect, fixed, and variable costs. Sumitomo Cable manufactures various types of aluminum and copper cables which it sells directly to retail outlets through its distribution channels. The manufacturing process for producing cables includes a process called wire draw in which the aluminum and copper rods are pulled through a series of synthetic dies, which gradually decrease in size. The wires are then passed through an extruder, where either a single or a double coating of plastic is applied. These insulated wires are twisted into pairs by the Twisting and Stranding Department. The final shape is given to the wires by the Jacketing and Packaging department after carrying out the process of quality control.

Required

1. Costs involved in the different processes are listed below. For each cost, indicate whether it is a direct variable, direct fixed, indirect variable, or indirect fixed cost, assuming that the "units of production of each kind of wire" is the cost object.

Costs:

Aluminum and copper rods	Quality control
Insulating materials	Repairs to machines
Wages for wire draw	Normal wastages and spoilages
Depreciation on machineries	Store-keeper's salary
Depreciation on factory building	Material testing
Insurance on factory building	Materials used by jacketing and packaging department
Consumable stores and dies	Factory general utilities
Wages for machine operators	Fuel for factory generator
Power	Supervisors' salaries

2. If the cost object were the "Jacketing and Packaging department" instead, which costs from requirement 1 would now be direct instead of indirect costs?

2-23 Classification of costs, service sector. Market Focus is a marketing research firm that organizes focus groups for consumer-product companies. Each focus group has eight individuals who are paid $60 per session to provide comments on new products. These focus groups meet in hotels and are led by a trained, independent marketing specialist hired by Market Focus. Each specialist is paid a fixed retainer to conduct a minimum number of sessions and a per session fee of $2,200. A Market Focus staff member attends each session to ensure that all the logistical aspects run smoothly.

Classify each cost item **(A–H)** as follows:

Required

a. Direct or indirect (D or I) costs of each individual focus group.
b. Variable or fixed (V or F) costs of how the total costs of Market Focus change as the number of focus groups conducted changes. (If in doubt, select on the basis of whether the total costs will change substantially if there is a large change in the number of groups conducted.)

You will have two answers (D or I; V or F) for each of the following items:

Cost Item	D or I	V or F
A. Payment to individuals in each focus group to provide comments on new products		
B. Annual subscription of Market Focus to *Consumer Reports* magazine		
C. Phone calls made by Market Focus staff member to confirm individuals will attend a focus group session (Records of individual calls are not kept.)		
D. Retainer paid to focus group leader to conduct 18 focus groups per year on new medical products		
E. Recruiting cost to hire marketing specialists		
F. Lease payment by Market Focus for corporate office		
G. Cost of tapes used to record comments made by individuals in a focus group session (These tapes are sent to the company whose products are being tested.)		
H. Gasoline costs of Market Focus staff for company-owned vehicles (Staff members submit monthly bills with no mileage breakdowns.)		
I. Costs incurred to improve the design of focus groups to make them more effective		

2-24 Classification of costs, merchandising sector. Band Box Entertainment (BBE) operates a large store in Atlanta, Georgia. The store has both a movie (DVD) section and a music (CD) section. BBE reports revenues for the movie section separately from the music section.

Classify each cost item **(A–H)** as follows:

Required

a. Direct or indirect (D or I) costs of the total number of DVDs sold.
b. Variable or fixed (V or F) costs of how the total costs of the movie section change as the total number of DVDs sold changes. (If in doubt, select on the basis of whether the total costs will change substantially if there is a large change in the total number of DVDs sold.)

You will have two answers (D or I; V or F) for each of the following items:

Cost Item	D or I	V or F
A. Annual retainer paid to a video distributor		
B. Cost of store manager's salary		
C. Costs of DVDs purchased for sale to customers		
D. Subscription to *DVD Trends* magazine		
E. Leasing of computer software used for financial budgeting at the BBE store		
F. Cost of popcorn provided free to all customers of the BBE store		
G. Cost of cleaning the store every night after closing		
H. Freight-in costs of DVDs purchased by BBE		

2-25 Classification of costs, manufacturing sector. The Cooper Furniture Company of Potomac, Maryland, assembles two types of chairs (Recliners and Rockers). Separate assembly lines are used for each type of chair.

Classify each cost item **(A–I)** as follows:

Required

a. Direct or indirect (D or I) cost for the total number of Recliners assembled.
b. Variable or fixed (V or F) cost depending on how total costs change as the total number of Recliners assembled changes. (If in doubt, select on the basis of whether the total costs will change substantially if there is a large change in the total number of Recliners assembled.)

You will have two answers (D or I; V or F) for each of the following items:

Cost Item	D or I	V or F
A. Cost of fabric used on Recliners		
B. Salary of public relations manager for Cooper Furniture		
C. Annual convention for furniture manufacturers; generally Cooper Furniture attends		
D. Cost of lubricant used on the Recliner assembly line		
E. Freight costs of Recliner frames shipped from Durham to Potomac, MD		
F. Electricity costs for Recliner assembly line (single bill covers entire plant)		
G. Wages paid to temporary assembly-line workers hired in periods of high Recliner production (paid on hourly basis)		
H. Annual fire-insurance policy cost for Potomac, MD plant		
I. Wages paid to plant manager who oversees the assembly lines for both chair types		

2-26 Variable costs, fixed costs, total costs. Bridget Ashton is getting ready to open a small restaurant. She is on a tight budget and must choose between the following long-distance phone plans:

Plan A: Pay 10 cents per minute of long-distance calling.

Plan B: Pay a fixed monthly fee of $15 for up to 240 long-distance minutes and 8 cents per minute thereafter (if she uses fewer than 240 minutes in any month, she still pays $15 for the month).

Plan C: Pay a fixed monthly fee of $22 for up to 510 long-distance minutes and 5 cents per minute thereafter (if she uses fewer than 510 minutes, she still pays $22 for the month).

Required
1. Draw a graph of the total monthly costs of the three plans for different levels of monthly long-distance calling.
2. Which plan should Ashton choose if she expects to make 100 minutes of long-distance calls? 240 minutes? 540 minutes?

2-27 Variable and fixed costs. Consolidated Motors specializes in producing one specialty vehicle. It is called Surfer and is styled to easily fit multiple surfboards in its back area and top-mounted storage racks.

Consolidated has the following manufacturing costs:

Plant management costs, $1,992,000 per year

Cost of leasing equipment, $1,932,000 per year

Workers' wages, $800 per Surfer vehicle produced

Direct materials costs: Steel, $1,400 per Surfer; Tires, $150 per tire, each Surfer takes 5 tires (one spare).

City license, which is charged monthly based on the number of tires used in production:

0–500 tires	$ 40,040
501–1,000 tires	$ 65,000
more than 1,000 tires	$249,870

Consolidated currently produces 170 vehicles per month.

Required
1. What is the variable manufacturing cost per vehicle? What is the fixed manufacturing cost per month?
2. Plot a graph for the variable manufacturing costs and a second for the fixed manufacturing costs per month. How does the concept of relevant range relate to your graphs? Explain.
3. What is the total manufacturing cost of each vehicle if 80 vehicles are produced each month? 205 vehicles? How do you explain the difference in the manufacturing cost per unit?

2-28 Variable costs, fixed costs, relevant range. Dotball Candies manufactures jaw-breaker candies in a fully automated process. The machine that produces candies was purchased recently and can make 4,400 per month. The machine costs $9,500 and is depreciated using straight-line depreciation over 10 years assuming zero residual value. Rent for the factory space and warehouse and other fixed manufacturing overhead costs total $1,300 per month.

Dotball currently makes and sells 3,100 jaw-breakers per month. Dotball buys just enough materials each month to make the jaw-breakers it needs to sell. Materials cost 10 cents per jawbreaker. Next year Dotball expects demand to increase by 100%. At this volume of materials purchased, it will get a 10% discount on price. Rent and other fixed manufacturing overhead costs will remain the same.

Required
1. What is Dotball's current annual relevant range of output?
2. What is Dotball's current annual fixed manufacturing cost within the relevant range? What is the annual variable manufacturing cost?
3. What will Dotball's relevant range of output be next year? How, if at all, will total annual fixed and variable manufacturing costs change next year? Assume that if it needs to Dotball could buy an identical machine at the same cost as the one it already has.

2-29 Cost drivers and value chain. Torrance Technology Company (TTC) is developing a new touchscreen smartphone to compete in the cellular phone industry. The company will sell the phones at wholesale prices to cell phone companies, which will in turn sell them in retail stores to the final customer. TTC has undertaken the following activities in its value chain to bring its product to market:

A. Perform market research on competing brands
B. Design a prototype of the TTC smartphone
C. Market the new design to cell phone companies
D. Manufacture the TTC smartphone
E. Process orders from cell phone companies
F. Deliver the TTC smartphones to the cell phone companies
G. Provide online assistance to cell phone users for use of the TTC smartphone
H. Make design changes to the smartphone based on customer feedback

During the process of product development, production, marketing, distribution, and customer service, TTC has kept track of the following cost drivers:

Number of smartphones shipped by TTC

Number of design changes

Number of deliveries made to cell phone companies

Engineering hours spent on initial product design

Hours spent researching competing market brands

Customer-service hours

Number of smartphone orders processed

Machine hours required to run the production equipment

1. Identify each value-chain activity listed at the beginning of the exercise with one of the following value-chain categories:
   a. Design of products and processes
   b. Production
   c. Marketing
   d. Distribution
   e. Customer service
2. Use the list of preceding cost drivers to find one or more reasonable cost drivers for each of the activities in TTC's value chain.

Required

2-30 Cost drivers and functions. The representative cost drivers in the right column of this table are randomized so they do not match the list of functions in the left column.

Function	Representative Cost Driver
1. Inspection of materials	A. Number of batches produced
2. Accounts receivable	B. Number of sales orders
3. Employee training	C. Number of machines repaired
4. Repairs of machines	D. Number of labors supervised
5. Testing of samples	E. Number of purchase orders
6. Dispatching	F. Number of bills issued to customers
7. Supervisions	G. Number of employees trained

1. Match each function with its representative cost driver.
2. Give a second example of a cost driver for each function.

Required

2-31 Total costs and unit costs, service setting. The Big Event (TBE) recently started a business organizing food and music at weddings and other large events. In order to better understand the profitability of the business, the owner has asked you for an analysis of costs—what costs are fixed, what costs are variable, and so on, for each event. You have the following cost information:

Music costs: $10,000 per event

Catering costs:

   Food: $65 per guest

   Setup/cleanup: $15 per guest

   Fixed fee: $4,000 per event

TBE has allowed the caterer, who is also new in business, to place business cards on each table as a form of advertising. This has proved quite effective, and the caterer gives TBE a discount of $5 per guest in exchange for allowing the caterer to advertise.

Required

1. Draw a graph depicting fixed costs, variable costs, and total costs for each event versus the number of guests.
2. Suppose 150 persons attend the next event. What is TBE's total net cost and the cost per attendee?
3. Suppose instead that 200 persons attend. What is TBE's total net cost and the cost per attendee.
4. How should TBE charge customers for its services? Explain briefly.

2-32 Total and unit cost, decision making. Gayle's Glassworks makes glass flanges for scientific use. Materials cost $1 per flange, and the glass blowers are paid a wage rate of $28 per hour. A glass blower blows 10 flanges per hour. Fixed manufacturing costs for flanges are $28,000 per period. Period (nonmanufacturing) costs associated with flanges are $10,000 per period and are fixed.

Required

1. Graph the fixed, variable, and total manufacturing cost for flanges, using units (number of flanges) on the x-axis.
2. Assume Gayle's Glassworks manufactures and sells 5,000 flanges this period. Its competitor, Flora's Flasks, sells flanges for $10 each. Can Gayle sell below Flora's price and still make a profit on the flanges?
3. How would your answer to requirement 2 differ if Gayle's Glassworks made and sold 10,000 flanges this period? Why? What does this indicate about the use of unit cost in decision making?

2-33 Inventoriable costs versus period costs. Each of the following cost items pertains to one of these companies: Best Buy (a merchandising-sector company), KitchenAid (a manufacturing-sector company), and HughesNet (a service-sector company):

a. Cost of phones and computers available for sale in Best Buy's electronics department
b. Electricity used to provide lighting for assembly-line workers at a KitchenAid manufacturing plant
c. Depreciation on HughesNet satellite equipment used to provide its services
d. Electricity used to provide lighting for Best Buy's store aisles
e. Wages for personnel responsible for quality testing of the KitchenAid products during the assembly process
f. Salaries of Best Buy's marketing personnel planning local-newspaper advertising campaigns
g. Perrier mineral water purchased by HughesNet for consumption by its software engineers
h. Salaries of HughesNet area sales managers
i. Depreciation on vehicles used to transport KitchenAid products to retail stores

Required

1. Distinguish between manufacturing-, merchandising-, and service-sector companies.
2. Distinguish between inventoriable costs and period costs.
3. Classify each of the cost items (a–i) as an inventoriable cost or a period cost. Explain your answers.

Problems

2-34 Computing cost of goods purchased and cost of goods sold. The following data are for Marvin Department Store. The account balances (in thousands) are for 2017.

Marketing, distribution, and customer-service costs	$ 37,000
Merchandise inventory, January 1, 2017	27,000
Utilities	17,000
General and administrative costs	43,000
Merchandise inventory, December 31, 2017	34,000
Purchases	155,000
Miscellaneous costs	4,000
Transportation-in	7,000
Purchase returns and allowances	4,000
Purchase discounts	6,000
Revenues	280,000

Required

1. Compute (a) the cost of goods purchased and (b) the cost of goods sold.
2. Prepare the income statement for 2017.

An Introduction to Cost Terms and Purposes

2-35 Cost of goods purchased, cost of goods sold, and income statement. The following data are for Huang Wong Ping Retail Outlet Stores. The account balances (in thousands) are for 2017.

Marketing and advertising costs	$ 54,300
Merchandise inventory, January 1, 2017	115,800
Shipping of merchandise to customers	5,700
Depreciation on store fixtures	10,420
Purchases	654,000
General and administrative costs	74,800
Merchandise inventory, December 31, 2017	124,200
Merchandise freight-in	25,000
Purchase returns and allowances	32,400
Purchase discounts	22,600
Revenues	798,000

Required

1. Compute **(a)** the cost of goods purchased and **(b)** the cost of goods sold.
2. Prepare the income statement for 2017.

2-36 Flow of Inventoriable Costs. Renka's Heaters selected data for October 2017 are presented here (in millions):

Direct materials inventory 10/1/2017	$ 105
Direct materials purchased	365
Direct materials used	385
Total manufacturing overhead costs	450
Variable manufacturing overhead costs	265
Total manufacturing costs incurred during October 2017	1,610
Work-in-process inventory 10/1/2017	230
Cost of goods manufactured	1,660
Finished-goods inventory 10/1/2017	130
Cost of goods sold	1,770

Calculate the following costs:

Required

1. Direct materials inventory 10/31/2017
2. Fixed manufacturing overhead costs for October 2017
3. Direct manufacturing labor costs for October 2017
4. Work-in-process inventory 10/31/2017
5. Cost of finished goods available for sale in October 2017
6. Finished goods inventory 10/31/2017

2-37 Cost of goods manufactured, income statement, manufacturing company. Consider the following account balances (in thousands) for the Peterson Company:

Peterson Company	Beginning of 2017	End of 2017
Direct materials inventory	21,000	23,000
Work-in-process inventory	26,000	25,000
Finished-goods inventory	13,000	20,000
Purchases of direct materials		74,000
Direct manufacturing labor		22,000
Indirect manufacturing labor		17,000
Plant insurance		7,000
Depreciation—plant, building, and equipment		11,000
Repairs and maintenance—plant		3,000
Marketing, distribution, and customer-service costs		91,000
General and administrative costs		24,000

Required

1. Prepare a schedule for the cost of goods manufactured for 2017.
2. Revenues for 2017 were $310 million. Prepare the income statement for 2017.

2-38 Cost of goods manufactured, income statement, manufacturing company. Consider the following account balances (in thousands) for the Carolina Corporation:

Carolina Corporation	Beginning of 2017	End of 2017
Direct materials inventory	124,000	73,000
Work-in-process inventory	173,000	145,000
Finished-goods inventory	240,000	206,000
Purchases of direct materials		262,000
Direct manufacturing labor		217,000
Indirect manufacturing labor		97,000
Plant insurance		9,000
Depreciation—plant, building, and equipment		45,000
Plant utilities		26,000
Repairs and maintenance—plant		12,000
Equipment leasing costs		65,000
Marketing, distribution, and customer-service costs		125,000
General and administrative costs		71,000

Required

1. Prepare a schedule for the cost of goods manufactured for 2017.
2. Revenues (in thousands) for 2017 were $1,300,000. Prepare the income statement for 2017.

2-39 Income statement and schedule of cost of goods manufactured. The Howell Corporation has the following account balances (in millions):

For Specific Date		For Year 2017	
Direct materials inventory, Jan. 1, 2017	$15	Purchases of direct materials	$325
Work-in-process inventory, Jan. 1, 2017	10	Direct manufacturing labor	100
Finished goods inventory, Jan. 1, 2017	70	Depreciation—plant and equipment	80
Direct materials inventory, Dec. 31, 2017	20	Plant supervisory salaries	5
Work-in-process inventory, Dec. 31, 2017	5	Miscellaneous plant overhead	35
Finished goods inventory, Dec. 31, 2017	55	Revenues	950
		Marketing, distribution, and customer-service costs	240
		Plant supplies used	10
		Plant utilities	30
		Indirect manufacturing labor	60

Required

Prepare an income statement and a supporting schedule of cost of goods manufactured for the year ended December 31, 2017. (For additional questions regarding these facts, see the next problem.)

2-40 Interpretation of statements (continuation of 2-39).

Required

1. How would the answer to Problem 2-39 be modified if you were asked for a schedule of cost of goods manufactured and sold instead of a schedule of cost of goods manufactured? Be specific.
2. Would the sales manager's salary (included in marketing, distribution, and customer-service costs) be accounted for any differently if the Howell Corporation were a merchandising-sector company instead of a manufacturing-sector company?
3. Using the flow of manufacturing costs outlined in Exhibit 2-9 (page 64), describe how the wages of an assembler in the plant would be accounted for in this manufacturing company.
4. Plant supervisory salaries are usually regarded as manufacturing overhead costs. When might some of these costs be regarded as direct manufacturing costs? Give an example.
5. Suppose that both the direct materials used and the plant and equipment depreciation are related to the manufacture of 1 million units of product. What is the unit cost for the direct materials assigned to those units? What is the unit cost for plant and equipment depreciation? Assume that yearly plant and equipment depreciation is computed on a straight-line basis.
6. Assume that the implied cost-behavior patterns in requirement 5 persist. That is, direct material costs behave as a variable cost and plant and equipment depreciation behaves as a fixed cost. Repeat the computations in requirement 5, assuming that the costs are being predicted for the manufacture of 1.2 million units of product. How would the total costs be affected?
7. As a management accountant, explain concisely to the president why the unit costs differed in requirements 5 and 6.

2-41 Income statement and schedule of cost of goods manufactured. The following items (in millions) pertain to Schaeffer Corporation:

Schaeffer's manufacturing costing system uses a three-part classification of direct materials, direct manufacturing labor, and manufacturing overhead costs.

For Specific Date		For Year 2017	
Work-in-process inventory, Jan. 1, 2017	$10	Plant utilities	$ 8
Direct materials inventory, Dec. 31, 2017	4	Indirect manufacturing labor	21
Finished-goods inventory, Dec. 31, 2017	16	Depreciation—plant and equipment	6
Accounts payable, Dec. 31, 2017	24	Revenues	359
Accounts receivable, Jan. 1, 2017	53	Miscellaneous manufacturing overhead	15
Work-in-process inventory, Dec. 31, 2017	5	Marketing, distribution, and customer-service costs	90
Finished-goods inventory, Jan 1, 2017	46	Direct materials purchased	88
Accounts receivable, Dec. 31, 2017	32	Direct manufacturing labor	40
Accounts payable, Jan. 1, 2017	45	Plant supplies used	9
Direct materials inventory, Jan. 1, 2017	34	Property taxes on plant	2

Prepare an income statement and a supporting schedule of cost of goods manufactured. (For additional questions regarding these facts, see the next problem.)

Required

2-42 Terminology, interpretation of statements (continuation of 2-41).

1. Calculate total prime costs and total conversion costs.
2. Calculate total inventoriable costs and period costs.
3. Design costs and R&D costs are not considered product costs for financial statement purposes. When might some of these costs be regarded as product costs? Give an example.
4. Suppose that both the direct materials used and the depreciation on plant and equipment are related to the manufacture of 2 million units of product. Determine the unit cost for the direct materials assigned to those units and the unit cost for depreciation on plant and equipment. Assume that yearly depreciation is computed on a straight-line basis.
5. Assume that the implied cost-behavior patterns in requirement 4 persist. That is, direct material costs behave as a variable cost and depreciation on plant and equipment behaves as a fixed cost. Repeat the computations in requirement 4, assuming that the costs are being predicted for the manufacture of 3 million units of product. Determine the effect on total costs.
6. Assume that depreciation on the equipment (but not the plant) is computed based on the number of units produced because the equipment deteriorates with units produced. The depreciation rate on equipment is $1.50 per unit. Calculate the depreciation on equipment assuming (a) 2 million units of product are produced and (b) 3 million units of product are produced.

Required

2-43 Labor cost, overtime, and idle time. Akua works in the manufacturing department of Impala Iron Works (IIW) as a machine operator. Akua, a long-time employee of IIW, is paid on an hourly basis at a rate of $25 per hour. She works five 8-hour shifts per week from Monday to Friday (40 hours). Any time Akua works beyond these 40 hours is considered overtime for which she is paid at a rate of 160% ($40 per hour). If the overtime falls on weekends, Akua is paid at a rate of double time ($50 per hour). She is also paid an additional $26 per hour for working on any holidays worked, even if it is part of her regular 40 hours. Akua is paid her regular wages even if the machines are down (not operating) due to regular machine maintenance, slow order periods, or unexpected mechanical problems. These hours are considered "idle time."

During December Akua worked the following hours:

	Hours worked including machine downtime	Machine downtime
Week 1	49	5.0
Week 2	51	6.0
Week 3	45	3.0
Week 4	47	4.0

Included in the total hours worked are two company holidays (Christmas Eve and Christmas Day) during Week 4. All overtime worked by Akua was Monday–Friday, except for the hours worked in Week 3; all of the Week 3 overtime hours were worked on a Saturday.

Required

1. Calculate (a) direct manufacturing labor, (b) idle time, (c) overtime and holiday premium, and (d) total earnings for Akua in December.
2. Is idle time and overtime premium a direct or indirect cost of the products that Akua worked on in December? Explain.

2-44 Missing records, computing inventory costs. Ron Howard recently took over as the controller of Johnson Brothers Manufacturing. Last month, the previous controller left the company with little notice and left the accounting records in disarray. Ron needs the ending inventory balances to report first-quarter numbers.

For the previous month (March 2017) Ron was able to piece together the following information:

Direct materials purchased	$120,000
Work-in-process inventory, 3/1/2017	$ 35,000
Direct materials inventory, 3/1/2017	$ 12,500
Finished-goods inventory, 3/1/2017	$160,000
Conversion costs	$330,000
Total manufacturing costs added during the period	$420,000
Cost of goods manufactured	4 times direct materials used
Gross margin as a percentage of revenues	20%
Revenues	$518,750

Calculate the cost of:

Required

1. Finished-goods inventory, 3/31/2017
2. Work-in-process inventory, 3/31/2017
3. Direct materials inventory, 3/31/2017

2-45 Comprehensive problem on unit costs, product costs. Atlanta Office Equipment manufactures and sells metal shelving. It began operations on January 1, 2017. Costs incurred for 2017 are as follows (V stands for variable; F stands for fixed):

Direct materials used	$149,500 V
Direct manufacturing labor costs	34,500 V
Plant energy costs	6,000 V
Indirect manufacturing labor costs	12,000 V
Indirect manufacturing labor costs	17,000 F
Other indirect manufacturing costs	7,000 V
Other indirect manufacturing costs	27,000 F
Marketing, distribution, and customer-service costs	126,000 V
Marketing, distribution, and customer-service costs	47,000 F
Administrative costs	58,000 F

Variable manufacturing costs are variable with respect to units produced. Variable marketing, distribution, and customer-service costs are variable with respect to units sold.

Inventory data are as follows:

	Beginning: January 1, 2017	Ending: December 31, 2017
Direct materials	0 lb	2,300 lbs
Work in process	0 units	0 units
Finished goods	0 units	? units

Production in 2017 was 115,000 units. Two pounds of direct materials are used to make one unit of finished product.

Revenues in 2017 were $540,000. The selling price per unit and the purchase price per pound of direct materials were stable throughout the year. The company's ending inventory of finished goods is carried at the average unit manufacturing cost for 2017. Finished-goods inventory at December 31, 2017, was $15,400.

Required

1. Calculate direct materials inventory, total cost, December 31, 2017.
2. Calculate finished-goods inventory, total units, December 31, 2017.
3. Calculate selling price in 2017.
4. Calculate operating income for 2017.

2-46 Different meanings of product costs. There are at least 3 different purposes for which we measure product costs. They are (1) pricing and product mix decisions, (2) determining the appropriate charge for a government contract, and (3) for preparing financial statements for external reporting following Generally Accepted Accounting Principles. On the following table, indicate whether the indicated cost would be included or excluded for the particular purpose. If your answer is not definitive (include or exclude), provide a short explanation of why.

Type of Cost	Purpose: Pricing/ Product Mix	Purpose: Government Contract	Purpose: Financial Statement (using GAAP)
Direct Material			
Direct Manufacturing Labor			
Manufacturing Overhead			
Marketing Costs			
Distribution Expense			
Customer Service			

2-47 Cost classification; ethics. Adalard Müller, the new plant manager of New Times Manufacturing Plant Number 12, has just reviewed a draft of his year-end financial statements. Müller receives a year-end bonus of 8% of the plant's operating income before tax. The year-end income statement provided by the plant's controller was disappointing to say the least. After reviewing the numbers, Müller demanded that his controller go back and "work the numbers" again. Müller insisted that if he didn't see a better operating income number the next time around he would be forced to look for a new controller.

New Times Manufacturing classifies all costs directly related to the manufacturing of its product as product costs. These costs are inventoried and later expensed as costs of goods sold when the product is sold. All other expenses, including finished goods warehousing costs of $3,570,000, are classified as period expenses. Müller had suggested that warehousing costs be included as product costs because they are "definitely related to our product." The company produced 210,000 units during the period and sold 190,000 units.

As the controller reworked the numbers, he discovered that if he included warehousing costs as product costs, he could improve operating income by $340,000. He was also sure these new numbers would make Müller happy.

Required

1. Show numerically how operating income would improve by $340,000 just by classifying the preceding costs as product costs instead of period expenses.
2. Is Müller correct in his justification that these costs are "definitely related to our product"?
3. By how much will Müller profit personally if the controller makes the adjustments in requirement 1?
4. What should the plant controller do?

2-48 Finding unknown amounts. An auditor for the Internal Revenue Service is trying to reconstruct some partially destroyed records of two taxpayers. For each case in the accompanying list, find the unknown elements designated by the letters A and B for Case 1 and C and D for Case 2.

	Case 1	Case 2
	(in thousands)	
Accounts receivable, 12/31	$ 10,250	$ 4,500
Cost of goods sold	A	33,400
Accounts payable, 1/1	5,900	2,850
Accounts payable, 12/31	2,700	2,250
Finished goods inventory, 12/31	B	6,300
Gross margin	26,000	C
Work-in-process inventory, 1/1	4,600	2,800
Work-in-process inventory, 12/31	2,300	5,500
Finished goods inventory, 1/1	6,600	5,100
Direct materials used	14,500	20,200
Direct manufacturing labor costs	5,200	7,300
Manufacturing overhead costs	10,400	D
Purchases of direct materials	13,500	10,500
Revenues	64,500	57,600
Accounts receivable, 1/1	6,400	3,200

3 Cost–Volume–Profit Analysis

LEARNING OBJECTIVES

1. Explain the features of cost–volume–profit (CVP) analysis
2. Determine the breakeven point and output level needed to achieve a target operating income
3. Understand how income taxes affect CVP analysis
4. Explain how managers use CVP analysis to make decisions
5. Explain how sensitivity analysis helps managers cope with uncertainty
6. Use CVP analysis to plan variable and fixed costs
7. Apply CVP analysis to a company producing multiple products
8. Apply CVP analysis in service and not-for-profit organizations
9. Distinguish contribution margin from gross margin

All managers want to know how profits will change as the units sold, selling price, or the cost per unit of a product or service change.

Home Depot managers, for example, might wonder how many units of a new power drill must be sold to break even or make a certain amount of profit. Procter & Gamble managers might ask themselves how expanding their business in Nigeria would affect costs, revenues, and profits. These questions have a common "what-if" theme: What if we sold more power drills? What if we started selling in Nigeria? Examining the results of these what-if possibilities and alternatives helps managers make better decisions.

The following article explains how Goldenvoice, the organizer of the Coachella music festival in California, generated additional revenues to cover its fixed costs and turn a loss into a profit.

HOW COACHELLA TUNES UP THE SWEET SOUND OF PROFITS[1]

Each year, the Coachella music festival in California features more than 150 of the biggest names in rock, hip-hop, and electronic dance music. Putting on this annual music extravaganza is a costly endeavor. Headlining acts such as Drake and Jack White command as much as $4 million to perform, and production—including stagehands, insurance, and security—costs up to $12 million before the first note is played.

To cover its high fixed costs and make a profit, Coachella needs to sell a lot of tickets. After struggling for years to turn a profit, Goldenvoice expanded Coachella to two identical editions taking place on consecutive weekends. Same venue, same lineup, and same ticket price. Goldenvoice also launched Stagecoach, a country music festival that occupies the same California venue one week after Coachella. This allowed temporary infrastructure costs such as stages and fencings to be shared across both events. With tickets prices from $375 to $889, the 2015 Coachella festival sold a staggering $84 million in tickets,

WENN Ltd/Alamy Stock Photo

[1] *Sources*: Chris Parker, "The Economics of Music Festivals: Who's Getting Rich? Who's Going Broke?" *L.A. Weekly*, April 17, 2013 (http://www.laweekly.com/music/the-economics-of-music-festivals-whos-getting-rich-whos-going-broke-4167927); Anil Patel, "Coachella: A Lesson in Strategic Growth," *Anil Patel's blog*, LinkedIn, April 17, 2015 (https://www.linkedin.com/pulse/coachella-lesson-strategic-growth-anil-patel); Ray Waddell, "Coachella Earns Over $84 Million, Breaks Attendance Records," *Billboard*, July 15, 2015 (http://www.billboard.com/articles/business/6633636/coachella-2015-earnings-84-million-breaks-attendance-records).

while the follow-on Stagecoach festival grossed more than $21 million in ticket sales. By expanding Coachella's volume, Goldenvoice was able to recover its fixed costs and tune up the sweet sound of profits.

Businesses that have high fixed costs, such as American Airlines and General Motors, have to pay particular attention to the "what-ifs" behind decisions because these companies need significant revenues just to break even. In the airline industry, for example, the profits most airlines make come from the last two to five passengers who board each flight! Consequently, when revenues at American Airlines dropped, it was forced to declare bankruptcy. In this chapter, you will see how cost–volume–profit (CVP) analysis helps managers minimize such risks.

Essentials of CVP Analysis

In Chapter 2, we discussed total revenues, total costs, and income. Managers use **cost–volume–profit (CVP) analysis** to study the behavior of and relationship among these elements as changes occur in the number of units sold, the selling price, the variable cost per unit, or the fixed costs of a product. Consider this example:

> Example: Emma Jones is a young entrepreneur who recently used *GMAT Success*, a test-prep book and software package for the business school admission test. Emma loved the book and program so much that after graduating she signed a contract with *GMAT Success*'s publisher to sell the learning materials. She recently sold them at a college fair in Boston and is now thinking of selling them at a college fair in Chicago. Emma can purchase each package (book and software) from the publisher for $120 per package, with the privilege of returning all unsold packages and receiving a full $120 refund per package. She must pay $2,000 to rent a booth at the fair. She will incur no other costs. Should she rent the booth or not?

Emma, like most managers who face such a situation, works through the series of steps introduced in Chapter 1 to make the most profitable decisions.

1. **Identify the problem and uncertainties.** Every managerial decision involves selecting a course of action. The decision to rent the booth hinges on how Emma resolves two important uncertainties: the price she can charge and the number of packages she can sell at that price. Emma must decide knowing that the outcome of the action she chooses is uncertain. The more confident she is about selling a large number of packages at a high price, the more willing she will be to rent the booth.

2. **Obtain information.** When faced with uncertainty, managers obtain information that might help them understand the uncertainties more clearly. For example, Emma gathers information about the type of individuals likely to attend the fair and other test-prep packages that might be sold at the fair. She also gathers data from her experience selling packages at the Boston fair.

3. **Make predictions about the future.** Managers make predictions using all the information available to them. Emma predicts she can charge $200 for the *GMAT Success* package. At that price, she is reasonably confident that she will be able to sell at least 30 packages and possibly as many as 60. Emma must be realistic and exercise judgment when making these predictions. If they are too optimistic, she will rent the booth when she should not. If they are too pessimistic, she will not rent the booth when she should.

    Emma's predictions rest on the belief that her experience at the Chicago fair will be similar to her experience at the Boston fair 4 months earlier. Yet Emma is uncertain about several aspects of her prediction. Are the fairs truly comparable? For example, will attendance at the two fairs be the same? Have market conditions changed over the past

> **LEARNING OBJECTIVE** 1
>
> Explain the features of cost–volume–profit (CVP) analysis
>
> ...how operating income changes with changes in output level, selling prices, variable costs, or fixed costs

4 months? Are there any biases creeping into her thinking? She is keen on selling at the Chicago fair because sales in the last couple of months have been lower than expected. Is this experience making her predictions overly optimistic? Has she ignored some of the competitive risks? Will the other test-prep vendors at the fair reduce their prices? If they do, should she? How many packages can she expect to sell if she does?

Emma rethinks her plan and retests her assumptions. She obtains data about student attendance and total sales in past years from the organizers of the fair. In the end, she feels quite confident that her predictions are reasonable, accurate, and carefully thought through.

4. **Make decisions by choosing among alternatives.** Emma uses the CVP analysis that follows and decides to rent the booth at the Chicago fair.
5. **Implement the decision, evaluate performance, and learn.** Thoughtful managers never stop learning. They compare their actual performance to predicted performance to understand why things worked out the way they did and what they might learn. At the end of the Chicago fair, for example, Emma would want to evaluate whether her predictions about price and the number of packages she could sell were correct. This will help her make better decisions about renting booths at future fairs.

How does Emma use CVP analysis in Step 4 to make her decision? She begins by identifying which costs are fixed and which costs are variable and then calculates *contribution margin*.

Contribution Margin

The booth-rental cost of $2,000 is a fixed cost because it will not change no matter how many packages Emma sells. The cost of the packages is a variable cost because it increases in proportion to the number of packages sold and she can return whatever she doesn't sell for a full refund.

To understand how her operating income will change by selling different quantities of packages, Emma calculates operating income if sales are 5 packages and if sales are 40 packages.

	5 packages sold	40 packages sold
Revenues	$ 1,000 ($200 per package × 5 packages)	$8,000 ($ 200 per package × 40 packages)
Variable purchase costs	600 ($120 per package × 5 packages)	4,800 ($120 per package × 40 packages)
Fixed costs	2,000	2,000
Operating income	$(1,600)	$1,200

The only numbers that change from selling different quantities of packages are *total revenues* and *total variable costs*. The difference between total revenues and total variable costs is called **contribution margin**. That is,

$$\text{Contribution margin} = \text{Total revenues} - \text{Total variable costs}$$

Contribution margin indicates why operating income changes as the number of units sold changes. The contribution margin when Emma sells 5 packages is $400 ($1,000 in total revenues minus $600 in total variable costs); the contribution margin when Emma sells 40 packages is $3,200 ($8,000 in total revenues minus $4,800 in total variable costs). When calculating the contribution margin, be sure to subtract all variable costs. For example, if Emma incurred some variable selling costs because she paid a commission to salespeople for each package they sold at the fair, variable costs would include the cost of each package plus the sales commission paid on it.

Contribution margin per unit is a useful tool for calculating contribution margin and operating income. It is defined as:

$$\text{Contribution margin per unit} = \text{Selling price} - \text{Variable cost per unit}$$

In the *GMAT Success* example, the contribution margin per package, or per unit, is $200 − $120 = $80. Contribution margin per unit recognizes the tight coupling of selling price and variable cost per unit. Unlike fixed costs, Emma will only incur the variable cost per unit of $120 when she sells a unit of *GMAT Success*.

Contribution margin per unit provides a second way to calculate contribution margin:

Contribution margin = Contribution margin per unit × Number of units sold

For example, when Emma sells 40 packages, contribution margin = $80 per unit × 40 units = $3,200.

Even before she gets to the fair, Emma incurs $2,000 in fixed costs. Because the contribution margin per unit is $80, Emma will recover $80 for each package that she sells at the fair. Emma hopes to sell enough packages to fully recover the $2,000 she spent renting the booth and to then make a profit.

To get a feel for how operating income will change for different quantities of packages sold, Emma can prepare a contribution income statement as in Exhibit 3-1. The income statement in Exhibit 3-1 is called a **contribution income statement** because it groups costs into variable costs and fixed costs to highlight contribution margin.

Operating income = Contribution margin − Fixed costs

Each additional package sold from 0 to 1 to 5 increases contribution margin by $80 per package and helps Emma recover more and more of her fixed costs and reduce her operating loss. If Emma sells 25 packages, contribution margin equals $2,000 ($80 per package × 25 packages). This quantity exactly recovers her fixed costs and results in $0 operating income. If Emma sells 40 packages, contribution margin increases by another $1,200 ($3,200 − $2,000), all of which becomes operating income. As you look across Exhibit 3-1 from left to right, you see that the increase in contribution margin exactly equals the increase in operating income (or the decrease in operating loss).

When companies, such as Samsung and Prada, sell multiple products, calculating contribution margin per unit is cumbersome. Instead of expressing contribution margin in dollars per unit, these companies express it as a percentage called **contribution margin percentage** (or **contribution margin ratio**):

$$\text{Contribution margin percentage (or contribution margin ratio)} = \frac{\text{Contribution margin}}{\text{Revenues}}$$

Consider a sales level such as the 40 units sold in Exhibit 3-1:

$$\text{Contribution margin percentage} = \frac{\$3,200}{\$8,000} = 0.40, \text{ or } 40\%$$

Contribution margin percentage is the contribution margin per dollar of revenue. Emma earns 40% for each dollar of revenue (40 cents) she takes in. Contribution margin percentage is a handy way to calculate contribution margin for different dollar amounts of revenue. Rearranging terms in the equation defining contribution margin percentage, we get:

Contribution margin = Contribution margin percentage × Revenues (in dollars)

EXHIBIT 3-1

Contribution Income Statement for Different Quantities of *GMAT Success* Packages Sold

	A	B	C	D	E	F	G	H
1				\multicolumn{5}{c}{Number of Packages Sold}				
2				0	1	5	25	40
3	Revenues	$ 200 per package	$ 0	$ 200	$ 1,000	$5,000	$8,000
4	Variable costs	$ 120 per package		0	120	600	3,000	4,800
5	Contribution margin	$ 80 per package		0	80	400	2,000	3,200
6	Fixed costs	$2,000		2,000	2,000	2,000	2,000	2,000
7	Operating income			$(2,000)	$(1,920)	$(1,600)	$ 0	$1,200

To derive the relationship between operating income and contribution margin percentage, recall that:

$$\text{Operating income} = \text{Contribution margin} - \text{Fixed costs}$$

Substituting for contribution margin in the above equation:

$$\text{Operating income} = \text{Contribution margin percentage} \times \text{Revenues} - \text{Fixed costs}$$

For example, in Exhibit 3-1, if Emma sells 40 packages:

Revenues	$8,000
Contribution margin percentage	40%
Contribution margin, 40% × $8,000	$3,200
Fixed costs	2,000
Operating income	$1,200

When there is only one product, as in our example, we can divide both the numerator and denominator of the contribution margin percentage equation by the quantity of units sold and calculate contribution margin percentage as follows:

$$\text{Contribution margin percentage} = \frac{\text{Contribution margin}/\text{Quantity of units sold}}{\text{Revenues}/\text{Quantity of units sold}}$$

$$= \frac{\text{Contribution margin per unit}}{\text{Selling price}}$$

In our example,

$$\text{Contribution margin percentage} = \frac{\$80}{\$200} = 0.40, \text{ or } 40\%$$

Contribution margin percentage is a useful tool for calculating how a change in revenues changes contribution margin. As Emma's revenues increase by $3,000 from $5,000 to $8,000, her contribution margin increases from $2,000 to $3,200 (by $1,200):

Contribution margin at revenue of $8,000, 0.40 × $8,000	$3,200
Contribution margin at revenue of $5,000, 0.40 × $5,000	2,000
Change in contribution margin when revenue increases by $3,000, 0.40 × $3,000	$1,200

$$\text{Change in contribution margin} = \text{Contribution margin percentage} \times \text{Change in revenues}$$

Contribution margin analysis is a widely used technique. For example, managers at Home Depot use contribution margin analysis to evaluate how sales fluctuations during a recession will affect the company's profitability.

Expressing CVP Relationships

How was the Excel spreadsheet in Exhibit 3-1 constructed? Underlying the exhibit are some equations that express the CVP relationships. To make good decisions using CVP analysis, we must understand these relationships and the structure of the contribution income statement in Exhibit 3-1. There are three related ways (we will call them "methods") to think more deeply about and model CVP relationships:

1. The equation method
2. The contribution margin method
3. The graph method

As you will learn later in the chapter, different methods are useful for different decisions.

The equation method and the contribution margin method are most useful when managers want to determine operating income at a few specific sales levels (for example, 5, 15, 25, and 40 units sold). The graph method helps managers visualize the relationship between units sold and operating income over a wide range of quantities.

Equation Method

Each column in Exhibit 3-1 is expressed as an equation.

$$\text{Revenues} - \text{Variable costs} - \text{Fixed costs} = \text{Operating income}$$

How are revenues in each column calculated?

$$\text{Revenues} = \text{Selling price (SP)} \times \text{Quantity of units sold (Q)}$$

How are variable costs in each column calculated?

$$\text{Variable costs} = \text{Variable cost per unit (VCU)} \times \text{Quantity of units sold (Q)}$$

So,

$$\left[\left(\begin{array}{c}\text{Selling}\\ \text{price}\end{array}\right) \times \left(\begin{array}{c}\text{Quantity of}\\ \text{units sold}\end{array}\right) - \left(\begin{array}{c}\text{Variable cost}\\ \text{per unit}\end{array}\right) \times \left(\begin{array}{c}\text{Quantity of}\\ \text{units sold}\end{array}\right)\right] - \begin{array}{c}\text{Fixed}\\ \text{costs}\end{array} = \begin{array}{c}\text{Operating}\\ \text{income}\end{array} \quad \text{(Equation 1)}$$

Equation 1 becomes the basis for calculating operating income for different quantities of units sold. For example, if you go to cell F7 in Exhibit 3-1, the calculation of operating income when Emma sells 5 packages is

$$(\$200 \times 5) - (\$120 \times 5) - \$2{,}000 = \$1{,}000 - \$600 - \$2{,}000 = -\$1{,}600$$

Contribution Margin Method

Rearranging equation 1,

$$\left[\left(\begin{array}{c}\text{Selling}\\ \text{price}\end{array} - \begin{array}{c}\text{Variable cost}\\ \text{per unit}\end{array}\right) \times \left(\begin{array}{c}\text{Quantity of}\\ \text{units sold}\end{array}\right)\right] - \begin{array}{c}\text{Fixed}\\ \text{costs}\end{array} = \begin{array}{c}\text{Operating}\\ \text{income}\end{array}$$

$$\left(\begin{array}{c}\text{Contribution margin}\\ \text{per unit}\end{array}\right) \times \left(\begin{array}{c}\text{Quantity of}\\ \text{units sold}\end{array}\right) - \begin{array}{c}\text{Fixed}\\ \text{costs}\end{array} = \begin{array}{c}\text{Operating}\\ \text{income}\end{array} \quad \text{(Equation 2)}$$

In our *GMAT Success* example, contribution margin per unit is $80 ($200 − $120), so when Emma sells 5 packages,

$$\text{Operating income} = (\$80 \times 5) - \$2{,}000 = -\$1{,}600$$

Equation 2 expresses the basic idea we described earlier—each unit sold helps Emma recover $80 (in contribution margin) of the $2,000 in fixed costs.

3-1 TRY IT!

Bernard Windows is a small company that installs windows. Its cost structure is as follows:

Selling price from each window installation	$ 500
Variable cost of each window installation	$ 400
Annual fixed costs	$150,000

Use (a) the equation method and (b) the contribution method to calculate operating income if Bernard installs 2,000 windows.

Graph Method

The graph method helps managers visualize the relationships between total revenues and total costs. The graph shows each relationship as a line. Exhibit 3-2 illustrates the graph method for selling *GMAT Success*. Because we have assumed that total costs and total revenues behave in a linear way, we need only two points to plot the line representing each of them.

1. **Total costs line.** The total costs line is the sum of fixed costs and variable costs. Fixed costs are $2,000 for all quantities of units sold within the relevant range. To plot the total costs line, use as one point the $2,000 fixed costs at zero units sold (point A) because variable costs are $0 when no units are sold. Select a second point by choosing any other output level (say, 40 units sold) and determine the corresponding total costs. Total variable costs at this output level are $4,800 (40 units × $120 per unit). Remember, fixed costs are $2,000 at all quantities of units sold within the relevant range, so total costs at 40 units sold equal $6,800 ($2,000 + $4,800), which is point B in Exhibit 3-2. The total costs line is the straight line from point A through point B.

2. **Total revenues line.** One convenient starting point is $0 revenues at 0 units sold, which is point C in Exhibit 3-2. Select a second point by choosing any other convenient output level and determining the corresponding total revenues. At 40 units sold, total revenues are $8,000 ($200 per unit × 40 units), which is point D in Exhibit 3-2. The total revenues line is the straight line from point C through point D.

   The profit or loss at any sales level can be determined by the vertical distance between the two lines at that level in Exhibit 3-2. For quantities fewer than 25 units sold, total costs exceed total revenues, and the purple area indicates operating losses. For quantities greater than 25 units sold, total revenues exceed total costs, and the blue-green area indicates operating incomes. At 25 units sold, total revenues equal total costs. Emma will break even by selling 25 packages.

Like Emma, many companies, particularly small- and medium-sized companies, use the graph method to see how their revenues and costs will change as the quantity of units sold changes. The graph helps them understand their regions of profitability and unprofitability.

DECISION POINT

How can CVP analysis help managers?

EXHIBIT 3-2

Cost–Volume Graph for *GMAT Success*

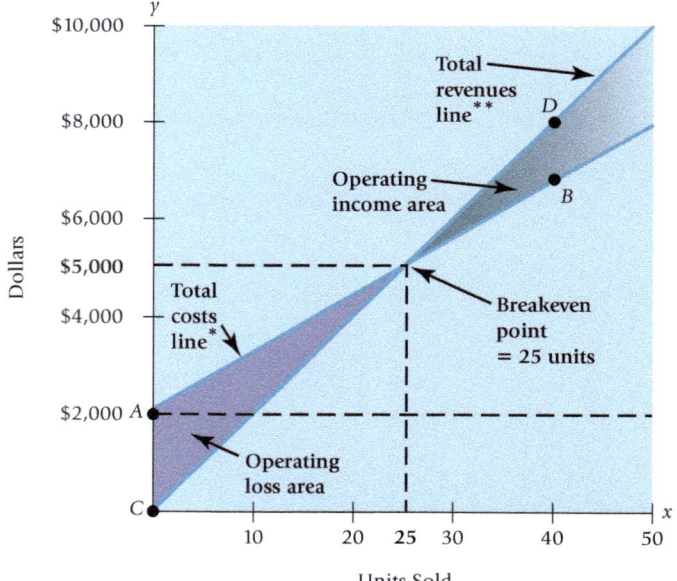

*Slope of the total costs line is the variable cost per unit = $120
**Slope of the total revenues line is the selling price = $200

Cost–Volume–Profit Assumptions

Now that you know how CVP analysis works, think about the following assumptions we made during the analysis:

1. Changes in revenues and costs arise only because of changes in the number of product (or service) units sold. The number of units sold is the only revenue driver and the only cost driver. Just as a cost driver is any factor that affects costs, a **revenue driver** is a variable, such as volume, that causally affects revenues.
2. Total costs can be separated into two components: a fixed component that does not vary with units sold (such as Emma's $2,000 booth fee) and a variable component that changes based on units sold (such as the $120 cost per *GMAT Success* package).
3. When represented graphically, the behaviors of total revenues and total costs are linear (meaning they can be represented as a straight line) in relation to units sold within a relevant range (and time period).
4. Selling price, variable cost per unit, and total fixed costs (within a relevant range and time period) are known and constant.

As you can tell from these assumptions, to conduct a CVP analysis, you need to correctly distinguish fixed from variable costs. Always keep in mind, however, that whether a cost is variable or fixed depends on the time period for a decision.

The shorter the time horizon, the higher the percentage of total costs considered fixed. For example, suppose an American Airlines plane will depart from its gate in the next hour and currently has 20 seats unsold. A potential passenger arrives with a transferable ticket from a competing airline. American's variable costs of placing one more passenger in an otherwise empty seat (such as the cost of providing the passenger with a free beverage) is negligible. With only an hour to go before the flight departs, virtually all costs (such as crew costs and baggage-handling costs) are fixed.

Alternatively, suppose American Airlines must decide whether to continue to offer this particular flight next year. If American Airlines decides to cancel this flight because very few passengers during the last year have taken it, many more of its costs, including crew costs, baggage-handling costs, and airport fees for the flight, would be considered variable: Over this longer 1-year time period, American Airlines would not have to incur these costs if the flight were no longer operating. Always consider the relevant range, the length of the time horizon, and the specific decision situation when classifying costs as variable or fixed.

Breakeven Point and Target Operating Income

In previous sections, we used the number of packages sold as an input to the contribution income statement, the equation method, the contribution margin method, and the graph method to calculate Emma's operating income for different quantities of packages sold. In this section we use the same tools to reverse the logic. We use as input the amount of operating income Emma wants to earn and then compute the number of packages Emma must sell to earn this income. A very important question is how much Emma must sell to avoid a loss.

LEARNING OBJECTIVE 2

Determine the breakeven point and output level needed to achieve a target operating income

...compare contribution margin and fixed costs

Breakeven Point

The **breakeven point (BEP)** is that quantity of output sold at which total revenues equal total costs—that is, the quantity of output sold that results in $0 of operating income. You have already learned how to use the graph method to calculate the breakeven point. Recall from Exhibit 3-1 that operating income was $0 when Emma sold 25 units; this is the breakeven point. But by understanding the equations underlying the calculations in Exhibit 3-1, we can calculate the breakeven point directly for selling *GMAT Success* rather than trying out different quantities and checking when operating income equals $0.

Recall the equation method (equation 1):

$$\left[\left(\begin{array}{c}\text{Selling}\\\text{price}\end{array} \times \begin{array}{c}\text{Quantity of}\\\text{units sold}\end{array}\right) - \left(\begin{array}{c}\text{Variable cost}\\\text{per unit}\end{array} \times \begin{array}{c}\text{Quantity of}\\\text{units sold}\end{array}\right)\right] - \begin{array}{c}\text{Fixed}\\\text{costs}\end{array} = \begin{array}{c}\text{Operating}\\\text{income}\end{array}$$

Setting operating income equal to $0 and denoting quantity of output units that must be sold by Q,

$$(\$200 \times Q) - (\$120 \times Q) - \$2{,}000 = \$0$$
$$\$80 \times Q = \$2{,}000$$
$$Q = \$2{,}000 \div \$80 \text{ per unit} = 25 \text{ units}$$

If Emma sells fewer than 25 units, she will incur a loss; if she sells 25 units, she will break even; and if she sells more than 25 units, she will make a profit. Although this breakeven point is expressed in units, it can also be expressed in revenues: 25 units × $200 selling price = $5,000. Recall the contribution margin method (equation 2):

$$\left(\begin{array}{c}\text{Contribution}\\\text{margin per unit}\end{array} \times \begin{array}{c}\text{Quantity of}\\\text{units sold}\end{array}\right) - \text{Fixed costs} = \text{Operating income}$$

At the breakeven point, operating income is by definition $0, and so,

Contribution margin per unit × Breakeven quantity of units = Fixed costs   (Equation 3)

Rearranging equation 3 and entering the data,

$$\frac{\text{Breakeven}}{\text{number of units}} = \frac{\text{Fixed costs}}{\text{Contribution margin per unit}} = \frac{\$2{,}000}{\$80 \text{ per unit}} = 25 \text{ units}$$

Breakeven revenues = Breakeven number of units × Selling price
= 25 units × $200 per unit = $5,000

In practice (because companies have multiple products), management accountants usually calculate the breakeven point directly in terms of revenues using contribution margin percentages. Recall that in the *GMAT Success* example, at revenues of $8,000, contribution margin is $3,200:

$$\frac{\text{Contribution margin}}{\text{percentage}} = \frac{\text{Contribution margin}}{\text{Revenues}} = \frac{\$3{,}200}{\$8{,}000} = 0.40, \text{ or } 40\%$$

That is, 40% of each dollar of revenue, or 40 cents, is the contribution margin. To break even, contribution margin must equal Emma's fixed costs, which are $2,000. To earn $2,000 of contribution margin, when $1 of revenue results in a $0.40 contribution margin, revenues must equal $2,000 ÷ 0.40 = $5,000.

$$\frac{\text{Breakeven}}{\text{revenues}} = \frac{\text{Fixed costs}}{\text{Contribution margin \%}} = \frac{\$2{,}000}{0.40} = \$5{,}000$$

While the breakeven point tells managers how much they must sell to avoid a loss, managers are equally interested in how they will achieve the operating income targets underlying their strategies and plans. In our example, selling 25 units at a price of $200 (equal to revenue of $5,000) assures Emma that she will not lose money if she rents the booth. While this news is comforting, how does Emma determine how much she needs to sell to achieve a targeted amount of operating income?

Target Operating Income

Suppose Emma wants to earn an operating income of $1,200? How many units must she sell? One approach is to keep plugging in different quantities into Exhibit 3-1 and check when operating income equals $1,200. Exhibit 3-1 shows that operating income is $1,200 when 40 packages are sold. A more convenient approach is to use equation 1 from page 91.

$$\left[\binom{\text{Selling}}{\text{price}} \times \binom{\text{Quantity of}}{\text{units sold}} - \binom{\text{Variable cost}}{\text{per unit}} \times \binom{\text{Quantity of}}{\text{units sold}}\right] - \binom{\text{Fixed}}{\text{costs}} = \binom{\text{Operating}}{\text{income}} \quad \text{(Equation 1)}$$

We denote by Q the unknown quantity of units Emma must sell to earn an operating income of $1,200. Selling price is $200, variable cost per package is $120, fixed costs are $2,000, and target operating income is $1,200. Substituting these values into equation 1, we have

$$(\$200 \times Q) - (\$120 \times Q) - \$2,000 = \$1,200$$
$$\$80 \times Q = \$2,000 + \$1,200 = \$3,200$$
$$Q = \$3,200 \div \$80 \text{ per unit} = 40 \text{ units}$$

Alternatively, we could use equation 2,

$$\binom{\text{Contribution margin}}{\text{per unit}} \times \binom{\text{Quantity of}}{\text{units sold}} - \binom{\text{Fixed}}{\text{costs}} = \binom{\text{Operating}}{\text{income}} \quad \text{(Equation 2)}$$

Given a target operating income ($1,200 in this case), we can rearrange terms to get equation 4.

$$\frac{\text{Quantity of units}}{\text{required to be sold}} = \frac{\text{Fixed costs} + \text{Target operating income}}{\text{Contribution margin per unit}} \quad \text{(Equation 4)}$$

$$\frac{\text{Quantity of units}}{\text{required to be sold}} = \frac{\$2,000 + \$1,200}{\$80 \text{ per unit}} = 40 \text{ units}$$

Proof:

	Revenues, $200 per unit × 40 units	$8,000
	Variable costs, $120 per unit × 40 units	4,800
	Contribution margin, $80 per unit × 40 units	3,200
	Fixed costs	2,000
	Operating income	$1,200

The revenues needed to earn an operating income of $1,200 can also be calculated directly by recognizing (1) that $3,200 of contribution margin must be earned (to cover the fixed costs of $2,000 plus earn an operating income of $1,200) and (2) that $1 of revenue earns $0.40 (40 cents) of contribution margin (the contribution margin percentage is 40%). To earn a contribution margin of $3,200, revenues must equal $3,200 ÷ 0.40 = $8,000. That is,

$$\frac{\text{Revenues needed to earn}}{\text{target operating income}} = \frac{\text{Fixed costs} + \text{Target operating income}}{\text{Contribution margin percentage}}$$

$$\text{Revenues needed to earn operating income of } \$1,200 = \frac{\$2,000 + \$1,200}{0.40} = \frac{\$3,200}{0.40} = \$8,000$$

3-2 TRY IT!

Bernard Windows is a small company that installs windows. Its cost structure is as follows:

Selling price from each window installation	$ 500
Variable cost of each window installation	$ 400
Annual fixed costs	$150,000

Calculate (a) the breakeven point in units and revenues and (b) the number of windows Bernard Windows must install and the revenues needed to earn a target operating income of $100,000.

EXHIBIT 3-3
Profit–Volume Graph for *GMAT Success*

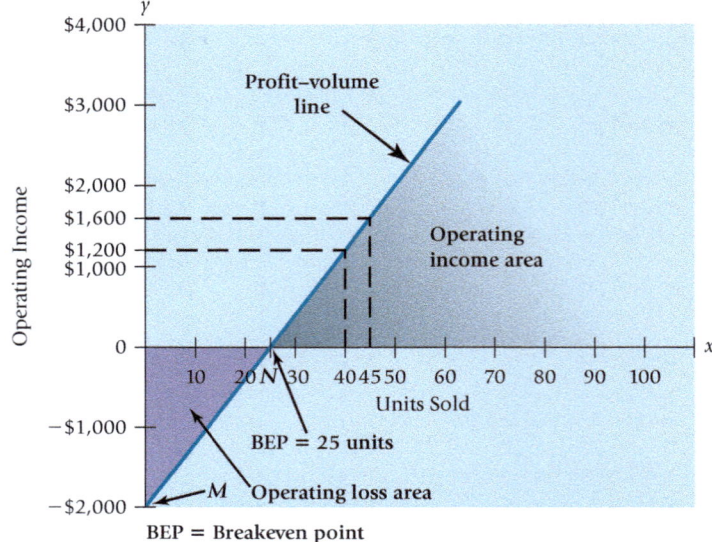

Could we use the graph method and the graph in Exhibit 3-2 to figure out how many units Emma must sell to earn an operating income of $1,200? Yes, but it is not as easy to determine the precise point at which the difference between the total revenues line and the total costs line equals $1,200. Recasting Exhibit 3-2 in the form of a profit–volume (PV) graph, however, makes it easier to answer this question.

A **PV graph** shows how changes in the quantity of units sold affect operating income. Exhibit 3-3 is the PV graph for *GMAT Success* (fixed costs, $2,000; selling price, $200; and variable cost per unit, $120). The PV line can be drawn using two points. One convenient point (M) is the operating loss at 0 units sold, which is equal to the fixed costs of $2,000 and is shown at −$2,000 on the vertical axis. A second convenient point (N) is the breakeven point, which is 25 units in our example (see page 94). The PV line is the straight line from point M through point N. To find the number of units Emma must sell to earn an operating income of $1,200, draw a horizontal line parallel to the *x*-axis corresponding to $1,200 on the vertical axis (the *y*-axis). At the point where this line intersects the PV line, draw a vertical line down to the horizontal axis (the *x*-axis). The vertical line intersects the *x*-axis at 40 units, indicating that by selling 40 units Emma will earn an operating income of $1,200.

Just like Emma, managers at larger companies such as California Pizza Kitchen use profit–volume analyses to understand how profits change with sales volumes. They use this understanding to target the sales levels they need to achieve to meet their profit plans.

Until now, we have ignored the effect of income taxes in our CVP analysis. In many companies, boards of directors want top executives and managers to consider the effect their decisions have on the company's operating income *after* income taxes because this is the measure that drives shareholders' dividends and returns. Some decisions might not result in a large operating income, but their favorable tax consequences make them attractive over other investments that have larger operating incomes but attract much higher taxes. CVP analysis can easily be adapted to consider the effect of taxes.

DECISION POINT

How can managers determine the breakeven point or the output needed to achieve a target operating income?

Income Taxes and Target Net Income

LEARNING OBJECTIVE 3

Understand how income taxes affect CVP analysis

...focus on net income

Net income is operating income plus nonoperating revenues (such as interest revenue) minus nonoperating costs (such as interest cost) minus income taxes. For simplicity, throughout this chapter we assume nonoperating revenues and nonoperating costs are zero. So, our net income equation is:

Net income = Operating income − Income taxes

To make net income evaluations, CVP calculations for target income must be stated in terms of target net income instead of target operating income. For example, Emma may be interested in knowing the quantity of units of *GMAT Success* she must sell to earn a net income of $960, assuming an income tax rate of 40%.

$$\text{Target net income} = \left(\begin{array}{c}\text{Target}\\ \text{operating income}\end{array}\right) - \left(\begin{array}{c}\text{Target}\\ \text{operating income}\end{array} \times \text{Tax rate}\right)$$

$$\text{Target net income} = (\text{Target operating income}) \times (1 - \text{Tax rate})$$

$$\text{Target operating income} = \frac{\text{Target net income}}{1 - \text{Tax rate}} = \frac{\$960}{1 - 0.40} = \$1{,}600$$

In other words, to earn a target net income of $960, Emma's target operating income is $1,600.

Proof:

Target operating income	$1,600
Tax at 40% (0.40 × $1,600)	640
Target net income	$ 960

The key step is to take the target net income number and convert it into the corresponding target operating income number. We can then use equation 1 to determine the target operating income and substitute numbers from our *GMAT Success* example.

$$\left[\left(\begin{array}{c}\text{Selling}\\ \text{price}\end{array} \times \begin{array}{c}\text{Quantity of}\\ \text{units sold}\end{array}\right) - \left(\begin{array}{c}\text{Variable cost}\\ \text{per unit}\end{array} \times \begin{array}{c}\text{Quantity of}\\ \text{units sold}\end{array}\right)\right] - \begin{array}{c}\text{Fixed}\\ \text{costs}\end{array} = \begin{array}{c}\text{Operating}\\ \text{income}\end{array} \quad \text{(Equation 1)}$$

$$(\$200 \times Q) - (\$120 \times Q) - \$2{,}000 = \$1{,}600$$
$$\$80 \times Q = \$3{,}600$$
$$Q = \$3{,}600 \div \$80 \text{ per unit} = 45 \text{ units}$$

Alternatively, we can calculate the number of units Emma must sell by using the contribution margin method and equation 4:

$$\begin{array}{c}\text{Quantity of units}\\ \text{required to be sold}\end{array} = \frac{\text{Fixed costs} + \text{Target operating income}}{\text{Contribution margin per unit}} \quad \text{(Equation 4)}$$

$$= \frac{\$2{,}000 + \$1{,}600}{\$80 \text{ per unit}} = 45 \text{ units}$$

Proof:

Revenues, $200 per unit × 45 units	$9,000
Variable costs, $120 per unit × 45 units	5,400
Contribution margin	3,600
Fixed costs	2,000
Operating income	1,600
Income taxes, $1,600 × 0.40	640
Net income	$ 960

Emma can also use the PV graph in Exhibit 3-3. To earn the target operating income of $1,600, Emma needs to sell 45 units.

Focusing the analysis on target net income instead of target operating income will not change the breakeven point because, by definition, operating income at the breakeven point is $0 and no income taxes are paid when there is no operating income.

DECISION POINT

How can managers incorporate income taxes into CVP analysis?

3-3 TRY IT!

Bernard Windows is a small company that installs windows. Its cost structure is as follows:

Selling price from each window installation	$ 500
Variable cost of each window installation	$ 400
Annual fixed costs	$150,000
Tax rate	30%

Calculate the number of windows Bernard Windows must install and the revenues needed to earn a target net income of $63,000.

LEARNING OBJECTIVE 4

Explain how managers use CVP analysis to make decisions

...choose the alternative that maximizes operating income

Using CVP Analysis for Decision Making

You have learned how CVP analysis is useful for calculating the units that need to be sold to break even or to achieve a target operating income or target net income. A manager can also use CVP analysis to make other strategic decisions. Consider a decision about choosing the features for a product, such as the engine size, transmission system, or steering system for a new car model. Different choices will affect the vehicle's selling price, variable cost per unit, fixed costs, units sold, and operating income. CVP analysis helps managers make product decisions by estimating the expected profitability of these choices. We return to our *GMAT Success* example to show how Emma can use CVP analysis to make decisions about advertising and selling price.

Decision to Advertise

Suppose Emma anticipates selling 40 units of the *GMAT Success* package at the fair. Exhibit 3-3 indicates that Emma's operating income will be $1,200. Emma is considering advertising the product and its features in the fair brochure. The advertisement will be a fixed cost of $500. Emma thinks that advertising will increase sales by 10% to 44 packages. Should Emma advertise? The following table presents the CVP analysis.

	40 Packages Sold with No Advertising (1)	44 Packages Sold with Advertising (2)	Difference (3) = (2) − (1)
Revenues ($200 × 40; $200 × 44)	$8,000	$8,800	$ 800
Variable costs ($120 × 40; $120 × 44)	4,800	5,280	480
Contribution margin ($80 × 40; $80 × 44)	3,200	3,520	320
Fixed costs	2,000	2,500	500
Operating income	$1,200	$1,020	$ (180)

Operating income will decrease from $1,200 to $1,020, so Emma should not advertise. Note that Emma could focus only on the difference column and come to the same conclusion: If Emma advertises, contribution margin will increase by $320 (revenues, $800 − variable costs, $480) and fixed costs will increase by $500, resulting in a $180 decrease in operating income.

When using CVP analysis, try evaluating your decisions based on differences rather than mechanically working through the contribution income statement. What if advertising costs were $400 or $600 instead of $500? Analyzing differences allows managers to get to the heart of CVP analysis and sharpens their intuition by focusing only on the revenues and costs that will change as a result of a decision.

Decision to Reduce the Selling Price

Having decided not to advertise, Emma is contemplating whether to reduce the selling price to $175. At this price, she thinks she will sell 50 units. At this quantity, the test-prep package company that supplies *GMAT Success* will sell the packages to Emma for $115 per unit instead of $120. Should Emma reduce the selling price?

Contribution margin from lowering price to $175: ($175 − $115) per unit × 50 units	$3,000
Contribution margin from maintaining price at $200: ($200 − $120) per unit × 40 units	3,200
Change in contribution margin from lowering price	$ (200)

Decreasing the price will reduce contribution margin by $200 and, because the fixed costs of $2,000 will not change, will also reduce Emma's operating income by $200. Emma should not reduce the selling price.

Determining Target Prices

Emma could also ask, "At what price can I sell 50 units (purchased at $115 per unit) and continue to earn an operating income of $1,200?" The answer is $179, as the following calculations show:

	Target operating income	$1,200
	Add fixed costs	2,000
	Target contribution margin	$3,200
	Divided by number of units sold	÷ 50 units
	Target contribution margin per unit	$ 64
	Add variable cost per unit	115
	Target selling price	$ 179
Proof:	Revenues, $179 per unit × 50 units	$8,950
	Variable costs, $115 per unit × 50 units	5,750
	Contribution margin	3,200
	Fixed costs	2,000
	Operating income	$1,200

Emma should also examine the effects of other decisions, such as simultaneously increasing her advertising costs and raising or lowering the price of *GMAT Success* packages. In each case, Emma will estimate the effects these actions are likely to have on the demand for *GMAT Success*. She will then compare the changes in contribution margin (through the effects on selling prices, variable costs, and quantities of units sold) to the changes in fixed costs and choose the alternative that provides the highest operating income. Concepts in Action: Cost–Volume–Profit Analysis Makes Subway's $5 Foot-Long Sandwiches a Success But Innovation

> **DECISION POINT**
> How do managers use CVP analysis to make decisions?

CONCEPTS IN ACTION > Cost–Volume–Profit Analysis Makes Subway's $5 Foot-Long Sandwiches a Success But Innovation Challenges Loom

Julian Stratenschulte/dpa/picture-alliance/Newscom

Since 2008, the 44,000-location Subway restaurant chain has done big business with the success of its $5 foot-long sandwich deal. Heavily advertised, the promotion lowered the price of many sandwiches, which attracted customers in droves and helped Subway significantly boost profits. Since introducing $5 foot-longs, Subway has sold billions of the sandwiches worldwide.

How did Subway lower prices *and* boost profits, you may ask? Through higher volume and incremental sales of other items. When the price of foot-long sandwiches was lowered to $5, contribution margin per sandwich dropped but customers flocked to Subway and sales skyrocketed increasing total contribution margin.

At least two-thirds of Subway customers purchase potato chips or a soft drink with their sandwich. Subway's contribution margin on these items is very high, frequently as high as 70%. As the number of customers increased, the total contribution margin from these other items also increased. Fixed costs increased but the increases in contribution margin resulted in big increases in operating income.

But Subway faces challenges going forward. Its rapid sales growth has slowed as customer preferences have changed, and competitors from McDonalds to Firehouse Subs, Jimmy John's, and Jersey Mike's have begun offering more healthy menu options. If Subway is to continue to grow, it needs to get closer to its customers and continue to innovate its product offerings and its marketing.

Sources: Wendy Rotelli, "How Does Subway Profit From The $5 Foot-Long Deal?" *Restaurant Business* blog, Restaurants.com, April 10, 2013 (https://www.restaurants.com/blog/how-does-subway-profit-from-the-5-foot-long-deal); Drew Harwell, "The Rise and Fall of Subway, the World's Biggest Food Chain," *Washington Post*, May 30, 2015 (https://www.washingtonpost.com/business/economy/the-rise-and-fall-of-subway-the-worlds-biggest-food-chain/2015/05/29/0ca0a84a-fa7a-11e4-a13c-193b1241d51a_story.html).

Challenges Loom describes how Subway restaurant chain reduced the prices of its sandwiches to increase contribution margin and operating income but must now innovate to sustain its growth.

Strategic decisions invariably entail risk. Managers can use CVP analysis to evaluate how the operating income of their companies will be affected if the outcomes they predict are not achieved—say, if sales are 10% lower than they estimated. Evaluating this risk affects other strategic decisions a manager might make. For example, if the probability of a decline in sales seems high, a manager may take actions to change the cost structure to have more variable costs and fewer fixed costs.

Sensitivity Analysis and Margin of Safety

LEARNING OBJECTIVE 5

Explain how sensitivity analysis helps managers cope with uncertainty

...determine the effect on operating income of different assumptions

Sensitivity analysis is a "what-if" technique managers use to examine how an outcome will change if the original predicted data are not achieved or if an underlying assumption changes. The analysis answers questions such as "What will operating income be if the quantity of units sold decreases by 5% from the original prediction?" and "What will operating income be if variable cost per unit increases by 10%?" This helps visualize the possible outcomes that might occur *before* the company commits to funding a project. For example, companies such as Boeing and Airbus use CVP analysis to evaluate how many airplanes they need to sell in order to recover the multibillion-dollar costs of designing and developing new ones. The managers then do a sensitivity analysis to test how sensitive their conclusions are to different assumptions, such as the size of the market for the airplane, its selling price, and the market share they think it can capture.

Electronic spreadsheets, such as Excel, enable managers to systematically and efficiently conduct CVP-based sensitivity analyses and to examine the effect and interaction of changes in selling price, variable cost per unit, and fixed costs on target operating income. Exhibit 3-4 displays a spreadsheet for the *GMAT Success* example.

Using the spreadsheet, Emma can immediately see how many units she needs to sell to achieve particular operating-income levels, given alternative levels of fixed costs and variable cost per unit that she may face. For example, she must sell 32 units to earn an operating

EXHIBIT 3-4

Spreadsheet Analysis of CVP Relationships for *GMAT Success*

D5 fx =($A5+D$3)/(F1-$B5)

	A	B	C	D	E	F
1			\multicolumn{4}{l	}{Number of units required to be sold at $200}
2			\multicolumn{4}{l	}{Selling Price to Earn Target Operating Income of}
3		Variable Costs	$0	$1,200	$1,600	$2,000
4	Fixed Costs	per Unit	(Breakeven point)			
5	$2,000	$100	20	32[a]	36	40
6	$2,000	$120	25	40	45	50
7	$2,000	$150	40	64	72	80
8	$2,400	$100	24	36	40	44
9	$2,400	$120	30	45	50	55
10	$2,400	$150	48	72	80	88
11	$2,800	$100	28	40	44	48
12	$2,800	$120	35	50	55	60
13	$2,800	$150	56	80	88	96
14						
15-16	[a]Number of units required to be sold					

$$^a\text{Number of units required to be sold} = \frac{\text{Fixed costs + Target operating income}}{\text{Contribution margin per unit}} = \frac{\$2{,}000 + \$1{,}200}{\$200 - \$100} = 32$$

income of $1,200 if fixed costs are $2,000 and variable cost per unit is $100. Emma can also use cell C13 of Exhibit 3-4 to determine that she needs to sell 56 units to break even if the fixed cost of the booth rental at the Chicago fair is raised to $2,800 and if the variable cost per unit charged by the test-prep package supplier increases to $150. Emma can use this information along with sensitivity analysis and her predictions about how much she can sell to decide if she should rent the booth.

An important aspect of sensitivity analysis is **margin of safety**:

$$\text{Margin of safety} = \text{Budgeted (or actual) revenues} - \text{Breakeven revenues}$$

$$\text{Margin of safety (in units)} = \text{Budgeted (or actual) sales quantity} - \text{Breakeven quantity}$$

The margin of safety answers the "what-if" question: If budgeted revenues are above the breakeven point and drop, how far can they fall below budget before the breakeven point is reached? Sales might decrease as a result of factors such as a poorly executed marketing program or a competitor introducing a better product. Assume that Emma has fixed costs of $2,000, a selling price of $200, and variable cost per unit of $120. From Exhibit 3-1, if Emma sells 40 units, budgeted revenues are $8,000 and budgeted operating income is $1,200. The breakeven point is 25 units or $5,000 in total revenues.

$$\text{Margin of safety} = \text{Budgeted revenues} - \text{Breakeven revenues} = \$8,000 - \$5,000 = \$3,000$$

$$\text{Margin of safety (in units)} = \text{Budgeted sales (units)} - \text{Breakeven sales (units)} = 40 - 25 = 15 \text{ units}$$

Sometimes margin of safety is expressed as a percentage:

$$\text{Margin of safety percentage} = \frac{\text{Margin of safety in dollars}}{\text{Budgeted (or actual) revenues}}$$

In our example, margin of safety percentage $= \frac{\$3,000}{\$8,000} = 37.5\%$

This result means that revenues would have to decrease substantially, by 37.5%, to reach the breakeven revenues. The high margin of safety gives Emma confidence that she is unlikely to suffer a loss.

If, however, Emma expects to sell only 30 units, budgeted revenues would be $6,000 ($200 per unit × 30 units) and the margin of safety would equal:

$$\text{Budgeted revenues} - \text{Breakeven revenues} = \$6,000 - \$5,000 = \$1,000$$

$$\text{Margin of safety percentage} = \frac{\text{Margin of safety in dollars}}{\text{Budgeted (or actual) revenues}} = \frac{\$1,000}{\$6,000} = 16.67\%$$

The analysis implies that if revenues fall by more than 16.67%, Emma would suffer a loss. A low margin of safety increases the risk of a loss, which means Emma would need to look for ways to lower the breakeven point by reducing fixed costs or increasing contribution margin. For example, she would need to evaluate if her product is attractive enough to customers to allow her to charge a higher price without reducing the demand for it or if she could purchase the software at a lower cost. If Emma can neither reduce her fixed costs nor increase contribution margin and if she does not have the tolerance for this level of risk, she will prefer not to rent a booth at the fair.

Sensitivity analysis gives managers a good feel for a decision's risks. It is a simple approach to recognizing **uncertainty**, which is the possibility that an actual amount will deviate from an expected amount. A more comprehensive approach to recognizing uncertainty is to compute expected values using probability distributions. This approach is illustrated in the appendix to this chapter.

DECISION POINT

What can managers do to cope with uncertainty or changes in underlying assumptions?

TRY IT! 3-4

Bernard Windows is a small company that installs windows. Its cost structure is as follows:

Selling price from each window installation	$ 500
Variable cost of each window installation	$ 400
Annual fixed costs	$150,000

Calculate the margin of safety in units and dollars and the margin of safety percentage if Bernard Windows expects to sell 2,400 windows in the year.

Cost Planning and CVP

LEARNING OBJECTIVE 6

Use CVP analysis to plan variable and fixed costs

...compare risk of losses versus higher returns

Managers have the ability to choose the levels of fixed and variable costs in their cost structures. This is a strategic decision that affects risk and returns. In this section, we describe how managers and management accountants think through this decision.

Alternative Fixed-Cost/Variable-Cost Structures

CVP-based sensitivity analysis highlights the risks and returns as fixed costs are substituted for variable costs in a company's cost structure. In Exhibit 3-4, compare line 6 and line 11.

			Number of units required to be sold at $200 selling price to earn target operating income of	
	Fixed Cost	Variable Cost	$0 (Breakeven point)	$2,000
Line 6	$2,000	$120	25	50
Line 11	$2,800	$100	28	48

Line 11, which has higher fixed costs and lower variable costs than line 6, has a higher breakeven point but requires fewer units to be sold (48 vs. 50) to earn an operating income of $2,000. CVP analysis can help managers evaluate various fixed-cost/variable-cost structures. We next consider the effects of these choices in more detail. Suppose the Chicago fair organizers offer Emma three rental alternatives:

Option 1: $2,000 fixed fee

Option 2: $800 fixed fee plus 15% of *GMAT Success* revenues

Option 3: 25% of *GMAT Success* revenues with no fixed fee

Emma is interested in how her choice of a rental agreement will affect the income she earns and the risks she faces. Exhibit 3-5 graphically depicts the profit–volume relationship for each option.

- The line representing the relationship between units sold and operating income for Option 1 is the same as the line in the PV graph shown in Exhibit 3-3 (fixed costs of $2,000 and contribution margin per unit of $80).
- The line representing Option 2 shows fixed costs of $800 and a contribution margin per unit of $50 [selling price, $200, minus variable cost per unit, $120, minus variable rental fees per unit, $30 (0.15 × $200)].
- The line representing Option 3 shows fixed costs of $0 and a contribution margin per unit of $30 [selling price, $200, minus variable cost per unit, $120, minus variable rental fees per unit, $50 (0.25 × $200)].

Option 3 has the lowest breakeven point (0 units), and Option 1 has the highest breakeven point (25 units). Option 1 is associated with the highest risk of loss if sales are low, but it also has the highest contribution margin per unit ($80) and therefore the highest operating income when sales are high (greater than 40 units).

The choice among Options 1, 2, and 3 is a strategic decision. As with most strategic decisions, what Emma decides will significantly affect her operating income (or loss), depending on the demand for the product. Faced with this uncertainty, Emma's choice will be influenced

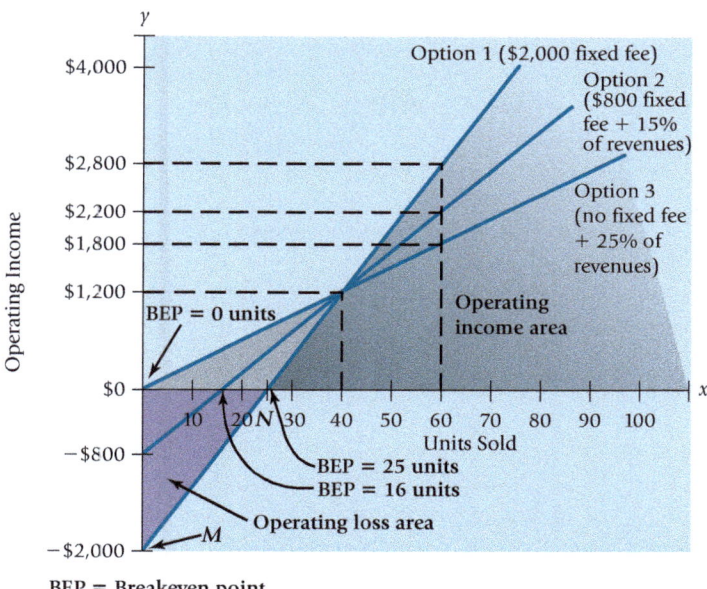

EXHIBIT 3-5

Profit–Volume Graph for Alternative Rental Options for *GMAT Success*

by her confidence in the level of demand for *GMAT Success* packages and her willingness to risk losses if demand is low. For example, if Emma's tolerance for risk is high, she will choose Option 1 with its high potential rewards. If, however, Emma is risk averse, she will prefer Option 3, where the rewards are smaller if sales are high but where she never suffers a loss if sales are low.

Operating Leverage

The risk-return tradeoff across alternative cost structures can be measured as *operating leverage*. **Operating leverage** describes the effects that fixed costs have on changes in operating income as changes occur in units sold and contribution margin. Organizations with a high proportion of fixed costs in their cost structures, as is the case with Option 1, have high operating leverage. The line representing Option 1 in Exhibit 3-5 is the steepest of the three lines. Small increases in sales lead to large increases in operating income. Small decreases in sales result in relatively large decreases in operating income, leading to a greater risk of operating losses. *At any given level of sales,*

$$\frac{\text{Degree of}}{\text{operating leverage}} = \frac{\text{Contribution margin}}{\text{Operating income}}$$

The following table shows the **degree of operating leverage** at sales of 40 units for the three rental options.

	Option 1	Option 2	Option 3
1. Contribution margin per unit (see page 102)	$ 80	$ 50	$ 30
2. Contribution margin (row 1 × 40 units)	$3,200	$2,000	$1,200
3. Operating income (from Exhibit 3-5)	$1,200	$1,200	$1,200
4. Degree of operating leverage (row 2 ÷ row 3)	$\frac{\$3{,}200}{\$1{,}200} = 2.67$	$\frac{\$2{,}000}{\$1{,}200} = 1.67$	$\frac{\$1{,}200}{\$1{,}200} = 1.00$

These results indicate that, when sales are 40 units, a 1% change in sales and contribution margin will result in 2.67% change in operating income for Option 1. For Option 3, a 1% change in sales and contribution margin will result in only a 1% change in operating income. Consider, for example, a sales increase of 50% from 40 to 60 units. Contribution margin will increase by 50% under each option. Operating income, however, will increase by 2.67 × 50% = 133% from $1,200 to $2,800 in Option 1, but it will increase by only

1.00 × 50% = 50% from $1,200 to $1,800 in Option 3 (see Exhibit 3-5). The degree of operating leverage at a given level of sales helps managers calculate the effect of sales fluctuations on operating income.

Keep in mind that, in the presence of fixed costs, the degree of operating leverage is different at different levels of sales. For example, at sales of 60 units, the degree of operating leverage under each of the three options is as follows:

	Option 1	Option 2	Option 3
1. Contribution margin per unit (page 102)	$ 80	$ 50	$ 30
2. Contribution margin (row 1 × 60 units)	$4,800	$3,000	$1,800
3. Operating income (from Exhibit 3-5)	$2,800	$2,200	$1,800
4. Degree of operating leverage (row 2 ÷ row 3)	$\frac{\$4,800}{\$2,800} = 1.71$	$\frac{\$3,000}{\$2,200} = 1.36$	$\frac{\$1,800}{\$1,800} = 1.00$

The degree of operating leverage decreases from 2.67 (at sales of 40 units) to 1.71 (at sales of 60 units) under Option 1 and from 1.67 to 1.36 under Option 2. In general, whenever there are fixed costs, the degree of operating leverage decreases as the level of sales increases beyond the breakeven point. If fixed costs are $0 as they are in Option 3, contribution margin equals operating income and the degree of operating leverage equals 1.00 at all sales levels.

It is important for managers to monitor operating leverage carefully. Consider companies such as General Motors and American Airlines. Their high operating leverage was a major reason for their financial problems. Anticipating high demand for their services, these companies borrowed money to acquire assets, resulting in high fixed costs. As their sales declined, they suffered losses and could not generate enough cash to service their interest and debt, causing them to seek bankruptcy protection. Managers and management accountants must manage the level of fixed costs and variable costs to balance the risk-return tradeoffs in their firms.

What can managers do to reduce fixed costs? Nike, the shoe and apparel company, does no manufacturing and incurs no fixed costs of operating and maintaining manufacturing plants. Instead, it outsources production and buys its products from suppliers in countries such as China, Indonesia, and Vietnam. As a result, all of Nike's production costs are variable costs. Nike reduces its risk of loss by increasing variable costs and reducing fixed costs.

Companies that continue to do their own manufacturing are moving their facilities from the United States to lower-cost countries, such as Mexico and China, to reduce both fixed costs and variable costs. Other companies, such as General Electric and Hewlett-Packard, have shifted service functions, such as after-sales customer service, to their customer call centers in countries such as India. These decisions by companies are often controversial. Some economists argue that outsourcing or building plants in other countries helps keep costs, and therefore prices, low and enables U.S. companies to remain globally competitive. Others argue that outsourcing and setting up manufacturing in other countries reduces job opportunities in the United States and hurts working-class families.

DECISION POINT

How should managers choose among different variable-cost/fixed-cost structures?

TRY IT! 3-5

Bernard Windows is a small company that installs windows. Its cost structure is as follows:

Selling price from each window installation	$ 500
Variable cost of each window installation	$ 400
Annual fixed costs	$150,000
Number of window units sold	2,500

Bernard is considering changing its sales compensation for next year. Bernard would pay salespeople a 5% commission next year and reduce fixed selling costs by $62,500.

Calculate the degree of operating leverage at sales of 2,500 units under the two options. Comment briefly on the result.

Effects of Sales Mix on Income

Sales mix is the quantities (or proportion) of various products (or services) that constitute a company's total unit sales. Suppose Emma is now budgeting for a subsequent college fair in New York. She plans to sell two different test-prep packages—*GMAT Success* and *GRE Guarantee*—and budgets the following:

	GMAT Success	*GRE Guarantee*	Total
Expected sales	60	40	100
Revenues, $200 and $100 per unit	$12,000	$4,000	$16,000
Variable costs, $120 and $70 per unit	7,200	2,800	10,000
Contribution margin, $80 and $30 per unit	$ 4,800	$1,200	6,000
Fixed costs			4,500
Operating income			$ 1,500

> **LEARNING OBJECTIVE 7**
>
> Apply CVP analysis to a company producing multiple products
>
> ...assume sales mix of products remains constant as total units sold changes

What is the breakeven point for Emma's business now? The total number of units that must be sold to break even in a multiproduct company depends on the sales mix. For Emma, this is the combination of the number of units of *GMAT Success* sold and the number of units of *GRE Guarantee* sold. We assume that the budgeted sales mix (60 units of *GMAT Success* sold for every 40 units of *GRE Guarantee* sold, that is, a ratio of 3:2) will not change at different levels of total unit sales. That is, we think of Emma selling a bundle of 3 units of *GMAT Success* and 2 units of *GRE Guarantee*. (Note that this does not mean that Emma physically bundles the two products together into one big package.)

Each bundle yields a contribution margin of $300, calculated as follows:

	Number of Units of *GMAT Success* and *GRE Guarantee* in Each Bundle	Contribution Margin per Unit for *GMAT Success* and *GRE Guarantee*	Contribution Margin of the Bundle
GMAT *Success*	3	$80	$240
GRE *Guarantee*	2	30	60
Total			$300

To compute the breakeven point, we calculate the number of bundles Emma needs to sell.

$$\text{Breakeven point in bundles} = \frac{\text{Fixed costs}}{\text{Contribution margin per bundle}} = \frac{\$4,500}{\$300 \text{ per bundle}} = 15 \text{ bundles}$$

The breakeven point in units of *GMAT Success* and *GRE Guarantee* is as follows:

GMAT *Success*: 15 bundles × 3 units per bundle	45 units
GRE *Guarantee*: 15 bundles × 2 units per bundle	30 units
Total number of units to break even	75 units

The breakeven point in dollars for *GMAT Success* and *GRE Guarantee* is as follows:

GMAT *Success*: 45 units × $200 per unit	$ 9,000
GRE *Guarantee*: 30 units × $100 per unit	3,000
Breakeven revenues	$12,000

When there are multiple products, it is often convenient to use the contribution margin percentage. Under this approach, Emma also calculates the revenues from selling a bundle of 3 units of *GMAT Success* and 2 units of *GRE Guarantee*:

	Number of Units of *GMAT Success* and *GRE Guarantee* in Each Bundle	Selling Price for *GMAT Success* and *GRE Guarantee*	Revenue of the Bundle
GMAT *Success*	3	$200	$600
GRE *Guarantee*	2	100	200
Total			$800

$$\text{Contribution margin percentage for the bundle} = \frac{\text{Contribution margin of the bundle}}{\text{Revenue of the bundle}} = \frac{\$300}{\$800} = 0.375, \text{ or } 37.5\%$$

$$\text{Breakeven revenues} = \frac{\text{Fixed costs}}{\text{Contribution margin \% for the bundle}} = \frac{\$4,500}{0.375} = \$12,000$$

$$\text{Number of bundles required to be sold to break even} = \frac{\text{Breakeven revenues}}{\text{Revenue per bundle}} = \frac{\$12,000}{\$800 \text{ per bundle}} = 15 \text{ bundles}$$

The breakeven point in units and dollars for *GMAT Success* and *GRE Guarantee* are as follows:

GMAT Success: 15 bundles × 3 units per bundle = 45 units × $200 per unit = $9,000

GRE Guarantee: 15 bundles × 2 units per bundle = 30 units × $100 per unit = $3,000

Recall that in all our calculations we have assumed that the budgeted sales mix (3 units of *GMAT Success* for every 2 units of *GRE Guarantee*) will not change at different levels of total unit sales.

Of course, there are many different sales mixes (in units) that can result in a contribution margin of $4,500 that leads to Emma breaking even, as the following table shows:

Sales Mix (Units)		Contribution Margin from		
GMAT Success (1)	GRE Guarantee (2)	GMAT Success (3) = $80 × (1)	GRE Guarantee (4) = $30 × (2)	Total Contribution Margin (5) = (3) + (4)
48	22	$3,840	$ 660	$4,500
36	54	2,880	1,620	4,500
30	70	2,400	2,100	4,500

If, for example, the sales mix changes to 3 units of *GMAT Success* for every 7 units of *GRE Guarantee*, the breakeven point increases from 75 units to 100 units, composed of 30 units of *GMAT Success* and 70 units of *GRE Guarantee*. The breakeven quantity increases because the sales mix has shifted toward the lower-contribution-margin product, *GRE Guarantee* (which is $30 per unit compared to *GMAT Success*'s $80 per unit). In general, for any given total quantity of units sold, a shift in sales mix towards units with lower contribution margins (more units of *GRE Guarantee* compared to *GMAT Success*), decreases operating income.

How do companies choose their sales mix? They adjust their mix to respond to demand changes. For example, when gasoline prices increased and customers wanted smaller cars, auto companies, such as Ford, Nissan, and Toyota, shifted their production mix to produce smaller cars. This shift to smaller cars increased the breakeven point because the sales mix had shifted toward lower-contribution-margin products. Despite this increase in the breakeven point, shifting the sales mix to smaller cars was the correct decision because the demand for larger cars had fallen. At no point should a manager focus on changing the sales mix to lower the breakeven point without taking into account customer preferences and demand. Of course, the shift in sales mix to smaller cars prompted managers at Ford, Nissan, and Toyota to increase the prices of these cars in line with demand.

The multiproduct case has two cost (and revenue) drivers, *GMAT Success* and *GRE Guarantee*. It illustrates how CVP and breakeven analyses can be adapted when there are multiple cost drivers. The key point is that many different combinations of cost drivers can result in a given contribution margin.

DECISION POINT

How can managers apply CVP analysis to a company producing multiple products?

3-6 TRY IT!

Bernard Windows plans to sell two different brands of windows—Chad and Musk—and budgets the following:

	Chad Windows	Musk Windows	Total
Expected sales	2,500	1,000	3,500
Revenues, $500 and $350 per unit	$1,250,000	$350,000	$1,600,000
Variable costs, $400 and $275 per unit	1,000,000	275,000	1,275,000
Contribution margin, $100 and $75 per unit	$ 250,000	$ 75,000	325,000
Fixed costs			195,000
Operating income			$ 130,000

Calculate the breakeven point for Bernard Windows in terms of (a) the number of units sold and (b) revenues.

CVP Analysis in Service and Not-for-Profit Organizations

So far, our CVP analysis has focused on Emma's merchandising company. Of course, managers at manufacturing companies such as BMW, service companies such as Bank of America, and not-for-profit organizations such as the United Way also use CVP analysis to make decisions. To apply CVP analysis in service and not-for-profit organizations, we need to focus on measuring their output, which is different from the tangible units sold by manufacturing and merchandising companies. Examples of output measures in various service industries (for example, airlines, hotels/motels, and hospitals) and not-for-profit organizations (for example, universities) are as follows:

LEARNING OBJECTIVE 8

Apply CVP analysis in service and not-for-profit organizations

...define appropriate output measures

Industry	Measure of Output
Airlines	Passenger miles
Hotels/motels	Room-nights occupied
Hospitals	Patient days
Universities	Student credit-hours

Variable and fixed costs are then defined with respect to the chosen output measure. The concepts of contribution margin, breakeven point, target operating income, target net income, sensitivity analysis, and operating leverage apply as we have described in the chapter.

To see the application of CVP analysis in the context of a service-sector example, consider Highbridge Consulting, a boutique management consulting firm. Highbridge measures output in terms of person-days of consulting services. It hires consultants to match the demand for consulting services. The greater the demand, the greater the number of consultants it hires.

Highbridge must hire and train new consultants before the consultants are deployed on assignments. At the start of each year, Highbridge allocates a recruiting budget for the number of employees it desires to recruit. In 2017, this budget is $1,250,000. On average, the annual cost of a consultant is $100,000. Fixed costs of recruiting including administrative salaries and expenses of the recruiting department are $250,000. How many consultants can Highbridge recruit in 2017? We can use CVP analysis to answer this question by setting the recruiting department's operating income to $0. Let Q be the number of consultants hired:

$$\text{Recruiting Budget} - \text{Variable costs} - \text{Fixed costs} = 0$$
$$\$1,250,000 - \$100,000\, Q - \$250,000 = 0$$
$$\$100,000\, Q = \$1,250,000 - \$250,000 = \$1,000,000$$
$$Q = \$1,000,000 \div \$100,000 \text{ per consultant} = 10 \text{ consultants}$$

Suppose Highbridge anticipates reduced demand for consulting services in 2018. It reduces its recruiting budget by 40% to $1,250,000 \times (1 - 0.40) = \$750,000$, expecting to hire 6 consultants (40% fewer consultants than 2017). Assuming the cost per consultant and the recruiting department's fixed costs remain the same as in 2017, is this budget correct? No, as the following calculation shows:

$$\$750{,}000 - \$100{,}000\, Q - \$250{,}000 = 0$$
$$\$100{,}000\, Q = \$750{,}000 - \$250{,}000 = \$500{,}000$$
$$Q = \$500{,}000 \div \$100{,}000 \text{ per consultant} = 5 \text{ consultants}$$

Highbridge will only be able to recruit 5 consultants. Note the following two characteristics of the CVP relationships in this service company situation:

1. The percentage decrease in the number of consultants hired, $(10 - 5) \div 10$, or 50%, is greater than the 40% reduction in the recruiting budget. It is greater because the $250,000 in fixed costs still must be paid, leaving a proportionately lower budget to hire consultants. In other words, the percentage drop in consultants hired exceeds the percentage drop in the recruiting budget because of the fixed costs.

2. Given the reduced recruiting budget of $750,000 in 2018, the manager can adjust recruiting activities to hire 6 consultants in one or more of the following ways: (a) by reducing the variable cost per person (the average compensation) from the current $100,000 per consultant, or (b) by reducing the recruiting department's total fixed costs from the current $250,000. For example if the recruiting department's fixed costs were reduced to $210,000 and the cost per consultant were reduced to $90,000, Highbridge would be able to hire the 6 consultants it needs, $(\$750{,}000 - \$210{,}000) \div \$90{,}000 = 6$ consultants.

If the fixed costs of the recruiting department remain $250,000 and Highbridge wants to hire 6 consultants at an average cost of $100,000, it would have to set the recruiting budget at $850,000 [(\$100{,}000 \times 6) + \$250{,}000]$ instead of $750,000. Again the percentage decrease in the number of consultants hired $40\% [(10 - 6) \div 10]$ is greater than the $32\% [(\$1{,}250{,}000 - \$850{,}000) \div \$1{,}250{,}000]$ reduction in the recruiting budget because of the fixed costs of the recruiting department.

> **DECISION POINT**
> How do managers apply CVP analysis in service and not-for-profit organizations?

Contribution Margin Versus Gross Margin

> **LEARNING OBJECTIVE**
>
> Distinguish contribution margin
>
> ...revenues minus all variable costs
>
> from gross margin
>
> ...revenues minus cost of goods sold

So far, we have developed two important concepts relating to profit margin—contribution margin, which was introduced in this chapter, and gross margin, which was discussed in Chapter 2. Is there a relationship between these two concepts? In the following equations, we clearly distinguish contribution margin, which provides information for CVP and risk analysis, from gross margin, a measure of competitiveness, described in Chapter 2.

$$\text{Gross margin} = \text{Revenues} - \text{Cost of goods sold}$$
$$\text{Contribution margin} = \text{Revenues} - \text{All variable costs}$$

The gross margin measures how much a company can charge for its products over and above the cost of acquiring or producing them. Companies, such as brand-name pharmaceuticals producers, have high gross margins because their products are often patented and provide unique and distinctive benefits to consumers. In contrast, manufacturers of generic medicines and basic chemicals have low gross margins because the market for these products is highly competitive. Contribution margin indicates how much of a company's revenues are available to cover fixed costs. It helps in assessing the risk of losses. For example, the risk of loss is low if the contribution margin exceeds a company's fixed costs even when sales are low. Gross margin and contribution margin are related but give different insights. For example, a company operating in a competitive market with a low gross margin will have a low risk of loss if its fixed costs are small.

Consider the distinction between gross margin and contribution margin in the manufacturing sector. The concepts differ in two ways: fixed manufacturing costs and variable nonmanufacturing costs. The following example (figures assumed) illustrates this difference:

Contribution Income Statement Emphasizing Contribution Margin (in thousands)			Financial Accounting Income Statement Emphasizing Gross Margin (in thousands)	
Revenues		$1,000	Revenues	$1,000
Variable manufacturing costs	$250		Cost of goods sold (variable manufacturing costs, $250 + fixed manufacturing costs, $160)	410
Variable nonmanufacturing costs	270	520		
Contribution margin		480	Gross margin	590
Fixed manufacturing costs	160			
Fixed nonmanufacturing costs	138	298	Nonmanufacturing costs (variable, $270 + fixed, $138)	408
Operating income		$ 182	Operating income	$ 182

Fixed manufacturing costs of $160,000 are not deducted from revenues when computing the contribution margin but are deducted when computing the gross margin. The cost of goods sold in a manufacturing company includes all variable manufacturing costs and all fixed manufacturing costs ($250,000 + $160,000). The company's variable nonmanufacturing costs (such as commissions paid to salespersons) of $270,000 are deducted from revenues when computing the contribution margin but are not deducted when computing gross margin.

Like contribution margin, gross margin can be expressed as a total, as an amount per unit, or as a percentage. For example, the **gross margin percentage** is the gross margin divided by revenues—59% ($590 ÷ $1,000) in our manufacturing-sector example.

One reason why managers sometimes confuse gross margin and contribution margin with each other is that the two are often identical in the case of merchandising companies because the cost of goods sold equals the variable cost of goods purchased (and subsequently sold).

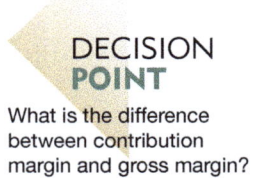

DECISION POINT

What is the difference between contribution margin and gross margin?

PROBLEM FOR SELF-STUDY

Wembley Travel Agency specializes in flights between Los Angeles and London. It books passengers on United Airlines at $900 per round-trip ticket. Until last month, United paid Wembley a commission of 10% of the ticket price paid by each passenger. This commission was Wembley's only source of revenues. Wembley's fixed costs are $14,000 per month (for salaries, rent, and so on), and its variable costs, such as sales commissions and bonuses, are $20 per ticket purchased for a passenger.

United Airlines has just announced a revised payment schedule for all travel agents. It will now pay travel agents a 10% commission per ticket up to a maximum of $50. Any ticket costing more than $500 generates only a $50 commission, regardless of the ticket price. Wembley's managers are concerned about how United's new payment schedule will affect its breakeven point and profitability.

1. Under the old 10% commission structure, how many round-trip tickets must Wembley sell each month (a) to break even and (b) to earn an operating income of $7,000?
2. How does United's revised payment schedule affect your answers to (a) and (b) in requirement 1?

Continued

Solution

1. Wembley receives a 10% commission on each ticket: 10% × $900 = $90. Thus,

$$\text{Selling price} = \$90 \text{ per ticket}$$
$$\text{Variable cost per unit} = \$20 \text{ per ticket}$$
$$\text{Contribution margin per unit} = \$90 - \$20 = \$70 \text{ per ticket}$$
$$\text{Fixed costs} = \$14{,}000 \text{ per month}$$

   a. $$\frac{\text{Breakeven number}}{\text{of tickets}} = \frac{\text{Fixed costs}}{\text{Contribution margin per unit}} = \frac{\$14{,}000}{\$70 \text{ per ticket}} = 200 \text{ tickets}$$

   b. When target operating income = $7,000 per month,

   $$\frac{\text{Quantity of tickets}}{\text{required to be sold}} = \frac{\text{Fixed costs} + \text{Target operating income}}{\text{Contribution margin per unit}}$$

   $$= \frac{\$14{,}000 + \$7{,}000}{\$70 \text{ per ticket}} = \frac{\$21{,}000}{\$70 \text{ per ticket}} = 300 \text{ tickets}$$

2. Under the new system, Wembley would receive only $50 on the $900 ticket. Thus,

$$\text{Selling price} = \$50 \text{ per ticket}$$
$$\text{Variable cost per unit} = \$20 \text{ per ticket}$$
$$\text{Contribution margin per unit} = \$50 - \$20 = \$30 \text{ per ticket}$$
$$\text{Fixed costs} = \$14{,}000 \text{ per month}$$

   a. $$\frac{\text{Breakeven number}}{\text{of tickets}} = \frac{\$14{,}000}{\$30 \text{ per ticket}} = 467 \text{ tickets (rounded up)}$$

   b. $$\frac{\text{Quantity of tickets}}{\text{required to be sold}} = \frac{\$21{,}000}{\$30 \text{ per ticket}} = 700 \text{ tickets}$$

The $50 cap on the commission paid per ticket causes the breakeven point to more than double (from 200 to 467 tickets) and the tickets required to be sold to earn $7,000 per month to also more than double (from 300 to 700 tickets). As would be expected, managers at Wembley reacted very negatively to the United Airlines announcement to change commission payments. Unfortunately for Wembley, other airlines also changed their commission structure in similar ways.

DECISION POINTS

The following question-and-answer format summarizes the chapter's learning objectives. Each decision presents a key question related to a learning objective. The guidelines are the answer to that question.

Decision	Guidelines
1. How can CVP analysis help managers?	CVP analysis assists managers in understanding the behavior of a product's or service's total costs, total revenues, and operating income as changes occur in the output level, selling price, variable costs, or fixed costs.
2. How can managers determine the breakeven point or the output needed to achieve a target operating income?	The breakeven point is the quantity of output at which total revenues equal total costs. The three methods for computing the breakeven point and the quantity of output to achieve target operating income are the equation method, the contribution margin method, and the graph method. Each method is merely a restatement of the others. Managers often select the method they find easiest to use in a specific decision situation.

Decision	Guidelines
3. How can managers incorporate income taxes into CVP analysis?	Income taxes can be incorporated into CVP analysis by using the target net income to calculate the target operating income. The breakeven point is unaffected by income taxes because no income taxes are paid when operating income equals zero.
4. How do managers use CVP analysis to make decisions?	Managers compare how revenues, costs, and contribution margins change across various alternatives. They then choose the alternative that maximizes operating income.
5. What can managers do to cope with uncertainty or changes in underlying assumptions?	Sensitivity analysis is a "what-if" technique that examines how an outcome will change if the original predicted data are not achieved or if an underlying assumption changes. When making decisions, managers use CVP analysis to compare contribution margins and fixed costs under different assumptions. Managers also calculate the margin of safety equal to budgeted revenues minus breakeven revenues.
6. How should managers choose among different variable-cost/fixed-cost structures?	Choosing the variable-cost/fixed-cost structure is a strategic decision for companies. CVP analysis helps managers compare the risk of losses when revenues are low and the upside profits when revenues are high for different proportions of variable and fixed costs in a company's cost structure.
7. How can managers apply CVP analysis to a company producing multiple products?	Managers apply CVP analysis in a company producing multiple products by assuming the sales mix of products sold remains constant as the total quantity of units sold changes.
8. How do managers apply CVP analysis in service and not-for-profit organizations?	Managers define output measures such as passenger-miles in the case of airlines or patient-days in the context of hospitals and identify costs that are fixed and those that vary with these measures of output.
9. What is the difference between contribution margin and gross margin?	Contribution margin is revenues minus all variable costs whereas gross margin is revenues minus cost of goods sold. Contribution margin measures the risk of a loss, whereas gross margin measures the competitiveness of a product.

APPENDIX

Decision Models and Uncertainty[2]

This appendix explores the characteristics of uncertainty, describes an approach managers can use to make decisions in a world of uncertainty, and illustrates the insights gained when uncertainty is recognized in CVP analysis. In the face of uncertainty, managers rely on decision models to help them make the right choices.

Role of a Decision Model

Uncertainty is the possibility that an actual amount will deviate from an expected amount. In the *GMAT Success* example, Emma might forecast sales at 42 units, but actual sales might turn out to be 30 units or 60 units. A decision model helps managers deal with such uncertainty. It is a formal method for making a choice, commonly involving both quantitative and qualitative analyses. This appendix focuses on the quantitative analysis that usually includes the following steps:

Step 1: Identify a choice criterion. A **choice criterion** is an objective that can be quantified, such as maximize income or minimize costs. Managers use the choice criterion to choose the

---
[2] *Source:* Based on teaching notes prepared by R. Williamson.

best alternative action. Emma's choice criterion is to maximize expected operating income at the Chicago college fair.

Step 2: Identify the set of alternative actions that can be taken. We use the letter a with subscripts $_1$, $_2$, and $_3$ to distinguish each of Emma's three possible actions:

a_1 = Pay $2,000 fixed fee
a_2 = Pay $800 fixed fee plus 15% of *GMAT Success* revenues
a_3 = Pay 25% of *GMAT Success* revenues with no fixed fee

Step 3: Identify the set of events that can occur. An **event** is a possible relevant occurrence, such as the actual number of *GMAT Success* packages Emma might sell at the fair. The set of events should be mutually exclusive and collectively exhaustive. Events are mutually exclusive if they cannot occur at the same time. Events are collectively exhaustive if, taken together, they make up the entire set of possible relevant occurrences (no other event can occur). Examples of mutually exclusive and collectively exhaustive events are growth, decline, or no change in industry demand and increase, decrease, or no change in interest rates. Only one event out of the entire set of mutually exclusive and collectively exhaustive events will actually occur.

Suppose Emma's only uncertainty is the number of units of *GMAT Success* that she can sell. For simplicity, suppose Emma estimates that sales will be either 30 or 60 units. This set of events is mutually exclusive because clearly sales of 30 units and 60 units cannot both occur at the same time. It is collectively exhaustive because under our assumptions sales cannot be anything other than 30 or 60 units. We use the letter x with subscripts $_1$ and $_2$ to distinguish the set of mutually exclusive and collectively exhaustive events:

x_1 = 30 units
x_2 = 60 units

Step 4: Assign a probability to each event that can occur. A **probability** is the likelihood or chance that an event will occur. The decision model approach to coping with uncertainty assigns probabilities to events. A **probability distribution** describes the likelihood, or the probability, that each of the mutually exclusive and collectively exhaustive set of events will occur. In some cases, there will be much evidence to guide the assignment of probabilities. For example, the probability of obtaining heads in the toss of a coin is 1/2 and that of drawing a particular playing card from a standard, well-shuffled deck is 1/52. In business, the probability of having a specified percentage of defective units may be assigned with great confidence on the basis of production experience with thousands of units. In other cases, there will be little evidence supporting estimated probabilities—for example, expected sales of a new pharmaceutical product next year. Suppose that Emma, on the basis of past experience, assesses a 60% chance, or a 6/10 probability, that she will sell 30 units and a 40% chance, or a 4/10 probability, that she will sell 60 units. Using $P(x)$ as the notation for the probability of an event, the probabilities are as follows:

$P(x_1) = 6/10 = 0.60$
$P(x_2) = 4/10 = 0.40$

The sum of these probabilities must equal 1.00 because these events are mutually exclusive and collectively exhaustive.

Step 5: Identify the set of possible outcomes. **Outcomes** specify, in terms of the choice criterion, the predicted economic results of the various possible combinations of actions and events. In the *GMAT Success* example, the outcomes are the six possible operating incomes displayed in the decision table in Exhibit 3-6. A **decision table** is a summary of the alternative actions, events, outcomes, and probabilities of events.

Distinguish among actions, events, and outcomes. Actions are decision choices available to managers—for example, the particular rental alternatives that Emma can choose. Events are the set of all relevant occurrences that can happen—for example, the different quantities of *GMAT Success* packages that may be sold at the fair. The outcome is operating income, which depends both on the action the manager selects (rental alternative chosen) and the event that occurs (the quantity of packages sold).

EXHIBIT 3-6 Decision Table for *GMAT Success*

	A	B	C	D	E F	G	H I
1		Selling price = $200				Operating Income	
2		Package cost = $120				Under Each Possible Event	
3			Percentage				
4		Fixed	of Fair	Event x_1: Units Sold = 30		Event x_2: Units Sold = 60	
5	**Actions**	Fee	Revenues	Probability(x_1) = 0.60		Probability(x_2) = 0.40	
6	a_1: Pay $2,000 fixed fee	$2,000	0%	$400^l		$2,800^m	
7	a_2: Pay $800 fixed fee plus 15% of revenues	$ 800	15%	$700^n		$2,200^p	
8	a_3: Pay 25% of revenues with no fixed fee	$ 0	25%	$900^q		$1,800^r	
9							
10	^{l}Operating income = ($200 − $120)(30) − $2,000	=	$ 400				
11	^{m}Operating income = ($200 − $120)(60) − $2,000	=	$2,800				
12	^{n}Operating income = ($200 − $120 − 15% × $200)(30) − $800	=	$ 700				
13	^{p}Operating income = ($200 − $120 − 15% × $200)(60) − $800	=	$2,200				
14	^{q}Operating income = ($200 − $120 − 25% × $200)(30)	=	$ 900				
15	^{r}Operating income = ($200 − $120 − 25% × $200)(60)	=	$1,800				

Exhibit 3-7 presents an overview of relationships among a decision model, the implementation of a chosen action, its outcome, and subsequent performance evaluation. Thoughtful managers step back and evaluate what happened and learn from their experiences. This learning serves as feedback for adapting the decision model for future actions.

Expected Value

An **expected value** is the weighted average of the outcomes, with the probability of each outcome serving as the weight. When the outcomes are measured in monetary terms, expected value is often called **expected monetary value**. Using information in Exhibit 3-6, the expected monetary value of each booth-rental alternative denoted by $E(a_1)$, $E(a_2)$, and $E(a_3)$ is as follows:

Pay $2,000 fixed fee: $E(a_1) = (0.60 \times \$400) + (0.40 \times \$2,800) = \$1,360$
Pay $800 fixed fee plus 15% of revenues: $E(a_2) = (0.60 \times \$700) + (0.40 \times \$2,200) = \$1,300$
Pay 25% of revenues with no fixed fee: $E(a_3) = (0.60 \times \$900) + (0.40 \times \$1,800) = \$1,260$

To maximize expected operating income, Emma should select action a_1—pay the Chicago fair organizers a $2,000 fixed fee.

To interpret the expected value of selecting action a_1, imagine that Emma attends many fairs, each with the probability distribution of operating incomes given in Exhibit 3-6. For a specific fair, Emma will earn operating income of either $400, if she sells 30 units, or $2,800, if she sells 60 units. But if Emma attends 100 fairs, she will expect to earn $400 operating income 60% of the time (at 60 fairs) and $2,800 operating income 40% of the time (at 40 fairs), for a total op-

EXHIBIT 3-7 A Decision Model and Its Link to Performance Evaluation

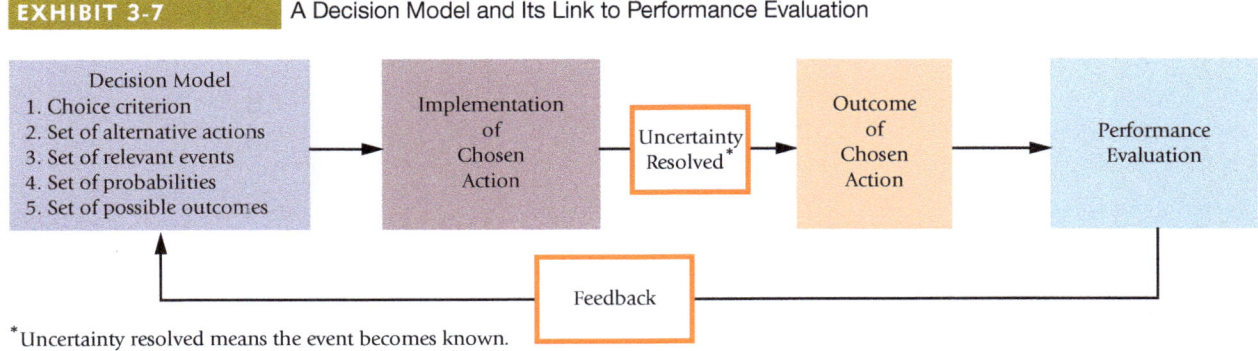

*Uncertainty resolved means the event becomes known.

erating income of $136,000 ($400 × 60 + $2,800 × 40). The expected value of $1,360 is the operating income per fair that Emma will earn when averaged across all fairs ($136,000 ÷ 100). Of course, in many real-world situations, managers must make one-time decisions under uncertainty. Even in these cases, expected value is a useful tool for choosing among alternatives.

Consider the effect of uncertainty on the preferred action choice. If Emma were certain she would sell only 30 units (that is, $P(x_1) = 1$), she would prefer alternative a_3—pay 25% of revenues with no fixed fee. To follow this reasoning, examine Exhibit 3-6. When 30 units are sold, alternative a_3 yields the maximum operating income of $900. Because fixed costs are $0, booth-rental costs are lower, equal to $1,500 (25% of revenues = 0.25 × $200 per unit × 30 units), when sales are low.

However, if Emma were certain she would sell 60 packages (that is, $P(x_2) = 1$), she would prefer alternative a_1—pay a $2,000 fixed fee. Exhibit 3-6 indicates that when 60 units are sold, alternative a_1 yields the maximum operating income of $2,800. That's because, when 60 units are sold, rental payments under a_2($800 + 0.15 × $200 per unit × 60 units = $2,600) and a_3(0.25 × $200 per unit × 60 units = $3,000) are more than the fixed $2,000 fee under a_1.

Despite the high probability of selling only 30 units, Emma still prefers to take action a_1, which is to pay a fixed fee of $2,000. That's because the high risk of low operating income (the 60% probability of selling only 30 units) is more than offset by the high return from selling 60 units, which has a 40% probability. If Emma were more averse to risk (measured in our example by the difference between operating incomes when 30 versus 60 units are sold), she might have preferred action a_2 or a_3. For example, action a_2 ensures an operating income of at least $700, greater than the operating income of $400 that she would earn under action a_1 if only 30 units were sold. Of course, choosing a_2 limits the upside potential to $2,200 relative to $2,800 under a_1, if 60 units are sold. If Emma is very concerned about downside risk, however, she may be willing to forgo some upside benefits to protect against a $400 outcome by choosing a_2.[3]

Good Decisions and Good Outcomes

Always distinguish between a good decision and a good outcome. One can exist without the other. Suppose you are offered a one-time-only gamble tossing a coin. You will win $20 if the outcome is heads, but you will lose $1 if the outcome is tails. As a decision maker, you proceed through the logical phases: gathering information, assessing outcomes, and making a choice. You accept the bet. Why? Because the expected value is $9.50 [0.5($20) + 0.5(−$1)]. The coin is tossed and the outcome is tails. You lose. From your viewpoint, this was a good decision but a bad outcome.

A decision can be made only on the basis of information that is available at the time of evaluating and making the decision. By definition, uncertainty rules out guaranteeing that the best outcome will always be obtained. As in our example, it is possible that bad luck will produce bad outcomes even when good decisions have been made. A bad outcome does not mean a bad decision was made. The best protection against a bad outcome is a good decision.

TERMS TO LEARN

This chapter and the Glossary at the end of the book contain definitions of the following important terms:

breakeven point (BEP)	decision table	operating leverage
choice criterion	degree of operating leverage	outcomes
contribution income statement	event	probability
contribution margin	expected monetary value	probability distribution
contribution margin per unit	expected value	PV graph
contribution margin percentage	gross margin percentage	revenue driver
contribution margin ratio	margin of safety	sales mix
cost–volume–profit (CVP) analysis	net income	sensitivity analysis
		uncertainty

---

[3] For more formal approaches, refer to J. Moore and L. Weatherford, *Decision Modeling with Microsoft Excel*, 6th ed. (Upper Saddle River, NJ: Prentice Hall, 2001).

ASSIGNMENT MATERIAL

Note: To underscore the basic CVP relationships, the assignment material ignores income taxes unless stated otherwise.

Questions

3-1 Define cost–volume–profit analysis.

3-2 Describe the assumptions underlying CVP analysis.

3-3 Distinguish between operating income and net income.

3-4 Define contribution margin, contribution margin per unit, and contribution margin percentage.

3-5 Describe three methods that managers can use to express CVP relationships.

3-6 Differentiate between breakeven analysis and CVP analysis.

3-7 With regard to making decisions, what do you think are the main limitations of CVP analysis? Explain.

3-8 How does an increase in the income tax rate affect the breakeven point?

3-9 Describe sensitivity analysis. How has the advent of the electronic spreadsheet affected the use of sensitivity analysis?

3-10 Is CVP analysis more focused on the short or the long term? Explain.

3-11 Is it possible to calculate the breakeven point for a company that produces and sells more than one type of product? Explain.

3-12 What is operating leverage? How is knowing the degree of operating leverage helpful to managers?

3-13 CVP analysis assumes that costs can be accurately divided into fixed and variable categories. Do you agree? Explain.

3-14 Give an example each of how a manager can decrease variable costs while increasing fixed costs and increase variable costs while decreasing fixed costs.

3-15 What is the main difference between gross margin and contribution margin? Which one is the main focus of CVP analysis? Explain briefly.

Multiple-Choice Questions

3-16 Jack's Jax has total fixed costs of $25,000. If the company's contribution margin is 60%, the income tax rate is 25% and the selling price of a box of Jax is $20, how many boxes of Jax would the company need to sell to produce a net income of $15,000?
- a. 5,625
- b. 4,445
- c. 3,750
- d. 3,333

3-17 During the current year, XYZ Company increased its variable SG&A expenses while keeping fixed SG&A expenses the same. As a result, XYZ's:
- a. Contribution margin and gross margin will be lower.
- b. Contribution margin will be higher, while its gross margin will remain the same.
- c. Operating income will be the same under both the financial accounting income statement and contribution income statement.
- d. Inventory amounts booked under the financial accounting income statement will be lower than under the contribution income statement.

3-18 Under the contribution income statement, a company's contribution margin will be:
- a. Higher if fixed SG&A costs decrease.
- b. Higher if variable SG&A costs increase.
- c. Lower if fixed manufacturing overhead costs decrease.
- d. Lower if variable manufacturing overhead costs increase.

3-19 A company needs to sell 10,000 units of its only product in order to break even. Fixed costs are $110,000, and the per unit selling price and variable costs are $20 and $9, respectively. If total sales are $220,000, the company's margin of safety will be equal to:
- a. $0
- b. $20,000
- c. $110,000
- d. $200,000

3-20 Once a company exceeds its breakeven level, operating income can be calculated by multiplying:

a. The sales price by unit sales in excess of breakeven units.
b. Unit sales by the difference between the sales price and fixed cost per unit.
c. The contribution margin ratio by the difference between unit sales and breakeven sales.
d. The contribution margin per unit by the difference between unit sales and breakeven sales.

©2016 DeVry/Becker Educational Development Corp. All Rights Reserved.

Exercises

3-21 CVP computations. Fill in the blanks for each of the following independent cases.

Case	Revenues	Variable Costs	Fixed Costs	Total Costs	Operating Income	Contribution Margin	Operating Income %	Contribution Margin %
a.	$4,250			$3,500			30.00	60.00
b.				$6,000		$3,000	25.00	
c.	$6,600	$3,500			$2,200			
d.		$2,400	$1,800		$3,200			

3-22 CVP computations. Simplex Inc. sells its product at $80 per unit with a contribution margin of 40%. During 2016, Simplex sold 540,000 units of its product; its total fixed costs are $2,100,000.

Required

1. Calculate the (a) contribution margin, (b) variable costs, and (c) operating income.
2. The production manager of Simplex has proposed modernizing the whole production process in order to save labor costs. However, the modernization of the production process will increase the annual fixed costs by $3,800,000. The variable costs are expected to decrease by 20%. Simplex Inc. expects to maintain the same sales volume and selling price next year. How would the acceptance of the production manager's proposal affect your answers to (a) and (c) in requirement 1?
3. Should Simplex accept the production manager's proposal? Explain.

3-23 CVP analysis, changing revenues, and costs. Brilliant Travel Agency specializes in flights between Toronto and Vishakhapatnam. It books passengers on EastWest Air. Brilliant's fixed costs are $36,000 per month. EastWest Air charges passengers $1,300 per round-trip ticket.

Calculate the number of tickets Brilliant must sell each month to (a) break even and (b) make a target operating income of $12,000 per month in each of the following independent cases.

Required

1. Brilliant's variable costs are $34 per ticket. EastWest Air pays Brilliant 10% commission on ticket price.
2. Brilliant's variable costs are $30 per ticket. EastWest Air pays Brilliant 10% commission on ticket price.
3. Brilliant's variable costs are $30 per ticket. EastWest Air pays $46 fixed commission per ticket to Brilliant. Comment on the results.
4. Brilliant's variable costs are $30 per ticket. It receives $46 commission per ticket from EastWest Air. It charges its customers a delivery fee of $8 per ticket. Comment on the results.

3-24 CVP exercises. The Patisserie Hartog owns and operates 10 puff pastry outlets in and around Amsterdam. You are given the following corporate budget data for next year:

Revenues	$12,500,000
Fixed costs	$ 2,240,000
Variable costs	$ 9,750,000

Variable costs change based on the number of puff pastries sold.
Compute the budgeted operating income for each of the following deviations from the original budget data. (Consider each case independently.)

Required

1. A 15% increase in contribution margin, holding revenues constant
2. A 15% decrease in contribution margin, holding revenues constant
3. A 10% increase in fixed costs
4. A 10% decrease in fixed costs
5. A 12% increase in units sold
6. A 12% decrease in units sold
7. An 8% increase in fixed costs and an 8% increase in units sold
8. A 6% increase in fixed costs and a 6% decrease in variable costs
9. Which of these alternatives yields the highest budgeted operating income? Explain why this is the case.

3-25 CVP exercises. The Unique Toys Company manufactures and sells toys. Currently, 300,000 units are sold per year at $12.50 per unit. Fixed costs are $880,000 per year. Variable costs are $7.00 per unit. Consider each case separately:

1. a. What is the current annual operating income?
   b. What is the present breakeven point in revenues?

Compute the new operating income for each of the following changes:

2. A 10% increase in variable costs
3. A $250,000 increase in fixed costs and a 2% increase in units sold
4. A 10% decrease in fixed costs, a 10% decrease in selling price, a 10% increase in variable cost per unit, and a 25% increase in units sold

Compute the new breakeven point in units for each of the following changes:

5. A 20% increase in fixed costs
6. A 12% increase in selling price and a $30,000 increase in fixed costs

3-26 CVP analysis, income taxes. Sonix Electronics is a dealer of industrial refrigerator. Its average selling price of an industrial refrigerator is $5,000, which it purchases from the manufacturer for $4,200. Each month, Sonix Electronics pays $52,800 in rent and other office expenditures and $75,200 for salespeople's salaries. In addition to their salaries, salespeople are paid a commission of 4% of sale price on each refrigerator they sell. Sonix Electronics also spends $18,400 each month for local advertisements. Its tax rate is 30%.

1. How many refrigerators must Sonix Electronics sell each month to break even?
2. Sonix Electronics has a target monthly net income of $63,000. What is its target monthly operating income? How many refrigerators must be sold each month to reach the target monthly net income of $63,000?

3-27 CVP analysis, income taxes. The Swift Meal has two restaurants that are open 24 hours a day. Fixed costs for the two restaurants together total $456,000 per year. Service varies from a cup of coffee to full meals. The average sales check per customer is $9.50. The average cost of food and other variable costs for each customer is $3.80. The income tax rate is 30%. Target net income is $159,600.

1. Compute the revenues needed to earn the target net income.
2. How many customers are needed to break even? To earn net income of $159,600?
3. Compute net income if the number of customers is 145,000.

3-28 CVP analysis, sensitivity analysis. Roughstyle Shirts Co. sells shirts wholesale to major retailers across Australia. Each shirt has a selling price of $40 with $26 in variable costs of goods sold. The company has fixed manufacturing costs of $1,600,000 and fixed marketing costs of $650,000. Sales commissions are paid to the wholesale sales reps at 10% of revenues. The company has an income tax rate of 30%.

1. How many shirts must Roughstyle sell in order to break even?
2. How many shirts must it sell in order to reach:
   a. a target operating income of $600,000?
   b. a net income of $600,000?
3. How many shirts would Roughstyle have to sell to earn the net income in part 2b if: (Consider each requirement independently.)
   a. the contribution margin per unit increases by 15%.
   b. the selling price is increased to $45.00.
   c. the company outsources manufacturing to an overseas company increasing variable costs per unit by $3.00 and saving 50% of fixed manufacturing costs.

3-29 CVP analysis, margin of safety. Ariba Corporation reaches its breakeven point at $3,200,000 of revenues. At present, it is selling 105,000 units and its variable costs are $30. Fixed manufacturing costs, administrative costs, and marketing costs are $400,000, $250,000, and $150,000 respectively.

1. Compute the contribution margin percentage.
2. Compute the selling price.
3. Compute the margin of safety in units and dollars.
4. What does this tell you about the risk of Ariba making a loss? What are the most likely reasons for this risk to increase?

3-30 Operating leverage. Broadpull Rugs is holding a 4-week carpet sale at Tryst's Club, a local warehouse store. Broadpull Rugs plans to sell carpets for $1,500 each. The company will purchase the carpets from a local distributor for $900 each, with the privilege of returning any unsold units for a full refund. Tryst's Club has offered Broadpull Rugs two payment alternatives for the use of space.

- Option 1: 25% of total revenues earned during the sale period
- Option 2: A fixed payment of $30,000 for the sale period

Assume Broadpull Rugs will incur no other costs.

Required

1. Calculate the breakeven point in units for (a) option 1 and (b) option 2.
2. At what level of revenues will Broadpull Rugs earn the same operating income under either option?
   a. For what range of unit sales will Broadpull Rugs prefer option 1?
   b. For what range of unit sales will Broadpull Rugs prefer option 2?
3. Calculate the degree of operating leverage at sales of 80 units for the two rental options.
4. Briefly explain and interpret your answer to requirement 3.

3-31 CVP analysis, international cost structure differences. Plush Decor, Inc., is considering three possible countries for the sole manufacturing site of its newest area rug: Italy, Spain, and Singapore. All area rugs are to be sold to retail outlets in Australia for $200 per unit. These retail outlets add their own markup when selling to final customers. Fixed costs and variable cost per unit (area rug) differ in the three countries.

Country	Sales Price to Retail Outlets	Annual Fixed Costs	Variable Manufacturing Cost per Area Rug	Variable Marketing & Distribution Cost per Area Rug
Italy	$200.00	$ 6,386,000.00	$70.00	$27.00
Spain	200.00	5,043,000.00	61.00	16.00
Singapore	200.00	12,240,000.00	84.00	14.00

Required

1. Compute the breakeven point for Plush Decor, Inc., in each country in (a) units sold and (b) revenues.
2. If Plush Decor, Inc., plans to produce and sell 80,000 rugs in 2014, what is the budgeted operating income for each of the three manufacturing locations? Comment on the results.

3-32 Sales mix, new and upgrade customers. Chartz 1-2-3 is a top-selling electronic spreadsheet product. Chartz is about to release version 5.0. It divides its customers into two groups: new customers and upgrade customers (those who previously purchased Chartz 1-2-3 4.0 or earlier versions). Although the same physical product is provided to each customer group, sizable differences exist in selling prices and variable marketing costs:

	New Customers		Upgrade Customers	
Selling price		$195		$115
Variable costs				
Manufacturing	$15		$15	
Marketing	50	65	20	35
Contribution margin		$130		$ 80

The fixed costs of Chartz 1-2-3 5.0 are $16,500,000. The planned sales mix in units is 60% new customers and 40% upgrade customers.

Required

1. What is the Chartz 1-2-3 5.0 breakeven point in units, assuming that the planned 60%/40% sales mix is attained?
2. If the sales mix is attained, what is the operating income when 170,000 total units are sold?
3. Show how the breakeven point in units changes with the following customer mixes:
   a. New 40% and upgrade 60%
   b. New 80% and upgrade 20%
   c. Comment on the results.

3-33 Sales mix, three products. The Belkin Company has three product lines of coffee mugs—A, B, and C—with contribution margins of $7, $5, and $4, respectively. The president foresees sales of 240,000 units in the coming period, consisting of 40,000 units of A, 120,000 units of B, and 80,000 units of C. The company's fixed costs for the period are $552,000.

Required

1. What is the company's breakeven point in units, assuming that the given sales mix is maintained?
2. If the sales mix is maintained, what is the total contribution margin when 220,000 units are sold? What is the operating income?
3. What would operating income be if the company sold 40,000 units of A, 100,000 units of B, and 100,000 units of C? What is the new breakeven point in units if these relationships persist in the next period?
4. Comparing the breakeven points in requirements 1 and 3, is it always better for a company to choose the sales mix that yields the lower breakeven point? Explain.

3-34 CVP, not-for-profit. Recreational Music Society is a not-for-profit organization that brings guest artists to the community's greater metropolitan area. The society just bought a small concert hall in the center of town to house its performances. The lease payments on the concert hall are expected to be $6,000 per month. The organization pays its guest performers $2,200 per concert and anticipates corresponding ticket sales to be $6,000 per concert. The society also incurs costs of approximately $1,400 per concert for marketing and advertising. The organization pays its artistic director $47,000 per year and expects to receive $23,000 in donations in addition to its ticket sales.

Required

1. If the Recreational Music Society just breaks even, how many concerts does it hold?
2. In addition to the organization's artistic director, the society would like to hire a marketing director for $36,000 per year. What is the breakeven point? The society anticipates that the addition of a marketing director would allow the organization to increase the number of concerts to 50 per year. What is the society's operating income/loss if it hires the new marketing director?
3. The society expects to receive a grant that would provide the organization with an additional $36,000 toward the payment of the marketing director's salary. What is the breakeven point if the society hires the marketing director and receives the grant?

3-35 Contribution margin, decision making. Brandon Harris has a small bakery business called Super Bakery. Revenues and cost data of Super Bakery for the year 2016 are as follows:

Sales revenues		$475,000
Cost of goods sold (40% of sales revenues)		190,000
Gross margin		285,000
Operating costs:		
Salaries fixed	$175,000	
Sales commissions (15% of sales)	71,250	
Depreciation of equipment and fixtures	22,000	
Insurance for the year	5,000	
Store rent ($5,000 per month)	60,000	
Other operating costs	50,000	383,250
Operating income (loss)		$(98,250)

An analysis of other operating costs reveals that 80% of it varies with sales volume, and remaining 20% does not vary with sales volume rather remains same irrespective of sales volume.

Required

1. Compute the contribution margin of Super Bakery.
2. Compute the contribution margin percentage.
3. Mr. Harris estimates that if he can spend an additional $15,000 toward sales promotion, sales revenues may increase by 30%. What should Mr. Harris' decision be?
4. What other actions can he take to improve the operating income?

3-36 Contribution margin, gross margin, and margin of safety. Roma Skincare manufactures and sells a face cream to small specialty stores in Victoria, Australia. It presents the monthly operating income statement shown here to Jacob Scott, a potential investor in the business. Help Mr. Scott understand Roma Skincare's cost structure.

	A	B	C	D
1		Roma Skincare		
2		Operating Income Statement June, 2017		
3	Units sold			15,000
4	Revenues			$1,20,000
5	Cost of goods sold			
6		Variable manufacturing costs	$60,000	
7		Fixed manufacturing costs	$22,000	
8		Total cost of goods sold		$ 82,000
9	Gross margin			$ 38,000
10	Operating costs			
11		Variable marketing costs	$ 6,000	
12		Fixed marketing & admin costs	$14,000	
13		Total operating costs		$ 20,000
14	Operating income			$ 18,000

Required

1. Recast the income statement to emphasize contribution margin.
2. Calculate the contribution margin percentage and breakeven point in units and revenues for June 2017.
3. What is the margin of safety (in units) for June 2017?
4. If sales in June were only 12,000 units and Roma Skincare's tax rate is 30%, calculate its net income.

3-37 Uncertainty and expected costs. Futuremart is an international retail store. They are considering implementing a new business-to-business (B2B) information system for processing merchandise orders. The current system costs Futuremart $2,500,000 per month and $62 per order. Futuremart has two options, a partially automated B2B and a fully automated B2B system. The partially automated B2B system will have a fixed cost of $7,200,000 per month and a variable cost of $50 per order. The fully automated B2B system has a fixed cost of $11,400,000 per month and $30 per order.

Based on data from the past two years, Futuremart has determined the following distribution on monthly orders:

Monthly Number of Orders	Probability
400,000	0.35
600,000	0.40
800,000	0.25

Required

1. Prepare a table showing the cost of each plan for each quantity of monthly orders.
2. What is the expected cost of each plan?
3. In addition to the information systems costs, what other factors should Futuremart consider before deciding to implement a new B2B system?

Problems

3-38 CVP analysis, service firm. Appolo Healthcare Solutions provides preventive health check-up packages for men and women over 40 years of age and charges $12,000 per package on an average. The average variable costs per package are as follows:

Doctor's fees	$1,000
Pathological tests and clinical examinations	3,500
Medicines	2,800
Refreshments and health drinks	300
Costs of miscellaneous services	800
Total	$8,400

Annual fixed costs total $900,000.

Required

1. Calculate the number of health check-up packages that must be sold to break even.
2. Calculate the revenue needed to earn a target operating income of $270,000.
3. If fixed costs increase by $25,000, what decrease in variable cost per person must be achieved to maintain the breakeven point calculated in requirement 1?
4. The managing director at Appolo proposes to increase the average price of the packages by $900 to decrease the breakeven point in units. Using information in the original problem, calculate the new breakeven point in units. What factors should the managing director consider before deciding to increase the price of the package?

3-39 CVP, target operating income, service firm. Modern Beauty Parlour provides beauty treatment for women. Its average monthly variable costs per woman are as follows:

Materials for beauty treatment	$110
Beautician's commission	50
Other supplies (soaps, napkins, etc.)	40
Total	$200

Monthly fixed costs consist of the following:

Rent	$1,250
Utilities	300
Advertisements on a local TV channel	250
Salaries	1,500
Miscellaneous	300
Total	$3,600

Modern Beauty charges $250 per woman on an average.

1. Calculate the breakeven point.
2. Modern Beauty's target operating income is $4,000 per month. Compute the number of customers required to achieve the target operating income.
3. The parlor wants to move to another building for geographical advantage. Monthly rent for the new building is $2,350. With the objective of better visibility for the prospective customers, it plans to advertise on another local TV channel, incurring a monthly cost of $420. By how much should the parlor increase its average fees per customer to meet the target operating income of $4,000 per month, assuming the same number of customers as in requirement 2?

3-40 CVP analysis, margin of safety. United Project Consultants (UPC) provides project consultancy services to new business projects. For 2017, it has a total budgeted revenue of $480,000, based on an average price of $240 per business project prepared. UPC would like to achieve at least 50% as a margin of safety. The company's current fixed costs are $241,956, and variable costs average $42 per project. (Consider each of the following separately.)

1. Calculate UPC's breakeven point and margin of safety in units.
2. Which of the following changes would help UPC achieve its desired margin of safety?
   a. Average revenue per business project increases to $276.
   b. Planned number of business projects prepared increases by 25%.
   c. United Project Consultants purchases new tax-software that results in a 7.5% increase in fixed costs, but makes project calculations easier. The software reduces variable costs by an average of $2 per project.

3-41 CVP analysis, income taxes. (CMA, adapted) J.T. Brooks and Company, a manufacturer of quality handmade walnut bowls, has had a steady growth in sales for the past 5 years. However, increased competition has led Mr. Brooks, the president, to believe that an aggressive marketing campaign will be necessary next year to maintain the company's present growth. To prepare for next year's marketing campaign, the company's controller has prepared and presented Mr. Brooks with the following data for the current year, 2017:

Variable cost (per bowl)		
Direct materials		$ 3.00
Direct manufacturing labor		8.00
Variable overhead (manufacturing, marketing, distribution, and customer service)		7.50
Total variable cost per bowl		$ 18.50
Fixed costs		
Manufacturing		$ 20,000
Marketing, distribution, and customer service		194,500
Total fixed costs		$214,500
Selling price		$ 35.00
Expected sales, 22,000 units		$770,000
Income tax rate		40%

1. What is the projected net income for 2017?
2. What is the breakeven point in units for 2017?
3. Mr. Brooks has set the revenue target for 2018 at a level of $875,000 (or 25,000 bowls). He believes an additional marketing cost of $16,500 for advertising in 2018, with all other costs remaining constant, will be necessary to attain the revenue target. What is the net income for 2018 if the additional $16,500 is spent and the revenue target is met?
4. What is the breakeven point in revenues for 2018 if the additional $16,500 is spent for advertising?
5. If the additional $16,500 is spent, what are the required 2018 revenues for 2018 net income to equal 2017 net income?
6. At a sales level of 25,000 units, what maximum amount can be spent on advertising if a 2018 net income of $108,450 is desired?

3-42 CVP, sensitivity analysis. Mundial Nails produces a famous nail polish with a unique glossy feature and sells it for $25 per unit. The operating income for 2017 is as follows:

	Per unit ($)	Total ($)
Sales revenue	$25	$750,000
Raw materials	5	150,000
Variable manufacturing costs	4	120,000
Other variable costs	6	180,000
Contribution margin	10	300,000
Fixed cost		174,000
Operating income		$126,000

Mundial Nails would like to increase its profitability over the next year by at least 20%. To do so, the company is considering the following options:

1. Replacing a portion of its variable labor with an automated machining process. This would result in a 25% decrease in variable manufacturing costs per unit, but a 20% increase in fixed costs. Sales would remain the same.
2. Spending $30,000 on a new advertising campaign, which would increase sales by 20%.
3. Increasing both selling price by $5 per unit and raw-material costs by $3 per unit by using a higher-quality raw materials in producing its nail polish. The higher-priced nail polish would cause demand to drop by approximately 20%.
4. Adding a second manufacturing facility that would double Mundial Nails' fixed costs, but would increase sales by 60%.

Evaluate each of the alternatives considered by Mundial Nails. Do any of the options meet or exceed Mundial's targeted increase in income of 25%? What should Mundial Nails do?

3-43 CVP analysis, shoe stores. The LadyStyle sells women's shoes across the country through its chain of shoe stores. It sells 20 different styles of shoes with identical unit costs and selling prices. A unit is defined as a pair of shoes. Each store has a store manager and a store supervisor who are paid a fixed salary. Shoes are sold by sales women who receive a fixed salary and a sales commission. LadyStyle is considering opening another store that is expected to have the revenue and cost relationships shown here.

	A	B	C	D	E
1	Unit Variable Data (per pair of shoes)			Annual Fixed Costs	
2	Selling price	$40.00		Rent	$ 25,000
3	Cost of shoes	$29.00		Salaries	96,000
4	Sales commission	$ 2.00		Advertising	35,000
5	Variable cost per unit	$31.00		Depreciation	6,000
6				Other fixed costs	9,000
				Total fixed costs	$171,000

Consider each question independently:

1. What is the annual breakeven point in (a) units sold and (b) revenues?
2. If 15,000 units are sold, what will be the store's operating income (loss)?
3. If sales commissions are discontinued and fixed salaries are raised by a total of $19,190, what would be the annual breakeven point in (a) units sold and (b) revenues?
4. Refer to the original data. If, in addition to his fixed salary, the store supervisor and store manager are paid a commission of $0.50 per unit sold and $1.00 per unit sold, respectively, what would be the annual breakeven point in (a) units sold and (b) revenues?
5. Refer to the original data. If, in addition to his fixed salary, the store supervisor and store manager are paid a commission of $0.50 per unit and $1.00 per unit sold, respectively, in excess of the breakeven point, what would be the store's operating income if 25,000 units were sold?

3-44 CVP analysis, shoe stores (continuation of 3-43). Refer to requirement 3 of Problem 3-43. In this problem, assume the role of the owner of LadyStyle.

1. As owner, which sales compensation plan would you choose if forecasted annual sales of the new store were at least 25,000 units? What do you think of the motivational aspect of your chosen compensation plan?
2. Suppose the target operating income is $99,000. How many units must be sold to reach the target operating income under (a) the original salary-plus-commissions plan and (b) the higher-fixed-salaries-only plan? Which method would you prefer? Explain briefly.
3. You open the new store on January 1, 2017, with the original salary-plus-commission compensation plan in place. Because you expect the cost of the shoes to rise due to inflation, you place a firm bulk order for 25,000 shoes and lock in the $29 price per unit. But toward the end of the year, only 20,000 shoes are sold, and you authorize a markdown of the remaining inventory to $35 per unit. Finally, all units are sold. The salespeople get paid a commission of 5% of revenues. What is the annual operating income for the store?

3-45 Alternate cost structures, uncertainty, and sensitivity analysis. Sunshine Printing Company currently leases its only copy machine for $1,500 a month. The company is considering replacing this leasing agreement with a new contract that is entirely commission based. Under the new agreement, Sunshine would pay a commission for its printing at a rate of $10 for every 500 pages printed. The company currently charges $0.20 per page to its customers. The paper used in printing costs the company $0.08 per page and other variable costs, including hourly labor, amount to $0.07 per page.

1. What is the company's breakeven point under the current leasing agreement? What is it under the new commission-based agreement?
2. For what range of sales levels will Sunshine prefer (a) the fixed lease agreement and (b) the commission agreement?
3. Do this question only if you have covered the chapter appendix in your class. Sunshine estimates that the company is equally likely to sell 30,000, 45,000, 60,000, 75,000, or 90,000 pages of print. Using information from the original problem, prepare a table that shows the expected profit at each sales level under the fixed leasing agreement and under the commission-based agreement. What is the expected value of each agreement? Which agreement should Sunshine choose?

3-46 CVP, alternative cost structures. TopHats operates a kiosk at a local mall, selling hats for $30 each. TopHats currently pays $900 a month to rent the space and pays three full-time employees to each work 160 hours a month at $12 per hour. The store shares a manager with a neighboring mall and pays 40% of the manager's annual salary of $60,000 and benefits equal to 18% of salary. The wholesale cost of the hats to the company is $10 a hat.

1. How many hats does TopHats need to sell each month to break even?
2. If TopHats wants to earn an operating income of $5,000 per month, how many hats does the store need to sell?
3. If the store's hourly employees agreed to a 20% sales-commission-only pay structure, instead of their hourly pay, how many hats would TopHats need to sell to earn an operating income of $5,000?
4. Assume TopHats pays its employees hourly under the original pay structure, but is able to pay the mall 5% of its monthly revenue instead of monthly rent. At what sales levels would TopHats prefer to pay a fixed amount of monthly rent, and at what sales levels would it prefer to pay 5% of its monthly revenue as rent?

3-47 CVP analysis, income taxes, sensitivity. (CMA, adapted) Carlisle Engine Company manufactures and sells diesel engines for use in small farming equipment. For its 2014 budget, Carlisle Engine Company estimates the following:

Selling price	$ 4,000
Variable cost per engine	$ 1,000
Annual fixed costs	$4,800,000
Net income	$1,200,000
Income tax rate	20%

The first-quarter income statement, as of March 31, reported that sales were not meeting expectations. During the first quarter, only 400 units had been sold at the current price of $4,000. The income statement showed that variable and fixed costs were as planned, which meant that the 2014 annual net income projection would not be met unless management took action. A management committee was formed and presented the following mutually exclusive alternatives to the president:

1. Reduce the selling price by 15%. The sales organization forecasts that at this significantly reduced price, 2,100 units can be sold during the remainder of the year. Total fixed costs and variable cost per unit will stay as budgeted.
2. Lower variable cost per unit by $300 through the use of less-expensive direct materials. The selling price will also be reduced by $400, and sales of 1,750 units are expected for the remainder of the year.
3. Reduce fixed costs by 10% and lower the selling price by 30%. Variable cost per unit will be unchanged. Sales of 2,200 units are expected for the remainder of the year.
    a. If no changes are made to the selling price or cost structure, determine the number of units that Carlisle Engine Company must sell (i) to break even and (ii) to achieve its net income objective.
    b. Determine which alternative Carlisle Engine should select to achieve its net income objective. Show your calculations.

3-48 Choosing between compensation plans, operating leverage. (CMA, adapted) AgroPharm Corporation manufactures pharmaceutical products that are sold through a network of external sales agents. The agents are paid a commission of 18% of revenues. AgroPharm is considering replacing the sales agents with its own salespeople, who would be paid a commission of 12% of revenues and total salaries of $7,950,000. The income statement for the year ending December 31, 2017, under the two scenarios is shown here.

	A	B	C	D	E
1		AgroPharm Corporation			
2		Income Statement			
3		For the Year Ended December 31, 2017			
4		Using Sales Agents		Using Own Sales Force	
5	Revenues		$45,000,000		$45,000,000
6	Cost of goods sold				
7	Variable	$15,750,000		$15,750,000	
8	Fixed	5,425,000	21,175,000	5,425,000	21,175,000
9	Gross margin		$23,825,000		$23,825,000
10	Marketing costs				
11	Commissions	$ 8,100,000		$ 5,400,000	
12	Fixed costs	5,250,000	13,350,000	7,950,000	13,350,000
13	Operating income		$10,475,000		$10,475,000

Required

1. Calculate AgroPharm's 2017 contribution margin percentage, breakeven revenues, and degree of operating leverage under the two scenarios.
2. Describe the advantages and disadvantages of each type of sales alternative.
3. In 2018, AgroPharm uses its own salespeople, who demand a 14% commission. If all other cost-behavior patterns are unchanged, how much revenue must the salespeople generate in order to earn the same operating income as in 2017?

3-49 Sales mix, three products. The Matrix Company has three product lines of belts—A, B, and C—with contribution margins of $7, $5, and $4, respectively. The president foresees sales of 400,000 units in the coming period, consisting of 40,000 units of A, 200,000 units of B, and 160,000 units of C. The company's fixed costs for the period are $1,020,000.

Required

1. What is the company's breakeven point in units, assuming that the given sales mix is maintained?
2. If the sales mix is maintained, what is the total contribution margin when 400,000 units are sold? What is the operating income?
3. What would operating income be if 40,000 units of A, 160,000 units of B, and 200,000 units of C were sold? What is the new breakeven point in units if these relationships persist in the next period?

3-50 Multiproduct CVP and decision making. Romi Filters produces two types of water filters. One attaches to the faucet and cleans all water that passes through the faucet; the other is a pitcher-cum-filter that only purifies water meant for drinking.

The unit that attaches to the faucet is sold for $150 and has variable costs of $90.
The pitcher-cum-filter sells for $160 and has variable costs of $80.

Romi Filters sells two faucet models for every three pitchers sold. Fixed costs equal $1,260,000.

Required

1. What is the breakeven point in unit sales and dollars for each type of filter at the current sales mix?
2. Romi Filters is considering buying new production equipment. The new equipment will increase fixed cost by $240,000 per year and will decrease the variable cost of the faucet and the pitcher units by $5 and $10, respectively. Assuming the same sales mix, how many of each type of filter does Romi Filters need to sell to break even?
3. Assuming the same sales mix, at what total sales level would Romi Filters be indifferent between using the old equipment and buying the new production equipment? If total sales are expected to be 28,000 units, should Romi Filters buy the new production equipment?

3-51 Sales mix, two products. The Stackpole Company retails two products: a standard and a deluxe version of a luggage carrier. The budgeted income statement for next period is as follows:

	Standard Carrier	Deluxe Carrier	Total
Units sold	187,500	62,500	250,000
Revenues at $28 and $50 per unit	$5,250,000	$3,125,000	$8,375,000
Variable costs at $18 and $30 per unit	3,375,000	1,875,000	5,250,000
Contribution margins at $10 and $20 per unit	$1,875,000	$1,250,000	3,125,000
Fixed costs			2,250,000
Operating income			$ 875,000

Required

1. Compute the breakeven point in units, assuming that the company achieves its planned sales mix.
2. Compute the breakeven point in units (a) if only standard carriers are sold and (b) if only deluxe carriers are sold.
3. Suppose 250,000 units are sold but only 50,000 of them are deluxe. Compute the operating income. Compute the breakeven point in units. Compare your answer with the answer to requirement 1. What is the major lesson of this problem?

3-52 Gross margin and contribution margin. The Garden Club is preparing for its annual meeting in which a magic show will be shown to its contributing members only. Last year, out of 1,500 members, only 600 contributed for the magic show. Tickets for the show were $30 per attendee. The profit report for last year's show follows.

Ticket sales	$18,000
Cost of magic show	20,000
Gross margin	(2,000)
Printing, invitations, and paperwork	1,800
Profit (loss)	$ (3,800)

This year, the club committee does not want to lose money on the magic show due to poor attendance and to achieve this goal, the committee analyzed last year's costs. It found that of the $20,000 cost of the magic show, 40% was fixed costs and the remaining 60% was variable costs. Of the $1,800 cost of printing, invitations, and paperwork, 50% was fixed and 50% variable.

Required

1. Prepare last year's profit report using the contribution margin format.
2. The club committee is considering expanding this year's magic show invitation list to include volunteer members (in addition to its contributing members). If the club committee expands the magic show invitation list, it expects an 80% increase in attendance. Calculate the effect this will have on the profitability of the show assuming that fixed costs will be the same as last year.

3-53 Ethics, CVP analysis. Megaphone Corporation produces a molded plastic casing, M&M101, for many cell phones currently on the market. Summary data from its 2017 income statement are as follows:

Revenues	$5,000,000
Variable costs	3,250,000
Fixed costs	1,890,000
Operating income	$ (140,000)

Joshua Kirby, Megaphone's president, is very concerned about Megaphone Corporation's poor profitability. He asks Leroy Gibbs, production manager, and Tony DiNunzo, controller, to see if there are ways to reduce costs.

After 2 weeks, Leroy returns with a proposal to reduce variable costs to 55% of revenues by reducing the costs Megaphone currently incurs for safe disposal of wasted plastic. Tony is concerned that this would expose the company to potential environmental liabilities. He tells Leroy, "We would need to estimate some of these potential environmental costs and include them in our analysis." "You can't do that," Leroy replies. "We are not violating any laws. There is some possibility that we may have to incur environmental costs in the future, but if we bring it up now, this proposal will not go through because our senior management always assumes these costs to be larger than they turn out to be. The market is very tough, and we are in danger of shutting down the company and costing all of us our jobs. The only reason our competitors are making money is because they are doing exactly what I am proposing."

Required

1. Calculate Megaphone Corporation's breakeven revenues for 2017.
2. Calculate Megaphone Corporation's breakeven revenues if variable costs are 55% of revenues.
3. Calculate Megaphone Corporation's operating income for 2017 if variable costs had been 55% of revenues.
4. Given Leroy Gibbs's comments, what should Tony DiNunzo do?

3-54 Deciding where to produce. (CMA, adapted) Central térmica, Inc., produces the same power generator in two Spanish plants, a new plant in Los Barrios and an older plant in Ascó. The following data are available for the two plants.

	A	Los Barrios		Ascó	
		B	C	D	E
1		Los Barrios		Ascó	
2	Selling price		$200.00		$200.00
3	Variable manufacturing cost per unit	$80.00		$100.00	
4	Fixed manufacturing cost per unit	35.00		26.00	
5	Variable marketing cost per unit	20.00		25.00	
6	Fixed marketing cost per unit	30.00		24.00	
7	Total cost per unit		165.00		175.00
8	Operating income per unit		$ 35.00		$ 25.00
9	Production rate per day		500 units		400 units
10	Normal annual capacity usage		240 days		240 days
11	Maximum annual capacity		300 days		300 days

All fixed costs per unit are calculated based on a normal capacity usage consisting of 240 working days. When the number of working days exceeds 240, overtime charges raise the variable manufacturing costs of additional units by $5.00 per unit in Los Barrios and $10.00 per unit in Ascó.

Central térmica, Inc., is expected to produce and sell 240,000 power generators during the coming year. Wanting to take advantage of the higher operating income per unit at Ascó, the company's production manager has decided to manufacture 120,000 units at each plant, resulting in a plan in which Ascó operates at maximum capacity (400 units per day × 300 days) and Los Barrios operates at its normal volume (500 units per day × 240 days).

Required

1. Calculate the breakeven point in units for the Los Barrios plant and for the Ascó plant.
2. Calculate the operating income that would result from the production manager's plan to produce 120,000 units at each plant.
3. Determine how the production of 240,000 units should be allocated between the Los Barrios and Ascó plants to maximize operating income for Central térmica, Inc. Show your calculations.

Job Costing

4

No one likes to lose money.

Whether a company is a new startup venture providing marketing consulting services or an established manufacturer of custom-built motorcycles, knowing how to job cost—that is, knowing how much it costs to produce an individual product—is critical if a company is to generate a profit. As the following article shows, Turner Construction Company knows this all too well.

JOB COSTING AND THE WORLD'S TALLEST BUILDING[1]

Turner Construction Company was responsible for constructing, costing and pricing the world's tallest building, the 2,716-foot high, 163-story Burj Khalifa in Dubai. Completed in 2010, the $1.5 billion Burj Khalifa features 49 floors of office space, more than 1,000 apartments, a 160-room Armani Hotel with a 76th floor swimming pool, and the world's highest outdoor observation deck on the 124th floor.

To construct the Burj Khalifa, Turner managers used historical data and marketplace information to carefully estimate all costs associated with the project: direct costs, indirect costs, and general administrative costs. Direct costs included the 45,000 cubic meters of concrete, 39,000 tons of steel rebar, 26,000 exterior glass panels, and 22 million man hours required for construction. Indirect costs included the cost of supervisory labor, company-owned equipment, and safety equipment. Finally, general administrative costs allocated to the Burj Khalifa included office rent, utilities, and insurance.

Throughout the seven-year construction process, job costing was critical as on-site managers reported on the status of the mega-building. Managers identified potential problems with the project and took corrective action to ensure the luxury skyscraper was delivered on time and within the original project budget.

Knowing the costs and profitability of jobs helps managers pursue their business strategies, develop pricing plans, and manage costs.

LEARNING OBJECTIVES

1. Describe the building-block concepts of costing systems
2. Distinguish job costing from process costing
3. Describe the approaches to evaluating and implementing job-costing systems
4. Outline the seven-step approach to normal costing
5. Distinguish actual costing from normal costing
6. Track the flow of costs in a job-costing system
7. Dispose of under- or overallocated manufacturing overhead costs at the end of the fiscal year using alternative methods
8. Understand variations from normal costing

Tomas Marek/123RF

---

[1] Sources: Bill Baker and James Pawlikowski, "The Design and Construction of the World's Tallest Building: The Burj Khalifa, Dubai," *Structural Engineering International* 25 (4 2015): 389–394 (http://www.iabse.org/Images/Publications_PDF/SEI/SEI.Burj%20Dubai.pdf); Burj Khalifa, "Building a Global Icon," http://www.burjkhalifa.ae/en/the-tower/construction.aspx, accessed March 2016; Turner Construction Company, "Burj Khalifa," http://www.turnerconstruction.com/experience/project/28/burj-khalifa, accessed March 2016; SkyscraperPage.com, "World Skyscraper Construction," http://skyscraperpage.com/diagrams/?searchID=202, accessed March 2016.

Building-Block Concepts of Costing Systems

LEARNING OBJECTIVE 1

Describe the building-block concepts of costing systems

...the building blocks are cost object, direct costs, indirect costs, cost pools, and cost-allocation bases

Before we begin our discussion of costing systems, let's review the cost-related terms from Chapter 2 and introduce some new terms.

1. A *cost object* is anything for which a measurement of costs is desired—for example, a product, such as an iMac computer, or a service, such as the cost of repairing an iMac computer.
2. The *direct costs of a cost object* are costs related to a particular cost object that can be traced to it in an economically feasible (cost-effective) way—for example, the cost of the main computer board and parts to make an iMac computer.
3. The *indirect costs of a cost object* are costs related to a particular cost object that cannot be traced to it in an economically feasible (cost-effective) way—for example, the salaries of supervisors who oversee multiple products, only one of which is the iMac, or the rent paid for the repair facility that repairs many different Apple computer products. Indirect costs are allocated to the cost object using a cost-allocation method. Recall that *cost assignment* is a general term for assigning costs, whether direct or indirect, to a cost object. *Cost tracing* is the process of assigning direct costs. *Cost allocation* is the process of assigning indirect costs. The relationship among these three concepts can be graphically represented as

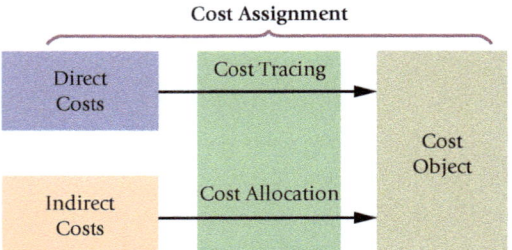

Throughout this chapter, the costs assigned to a cost object, such as a BMW Mini Cooper car, or a service, such as an audit of the MTV network, include both variable costs and costs that are fixed in the short run. Managers cost products and services to guide their long-run strategic decisions; for example: "What mix of products and services should we produce?" or "What price should we charge for each product?" In the long run, managers want revenues to exceed total (variable plus fixed) costs.

We also need to introduce and explain two more terms to understand costing systems:

4. **Cost pool.** A **cost pool** is a grouping of individual indirect cost items. Cost pools can range from broad, such as all manufacturing-plant costs, to narrow, such as the costs of operating metal-cutting machines. Cost pools simplify the allocation of indirect costs because the costing system does not have to allocate each cost individually. Instead costs that have the same cost-allocation base are grouped together and allocated to cost objects.
5. **Cost-allocation base.** How should a company allocate the costs of operating metal-cutting machines among different products? One way is to determine the number of machine-hours used to produce different products. The **cost-allocation base** (number of machine-hours) is a systematic way to link an indirect cost or group of indirect costs (operating costs of all metal-cutting machines) to cost objects (different products). For example, if the indirect costs of operating metal-cutting machines is $500,000 based on running these machines for 10,000 hours, the cost-allocation rate is $500,000 ÷ 10,000 hours = $50 per machine-hour, where machine-hours is the cost-allocation base. If a product uses 800 machine-hours, it will be allocated $40,000, or $50 per machine-hour × 800 machine-hours. The ideal cost-allocation base is the cost driver of the indirect costs because there is a cause-and-effect relationship between the cost-allocation base and the indirect costs. A cost-allocation base can be either financial (such as direct labor costs) or nonfinancial (such as the number of machine-hours). When the cost object is a job, product, service, or customer, the cost-allocation base is also called a **cost-application base**. However, when the cost object is a department or another cost pool, the cost-allocation base is *not* called a cost-application base.

Sometimes a cost may need to be allocated in a situation where the cause-and-effect relationship is not clear-cut. Consider a corporate-wide advertising program that promotes the general image of a company and its various divisions, rather than the image of an individual product. Many companies, such as PepsiCo, allocate costs like these to their individual divisions on the basis of revenues: The higher a division's revenue, the higher the business's allocated cost of the advertising program. Allocating costs this way is based on the criterion of *benefits received* rather than cause-and-effect. Divisions with higher revenues benefit from the advertising more than divisions with lower revenues and, therefore, are allocated more of the advertising costs.

Another criterion for allocating some costs is the cost object's *ability to bear* the costs allocated to it. The city government of Houston, Texas, for example, distributes the costs of the city manager's office to other city departments—including the police department, fire department, library system, and others—based on the size of their budgets. The city's rationale is that larger departments should absorb a larger share of the overhead costs. Organizations generally use the cause-and-effect criterion to allocate costs, followed by benefits received, and finally, and more rarely, by ability to bear.

The concepts represented by these five terms constitute the building blocks we will use to design the costing systems described in this chapter.

> **DECISION POINT**
> What are the building block concepts of a costing system?

Job-Costing and Process-Costing Systems

Management accountants use two basic types of costing systems to assign costs to products or services.

1. **Job-costing system.** In a job-costing system, the cost object is a unit or multiple units of a distinct product or service called a **job**. Each job generally uses different amounts of resources. The product or service is often a single unit, such as a specialized machine made at Hitachi, a construction project managed by Bechtel Corporation, a repair job done at an Audi Service Center, or an advertising campaign produced by Saatchi & Saatchi. Each special machine made by Hitachi is unique and distinct from the other machines made at the plant. An advertising campaign for one client at Saatchi & Saatchi is unique and distinct from advertising campaigns for other clients. Job costing is also used by companies such as Ethan Allen to cost multiple identical units of distinct furniture products. Because the products and services are distinct, job-costing systems are used to accumulate costs separately for each product or service.

2. **Process-costing system.** In a process-costing system, the cost object is masses of identical or similar units of a product or service. For example, Citibank provides the same service to all its customers when processing customer deposits. Intel provides the same product (say, a Core i5 chip) to each of its customers. All Minute Maid consumers receive the same frozen orange juice product. In each period, process-costing systems divide the total costs of producing an identical or similar product or service by the total number of units produced to obtain a per-unit cost. This per-unit cost is the average unit cost that applies to each of the identical or similar units produced in that period.

> **LEARNING OBJECTIVE 2**
> Distinguish job costing
> ...job costing is used to cost a distinct product
> from process costing
> ...process costing is used to cost masses of identical or similar units

Exhibit 4-1 presents examples of job costing and process costing in the service, merchandising, and manufacturing sectors. These two types of costing systems lie at opposite ends of a continuum; in between, one type of system can blur into the other to some degree.

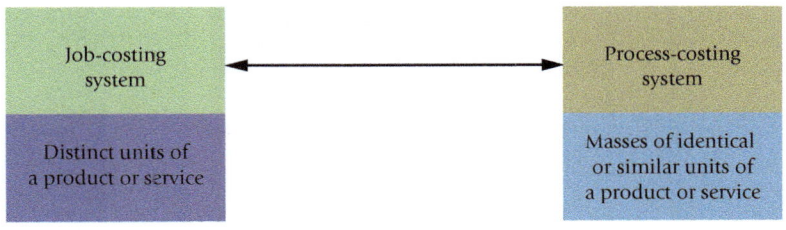

EXHIBIT 4-1

Examples of Job Costing and Process Costing in the Service, Merchandising, and Manufacturing Sectors

	Service Sector	Merchandising Sector	Manufacturing Sector
Job Costing Used	• Audit engagements done by PricewaterhouseCoopers • Consulting engagements done by McKinsey & Co. • Advertising-agency campaigns run by Ogilvy & Mather • Legal cases argued by Hale & Dorr • Computer-repair jobs done by CompUSA • Movies produced by Universal Studios	• L. L. Bean sending individual items by mail order • Special promotion of new products by Walmart	• Assembly of individual aircrafts at Boeing • Construction of ships at Litton Industries
Process Costing Used	• Bank-check clearing at Bank of America • Postal delivery (standard items) by U.S. Postal Service	• Grain dealing by Arthur Daniel Midlands • Lumber dealing by Weyerhauser	• Oil refining by Shell Oil • Beverage production by PepsiCo

DECISION POINT

How do you distinguish job costing from process costing?

Many companies have costing systems that are neither pure job-costing systems nor pure process-costing systems but—instead—have elements of both, tailored to the underlying operations. For example, Kellogg Corporation uses job costing to calculate the total cost to manufacture each of its different and distinct types of products—such as Corn Flakes, Crispix, and Froot Loops—and process costing to calculate the per-unit cost of producing each identical box of Corn Flakes, each identical box of Crispix, and so on. In this chapter, we focus on job-costing systems. Chapters 17 and 18 discuss process-costing systems.

Job Costing: Evaluation and Implementation

LEARNING OBJECTIVE 3

Describe the approaches to evaluating and implementing job-costing systems

...to determine costs of jobs in a timely manner

We will illustrate job costing using the example of Robinson Company, which manufactures and installs specialized machinery for the paper-making industry. In early 2017, Robinson receives a request to bid on the manufacturing and installation of a new paper-making machine for the Western Pulp and Paper Company (WPP). Robinson had never made a machine quite like this one, and its managers wonder what to bid for the job. In order to make decisions about the job, Robinson's management team works through the five-step decision-making process.

1. **Identify the problems and uncertainties.** The decision of whether and how much to bid for the WPP job depends on how management resolves two critical uncertainties: (1) what it will cost to complete the job; and (2) the prices Robinson's competitors are likely to bid.

2. **Obtain information.** Robinson's managers first evaluate whether doing the WPP job is consistent with the company's strategy. Do they want to do more of these kinds of jobs? Is this an attractive segment of the market? Will Robinson be able to develop a competitive advantage over its competitors and satisfy customers such as WPP? After completing their research, Robinson's managers conclude that the WPP job fits well with the company's strategy and capabilities.

    Robinson's managers study the drawings and engineering specifications provided by WPP and decide on the technical details of the machine. They compare the specifications of this machine to similar machines they have made in the past, identify competitors that might bid on the job, and gather information on what these bids might be.

3. **Make predictions about the future.** Robinson's managers estimate the cost of direct materials, direct manufacturing labor, and overhead for the WPP job. They also consider qualitative factors and risk factors and evaluate any biases they might have. For example, do engineers and employees working on the WPP job have the necessary skills and technical competence? Would they find the experience valuable and challenging? How accurate are the cost estimates, and what is the likelihood of cost overruns? What biases do Robinson's managers have to be careful about?

4. **Make decisions by choosing among alternatives.** Robinson's managers consider several alternative bids based on what they believe competing firms will bid, the technical expertise needed for the job, business risks, and other qualitative factors. Ultimately Robinson decides to bid $15,000. The manufacturing cost estimate is $9,800, which yields a markup of more than 50% on manufacturing cost.

5. **Implement the decision, evaluate performance, and learn.** Robinson wins the bid for the WPP job. As Robinson works on the job, management accountants carefully track all of the costs incurred (which are detailed later in this chapter). Ultimately, Robinson's managers will compare the predicted amounts against actual costs to evaluate how well the company did on the WPP job.

In its job-costing system, Robinson accumulates the costs incurred for a job in different parts of the value chain, such as manufacturing, marketing, and customer service. We focus here on Robinson's manufacturing function (which also includes the installation of the machine). To make a machine, Robinson purchases some components from outside suppliers and makes other components itself. Each of Robinson's jobs also has a service element: installing a machine at a customer's site and integrating it with the customer's other machines and processes.

One form of a job-costing system that Robinson can use is **actual costing**, which is a costing system that traces direct costs to a cost object based on the *actual direct-cost rate*s times the actual quantities of the direct-cost inputs used. Indirect costs are allocated based on the *actual indirect-cost rates* times the actual quantities of the cost-allocation bases. An actual indirect-cost rate is calculated by dividing actual annual indirect costs by the actual annual quantity of the cost-allocation base.

$$\frac{\text{Actual indirect}}{\text{cost rate}} = \frac{\text{Actual annual indirect costs}}{\text{Actual annual quantity of the cost-allocation base}}$$

As its name suggests, actual costing systems calculate the actual costs of jobs. Yet actual costing systems are not commonly found in practice because actual costs cannot be computed in a *timely* manner.[2] The problem is not with computing direct-cost rates for direct materials and direct manufacturing labor. For example, Robinson records the actual prices paid for materials. As it uses these materials, the prices paid serve as actual direct-cost rates for charging material costs to jobs. As we discuss next, calculating actual indirect-cost rates on a timely basis each week or each month is, however, a problem. Robinson can only calculate actual indirect-cost rates at the end of the fiscal year. However, the firm's managers are unwilling to wait that long to learn the costs of various jobs because they need cost information to monitor and manage the cost of jobs while they are in progress. Ongoing cost information about jobs also helps managers bid on new jobs while working on current jobs.

Time Period Used to Compute Indirect-Cost Rates

There are two reasons for using longer periods, such as a year, to calculate indirect-cost rates.

1. **The numerator reason (indirect-cost pool).** The shorter the period, the greater is the influence of seasonal patterns on the amount of costs. For example, if indirect-cost rates were calculated each month, the costs of heating (included in the numerator) would be charged to production only during the winter months. An annual period incorporates the effects of all four seasons into a single, annual indirect-cost rate.

---

[2] Actual costing is presented in more detail on pages 138–140.

Levels of total indirect costs are also affected by nonseasonal erratic costs. Nonseasonal erratic costs are the costs incurred in a particular month that benefit operations during future months, such as equipment-repair costs and the costs of vacation and holiday pay for employees. If monthly indirect-cost rates were calculated, the jobs done in a month in which there were high, nonseasonal erratic costs would be charged with these higher costs. Pooling all indirect costs together over the course of a full year and calculating a single annual indirect-cost rate helps smooth some of the erratic bumps in costs associated with shorter periods.

2. **The denominator reason (quantity of the cost-allocation base).** Another reason for longer periods is to avoid spreading monthly fixed indirect costs over fluctuating levels of monthly output and fluctuating quantities of the cost-allocation base. Consider the following example.

Reardon and Pane is a firm of tax accountants whose work follows a highly seasonal pattern. Tax season (January–April) is very busy. Other times of the year are less busy. The firm has both variable indirect costs and fixed indirect costs. Variable indirect costs (such as supplies, power, and indirect support labor) vary with the quantity of the cost-allocation base (direct professional labor-hours). Monthly fixed indirect costs (depreciation and general administrative support) do not vary with short-run fluctuations in the quantity of the cost-allocation base:

	Indirect Costs			Direct Professional Labor-Hours (4)	Variable Indirect Cost Rate per Direct Professional Labor-Hour (5) = (1) ÷ (4)	Fixed Indirect Cost Rate per Direct Professional Labor-Hour (6) = (2) ÷ (4)	Total Allocation Rate per Direct Professional Labor-Hour (7) = (3) ÷ (4)
	Variable (1)	Fixed (2)	Total (3)				
High-output month	$40,000	$60,000	$100,000	3,200	$12.50	$18.75	$31.25
Low-output month	10,000	60,000	70,000	800	$12.50	$75.00	87.50

Variable indirect costs change in proportion to changes in the number of direct professional labor-hours worked. Therefore, the variable indirect-cost rate is the same in both the high-output months and the low-output months ($12.50 in both as the table shows). Sometimes overtime payments can cause the variable indirect-cost rate to be higher in high-output months. In such cases, variable indirect costs will be allocated at a higher rate to production in high-output months relative to production in low-output months.

Now consider the fixed costs of $60,000. Reardon and Pane chooses this level of monthly fixed costs for the year recognizing that it needs to support higher professional labor-hours during some periods of the year and lower professional labor-hours during other periods. The fixed costs cause monthly total indirect-cost rates to vary considerably—from $31.25 per hour to $87.50 per hour. Few managers believe that identical jobs done in different months should be allocated such significantly different indirect-cost charges per hour ($87.50 ÷ $31.25 = 2.80, or 280%) because of fixed costs. Furthermore, if fees for preparing tax returns are based on costs, fees would be high in low-output months leading to lost business, when in fact management wants to accept more business to use the idle capacity during these months (for more details, see Chapter 9). Reardon and Pane chose a specific level of capacity based on a time horizon far beyond a mere month. An average, annualized rate based on the relationship between total annual indirect costs and the total annual level of output smoothes the effect of monthly variations in output levels. This rate is more representative of the total costs and total output the company's managers considered when choosing the level of capacity and, therefore, fixed costs.

Another denominator reason for using annual overhead rates is because the number of Monday-to-Friday workdays in a month affects the calculation of monthly indirect-cost rates. The number of workdays per month varies from 20 to 23 during a year. Because February has the fewest workdays (and consequently labor-hours), if separate rates are computed each month, jobs done in February would bear a greater share of the firm's indirect costs (such as depreciation and property taxes) than identical jobs in other months. An annual period is consistent with how managers decide on the level of fixed costs and reduces the effect that the number of working days per month has on unit costs.

DECISION POINT

What is the main challenge of implementing job-costing systems?

Normal Costing

As we indicated, because it's hard to calculate actual indirect-cost rates on a weekly or monthly basis, managers cannot calculate the actual costs of jobs as they are completed. Nonetheless, managers want a close approximation of the costs of various jobs regularly during the year, not just at the end of the fiscal year. They want to know manufacturing costs (and other costs, such as marketing costs) to price jobs, monitor and manage costs, evaluate the success of jobs, learn about what did and did not work, bid on new jobs, and prepare interim financial statements. Because companies need immediate access to job costs, few wait to allocate overhead costs until the end of the accounting year. Instead, a *predetermined* or *budgeted* indirect-cost rate is calculated for each cost pool at the beginning of a fiscal year, and overhead costs are allocated to jobs as work progresses. For the numerator and denominator reasons described previously, the **budgeted indirect-cost rate** for each cost pool is computed as:

$$\text{Budgeted indirect cost rate} = \frac{\text{Budgeted annual indirect costs}}{\text{Budgeted annual quantity of the cost-allocation base}}$$

Using budgeted indirect-cost rates gives rise to normal costing.

Normal costing is a costing system that (1) traces direct costs to a cost object by using the actual direct-cost rates times the actual quantities of the direct-cost inputs and (2) allocates indirect costs based on the *budgeted* indirect-cost rates times the actual quantities of the cost-allocation bases.

General Approach to Job Costing Using Normal Costing

We illustrate normal costing for the Robinson Company example using the following seven steps to assign costs to an individual job. This approach is commonly used by companies in the manufacturing, merchandising, and service sectors.

Step 1: Identify the Job That Is the Chosen Cost Object.
The cost object in the Robinson Company example is Job WPP 298, manufacturing a paper-making machine for Western Pulp and Paper (WPP) in 2017. Robinson's managers and management accountants gather information to cost jobs through source documents. A **source document** is an original record (such as a labor time card on which an employee's work hours are recorded) that supports journal entries in an accounting system. The main source document for Job WPP 298 is a job-cost record. A **job-cost record**, also called a **job-cost sheet**, is used to record and accumulate all the costs assigned to a specific job, starting when work begins. Exhibit 4-2 shows the job-cost record for the paper-making machine ordered by WPP. Follow the various steps in costing Job WPP 298 on the job-cost record in Exhibit 4-2.

Step 2: Identify the Direct Costs of the Job.
Robinson identifies two direct-manufacturing cost categories: direct materials and direct manufacturing labor.

- **Direct materials:** On the basis of the engineering specifications and drawings provided by WPP, a manufacturing engineer orders materials from the storeroom using a basic source document called a **materials-requisition record**, which contains information about the cost of direct materials used on a specific job and in a specific department. Exhibit 4-3, Panel A, shows a materials-requisition record for the Robinson Company. See how the record specifies the job for which the material is requested (WPP 298) and describes the material (Part Number MB 468-A, metal brackets), the actual quantity (8), the actual unit cost ($14), and the actual total cost ($112). The $112 actual total cost also appears on the job-cost record in Exhibit 4-2. If we add the cost of all materials requisitions, the total actual direct materials cost is $4,606, which is shown in the Direct Materials panel of the job-cost record in Exhibit 4-2.

- **Direct manufacturing labor:** Accounting for direct manufacturing labor is similar to accounting for direct materials. The source document for direct manufacturing labor is a **labor-time sheet**, which contains information about the amount of labor time used

LEARNING OBJECTIVE 4

Outline the seven-step approach to normal costing

...the seven-step approach is used to compute direct and indirect costs of a job

EXHIBIT 4-2   Source Documents at Robinson Company: Job-Cost Record

	A	B	C	D	E	F
1			JOB-COST RECORD			
2	JOB NO:	WPP 298		CUSTOMER:	Western Pulp and Paper	
3	Date Started:	Feb. 6, 2017		Date Completed	Feb. 28, 2017	
4						
5						
6	DIRECT MATERIALS					
7	Date	Materials		Quantity	Unit	Total
8	Received	Requisition No.	Part No.	Used	Cost	Costs
9	Feb. 6, 2017	2017: 198	MB 468-A	8	$14	$ 112
10	Feb. 6, 2017	2017: 199	TB 267-F	12	63	756
11						•
12						•
13	Total					$ 4,606
14						
15	DIRECT MANUFACTURING LABOR					
16	Period	Labor Time	Employee	Hours	Hourly	Total
17	Covered	Record No.	No.	Used	Rate	Costs
18	Feb. 6-12, 2017	LT 232	551-87-3076	25	$18	$ 450
19	Feb. 6-12, 2017	LT 247	287-31-4671	5	19	95
20	•	•	•	•	•	•
21	•	•	•	•	•	•
22	Total			88		$ 1,579
23						
24	MANUFACTURING OVERHEAD*					
25		Cost Pool		Allocation Base	Allocation-	Total
26	Date	Category	Allocation Base	Quantity Used	Base Rate	Costs
27	Feb. 28, 2017	Manufacturing	Direct Manufacturing	88 hours	$40	$ 3,520
28			Labor-Hours			
29						
30	Total					$ 3,520
31	TOTAL MANUFACTURING COST OF JOB					$ 9,705
32						
33						
34	*The Robinson Company uses a single manufacturing-overhead cost pool. The use of multiple overhead cost pools					
35	would mean multiple entries in the "Manufacturing Overhead" section of the job-cost record.					
36						

for a specific job in a specific department. Exhibit 4-3, Panel B, shows a typical weekly labor-time sheet for a particular employee (G. L. Cook). Each day Cook records the time spent on individual jobs (in this case WPP 298 and JL 256), as well as the time spent on other tasks, such as the maintenance of machines and cleaning, that are not related to a specific job.

The 25 hours that Cook spent on Job WPP 298 appears on the job-cost record in Exhibit 4-2 at a cost of $450 (25 hours × $18 per hour). Similarly, the job-cost record for Job JL 256 will show a cost of $216 (12 hours × $18 per hour). The three hours of time spent on maintenance and cleaning at $18 per hour equals $54. This cost is part of indirect manufacturing costs because it is not traceable to any particular job. This indirect cost is included as part of the manufacturing-overhead cost pool allocated to jobs. The total direct manufacturing labor costs of $1,579 for the paper-making machine that

EXHIBIT 4-3 Source Documents at Robinson Company: Materials-Requisition Record and Labor-Time Sheet

PANEL A:

MATERIALS-REQUISITION RECORD				
Materials-Requisition Record No.			2017: 198	
Job No. WPP 298		Date:	FEB. 6, 2017	
Part No.	Part Description	Quantity	Unit Cost	Total Cost
MB 468-A	Metal Brackets	8	$14	$112
Issued By: B. Clyde		Date:	Feb. 6, 2017	
Received By: L. Daley		Date:	Feb. 6, 2017	

PANEL B:

LABOR-TIME SHEET								
Labor-Time Record No: LT 232								
Employee Name: G. L. Cook Employee No: 551-87-3076								
Employee Classification Code: Grade 3 Machinist								
Hourly Rate: $18								
Week Start: Feb. 6, 2017 Week End: Feb. 12, 2017								
Job. No.	M	T	W	Th	F	S	Su	Total
WPP 298	4	8	3	6	4	0	0	25
JL 256	3	0	4	2	3	0	0	12
Maintenance	1	0	1	0	1	0	0	3
Total	8	8	8	8	8	0	0	40
Supervisor: R. Stuart Date: Feb. 12, 2017								

appears in the Direct Manufacturing Labor panel of the job-cost record in Exhibit 4-2 is the sum of all the direct manufacturing labor costs charged by different employees for producing and installing Job WPP 298.

All costs other than direct materials and direct manufacturing labor are classified as indirect costs.

Step 3: Select the Cost-Allocation Bases to Use for Allocating Indirect Costs to the Job. Recall that indirect manufacturing costs are those costs that are necessary to do a job, but that cannot be traced to a specific job. It would be impossible to complete a job without incurring indirect costs such as supervision, manufacturing engineering, utilities, and repairs. Moreover, different jobs require different quantities of indirect resources. Because these costs cannot be traced to a specific job, managers must allocate them to jobs in a systematic way.

Companies often use multiple cost-allocation bases to allocate indirect costs because different indirect costs have different cost drivers. For example, some indirect costs such as depreciation and repairs of machines are more closely related to machine-hours. Other indirect costs such as supervision and production support are more closely related to direct manufacturing labor-hours. Robinson, however, chooses direct manufacturing labor-hours as the sole allocation base for linking all indirect manufacturing costs to jobs. The managers do so because, in Robinson's labor-intensive environment, they believe the number of direct manufacturing labor-hours drives the manufacturing overhead resources required by individual jobs. (We will see in Chapter 5 that managers in many manufacturing environments often need to broaden the set of cost drivers.) In 2017, Robinson budgets 28,000 direct manufacturing labor-hours.

Step 4: Identify the Indirect Costs Associated with Each Cost-Allocation Base. Because Robinson believes that a single cost-allocation base—direct manufacturing labor-hours—can be used to allocate indirect manufacturing costs to jobs, Robinson creates a single cost pool called manufacturing overhead costs. This pool represents all indirect costs of the Manufacturing Department that are difficult to trace directly to individual jobs. In 2017, budgeted manufacturing overhead costs total $1,120,000.

As we saw in Steps 3 and 4, managers first identify cost-allocation bases and then identify the costs related to each cost-allocation base, not the other way around. They choose this order because managers must first understand their companies' cost drivers (the reasons why costs are being incurred) before they can determine the costs associated with each cost driver. Otherwise, there is nothing to guide the creation of cost pools. Of course, Steps 3 and 4 are often done almost simultaneously.

Step 5: Compute the Rate per Unit of Each Cost-Allocation Base Used to Allocate Indirect Costs to the Job. For each cost pool, the budgeted indirect-cost rate is calculated by dividing the budgeted total indirect costs in the pool (determined in Step 4) by the budgeted total quantity of the cost-allocation base (determined in Step 3). Robinson calculates the allocation rate for its single manufacturing overhead cost pool as follows:

$$\text{Budgeted manufacturing overhead rate} = \frac{\text{Budgeted manufacturing overhead costs}}{\text{Budgeted total quantity of cost-allocation base}}$$

$$= \frac{\$1,120,000}{28,000 \text{ direct manufacturing labor-hours}}$$

$$= \$40 \text{ per direct manufacturing labor-hour}$$

Step 6: Compute the Indirect Costs Allocated to the Job. The indirect costs of a job are calculated by multiplying the *actual* quantity of each different allocation base (one allocation base for each cost pool) associated with the job by the *budgeted* indirect cost rate of each allocation base (computed in Step 5). Recall that Robinson's managers selected direct manufacturing labor-hours as the only cost-allocation base. Robinson uses 88 direct manufacturing labor-hours on the WPP 298 job. Consequently, the manufacturing overhead costs allocated to WPP 298 equal $3,520 ($40 per direct manufacturing labor-hour × 88 hours) and appear in the Manufacturing Overhead panel of the WPP 298 job-cost record in Exhibit 4-2.

Step 7: Compute the Total Cost of the Job by Adding All Direct and Indirect Costs Assigned to the Job. Exhibit 4-2 shows that the total manufacturing costs of the WPP job are $9,705.

Direct manufacturing costs		
Direct materials	$4,606	
Direct manufacturing labor	1,579	$ 6,185
Manufacturing overhead costs		
($40 per direct manufacturing labor-hour × 88 hours)		3,520
Total manufacturing costs of job WPP 298		$9,705

Recall that Robinson bid a price of $15,000 for the job. At that revenue, the normal-costing system shows the job's gross margin is $5,295 ($15,000 − $9,705) and its gross-margin percentage is 35.3% ($5,295 ÷ $15,000 = 0.353).

CONCEPTS IN ACTION: The Job-Costing "Game Plan" at AT&T Stadium

Tony Gutierrez/AP Images

While the Dallas Cowboys have won five Super Bowls, many football fans recognize the team for its futuristic home, AT&T Stadium in Arlington, Texas. The 80,000-seat stadium, built in 3 years, features two arches spanning a quarter-mile in length over the dome, a retractable roof, the largest retractable glass doors in the world (in each end zone), canted glass exterior walls, and a 600-ton video screen. To manage costs and make a profit, Manhattan Construction estimated and then evaluated the cost of building each feature.

The AT&T Stadium project had five stages: (1) conceptualization, (2) design and planning, (3) preconstruction, (4) construction, and (5) finalization and delivery. At each stage, the job-costing system tracked actual costs of direct materials, direct labor, and overhead costs (supervisor salaries, rent, materials handling, and so on). These costs were compared to budgeted costs to evaluate how well materials, labor and overhead resources were used. Without disciplined job costing, managing costs on this complex project would be extremely difficult. Job costing was key to Manhattan Construction turning a profit on AT&T Stadium.

Sources: Based on interview with Mark Penny, Project Manager, Manhattan Construction Co., 2010; David Dillon, "New Cowboys Stadium Has Grand Design, but Discipline Isn't Compromised," *The Dallas Morning News* (June 3, 2009); Brooke Knudson, "Profile: Dallas Cowboys Stadium," *Construction Today* (December 22, 2008); and Dallas Cowboys, "Cowboys Stadium: Architecture Fact Sheet," accessed March 2016 (http://stadium.dallascowboys.com/assets/pdf/mediaArchitectureFactSheet.pdf).

4-1 TRY IT!

Donna Corporation manufactures custom cabinets for kitchens. It uses a normal-costing system with two direct-cost categories—direct materials and direct manufacturing labor—and one indirect-cost pool, manufacturing overhead costs. It provides the following information for 2017.

Budgeted manufacturing overhead costs	$960,000
Budgeted direct manufacturing labor-hours	32,000 hours
Actual manufacturing overhead costs	$992,000
Actual direct manufacturing labor-hours	31,000 hours

Calculate the total manufacturing costs of the 32 Berndale Drive job using normal costing based on the following information:

Actual direct materials costs	$3,500
Actual direct manufacturing labor	160 hours
Actual direct manufacturing labor rate	$ 20 per hour

Robinson's manufacturing managers and sales managers can use the gross margin and gross-margin percentage calculations to compare the different jobs to try to understand why some jobs aren't as profitable as others. Were direct materials wasted? Was the direct manufacturing labor cost of the jobs too high? Were the jobs simply underpriced? A job-cost analysis provides the information managers needed to gauge the manufacturing and sales performance of their firms (see Concepts in Action: The Job Costing "Game Plan" at AT&T Stadium).

Exhibit 4-4 is an overview of Robinson Company's job-costing system. This exhibit represents the concepts comprising the five building blocks of job-costing systems introduced

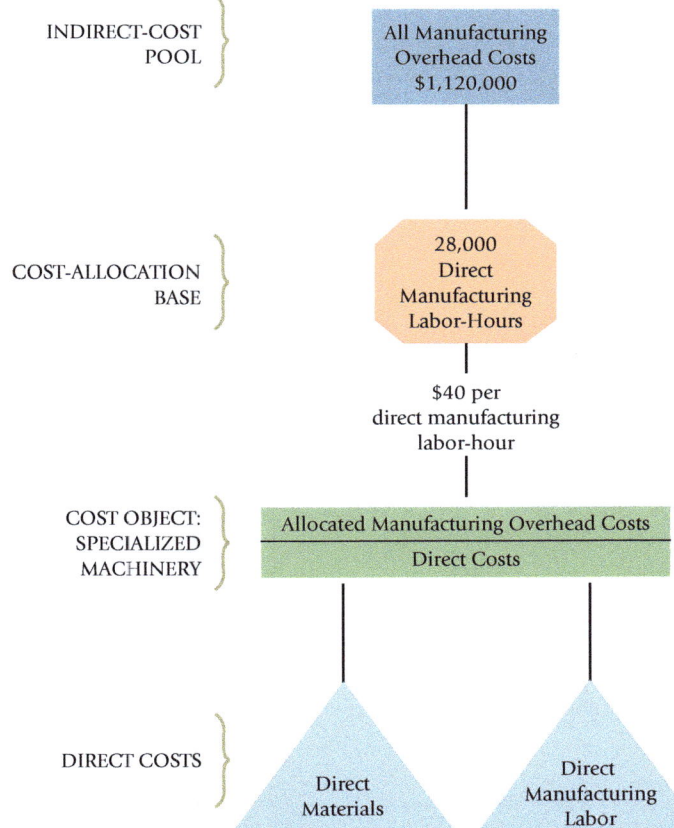

EXHIBIT 4-4

Job-Costing Overview for Determining Manufacturing Costs of Jobs at Robinson Company at the beginning of this chapter: (1) cost objects, (2) the direct costs of a cost object, (3) the indirect (overhead) costs of a cost object, (4) the indirect-cost pool, and (5) the cost-allocation base. (The symbols in the exhibit are used consistently in the costing-system overviews presented in this book. A triangle always identifies a direct cost, a rectangle represents the indirect-cost pool, and an octagon describes the cost-allocation base.) Costing-system overviews such as Exhibit 4-4 are important learning tools. We urge you to sketch one when you need to understand a costing system.

DECISION POINT

How do you implement a normal-costing system?

Note the similarities between Exhibit 4-4 and the cost of the WPP 298 job described in Step 7. Exhibit 4-4 shows two direct-cost categories (direct materials and direct manufacturing labor) and one indirect-cost category (manufacturing overhead) used to allocate indirect costs. The costs in Step 7 also have three dollar amounts, each corresponding respectively to the two direct-cost and one indirect-cost categories.

The Role of Technology

Information technology gives managers quick and accurate job-costing information, making it easier for them to manage and control jobs. Consider, for example, the direct materials charged to jobs. Managers control these costs as materials are purchased and used. Using Electronic Data Interchange (EDI) technology, companies like Robinson order materials from their suppliers by clicking a few keys on a computer keyboard. EDI, an electronic computer link between a company and its suppliers, ensures that the order is transmitted quickly and accurately with minimal paperwork and costs. A bar code scanner records the receipt of incoming materials, and a computer matches the receipt with the order, prints out a check to the supplier, and records the materials received. When an operator on the production floor transmits a request for materials via a computer terminal, the computer prepares a materials-requisition record, instantly recording the issue of materials in the materials and job-cost records. Each day, the computer sums the materials-requisition records charged to a particular job or manufacturing department. A performance report is then prepared monitoring the actual costs of direct materials. The use of direct materials can be reported hourly if managers believe the benefits exceed the cost of such frequent reporting.

Similarly, information about direct manufacturing labor is obtained as employees log into computer terminals and key in job numbers, their employee numbers, and the start and end times of their work on different jobs. The computer automatically prints the labor time record and, using hourly rates stored for each employee, calculates the direct manufacturing labor costs of individual jobs. Information technology can also give managers instant feedback to help them control manufacturing overhead costs, jobs in process, jobs completed, and jobs shipped and installed at customer sites.

Actual Costing

LEARNING OBJECTIVE 5

Distinguish actual costing

...actual costing uses actual indirect-cost rates

from normal costing

...normal costing uses budgeted indirect-cost rates

How would the cost of Job WPP 298 change if Robinson had used actual costing rather than normal costing? Both actual costing and normal costing trace direct costs to jobs in the same way because source documents identify the actual quantities and actual rates of direct materials and direct manufacturing labor for a job as the work is being done. The only difference between costing a job with normal costing and actual costing is that normal costing uses *budgeted* indirect-cost rates, whereas actual costing uses *actual* indirect-cost rates calculated annually at the end of the year. Exhibit 4-5 distinguishes actual costing from normal costing.

The following actual data for 2017 are for Robinson's manufacturing operations:

	Actual
Total manufacturing overhead costs	$1,215,000
Total direct manufacturing labor-hours	27,000

Steps 1 and 2 are the same in both normal and actual costing: Step 1 identifies WPP 298 as the cost object; Step 2 calculates actual direct materials costs of $4,606 and actual direct

EXHIBIT 4-5 Actual Costing and Normal Costing Methods

	Actual Costing	Normal Costing
Direct Costs	Actual direct-cost rates × actual quantities of direct-cost inputs	Actual direct-cost rates × actual quantities of direct-cost inputs
Indirect Costs	Actual indirect-cost rates × actual quantities of cost-allocation bases	Budgeted indirect-cost rates × actual quantities of cost-allocation bases

manufacturing labor costs of $1,579. Recall from Step 3 that Robinson uses a single cost-allocation base, direct manufacturing labor-hours, to allocate all manufacturing overhead costs to jobs. The actual quantity of direct manufacturing labor-hours for 2017 is 27,000 hours. In Step 4, Robinson groups all actual indirect manufacturing costs of $1,215,000 into a single manufacturing overhead cost pool. In Step 5, the **actual indirect-cost rate** is calculated by dividing actual total indirect costs in the pool (determined in Step 4) by the actual total quantity of the cost-allocation base (determined in Step 3). Robinson calculates the actual manufacturing overhead rate in 2017 for its single manufacturing overhead cost pool as follows:

$$\text{Actual manufacturing overhead rate} = \frac{\text{Actual annual manufacturing overhead costs}}{\text{Actual annual quantity of the cost-allocation base}}$$

$$= \frac{\$1,215,000}{27,000 \text{ direct manufacturing labor-hours}}$$

$$= \$45 \text{ per direct manufacturing labor-hour}$$

In Step 6, under an actual-costing system,

$$\text{Manufacturing overhead costs allocated to WPP 298} = \text{Actual manufacturing overhead rate} \times \text{Actual quantity of direct manufacturing labor-hours}$$

$$= \$45 \text{ per direct manuf. labor-hour} \times 88 \text{ direct manufacturing labor-hours}$$

$$= \$3,960$$

In Step 7, the cost of the job under actual costing is $10,145, calculated as follows:

Direct manufacturing costs		
Direct materials	$4,606	
Direct manufacturing labor	1,579	$ 6,185
Manufacturing overhead costs		
($45 per direct manufacturing labor-hour × 88 actual		
direct manufacturing labor-hours)		3,960
Total manufacturing costs of job		$10,145

The manufacturing cost of the WPP 298 job is higher by $440 under actual costing ($10,145) than it is under normal costing ($9,705) because the actual indirect-cost rate is $45 per hour, whereas the budgeted indirect-cost rate is $40 per hour. That is, ($45 − $40) × 88 actual direct manufacturing labor-hours = $440.

As we discussed previously, the manufacturing costs of a job are available much earlier in a normal-costing system. Consequently, Robinson's manufacturing and sales managers can evaluate the profitability of different jobs, the efficiency with which the jobs are done, and the pricing of different jobs as soon as they are completed, while the experience is still fresh in everyone's mind. Another advantage of normal costing is that it provides managers with information earlier—while there is still time to take corrective actions, such as improving the company's labor efficiency or reducing the company's overhead costs. At the end of the year, though, costs allocated using normal costing will not, in general, equal actual costs incurred. If the differences are significant, adjustments will need to be made so that the cost of jobs and the costs in various inventory accounts are based on actual rather than normal costing because

DECISION POINT

How do you distinguish actual costing from normal costing?

companies need to prepare financial statements based on what actually happened rather than on what was expected to happen at the beginning of the year. We describe these adjustments later in the chapter.

The next section explains how a normal job-costing system aggregates the costs and revenues for all jobs worked on during a particular month. *Instructors and students who do not wish to explore these details can go directly to page 148 to the section "Budgeted Indirect Costs and End-of-Accounting-Year Adjustments."*

TRY IT! 4-2

Donna Corporation manufactures custom cabinets for kitchens. It uses a normal-costing system with two direct-cost categories—direct materials and direct manufacturing labor—and one indirect-cost pool, manufacturing overhead costs. It provides the following information for 2017.

Budgeted manufacturing overhead costs	$960,000
Budgeted direct manufacturing labor-hours	32,000 hours
Actual manufacturing overhead costs	$992,000
Actual direct manufacturing labor-hours	31,000 hours

Calculate the total manufacturing costs of the 32 Berndale Drive job using actual costing based on the following information:

Actual direct materials costs	$3,500
Actual direct manufacturing labor	160 hours
Actual direct manufacturing labor rate	$ 20 per hour

A Normal Job-Costing System in Manufacturing

LEARNING OBJECTIVE 6

Track the flow of costs in a job-costing system

...from purchase of materials to sale of finished goods

The following example looks at events that occurred at Robinson Company in February 2017. Before getting into the details of normal costing, study Exhibit 4-6, which provides a broad framework for understanding the flow of costs in job costing.

The upper part of Exhibit 4-6 shows the flow of inventoriable costs from the purchase of materials and other manufacturing inputs to their conversion into work-in-process and finished goods, to the sale of finished goods.

Direct materials used and direct manufacturing labor can be easily traced to jobs. They become part of work-in-process inventory on the balance sheet because direct manufacturing labor transforms direct materials into another asset, work-in-process inventory. Robinson also incurs manufacturing overhead costs (including indirect materials and indirect manufacturing labor) to convert direct materials into work-in-process inventory. The overhead (indirect) costs, however, cannot be easily traced to individual jobs. As we described earlier in this chapter, manufacturing overhead costs are first accumulated in a manufacturing overhead account and then allocated to individual jobs. As manufacturing overhead costs are allocated, they become part of work-in-process inventory.

As we described in Chapter 2, when individual jobs are completed, work-in-process inventory becomes another balance sheet asset, finished-goods inventory. Only when finished goods are sold is the expense of cost of goods sold recognized in the income statement and matched against revenues earned.

The lower part of Exhibit 4-6 shows the period costs—marketing and customer-service costs. These costs do not create any assets on the balance sheet because they are not incurred to transform materials into a finished product. Instead, they are expensed in the income statement as they are incurred to best match revenues.

We next describe the entries made in the general ledger.

EXHIBIT 4-6 Flow of Costs in Job Costing

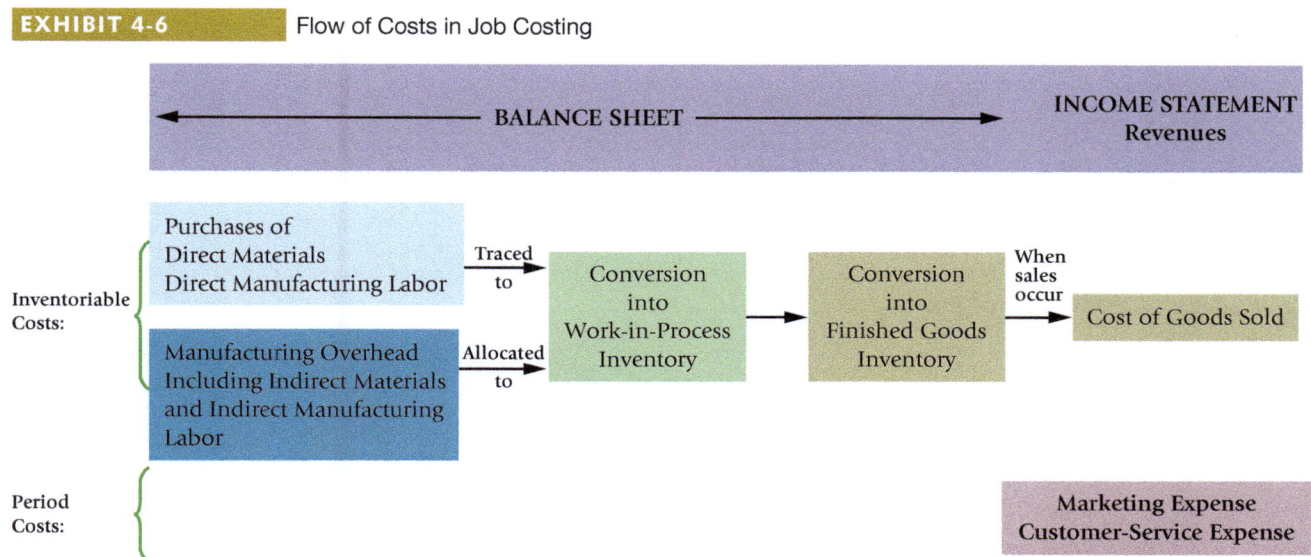

General Ledger

You know by this point that a job-costing system has a separate job-cost record for each job. A summary of the job-cost record is typically found in a subsidiary ledger. The general ledger account—Work-in-Process Control—presents the total of these separate job-cost records pertaining to all unfinished jobs. The job-cost records and Work-in-Process Control account track job costs from when jobs start until they are complete. When jobs are completed or sold, they are recorded in the finished-goods inventory records of jobs in the subsidiary ledger. The general ledger account Finished Goods Control records the total of these separate job-cost records for all jobs completed and subsequently for all jobs sold.

Exhibit 4-7 shows T-account relationships for Robinson Company's general ledger. The general ledger gives a "bird's-eye view" of the costing system. The amounts shown in Exhibit 4-7 are based on the monthly transactions and journal entries that follow. As you go through each journal entry, use Exhibit 4-7 to see how the various entries being made come together. General ledger accounts with "Control" in their titles (for example, Materials Control and Accounts Payable Control) have underlying subsidiary ledgers that contain additional details, such as each type of material in inventory and individual suppliers Robinson must pay.

Some companies simultaneously make entries in the general ledger and subsidiary ledger accounts. Others, such as Robinson, simplify their accounting by making entries in the subsidiary ledger when transactions occur and entries in the general ledger less frequently, often on a monthly basis, only when monthly financial statements are prepared.

A general ledger should be viewed as only one of many tools managers can use for planning and control. To control operations, managers rely on not only the source documents used to record amounts in the subsidiary ledgers, but also on nonfinancial information such as the percentage of jobs requiring rework or behind schedule.

Explanations of Transactions

We next look at a summary of Robinson Company's transactions for February 2017 and the corresponding journal entries for those transactions.

1. Purchases of materials (direct and indirect) on credit, $89,000

    Materials Control   89,000
        Accounts Payable Control   89,000

EXHIBIT 4-7 Manufacturing Job-Costing System Using Normal Costing: Diagram of General Ledger Relationships for February 2017

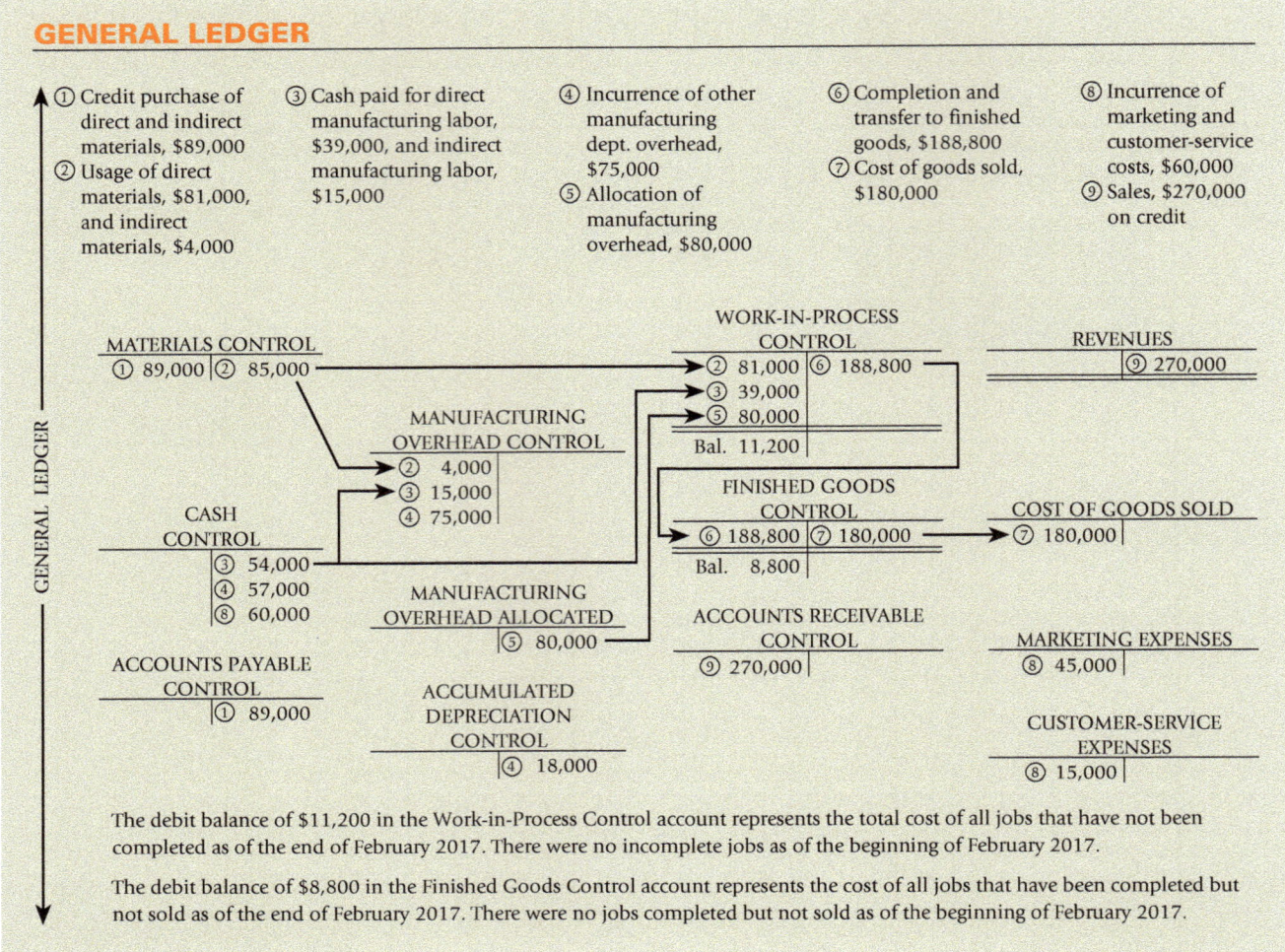

The debit balance of $11,200 in the Work-in-Process Control account represents the total cost of all jobs that have not been completed as of the end of February 2017. There were no incomplete jobs as of the beginning of February 2017.

The debit balance of $8,800 in the Finished Goods Control account represents the cost of all jobs that have been completed but not sold as of the end of February 2017. There were no jobs completed but not sold as of the beginning of February 2017.

2. Usage of direct materials, $81,000, and indirect materials, $4,000

Work-in-Process Control	81,000	
Manufacturing Overhead Control	4,000	
Materials Control		85,000

3. Manufacturing payroll for February: direct labor, $39,000, and indirect labor, $15,000, paid in cash

Work-in-Process Control	39,000	
Manufacturing Overhead Control	15,000	
Cash Control		54,000

4. Other manufacturing overhead costs incurred during February, $75,000, consisting of
   - supervision and engineering salaries, $44,000 (paid in cash);
   - plant utilities, repairs, and insurance, $13,000 (paid in cash); and
   - plant depreciation, $18,000

Manufacturing Overhead Control	75,000	
Cash Control		57,000
Accumulated Depreciation Control		18,000

5. Allocation of manufacturing overhead to jobs, $80,000

Work-in-Process Control	80,000	
Manufacturing Overhead Allocated		80,000

Under normal costing, **manufacturing overhead allocated**—or **manufacturing overhead applied**—is the amount of manufacturing overhead costs allocated to individual jobs based on the budgeted rate ($40 per direct manufacturing labor-hour) multiplied by the actual quantity of the allocation base used for each job. (The total actual direct manufacturing labor-hours across all jobs in February 2017 total 2,000.) Manufacturing overhead allocated contains all manufacturing overhead costs assigned to jobs using a cost-allocation base because overhead costs cannot be traced specifically to jobs in an economically feasible way.

Keep in mind the distinct difference between transactions 4 and 5. In transaction 4, actual overhead costs incurred throughout the month are added (debited) to the Manufacturing Overhead Control account. These costs are not debited to Work-in-Process Control because, unlike direct costs, they cannot be traced to individual jobs. Manufacturing overhead costs are added (debited) to individual jobs and to Work-in-Process Control *only when* manufacturing overhead costs are allocated in transaction 5. At the time these costs are allocated, Manufacturing Overhead Control is, *in effect*, decreased (credited) via its contra account, Manufacturing Overhead Allocated. Manufacturing Overhead Allocated is referred to as a *contra account* because the amounts debited to it represent the amounts credited to the Manufacturing Overhead Control account. Having Manufacturing Overhead Allocated as a contra account allows the job-costing system to separately retain information about the manufacturing overhead costs the company has *incurred* (in the Manufacturing Overhead Control account) as well as the amount of manufacturing overhead costs it has *allocated* (in the Manufacturing Overhead Allocated account). If the allocated manufacturing overhead had been credited to manufacturing overhead control, the company would lose information about the actual manufacturing overhead costs it is incurring.

Under the normal-costing system described in our Robinson Company example, at the beginning of the year, the company calculated the budgeted manufacturing overhead rate of $40 per direct manufacturing labor-hour by predicting the company's annual manufacturing overhead costs and annual quantity of the cost-allocation base. Almost certainly, the actual amounts allocated will differ from the predictions. We discuss what to do with this difference later in the chapter.

6. The sum of all individual jobs completed and transferred to finished goods in February 2017 is $188,800

Finished Goods Control	188,800	
Work-in-Process Control		188,800

7. Cost of goods sold, $180,000

Cost of Goods Sold	180,000	
Finished Goods Control		180,000

8. Marketing costs for February 2017, $45,000, and customer-service costs for February 2017, $15,000, paid in cash

Marketing Expenses	45,000	
Customer-Service Expenses	15,000	
Cash Control		60,000

9. Sales revenues from all jobs sold and delivered in February 2017, all on credit, $270,000

Accounts Receivable Control	270,000	
Revenues		270,000

TRY IT! 4-3

Donna Corporation manufactures custom cabinets for kitchens. It uses a normal-costing system with two direct-cost categories—direct materials and direct manufacturing labor—and one indirect-cost pool, manufacturing overhead costs. It provides the following information about manufacturing overhead costs for April 2017.

Actual direct materials used	$60,000
Actual direct manufacturing labor costs paid in cash	54,000
Indirect materials used	$3,000
Supervision and engineering salaries paid in cash	$50,000
Plant utilities and repairs paid in cash	10,000
Plant depreciation	$16,000
Actual direct manufacturing labor-hours	2,700
Cost of individual jobs completed and transferred to finished goods	$180,000
Cost of goods sold	$175,000

The following information is also available for 2017:

Budgeted manufacturing overhead costs for 2017	$960,000
Direct manufacturing labor-hours for 2017	32,000 hours

Present journal entries for (a) usage of direct and indirect materials, (b) manufacturing labor incurred, (c) manufacturing overhead costs incurred, (d) allocation of manufacturing overhead costs to jobs, (e) cost of jobs completed and transferred to finished goods, and (f) cost of goods sold.

Subsidiary Ledgers

Exhibits 4-8 and 4-9 present subsidiary ledgers that contain the underlying details—the "worm's-eye view"—that help Robinson's managers keep track of the WPP 298 job, as opposed to the "bird's-eye view" of the general ledger. The sum of all entries in underlying subsidiary ledgers equals the total amount in the corresponding general ledger control accounts.

Materials Records by Type of Material

The subsidiary ledger for materials at Robinson Company—called *Materials Records*—is used to continuously record the quantity of materials received, issued to jobs, and the inventory balances for each type of material. Panel A of Exhibit 4-8 shows the Materials Record for Metal Brackets (Part No. MB 468-A). In many companies, the source documents supporting the receipt and issue of materials [the material requisition record in Exhibit 4-3, Panel A, (page 135)] are scanned into a computer. Software programs then automatically update the Materials Records and make all the necessary accounting entries in the subsidiary and general ledgers. The cost of materials received across all types of direct and indirect material records for February 2017 is $89,000 (Exhibit 4-8, Panel A). The cost of materials issued across all types of direct and indirect material records for February 2017 is $85,000 (Exhibit 4-8, Panel A).

As direct materials are used, they are recorded as issued in the Materials Records (see Exhibit 4-8, Panel A, for a record of the Metal Brackets issued for the WPP machine job). Direct materials are also charged to Work-in-Process Inventory Records for Jobs, which are the subsidiary ledger accounts for the Work-in-Process Control account in the general ledger. For example, the metal brackets used in the WPP machine job appear as direct material costs of $112 in the subsidiary ledger under the work-in-process inventory record for WPP 298 [Exhibit 4-9, Panel A, which is based on the job-cost record source document in Exhibit 4-2, (page 134)]. The cost of direct materials used across all job-cost records for February 2017 is $81,000 (Exhibit 4-9, Panel A).

As indirect materials (for example, lubricants) are used, they are charged to the Manufacturing Department overhead records (Exhibit 4-8, Panel C), which comprise the

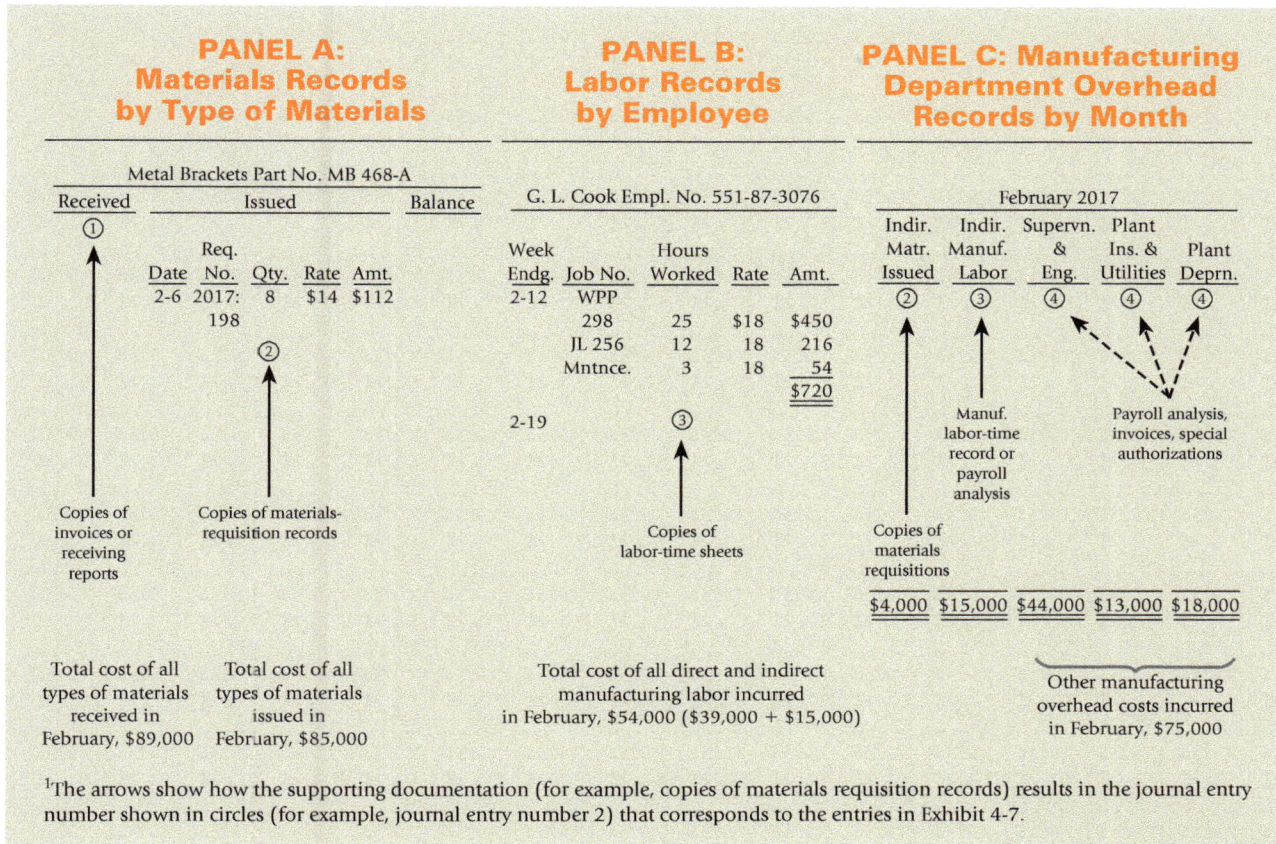

EXHIBIT 4-8 Subsidiary Ledgers for Materials, Labor, and Manufacturing Department Overhead[1]

[1]The arrows show how the supporting documentation (for example, copies of materials requisition records) results in the journal entry number shown in circles (for example, journal entry number 2) that corresponds to the entries in Exhibit 4-7.

subsidiary ledger for the Manufacturing Overhead Control account. The Manufacturing Department overhead records are used to accumulate actual costs in individual overhead categories by each indirect-cost-pool account in the general ledger. Recall that Robinson has only one indirect-cost pool: Manufacturing Overhead. The cost of indirect materials used is not added directly to individual job records. Instead, this cost is allocated to individual job records as a part of manufacturing overhead.

Labor Records by Employee

Labor records by employee (see Exhibit 4-8, Panel B, for G. L. Cook) are used to trace the costs of direct manufacturing labor to individual jobs and to accumulate the costs of indirect manufacturing labor in the Manufacturing Department overhead records (Exhibit 4-8, Panel C). The labor records are based on the labor-time sheet source documents [see Exhibit 4-3, Panel B, (page 135)]. The subsidiary ledger for employee labor records (Exhibit 4-8, Panel B) shows the different jobs that G. L. Cook, Employee No. 551-87-3076, worked on and the $720 of wages owed to Cook, for the week ending February 12. The sum of total wages owed to all employees for February 2017 is $54,000. The job-cost record for WPP 298 shows direct manufacturing labor costs of $450 for the time Cook spent on the WPP machine job during that week (Exhibit 4-9, Panel A). Total direct manufacturing labor costs recorded in all job-cost records (the subsidiary ledger for Work-in-Process Control) for February 2017 is $39,000.

G. L. Cook's employee record shows $54 for maintenance, which is an indirect manufacturing labor cost. The total indirect manufacturing labor costs of $15,000 for February 2017 appear in the Manufacturing Department overhead records in the subsidiary ledger (Exhibit 4-8, Panel C). These costs, by definition, cannot be traced to an individual job. Instead, they are allocated to individual jobs as a part of manufacturing overhead.

EXHIBIT 4-9 Subsidiary Ledgers for Individual Jobs[1]

PANEL A: Work-in-Process Inventory Records by Jobs

Job No. WPP 298

	In-Process				Completed		Balance	
Date	Direct Materials	Direct Manuf. Labor	Allocated Manuf. Overhead	Total Cost	Date	Total Cost	Date	Total Cost
2-6	$112			$112				
2-12		$450		$450				
...	...	...	...					
2-28	$4,606	$1,579	$3,520	$9,705	2-28	$9,705	2-28	$0
	②	③	⑤			⑥		

↑ Copies of materials-requisition records

↑ Copies of labor-time sheets

↑ Budgeted rate × actual direct manuf. labor-hours

↑ Completed job-cost record

Total cost of direct materials issued to all jobs in Feb., $81,000

Total cost of direct manuf. labor used on all jobs in Feb., $39,000

Total manuf. overhead allocated to all jobs in Feb., $80,000

Total cost of all jobs completed and transferred to finished goods in Feb., $188,800

PANEL B: Finished Goods Inventory Records by Job

Job No. WPP 298

Received		Issued		Balance	
Date	Amt.	Date	Amt.	Date	Amt.
2-28	$9,705	2-28	$9,705	2-28	$0
⑥					

↑ Completed job-cost record

↑ Costed sales invoice

Total cost of all jobs transferred to finished goods in Feb., $188,800

Total cost of all jobs sold and invoiced in Feb., $180,000

[1]The arrows show how the supporting documentation (for example, copies of materials requisition records) results in the journal entry number shown in circles (for example, journal entry number 2) that corresponds to the entries in Exhibit 4-7.

Manufacturing Department Overhead Records by Month

The Manufacturing Department overhead records (see Exhibit 4-8, Panel C) that make up the subsidiary ledger for the Manufacturing Overhead Control account show details of different categories of overhead costs such as indirect materials, indirect manufacturing labor, supervision and engineering, plant insurance and utilities, and plant depreciation. The source documents for these entries include invoices (for example, a utility bill) and special schedules (for example, a depreciation schedule) from the responsible accounting officer. Manufacturing department overhead for February 2017 is indirect materials, $4,000; indirect manufacturing labor, $15,000; and other manufacturing overhead, $75,000 (Exhibit 4-8, Panel C).

Work-in-Process Inventory Records by Jobs

As we have already discussed, the job-cost record for each individual job in the subsidiary ledger is debited by the actual cost of direct materials and direct manufacturing labor used by individual jobs. In Robinson's normal-costing system, the job-cost record for each individual job in the subsidiary ledger is also debited for manufacturing overhead allocated based on the budgeted manufacturing overhead rate times the actual direct manufacturing labor-hours used in that job. For example, the job-cost record for Job WPP 298 (Exhibit 4-9, Panel A) shows Manufacturing Overhead Allocated of $3,520 (the budgeted rate of $40 per labor-hour × 88 actual direct manufacturing labor-hours used). For the

2,000 actual direct manufacturing labor-hours used for all jobs in February 2017, the total manufacturing overhead allocated equals $40 per labor-hour × 2,000 direct manufacturing labor-hours = $80,000.

Finished Goods Inventory Records by Jobs

Exhibit 4-9, Panel A, shows that Job WPP 298 was completed at a cost of $9,705. Job WPP 298 also simultaneously appears in the finished-goods records of the subsidiary ledger. The total cost of all jobs completed and transferred to finished goods in February 2017 is $188,800 (Exhibit 4-9, Panels A and B). Exhibit 4-9, Panel B, indicates that Job WPP 298 was sold and delivered to the customer on February 28, 2017, at which time $9,705 was transferred from finished goods to cost of goods sold. The total cost of all jobs sold and invoiced in February 2017 is $180,000 (Exhibit 4-9, Panel B).

Other Subsidiary Records

Just as it does for manufacturing payroll, Robinson maintains employee labor records in subsidiary ledgers for marketing and customer-service payroll as well as records for different types of advertising costs (print, television, and radio). An accounts receivable subsidiary ledger is also used to record the February 2017 amounts due from each customer, including the $15,000 due from the sale of Job WPP 298.

At this point, pause and review the nine entries in this example. Exhibit 4-7 is a handy summary of all nine general-ledger entries presented in the form of T-accounts. Be sure to trace each journal entry, step by step, to T-accounts in the general ledger presented in Exhibit 4-7. Robinson's managers will use this information to evaluate how Robinson has performed on the WPP job.

Exhibit 4-10 provides Robinson's income statement for February 2017 using information from entries 7, 8, and 9. Managers could further subdivide the cost of goods sold calculations and present them in the format of Exhibit 2-8 [(page 62)]. The benefit of using the subdivided format is that it allows managers to discern detailed performance trends that can help them improve the efficiency on future jobs.

Nonmanufacturing Costs and Job Costing

In Chapter 2 (pages 68–69), you learned that companies use product costs for different purposes. The product costs reported as inventoriable costs to shareholders may differ from the product costs reported to managers to guide their pricing and product-mix decisions. Managers must keep in mind that even though marketing and customer-service costs are expensed when incurred for financial accounting purposes, companies often trace or allocate these costs to individual jobs for pricing, product-mix, and cost-management decisions.

EXHIBIT 4-10 Robinson Company Income Statement for the Month Ending February 2017

Revenues		$270,000
Cost of goods sold ($180,000 + $14,000[1])		194,000
Gross margin		76,000
Operating costs		
Marketing costs	$45,000	
Customer-service costs	15,000	
Total operating costs		60,000
Operating income		$ 16,000

[1] Cost of goods sold has been increased by $14,000, the difference between the Manufacturing overhead control account ($94,000) and the Manufacturing overhead allocated ($80,000). In a later section of this chapter, we discuss this adjustment, which represents the amount by which actual manufacturing overhead cost exceeds the manufacturing overhead allocated to jobs during February 2017.

DECISION POINT

How are transactions recorded in a manufacturing job-costing system?

Robinson can trace direct marketing costs and customer-service costs to jobs the same way in which it traces direct manufacturing costs to jobs. What about indirect marketing and customer-service costs? Assume these costs have the same cost-allocation base, revenues, and are included in a single cost pool. Robinson can then calculate a budgeted indirect-cost rate by dividing budgeted indirect marketing costs plus budgeted indirect customer-service costs by budgeted revenues. Robinson can use this rate to allocate these indirect costs to jobs. For example, if this rate were 15% of revenues, Robinson would allocate $2,250 to Job WPP 298 (0.15 × $15,000, the revenue from the job). By assigning both manufacturing costs and nonmanufacturing costs to jobs, Robinson can compare all costs against the revenues of different jobs.

Budgeted Indirect Costs and End-of-Accounting-Year Adjustments

LEARNING OBJECTIVE 7

Dispose of under- or overallocated manufacturing overhead costs at the end of the fiscal year using alternative methods

...for example, writing off this amount to the Cost of Goods Sold account

Managers try to closely approximate actual manufacturing overhead costs and actual direct manufacturing labor-hours when calculating the budgeted indirect cost rate. However, for the numerator and denominator reasons explained earlier in the chapter, under normal costing, a company's actual overhead costs incurred each month are not likely to equal its overhead costs allocated each month. Even at the end of the year, allocated costs are unlikely to equal actual costs because they are based on estimates made up to 12 months before actual costs are incurred. For financial statement purposes, companies are required under Generally Accepted Accounting Principles to report results based on actual costs. We now describe adjustments that management accountants need to make when, at the end of the fiscal year, indirect costs allocated differ from actual indirect costs incurred.

Underallocated and Overallocated Indirect Costs

Underallocated indirect costs occur when the allocated amount of indirect costs in an accounting period is less than the actual (incurred) amount. **Overallocated indirect costs** occur when the allocated amount of indirect costs in an accounting period is greater than the actual (incurred) amount.

Underallocated (overallocated) indirect costs = Actual indirect costs incurred − Indirect costs allocated

Underallocated (overallocated) indirect costs are also called **underapplied (overapplied) indirect costs** and **underabsorbed (overabsorbed) indirect costs**.

Consider the manufacturing overhead cost pool at Robinson Company. There are two indirect-cost accounts in the general ledger related to manufacturing overhead:

1. Manufacturing Overhead Control, the record of the actual costs in all the individual overhead categories (such as indirect materials, indirect manufacturing labor, supervision, engineering, utilities, and plant depreciation)
2. Manufacturing Overhead Allocated, the record of the manufacturing overhead allocated to individual jobs on the basis of the budgeted rate multiplied by actual direct manufacturing labor-hours

At the end of the year, the overhead accounts show the following amounts.

Manufacturing Overhead Control		Manufacturing Overhead Allocated	
Bal. Dec. 31, 2017	1,215,000	Bal. Dec. 31, 2017	1,080,000

The $1,080,000 credit balance in Manufacturing Overhead Allocated results from multiplying the 27,000 actual direct manufacturing labor-hours worked on all jobs in 2017 by the budgeted rate of $40 per direct manufacturing labor-hour.

The $135,000 ($1,215,000 − $1,080,000) difference (a net debit) is an underallocated amount because actual manufacturing overhead costs are greater than the allocated amount. This difference arises for two reasons related to the computation of the $40 budgeted hourly rate:

1. **Numerator reason (indirect-cost pool).** Actual manufacturing overhead costs of $1,215,000 are greater than the budgeted amount of $1,120,000.
2. **Denominator reason (quantity of allocation base).** Actual direct manufacturing labor-hours of 27,000 are fewer than the budgeted 28,000 hours.

There are three main approaches to accounting for the $135,000 underallocated manufacturing overhead caused by Robinson underestimating manufacturing overhead costs and overestimating the quantity of the cost-allocation base: (1) adjusted allocation-rate approach, (2) proration approach, and (3) write-off to cost of goods sold approach.

Adjusted Allocation-Rate Approach

The **adjusted allocation-rate approach** restates all overhead entries in the general ledger and subsidiary ledgers using actual cost rates rather than budgeted cost rates. First, the actual manufacturing overhead rate is computed at the end of the fiscal year. Then the manufacturing overhead costs allocated to every job during the year are recomputed using the actual manufacturing overhead rate (rather than the budgeted manufacturing overhead rate). Finally, end-of-year closing entries are made. The result is that at year-end, every job-cost record and finished-goods record—as well as the ending Work-in-Process Control, Finished Goods Control, and Cost of Goods Sold accounts—represent actual manufacturing overhead costs incurred.

The widespread adoption of computerized accounting systems has greatly reduced the cost of using the adjusted allocation-rate approach. In our Robinson example, the actual manufacturing overhead ($1,215,000) exceeds the manufacturing overhead allocated ($1,080,000) by 12.5% [($1,215,000 − $1,080,000) ÷ $1,080,000]. At year-end, Robinson could increase the manufacturing overhead allocated to each job in 2017 by 12.5% using a single software command. The command would adjust both the subsidiary ledgers and the general ledger.

Consider the Western Pulp and Paper machine job, WPP 298. Under normal costing, the manufacturing overhead allocated to the job is $3,520 (the budgeted rate of $40 per direct manufacturing labor-hour × 88 hours). Increasing the manufacturing overhead allocated by 12.5%, or $440 ($3,520 × 0.125), means the adjusted amount of manufacturing overhead allocated to Job WPP 298 equals $3,960 ($3,520+$440). Note from page 139 that using actual costing, manufacturing overhead allocated to this job is $3,960 (the actual rate of $45 per direct manufacturing labor-hour × 88 hours). Making this adjustment under normal costing for each job in the subsidiary ledgers ensures that actual manufacturing overhead costs of $1,215,000 are allocated to jobs.

The adjusted allocation-rate approach yields the benefits of both the *timeliness and convenience of normal costing during the year and the allocation of actual manufacturing overhead costs at year-end*. Each individual job-cost record and the end-of-year account balances for inventories and cost of goods sold are adjusted to actual costs. These adjustments, in turn, will affect the income Robinson reports. Knowing the actual profitability of individual jobs after they are completed provides managers with accurate and useful insights for future decisions about which jobs to undertake, how to price them, and how to manage their costs.

Proration Approach

The **proration** approach spreads underallocated overhead or overallocated overhead among ending work-in-process inventory, finished-goods inventory, and cost of goods sold. Materials inventory is not included in this proration because no manufacturing overhead costs have been allocated to it. We illustrate end-of-year proration in the Robinson Company example. Assume the following actual results for Robinson Company in 2017:

	A	B	C
1	Account	Account Balance (Before Proration)	Manufacturing Overhead in Each Account Balance Allocated in the Current Year (Before Proration)
2	Work-in-process control	$ 50,000	$ 16,200
3	Finished goods control	75,000	31,320
4	Cost of goods sold	2,375,000	1,032,480
5		$2,500,000	$1,080,000

How should Robinson prorate the underallocated $135,000 of manufacturing overhead at the end of 2017?

On the basis of the total amount of manufacturing overhead allocated in 2017 (before proration) in the ending balances of Work-in-Process Control, Finished Goods Control, and Cost of Goods Sold accounts. The $135,000 underallocated overhead is prorated over the three accounts in proportion to the total amount of manufacturing overhead allocated (before proration) in column 2 of the following table, resulting in the ending balances (after proration) in column 5 at actual costs.

	A	B	C	D	E	F	G
10		Account Balance (Before Proration)	Manufacturing Overhead in Each Account Balance Allocated in the Current Year (Before Proration)	Manufacturing Overhead in Each Account Balance Allocated in the Current Year as a Percent of Total	Proration of $135,000 of Underallocated Manufacturing Overhead		Account Balance (After Proration)
11	Account	(1)	(2)	(3) = (2) / $1,080,000	(4) = (3) × $135,000		(5) = (1) + (4)
12	Work-in-process control	$ 50,000	$ 16,200	1.5%	0.015 × $135,000 =	$ 2,025	$ 52,025
13	Finished goods control	75,000	31,320	2.9%	0.029 × 135,000 =	3,915	78,915
14	Cost of goods sold	2,375,000	1,032,480	95.6%	0.956 × 135,000 =	129,060	2,504,060
15	Total	$2,500,000	$1,080,000	100.0%		$135,000	$2,635,000

Prorating on the basis of the manufacturing overhead allocated (before proration) results in Robinson allocating manufacturing overhead based on actual manufacturing overhead costs. Recall that Robinson's actual manufacturing overhead ($1,215,000) in 2017 exceeds its manufacturing overhead allocated ($1,080,000) in 2017 by 12.5%. The proration amounts in column 4 can also be derived by multiplying the balances in column 2 by 0.125. For example, the $3,915 proration to Finished Goods is 0.125 × $31,320. Adding these amounts effectively means allocating manufacturing overhead at 112.5% of what had been allocated before. The journal entry to record this proration is:

Work-in-Process Control	2,025	
Finished Goods Control	3,915	
Cost of Goods Sold	129,060	
Manufacturing Overhead Allocated	1,080,000	
Manufacturing Overhead Control		1,215,000

If manufacturing overhead had been overallocated, the Work-in-Process Control, Finished Goods Control, and Cost of Goods Sold accounts would be decreased (credited) instead of increased (debited).

This journal entry closes (brings to zero) the manufacturing overhead-related accounts and restates the 2017 ending balances for Work-in-Process Control, Finished Goods Control, and Cost of Goods Sold to what they would have been if actual manufacturing overhead rates had been used rather than budgeted manufacturing overhead rates. This method reports the same 2017 ending balances in the general ledger as the adjusted allocation-rate approach. However, unlike the adjusted allocation-rate approach, the sum of the amounts shown in the subsidiary ledgers will not match the amounts shown in the general ledger after proration because no adjustments from budgeted to actual manufacturing overhead rates are made in the individual job-cost records. The objective of the proration approach is to only adjust the general ledger to actual manufacturing overhead rates for purposes of financial reporting. The increase in cost of goods sold expense by $129,060 as a result of the proration causes Robinson's reported operating income to decrease by the same amount.

Some companies use the proration approach, but base it on the ending balances of Work-in-Process Control, Finished Goods Control, and Cost of Goods Sold accounts prior to proration (see column 1 of the preceding table). The following table shows that prorations based on ending account balances are not the same as the more accurate prorations calculated earlier based on the amount of manufacturing overhead allocated to the accounts because the proportions of manufacturing overhead costs to total costs in these accounts are not the same.

	A	B	C	D	E	F
1		Account Balance (Before Proration)	Account Balance as a Percent of Total	Proration of $135,000 of Underallocated Manufacturing Overhead		Account Balance (After Proration)
2	Account	(1)	(2) = (1) / $2,500,000	(3) = (2) × $135,000		(4) = (1) + (3)
3	Work-in-process control	$ 50,000	2.0%	0.02 × $135,000 =	$ 2,700	$ 52,700
4	Finished goods control	75,000	3.0%	0.03 × 135,000 =	4,050	79,050
5	Cost of goods sold	2,375,000	95.0%	0.95 × 135,000 =	128,250	2,503,250
6	Total	$2,500,000	100.0%		$135,000	$2,635,000

However, proration based on ending balances is frequently justified as being an expedient way of approximating the more accurate results from using manufacturing overhead costs allocated.

Write-off to Cost of Goods Sold Approach

Under the write-off approach, the total under- or overallocated manufacturing overhead is included in this year's Cost of Goods Sold. For Robinson, the journal entry would be as follows:

Cost of Goods Sold	135,000	
Manufacturing Overhead Allocated	1,080,000	
Manufacturing Overhead Control		1,215,000

Robinson's two Manufacturing Overhead accounts—Manufacturing Overhead Control and Manufacturing Overhead Allocated—are closed with the difference between them included in Cost of Goods Sold. The Cost of Goods Sold account after the write-off equals $2,510,000, the balance before the write-off of $2,375,000 *plus the underallocated* manufacturing overhead amount of $135,000. This results in operating income decreasing by $135,000.

TRY IT! 4-4

Donna Corporation manufactures custom cabinets for kitchens. It uses a normal-costing system with two direct-cost categories—direct materials and direct manufacturing labor—and one indirect-cost pool, manufacturing overhead costs. It provides the following information about manufacturing overhead costs for 2017.

Budgeted manufacturing overhead costs	$960,000
Budgeted direct manufacturing labor-hours	32,000 hours
Actual manufacturing overhead costs	$992,000
Actual direct manufacturing labor-hours	31,000 hours

The following information is available as of December 31, 2017.

Account	Account Balance (Before Proration)	Manufacturing Overhead in Each Account Balance Allocated in the Current Year (Before Proration)
Work-in-Process Control	$ 40,000	$ 14,400
Finished Goods Control	60,000	24,000
Cost of Goods Sold	1,900,000	921,600
	$2,000,000	$960,000

Calculate the underallocated or overallocated manufacturing overhead at the end of 2017 and prorate it to Work-in-Process Control, Finished Goods Control, and Cost of Goods Sold accounts based on the allocated manufacturing overhead in each account balance using normal costing.

Choosing Among Approaches

Which of the three approaches of dealing with underallocated overhead and overallocated overhead is the best one to use? When making this decision, managers should consider the amount of underallocated or overallocated overhead and the purpose of the adjustment, as the following table indicates.

If the purpose of the adjustment is to…	and the total amount of underallocation or overallocation is…	then managers prefer to use the…
state the balance sheet and income statements based on actual rather than budgeted manufacturing overhead rates	big, relative to total operating income, and inventory levels are high	proration method because it is the most accurate method of allocating actual manufacturing overhead costs to the general ledger accounts.
state the balance sheet and income statements based on actual rather than budgeted manufacturing overhead rates	small, relative to total operating income, or inventory levels are low	write-off to cost of goods sold approach because it is a good approximation of the more accurate proration method.
provide an accurate record of actual individual job costs in order to conduct a profitability analysis, learn how to better manage the costs of jobs, and bid on future jobs	big, relative to total operating income,	adjusted allocation-rate method because it makes adjustments in individual job records in addition to the general ledger accounts.

Many management accountants and managers argue that to the extent that the underallocated overhead cost measures inefficiency during the period, it should be written off to the Cost of Goods Sold account instead of being prorated to the Work-in-Process or Finished-Goods inventory accounts. This line of reasoning favors applying a combination of the write-off and proration methods. For example, the portion of the underallocated overhead cost that is due to inefficiency (say, because of excessive spending or idle capacity) and that could have been avoided should be written off to the Cost of Goods Sold account, whereas the portion that is unavoidable should be prorated. Unlike full proration, this approach avoids making the costs of inefficiency part of inventory assets.

As our discussion suggests, choosing which method to use and determining the amount to be written off is often a matter of judgment. The method managers choose affects the operating income a company reports. In the case of underallocated overhead, the method of writing off to cost of goods sold results in lower operating income compared to proration. In the case of overallocated overhead, proration results in lower operating income compared to writing the overhead off to cost of goods sold.

Do managers prefer to report lower or higher operating income? Reporting lower operating income lowers the company's taxes, saving the company cash and increasing company value. But managers are often compensated based on operating income and so favor reporting higher operating incomes even if it results in higher taxes. Managers of companies in financial difficulty also tend to report higher incomes to avoid violating financial covenants. Shareholders and boards of directors seek to motivate managerial actions that increase company value. For this reason, many compensation plans include metrics such as after-tax cash flow, in addition to operating income. At no time should managers make choices that are illegal or unethical. We discuss these issues in more detail in Chapter 23.

Robinson's managers believed that a single manufacturing overhead cost pool with direct manufacturing labor-hours as the cost-allocation base was appropriate for allocating all manufacturing overhead costs to jobs. Had Robinson's managers felt that different manufacturing departments (for example, machining and assembly) used overhead resources differently, they would have assigned overhead costs to each department and calculated a separate overhead allocation rate for each department based on the cost driver of the overhead costs in each department. The general ledger would contain Manufacturing Overhead Control and Manufacturing Overhead Allocated accounts for each department, resulting in end-of-year adjustments for underallocated or overallocated overhead costs for each department.

Instructors and students interested in exploring these more detailed allocations can go to Chapter 15, where we continue the Robinson Company example.

> **DECISION POINT**
> How should managers dispose of under- or overallocated manufacturing overhead costs at the end of the accounting year?

Variations from Normal Costing: A Service-Sector Example

Job costing is also very useful in service organizations such as accounting and consulting firms, advertising agencies, auto repair shops, and hospitals. In an accounting firm, each audit is a job. The costs of each audit are accumulated in a job-cost record, much like the document used by Robinson Company, based on the seven-step approach described earlier. On the basis of labor-time sheets, direct labor costs of the professional staff—audit partners, audit managers, and audit staff—are traced to individual jobs. Other direct costs, such as travel, out-of-town meals and lodging, phone, fax, and copying, are also traced to jobs. The costs of secretarial support, office staff, rent, and depreciation of furniture and equipment are indirect costs because these costs cannot be traced to jobs in an economically feasible way. Indirect costs are allocated to jobs, for example, using a cost-allocation base such as number of professional labor-hours.

In some service organizations, a variation from normal costing is helpful because actual direct-labor costs, the largest component of total costs, can be difficult to trace to jobs as they are completed. For example, the actual direct-labor costs of an audit may include bonuses that become known only at the end of the year (a numerator reason). Also, the hours worked each period might vary significantly depending on the number of working days each

> **LEARNING OBJECTIVE** 8
> Understand variations from normal costing
> ...some variations from normal costing use budgeted direct-cost rates

month and the demand for services (a denominator reason) while the direct-labor costs remain largely fixed. It would be inappropriate to charge a job with higher actual direct labor costs simply because a month had fewer working days or demand for services was low in that month. Using budgeted rates gives a better picture of the direct labor cost per hour that the company had planned when it hired the workers. In situations like these, a company needing timely information during the progress of an audit will use budgeted rates for some direct costs and budgeted rates for other indirect costs. All budgeted rates are calculated at the start of the fiscal year. In contrast, normal costing uses actual cost rates for all direct costs and budgeted cost rates only for indirect costs.

The mechanics of using budgeted rates for direct costs are similar to the methods employed when using budgeted rates for indirect costs in normal costing. We illustrate this for Donahue and Associates, a public accounting firm. For 2017, Donahue budgets total direct-labor costs of $14,400,000, total indirect costs of $12,960,000, and total direct (professional) labor-hours of 288,000. In this case,

$$\text{Budgeted direct-labor cost rate} = \frac{\text{Budgeted total direct-labor costs}}{\text{Budgeted total direct-labor hours}}$$

$$= \frac{\$14,400,000}{288,000 \text{ direct labor-hours}} = \$50 \text{ per direct labor-hour}$$

Assuming only one indirect-cost pool and total direct-labor costs as the cost-allocation base,

$$\text{Budgeted indirect cost rate} = \frac{\text{Budgeted total costs in indirect cost pool}}{\text{Budgeted total quantity of cost-allocation base (direct-labor costs)}}$$

$$= \frac{\$12,960,000}{\$14,400,000} = 0.90, \text{ or } 90\% \text{ of direct-labor costs}$$

Suppose that in March 2017, an audit of Hanley Transport, a client of Donahue, uses 800 direct labor-hours. Donahue calculates the direct-labor costs of the audit by multiplying the budgeted direct-labor cost rate, $50 per direct labor-hour, by 800, the actual quantity of direct labor-hours. The indirect costs allocated to the Hanley Transport audit are determined by multiplying the budgeted indirect-cost rate (90%) by the direct-labor costs assigned to the job ($40,000). Assuming no other direct costs for travel and the like, the cost of the Hanley Transport audit is:

Direct-labor costs, $50 × 800	$40,000
Indirect costs allocated, 90% × $40,000	36,000
Total	$76,000

At the end of the fiscal year, the direct costs traced to jobs using budgeted rates will generally not equal actual direct costs because the actual rate and the budgeted rate are developed at different times using different information. End-of-year adjustments for underallocated or overallocated direct costs would need to be made in the same way that adjustments are made for underallocated or overallocated indirect costs.

The Donahue and Associates example illustrates that all costing systems do not exactly match either the actual-costing system or the normal-costing system described earlier in the chapter. As another example, engineering consulting firms, such as Tata Consulting Engineers in India and Terracon Consulting Engineers in the United States, often use budgeted rates to allocate indirect costs (such as engineering and office-support costs) as well as some direct costs (such as professional labor-hours) and trace some actual direct costs (such as the cost of making blueprints and fees paid to outside experts). Users of costing systems should be aware of the different systems that they may encounter.

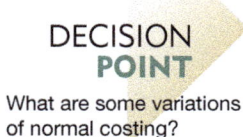

DECISION POINT

What are some variations of normal costing?

PROBLEM FOR SELF-STUDY

Your manager asks you to bring the following incomplete accounts of Endeavor Printing, Inc., up to date through January 31, 2017. Consider the data that appear in the T-accounts as well as the following information in items (a) through (j).

Endeavor's normal-costing system has two direct-cost categories (direct material costs and direct manufacturing labor costs) and one indirect-cost pool (manufacturing overhead costs, which are allocated using direct manufacturing labor costs).

Materials Control		Wages Payable Control	
12-31-2016 Bal. 30,000			1-31-2017 Bal. 6,000

Work-in-Process Control		Manufacturing Overhead Control	
		1-31-2017 Bal. 114,000	

Finished Goods Control		Costs of Goods Sold	
12-31-2016 Bal. 40,000			

Additional information follows:

a. Manufacturing overhead is allocated using a budgeted rate that is set every December. You forecast next year's manufacturing overhead costs and next year's direct manufacturing labor costs. The budget for 2017 is $1,200,000 for manufacturing overhead costs and $800,000 for direct manufacturing labor costs.
b. The only job unfinished on January 31, 2017, is No. 419, on which direct manufacturing labor costs are $4,000 (250 direct manufacturing labor-hours) and direct material costs are $16,000.
c. Total direct materials issued to production during January 2017 are $180,000.
d. Cost of goods completed during January is $360,000.
e. Materials inventory as of January 31, 2017, is $40,000.
f. Finished-goods inventory as of January 31, 2017, is $30,000.
g. All plant workers earn the same wage rate. Direct manufacturing labor-hours used for January total 5,000 hours. Other labor costs total $20,000.
h. The gross plant payroll paid in January equals $104,000. Ignore withholdings.
i. All "actual" manufacturing overhead cost incurred during January has already been posted.
j. All materials are direct materials.

Calculate the following:

1. Materials purchased during January
2. Cost of Goods Sold during January
3. Direct manufacturing labor costs incurred during January
4. Manufacturing Overhead Allocated during January
5. Balance, Wages Payable Control, December 31, 2016
6. Balance, Work-in-Process Control, January 31, 2017
7. Balance, Work-in-Process Control, December 31, 2016
8. Manufacturing Overhead Underallocated or Overallocated for January 2017

Solution

Amounts from the T-accounts are labeled "(T)."

1. From Materials Control T-account, Materials purchased: $180,000 (c) + $40,000 (e) − $30,000 (T) = $190,000
2. From Finished Goods Control T-account, Cost of Goods Sold: $40,000 (T) + $360,000 (d) − $30,000 (f) = $370,000

3. Direct manufacturing wage rate: $4,000 (b) ÷ 250 direct manufacturing labor-hours (b) = $16 per direct manufacturing labor-hour
   Direct manufacturing labor costs: 5,000 direct manufacturing labor-hours (g) × $16 per direct manufacturing labor-hour = $80,000
4. Manufacturing overhead rate: $1,200,000 (a) ÷ $800,000 (a) = 150%
   Manufacturing Overhead Allocated: 150% of $80,000 (see 3) = 1.50 × $80,000 = $120,000
5. From Wages Payable Control T-account, Wages Payable Control, December 31, 2016: $104,000 (h) + $6,000 (T) − $80,000 (see 3) − $20,000 (g) = $10,000
6. Work-in-Process Control, January 31, 2017: $16,000 (b) + $4,000 (b) + 150% of $4,000 (b) = $26,000 (This answer is used in item 7.)
7. From Work-in-Process Control T-account, Work-in-Process Control, December 31, 2016: $360,000 (d) + $26,000 (see 6) − $180,000 (c) − $80,000 (see 3) − $120,000 (see 4) = $6,000
8. Manufacturing overhead overallocated: $120,000 (see 4) − $114,000 (T) = $6,000.

Letters alongside entries in T-accounts correspond to letters in the preceding additional information. Numbers alongside entries in T-accounts correspond to numbers in the preceding requirements.

Materials Control

December 31, 2016, Bal.	(given)	30,000			
	(1)	190,000*		(c)	180,000
January 31, 2017, Bal.	(e)	40,000			

Work-in-Process Control

December 31, 2016, Bal.	(7)	6,000		(d)	360,000
Direct materials	(c)	180,000			
Direct manufacturing labor	(b) (g) (3)	80,000			
Manufacturing overhead allocated	(3) (a) (4)	120,000			
January 31, 2017, Bal.	(b) (6)	26,000			

Finished Goods Control

December 31, 2016, Bal.	(given)	40,000		(2)	370,000
	(d)	360,000			
January 31, 2017, Bal.	(f)	30,000			

Wages Payable Control

	(h)	104,000	December 31, 2016, Bal.	(5)	10,000
				(g) (3)	80,000
				(g)	20,000
			January 31, 2017	(given)	6,000

Manufacturing Overhead Control

Total January charges	(given)	114,000

Manufacturing Overhead Allocated

	(3) (a) (4)	120,000

Cost of Goods Sold

(d) (f) (2)	370,000	

---

*Can be computed only after all other postings in the account have been made.

DECISION POINTS

The following question-and-answer format summarizes the chapter's learning objectives. Each decision presents a key question related to a learning objective. The guidelines are the answer to that question.

Decision	Guidelines
1. What are the building-block concepts of a costing system?	The building-block concepts of a costing system are a cost object, direct costs of a cost object, indirect costs of a cost object, cost pool, and cost-allocation base. Costing-system overview diagrams represent these concepts in a systematic way. Costing systems aim to report cost numbers that reflect the way cost objects (such as products or services) use the resources of an organization.
2. How do you distinguish job costing from process costing?	Job-costing systems assign costs to distinct units of a product or service. Process-costing systems assign costs to masses of identical or similar units and compute unit costs on an average basis. These two costing systems represent opposite ends of a continuum. The costing systems of many companies combine some elements of both job costing and process costing.
3. What is the main challenge of implementing job-costing systems?	The main challenge of implementing job-costing systems is estimating actual costs of jobs in a timely manner.
4. How do you implement a normal-costing system?	A general seven-step approach to normal costing requires identifying (1) the job, (2) the actual direct costs, (3) the budgeted cost-allocation bases, (4) the budgeted indirect-cost pools, (5) the budgeted cost-allocation rates, (6) the allocated indirect costs (budgeted rates times actual quantities of the cost-allocation bases), and (7) the total direct and indirect costs of a job.
5. How do you distinguish actual costing from normal costing?	Actual costing and normal costing differ in the type of indirect-cost rates used:

	Actual Costing	Normal Costing
Direct-cost rates	Actual rates	Actual rates
Indirect-cost rates	Actual rates	Budgeted rates

Both systems use actual quantities of inputs for tracing direct costs and actual quantities of the cost-allocation bases for allocating indirect costs.

Decision	Guidelines
6. How are transactions recorded in a manufacturing job-costing system?	A job-costing system in manufacturing records the flow of inventoriable costs in the general and subsidiary ledgers for (a) acquisition of materials and other manufacturing inputs, (b) their conversion into work in process, (c) their conversion into finished goods, and (d) the sale of finished goods. The job-costing system expenses period costs, such as marketing costs, as they are incurred.

Decision	Guidelines
7. How should managers dispose of under- or overallocated manufacturing overhead costs at the end of the accounting year?	The two standard approaches to disposing of under- or overallocated manufacturing overhead costs at the end of the accounting year for the purposes of stating balance sheet and income statement amounts at actual costs are: (1) to adjust the allocation rate and (2) to prorate on the basis of the total amount of the allocated manufacturing overhead cost in the ending balances of Work-in-Process Control, Finished Goods Control, and Cost of Goods Sold accounts. Many companies write off amounts of under- or overallocated manufacturing overhead to Cost of Goods Sold when amounts are immaterial or underallocated overhead costs are the result of inefficiencies.
8. What are some variations of normal costing?	In some variations from normal costing, organizations use budgeted rates to assign direct costs, as well as indirect costs, to jobs.

TERMS TO LEARN

This chapter and the Glossary at the end of the book contain definitions of the following important terms:

- actual costing
- actual indirect-cost rate
- adjusted allocation-rate approach
- budgeted indirect-cost rate
- cost-allocation base
- cost-application base
- cost pool
- job
- job-cost record
- job-cost sheet
- job-costing system
- labor-time sheet
- manufacturing overhead allocated
- manufacturing overhead applied
- materials-requisition record
- normal costing
- overabsorbed indirect costs
- overallocated indirect costs
- overapplied indirect costs
- process-costing system
- proration
- source document
- underabsorbed indirect costs
- underallocated indirect costs
- underapplied indirect costs

ASSIGNMENT MATERIAL

Pearson MyLab Accounting

Questions

4-1 Define cost pool, cost tracing, cost allocation, and cost-allocation base.
4-2 What is the main difference between job costing and process costing? Provide one example for each costing method.
4-3 Why might an advertising agency use job costing for an advertising campaign by PepsiCo, whereas a bank might use process costing to determine the cost of checking account deposits?
4-4 Explain how you can determine the cost of a cost object/job under job-costing system.
4-5 Give examples of two cost objects in companies using job costing.
4-6 Describe three major source documents used in job-costing systems.
4-7 What is the role of information technology in job costing?
4-8 Seasonal patterns and fluctuating levels of monthly outputs are the two main factors for most organizations to use an annual period rather than a weekly or a monthly period to compute budgeted indirect-cost rates. Explain how annual indirect rates alleviate the impacts of these two factors.
4-9 Distinguish between actual costing and normal costing.
4-10 Explain how job-costing information may be used for decision making.
4-11 Comment on the following statement: There is no difference between "actual costing" and "normal costing" systems as both use the product of actual direct-cost rates and actual quantities of direct-cost inputs.
4-12 Describe the flow of costs in a normal job-costing system.

4-13 Describe three alternative ways to dispose of under- or overallocated overhead costs.

4-14 When might a company use budgeted costs rather than actual costs to compute direct-labor rates?

4-15 Describe briefly why Electronic Data Interchange (EDI) is helpful to managers.

Multiple-Choice Questions

Pearson MyLab Accounting

4-16 Which of the following does not accurately describe the application of job-order costing?
a. Finished goods that are purchased by customers will directly impact cost of goods sold.
b. Indirect manufacturing labor and indirect materials are part of the actual manufacturing costs incurred.
c. Direct materials and direct manufacturing labor are included in total manufacturing costs.
d. Manufacturing overhead costs incurred is used to determine total manufacturing costs.

4-17 Sturdy Manufacturing Co. assembled the following cost data for job order #23:

Direct manufacturing labor	$80,000
Indirect manufacturing labor	12,000
Equipment depreciation	1,000
Other indirect manufacturing costs	1,500
Direct materials	95,000
Indirect materials	4,000
Manufacturing overhead overapplied	2,000

What are the total manufacturing costs for job order #23 if the company uses normal job-order costing?
a. $191,500
b. $193,500
c. $194,500
d. $195,500

4-18 For which of the following industries would job-order costing most likely not be appropriate?
a. Small business printing.
b. Cereal production.
c. Home construction.
d. Aircraft assembly.

4-19 ABC Company uses job-order costing and has assembled the following cost data for the production and assembly of item X:

Direct manufacturing labor wages	$35,000
Direct material used	70,000
Indirect manufacturing labor	4,000
Utilities	400
Fire insurance	500
Manufacturing overhead applied	11,000
Indirect materials	6,000
Depreciation on equipment	600

Based on the above cost data, the manufacturing overhead for item X is:
a. $500 overallocated.
b. $600 underallocated.
c. $500 underallocated
d. $600 overallocated.

4-20 Under Stanford Corporation's job costing system, manufacturing overhead is applied to work in process using a predetermined annual overhead rate. During November, Year 1, Stanford's transactions included the following:

Direct materials issued to production	$180,000
Indirect materials issued to production	16,000
Manufacturing overhead incurred	250,000
Manufacturing overhead applied	226,000
Direct manufacturing labor costs	214,000

Stanford had neither beginning nor ending work-in-process inventory. What was the cost of jobs completed and transferred to finished goods in November 20X1?

1. $604,000
2. $644,000
3. $620,000
4. $660,000

©2016 DeVry/Becker Educational Development Corp. All Rights Reserved.

Exercises

4-21 Job order costing, process costing. In each of the following situations, determine whether job costing or process costing would be more appropriate.

a. A hospital
b. A car manufacturer
c. A computer manufacturer
d. A road construction firm
e. A soap manufacturer
f. A solicitor firm
g. A glassware manufacturer
h. A land development company
i. An event management company
j. An oil mill
k. A wine manufacturer
l. An advertisement film producer
m. A travel agent company
n. A health drink manufacturer
o. A cost audit firm
p. A boiler manufacturer
q. A electric lamp manufacturer
r. A courier service agency
s. A pharmaceutical company
t. A cosmetic products manufacturer
u. A cell phone manufacturer

4-22 Actual costing, normal costing, accounting for manufacturing overhead. Carolin Chemicals produces a range of chemical products for industries on getting bulk orders. It uses a job-costing system to calculate the cost of a particular job. Materials and labors used in the manufacturing process are direct in nature, but manufacturing overhead is allocated to different jobs using direct manufacturing labor costs. Carolin provides the following information:

	Budget for 2017	Actual Results for 2017
Direct material costs	$2,750,000	$3,000,000
Direct manufacturing labor costs	1,830,000	2,250,000
Manufacturing overhead costs	3,294,000	3,780,000

Required

1. Compute the actual and budgeted manufacturing overhead rates for 2017.
2. During March, the job-cost records for Job 635 contained the following information:

Direct materials used	$73,500
Direct manufacturing labor costs	$51,000

Compute the cost of Job 635 using (a) actual costing and (b) normal costing.

3. At the end of 2017, compute the under- or overallocated manufacturing overhead under normal costing. Why is there no under- or overallocated overhead under actual costing?
4. Why might managers at Carolin Chemicals prefer to use normal costing?

4-23 Job costing, normal and actual costing. Caldwell Toys produces toys mainly for the domestic market. The company uses a job-costing system under which materials and labors used in the manufacturing process are directly allocated to different jobs. Whereas costs incurred in the manufacturing support department are indirect in nature and allocated to different jobs on the basis of direct labor-hours. Caldwell budgets 2017 manufacturing-support costs to be $5,100,000 and 2017 direct labor-hours to be 150,000.

At the end of 2017, Caldwell collects the cost-related data of different jobs that were started and completed in 2017 for comparison. They are as follows:

	Steel Wheels	Magic Wheels
Production period	Jan–May 2017	May–Sept 2017
Direct material costs	$78,290	$94,650
Direct labor costs	$25,445	$32,752
Direct labor-hours	840	960

Direct materials and direct labor are paid for on a contractual basis. The costs of each are known when direct materials are used or when direct labor-hours are worked. The 2017 actual manufacturing-support costs were $5,355,000 and the actual direct labor-hours were 153,000.

Required

1. Compute the (a) budgeted indirect-cost rate and (b) actual indirect-cost rate. Why do they differ?
2. What are the job costs of the Steel Wheels and the Magic Wheels using (a) normal costing and (b) actual costing?
3. Why might Caldwell Toys prefer normal costing over actual costing?

4-24 Budgeted manufacturing overhead rate, allocated manufacturing overhead. Gammaro Company uses normal costing. It allocates manufacturing overhead costs using a budgeted rate per machine-hour. The following data are available for 2017:

Budgeted manufacturing overhead costs	$4,600,000
Budgeted machine-hours	184,000
Actual manufacturing overhead costs	$4,830,000
Actual machine-hours	180,000

Required

1. Calculate the budgeted manufacturing overhead rate.
2. Calculate the manufacturing overhead allocated during 2017.
3. Calculate the amount of under- or overallocated manufacturing overhead. Why do Gammaro's managers need to calculate this amount?

4-25 Job costing, accounting for manufacturing overhead, budgeted rates. The Lynn Company uses a normal job-costing system at its Minneapolis plant. The plant has a machining department and an assembly department. Its job-costing system has two direct-cost categories (direct materials and direct manufacturing labor) and two manufacturing overhead cost pools (the machining department overhead, allocated to jobs based on actual machine-hours, and the assembly department overhead, allocated to jobs based on actual direct manufacturing labor costs). The 2014 budget for the plant is as follows:

	Machining Department	Assembly Department
Manufacturing overhead	$1,800,000	$3,600,000
Direct manufacturing labor costs	$1,400,000	$2,000,000
Direct manufacturing labor-hours	100,000	200,000
Machine-hours	50,000	200,000

Required

1. Present an overview diagram of Lynn's job-costing system. Compute the budgeted manufacturing overhead rate for each department.
2. During February, the job-cost record for Job 494 contained the following:

	Machining Department	Assembly Department
Direct materials used	$45,000	$70,000
Direct manufacturing labor costs	$14,000	$15,000
Direct manufacturing labor-hours	1,000	1,500
Machine-hours	2,000	1,000

Compute the total manufacturing overhead costs allocated to Job 494.
3. At the end of 2014, the actual manufacturing overhead costs were $2,100,000 in machining and $3,700,000 in assembly. Assume that 55,000 actual machine-hours were used in machining and that actual direct manufacturing labor costs in assembly were $2,200,000. Compute the over- or underallocated manufacturing overhead for each department.

4-26 Job costing, consulting firm. Global Enterprize, a management consulting firm, has the following condensed budget for 2017:

Revenues		$42,000,000
Total costs:		
Direct costs		
Professional Labor	$15,000,000	
Indirect costs		
Client support	22,170,000	37,170,000
Operating income		$ 4,830,000

Global Enterprize has a single direct-cost category (professional labor) and a single indirect-cost pool (client support). Indirect costs are allocated to jobs on the basis of professional labor costs.

Required

1. Prepare an overview diagram of the job-costing system. Calculate the 2017 budgeted indirect-cost rate for Global Enterprize.
2. The markup rate for pricing jobs is intended to produce operating income equal to 11.50% of revenues. Calculate the markup rate as a percentage of professional labor costs.
3. Global Enterprize is bidding on a consulting job for Horizon Telecommunications, a wireless communications company. The budgeted breakdown of professional labor on the job is as follows:

Professional Labor Category	Budgeted Rate per Hour	Budgeted Hours
Director	$175	8
Partner	80	20
Associate	40	75
Assistant	25	180

Calculate the budgeted cost of the Horizon Telecommunications job. How much will Global Enterprize bid for the job if it is to earn its target operating income of 11.50% of revenues?

4-27 Time period used to compute indirect cost rates. Plunge Manufacturing produces outdoor wading and slide pools. The company uses a normal-costing system and allocates manufacturing overhead on the basis of direct manufacturing labor-hours. Most of the company's production and sales occur in the first and second quarters of the year. The company is in danger of losing one of its larger customers, Socha Wholesale, due to large fluctuations in price. The owner of Plunge has requested an analysis of the manufacturing cost per unit in the second and third quarters. You have been provided the following budgeted information for the coming year:

	Quarter			
	1	2	3	4
Pools manufactured and sold	565	490	245	100

It takes 1 direct manufacturing labor-hour to make each pool. The actual direct material cost is $14.00 per pool. The actual direct manufacturing labor rate is $20 per hour. The budgeted variable manufacturing overhead rate is $15 per direct manufacturing labor-hour. Budgeted fixed manufacturing overhead costs are $12,250 each quarter.

Required

1. Calculate the total manufacturing cost per unit for the second and third quarter assuming the company allocates manufacturing overhead costs based on the budgeted manufacturing overhead rate determined for each quarter.
2. Calculate the total manufacturing cost per unit for the second and third quarter assuming the company allocates manufacturing overhead costs based on an annual budgeted manufacturing overhead rate.
3. Plunge Manufacturing prices its pools at manufacturing cost plus 30%. Why might Socha Wholesale be seeing large fluctuations in the prices of pools? Which of the methods described in requirements 1 and 2 would you recommend Plunge use? Explain.

4-28 Accounting for manufacturing overhead. Holland Woodworking uses normal costing and allocates manufacturing overhead to jobs based on a budgeted labor-hour rate and actual direct labor-hours. Under- or overallocated overhead, if immaterial, is written off to cost of goods sold. During 2014, Holland recorded the following:

Budgeted manufacturing overhead costs	$4,400,000
Budgeted direct labor-hours	200,000
Actual manufacturing overhead costs	$4,650,000
Actual direct labor-hours	212,000

Required

1. Compute the budgeted manufacturing overhead rate.
2. Prepare the summary journal entry to record the allocation of manufacturing overhead.
3. Compute the amount of under- or overallocated manufacturing overhead. Is the amount significant enough to warrant proration of overhead costs, or would it be permissible to write it off to cost of goods sold? Prepare the journal entry to dispose of the under- or overallocated overhead.

4-29 Job costing, journal entries. The University of Chicago Press is wholly owned by the university. It performs the bulk of its work for other university departments, which pay as though the press were an outside business enterprise. The press also publishes and maintains a stock of books for general sale. The press uses normal costing to cost each job. Its job-costing system has two direct-cost categories (direct materials and direct manufacturing labor) and one indirect-cost pool (manufacturing overhead, allocated on the basis of direct manufacturing labor costs).

The following data (in thousands) pertain to 2017:

Direct materials and supplies purchased on credit	$ 800
Direct materials used	710
Indirect materials issued to various production departments	100
Direct manufacturing labor	1,300
Indirect manufacturing labor incurred by various production departments	900
Depreciation on building and manufacturing equipment	400
Miscellaneous manufacturing overhead* incurred by various production departments (ordinarily would be detailed as repairs, photocopying, utilities, etc.)	550
Manufacturing overhead allocated at 160% of direct manufacturing labor costs	?
Cost of goods manufactured	4,120
Revenues	8,000
Cost of goods sold (before adjustment for under- or overallocated manufacturing overhead)	4,020
Inventories, December 31, 2016 (not 2017):	
Materials Control	100
Work-in-Process Control	60
Finished Goods Control	500

Required

1. Prepare an overview diagram of the job-costing system at the University of Chicago Press.
2. Prepare journal entries to summarize the 2017 transactions. As your final entry, dispose of the year-end under- or overallocated manufacturing overhead as a write-off to Cost of Goods Sold. Number your entries. Explanations for each entry may be omitted.
3. Show posted T-accounts for all inventories, Cost of Goods Sold, Manufacturing Overhead Control, and Manufacturing Overhead Allocated.
4. How did the University of Chicago Press perform in 2017?

4-30 Journal entries, T-accounts, and source documents. Visual Company produces gadgets for the coveted small appliance market. The following data reflect activity for the year 2017:

Costs incurred:	
Purchases of direct materials (net) on credit	$121,000
Direct manufacturing labor cost	87,000
Indirect labor	54,400
Depreciation, factory equipment	53,000
Depreciation, office equipment	7,700
Maintenance, factory equipment	46,000
Miscellaneous factory overhead	9,100
Rent, factory building	99,000
Advertising expense	97,000
Sales commissions	39,000

Inventories:

	January 1, 2017	December 31, 2017
Direct materials	$ 9,400	$18,000
Work in process	6,500	26,000
Finished goods	60,000	31,000

Visual Co. uses a normal-costing system and allocates overhead to work in process at a rate of $3.10 per direct manufacturing labor dollar. Indirect materials are insignificant so there is no inventory account for indirect materials.

Required

1. Prepare journal entries to record the transactions for 2017 including an entry to close out over- or underallocated overhead to cost of goods sold. For each journal entry indicate the source document that

---
* The term *manufacturing overhead* is not used uniformly. Other terms that are often encountered in printing companies include *job overhead* and *shop overhead*.

would be used to authorize each entry. Also note which subsidiary ledger, if any, should be referenced as backup for the entry.
2. Post the journal entries to T-accounts for all of the inventories, Cost of Goods Sold, the Manufacturing Overhead Control Account, and the Manufacturing Overhead Allocated Account.

4-31 Job costing, journal entries. Donald Transport assembles prestige manufactured homes. Its job-costing system has two direct-cost categories (direct materials and direct manufacturing labor) and one indirect-cost pool (manufacturing overhead allocated at a budgeted $31 per machine-hour in 2017). The following data (in millions) show operation costs for 2017:

Materials Control, beginning balance, January 1, 2017	$ 18
Work-in-Process Control, beginning balance, January 1, 2017	9
Finished Goods Control, beginning balance, January 1, 2017	10
Materials and supplies purchased on credit	154
Direct materials used	152
Indirect materials (supplies) issued to various production departments	19
Direct manufacturing labor	96
Indirect manufacturing labor incurred by various production departments	34
Depreciation on plant and manufacturing equipment	28
Miscellaneous manufacturing overhead incurred (ordinarily would be detailed as repairs, utilities, etc., with a corresponding credit to various liability accounts)	13
Manufacturing overhead allocated, 3,000,000 actual machine-hours	?
Cost of goods manufactured	298
Revenues	410
Cost of goods sold	294

Required

1. Prepare an overview diagram of Donald Transport's job-costing system.
2. Prepare journal entries. Number your entries. Explanations for each entry may be omitted. Post to T-accounts. What is the ending balance of Work-in-Process Control?
3. Show the journal entry for disposing of under- or overallocated manufacturing overhead directly as a year-end writeoff to Cost of Goods Sold. Post the entry to T-accounts.
4. How did Donald Transport perform in 2017?

4-32 Job costing, unit cost, ending work in process. Rafael Company produces pipes for concert-quality organs. Each job is unique. In April 2013, it completed all outstanding orders, and then, in May 2013, it worked on only two jobs, M1 and M2:

	A	B	C
1	Rafael Company, May 2013	Job M1	Job M2
2	Direct materials	$ 78,000	$ 51,000
3	Direct manufacturing labor	273,000	208,000

Direct manufacturing labor is paid at the rate of $26 per hour. Manufacturing overhead costs are allocated at a budgeted rate of $20 per direct manufacturing labor-hour. Only Job M1 was completed in May.

Required

1. Calculate the total cost for Job M1.
2. 1,100 pipes were produced for Job M1. Calculate the cost per pipe.
3. Prepare the journal entry transferring Job M1 to finished goods.
4. What is the ending balance in the work-in-process control account?

4-33 Job costing; actual, normal, and variation from normal costing. Cheney & Partners, a Quebecbased public accounting partnership, specializes in audit services. Its job-costing system has a single direct-cost category (professional labor) and a single indirect-cost pool (audit support, which contains all costs of the Audit Support Department). Audit support costs are allocated to individual jobs using actual professional labor-hours. Cheney & Partners employs 10 professionals to perform audit services

Budgeted and actual amounts for 2017 are as follows:

	A	B	C
1	**Cheney & Partners**		
2	**Budget for 2017**		
3	Professional labor compensation	$960,000	
4	Audit support department costs	720,000	
5	Professional labor-hours billed to clients	16,000	hours
6			
7	**Actual results for 2017**		
8	Audit support department costs	$744,000	
9	Professional labor-hours billed to clients	15,500	hours
10	Actual professional labor cost rate	$ 53	per hour

Required

1. Compute the direct-cost rate and the indirect-cost rate per professional labor-hour for 2017 under (a) actual costing, (b) normal costing, and (c) the variation from normal costing that uses budgeted rates for direct costs.
2. Which job-costing system would you recommend Cheney & Partners use? Explain.
3. Cheney's 2017 audit of Pierre & Co. was budgeted to take 170 hours of professional labor time. The actual professional labor time spent on the audit was 185 hours. Compute the cost of the Pierre & Co. audit using (a) actual costing, (b) normal costing, and (c) the variation from normal costing that uses budgeted rates for direct costs. Explain any differences in the job cost.

4-34 Job costing; variation on actual, normal, and variation from normal costing. Creative Solutions designs Web pages for clients in the education sector. The company's job-costing system has a single direct cost category (Web-designing labor) and a single indirect cost pool composed of all overhead costs. Overhead costs are allocated to individual jobs based on direct labor-hours. The company employs six Web designers. Budgeted and actual information regarding Creative Solutions follows:

Budget for 2017:
Direct labor costs $273,000
Direct labor-hours   10,500
Overhead costs $157,500

Actual results for 2017:
Direct labor costs $285,000
Direct labor-hours   11,400
Overhead costs $159,600

Required

1. Compute the direct-cost rate and the indirect-cost rate per Web-designing labor-hour for 2017 under (a) actual costing, (b) normal costing, and (c) the variation from normal costing that uses budgeted rates for direct costs.
2. Which method would you suggest Creative Solutions use? Explain.
3. Creative Solutions' Web design for Greenville Day School was budgeted to take 86 direct labor-hours. The actual time spent on the project was 79 hours. Compute the cost of the Greenville Day School job using (a) actual costing, (b) normal costing, and (c) the variation from normal costing that uses budgeted rates for direct costs.

4-35 Proration of overhead. The Ride-On-Wave Company (ROW) produces a line of non-motorized boats. ROW uses a normal-costing system and allocates manufacturing overhead using direct manufacturing labor cost. The following data are for 2017:

Budgeted manufacturing overhead cost $125,000
Budgeted direct manufacturing labor cost $250,000
Actual manufacturing overhead cost $117,000
Actual direct manufacturing labor cost $228,000

Inventory balances on December 31, 2017, were as follows:

Account	Ending balance	2017 direct manufacturing labor cost in ending balance
Work in process	$ 50,700	$ 20,520
Finished goods	245,050	59,280
Cost of goods sold	549,250	148,200

Required

1. Calculate the manufacturing overhead allocation rate.
2. Compute the amount of under- or overallocated manufacturing overhead.
3. Calculate the ending balances in work in process, finished goods, and cost of goods sold if under- or overallocated manufacturing overhead is as follows:
   a. Written off to cost of goods sold
   b. Prorated based on ending balances (before proration) in each of the three accounts
   c. Prorated based on the overhead allocated in 2017 in the ending balances (before proration) in each of the three accounts
4. Which method would you choose? Justify your answer.

Problems

4-36 Job costing, accounting for manufacturing overhead, budgeted rates. The Pisano Company uses a job-costing system at its Dover, Delaware, plant. The plant has a machining department and a finishing department. Pisano uses normal costing with two direct-cost categories (direct materials and direct manufacturing labor) and two manufacturing overhead cost pools (the machining department with machine-hours as the allocation base and the finishing department with direct manufacturing labor costs as the allocation base). The 2014 budget for the plant is as follows:

	Machining Department	Finishing Department
Manufacturing overhead costs	$9,065,000	$8,181,000
Direct manufacturing labor costs	$ 970,000	$4,050,000
Direct manufacturing labor-hours	36,000	155,000
Machine-hours	185,000	37,000

Required

1. Prepare an overview diagram of Pisano's job-costing system.
2. What is the budgeted manufacturing overhead rate in the machining department? In the finishing department?
3. During the month of January, the job-cost record for Job 431 shows the following:

	Machining Department	Finishing Department
Direct materials used	$13,000	$5,000
Direct manufacturing labor costs	$ 900	$1,250
Direct manufacturing labor-hours	20	70
Machine-hours	140	20

Compute the total manufacturing overhead cost allocated to Job 431.
4. Assuming that Job 431 consisted of 300 units of product, what is the cost per unit?
5. Amounts at the end of 2014 are as follows:

	Machining Department	Finishing Department
Manufacturing overhead incurred	$10,000,000	$7,982,000
Direct manufacturing labor costs	$ 1,030,000	$4,100,000
Machine-hours	200,000	34,000

Compute the under- or overallocated manufacturing overhead for each department and for the Dover plant as a whole.
6. Why might Pisano use two different manufacturing overhead cost pools in its job-costing system?

4-37 Service industry, job costing, law firm. Kidman & Associates is a law firm specializing in labor relations and employee-related work. It employs 30 professionals (5 partners and 25 associates) who work directly with its clients. The average budgeted total compensation per professional for 2017 is $97,500. Each professional is budgeted to have 1,500 billable hours to clients in 2017. All professionals work for clients to their maximum 1,500 billable hours available. All professional labor costs are included in a single direct-cost category and are traced to jobs on a per-hour basis. All costs of Kidman & Associates other than professional labor costs are included in a single indirect-cost pool (legal support) and are allocated to jobs using professional labor-hours as the allocation base. The budgeted level of indirect costs in 2017 is $2,475,000.

Required

1. Prepare an overview diagram of Kidman's job-costing system.
2. Compute the 2017 budgeted direct-cost rate per hour of professional labor.
3. Compute the 2017 budgeted indirect-cost rate per hour of professional labor.
4. Kidman & Associates is considering bidding on two jobs:
   a. Litigation work for Richardson, Inc., which requires 120 budgeted hours of professional labor
   b. Labor contract work for Punch, Inc., which requires 160 budgeted hours of professional labor.
   Prepare a cost estimate for each job.

4-38 Service industry, job costing, two direct- and two indirect-cost categories, law firm (continuation of 4-37). Kidman has just completed a review of its job-costing system. This review included a detailed analysis of how past jobs used the firm's resources and interviews with personnel about what factors drive the level of indirect costs. Management concluded that a system with two direct-cost categories (professional partner labor and professional associate labor) and two indirect-cost categories (general support and secretarial support) would yield more accurate job costs. Budgeted information for 2017 related to the two direct-cost categories is as follows:

	Professional Partner Labor	Professional Associate Labor
Number of professionals	5	25
Hours of billable time per professional	1,500 per year	1,500 per year
Total compensation (average per professional)	$210,000	$75,000

Budgeted information for 2017 relating to the two indirect-cost categories is as follows:

	General Support	Secretarial Support
Total costs	$2,025,000	$450,000
Cost-allocation base	Professional labor-hours	Partner labor-hours

Required

1. Compute the 2017 budgeted direct-cost rates for (a) professional partners and (b) professional associates.
2. Compute the 2017 budgeted indirect-cost rates for (a) general support and (b) secretarial support.
3. Compute the budgeted costs for the Richardson and Punch jobs, given the following information:

	Richardson, Inc.	Punch, Inc.
Professional partners	48 hours	32 hours
Professional associates	72 hours	128 hours

4. Comment on the results in requirement 3. Why are the job costs different from those computed in Problem 4-37?
5. Would you recommend Kidman & Associates use the job-costing system in Problem 4-37 or the job-costing system in this problem? Explain.

4-39 Proration of overhead. (Z. Iqbal, adapted) The Zaf Radiator Company uses a normal-costing system with a single manufacturing overhead cost pool and machine-hours as the cost-allocation base. The following data are for 2017:

Budgeted manufacturing overhead costs	$4,800,000
Overhead allocation base	Machine-hours
Budgeted machine-hours	80,000
Manufacturing overhead costs incurred	$4,900,000
Actual machine-hours	75,000

Machine-hours data and the ending balances (before proration of under- or overallocated overhead) are as follows:

	Actual Machine-Hours	2017 End-of-Year Balance
Cost of Goods Sold	60,000	$8,000,000
Finished Goods Control	11,000	1,250,000
Work-in-Process Control	4,000	750,000

Required

1. Compute the budgeted manufacturing overhead rate for 2017.
2. Compute the under- or overallocated manufacturing overhead of Zaf Radiator in 2017. Dispose of this amount using the following:
   a. Write-off to Cost of Goods Sold
   b. Proration based on ending balances (before proration) in Work-in-Process Control, Finished Goods Control, and Cost of Goods Sold
   c. Proration based on the overhead allocated in 2017 (before proration) in the ending balances of Work-in-Process Control, Finished Goods Control, and Cost of Goods Sold
3. Which method do you prefer in requirement 2? Explain.

4-40 Normal costing, overhead allocation, working backward. Gardi Manufacturing uses normal costing for its job-costing system, which has two direct-cost categories (direct materials and direct manufacturing labor) and one indirect-cost category (manufacturing overhead). The following information is obtained for 2017:

- Total manufacturing costs, $8,300,000
- Manufacturing overhead allocated, $4,100,000 (allocated at a rate of 250% of direct manufacturing labor costs)
- Work-in-process inventory on January 1, 2017, $420,000
- Cost of finished goods manufactured, $8,100,000

Required

1. Use information in the first two bullet points to calculate (a) direct manufacturing labor costs in 2017 and (b) cost of direct materials used in 2017.
2. Calculate the ending work-in-process inventory on December 31, 2017.

4-41 Proration of overhead with two indirect cost pools. Premier Golf Carts makes custom golf carts that it sells to dealers across the Southeast. The carts are produced in two departments, fabrication (a mostly automated department) and custom finishing (a mostly manual department). The company uses a normal-costing system in which overhead in the fabrication department is allocated to jobs on the basis of machine-hours and overhead in the finishing department is allocated to jobs based on direct labor-hours. During May, Premier Golf Carts reported actual overhead of $49,500 in the fabrication department and $22,200 in the finishing department. Additional information follows:

Manufacturing overhead rate (fabrication department)	$20 per machine-hour
Manufacturing overhead rate (finishing department)	$16 per direct labor-hour
Machine-hours (fabrication department) for May	2,000 machine-hours
Direct labor-hours (finishing department) for May	1,200 labor-hours
Work in process inventory, May 31	$50,000
Finished goods inventory, May 31	$150,000
Cost of goods sold, May 31	$300,000

Premier Golf Carts prorates under- and overallocated overhead monthly to work in process, finished goods, and cost of goods sold based on the ending balance in each account.

Required

1. Calculate the amount of overhead allocated in the fabrication department and the finishing department in May.
2. Calculate the amount of under- or overallocated overhead in each department and in total.
3. How much of the under- or overallocated overhead will be prorated to (a) work in process inventory, (b) finished goods inventory, and (c) cost of goods sold based on the ending balance (before proration) in each of the three accounts? What will be the balance in work in process, finished goods, and cost of goods sold after proration?
4. What would be the effect of writing off under- and overallocated overhead to cost of goods sold? Would it be reasonable for Premier Golf Carts to change to this simpler method?

4-42 General ledger relationships, under- and overallocation. (S. Sridhar, adapted) Keezel Company uses normal costing in its job-costing system. Partially completed T-accounts and additional information for Keezel for 2017 are as follows:

Direct Materials Control		Work-in-Process Control		Finished Goods Control	
1-1-2017 42,000	148,000	1-1-2017 82,000		1-1-2017 105,000	700,000
135,000		Dir. manuf. labor 285,000		705,000	

Manufacturing Overhead Control	Manufacturing Overhead Allocated	Cost of Goods Sold
425,000		

Additional information follows:

a. Direct manufacturing labor wage rate was $15 per hour.
b. Manufacturing overhead was allocated at $20 per direct manufacturing labor-hour.
c. During the year, sales revenues were $1,550,000, and marketing and distribution costs were $810,000.

Required

1. What was the amount of direct materials issued to production during 2017?
2. What was the amount of manufacturing overhead allocated to jobs during 2017?
3. What was the total cost of jobs completed during 2017?
4. What was the balance of work-in-process inventory on December 31, 2017?
5. What was the cost of goods sold before proration of under- or overallocated overhead?
6. What was the under- or overallocated manufacturing overhead in 2017?
7. Dispose of the under- or overallocated manufacturing overhead using the following:
    a. Write-off to Cost of Goods Sold
    b. Proration based on ending balances (before proration) in Work-in-Process Control, Finished Goods Control, and Cost of Goods Sold
8. Using each of the approaches in requirement 7, calculate Keezel's operating income for 2017.
9. Which approach in requirement 7 do you recommend Keezel use? Explain your answer briefly.

4-43 Overview of general ledger relationships. Brandon Company uses normal costing in its job-costing system. The company produces custom bikes for toddlers. The beginning balances (December 1) and ending balances (as of December 30) in their inventory accounts are as follows:

	Beginning Balance 12/1	Ending Balance 12/31
Materials control	$2,100	$ 8,500
Work-in-process control	6,700	9,000
Manufacturing department overhead control	——	94,000
Finished goods control	4,400	19,400

Additional information follows:

a. Direct materials purchased during December were $66,300.
b. Cost of goods manufactured for December was $234,000.
c. No direct materials were returned to suppliers.
d. No units were started or completed on December 31 and no direct materials were requisitioned on December 31.
e. The manufacturing labor costs for the December 31 working day: direct manufacturing labor, $4,300, and indirect manufacturing labor, $1,400.
f. Manufacturing overhead has been allocated at 110% of direct manufacturing labor costs through December 31.

Required

1. Prepare journal entries for the December 31 payroll.
2. Use T-accounts to compute the following:
    a. The total amount of materials requisitioned into work in process during December
    b. The total amount of direct manufacturing labor recorded in work in process during December (Hint: You have to solve requirements 2b and 2c simultaneously)
    c. The total amount of manufacturing overhead recorded in work in process during December
    d. Ending balance in work in process, December 31
    e. Cost of goods sold for December before adjustments for under- or overallocated manufacturing overhead
3. Prepare closing journal entries related to manufacturing overhead. Assume that all under- or overallocated manufacturing overhead is closed directly to cost of goods sold.

4-44 Allocation and proration of overhead. InStep Company prints custom training material for corporations. The business was started January 1, 2017. The company uses a normal-costing system. It has two direct cost pools, materials and labor, and one indirect cost pool, overhead. Overhead is charged to printing jobs on the basis of direct labor cost. The following information is available for 2017.

Budgeted direct labor costs	$225,000
Budgeted overhead costs	$315,000
Costs of actual material used	$148,500
Actual direct labor costs	$213,500
Actual overhead costs	$302,100

There were two jobs in process on December 31, 2017: Job 11 and Job 12. Costs added to each job as of December 31 are as follows:

	Direct materials	Direct labor
Job 11	$4,870	$5,100
Job 12	$5,910	$6,800

InStep Company has no finished goods inventories because all printing jobs are transferred to cost of goods sold when completed.

Required

1. Compute the overhead allocation rate.
2. Calculate the balance in ending work in process and cost of goods sold before any adjustments for under- or overallocated overhead.
3. Calculate under- or overallocated overhead.
4. Calculate the ending balances in work in process and cost of goods sold if the under- or overallocated overhead amount is as follows:
   a. Written off to cost of goods sold
   b. Prorated using the overhead allocated in 2017 (before proration) in the ending balances of cost of goods sold and work-in-process control accounts
5. Which of the methods in requirement 4 would you choose? Explain.

4-45 (25–30 min.) **Job costing, ethics.** Joseph Underwood joined Anderson Enterprises as controller in October 2016. Anderson Enterprises manufactures and installs home greenhouses. The company uses a normal-costing system with two direct-cost pools, direct materials and direct manufacturing labor, and one indirect-cost pool, manufacturing overhead. In 2016, manufacturing overhead was allocated to jobs at 150% of direct manufacturing labor cost. At the end of 2016, an immaterial amount of underallocated overhead was closed out to cost of goods sold, and the company showed a small loss.

Underwood is eager to impress his new employer, and he knows that in 2017, Anderson's upper management is under pressure to show a profit in a challenging competitive environment because they are hoping to be acquired by a large private equity firm sometime in 2018. At the end of 2016, Underwood decides to adjust the manufacturing overhead rate to 160% of direct labor cost. He explains to the company president that, because overhead was underallocated in 2016, this adjustment is necessary. Cost information for 2017 follows:

Direct materials control, 1/1/2017	25,000
Direct materials purchased, 2017	650,000
Direct materials added to production, 2017	630,000
Work in process control, 1/1/2017	280,000
Direct manufacturing labor, 2017	880,000
Cost of goods manufactured, 2017	2,900,000
Finished goods control, 1/1/2017	320,000
Finished goods control, 12/31/2017	290,000
Manufacturing overhead costs, 2017	1,300,000

Anderson's revenue for 2017 was $5,550,000, and the company's selling and administrative expenses were $2,720,000.

Required

1. Insert the given information in the T-accounts below. Calculate the following amounts to complete the T-accounts:
   a. Direct materials control, 12/31/2017
   b. Manufacturing overhead allocated, 2017
   c. Cost of goods sold, 2017

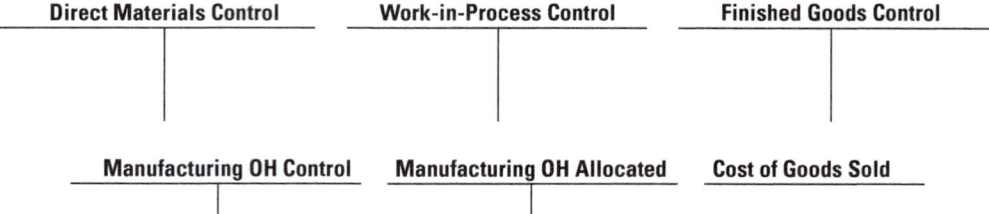

2. Calculate the amount of under- or overallocated manufacturing overhead.

3. Calculate Anderson's net operating income under the following:
   a. Under- or overallocated manufacturing overhead is written off to cost of goods sold.
   b. Under- or overallocated manufacturing overhead is prorated based on the ending balances in work in process, finished goods, and cost of goods sold.
4. Underwood chooses option 3a above, stating that the amount is immaterial. Comment on the ethical implications of his choice. Do you think that there were any ethical issues when he established the manufacturing overhead rate for 2017 back in late 2016? Refer to the IMA Statement of Ethical Professional Practice.

4-46 Job costing—service industry. Market Pulse performs market research for consumer product companies across the country. The company conducts telephone surveys and gathers consumers together in focus groups to review foods, cleaning products, and toiletries. Market Pulse uses a normal-costing system with one direct-cost pool, labor, and one indirect-cost pool, general overhead. General overhead is allocated to each job based on 150% of direct labor cost. Actual overhead equaled allocated overhead as of April 30, 2017. Actual overhead in May was $122,000. All costs incurred during the planning stage for a market research job and during the job are gathered in a balance sheet account called "Jobs in Progress (JIP)." When a job is completed, the costs are transferred to an income statement account called "Cost of Completed Jobs (CCJ)." Following is cost information for May 2017:

Band	From Beginning JIP		Incurred in May
	Labor	General Overhead Allocated	Labor
Cococrunch Candy Bars	$18,000	$27,000	$16,000
Brite Toothpaste	4,000	6,000	34,000
Verde Organic Salsa	—	—	22,400
Sparkle Dish Liquid	—	—	5,600

As of May 1, there were two jobs in progress: *Cococrunch Candy Bars*, and *Brite Toothpaste*. The jobs for *Verde Organic Salsa* and *Sparkle Dish Liquid* were started during May. The jobs for *Cococrunch Candy Bars* and *Sparkle Dish Liquid* were completed during May.

Required

1. Calculate JIP at the end of May.
2. Calculate CCJ for May.
3. Calculate under- or overallocated overhead at the end of May.
4. Calculate the ending balances in JIP and CCJ if the under- or overallocated overhead amount is as follows:
   a. Written off to CCJ
   b. Prorated based on the ending balances (before proration) in JIP and CCJ
   c. Prorated based on the overhead allocated in May in the ending balances of JIP and CCJ (before proration)
5. Which method would you choose? Explain. Would your choice depend on whether overhead cost is underallocated or overallocated? Explain.

5 Activity-Based Costing and Activity-Based Management

LEARNING OBJECTIVES

1. Explain how broad averaging undercosts and overcosts products or services

2. Present three guidelines for refining a costing system

3. Distinguish between simple and activity-based costing systems

4. Describe a four-part cost hierarchy

5. Cost products or services using activity-based costing

6. Evaluate the benefits and costs of implementing activity-based costing systems

7. Explain how managers use activity-based costing systems in activity-based management

8. Compare activity-based costing systems and department costing systems

A good mystery never fails to capture the imagination.

Business and organizations are like a good mystery. Their costing systems are often filled with unresolved questions: Why are we bleeding red ink? Are we pricing our products accurately? Activity-based costing can help unravel the mystery and result in improved operations. General Motors uses activity-based costing to evaluate the cost of its suppliers' products.

GENERAL MOTORS AND ACTIVITY-BASED COSTING[1]

In 2015, General Motors (GM) launched an automotive parts-buying program that forgoes conventional supplier bidding. Under the new program, any automotive parts supplier that wants GM's business agrees to let a team of GM engineers and purchasing managers evaluate the supplier's factories and cost data using activity-based costing. This evaluation assesses material costs, labor, scrap, production cycle times, and other factors that, in turn, help GM attach activity costs to each of the tens of thousands of parts needed to build its lineup of cars, trucks, and SUVs.

This new program allows GM, which spent approximately $85 billion in 2005 on parts and supplies, to develop more realistic cost estimates for its vehicles. Each year, GM can update its activity-based costing analyses to see whether suppliers can cut costs by more efficient production. Suppliers in the program benefit by receiving long-term contracts from GM, who agrees not to seek competing bids from other vendors.

In this chapter, we show how ABC systems help managers make cost-management decisions by improving product designs, processes, and efficiency.

Drive Images/Alamy Stock Photo

---

[1] *Sources:* David Sedgwick, "GM to Suppliers: Let's See Books, Not Bids," *Automotive News*, May 11, 2015 (http://www.autonews.com/article/20150511/OEM10/305119952/gm-to-suppliers:-lets-see-books-not-bids); General Motors Company, 2015 Annual Report.

Broad Averaging and Its Consequences

Historically, companies (such as television and automobile manufacturers) produced a limited variety of products. These companies used few overhead resources to support these simple operations, so indirect (or overhead) costs were a relatively small percentage of total costs. Managers used simple costing systems to allocate overhead costs broadly in an easy, inexpensive, and reasonably accurate way. But as product diversity and indirect costs increased, broad averaging led to inaccurate product costs. That's because simple *peanut-butter costing* (yes, that's what it's called) broadly averages or spreads the cost of resources uniformly to cost objects (such as products or services) when, in fact, the individual products or services use those resources in nonuniform ways.

> **LEARNING OBJECTIVE 1**
>
> Explain how broad averaging undercosts and overcosts products or services
>
> ... it does not measure the different resources consumed by different products and services

Undercosting and Overcosting

The following example illustrates how averaging can result in inaccurate and misleading cost data. Consider the cost of a restaurant bill for four colleagues who meet monthly to discuss business developments. Each diner orders separate entrees, desserts, and drinks. The restaurant bill for the most recent meeting is as follows.

	Emma	James	Jessica	Matthew	Total	Average
Entree	$11	$20	$15	$14	$ 60	$15
Dessert	0	8	4	4	16	4
Drinks	4	14	8	6	32	8
Total	$15	$42	$27	$24	$108	$27

If the $108 total restaurant bill is divided evenly, $27 is the average cost per diner. This cost-averaging approach treats each diner the same. When costs are averaged across all four diners, both Emma and Matthew are overcosted (the cost allocated to them is higher than their individual cost), James is undercosted (the cost allocated to him is lower than his individual cost), and Jessica is (by coincidence) accurately costed. Emma, especially, may object to paying the average bill of $27 because her individual bill is only $15.

Broad averaging often leads to undercosting or overcosting of products or services:

- **Product undercosting**—a product is reported to have a low cost per unit but consumes a higher level of resources per unit (James's dinner).
- **Product overcosting**—a product is reported to have a high cost per unit but consumes a lower level of resources per unit (Emma's dinner).

What are the strategic consequences of product undercosting and overcosting? Suppose a manager uses cost information about products to guide pricing decisions. Undercosted products will be underpriced and may even lead to sales that actually result in losses because the sales may bring in less revenue than the cost of resources they use. Overcosted products will lead to overpricing, causing those products to lose market share to competitors producing similar products. But what if prices of products, such as refrigerators, are determined by the market based on consumer demand and competition among companies? Consider a company manufacturing refrigerators with different features and complexities (such as different types of internal compartments, cooling systems, and vents). Suppose the complex refrigerator is undercosted and the simple refrigerator is overcosted. In this case, the complex refrigerator will appear to be more profitable than it actually is while the simple refrigerator will appear to be less profitable than it actually is. Managers may strategically promote the complex undercosted refrigerators thinking they are highly profitable, when in fact these refrigerators consume large amounts of resources and are far less profitable than they appear. They may underinvest in the simple overcosted refrigerator, which shows low profits when in fact the profits from this refrigerator may be considerably better. Alternatively, they may focus on trying to reduce the cost of the simple refrigerator to make it more profitable when, in fact, this refrigerator is reasonably profitable and the opportunities to reduce its costs may be quite limited.

Product-Cost Cross-Subsidization

Product-cost cross-subsidization means that if a company undercosts one of its products, it will overcost at least one of its other products. Similarly, if a company overcosts one of its products, it will undercost at least one of its other products. Product-cost cross-subsidization is very common when a cost is uniformly spread—meaning it is broadly averaged—across multiple products without managers recognizing the amount of resources each product consumes.

In the restaurant-bill example, the amount of cost cross-subsidization of each diner can be readily computed *because all cost items can be traced as direct costs to each diner*. If all diners pay $27, Emma is paying $12 more than her actual cost of $15. She is cross-subsidizing James who is paying $15 less than his actual cost of $42. Calculating the amount of cost cross-subsidization takes more work when there are indirect costs to be considered. Why? Because when two or more diners use the resources represented by indirect costs, we need to find a way to allocate costs to each diner. Consider, for example, a $40 bottle of wine whose cost is shared equally. Each diner would pay $10 ($40 ÷ 4). Suppose Matthew drinks two glasses of wine, while Emma, James, and Jessica drink one glass each for a total of five glasses. Allocating the cost of the bottle of wine on the basis of the glasses of wine that each diner drinks would result in Matthew paying $16 ($40 × 2/5) and each of the others paying $8 ($40 × 1/5). In this case, by sharing the cost equally, Emma, James, and Jessica are each paying $2 ($10 − $8) more and are cross-subsidizing Matthew who is paying $6 ($16 − $10) less for his wine for the night.

To see the effects of broad averaging on direct and indirect costs, we next consider Plastim Corporation's costing system.

> **DECISION POINT**
> When does product undercosting or overcosting occur?

Simple Costing System at Plastim Corporation

Plastim Corporation manufactures lenses for the rear taillights of automobiles. A lens, made from black, red, orange, or white plastic, is the part of the taillight visible on the automobile's exterior. Lenses are made by injecting molten plastic into a mold, which gives the lens its desired shape. The mold is cooled to allow the molten plastic to solidify, and the lens is removed.

Plastim sells all its lenses to Giovanni Motors, a major automobile manufacturer. Under the contract, Plastim manufactures two types of lenses for Giovanni: a simple lens called S3 and a complex lens called C5. The complex lens is large and has special features, such as multicolor molding (when more than one color is injected into the mold) and a complex shape that wraps around the corner of the car. Manufacturing C5 lenses is complicated because various parts in the mold must align and fit precisely. The S3 lens is simpler to make because it has a single color and few special features.

Design, Manufacturing, and Distribution Processes

Whether lenses are simple or complex, Plastim follows this sequence of steps to design, produce, and distribute them:

- **Design products and processes.** Each year Giovanni Motors specifies details of the simple and complex lenses it needs for its new models of cars. Plastim's design department designs the new molds and specifies the manufacturing process to make the lenses.
- **Manufacture lenses.** The lenses are molded, finished, cleaned, and inspected.
- **Distribute lenses.** Finished lenses are packed and sent to Giovanni Motors' plants.

Plastim is operating at capacity and incurs very low marketing costs. Because of its high-quality products, Plastim has minimal customer-service costs. Plastim competes with several other companies who also manufacture simple lenses. At a recent meeting, Giovanni's purchasing manager informed Plastim's sales manager that Bandix, which makes only simple lenses, is offering to supply the S3 lens to Giovanni at a price of $53, well below the $63 price that Plastim is currently projecting and budgeting for 2017. Unless Plastim can lower its selling price, it will lose the Giovanni business for the simple lens for the upcoming model year. Fortunately, the same competitive pressures do not exist for the complex lens, which Plastim currently sells to Giovanni at $137 per lens.

Plastim's managers have two primary options:

- Give up the Giovanni business in simple lenses if selling them is unprofitable. Bandix makes only simple lenses and perhaps, therefore, uses simpler technology and processes than Plastim. The simpler operations may give Bandix a cost advantage that Plastim cannot match. If so, it is better for Plastim to not supply the S3 lens to Giovanni.
- Reduce the price of the simple lens and either accept a lower margin or aggressively seek to reduce costs.

To make these long-run strategic decisions, managers first need to understand the costs to design, make, and distribute the S3 and C5 lenses.

Bandix makes only simple lenses and can fairly accurately calculate the cost of a lens by dividing total costs by the number of simple lenses produced. Plastim's costing environment is more challenging because the manufacturing overhead costs support the production of both simple and complex lenses. Plastim's managers and management accountants need to find a way to allocate overhead costs to each type of lens.

In computing costs, Plastim assigns both variable costs and costs that are fixed in the short run to the S3 and C5 lenses. Managers cost products and services to guide long-run strategic decisions, such as what mix of products and services to produce and sell and what prices to charge for them. In the long run, managers have the ability to influence all costs. The firm will only survive in the long run if revenues exceed total costs, regardless of whether these costs are variable or fixed in the short run.

To guide pricing and cost-management decisions, Plastim's managers need to consider all costs and therefore assign both manufacturing and nonmanufacturing costs to the S3 and C5 lenses. If managers had wanted to calculate the cost of inventory, Plastim's management accountants would have assigned only manufacturing costs to the lenses, as required by Generally Accepted Accounting Principles. Surveys of company practice across the globe indicate that the vast majority of companies use costing systems not just for inventory costing but also for strategic purposes, such as pricing and product-mix decisions and decisions about cost reduction, process improvement, design, and planning and budgeting. Managers of these companies assign all costs to products and services. Even merchandising-sector companies (for whom inventory costing is straightforward) and service-sector companies (who have no inventory) expend considerable resources in designing and operating their costing systems to allocate costs for strategic purposes.

Simple Costing System Using a Single Indirect-Cost Pool

Plastim currently has a simple costing system that allocates indirect costs using a single indirect-cost rate, the type of system described in Chapter 4. The only difference between these two chapters is that Chapter 4 focuses on jobs while here the cost objects are products. Exhibit 5-1 shows an overview of Plastim's simple costing system. Use this exhibit as a guide as you study the following steps, each of which is marked in Exhibit 5-1.

Step 1: Identify the Products That Are the Chosen Cost Objects. The cost objects are the 60,000 simple S3 lenses and the 15,000 complex C5 lenses that Plastim will produce in 2017. Plastim's management accountants first calculate the total costs and then the unit cost of designing, manufacturing, and distributing lenses.

Step 2: Identify the Direct Costs of the Products. The direct costs are direct materials and direct manufacturing labor. Exhibit 5-2 shows the direct and indirect costs for the S3 and the C5 lenses using the simple costing system. The direct-cost calculations appear on lines 5, 6, and 7 in Exhibit 5-2. Plastim's simple costing system classifies all costs other than direct materials and direct manufacturing labor as indirect costs.

Step 3: Select the Cost-Allocation Bases to Use for Allocating Indirect (or Overhead) Costs to the Products. A majority of the indirect costs consists of salaries paid to supervisors, engineers, manufacturing support, and maintenance staff that support direct manufacturing labor. Plastim's managers use direct manufacturing labor-hours as the only

EXHIBIT 5-1 Overview of Plastim's Simple Costing System

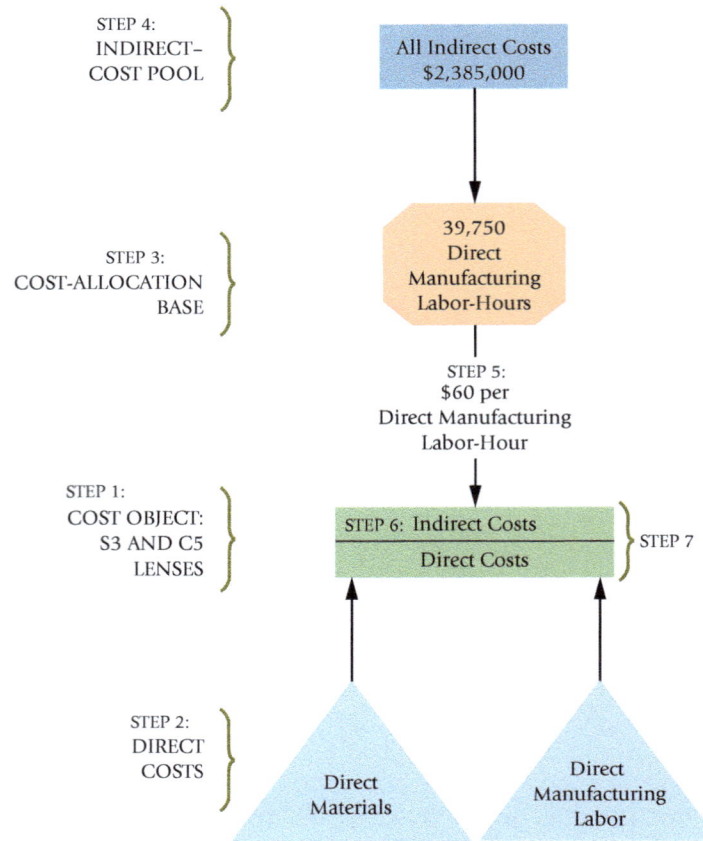

allocation base to allocate all manufacturing and nonmanufacturing indirect costs to S3 and C5. Historically, many companies used such simple costing systems because overhead costs were only a small component of costs and because a single cost driver accurately reflected how overhead resources were used. In 2017, Plastim's managers budget 39,750 direct manufacturing labor-hours.

Step 4: Identify the Indirect Costs Associated with Each Cost-Allocation Base. Because Plastim uses only a single cost-allocation base, Plastim's management accountants group all budgeted indirect costs of $2,385,000 for 2017 into a single overhead cost pool.

EXHIBIT 5-2 Plastim's Product Costs Using the Simple Costing System

	A	B	C	D	E	F	G
1		60,000			15,000		
2		Simple Lenses (S3)			Complex Lenses (C5)		
3		Total	per Unit		Total	per Unit	Total
4		(1)	(2) = (1) ÷ 60,000		(3)	(4) = (3) ÷ 15,000	(5) = (1) + (3)
5	Direct materials	$1,125,000	$18.75		$ 675,000	$45.00	$1,800,000
6	Direct manufacturing labor	600,000	10.00		195,000	13.00	795,000
7	Total direct costs (Step 2)	1,725,000	28.75		870,000	58.00	2,595,000
8	Indirect costs allocated (Step 6)	1,800,000	30.00		585,000	39.00	2,385,000
9	Total costs (Step 7)	$3,525,000	$58.75		$1,455,000	$97.00	$4,980,000
10							

Step 5: Compute the Rate per Unit of Each Cost-Allocation Base.

$$\text{Budgeted indirect-cost rate} = \frac{\text{Budgeted total costs in indirect-cost pool}}{\text{Budgeted total quantity of cost-allocation base}}$$

$$= \frac{\$2,385,000}{39,750 \text{ direct manufacturing labor-hours}}$$

$$= \$60 \text{ per direct manufacturing labor-hour}$$

Step 6: Compute the Indirect Costs Allocated to the Products.
Plastim's managers budget 30,000 total direct manufacturing labor-hours to make the 60,000 S3 lenses and 9,750 total direct manufacturing labor-hours to make the 15,000 C5 lenses. Exhibit 5-2 shows indirect costs of $1,800,000 ($60 per direct manufacturing labor-hour × 30,000 direct manufacturing labor-hours) allocated to the simple lens and $585,000 ($60 per direct manufacturing labor-hour × 9,750 direct manufacturing labor-hours) allocated to the complex lens.

Step 7: Compute the Total Cost of the Products by Adding All Direct and Indirect Costs Assigned to the Products.
Exhibit 5-2 presents the product costs for the simple and complex lenses. The direct costs are calculated in Step 2 and the indirect costs in Step 6. Be sure you see the parallel between the simple costing system overview diagram (Exhibit 5-1) and the costs calculated in Step 7. Exhibit 5-1 shows two direct-cost categories and one indirect-cost category. Therefore, the budgeted cost of each type of lens in Step 7 (Exhibit 5-2) has three line items: two for direct costs and one for allocated indirect costs. It is very helpful to draw overview diagrams to see the big picture of costing systems before getting into the detailed costing of products and services. The budgeted cost per S3 lens is $58.75, well above the $53 selling price quoted by Bandix. The budgeted cost per C5 lens is $97.

5-1 TRY IT!

Amherst Metal Works produces two types of metal lamps. Amherst manufactures 20,000 basic lamps and 5,000 designer lamps. Its simple costing system uses a single indirect-cost pool and allocates costs to the two lamps on the basis of direct manufacturing labor-hours. It provides the following budgeted cost information:

	Basic Lamps	Designer Lamps	Total
Direct materials per lamp	$9	$15	
Direct manufacturing labor per lamp	0.5 hours	0.6 hours	
Direct manufacturing labor rate per hour	$20	$20	
Indirect manufacturing costs			$234,000

Calculate the total budgeted costs of the basic and designer lamps using Amherst's simple costing system.

Applying the Five-Step Decision-Making Process at Plastim

To decide how it should respond to the threat that Bandix poses to its S3 lens business, Plastim's managers work through the five-step decision-making process introduced in Chapter 1.

Step 1: Identify the Problem and Uncertainties. The problem is clear: If Plastim wants to retain the Giovanni business for S3 lenses and make a profit, it must find a way to reduce the price and costs of the S3 lens. The two major uncertainties Plastim faces are (1) whether its technology and processes for the S3 lens are competitive with Bandix's and (2) whether Plastim's S3 lens is overcosted by the simple costing system.

Step 2: Obtain Information. Senior management asks a team of design and process engineers to analyze and evaluate the design, manufacturing, and distribution operations for the S3 lens. The team is very confident that the technology and processes for the S3 lens are not inferior to those of Bandix and other competitors because Plastim has many years of experience in manufacturing and distributing the S3 lens with a history and culture of continuous process improvements. The team is less certain about Plastim's capabilities in manufacturing and distributing complex lenses because it only recently started making this type of lens. Given these doubts, senior management is happy that Giovanni Motors considers the price of the C5 lens to be competitive. Plastim's managers are puzzled, though, by how, at the currently budgeted prices, Plastim is expected to earn a very large profit margin percentage (operating income ÷ revenues) on the C5 lenses and a small profit margin on the S3 lenses:

	60,000 Simple Lenses (S3)		15,000 Complex Lenses (C5)		
	Total (1)	per Unit (2) = (1) ÷ 60,000	Total (3)	per Unit (4) = (3) ÷ 15,000	Total (5) = (1)+(3)
Revenues	$3,780,000	$63.00	$2,055,000	$137.00	$5,835,000
Total costs	3,525,000	58.75	1,455,000	97.00	4,980,000
Operating income	$ 255,000	$ 4.25	$ 600,000	$ 40.00	$ 855,000
Profit margin percentage		6.75%		29.20%	

As they continue to gather information, Plastim's managers begin to ponder why the profit margins are under so much pressure for the S3 lens, where the company has strong capabilities, but not on the newer, less-established C5 lens. Plastim is not deliberately charging a low price for S3, so managers begin to evaluate the costing system. Plastim's simple costing system may be overcosting the simple S3 lens (assigning too much cost to it) and undercosting the complex C5 lens (assigning too little cost to it).

Step 3: Make Predictions About the Future. Plastim's key challenge is to get a better estimate of what it will cost to design, make, and distribute the S3 and C5 lenses. Managers are fairly confident about the direct material and direct manufacturing labor cost of each lens because these costs are easily traced to the lenses. Of greater concern is how accurately the simple costing system measures the indirect resources used by each type of lens. The managers believe the costing system can be substantially improved.

Even as they come to this conclusion, managers want to avoid biased thinking. In particular, they want to be careful that the desire to be competitive on the S3 lens does not lead to assumptions that bias them in favor of lowering costs of the S3 lens.

Step 4: Make Decisions by Choosing Among Alternatives. On the basis of predicted costs and taking into account how Bandix might respond, Plastim's managers must decide whether they should bid for Giovanni Motors' S3 lens business and, if they do bid, what price they should offer.

Step 5: Implement the Decision, Evaluate Performance, and Learn. If Plastim bids and wins Giovanni's S3 lens business, it must compare actual costs as it makes and ships the S3 lenses to predicted costs and learn why actual costs deviate from predicted costs. Such evaluation and learning form the basis for future improvements.

The next few sections focus on Steps 3, 4, and 5: (3) how Plastim improves the allocation of indirect costs to the S3 and C5 lenses, (4) how it uses these predictions to bid for the S3 lens business, and (5) how it evaluates performance, makes product design and process improvements, and learns using the new system.

LEARNING OBJECTIVE 2

Present three guidelines for refining a costing system

...classify more costs as direct costs, expand the number of indirect-cost pools, and identify cost drivers

Refining a Costing System

A **refined costing system** reduces the use of broad averages for assigning the cost of resources to cost objects (such as jobs, products, and services) and provides better measurement of the costs of indirect resources used by different cost objects, no matter how differently various cost objects use indirect resources. Refining a costing system helps managers make better decisions about how to allocate resources and which products to produce.

Reasons for Refining a Costing System

Three principal reasons have accelerated the demand for refinements to the costing system.

1. **Increase in product diversity.** The growing demand for customized products has led managers to increase the variety of products and services their companies offer. Kanthal, a Swedish manufacturer of heating elements, for example, produces more than 10,000 different types of electrical heating wires and thermostats. Banks, such as Barclays Bank in the United Kingdom, offer many different types of accounts and services: special passbook accounts, ATMs, credit cards, and electronic banking products. Producing these products places different demands on resources because of differences in volume, process, technology, and complexity. For example, the computer and network resources needed to support electronic banking products are much greater than the computer and network resources needed to support a passbook savings account. The use of broad averages fails to capture these differences in demand and leads to distorted and inaccurate cost information.

2. **Increase in indirect costs with different cost drivers.** The use of product and process technology such as computer-integrated manufacturing (CIM) and flexible manufacturing systems (FMS) has led to an increase in indirect costs and a decrease in direct costs, particularly direct manufacturing labor costs. In CIM and FMS, computers on the manufacturing floor instruct equipment to set up and run quickly and automatically. The computers accurately measure hundreds of production parameters and directly control the manufacturing processes to achieve high-quality output. Managing complex technology and producing diverse products also require additional support function resources for activities such as production scheduling, product and process design, and engineering. Because direct manufacturing labor is not a cost driver of these costs, allocating indirect costs on the basis of direct manufacturing labor (as in Plastim's simple costing system) does not accurately measure how resources are being used by different products.

3. **Competition in product markets.** As markets have become more competitive, managers have felt the need to obtain more accurate cost information to help them make important strategic decisions, such as how to price products and which products to sell. Making correct decisions about pricing and product mix is critical in competitive markets because competitors quickly capitalize on a manager's mistakes. For example, if Plastim overcosts the S3 lens and charges a higher price, a competitor aware of the true costs of making the lens could charge a lower price and gain the S3 business as Bandix is attempting to do.

The preceding factors explain why managers want to refine cost systems. Refining costing systems requires gathering, validating, analyzing, and storing vast quantities of data. Advances in information technology have drastically reduced the costs of performing these activities.

Guidelines for Refining a Costing System

There are three main guidelines for refining a costing system:

1. **Direct-cost tracing.** Identify as many direct costs as is economically feasible. This guideline aims to reduce the amount of costs classified as indirect, thereby minimizing the extent to which costs have to be allocated rather than traced.

2. **Indirect-cost pools.** Expand the number of indirect-cost pools until each pool is more homogeneous. All costs in a *homogeneous cost pool* have the same or a similar cause-and-effect (or benefits-received) relationship with a single cost driver that is used as the cost-allocation base. Consider, for example, a single indirect-cost pool containing both indirect machining costs and indirect distribution costs that are allocated to products using machine-hours. This pool is not homogeneous because machine-hours are a cost driver of machining costs but not of distribution costs, which has a different cost driver, cubic feet of product delivered. If, instead, machining costs and distribution costs are separated into two indirect-cost pools, with machine-hours as the cost-allocation base for the machining cost pool and cubic feet of product delivered as the cost-allocation base for the distribution cost pool, each indirect-cost pool would become homogeneous.

DECISION POINT

How do managers refine a costing system?

3. **Cost-allocation bases.** As we describe later in the chapter, whenever possible, managers should use the cost driver (the cause of indirect costs) as the cost-allocation base for each homogeneous indirect-cost pool (the effect).

Activity-Based Costing Systems

LEARNING OBJECTIVE 3

Distinguish between simple and activity-based costing systems

...unlike simple systems, activity-based costing systems calculate costs of individual activities to cost products

One of the best tools for refining a costing system is *activity-based costing*. **Activity-based costing (ABC)** refines a costing system by identifying individual activities as the fundamental cost objects. An **activity** is an event, task, or unit of work with a specified purpose—for example, designing products, setting up machines, operating machines, or distributing products. More informally, activities are verbs; they are things that a firm does. To help make strategic decisions, ABC systems identify activities in all functions of the value chain, calculate costs of individual activities, and assign costs to cost objects such as products and services on the basis of the mix of activities needed to produce each product or service.[2]

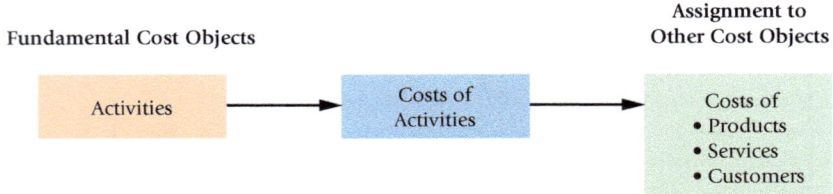

Plastim's ABC System

After reviewing its simple costing system and the potential miscosting of product costs, Plastim's managers decide to implement an ABC system. Direct material costs and direct manufacturing labor costs can be traced to products easily, so the ABC system focuses on refining the assignment of indirect costs to departments, processes, products, or other cost objects. To identify activities, Plastim organizes a team of managers from design, manufacturing, distribution, accounting, and administration. Plastim's ABC system then uses activities to break down its current single indirect-cost pool into finer pools of costs related to the various activities.

Defining activities is difficult. The team evaluates hundreds of tasks performed at Plastim. It must decide which tasks should be classified as separate activities and which should be combined. For example, should maintenance of molding machines, operations of molding machines, and process control be regarded as separate activities or combined into a single activity? An activity-based costing system with many activities becomes overly detailed and unwieldy to operate. An activity-based costing system with too few activities may not be refined enough to measure cause-and-effect relationships between cost drivers and various indirect costs. To achieve an effective balance, Plastim's team focuses on activities that account for a sizable fraction of indirect costs and combines activities that have the same cost driver into a single activity. For example, the team decides to combine maintenance of molding machines, operations of molding machines, and process control into a single activity—molding machine operations—because all these activities have the same cost driver: molding machine-hours.

The team identifies the following seven activities based on the steps and processes needed to design, manufacture, and distribute S3 and C5 lenses.

a. Design products and processes
b. Set up molding machines to ensure that the molds are properly held in place and parts are properly aligned before manufacturing starts

---

[2] For more details on ABC systems, see R. Cooper and R. S. Kaplan, *The Design of Cost Management Systems* (Upper Saddle River, NJ: Prentice Hall, 1999); G. Cokins, *Activity-Based Cost Management: An Executive's Guide* (Hoboken, NJ: John Wiley & Sons, 2001); and R. S. Kaplan and S. Anderson, *Time-Driven Activity-Based Costing: A Simpler and More Powerful Path to Higher Profits* (Boston: Harvard Business School Press, 2007).

c. Operate molding machines to manufacture lenses
d. Clean and maintain the molds after lenses are manufactured
e. Prepare batches of finished lenses for shipment
f. Distribute lenses to customers
g. Administer and manage all processes at Plastim

These activity descriptions (or *activity list* or *activity dictionary*) form the basis of the activity-based costing system. Compiling the list of tasks, however, is only the first step in implementing activity-based costing systems. Plastim must also identify the cost of each activity and the related cost driver by using the three guidelines for refining a costing system described on pages 179–180.

1. **Direct-cost tracing.** Plastim's ABC system subdivides the single indirect-cost pool into seven smaller cost pools related to the different activities. The costs in the cleaning and maintenance activity cost pool (item d) consist of salaries and wages paid to workers who clean the mold. These costs are direct costs because they can be economically traced to a specific mold and lens.

2. **Indirect-cost pools.** The remaining six activity cost pools are indirect-cost pools. Unlike the single indirect-cost pool of Plastim's simple costing system, each of the activity-related cost pools is homogeneous. That is, each activity cost pool includes only those narrow and focused sets of costs that have the same cost driver. Consider, for example, distribution costs. Managers identify cubic feet of packages delivered as the only cost driver of distribution costs because all distribution costs (such as wages of truck drivers) vary with the cubic feet of packages delivered. In the simple costing system, Plastim pooled all indirect costs together and used a single cost-allocation base, direct manufacturing labor-hours, which was not a cost driver of all indirect costs. Managers were therefore unable to measure how different cost objects (the S3 and C5 lenses) used resources.

    To determine the costs of activity pools, managers assign costs accumulated in various account classifications (such as salaries, wages, maintenance, and electricity) to each of the activity cost pools. This process is commonly called *first-stage allocation*. For example, as we will see later in the chapter, of the $2,385,000 in the total indirect-cost pool, Plastim identifies setup costs of $300,000. Setup costs include depreciation and maintenance costs of setup equipment, wages of setup workers, and allocated salaries of design engineers, process engineers, and supervisors. We discuss *first-stage allocation* in more detail in Chapters 14 and 15. We focus here on the *second-stage allocation*, the allocation of costs of activity cost pools to products.

3. **Cost-allocation bases.** For each activity cost pool, Plastim uses the cost driver (whenever possible) as the cost-allocation base. To identify cost drivers, Plastim's managers consider various alternatives and use their knowledge of operations to choose among them. For example, Plastim's managers choose setup-hours rather than the number of setups as the cost driver of setup costs because Plastim's managers believe that the more complex setups of C5 lenses take more time and are more costly. Over time, Plastim's managers can use data to test their beliefs. (Chapter 10 discusses several methods to estimate the relationship between a cost driver and costs.)

The logic of ABC systems is twofold. First, when managers structure activity cost pools more finely, using cost drivers for each activity cost pool as the cost-allocation base, it leads to more accurate costing of activities. Second, allocating these costs to products by measuring the cost-allocation bases of different activities used by different products leads to more accurate product costs. We illustrate this logic by focusing on the setup activity at Plastim.

Setting up molding machines frequently entails trial runs, fine-tuning, and adjustments. Improper setups cause quality problems such as scratches on the surface of the lens. The resources needed for each setup depend on the complexity of the manufacturing operation. Complex lenses require more setup resources (setup-hours) per setup than simple lenses. Furthermore, complex lenses can be produced only in small batches because the molds for complex lenses need to be cleaned more often than molds for simple lenses. Relative to simple lenses, complex lenses therefore not only use more setup-hours per setup, but also require more frequent setups.

Setup data for the simple S3 lens and the complex C5 lens are as follows.

		Simple S3 Lens	Complex C5 Lens	Total
1	Quantity of lenses produced	60,000	15,000	
2	Number of lenses produced per batch	240	50	
3 = (1) ÷ (2)	Number of batches	250	300	
4	Setup time per batch	2 hours	5 hours	
5 = (3) × (4)	Total setup-hours	500 hours	1,500 hours	2,000 hours

Recall that in its simple costing system, Plastim uses direct manufacturing labor-hours to allocate all $2,385,000 of indirect costs (which includes $300,000 of indirect setup costs) to products. The following table compares how setup costs allocated to simple and complex lenses will be different if Plastim allocates setup costs to lenses based on setup-hours rather than direct manufacturing labor-hours. Of the $60 total rate per direct manufacturing labor-hour (page 177), the setup cost per direct manufacturing labor-hour amounts to $7.54717 ($300,000 ÷ 39,750 total direct manufacturing labor-hours). The setup cost per setup-hour equals $150 ($300,000 ÷ 2,000 total setup-hours).

	Simple S3 Lens	Complex C5 Lens	Total
Setup cost allocated using direct manufacturing labor-hours: $7.54717 × 30,000; $7.54717 × 9,750	$226,415	$ 73,585	$300,000
Setup cost allocated using setup-hours: $150 × 500; $150 × 1,500	$ 75,000	$225,000	$300,000

ABC systems that use available time (setup-hours in our example) to calculate the cost of a resource and to allocate costs to cost objects are sometimes called *time-driven activity-based costing (TDABC) systems*. Following guidelines 2 and 3, Plastim should use setup hours, the cost driver of set up costs, and not direct manufacturing labor hours, to allocate setup costs to products. The C5 lens uses substantially more setup-hours than the S3 lens (1,500 hours ÷ 2,000 hours = 75% of the total setup-hours) because the C5 requires a greater number of setups (batches) and each setup is more challenging and requires more setup-hours.

The ABC system therefore allocates significantly more setup costs to C5 than to S3. When direct manufacturing labor-hours rather than setup-hours are used to allocate setup costs in the simple costing system, the S3 lens is allocated a very large share of the setup costs because the S3 lens uses a larger proportion of direct manufacturing labor-hours (30,000 ÷ 39,750 = 75.47%). As a result, the simple costing system overcosts the S3 lens with regard to setup costs.

As we will see later in the chapter, ABC systems provide valuable information to managers beyond more accurate product costs. For example, identifying setup-hours as the cost driver correctly orients managers' cost reduction efforts on reducing setup-hours and cost per setup-hour. Note that setup-hours are related to batches (or groups) of lenses made, not the number of individual lenses. Activity-based costing attempts to identify the most relevant cause-and-effect relationship for each activity pool without restricting the cost driver to be units of output or variables related to units of output (such as direct manufacturing labor-hours). As our discussion of setups illustrates, limiting cost-allocation bases to only units of output weakens the cause-and-effect relationship between the cost-allocation base and the costs in a cost pool. Broadening cost drivers to batches (or groups) of lenses, not just individual lenses, leads us to *cost hierarchies*.

DECISION POINT

What is the difference between the design of a simple costing system and an activity-based costing (ABC) system?

LEARNING OBJECTIVE 4

Describe a four-part cost hierarchy

...a four-part cost hierarchy is used to categorize costs based on different types of cost drivers—for example, costs that vary with each unit of a product versus costs that vary with each batch of products

Cost Hierarchies

A **cost hierarchy** categorizes various activity cost pools on the basis of the different types of cost drivers, cost-allocation bases, or different degrees of difficulty in determining cause-and-effect (or benefits-received) relationships. ABC systems commonly use a cost hierarchy with four levels to identify cost-allocation bases that are cost drivers of the activity cost pools: (1) output unit–level costs, (2) batch-level costs, (3) product-sustaining costs, and (4) facility-sustaining costs.

Output unit–level costs are the costs of activities performed on each individual unit of a product or service. Machine operations costs (such as the cost of energy, machine depreciation, and repair) related to the activity of running the automated molding machines are output unit–level costs because, over time, the cost of this activity increases with additional units of output produced (or machine-hours used). Plastim's ABC system uses molding machine-hours, an output unit–level cost-allocation base, to allocate machine operations costs to products.

Batch-level costs are the costs of activities related to a group of units of a product or service rather than each individual unit of product or service. In the Plastim example, setup costs are batch-level costs because, over time, the cost of this setup activity varies with the setup-hours needed to produce batches (groups) of lenses regardless of the total number of lenses produced. For example, if Plastim produces 20% fewer lenses using the same number of setup hours, would setup costs change? No, because setup hours not the number of lenses produced drive setup costs.

As described in the table on page 182, the S3 lens requires 500 setup-hours (2 setup-hours per batch × 250 batches). The C5 lens requires 1,500 setup-hours (5 setup-hours per batch × 300 batches). The total setup costs allocated to S3 and C5 depend on the total setup-hours required by each type of lens, not on the number of lenses of S3 and C5 produced. Plastim's ABC system uses setup-hours, a batch-level cost-allocation base, to allocate setup costs to products. Other examples of batch-level costs are material-handling and quality-inspection costs associated with batches (not the quantities) of products produced and costs of placing purchase orders, receiving materials, and paying invoices related to the number of purchase orders placed rather than the quantity or value of materials purchased.

Product-sustaining costs (service-sustaining costs) are the costs of activities undertaken to support individual products or services regardless of the number of units or batches in which the units are produced or services provided. In the Plastim example, design costs are product-sustaining costs. Over time, design costs depend largely on the time designers spend on designing and modifying the product, mold, and process, not on the number of lenses subsequently produced or the number of batches in which the lenses are produced using the mold. These design costs are a function of the complexity of the mold, measured by the number of parts in the mold multiplied by the area (in square feet) over which the molten plastic must flow (12 parts × 2.5 square feet, or 30 parts-square feet for the S3 lens; and 14 parts × 5 square feet, or 70 parts-square feet for the C5 lens). Plastim's ABC system uses parts-square feet, a product-sustaining cost-allocation base, to allocate design costs to products. Other examples of product-sustaining costs are product research and development costs, costs of making engineering changes, and marketing costs to launch new products.

Facility-sustaining costs are the costs of activities that managers cannot trace to individual products or services but that support the organization as a whole. In the Plastim example and at companies such as Volvo, Samsung, and General Electric, the general administration costs (including top management compensation, rent, and building security) are facility-sustaining costs. It is usually difficult to find a good cause-and-effect relationship between these costs and the cost-allocation base, so some companies deduct facility-sustaining costs as a separate lump-sum amount from operating income rather than allocate these costs to products. Managers who follow this approach need to keep in mind that when making decisions based on costs (such as pricing), some lump-sum costs have not been allocated. They must set prices that are much greater than the allocated costs to recover some of the unallocated facility-sustaining costs. Other companies, such as Plastim, allocate facility-sustaining costs to products on some basis—for example, direct manufacturing labor-hours—because management believes all costs should be allocated to products even if it's done in a somewhat arbitrary way. Allocating all costs to products or services ensures that managers take into account all costs when making decisions based on costs. So long as managers are aware of the nature of facility-sustaining costs and the pros and cons of allocating them, which method a manager chooses is a matter of personal preference.

DECISION POINT

What is a cost hierarchy?

LEARNING OBJECTIVE 5

Cost products or services using activity-based costing

...use cost rates for different activities to compute indirect costs of a product

Implementing Activity-Based Costing

Now that you understand the basic concepts of ABC, let's see how Plastim's managers refine the simple costing system, evaluate the two systems, and identify the factors to consider when deciding whether to develop the ABC system.

Implementing ABC at Plastim

To implement ABC, Plastim's managers follow the seven-step approach to costing and the three guidelines for refining costing systems (increase direct-cost tracing, create homogeneous indirect-cost pools, and identify cost-allocation bases that have cause-and-effect relationships with costs in the cost pool). Exhibit 5-3 shows an overview of Plastim's ABC system. Use this exhibit as a guide as you study the following steps, each of which is marked in Exhibit 5-3.

Step 1: Identify the Products That Are the Chosen Cost Objects. The cost objects are the 60,000 S3 and the 15,000 C5 lenses that Plastim will produce in 2017. Plastim's managers want to determine the total costs and then the per-unit cost of designing, manufacturing, and distributing these lenses.

Step 2: Identify the Direct Costs of the Products. The managers identify the following direct costs of the lenses because these costs can be economically traced to a specific mold and lens: direct material costs, direct manufacturing labor costs, and mold cleaning and maintenance costs.

Exhibit 5-5 shows the direct and indirect costs for the S3 and C5 lenses using the ABC system. The direct costs calculations appear on lines 6, 7, 8, and 9 in Exhibit 5-5. Plastim's managers classify all other costs as indirect costs, as we will see in Exhibit 5-4.

Step 3: Select the Activities and Cost-Allocation Bases to Use for Allocating Indirect Costs to the Products. Following guideline 2 (subdivide into homogeneous cost pools) and guideline

EXHIBIT 5-3 Overview of Plastim's Activity-Based Costing System

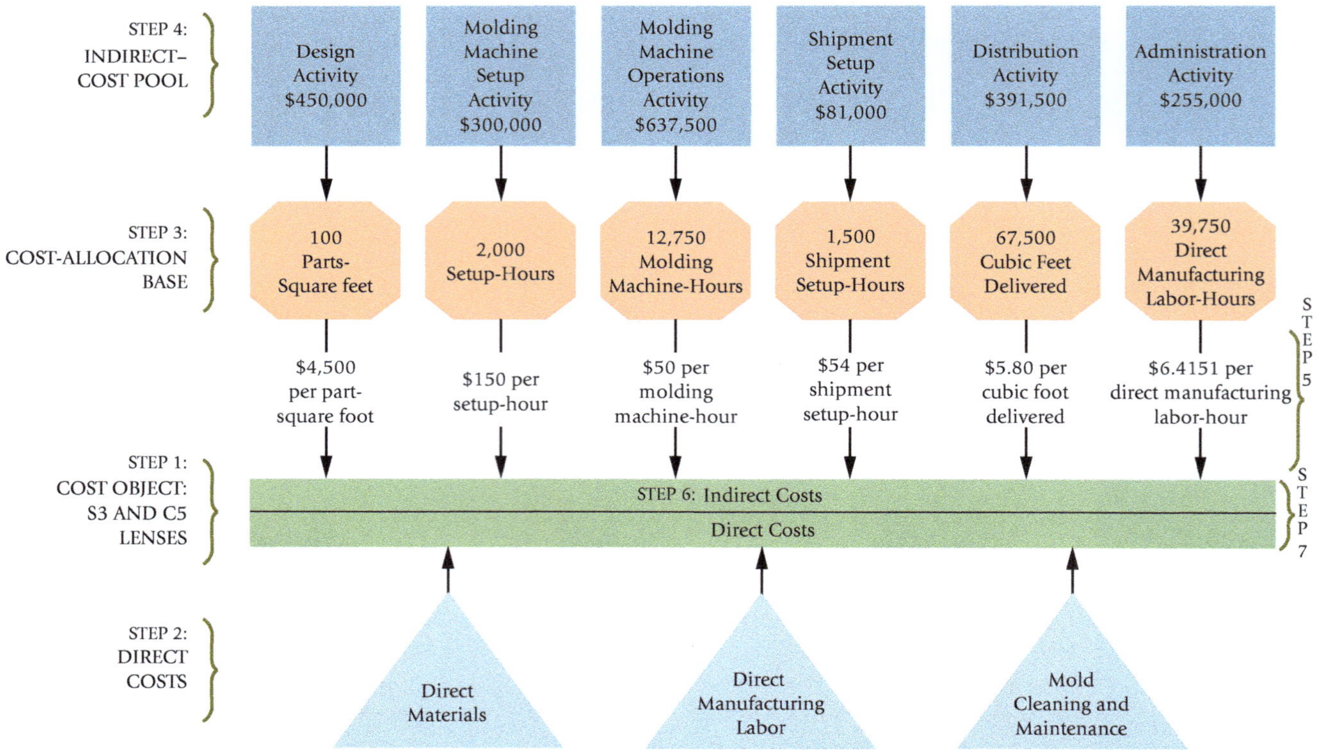

EXHIBIT 5-4 Activity-Cost Rates for Indirect-Cost Pools

A	B	C	D	E	F	G	H
		(Step 4)	(Step 3)		(Step 5)		
Activity	Cost Hierarchy Category	Total Budgeted Indirect Costs	Budgeted Quantity of Cost-Allocation Base		Budgeted Indirect Cost Rate		Cause-and-Effect Relationship Between Allocation Base and Activity Cost
(1)	(2)	(3)	(4)		(5) = (3) ÷ (4)		(6)
Design	Product-sustaining	$450,000	100	parts-square feet	$4,500	per part-square foot	Design Department indirect costs increase with more complex molds (more parts, larger surface area).
Molding machine setup	Batch-level	$300,000	2,000	setup-hours	$150	per setup-hour	Indirect setup costs increase with setup-hours.
Machine operations	Output unit-level	$637,500	12,750	molding machine-hours	$50	per molding machine-hour	Indirect costs of operating molding machines increases with molding machine-hours.
Shipment setup	Batch-level	$81,000	1,500	shipment setup-hours	$54	per shipment setup-hour	Shipping costs incurred to prepare batches for shipment increase with the number of shipment setup-hours.
Distribution	Output-unit-level	$391,500	67,500	cubic feet delivered	$5.80	per cubic foot delivered	Distribution costs increase with the cubic feet of packages delivered.
Administration	Facility sustaining	$255,000	39,750	direct manuf. labor-hours	$6.4151	per direct manuf. labor-hour	The demand for administrative resources increases with direct manufacturing labor-hours.

3 (identify relevant cost-allocation bases) for refining a costing system (pages 179–180), Plastim's managers identify six activities for allocating indirect costs to products: (a) design, (b) molding machine setup, (c) machine operations, (d) shipment setup, (e) distribution, and (f) administration. Exhibit 5-4, column 2, shows the cost hierarchy category, and column 4 shows the cost-allocation base and the budgeted quantity of the cost-allocation base for each activity described in column 1.

Identifying the cost-allocation bases defines the number of activity pools into which costs must be grouped in an ABC system. For example, rather than define the design activities of product design, process design, and prototyping as separate activities, Plastim's managers define these three activities together as a combined "design" activity and form a homogeneous design cost pool. Why? Because the same cost driver—the complexity of the mold—drives the costs of each design activity. A second consideration for choosing a cost-allocation base is the availability of reliable data and measures. For example, in its ABC system, Plastim's managers measure mold complexity in terms of the number of parts in the mold and the surface area of the mold (parts-square feet). If these data are difficult to obtain or measure, Plastim's managers may be forced to use some other measure of complexity, such as the amount of material flowing through the mold that may only be weakly related to the cost of the design activity.

Step 4: Identify the Indirect Costs Associated with Each Cost-Allocation Base. In this step, Plastim's managers try to assign budgeted indirect costs for 2017 to activities (see Exhibit 5-4, column 3) on the basis of a cause-and-effect relationship between the cost-allocation base for an activity and the cost. For example, all costs that have a cause-and-effect relationship to cubic feet of packages moved are assigned to the distribution cost pool. Of course, the strength of the cause-and-effect relationship between the cost-allocation base and the cost of an activity varies across cost pools. For example, the cause-and-effect relationship between direct manufacturing labor-hours and administration activity costs, which as we discussed earlier is somewhat arbitrary, is not as strong as the relationship between setup-hours and setup activity costs, where setup-hours is the cost driver of setup costs.

Some costs can be directly identified with a particular activity. For example, salaries paid to design engineers and depreciation of equipment used in the design department are directly identified with the design activity. Other costs need to be allocated across activities. For example, on the basis of interviews or time records, manufacturing engineers and supervisors estimate the time they will spend on design, molding machine setup, and molding machine operations. If a manufacturing engineer spends 15% of her time on design, 45% of her time managing molding machine setups, and 40% of her time on molding operations, the company will allocate the manufacturing engineer's salary to each of these activities in proportion to the time spent. Still other costs are allocated to activity-cost pools using allocation bases that measure how these costs support different activities. For example, rent costs are allocated to activity-cost pools on the basis of square-feet area used by different activities.

As you can see, most costs do not fit neatly into activity categories. Often, costs may first need to be allocated to activities (Stage 1 of the two-stage cost-allocation model) before the costs of the activities can be allocated to products (Stage 2).

The following table shows the assignment of costs to the seven activities identified earlier. Recall that Plastim's management accountants reclassify mold cleaning costs as a direct cost because these costs can be easily traced to a specific mold and lens.

	Design	Molding Machine Setups	Molding Operations	Mold Cleaning	Shipment Setup	Distribution	Administration	Total
Salaries (supervisors, design engineers, process engineers)	$320,000	$105,000	$137,500	$ 0	$21,000	$ 61,500	$165,000	$ 810,000
Wages of support staff	65,000	115,000	70,000	234,000	34,000	125,000	40,000	683,000
Depreciation	24,000	30,000	290,000	18,000	11,000	140,000	15,000	528,000
Maintenance	13,000	16,000	45,000	12,000	6,000	25,000	5,000	122,000
Power and fuel	18,000	20,000	35,000	6,000	5,000	30,000	10,000	124,000
Rent	10,000	14,000	60,000	0	4,000	10,000	20,000	118,000
Total	$450,000	$300,000	$637,500	$270,000	$81,000	$391,500	$255,000	$2,385,000

Step 5: Compute the Rate per Unit of Each Cost-Allocation Base. Exhibit 5-4, column 5, summarizes the calculation of the budgeted indirect-cost rates using the budgeted quantity of the cost-allocation base from Step 3 and the total budgeted indirect costs of each activity from Step 4.

Step 6: Compute the Indirect Costs Allocated to the Products. Exhibit 5-5 shows total budgeted indirect costs of $1,153,953 allocated to the simple lens and $961,047 allocated to the complex lens. Follow the budgeted indirect-cost calculations for each lens in Exhibit 5-5. For each activity, Plastim's operations personnel indicate the total quantity of the cost-allocation base that will be used by each type of lens (recall that Plastim operates at capacity). For example, lines 15 and 16 in Exhibit 5-5 show that of the 2,000 total setup-hours, the S3 lens is budgeted to use 500 hours and the C5 lens 1,500 hours. The budgeted indirect-cost rate is $150 per setup-hour (Exhibit 5-4, column 5, line 5). Therefore, the total budgeted cost of the setup activity allocated to the S3 lens is $75,000 (500 setup-hours × $150 per setup-hour) and to the C5 lens is $225,000 (1,500 setup-hours × $150 per setup-hour). Budgeted setup cost per unit equals $1.25 ($75,000 ÷ 60,000 units) for the S3 lens and $15 ($225,000 ÷ 15,000 units) for the C5 lens.

Next consider shipment setup costs. Plastim supplies its S3 and C5 lenses to two different Giovanni plants. One of these is an international plant in Mexico. Preparing for these

EXHIBIT 5-5 Plastim's Product Costs Using Activity-Based Costing System

A	B	C	D	E	F	G
	60,000			15,000		
	Simple Lenses (S3)			Complex Lenses (C5)		
	Total	per Unit		Total	per Unit	Total
Cost Description	(1)	(2) = (1) ÷ 60,000		(3)	(4) = (3) ÷ 15,000	(5) = (1) + (3)
Direct costs						
Direct materials	$1,125,000	$18.75		$675,000	$45.00	$1,800,000
Direct manufacturing labor	600,000	10.00		195,000	13.00	795,000
Direct mold cleaning and maintenance costs	120,000	2.00		150,000	10.00	270,000
Total direct costs (Step 2)	1,845,000	30.75		1,020,000	68.00	2,865,000
Indirect Costs of Activities						
Design						
S3, 30 parts-sq.ft. × $4,500	135,000	2.25				} 450,000
C5, 70 parts-sq.ft. × $4,500				315,000	21.00	
Setup of molding machines						
S3, 500 setup-hours × $150	75,000	1.25				} 300,000
C5, 1,500 setup-hours × $150				225,000	15.00	
Machine operations						
S3, 9,000 molding machine-hours × $50	450,000	7.50				} 637,500
C5, 3,750 molding machine-hours × $50				187,500	12.50	
Shipment setup						
S3, 750 shipment setup hours × $54	40,500	0.67				} 81,000
C5, 750 shipment setup hours × $54				40,500	2.70	
Distribution						
S3, 45,000 cubic feet delivered × $5.80	261,000	4.35				} 391,500
C5, 22,500 cubic feet delivered × $5.80				130,500	8.70	
Administration						
S3, 30,000 dir. manuf. labor-hours × $6.4151	192,453	3.21				} 255,000
C5, 9,750 dir. manuf. labor-hours × $6.4151				62,547	4.17	
Total indirect costs allocated (Step 6)	1,153,953	19.23		961,047	64.07	2,115,000
Total Costs (Step 7)	$2,998,953	$49.98		$1,981,047	$132.07	$4,980,000

shipments is more time consuming than preparing shipments to the local plant in Indiana because of additional documents related to customs, taxes, and insurance. The following table shows the budgeted number of shipments of S3 and C5 lenses to each plant.

	Mexico Plant Shipments	Indiana Plant Shipments	Total Shipments
Simple S3 lens shipments	10	100	110
Complex C5 lens shipments	30	60	90
			200

Each shipment to the Mexico plant requires 12.5 hours of the shipment department personnel's time while each shipment to the Indiana plant requires half that time, 6.25 hours. The following table indicates the budgeted shipping setup-hours for the S3 and C5 lenses.

	Shipment Setup-Hours for Mexico Plant	Shipment Setup-Hours for Indiana Plant	Total Shipment Setup-Hours
Simple S3 lens shipment setup-hours (12.5 hours × 10; 6.25 hours × 100)	125	625	750
Complex C5 lens shipment setup-hours (12.5 hours × 30; 6.25 hours × 60)	375	375	750
			1,500

The budgeted indirect-cost rate is $54 per shipment setup-hour (Exhibit 5-4, column 5, line 7). Therefore, lines 21 and 22 in Exhibit 5-5 show that the total budgeted cost of the shipment setup activity allocated to the S3 lens is $40,500 (750 shipment setup-hours × $54 per shipment setup-hour) and to the C5 lens is $40,500 (750 shipment setup-hours × $54 per shipment setup-hour). Budgeted setup cost per unit equals $0.67 ($40,500 ÷ 60,000 units) for the S3 lens and $2.70 ($40,500 ÷ 15,000 units) for the C5 lens.

Costing for shipment setups using shipment setup-hours as the cost driver is another example of time-driven activity-based costing (TDABC) because it leverages the time taken for different activities within a cost pool. TDABC allows Plastim's managers to account for different complexities of shipments of S3 and C5 lenses. Notice that if Plastim had ignored the complexity of different shipments and allocated costs to lenses based only on the number of shipments, it would have calculated a budgeted indirect-cost rate of $405 per shipment in Exhibit 5-4 ($81,000 ÷ 200 shipments). Using this rate the total budgeted cost of the shipment setup activity allocated to the S3 lens is $44,550 (110 shipments × $405 per shipment) and to the C5 lens is $36,450 (90 shipments × $54 per shipment). The budgeted setup cost per unit equals $0.74 ($44,550 ÷ 60,000 units) for the S3 lens and $2.43 ($36,450 ÷ 15,000 units) for the C5 lens. Using the number of shipments, rather than shipment setup-hours, as the cost driver would overcost the simple S3 lens and undercost the complex C5 lens.

Step 7: Compute the Total Cost of the Products by Adding All Direct and Indirect Costs Assigned to the Products. Exhibit 5-5 presents the product costs for the simple and complex lenses. The direct costs are calculated in Step 2, and the indirect costs are calculated in Step 6. The ABC system overview in Exhibit 5-3 shows three direct-cost categories and six indirect-cost categories. The budgeted cost of each lens type in Exhibit 5-5 has nine line items, three for direct costs and six for indirect costs. The differences between the ABC product costs of S3 and C5 calculated in Exhibit 5-5 highlight how each of these products uses different amounts of direct and indirect costs in each activity area.

TRY IT! 5-2

Amherst Metal Works produces two types of metal lamps. Amherst manufactures 20,000 basic lamps and 5,000 designer lamps. Its activity-based costing system uses two indirect-cost pools. One cost pool is for setup costs and the other for general manufacturing overhead. Amherst allocates setup costs to the two lamps based on setup labor-hours and general manufacturing overhead costs on the basis of direct manufacturing labor-hours. It provides the following budgeted cost information:

	Basic Lamps	Designer Lamps	Total
Direct materials per lamp	$9	$15	
Direct manufacturing labor-hours per lamp	0.5 hours	0.6 hours	
Direct manufacturing labor rate per hour	$20	$20	
Setup costs			$114,000
Lamps produced per batch	250	50	
Setup-hours per batch	1 hour	3 hours	
General manufacturing overhead costs			$120,000

Calculate the total budgeted costs of the basic and designer lamps using Amherst's activity-based costing system.

We emphasize two features of ABC systems. First, these systems identify all costs used by products, whether the costs are variable or fixed in the short run. When making long-run strategic decisions using ABC information, managers want revenues to exceed total costs. Otherwise, a company will make losses and will be unable to continue in business. Second, recognizing the hierarchy of costs is critical when allocating costs to products. Management accountants use the cost hierarchy to first calculate the total costs of each product. They then derive per-unit costs by dividing total costs by the number of units produced.

> **DECISION POINT**
>
> How do managers cost products or services using ABC systems?

Comparing Alternative Costing Systems

Exhibit 5-6 compares the simple costing system using a single indirect-cost pool (Exhibits 5-1 and 5-2) that Plastim had been using and the ABC system (Exhibits 5-3 and 5-5). Note three points in Exhibit 5-6, consistent with the guidelines for refining a costing system: (1) ABC systems trace more costs as direct costs; (2) ABC systems create homogeneous cost pools linked to different activities; and (3) for each activity-cost pool, ABC systems seek a cost-allocation base that has a cause-and-effect relationship with costs in the cost pool.

The homogeneous cost pools and the choice of cost-allocation bases, tied to the cost hierarchy, give Plastim's managers greater confidence in the activity and product cost numbers from the ABC system. The bottom part of Exhibit 5-6 shows that allocating costs to lenses

EXHIBIT 5-6 Comparing Alternative Costing Systems

	Simple Costing System Using a Single Indirect-Cost Pool (1)	ABC System (2)	Difference (3) = (2) − (1)
Direct-cost categories	2	3	1
	Direct materials	Direct materials	
	Direct manufacturing labor	Direct manufacturing labor	
		Direct mold cleaning and maintenance labor	
Total direct costs	$2,595,000	$2,865,000	$270,000
Indirect-cost pools	1	6	5
	Single indirect-cost pool allocated using direct manufacturing labor-hours	Design (parts-square feet)[1]	
		Molding machine setup (setup-hours)	
		Machine operations (molding machine-hours)	
		Shipment setup (shipment setup-hours)	
		Distribution (cubic feet delivered)	
		Administration (direct manufacturing labor-hours)	
Total indirect costs	$2,385,000	$2,115,000	($270,000)
Total costs assigned to simple (S3) lens	$3,525,000	$2,998,953	($526,047)
Cost per unit of simple (S3) lens	$58.75	$49.98	($8.77)
Total costs assigned to complex (C5) lens	$1,455,000	$1,981,047	$526,047
Cost per unit of complex (C5) lens	$97.00	$132.07	$35.07

[1]Cost drivers for the various indirect-cost pools are shown in parentheses.

using only an output unit–level allocation base—direct manufacturing labor-hours, as in the single indirect-cost pool system used prior to ABC—overcosts the simple S3 lens by $8.77 per unit and undercosts the complex C5 lens by $35.07 per unit. The C5 lens uses a disproportionately larger amount of output unit–level, batch-level, and product-sustaining costs than is represented by the direct manufacturing labor-hour cost-allocation base. The S3 lens uses a disproportionately smaller amount of these costs.

The benefit of an ABC system is that it provides information to make better decisions. But managers must weigh this benefit against the measurement and implementation costs of an ABC system.

Considerations in Implementing Activity-Based Costing Systems

LEARNING OBJECTIVE 6

Evaluate the benefits and costs of implementing activity-based costing systems

...more accurate costs that aid in decision making when products make diverse demands on indirect resources versus measurement difficulties

Managers choose the level of detail to use in a costing system by evaluating the expected costs of the system against the expected benefits that result from better decisions.

Benefits and Costs of Activity-Based Costing Systems

Here are some of the telltale signs when an ABC system is likely to provide the most benefits:

- Significant amounts of indirect costs are allocated using only one or two cost pools.
- All or most indirect costs are identified as output unit–level costs (few indirect costs are described as batch-level costs, product-sustaining costs, or facility-sustaining costs).
- Products make diverse demands on resources because of differences in volume, process steps, batch size, or complexity.
- Products that a company is well suited to make and sell show small profits; whereas products that a company is less suited to make and sell show large profits.
- Operations staff has substantial disagreement with the reported costs of manufacturing and marketing products and services.

When managers decide to implement ABC, they must make important choices about the level of detail to use. Should managers choose many finely specified activities, cost drivers, and cost pools, or would a few suffice? For example, Plastim's managers could identify a different molding machine-hour rate for each different type of molding machine. In making such choices, managers weigh the benefits against the costs and limitations of implementing a more detailed costing system.

The main costs and limitations of an ABC system are the measurements necessary to implement it. ABC systems require managers to estimate costs of activity pools and to identify and measure cost drivers for these pools to serve as cost-allocation bases. Even basic ABC systems require many calculations to determine costs of products and services. These measurements are costly. Activity-cost rates also need to be updated regularly.

As ABC systems get very detailed and more cost pools are created, more allocations are necessary to calculate activity costs for each cost pool, which increases the chances of misidentifying the costs of different activity cost pools. For example, supervisors are more prone to incorrectly identify the time they spend on different activities if they have to allocate their time over five activities rather than only two activities.

Occasionally, managers are also forced to use allocation bases for which data are readily available rather than allocation bases they would have liked to use. For example, a manager might be forced to use the number of loads moved, instead of the degree of difficulty and distance of different loads moved, as the allocation base for material-handling costs because data on degree of difficulty and distance of moves are difficult to obtain. When incorrect cost-allocation bases are used, activity-cost information can be misleading. For example, if the cost per load moved decreases, a company may conclude that it has become more efficient in its materials-handling operations. In fact, the lower cost per load moved may have resulted solely from moving many lighter loads over shorter distances.

Many companies, such as Kanthal, a Swedish heating elements manufacturer, have found the strategic and operational benefits of a less-detailed ABC system to be good enough to not warrant incurring the costs and challenges of operating a more detailed system. Other organizations, such as Hewlett-Packard, have implemented ABC in only certain divisions (such as the Roseville Networks Division, which manufactures printed circuit boards) or functions (such as procurement and production). As improvements in information technology and accompanying declines in measurement costs continue, more detailed ABC systems have become a practical alternative in many companies. As these advancements become more widespread, more detailed ABC systems will be better able to pass the cost–benefit test.

Global surveys of company practice suggest that ABC implementation varies among companies. Nevertheless, its framework and ideas provide a standard for judging whether any simple costing system is good enough for a particular management's purposes. ABC thinking can help managers improve any simple costing system.

Behavioral Issues in Implementing Activity-Based Costing Systems

Successfully implementing ABC systems requires more than an understanding of the technical details. ABC implementation often represents a significant change in the costing system and, as the chapter indicates, requires a manager to choose how to define activities and the level of detail. What then are some of the behavioral issues to which managers and management accountants must be sensitive?

1. **Gaining support of top management and creating a sense of urgency for the ABC effort.** This requires managers and management accountants to clearly communicate the strategic benefits of ABC, such as improvements in product and process design. For example, at USAA Federal Savings Bank, managers calculated the cost of individual activities such as opening and closing accounts and demonstrated how the information gained from ABC provided insights into ways of improving the efficiency of bank operations that were previously unavailable.

2. **Creating a guiding coalition of managers throughout the value chain for the ABC effort.** ABC systems measure how the resources of an organization are used. Managers responsible for these resources have the best knowledge about activities and cost drivers. Getting managers to cooperate and take the initiative for implementing ABC is essential for gaining the required expertise, the proper credibility, greater commitment, valuable coordination, and the necessary leadership.

3. **Educating and training employees in ABC as a basis for employee empowerment.** Management accountants must disseminate information about ABC throughout the organization to enable employees in all areas of a business to use their knowledge of ABC to make improvements. For example, WS Industries, an Indian manufacturer of insulators, not only shared ABC information with its workers but also established an incentive plan that gave them a percentage of the cost savings. The results were dramatic because employees were empowered and motivated to implement numerous cost-saving projects.

4. **Seeking small short-run successes as proof that the ABC implementation is yielding results.** Too often, managers and management accountants seek big results and major changes far too quickly. In many situations, achieving a significant change overnight is difficult. However, showing how ABC information has helped improve a process and save costs, even if only in small ways, motivates the team to stay on course and build momentum. The credibility gained from small victories leads to additional and bigger improvements involving larger numbers of people and different parts of the organization. Eventually ABC becomes rooted in the culture of the organization. Sharing short-term successes also helps motivate employees to be innovative. At USAA Federal Savings Bank, managers created a "process improvement" mailbox in Microsoft Outlook to facilitate the sharing of process improvement ideas.

DECISION POINT

What should managers consider when deciding to implement ABC systems?

5. **Recognizing that ABC information is not perfect because it balances the need for better information against the costs of creating a complex system that few managers and employees can understand.** The management accountant must help managers recognize both the value and the limitations of ABC and not oversell it. Open and honest communication about ABC ensures that managers use ABC thoughtfully to make good decisions. Managers can then make critical judgments without being adversarial and can ask tough questions to help drive better decisions about the system.

Activity-Based Management

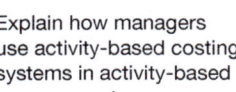

LEARNING OBJECTIVE 7

Explain how managers use activity-based costing systems in activity-based management

...such as pricing decisions, product-mix decisions, and cost reduction

The emphasis of this chapter so far has been on the role of ABC systems in obtaining better product costs. However, Plastim's managers must now use this information to make decisions (Step 4 of the five-step decision process, page 178) and to implement the decision, evaluate performance, and learn (Step 5, page 178). **Activity-based management (ABM)** is a method of management decision making that uses activity-based costing information to improve customer satisfaction and profitability. We define ABM broadly to include decisions about pricing and product mix, cost reduction, process improvement, and product and process design.

Pricing and Product-Mix Decisions

An ABC system gives managers information about the costs of making and selling diverse products. With this information, managers can make pricing and product-mix decisions. For example, the ABC system indicates that Plastim can match its competitor's price of $53 for the S3 lens and still make a profit because the ABC cost of S3 is $49.98 (see Exhibit 5-5).

Plastim's managers offer Giovanni Motors a price of $52 for the S3 lens. Plastim's managers are confident that they can use the deeper understanding of costs that the ABC system provides to improve efficiency and further reduce the cost of the S3 lens. Without information from the ABC system, Plastim managers might have erroneously concluded that they would incur an operating loss on the S3 lens at a price of $53. This incorrect conclusion would have probably caused Plastim to reduce or exit its business in simple lenses and focus instead on complex lenses, where its single indirect-cost-pool system indicated it is very profitable.

Focusing on complex lenses would have been a mistake. The ABC system indicates that the cost of making the complex lens is much higher—$132.07 versus $97 indicated by the direct manufacturing labor-hour-based costing system Plastim had been using. As Plastim's operations staff had thought all along, Plastim has no competitive advantage in making C5 lenses. At a price of $137 per lens for C5, the profit margin is very small ($137.00 − $132.07 = $4.93). As Plastim reduces its prices on simple lenses, it would need to negotiate a higher price for complex lenses while also reducing costs.

Cost Reduction and Process Improvement Decisions

Managers use ABC systems to focus on how and where to reduce costs. They set cost reduction targets for the cost per unit of the cost-allocation base in different activity areas. For example, the supervisor of the distribution activity area at Plastim could have a performance target of decreasing distribution cost per cubic foot of products delivered from $5.80 to $5.40 by reducing distribution labor and warehouse rental costs. The goal is to reduce these costs by improving the way work is done without compromising customer service or the actual or perceived value (usefulness) customers obtain from the product or service. That is, the supervisor will attempt to take out only those costs that are *nonvalue added*.

Controlling cost drivers, such as setup-hours or cubic feet delivered, is another fundamental way that operating personnel manage costs. For example, the distribution department can decrease distribution costs by packing the lenses in a way that reduces the bulkiness of the packages delivered.

The following table shows the reduction in distribution costs of the S3 and C5 lenses as a result of actions that lower cost per cubic foot delivered (from $5.80 to $5.40) and total cubic feet of deliveries (from 45,000 to 40,000 for S3 and 22,500 to 20,000 for C5).

	60,000 (S3) Lenses		15,000 (C5) Lenses	
	Total (1)	per Unit (2) = (1) ÷ 60,000	Total (3)	per Unit (4) = (3) ÷ 15,000
Distribution costs (from Exhibit 5-5)				
S3: 45,000 cubic feet × $5.80/cubic feet	$261,000	$4.35		
C5: 22,500 cubic feet × $5.80/cubic feet			$130,500	$8.70
Distribution costs as a result of process improvements				
S3: 40,000 cubic feet × $5.40/cubic feet	216,000	3.60		
C5: 20,000 cubic feet × $5.40/cubic feet			108,000	7.20
Savings in distribution costs from process improvements	$ 45,000	$0.75	$ 22,500	$1.50

In the long run, total distribution costs will decrease from $391,500 ($261,000 + $130,500) to $324,000 ($216,000 + $108,000). In the short run, however, distribution costs may be fixed and may not decrease. Suppose all $391,500 of distribution costs are fixed costs in the short run. The efficiency improvements (using less distribution labor and space) mean that the same $391,500 of distribution costs can now be used to distribute $72,500 \left(= \dfrac{\$391,500}{\$5.40 \text{ per cubic feet}} \right)$ cubic feet of lenses compared to the 67,500 cubic feet of lenses it currently distributes (see Exhibit 5-4). In this case, how should costs be allocated to the S3 and C5 lenses?

ABC systems distinguish costs incurred from resources used to design, manufacture, and deliver products and services. For the distribution activity, after process improvements,

Costs incurred = $391,500
Resources used = $216,000 (for S3 lens) + $108,000 (for C5 lens) = $324,000

On the basis of the resources used by each product, Plastim's ABC system allocates $216,000 to S3 and $108,000 to C5 for a total of $324,000. The difference of $67,500 ($391,500 − $324,000) is shown as costs of unused but available distribution capacity. Plastim's ABC system does not allocate the costs of unused capacity to products so as not to burden the product costs of S3 and C5 with the cost of resources not used by these products. Instead, the system highlights the amount of unused capacity as a separate line item to alert managers to reduce these costs, such as by redeploying labor to other uses or laying off workers. Chapter 9 discusses issues related to unused capacity in more detail.

Design Decisions

ABC systems help managers to evaluate the effect of current product and process designs on activities and costs and to identify new designs to reduce costs. For example, design decisions that decrease the complexity of the mold reduce costs of design, but also materials, labor, machine setups, machine operations, and mold cleaning and maintenance because a less-complex design reduces scrap and the time for setups and operations of the molding machine. Plastim's customers may be willing to give up some features of the lens in exchange for a lower price. Note that Plastim's previous costing system, which used direct manufacturing labor-hours as the cost-allocation base for all indirect costs, would have mistakenly signaled that Plastim choose designs that most reduce direct manufacturing labor-hours. In fact, there is a weak cause-and-effect relationship between direct manufacturing labor-hours and indirect costs.

Planning and Managing Activities

Most managers implementing ABC systems for the first time start by analyzing actual costs to identify activity-cost pools and activity-cost rates. Managers then calculate a budgeted rate (as in the Plastim example) that they use for planning, making decisions, and managing activities. At year-end, managers compare budgeted costs and actual costs to evaluate how well activities were managed. Management accountants make adjustments for underallocated or overallocated indirect costs for each activity using methods described in Chapter 4. As activities and processes change, managers calculate new activity-cost rates.

We return to activity-based management in later chapters. Management decisions that use activity-based costing information are described in Chapter 6, where we discuss activity-based budgeting; in Chapter 11, where we discuss outsourcing and adding or dropping business segments; in Chapter 12, where we present reengineering and downsizing; in Chapter 13, where we evaluate alternative design choices to improve efficiency and reduce nonvalue-added costs; in Chapter 14, where we explore managing customer profitability; in Chapter 19, where we explain quality improvements; and in Chapter 20, where we describe how to evaluate suppliers.

DECISION POINT
How can ABC systems be used to manage better?

Activity-Based Costing and Department Costing Systems

LEARNING OBJECTIVE

Compare activity-based costing systems and department costing systems

...activity-based costing systems refine department costing systems into more-focused and homogenous cost pools

Companies often use costing systems that have features of ABC systems—such as multiple cost pools and multiple cost-allocation bases—but that do not emphasize individual activities. Many companies have evolved their costing systems from using a single indirect cost rate system to using separate indirect cost rates for each department (such as design, manufacturing, and distribution) or each subdepartment (such as machining and assembly departments within manufacturing) that often represent broad tasks. ABC systems, with their focus on specific activities, are a further refinement of department costing systems. In this section, we compare ABC systems and department costing systems.

Plastim uses the design department indirect cost rate to cost its design activity. To do so Plastim calculates the design activity rate by dividing total design department costs by total parts-square feet, a measure of the complexity of the mold and the driver of design department costs. Plastim does not find it worthwhile to calculate separate activity rates within the design department for the different design activities, such as designing products, making temporary molds, and designing processes. The complexity of a mold is an appropriate cost-allocation base for costs incurred in each design activity because design department costs are homogeneous with respect to this cost-allocation base.

In contrast, the manufacturing department identifies two activity cost pools—a setup cost pool and a machine operations cost pool—instead of a single manufacturing department overhead cost pool. It identifies these activity-cost pools for two reasons. First, each of these activities within manufacturing incurs significant costs and has a different cost driver, setup-hours for the setup cost pool and machine-hours for the machine operations cost pool. Second, the S3 and C5 lenses do not use resources from these two activity areas in the same proportion. For example, C5 uses 75% (1,500 ÷ 2,000) of the setup-hours but only 29.4% (3,750 ÷ 12,750) of the machine-hours. Using only machine-hours, say, to allocate all manufacturing department costs at Plastim would result in C5 being undercosted because it would not be charged for the significant amounts of setup resources it actually uses.

For the reasons we just explained, using department indirect-cost rates to allocate costs to products results in similar information as activity cost rates if (1) a single activity accounts for a sizable proportion of the department's costs; or (2) significant costs are incurred on different activities within a department, but each activity has the same cost driver and therefore cost-allocation base (as was the case in Plastim's design department). From a purely product costing standpoint, department and activity indirect-cost rates will also result in the same product costs if (1) significant costs are incurred for different activities with different cost-allocation bases within a department but (2) different products use resources from the different activity areas in the same proportions (for example, if C5 had used 65%, say, of the setup-hours and 65% of the machine-hours). In this case, though, not identifying activities and cost drivers within departments conceals activity cost information that would help managers manage costs and improve design and processes.

We close this section with a note of caution: Do not assume that because department costing systems require the creation of multiple indirect-cost pools that they properly recognize the drivers of costs within departments as well as how resources are used by products. As we have indicated, in many situations, department costing systems can be refined using ABC. Emphasizing activities leads to more-focused and homogeneous cost pools, aids in identifying cost-allocation bases for activities that have a better cause-and-effect relationship with the costs in activity-cost pools, and leads to better design and process decisions. But these benefits of an ABC system would need to be balanced against its costs and limitations.

> **DECISION POINT**
> When can department costing systems be used instead of ABC systems?

ABC in Service and Merchandising Companies

Although many early examples of ABC originated in manufacturing, managers also use ABC in service and merchandising companies. For instance, the Plastim example includes the application of ABC to a service activity—design—and to a merchandising activity—distribution. Companies such as USAA Federal Savings Bank, Braintree Hospital, BCTel in the telecommunications industry, and Union Pacific in the railroad industry have implemented some form of ABC system to identify profitable product mixes, improve efficiency, and satisfy customers. Similarly, many retail and wholesale companies—for example, Supervalu, a retailer and distributor of grocery store products, and Owens and Minor, a medical supplies distributor—have used ABC systems. As we describe in Chapter 14, a large number of financial services companies (as well as other companies) employ variations of ABC systems to analyze and improve the profitability of their customer interactions.

The widespread use of ABC systems in service and merchandising companies reinforces the idea that ABC systems are used by managers for strategic decisions rather than for inventory valuation. (Inventory valuation is fairly straightforward in merchandising companies and not needed in service companies.) Service companies, in particular, find great value from ABC because a vast majority of their cost structure is composed of indirect costs. After all, there are few direct costs when a bank makes a loan or when a representative answers a phone call at a call center. As we have seen, a major benefit of ABC is its ability to assign indirect costs to cost objects by identifying activities and cost drivers. As a result, ABC systems provide greater insight than traditional systems into the management of these indirect costs. The general approach to ABC in service and merchandising companies is similar to the ABC approach in manufacturing.

USAA Federal Savings Bank followed the approach described in this chapter when it implemented ABC in its banking operations. Managers calculated the cost rates of various activities, such as performing ATM transactions, opening and closing accounts, administering mortgages, and processing Visa transactions by dividing the cost of these activities by the time available to do them. Managers used these time-based rates to cost individual products, such as checking accounts, mortgages, and Visa cards, and to calculate the costs of supporting different types of customers. Information from this time-driven activity-based costing system helped USAA Federal Savings Bank to improve its processes and to identify profitable products and customer segments. Concepts in Action: Mayo Clinic Uses Time-Driven Activity-Based Costing to Reduce Costs and Improve Care describes how the Mayo Clinic has similarly benefited from ABC analysis.

Activity-based costing raises some interesting issues when it is applied to a public service institution, such as the U.S. Postal Service. The costs of delivering mail to remote locations are far greater than the costs of delivering mail within urban areas. However, for fairness and community-building reasons, the Postal Service does not charge higher prices to customers in remote areas. In this case, activity-based costing is valuable for understanding, managing, and reducing costs but not for pricing decisions.

CONCEPTS IN ACTION: Mayo Clinic Uses Time-Driven Activity-Based Costing to Reduce Costs and Improve Care

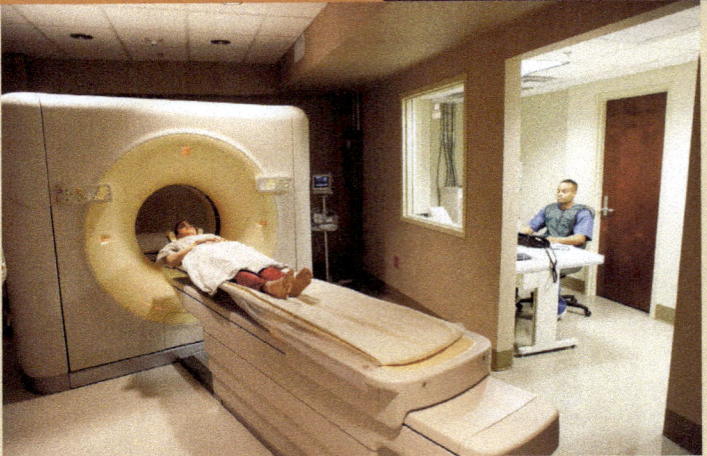

Fuse/Corbis/Getty Images

By 2024, $1 of every $5 spent in the United States will be on health care. Several medical centers, such as the Mayo Clinic in Rochester, Minnesota, are using time-driven activity-based costing (TDABC) to help bring accurate cost and value measurement practices into the health care delivery system.

TDABC assigns all of the organization's resource costs to cost objects using a framework that requires two sets of estimates. TDABC first calculates the cost of supplying resource capacity, such as a doctor's time. The total cost of resources—including personnel, supervision, insurance, space occupancy, technology, and supplies—is divided by the available capacity—the time available for doctors to do their work—to obtain the capacity cost rate. Next, TDABC uses the capacity cost rate to drive resource costs to cost objects, such as the number of patients seen, by estimating the demand for resource capacity (time) that the cost object requires.

Medical centers implementing TDABC have succeeded in reducing costs. For orthopedic procedures at the Mayo Clinic, the TDABC-modified process resulted in shorter stays for patients, a 24% decrease in patients discharged to expensive skilled nursing facilities, and a 15% decrease in cost. Follow-on improvements have included obtaining patient-reported outcomes from tablets and smartphones and eliminating major variations in the cost of prostheses and other supplies.

More broadly, health care providers implementing TDABC have found that better outcomes for patients often go hand in hand with lower total costs. For example, spending more on early detection and better diagnosis of disease reduces patient suffering and often leads to less-complex and less-expensive care. With the insights from TDABC, health care providers can utilize medical staff, equipment, facilities, and administrative resources far more efficiently; streamline the path of patients through the system; and select treatment approaches that improve outcomes while eliminating services that do not.

Sources: Derek A. Haas, Richard A. Helmers, March Rucci, Meredith Brady, and Robert S. Kaplan, "The Mayo Clinic Model for Running a Value-Improvement Program," HBR.org, October 22, 2015 (https://hbr.org/2015/10/the-mayo-clinic-model-for-running-a-value-improvement-program); Dan Mangan, "$1 of Every $5 Spent in US Will Be on Health Care," CNBC, July 28, 2015 (http://www.cnbc.com/2015/07/28/1-of-every-5-spent-in-us-will-be-on-health-care.html); Robert S. Kaplan and Michael E. Porter, "How to Solve the Cost Crisis in Health Care," *Harvard Business Review*, September 2011 (https://hbr.org/2011/09/how-to-solve-the-cost-crisis-in-health-care); Robert S. Kaplan and Steven R. Anderson, "The Innovation of Time-Driven Activity-Based Costing," *Journal of Cost Management*, 21, no. 2 (March–April 2007): 5–15.

PROBLEM FOR SELF-STUDY

Family Supermarkets (FS) has decided to increase the size of its Memphis store. It wants information about the profitability of individual product lines: soft drinks, fresh produce, and packaged food. FS provides the following data for 2017 for each product line:

	Soft Drinks	Fresh Produce	Packaged Food
Revenues	$317,400	$840,240	$483,960
Cost of goods sold	$240,000	$600,000	$360,000
Cost of bottles returned	$ 4,800	$ 0	$ 0
Number of purchase orders placed	144	336	144
Number of deliveries received	120	876	264
Hours of shelf-stocking time	216	2,160	1,080
Items sold	50,400	441,600	122,400

FS also provides the following information for 2017:

Activity (1)	Description of Activity (2)	Total Support Costs (3)	Cost-Allocation Base (4)
1. Bottle returns	Returning of empty bottles to store	$ 4,800	Direct tracing to soft-drink line
2. Ordering	Placing of orders for purchases	$ 62,400	624 purchase orders
3. Delivery	Physical delivery and receipt of merchandise	$100,800	1,260 deliveries
4. Shelf-stocking	Stocking of merchandise on store shelves and ongoing restocking	$ 69,120	3,456 hours of shelf-stocking time
5. Customer support	Assistance provided to customers, including checkout and bagging	$122,880	614,400 items sold
Total		$360,000	

Required

1. Family Supermarkets currently allocates store support costs (all costs other than cost of goods sold) to product lines on the basis of cost of goods sold of each product line. Calculate the operating income and operating income as a percentage of revenues for each product line.
2. If Family Supermarkets allocates store support costs (all costs other than cost of goods sold) to product lines using an ABC system, calculate the operating income and operating income as a percentage of revenues for each product line.
3. Comment on your answers in requirements 1 and 2.

Solution

1. The following table shows the operating income and operating income as a percentage of revenues for each product line. All store support costs (all costs other than cost of goods sold) are allocated to product lines using cost of goods sold of each product line as the cost-allocation base. Total store support costs equal $360,000 (cost of bottles returned, $4,800 + cost of purchase orders, $62,400 + cost of deliveries, $100,800 + cost of shelf-stocking, $69,120 + cost of customer support, $122,880). The allocation rate for store support costs = $360,000 ÷ $1,200,000 (soft drinks $240,000 + fresh produce $600,000 + packaged food, $360,000) = 30% of cost of goods sold. To allocate support costs to each product line, FS multiplies the cost of goods sold of each product line by 0.30.

	Soft Drinks	Fresh Produce	Packaged Food	Total
Revenues	$317,400	$840,240	$483,960	$1,641,600
Cost of goods sold	240,000	600,000	360,000	1,200,000
Store support cost ($240,000; $600,000; $360,000) × 0.30	72,000	180,000	108,000	360,000
Total costs	312,000	780,000	468,000	1,560,000
Operating income	$ 5,400	$ 60,240	$ 15,960	$ 81,600
Operating income ÷ Revenues	1.70%	7.17%	3.30%	4.97%

2. The ABC system identifies bottle-return costs as a direct cost because these costs can be traced to the soft-drink product line. FS then calculates cost-allocation rates for each activity area (as in Step 5 of the seven-step costing system, described earlier on page 186). The activity rates are as follows.

Activity (1)	Cost Hierarchy (2)	Total Costs (3)	Quantity of Cost-Allocation Base (4)	Overhead Allocation Rate (5) = (3) ÷ (4)
Ordering	Batch-level	$ 62,400	624 purchase orders	$100 per purchase order
Delivery	Batch-level	$100,800	1,260 deliveries	$80 per delivery
Shelf-stocking	Output unit–level	$ 69,120	3,456 shelf-stocking hours	$20 per stocking-hour
Customer support	Output unit–level	$122,880	614,400 items sold	$0.20 per item sold

Store support costs for each product line by activity are obtained by multiplying the total quantity of the cost-allocation base for each product line by the activity-cost rate. Operating income and operating income as a percentage of revenues for each product line are as follows:

	Soft Drinks	Fresh Produce	Packaged Food	Total
Revenues	$317,400	$840,240	$483,960	$1,641,600
Cost of goods sold	240,000	600,000	360,000	1,200,000
Bottle-return costs	4,800	0	0	4,800
Ordering costs	14,400	33,600	14,400	62,400
(144; 336; 144) purchase orders × $100				
Delivery costs				
(120; 876; 264) deliveries × $80	9,600	70,080	21,120	100,800
Shelf-stocking costs	4,320	43,200	21,600	69,120
(216; 2,160; 1,080) stocking-hours × $20				
Customer-support costs				
(50,400; 441,600; 122,400) items sold × $0.20	10,080	88,320	24,480	122,880
Total costs	283,200	835,200	441,600	1,560,000
Operating income	$ 34,200	$ 5,040	$ 42,360	$ 81,600
Operating income ÷ Revenues	10.78%	0.60%	8.75%	4.97%

3. Managers believe the ABC system is more credible than the simple costing system. The ABC system distinguishes the different types of activities at FS more precisely. It also tracks more accurately how individual product lines use resources. Rankings of relative profitability—operating income as a percentage of revenues—of the three product lines under the simple costing system and under the ABC system are as follows.

Simple Costing System		ABC System	
1. Fresh produce	7.17%	1. Soft drinks	10.78%
2. Packaged food	3.30%	2. Packaged food	8.75%
3. Soft drinks	1.70%	3. Fresh produce	0.60%

The percentage of revenues, cost of goods sold, and activity costs for each product line are as follows.

	Soft Drinks	Fresh Produce	Packaged Food
Revenues	19.34%	51.18%	29.48%
Cost of goods sold	20.00	50.00	30.00
Bottle returns	100.00	0	0
Activity areas:			
Ordering	23.08	53.84	23.08
Delivery	9.53	69.52	20.95
Shelf-stocking	6.25	62.50	31.25
Customer support	8.20	71.88	19.92

Soft drinks have fewer deliveries and require less shelf-stocking time and customer support than either fresh produce or packaged food. Most major soft-drink suppliers deliver merchandise to the store shelves and stock the shelves themselves. In contrast, the fresh produce area has the most deliveries and consumes a large percentage of shelf-stocking time. It also has the highest number of individual sales items and so requires the most customer support. The simple costing system assumed that each product line used the resources in each activity area in the same ratio as their respective individual cost of goods sold to total cost of goods sold. Clearly, this assumption is incorrect. Relative to cost of goods sold, soft drinks and packaged food use fewer resources while fresh produce uses more resources. As a result, the ABC system reduces the costs assigned to soft drinks and packaged food and increases the costs assigned to fresh produce. The simple costing system is an example of averaging that is too broad.

FS managers can use the ABC information to guide decisions such as how to allocate a planned increase in floor space. An increase in the percentage of space allocated to soft drinks is warranted. Note, however, that ABC information is only one input into decisions about shelf-space allocation. In many situations, companies cannot make product decisions in isolation but must consider the effect that dropping or de-emphasizing a product might have on customer demand for other products. For example, FS will have a minimum limit on the shelf space allocated to fresh produce because reducing the choice of fresh produce will lead to customers not shopping at FS, resulting in loss of sales of other, more profitable products.

Pricing decisions can also be made in a more informed way with ABC information. For example, suppose a competitor announces a 5% reduction in soft-drink prices. Given the 10.78% margin FS currently earns on its soft-drink product line, it has flexibility to reduce prices and still make a profit on this product line. In contrast, the simple costing system erroneously implied that soft drinks only had a 1.70% margin, leaving little room to counter a competitor's pricing initiatives.

DECISION POINTS

The following question-and-answer format summarizes the chapter's learning objectives. Each decision presents a key question related to a learning objective. The guidelines are the answer to that question.

Decision	Guidelines
1. When does product undercosting or overcosting occur?	Product undercosting (overcosting) occurs when a product or service is reported to have a low (high) cost but consumes a high (low) level of resources. Broad averaging, or peanut-butter costing, a common cause of undercosting or overcosting, is the result of using broad averages that uniformly assign, or spread, the cost of resources to products when the individual products use those resources in a nonuniform way. Product-cost cross-subsidization exists when one undercosted (overcosted) product results in at least one other product being overcosted (undercosted).
2. How do managers refine a costing system?	Refining a costing system means making changes that result in cost numbers better measuring the way different cost objects, such as products, use different amounts of resources of the company. These changes can require additional direct-cost tracing, the choice of more-homogeneous indirect-cost pools, or the use of cost drivers as cost-allocation bases.
3. What is the difference between the design of a simple costing system and an activity-based costing (ABC) system?	The ABC system differs from the simple system by its fundamental focus on activities. The ABC system typically has more homogeneous indirect-cost pools than the simple system, and more cost drivers are used as cost-allocation bases.
4. What is a cost hierarchy?	A cost hierarchy categorizes costs into different cost pools on the basis of the different types of cost-allocation bases or different degrees of difficulty in determining cause-and-effect (or benefits-received) relationships. A four-part hierarchy to cost products consists of output unit–level costs, batch-level costs, product-sustaining or service-sustaining costs, and facility-sustaining costs.
5. How do managers cost products or services using ABC systems?	In ABC, costs of activities are used to assign costs to other cost objects such as products or services based on the activities the products or services consume.

Decision	Guidelines
6. What should managers consider when deciding to implement ABC systems?	ABC systems are likely to yield the most decision-making benefits when indirect costs are a high percentage of total costs or when products and services make diverse demands on indirect resources. The main costs of ABC systems are the difficulties of the measurements necessary to implement and update the systems.
7. How can ABC systems be used to manage better?	Activity-based management (ABM) is a management method of decision making that uses ABC information to satisfy customers and improve profits. ABC systems are used for such management decisions as pricing, product-mix, cost reduction, process improvement, product and process redesign, and planning and managing activities.
8. When can department costing systems be used instead of ABC systems?	Activity-based costing systems are a refinement of department costing systems into more-focused and homogeneous cost pools. Cost information in department costing systems approximates cost information in ABC systems only when each department has a single activity (or a single activity accounts for a significant proportion of department costs) or a single cost driver for different activities or when different products use the different activities of the department in the same proportions.

TERMS TO LEARN

This chapter and the Glossary at the end of this book contain definitions of the following important terms:

- activity
- activity-based costing (ABC)
- activity-based management (ABM)
- batch-level costs
- cost hierarchy
- facility-sustaining costs
- output unit–level costs
- product-cost cross-subsidization
- product overcosting
- product-sustaining costs
- product undercosting
- refined costing system
- service-sustaining costs

ASSIGNMENT MATERIAL

Pearson MyLab Accounting

Questions

5-1 What is broad averaging, and what consequences can it have on costs?

5-2 Inaccurate costing can result in two deviations. Name the two deviations and explain how they can impact a business.

5-3 What is costing system refinement? Describe three guidelines for refinement.

5-4 What are the fundamental cost objects in activity-based costing? How does activity-based costing work?

5-5 How can a cost hierarchy lead to a more accurate costing system?

5-6 Which levels of cost hierarchy (under activity-based costing) are not used in simple costing systems and why are they important?

5-7 Differentiate between simple costing systems and ABC systems.

5-8 How can ABC help with cost reduction and process improvement decisions?

5-9 "The cost of cost objects under simple costing systems and under activity-based costing are never the same." Do you agree? Explain.

5-10 Describe the main barriers for adopting an ABC system.

5-11 What are the main behavioral issues in implementing ABC systems?

5-12 Explain why ABC is equally important for both manufacturing and service companies.

5-13 "Activity-based costing is providing more accurate and detailed information and should replace simple costing." Do you agree? Explain.

5-14 What are the main factors determining the number of indirect-cost pools in a costing system, to increase the accuracy of product or service costs? Explain.

5-15 The total annual production cost of a manufacturing company that produces three different USB devices is $10,000,000. The manager of the company states that the contribution margins of all three products guarantee and justify their productions and, therefore, there is no need to adopt ABC as the total manufacturing costs of the company would remain the same if the company did adopt ABC. How can you convince the manager to change his mind?

Multiple-Choice Questions

5-16 Conroe Company is reviewing the data provided by its management accounting system. Which of the following statements is/are correct?

I. A cost driver is a causal factor that increases the total cost of a cost object.
II. Cost drivers may be volume based or activity based.
III. Cost drivers are normally the largest cost in the manufacturing process.

1. I, II, and III are correct.
2. I and II only are correct.
3. I only is correct.
4. II and III only are correct.

5-17 Nobis Company uses an ABC system. Which of the following statements is/are correct with respect to ABC?

I. Departmental costing systems are a refinement of ABC systems.
II. ABC systems are useful in manufacturing, but not in merchandising or service industries.
III. ABC systems can eliminate cost distortions because ABC develops cost drivers that have a cause-and-effect relationship with the activities performed.

1. I, II, and III are correct.
2. II and III only are correct.
3. III only is correct.
4. None of the listed choices is correct.

©2016 DeVry/Becker Educational Development Corp. All Rights Reserved.

Exercises

5-18 Cost hierarchy. SharpPitch, Inc., manufactures karaoke machines for several well-known companies. The machines differ significantly in their complexity and their manufacturing batch sizes. The following costs were incurred in 2014:

a. Indirect manufacturing labor costs such as supervision that supports direct manufacturing labor, $950,000.
b. Procurement costs of placing purchase orders, receiving materials, and paying suppliers related to the number of purchase orders placed, $675,000.
c. Cost of indirect materials, $180,000.
d. Costs incurred to set up machines each time a different product needs to be manufactured, $450,000.
e. Designing processes, drawing process charts, and making engineering process changes for products, $315,000.
f. Machine-related overhead costs such as depreciation, maintenance, and production engineering, $975,500. (These resources relate to the activity of running the machines.)
g. Plant management, plant rent, and plant insurance, $578,000.

1. Classify each of the preceding costs as output unit-level, batch-level, product-sustaining, or facility-sustaining. Explain each answer.
2. Consider two types of karaoke machines made by SharpPitch, Inc. One machine, designed for professional use, is complex to make and is produced in many batches. The other machine, designed for home use, is simple to make and is produced in few batches. Suppose that SharpPitch needs the same number of machine-hours to make each type of karaoke machine and that SharpPitch allocates all overhead costs using machine-hours as the only allocation base. How, if at all, would the machines be miscosted? Briefly explain why.
3. How is the cost hierarchy helpful to SharpPitch in managing its business?

5-19 ABC, cost hierarchy, service. (CMA, adapted) CoreTech Laboratories does heat testing (HT) and stress testing (ST) on materials and operates at capacity. Under its current simple costing system, CoreTech aggregates all operating costs of $1,800,000 into a single overhead cost pool. CoreTech calculates a rate per test-hour of $20 ($1,800,000 ÷ 90,000 total test-hours). HT uses 50,000 test-hours, and ST uses 40,000 test-hours. Gary Celeste, CoreTech's controller, believes that there is enough variation in test procedures and cost structures to establish separate costing and billing rates for HT and ST. The market for test services is becoming competitive. Without this information, any miscosting and mispricing of its services could cause CoreTech to lose business. Celeste divides CoreTech's costs into four activity-cost categories.

a. Direct-labor costs, $276,000. These costs can be directly traced to HT, $204,000, and ST, $72,000.
b. Equipment-related costs (rent, maintenance, energy, and so on), $495,000. These costs are allocated to HT and ST on the basis of test-hours.
c. Setup costs, $630,000. These costs are allocated to HT and ST on the basis of the number of setup-hours required. HT requires 15,000 setup-hours, and ST requires 6,000 setup-hours.
d. Costs of designing tests, $399,000. These costs are allocated to HT and ST on the basis of the time required for designing the tests. HT requires 4,000 hours, and ST requires 2,000 hours.

Required

1. Classify each activity cost as output unit-level, batch-level, product- or service-sustaining, or facility-sustaining. Explain each answer.
2. Calculate the cost per test-hour for HT and ST. Explain briefly the reasons why these numbers differ from the $20 per test-hour that CoreTech calculated using its simple costing system.
3. Explain the accuracy of the product costs calculated using the simple costing system and the ABC system. How might CoreTech's management use the cost hierarchy and ABC information to better manage its business?

5-20 Alternative allocation bases for a professional services firm. The Walliston Group (WG) provides tax advice to multinational firms. WG charges clients for (a) direct professional time (at an hourly rate) and (b) support services (at 30% of the direct professional costs billed). The three professionals in WG and their rates per professional hour are as follows:

Professional	Billing Rate per Hour
Max Walliston	$640
Alexa Boutin	220
Jacob Abbington	100

WG has just prepared the May 2017 bills for two clients. The hours of professional time spent on each client are as follows:

	Hours per Client	
Professional	San Antonio Dominion	Amsterdam Enterprises
Walliston	26	4
Boutin	5	14
Abbington	39	52
Total	70	70

Required

1. What amounts did WG bill to San Antonio Dominion and Amsterdam Enterprises for May 2017?
2. Suppose support services were billed at $75 per professional labor-hour (instead of 30% of professional labor costs). How would this change affect the amounts WG billed to the two clients for May 2017? Comment on the differences between the amounts billed in requirements 1 and 2.
3. How would you determine whether professional labor costs or professional labor-hours is the more appropriate allocation base for WG's support services?

5-21 Plant-wide, department, and ABC indirect-cost rates. Automotive Products (AP) designs and produces automotive parts. In 2017, actual variable manufacturing overhead is $308,600. AP's simple costing system allocates variable manufacturing overhead to its three customers based on machine-hours and prices its contracts based on full costs. One of its customers has regularly complained of being charged noncompetitive prices, so AP's controller Devon Smith realizes that it is time to examine the consumption of overhead resources more closely. He knows that there are three main departments that consume overhead resources: design, production, and engineering. Interviews with the department personnel and examination of time records yield the following detailed information:

Activity-Based Costing and Activity-Based Management

	A	B	C	D	E	F
1				Usage of Cost Drivers by Customer Contract		
2	Department	Cost Driver	Manufacturing Overhead in 2017	United Motors	Holden Motors	Leland Auto
3	Design	CAD–design–hours	$ 39,000	110	200	80
4	Production	Engineering–hours	29,600	70	60	240
5	Engineering	Machine–hours	240,000	120	2,800	1,080
6	Total		$308,600			

Required

1. Compute the manufacturing overhead allocated to each customer in 2017 using the simple costing system that uses machine-hours as the allocation base.
2. Compute the manufacturing overhead allocated to each customer in 2017 using department-based manufacturing overhead rates.
3. Comment on your answers in requirements 1 and 2. Which customer do you think was complaining about being overcharged in the simple system? If the new department-based rates are used to price contracts, which customer(s) will be unhappy? How would you respond to these concerns?
4. How else might AP use the information available from its department-by-department analysis of manufacturing overhead costs?
5. AP's managers are wondering if they should further refine the department-by-department costing system into an ABC system by identifying different activities within each department. Under what conditions would it not be worthwhile to further refine the department costing system into an ABC system?

5-22 Plant-wide, department, and activity-cost rates. Triumph Trophies makes trophies and plaques and operates at capacity. Triumph does large custom orders, such as the participant trophies for the Minnetonka Little League. The controller has asked you to compare plant-wide, department, and activity-based cost allocation.

Triumph Trophies Budgeted Information for the Year Ended November 30, 2014

Forming Department	Trophies	Plaques	Total
Direct materials	$26,000	$22,500	$48,500
Direct manufacturing labor	31,200	18,000	49,200
Overhead costs			
Setup			24,000
General overhead			20,772
Assembly Department	**Trophies**	**Plaques**	**Total**
Direct materials	$ 5,200	$18,750	$23,950
Direct manufacturing labor	15,600	21,000	36,600
Overhead costs			
Set up			46,000
Supervision			21,920

Other information follows:
Setup costs in each department vary with the number of batches processed in each department. The budgeted number of batches for each product line in each department is as follows:

	Trophies	Plaques
Forming department	40	116
Assembly department	43	103

Supervision costs in each department vary with direct manufacturing labor costs in each department

Required

1. Calculate the budgeted cost of trophies and plaques based on a single plant-wide overhead rate, if total overhead is allocated based on total direct costs
2. Calculate the budgeted cost of trophies and plaques based on departmental overhead rates, where forming department overhead costs are allocated based on direct manufacturing labor costs of the forming department and assembly department overhead costs are allocated based on total direct costs of the assembly department.

3. Calculate the budgeted cost of trophies and plaques if Triumph allocates overhead costs in each department using activity-based costing.
4. Explain how the disaggregation of information could improve or reduce decision quality.

5-23 ABC, process costing. Parker Company produces mathematical and financial calculators and operates at capacity. Data related to the two products are presented here:

	Mathematical	Financial
Annual production in units	60,000	120,000
Direct material costs	$240,000	$480,000
Direct manufacturing labor costs	$ 75,000	$150,000
Direct manufacturing labor-hours	5,000	10,000
Machine-hours	40,000	80,000
Number of production runs	60	60
Inspection hours	1,500	750

Total manufacturing overhead costs are as follows:

	Total
Machining costs	$720,000
Setup costs	150,000
Inspection costs	135,000

Required

1. Choose a cost driver for each overhead cost pool and calculate the manufacturing overhead cost per unit for each product.
2. Compute the manufacturing cost per unit for each product.
3. How might Parker's managers use the new cost information from its activity-based costing system to better manage its business?

5-24 Department costing, service company. CKM is an architectural firm that designs and builds buildings. It prices each job on a cost plus 20% basis. Overhead costs in 2017 are $4,011,780. CKM's simple costing system allocates overhead costs to its jobs based on number of jobs. There were three jobs in 2017. One customer, Sanders, has complained that the cost of its building in Chicago was not competitive. As a result, the controller has initiated a detailed review of the overhead allocation to determine if overhead costs are charged to jobs in proportion to consumption of overhead resources by jobs. She gathers the following information:

			Quantity of Cost Drivers Used by Each Project		
Department	Cost Driver	Overhead Costs in 2017	Sanders	Hanley	Stanley
Design	Design department hours	$1,500,000	1,000	5,000	4,000
Engineering	Number of engineering hours	$ 500,030	2,000	2,000	2,200
Construction	Labor-hours	$2,011,750	20,800	21,500	19,600
		$4,011,780			

Required

1. Compute the overhead allocated to each project in 2017 using the simple costing system.
2. Compute the overhead allocated to each project in 2017 using department overhead cost rates.
3. Do you think Sanders had a valid reason for dissatisfaction with the cost? How does the allocation, based on department rates, change costs for each project?
4. What value, if any, would CKM get by allocating costs of each department based on the activities done in that department?

5-25 Activity-based costing, service company. Speediprint Corporation owns a small printing press that prints leaflets, brochures, and advertising materials. Speediprint classifies its various printing jobs as standard jobs or special jobs. Speediprint's simple job-costing system has two direct-cost categories (direct materials and direct labor) and a single indirect-cost pool. Speediprint operates at capacity and allocates all indirect costs using printing machine-hours as the allocation base.

Speediprint is concerned about the accuracy of the costs assigned to standard and special jobs and therefore is planning to implement an activity-based costing system. Speediprint's ABC system would have the same direct-cost categories as its simple costing system. However, instead of a single indirect-cost pool there would now be six categories for assigning indirect costs: design, purchasing, setup, printing machine operations, marketing, and administration. To see how activity-based costing would affect the costs of standard and special jobs, Speediprint collects the following information for the fiscal year 2017 that just ended.

	A	B	C	D	E F G H
1		Standard Job	Special Job	Total	Cause-and-Effect Relationship Between Allocation Base and Activity Cost
2	Number of printing jobs	400	200		
3	Price per job	$ 600	$ 750		
4	Cost of supplies per job	$ 100	$ 125		
5	Direct labor costs per job	$ 90	$ 100		
6	Printing machine-hours per job	10	10		
7	Cost of printing machine operations			$ 75,000	Indirect costs of operating printing machines
8					increase with printing machine-hours
9	Setup-hours per job	4	7		
10	Setup costs			$ 45,000	Indirect setup costs increase with setup-hours
11	Total number of purchase orders	400	500		
12	Purchase order costs			$ 18,000	Indirect purchase order costs increase with
13					number of purchase orders
14	Design costs	$4,000	$16,000	$ 20,000	Design costs are allocated to standard and special
15					jobs based on a special study of the design department
16	Marketing costs as a percentage of revenues	5%	5%	$ 19,500	
17	Administration costs			$ 24,000	Demand for administrative resources increases with direct labor costs

Required

1. Calculate the cost of a standard job and a special job under the simple costing system.
2. Calculate the cost of a standard job and a special job under the activity-based costing system.
3. Compare the costs of a standard job and a special job in requirements 1 and 2. Why do the simple and activity-based costing systems differ in the cost of a standard job and a special job?
4. How might Speediprint use the new cost information from its activity-based costing system to better manage its business?

5-26 Activity-based costing, manufacturing. Decorative Doors, Inc., produces two types of doors, interior and exterior. The company's simple costing system has two direct-cost categories (materials and labor) and one indirect-cost pool. The simple costing system allocates indirect costs on the basis of machine-hours. Recently, the owners of Decorative Doors have been concerned about a decline in the market share for their interior doors, usually their biggest seller. Information related to Decorative Doors production for the most recent year follows:

	Interior	Exterior
Units sold	3,200	1,800
Selling price	$ 125	$ 200
Direct material cost per unit	$ 30	$ 45
Direct manufacturing labor cost per hour	$ 16	$ 16
Direct manufacturing labor-hours per unit	1.50	2.25
Production runs	40	85
Material moves	72	168
Machine setups	45	155
Machine-hours	5,500	4,500
Number of inspections	250	150

The owners have heard of other companies in the industry that are now using an activity-based costing system and are curious how an ABC system would affect their product costing decisions. After analyzing the indirect-cost pool for Decorative Doors, the owners identify six activities as generating indirect costs: production scheduling, material handling, machine setup, assembly, inspection, and marketing. Decorative Doors collected the following data related to the indirect-cost activities:

Activity	Activity Cost	Activity Cost Driver
Production scheduling	$95,000	Production runs
Material handling	$45,000	Material moves
Machine setup	$25,000	Machine setups
Assembly	$60,000	Machine-hours
Inspection	$ 8,000	Number of inspections

Marketing costs were determined to be 3% of the sales revenue for each type of door.

Required

1. Calculate the cost of an interior door and an exterior door under the existing simple costing system.
2. Calculate the cost of an interior door and an exterior door under an activity-based costing system.
3. Compare the costs of the doors in requirements 1 and 2. Why do the simple and activity-based costing systems differ in the cost of an interior door and an exterior door?
4. How might Decorative Doors, Inc., use the new cost information from its activity-based costing system to address the declining market share for interior doors?

5-27 ABC, retail product-line profitability. Henderson Supermarkets (HS) operates at capacity and decides to apply ABC analysis to three product lines: baked goods, milk and fruit juice, and frozen foods. It identifies four activities and their activity cost rates as follows:

Ordering	$ 104 per purchase order
Delivery and receipt of merchandise	$ 80 per delivery
Shelf-stocking	$ 22 per hour
Customer support and assistance	$0.25 per item sold

The revenues, cost of goods sold, store support costs, activities that account for the store support costs, and activity-area usage of the three product lines are as follows:

	Baked Goods	Milk and Fruit Juice	Frozen Products
Financial data			
Revenues	$63,000	$68,500	$54,000
Cost of goods sold	$39,000	$52,000	$36,000
Store support	$11,700	$15,600	$10,800
Activity-area usage (cost-allocation base)			
Ordering (purchase orders)	21	18	13
Delivery (deliveries)	88	32	26
Shelf-stocking (hours)	185	176	38
Customer support (items sold)	12,200	16,400	7,600

Under its simple costing system, HS allocated support costs to products at the rate of 30% of cost of goods sold.

Required

1. Use the simple costing system to prepare a product-line profitability report for HS.
2. Use the ABC system to prepare a product-line profitability report for HS.
3. What new insights does the ABC system in requirement 2 provide to HS managers?

5-28 ABC, wholesale, customer profitability. Ramirez Wholesalers operates at capacity and sells furniture items to four department-store chains (customers). Mr. Ramirez commented, "We apply ABC to determine product-line profitability. The same ideas apply to customer profitability, and we should find out our customer profitability as well." Ramirez Wholesalers sends catalogs to corporate purchasing departments on a monthly basis. The customers are entitled to return unsold merchandise within a six-month period from the purchase date and receive a full purchase price refund. The following data were collected from last year's operations:

	Chain			
	1	2	3	4
Gross sales	$50,000	$30,000	$100,000	$70,000
Sales returns:				
Number of items	100	26	60	40
Amount	$10,000	$ 5,000	$ 7,000	$ 6,000
Number of orders:				
Regular	40	150	50	70
Rush	10	50	10	30

Ramirez has calculated the following activity rates:

Activity	Cost-Driver Rate
Regular order processing	$20 per regular order
Rush order processing	$100 per rush order
Returned items processing	$10 per item
Catalogs and customer support	$1,000 per customer

1. Customers pay the transportation costs. The cost of goods sold averages 80% of sales.
2. Determine the contribution to profit from each chain last year. Comment on your solution.

5-29 Activity-based costing. The job costing system at Sheri's Custom Framing has five indirect-cost pools (purchasing, material handling, machine maintenance, product inspection, and packaging). The company is in the process of bidding on two jobs: Job 215, an order of 15 intricate personalized frames, and Job 325, an order of 6 standard personalized frames. The controller wants you to compare overhead allocated under the current simple job-costing system and a newly designed activity-based job-costing system. Total budgeted costs in each indirect-cost pool and the budgeted quantity of activity driver are as follows:

	Budgeted Overhead	Activity Driver	Budgeted Quantity of Activity Driver
Purchasing	$ 35,000	Purchase orders processed	2,000
Material handling	43,750	Material moves	5,000
Machine maintenance	118,650	Machine-hours	10,500
Product inspection	9,450	Inspections	1,200
Packaging	19,950	Units produced	3,800
	$226,800		

Information related to Job 215 and Job 325 follows. Job 215 incurs more batch-level costs because it uses more types of materials that need to be purchased, moved, and inspected relative to Job 325.

	Job 215	Job 325
Number of purchase orders	25	8
Number of material moves	10	4
Machine-hours	40	60
Number of inspections	9	3
Units produced	15	6

1. Compute the total overhead allocated to each job under a simple costing system, where overhead is allocated based on machine-hours.
2. Compute the total overhead allocated to each job under an activity-based costing system using the appropriate activity drivers.
3. Explain why Sheri's Custom Framing might favor the ABC job-costing system over the simple job-costing system, especially in its bidding process.

5-30 ABC, product costing at banks, cross-subsidization. Legion Bank (LB) is examining the profitability of its Star Account, a combined savings and checking account. Depositors receive a 6% annual interest rate on their average deposit. LB earns an interest rate spread of 3% (the difference between the rate at which it lends money and the rate it pays depositors) by lending money for home-loan purposes at 9%. Thus, LB would gain $150 on the interest spread if a depositor had an average Star Account balance of $5,000 in 2017 ($5,000 × 3% = $150).

The Star Account allows depositors unlimited use of services such as deposits, withdrawals, checking accounts, and foreign currency drafts. Depositors with Star Account balances of $1,000 or more receive unlimited free use of services. Depositors with minimum balances of less than $1,000 pay a $25-a-month service fee for their Star Account.

LB recently conducted an activity-based costing study of its services. It assessed the following costs for six individual services. The use of these services in 2017 by three customers is as follows:

	Activity-Based Cost per "Transaction"	Lindell	Welker	Colston
Deposit/withdrawal with teller	$2.75	46	53	5
Deposit/withdrawal with automatic teller machine (ATM)	0.75	14	25	12
Deposit/withdrawal on prearranged monthly basis	0.6	0	16	55
Bank checks written	8.5	10	3	4
Foreign currency drafts	12.25	7	2	7
Inquiries about account balance	1.8	8	14	5
Average Star Account balance for 2017		$1,500	$800	$26,600

Assume Lindell and Colston always maintain a balance above $1,000, whereas Welker always has a balance below $1,000.

Required

1. Compute the 2017 profitability of the Lindell, Welker, and Colston Star Accounts at LB.
2. Why might LB worry about the profitability of individual customers if the Star Account product offering is profitable as a whole?
3. What changes would you recommend for LB's Star Account?

Problems

5-31 Job costing with single direct-cost category, single indirect-cost pool, law firm. Bradley Associates is a recently formed law partnership. Emmit Harrington, the managing partner of Bradley Associates, has just finished a tense phone call with Martin Omar, president of Campa Coal. Omar strongly complained about the price Bradley charged for some legal work done for Campa Coal.

Harrington also received a phone call from its only other client (St. Edith's Glass), which was very pleased with both the quality of the work and the price charged on its most recent job.

Bradley Associates operates at capacity and uses a cost-based approach to pricing (billing) each job. Currently it uses a simple costing system with a single direct-cost category (professional labor-hours) and a single indirect-cost pool (general support). Indirect costs are allocated to cases on the basis of professional labor-hours per case. The job files show the following:

	Campa Coal	St. Edith's Glass
Professional labor	150 hours	100 hours

Professional labor costs at Bradley Associates are $80 an hour. Indirect costs are allocated to cases at $100 an hour. Total indirect costs in the most recent period were $25,000.

Required

1. Why is it important for Bradley Associates to understand the costs associated with individual jobs?
2. Compute the costs of the Campa Coal and St. Edith's Glass jobs using Bradley's simple costing system.

5-32 Job costing with multiple direct-cost categories, single indirect-cost pool, law firm (continuation of 5-31). Harrington asks his assistant to collect details on those costs included in the $25,000 indirect-cost pool that can be traced to each individual job. After analysis, Bradley is able to reclassify $15,000 of the $25,000 as direct costs:

Other Direct Costs	Campa Coal	St. Edith's Glass
Research support labor	$1,800	$ 3,850
Computer time	400	1,600
Travel and allowances	700	4,200
Telephones/faxes	250	1,200
Photocopying	300	700
Total	$3,450	$11,550

Harrington decides to calculate the costs of each job as if Bradley had used six direct-cost pools and a single indirect-cost pool. The single indirect-cost pool would have $10,000 of costs and would be allocated to each case using the professional labor-hours base.

Required

1. Calculate the revised indirect-cost allocation rate per professional labor-hour for Bradley Associates when total indirect costs are $10,000.
2. Compute the costs of the Campa and St. Edith's jobs if Bradley Associates had used its refined costing system with multiple direct-cost categories and one indirect-cost pool.
3. Compare the costs of Campa and St. Edith's jobs in requirement 2 with those in requirement 2 of Problem 5-31. Comment on the results.

5-33 Job costing with multiple direct-cost categories, multiple indirect-cost pools, law firm (continuation of 5-31 and 5-32). Bradley has two classifications of professional staff: partners and associates. Harrington asks his assistant to examine the relative use of partners and associates on the recent Campa Coal and St. Edith's jobs. The Campa job used 50 partner-hours and 100 associate-hours. The St. Edith's job used 75 partner-hours and 25 associate-hours. Therefore, totals of the two jobs together were 125 partner-hours and 125 associate-hours. Harrington decides to examine how using separate direct-cost rates for partners and associates and using separate indirect-cost pools for partners and associates would have affected the costs of the Campa and St. Edith's jobs. Indirect costs in each indirect-cost pool would be allocated on the basis of total hours of that category of professional labor. From the total indirect-cost pool of $10,000, $6,000 is attributable to the activities of partners and $4,000 is attributable to the activities of associates. The rates per category of professional labor are as follows:

Category of Professional Labor	Direct Cost per Hour	Indirect Cost per Hour
Partner	$100	$6,000 ÷ 125 hours = $48
Associate	$ 60	$4,000 ÷ 125 hours = $32

Required

1. Compute the costs of the Campa and St. Edith's cases using Bradley's further refined system, with multiple direct-cost categories and multiple indirect-cost pools.
2. For what decisions might Bradley Associates find it more useful to use this job-costing approach rather than the approaches in Problem 5-31 or 5-32?

5-34 First stage allocation, activity-based costing, manufacturing sector. Marshall's Devices uses activity-based costing to allocate overhead costs to customer orders for pricing purposes. Many customer orders are won through competitive bidding. Direct material and direct manufacturing labor costs are traced directly to each order. Marshall's Devices direct manufacturing labor rate is $25 per hour. The company reports the following yearly overhead costs:

Wages and salaries	$ 600,000
Depreciation	72,000
Rent	128,000
Other overhead	280,000
Total overhead costs	$1,080,000

Marshall's Devices has established four activity cost pools:

Activity Cost Pool	Activity Measure	Budgeted Total Activity for the Year
Direct manufacturing labor support	Number of direct manufacturing labor-hours	32,000 direct manufacturing labor-hours
Order processing	Number of customer orders	440 orders
Design support	Number of custom design-hours	2,500 custom design-hours
Other	Facility-sustaining costs allocated to orders based on direct manufacturing labor-hours	32,000 direct manufacturing labor-hours

Some customer orders require more complex designs, while others need simple designs. Marshall estimates that it will do 100 complex designs during a year, which will each take 13 hours for a total of 1,300 design-hours. It estimates it will do 150 simple designs, which will each take 8 hours for a total of 1,200 design-hours.

Paul Napoli, Marshall's Devices' controller, has prepared the following estimates for distribution of the overhead costs across the four activity cost pools:

	Direct Manufacturing Labor Support	Order Processing	Design Support	Other	Total
Wages	35%	30%	25%	10%	100%
Depreciation	20%	15%	15%	50%	100%
Rent	25%	30%	15%	30%	100%
Other	25%	25%	40%	10%	100%

Order 277100 consists of six different metal products. Four products require a complex design and two require a simple design. Order 277100 requires $5,500 of direct materials and 100 direct manufacturing labor-hours.

Required

1. Allocate the overhead costs to each activity cost pool. Calculate the activity rate for each pool.
2. Determine the cost of Order 277100.
3. How does activity-based costing enhance Marshall's Devices' ability to price its orders? Suppose Marshall's Devices used a traditional costing system to allocate all overhead costs to orders on the basis of direct manufacturing labor-hours. How might this have affected Marshall's Devices' pricing decisions?
4. When designing its activity-based costing system, Marshall uses time-driven activity-based costing (TDABC) system for its design department. What does this approach allow Marshall to do? How would the cost of Order 277100 have been different if Marshall has used the number of customer designs rather than the number of custom design-hours to allocate costs to different customer orders? Which cost driver do you prefer for design support? Why?

5-35 First-stage allocation, time-driven activity-based costing, service sector. LawnCare USA provides lawn care and landscaping services to commercial clients. LawnCare USA uses activity-based costing to bid on jobs and to evaluate their profitability. LawnCare USA reports the following budgeted annual costs:

Wages and salaries	$360,000
Depreciation	72,000
Supplies	120,000
Other overhead	288,000
Total overhead costs	$840,000

John Gilroy, controller of LawnCare USA, has established four activity cost pools and the following budgeted activity for each cost pool:

Activity Cost Pool	Activity Measure	Total Activity for the Year
Estimating jobs	Number of job estimates	250 estimates
Lawn care	Number of direct labor-hours	10,000 direct labor-hours
Landscape design	Number of design hours	500 design hours
Other	Facility-sustaining costs that are not allocated to jobs	Not applicable

Gilroy estimates that LawnCare USA's costs are distributed to the activity-cost pools as follows:

	Estimating Jobs	Lawn Care	Landscape Design	Other	Total
Wages and salaries	5%	70%	15%	10%	100%
Depreciation	10%	65%	10%	15%	100%
Supplies	0%	100%	0%	0%	100%
Other overhead	15%	50%	20%	15%	100%

Sunset Office Park, a new development in a nearby community, has contacted LawnCare USA to provide an estimate on landscape design and annual lawn maintenance. The job is estimated to require a single landscape design requiring 40 design hours in total and 250 direct labor-hours annually. LawnCare USA has a policy of pricing estimates at 150% of cost.

Required

1. Allocate LawnCare USA's costs to the activity-cost pools and determine the activity rate for each pool.
2. Estimate total cost for the Sunset Office Park job. How much would LawnCare USA bid to perform the job?
3. LawnCare USA does 30 landscape designs for its customers each year. Estimate the total cost for the Sunset Office park job if LawnCare USA allocated costs of the Landscape Design activity based on the number of landscape designs rather than the number of landscape design-hours. How much would LawnCare USA bid to perform the job? Which cost driver do you prefer for the Landscape Design activity? Why?
4. Sunset Office Park asks LawnCare USA to give an estimate for providing its services for a 2-year period. What are the advantages and disadvantages for LawnCare USA to provide a 2-year estimate?

5-36 Department and activity-cost rates, service sector. Vital Dimension's Radiology Center (VDRC) performs X-rays, ultrasounds, computer tomography (CT) scans, and magnetic resonance imaging (MRI). VDRC has developed a reputation as a top radiology center in the state. VDRC has achieved this status because it constantly reexamines its processes and procedures. VDRC has been using a single, facility-wide overhead allocation rate. The vice president of finance believes that VDRC can make better process improvements if it uses more disaggregated cost information. She says, "We have state-of-the-art medical imaging technology. Can't we have state-of-the-art accounting technology?"

	X-rays	Ultrasound	CT Scan	MRI	Total
Technician labor	$ 74,000	$122,000	$178,000	$ 118,000	$ 492,000
Depreciation	45,230	264,320	432,550	895,900	1,638,000
Materials	24,500	21,400	26,300	36,800	109,000
Administration					24,000
Maintenance					275,500
Sanitation					276,200
Utilities					162,300
	$143,730	$407,720	$636,850	$1,050,700	$2,977,000
Number of procedures	4,254	4,024	3,344	2,698	
Minutes to clean after each procedure	10	15	20	30	
Minutes for each procedure	15	20	30	35	

VDRC operates at capacity. The proposed allocation bases for overhead are as follows:

Administration	Number of procedures
Maintenance (including parts)	Capital cost of the equipment (use depreciation)
Sanitation	Total cleaning minutes
Utilities	Total procedure minutes

Required

1. Calculate the budgeted cost per service for X-rays, ultrasounds, CT scans, and MRI using direct technician labor costs as the allocation basis.
2. Calculate the budgeted cost per service of X-rays, ultrasounds, CT scans, and MRI if VDRC allocated overhead costs using activity-based costing.
3. Explain how the disaggregation of information could be helpful to VDRC's intention to continuously improve its services.

5-37 Activity-based costing, merchandising. Pharmahelp, Inc., a distributor of special pharmaceutical products, operates at capacity and has three main market segments:
a. General supermarket chains
b. Drugstore chains
c. Mom-and-pop single-store pharmacies

Rick Flair, the new controller of Pharmahelp, reported the following data for 2017.

A	B	C	D	E
Pharmahelp, 2017	General Supermarket Chains	Drugstore Chains	Mom-and-Pop Single Stores	Total For Pharmahelp
Revenues	$3,708,000	$3,150,000	$1,980,000	$8,838,000
Cost of goods sold	3,600,000	3,000,000	1,800,000	8,400,000
Gross margin	$ 108,000	$ 150,000	$ 180,000	438,000
Other operating costs				301,080
Operating income				$ 136,920

For many years, Pharmahelp has used gross margin percentage [(Revenue − Cost of goods sold) ÷ Revenue] to evaluate the relative profitability of its market segments. But Flair recently attended a seminar on activity-based costing and is considering using it at Pharmahelp to analyze and allocate "other operating costs." He meets with all the key managers and several of his operations and sales staff, and they agree that there are five key activities that drive other operating costs at Pharmahelp:

Activity Area	Cost Driver
Order processing	Number of customer purchase orders
Line-item processing	Number of line items ordered by customers
Delivering to stores	Number of store deliveries
Cartons shipped to store	Number of cartons shipped
Stocking of customer store shelves	Hours of shelf-stocking

Each customer order consists of one or more line items. A line item represents a single product (such as Extra-Strength Tylenol Tablets). Each product line item is delivered in one or more separate cartons. Each store delivery entails the delivery of one or more cartons of products to a customer. Pharmahelp's staff stacks cartons directly onto display shelves in customers' stores. Currently, there is no additional charge to the customer for shelf-stocking and not all customers use Pharmahelp for this activity. The level of each activity in the three market segments and the total cost incurred for each activity in 2017 is as follows:

	A	B	C	D	E
13					
14	Activity-based Cost Data		Activity Level		
15	Pharmahelp 2017	General			Total Cost
16		Supermarket	Drugstore	Mom-and-Pop	of Activity
17	Activity	Chains	Chains	Single Stores	in 2017
18	Orders processed (number)	140	360	1,500	$ 80,000
19	Line-items ordered (number)	1,960	4,320	15,000	63,840
20	Store deliveries made (number)	120	360	1,000	71,000
21	Cartons shipped to stores (number)	36,000	24,000	16,000	76,000
22	Shelf stocking (hours)	360	180	100	10,240
23					$301,080

Required

1. Compute the 2017 gross-margin percentage for each of Pharmahelp's three market segments.
2. Compute the cost driver rates for each of the five activity areas.
3. Use the activity-based costing information to allocate the $301,080 of "other operating costs" to each of the market segments. Compute the operating income for each market segment.
4. Comment on the results. What new insights are available with the activity-based costing information?

5-38 Choosing cost drivers, activity-based costing, activity-based management. Shades & Hues (S&H) is a designer of high-quality curtains and bedsheets. Each design is made in small batches. Each spring, S&H comes out with new designs for the curtains and for the bedsheets. The company uses these designs for a year and then moves on to the next trend. The products are all made on the same fabrication equipment that is expected to operate at capacity. The equipment must be switched over to a new design and set up to prepare for the production of each new batch of products. When completed, each batch of products is immediately shipped to a wholesaler. Shipping costs vary with the number of shipments. Budgeted information for the year is as follows:

Shades & Hues
Budget for Costs and Activities
For the Year Ended February 28, 2017

Direct materials—bedsheets	$ 3,82,260
Direct materials—curtains	5,10,425
Direct manufacturing labor—bedsheets	1,12,500
Direct manufacturing labor—curtains	1,26,000
Setup	78,250
Shipping	84,500
Design	1,93,200
Plant utilities and administration	2,55,775
Total	$17,42,910

Other budget information follows:

	Curtains	Bedsheets	Total
Number of products	6,240	3,075	9,315
Hours of production	1,755	2,655	4,410
Number of batches	150	100	250
Number of designs	4	6	10

Required

1. Identify the cost hierarchy level for each cost category.
2. Identify the most appropriate cost driver for each cost category. Explain briefly your choice of cost driver.
3. Calculate the budgeted cost per unit of cost driver for each cost category.
4. Calculate the budgeted total costs and cost per unit for each product line.
5. Explain how you could use the information in requirement 4 to reduce costs.

5-39 ABC, health care. Crosstown Health Center runs two programs: drug addict rehabilitation and aftercare (counseling and support of patients after release from a mental hospital). The center's budget for 2017 follows.

Professional salaries:		
4 physicians × $150,000	$600,000	
12 psychologists × $75,000	900,000	
16 nurses × $30,000	480,000	$1,980,000
Medical supplies		242,000
Rent and clinic maintenance		138,600
Administrative costs to manage patient charts, food, laundry		484,000
Laboratory services		92,400
Total		$2,937,000

Kim Yu, the director of the center, is keen on determining the cost of each program. Yu compiles the following data describing employee allocations to individual programs:

	Drug	Aftercare	Total Employees
Physicians	4		4
Psychologists	4	8	12
Nurses	6	10	16

Yu has recently become aware of activity-based costing as a method to refine costing systems. She asks her accountant, Gus Gates, how she should apply this technique. Gates obtains the following budgeted information for 2017:

	Drug	Aftercare	Total
Square feet of space occupied by each program	9,000	12,000	21,000
Patient-years of service	50	60	110
Number of laboratory tests	1,400	700	2,100

Required

1. a. Selecting cost-allocation bases that you believe are the most appropriate for allocating indirect costs to programs, calculate the budgeted indirect cost rates for medical supplies; rent and clinic maintenance; administrative costs for patient charts, food, and laundry; and laboratory services.
   b. Using an activity-based costing approach to cost analysis, calculate the budgeted cost of each program and the budgeted cost per patient-year of the drug program.
   c. What benefits can Crosstown Health Center obtain by implementing the ABC system?
2. What factors, other than cost, do you think Crosstown Health Center should consider in allocating resources to its programs?

5-40 Unused capacity, activity-based costing, activity-based management. Zarson's Netballs is a manufacturer of high-quality basketballs and volleyballs. Setup costs are driven by the number of setups. Equipment and maintenance costs increase with the number of machine-hours, and lease rent is paid per square foot. Capacity of the facility is 14,000 square feet, and Zarson is using only 80% of this capacity.

Zarson records the cost of unused capacity as a separate line item and not as a product cost. The following is the budgeted information for Zarson:

Zarson's Netballs
Budgeted Costs and Activities
For the Year Ended December 31, 2017

Direct materials—basketballs	$ 168,100
Direct materials—volleyballs	303,280
Direct manufacturing labor—basketballs	111,800
Direct manufacturing labor—volleyballs	100,820
Setup	157,500
Equipment and maintenance costs	115,200
Lease rent	210,000
Total	$1,166,700

Other budget information follows:

	Basketballs	Volleyballs
Number of balls	58,000	85,000
Machine-hours	13,500	10,500
Number of setups	450	300
Square footage of production space used	3,200	8,000

Required

1. Calculate the budgeted cost per unit of cost driver for each indirect cost pool.
2. What is the budgeted cost of unused capacity?
3. What is the budgeted total cost and the cost per unit of resources used to produce (a) basketballs and (b) volleyballs?
4. Why might excess capacity be beneficial for Zarson? What are some of the issues Zarson should consider before increasing production to use the space?

5-41 Unused capacity, activity-based costing, activity-based management. Whitewater Adventures manufactures two models of kayaks, Basic and Deluxe, using a combination of machining and hand finishing. Machine setup costs are driven by the number of setups. Indirect manufacturing labor costs increase with direct manufacturing labor costs. Equipment and maintenance costs increase with the number of machine-hours, and facility rent is paid per square foot. Capacity of the facility is 6,250 square feet, and Whitewater is using only 80% of this capacity. Whitewater records the cost of unused capacity as a separate line item and not as a product cost. For the current year, Whitewater has budgeted the following:

Whitewater Adventures
Budgeted Costs and Activities
For the Year Ended December 31, 2017

Direct materials—Basic kayaks	$ 325,000
Direct materials—Deluxe kayaks	240,000
Direct manufacturing labor—Basic kayaks	110,000
Direct manufacturing labor—Deluxe kayaks	130,000
Indirect manufacturing labor costs	72,000
Machine setup costs	40,500
Equipment and maintenance costs	235,000
Facility rent	200,000
Total	$1,352,500

Other budget information follows:

	Basic	Deluxe
Number of kayaks	5,000	3,000
Machine-hours	11,000	12,500
Number of setups	300	200
Square footage of production space used	2,860	2,140

Required

1. Calculate the cost per unit of each cost-allocation base.
2. What is the budgeted cost of unused capacity?

3. Calculate the budgeted total cost and the cost per unit for each model.
4. Why might excess capacity be beneficial for Whitewater? What are some of the issues Whitewater should consider before increasing production to use the space?

5-42 ABC, implementation, ethics. (CMA, adapted) Plum Electronics, a division of Berry Corporation, manufactures two large-screen television models: the Mammoth, which has been produced since 2013 and sells for $990, and the Maximum, a newer model introduced in early 2015 that sells for $1,254. Based on the following income statement for the year ended November 30, 2017, senior management at Berry have decided to concentrate Plum's marketing resources on the Maximum model and to begin to phase out the Mammoth model because Maximum generates a much bigger operating income per unit.

Plum Electronics
Income Statement for the
Fiscal Year Ended November 30, 2017

	Mammoth	Maximum	Total
Revenues	$21,780,000	$5,016,000	$26,796,000
Cost of goods sold	13,794,000	3,511,200	17,305,200
Gross margin	7,986,000	1,504,800	9,490,800
Selling and administrative expense	6,413,000	1,075,800	7,488,800
Operating income	$ 1,573,000	$ 429,000	$ 2,002,000
Units produced and sold	22,000	4,000	
Operating income per unit sold	$ 71.50	$ 107.25	

Details for cost of goods sold for Mammoth and Maximum are as follows:

	Mammoth		Maximum	
	Total	Per Unit	Total	Per Unit
Direct materials	$ 5,033,600	$ 228.80	$2,569,600	$642.40
Direct manufacturing labor[a]	435,600	19.80	184,800	46.20
Machine costs[b]	3,484,800	158.40	316,800	79.20
Total direct costs	$ 8,954,000	$ 407.00	$3,071,200	$767.80
Manufacturing overhead costs[c]	$ 4,840,000	$ 220.00	$ 440,000	$110.00
Total cost of goods sold	$13,794,000	$ 627.00	$3,511,200	$877.80

[a] Mammoth requires 1.5 hours per unit and Maximum requires 3.5 hours per unit. The direct manufacturing labor cost is $13.20 per hour.

[b] Machine costs include lease costs of the machine, repairs, and maintenance. Mammoth requires 8 machine-hours per unit and Maximum requires 4 machine-hours per unit. The machine-hour rate is $19.80 per hour.

[c] Manufacturing overhead costs are allocated to products based on machine-hours at the rate of $27.50 per hour.

Plum's controller, Steve Jacobs, is advocating the use of activity-based costing and activity-based management and has gathered the following information about the company's manufacturing overhead costs for the year ended November 30, 2017.

		Units of the Cost-Allocation Base		
Activity Center (Cost-Allocation Base)	Total Activity Costs	Mammoth	Maximum	Total
Soldering (number of solder points)	$1,036,200	1,185,000	385,000	1,570,000
Shipments (number of shipments)	946,000	16,200	3,800	20,000
Quality control (number of inspections)	1,364,000	56,200	21,300	77,500
Purchase orders (number of orders)	1,045,440	80,100	109,980	190,080
Machine power (machine-hours)	63,360	176,000	16,000	192,000
Machine setups (number of setups)	825,000	16,000	14,000	30,000
Total manufacturing overhead	$5,280,000			

After completing his analysis, Jacobs shows the results to Charles Clark, the Plum division president. Clark does not like what he sees. "If you show headquarters this analysis, they are going to ask us to phase out the Maximum line, which we have just introduced. This whole costing stuff has been a major problem for us. First Mammoth was not profitable and now Maximum.

"Looking at the ABC analysis, I see two problems. First, we do many more activities than the ones you have listed. If you had included all activities, maybe your conclusions would be different. Second, you used number of setups and number of inspections as allocation bases. The numbers would be different had you used setup-hours and inspection-hours instead. I know that measurement problems precluded you from using these other cost-allocation bases, but I believe you ought to make some adjustments to our current numbers to compensate for these issues. I know you can do better. We can't afford to phase out either product."

Jacobs knows that his numbers are fairly accurate. As a quick check, he calculates the profitability of Maximum and Mammoth using more and different allocation bases. The set of activities and activity rates he had used results in numbers that closely approximate those based on more detailed analyses. He is confident that headquarters, knowing that Maximum was introduced only recently, will not ask Plum to phase it out. He is also aware that a sizable portion of Clark's bonus is based on division revenues. Phasing out either product would adversely affect his bonus. Still, he feels some pressure from Clark to do something.

Required

1. Using activity-based costing, calculate the gross margin per unit of the Maximum and Mammoth models.
2. Explain briefly why these numbers differ from the gross margin per unit of the Maximum and Mammoth models calculated using Plum's existing simple costing system.
3. Comment on Clark's concerns about the accuracy and limitations of ABC.
4. How might Plum find the ABC information helpful in managing its business?
5. What should Steve Jacobs do in response to Clark's comments?

5-43 Activity-based costing, activity-based management, merchandising. Main Street Books and Café (MSBC) is a large city bookstore that sells books and music CDs and has a café. MSBC operates at capacity and allocates selling, general, and administration (S, G, & A) costs to each product line using the cost of merchandise of each product line. MSBC wants to optimize the pricing and cost management of each product line. MSBC is wondering if its accounting system is providing it with the best information for making such decisions.

Main Street Books and Café
Product Line Information
For the Year Ended December 31, 2017

	Books	CDs	Café
Revenues	$3,720,480	$2,315,360	$736,216
Cost of merchandise	$2,656,727	$1,722,311	$556,685
Cost of café cleaning			$ 18,250
Number of purchase orders placed	2,800	2,500	2,000
Number of deliveries received	1,400	1,700	1,600
Hours of shelf stocking time	15,000	10,000	10,000
Items sold	124,016	115,768	368,108

Main Street Books and Café incurs the following selling, general, and administration costs:

Main Street Books and Café
Selling, General, and Administration (S, G, & A) Costs
For the Year Ended December 31, 2017

Purchasing department exercise	$ 474,500
Receiving department expense	432,400
Shelf stocking labor expense	487,500
Customer support expense (cashiers and floor employees)	91,184
	$1,485,584

Required

1. Suppose MSBC uses cost of merchandise to allocate all S, G, & A costs. Prepare product line and total company income statements.
2. Identify an improved method for allocating costs to the three product lines. Explain. Use the method for allocating S, G, & A costs that you propose to prepare new product line and total company income statements. Compare your results to the results in requirement 1.
3. Write a memo to MSBC management describing how the improved system might be useful for managing the store.

Master Budget and Responsibility Accounting

6

No one likes to run out of cash.

To manage their spending, businesses, like individuals, need budgets. Budgets help managers and their employees know whether they're on target for their growth and spending goals. Budgets are important for all types of companies: large financial institutions, such as Citigroup, which suffered big financial losses after the housing bubble burst in the mid-2000s; large retailers, such as Home Depot, whose profit margins are thin; profitable computer companies, such as Apple, which sell high dollar-value goods; and luxury hotels, such as the Ritz-Carlton, which sell high dollar-value services.

"SCRIMPING" AT THE RITZ: MASTER BUDGETS

"Ladies and gentlemen serving ladies and gentlemen." That's the motto of the Ritz-Carlton. However, the aura of the chain's old-world elegance stands in contrast to its emphasis—behind the scenes, of course—on cost control and budgets. A Ritz hotel's performance is the responsibility of its general manager and controller at each location. Local forecasts and budgets are prepared annually and are the basis of subsequent performance evaluations for the hotel and people who work there. The budget comprises revenue forecasts and standard costs for hotel rooms, conventions, weddings, meeting facilities, merchandise, and food and beverages. Managers monitor the revenue budget daily, review occupancy rates and adjust prices if necessary. Corporate headquarters monitors actual performance each month against the approved budget and other Ritz hotels. Any ideas for boosting revenues and reducing costs are regularly shared among hotels.

Why do successful companies budget? Because, as the Ritz-Carlton example illustrates, budgeting is a critical function in an organization's decision-making process. Southwest Airlines, for example, uses budgets to monitor and manage fluctuating fuel costs. Walmart depends on its budget to maintain razor-thin margins as it competes with Target. Gillette uses budgets to plan marketing campaigns for its razors and blades.

Even though budgeting is essential for businesses, many managers are often frustrated by the budgeting process. They find it difficult to predict the future and dislike superiors challenging them to improve the performance of their departments. They also dislike being personally evaluated on targets that are challenging and prefer to develop budgets that they can beat. We discuss these issues and the ways thoughtful managers deal with them later in this chapter. For now, we highlight some of the benefits managers get from budgeting.

LEARNING OBJECTIVES

1. Describe the master budget and explain its benefits
2. Describe the advantages of budgets
3. Prepare the operating budget and its supporting schedules
4. Use computer-based financial planning models for sensitivity analysis
5. Describe responsibility centers and responsibility accounting
6. Recognize the human aspects of budgeting
7. Appreciate the special challenges of budgeting in multinational companies

Suzanne Porter/Rough Guides/Dorling Kindersley, Ltd.

Budgets help managers:

1. Communicate directions and goals to different departments of a company to help them coordinate the actions they must pursue to satisfy customers and succeed in the marketplace.
2. Judge performance by measuring financial results against planned objectives, activities, and timelines and learn about potential problems.
3. Motivate employees to achieve their goals.

Interestingly, even when it comes to entrepreneurial activities, research shows that business planning increases a new venture's probability of survival, as well as its product development and venture-organizing activities.[1] As the old adage goes: "If you fail to plan, you plan to fail."

In this chapter, you will see that a budget is based on an organization's strategy and expresses its operating and financial plans. Most importantly, you will see that budgeting is a human activity that requires judgment and wise interpretation.

Budgets and the Budgeting Cycle

LEARNING OBJECTIVE 1

Describe the master budget

...the master budget is the initial budget prepared before the start of a period

and explain its benefits

...benefits include planning, coordination, and control

A *budget* is (a) the quantitative expression of a proposed plan of action by management for a specified period and (b) an aid to coordinate what needs to be done to implement that plan. The budget generally includes both the plan's financial and nonfinancial aspects and serves as a road map for the company to follow in an upcoming period. A financial budget quantifies managers' expectations regarding a company's income, cash flows, and financial position. Just as financial statements are prepared for past periods, financial statements can be prepared for future periods—for example, a budgeted income statement, a budgeted statement of cash flows, or a budgeted balance sheet. Managers develop financial budgets using supporting information from nonfinancial budgets for, say, units manufactured or sold, number of employees, and number of new products being introduced to the marketplace.

Strategic Plans and Operating Plans

Budgeting is most useful when it is integrated with a company's strategy. *Strategy* specifies how an organization matches its capabilities with the opportunities in the marketplace to accomplish its objectives. To develop successful strategies, managers must consider questions such as the following:

- What are our objectives?
- How do we create value for our customers while distinguishing ourselves from our competitors?
- Are the markets for our products local, regional, national, or global? What trends affect our markets? How do the economy, our industry, and our competitors affect us?
- What organizational and financial structures serve us best?
- What are the risks and opportunities of alternative strategies, and what are our contingency plans if our preferred plan fails?

A company, such as Home Depot, can have a strategy of providing quality products or services at a low price. Another company, such as Porsche or the Ritz-Carlton, can have a strategy of providing a unique product or service that is priced higher than the products or services of competitors. Exhibit 6-1 shows that strategic plans are expressed through long-run budgets and operating plans are expressed via short-run budgets. But there is more to the story! The exhibit shows arrows pointing backward as well as forward. The backward arrows show that budgets can lead to changes in plans and strategies. Budgets help managers assess strategic risks and opportunities by providing them with feedback about the likely effects of their strategies and plans. Sometimes that feedback prompts managers to revise their plans and possibly their strategies.

---

[1] For more details, see Frederic Delmar and Scott Shane, "Does Business Planning Facilitate the Development of New Ventures?" *Strategic Management Journal* (December 2003).

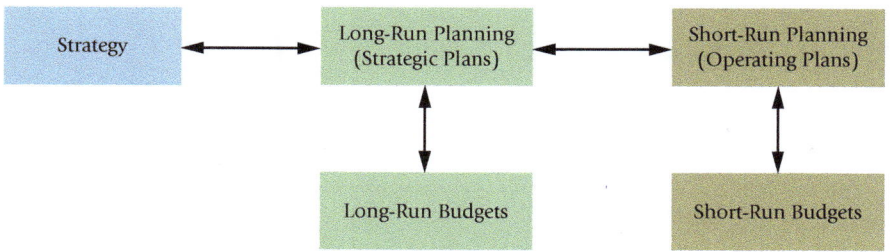

EXHIBIT 6-1

Strategy, Planning, and Budgets

Boeing's experience with the 747-8 program illustrates how budgets can help managers rework their operating plans. Boeing believed that utilizing some of the design concepts it was implementing in its 787 Dreamliner program would be a relatively inexpensive way to reconfigure its 747-8 jet. However, continued cost overruns and delays undermined that strategy: In early 2012, the 747-8 program was already $2 billion over budget and a year behind schedule. As a result, the company expected to earn no profit on any of the more than 100 orders for 747-8 planes it had on its books. And with the budget revealing higher-than-expected costs in design, rework, and production, Boeing postponed production plans for the 747-8 program. The problems with the 747-8 continue. Boeing plans to manufacture less than ten 747-8 aircraft each year.

Budgeting Cycle and Master Budget

Well-managed companies usually cycle through the following steps during the course of the fiscal year:

1. Before the start of the fiscal year, managers at all levels take into account the company's past performance, market feedback, and anticipated future changes to initiate plans for the next period. For example, an anticipated economic recovery from a recession may cause managers to plan for sales increases, higher production, and greater promotion expenses. Managers and management accountants work together to develop plans for the company as a whole and the performance of its subunits, such as departments or divisions.

2. At the beginning of the fiscal year, senior managers give subordinate managers a frame of reference, a set of specific financial or nonfinancial expectations against which they will compare actual results.

3. During the course of the year, management accountants help managers investigate any deviations from the plans, such as an unexpected decline in sales. If necessary, corrective action follows—changes in a product's features, a reduction in prices to boost sales, or cutting of costs to maintain profitability.

The preceding three steps describe the ongoing budget-related processes. The working document at the core of this process is called the *master budget*. The **master budget** expresses management's operating and financial plans for a specified period, usually a fiscal year, and it includes a set of budgeted financial statements. The master budget is the initial plan of what the company intends to accomplish in the period and evolves from both the operating and financing decisions managers make as they prepare the budget.

- Operating decisions deal with how to best use the limited resources of an organization.
- Financing decisions deal with how to obtain the funds to acquire those resources.

The terminology used to describe budgets varies among companies. For example, budgeted financial statements are sometimes called **pro forma statements**. Some companies, such as Hewlett-Packard, refer to budgeting as *targeting*. And many companies, such as Nissan Motor Company and Owens Corning, refer to the budget as a *profit plan*. Microsoft refers to goals as *commitments* and distributes firm-level goals across the company, connecting them to organizational, team, and—ultimately—individual commitments.

This book focuses on how management accounting helps managers make operating decisions, which is why operating budgets are emphasized here. Managers spend a significant part of their time preparing and analyzing budgets because budgeting yields many advantages.

What is the master budget and why is it useful?

Advantages and Challenges of Implementing Budgets

LEARNING OBJECTIVE 2

Describe the advantages of budgets

...advantages include coordination, communication, performance evaluation, and managerial motivation

Budgets are an integral part of management control systems. As we have discussed at the start of this chapter, when administered thoughtfully by managers, budgets do the following:

- Promote coordination and communication among subunits within the company
- Provide a framework for judging performance and facilitating learning
- Motivate managers and other employees

Promoting Coordination and Communication

Coordination is meshing and balancing all aspects of production or service and all departments in a company in the best way for the company to meet its goals. *Communication* is making sure all employees understand those goals. Coordination forces executives to think about the relationships among individual departments within the company, as well as between the company and its supply-chain partners.

Consider budgeting at Pace, a United Kingdom–based manufacturer of electronic products. A key product is Pace's digital set-top box for decoding satellite broadcasts. The production manager can achieve more timely production by coordinating and communicating with the company's marketing team to understand when set-top boxes need to be shipped to customers. In turn, the marketing team can make better predictions of future demand for set-top boxes by coordinating and communicating with Pace's customers.

Suppose BSkyB, one of Pace's largest customers, is planning to launch a new high-definition personal video recorder service. If Pace's marketing group is able to obtain information about the launch date for the service, it can share this information with Pace's manufacturing group. The manufacturing group must then coordinate and communicate with Pace's materials-procurement group, and so on. The point to understand is that Pace is more likely to have personal video recorders in the quantities customers demand if Pace coordinates and communicates both within its business functions and with its customers and suppliers during the budgeting and production processes.

Providing a Framework for Judging Performance and Facilitating Learning

Budgets enable a company's managers to measure actual performance against predicted performance. Budgets can overcome two limitations of using past performance as a basis for judging actual results. One limitation is that past results often incorporate past miscues and substandard performance. Suppose the cellular telephone company Mobile Communications is examining the current-year (2017) performance of its sales force. The sales force's 2016 performance incorporated the efforts of an unusually high number of salespeople who have since left the company because they did not have a good understanding of the marketplace. The president of Mobile said of those salespeople, "They could not sell ice cream in a heat wave." Using the sales record of those departed employees would set the performance bar for 2017 much too low.

The other limitation of using past performance is that future conditions can be expected to differ from the past. Suppose, in 2017, Mobile had a 20% revenue increase, compared with a 10% revenue increase in 2016. Does this increase indicate outstanding sales performance? Not if the forecasted and actual 2017 industry growth rate was 40%. In this case, Mobile's 20% actual revenue gain in 2017 doesn't look so good, even though it exceeded the 2016 actual growth rate of 10%. Using the 40% budgeted growth rate for the industry provides Mobile Communications with a better benchmark against which to evaluate its 2017 sales performance than using the 2016 actual growth rate of 10%. This is why many companies also evaluate their performance relative to their peers. Using only the budget to evaluate performance creates an incentive for subordinates to set targets that are relatively easy to achieve.[2] Of course, managers at all levels recognize this incentive and therefore work to make the budget more challenging to achieve for the individuals who report to them. Still, the budget is the end product of negotiations among senior and subordinate managers. At the end of the year, senior managers gain information about the performance of competitors and external market conditions. This is valuable information that they can use to judge the performance of subordinate managers.

One of the most valuable benefits of budgeting is that it helps managers gather information for improving future performance. When actual outcomes fall short of budgeted or planned results, it prompts thoughtful senior managers to ask questions about what happened and why and how this knowledge can be used to ensure that such shortfalls do not occur again. This probing and learning is one of the most important reasons why budgeting helps improve performance.

Motivating Managers and Other Employees

Research shows that the performance of employees improves when they receive a challenging budget. Why? Because they view not meeting it as a failure. Most employees are motivated to work more intensely to avoid failure than to achieve success (they are loss-averse). As employees get closer to a goal, they work harder to achieve it. Creating a little anxiety improves performance. However, overly ambitious and unachievable budgets can actually de-motivate employees because they see little chance of avoiding failure. As a result, many executives like to set demanding, but achievable, goals for their subordinate managers and employees.[3] General Electric's former CEO Jack Welch describes challenging, yet achievable, budgets as energizing, motivating, and satisfying for managers and other employees and capable of unleashing out-of-the-box and creative thinking. We will return to the topic of setting difficult-to-achieve targets and how it affects employees later in the chapter.

Challenges in Administering Budgets

The budgeting process involves all levels of management. Top managers want lower-level managers to participate in the budgeting process because they have more specialized knowledge and firsthand experience with the day-to-day aspects of running the business. Participation also creates greater commitment and accountability toward the budget among lower-level managers. This is the bottom-up aspect of the budgeting process. This is counterbalanced by the top-down feature of budgeting where senior managers probe and debate the budgets submitted by subordinates with the goal of setting demanding, but achievable, budget targets.

The budgeting process, however, is time-consuming. Estimates suggest that senior managers spend about 10–20% of their time on budgeting, and financial planning departments spend as much as 50% of their time on it.[4] For most organizations, the annual budget process is a months-long exercise that consumes a tremendous amount of resources.

The widespread use of budgets in companies ranging from major multinational corporations to small local businesses indicates that the advantages of budgeting systems outweigh the costs. To gain the benefits of budgeting, however, management at all levels of a company, particularly senior managers, should understand and support the budget and all aspects of the management control system. Lower-level managers who feel that top managers do not "believe" in budgets are unlikely to be active participants in the formulation and successful administration of budgets.

Budgets should not be administered rigidly. Attaining the budget is not an end in itself, especially when conditions change dramatically. A manager may commit to a budget, but if a situation arises in which some unplanned repairs or an unplanned advertising program would serve the long-run interests of the company, the manager should undertake the additional spending. For example, Chipotle, devastated by food-safety issues that sickened about 500 diners in the

---

[2] For several examples, see Jeremy Hope and Robin Fraser, *Beyond Budgeting* (Boston: Harvard Business School Press, 2003). The authors also criticize the tendency for managers to administer budgets rigidly even when changing market conditions have rendered the budgets obsolete.
[3] For a detailed discussion and several examples of the merits of setting specific hard goals, see Gary P. Latham, "The Motivational Benefits of Goal-Setting," *Academy of Management Executive* 18, no. 4 (2004).
[4] See Peter Horvath and Ralf Sauter, "Why Budgeting Fails: One Management System Is Not Enough," *Balanced Scorecard Report* (September 2004).

DECISION POINT

When should a company prepare budgets? What are the advantages of preparing budgets?

second half of 2015 and resulted in a halving of its stock price, has responded with a new marketing campaign and the largest media buy in its history in an effort to woo customers back. On the flip side, the dramatic decline in consumer demand during the 2007–2009 recession led designers such as Gucci to slash their ad budgets and put on hold planned new boutiques. Macy's and other retailers, stuck with shelves of merchandise ordered before the financial crisis, had no recourse but to slash prices and cut their workforces. J. C. Penney eventually missed its sales projections for 2009 by $2 billion. However, its aggressive actions during the year enabled it to survive the recession. Unfortunately, in 2012, J. C. Penney suffered steep declines in sales as a result of changing its strategy away from offering discounts and deals to everyday low pricing.

Developing an Operating Budget

LEARNING OBJECTIVE 3

Prepare the operating budget

...the budgeted income statement

and its supporting schedules

...such as cost of goods sold and nonmanufacturing costs

Budgets are typically developed for a set period, such as a month, quarter, or year, which can be then broken into subperiods. For example, a 12-month cash budget may be broken into 12 monthly periods so that cash inflows and outflows can be better coordinated.

Time Coverage of Budgets

The motive for creating a budget should guide a manager in choosing the period for the budget. For example, consider budgeting for a new Harley-Davidson 500-cc motorcycle. If the purpose is to budget for the total profitability of this new model, a 5-year period (or more) may be suitable and long enough to cover the product from design to manufacturing, sales, and after-sales support. In contrast, consider budgeting for a seasonal theater production, which is expected to run for a few months. If the purpose is to estimate all cash outlays, a 6-month period from the planning stage to the final performance should suffice.

The most frequently used budget period is 1 year, which is often subdivided into quarters and months. The budgeted data for a year are frequently revised as the year goes on. At the end of the second quarter, management may change the budget for the next two quarters in light of new information obtained during the first 6 months. For example, with the decline in the value of the pound against the euro following Britain's vote to exit the European Union, sales of Opel's Corsa and Insignia models have been sluggish in Britain. In order to reduce its cost of operations by around $400 million to deal with the sudden turn of events, General Motors recently decided to reduce work hours and production in its Opel plants in Germany.

Businesses are increasingly using *rolling budgets*. A **rolling budget**, also called a **continuous budget** or **rolling forecast**, is a budget that is always available for a specified future period. It is created by continually adding a month, quarter, or year to the period that just ended. Consider Electrolux, a global appliance company, which has a 3- to 5-year strategic plan and a 4-quarter rolling budget. A 4-quarter rolling budget for the April 2016 to March 2017 period is superseded in the next quarter—that is, in June 2016—by a 4-quarter rolling budget for July 2016 to June 2017, and so on. There is always a 12-month budget (for the next year) in place. Rolling budgets constantly force Electrolux's management to think about the forthcoming 12 months, regardless of the quarter at hand. Some companies, such as Borealis, Europe's leading polyolefin plastics manufacturer; Millipore, a life sciences research and manufacturing firm headquartered in Massachusetts; and Nordea, the largest financial services group in the Nordic and Baltic Sea region, prepare rolling financial forecasts that look ahead five quarters. Other companies, such as EMC Corporation, the information infrastructure giant, employ a 6-quarter rolling-forecast process so that budget allocations can be constantly adjusted to meet changing market conditions.

Steps in Preparing an Operating Budget

The best way to learn how to prepare an operating budget is by walking through the steps a company would take to develop it. Consider Stylistic Furniture, a company that makes two types of granite-top coffee tables: Casual and Deluxe. It is late 2016 and Stylistic's CEO, Rex Jordan, is very concerned about how to respond to the board of directors' mandate to increase profits by 10% in the coming year. Jordan goes through the five-step decision-making process introduced in Chapter 1.

1. **Identify the Problem and Uncertainties.** The problem is to identify a strategy and to build a budget to achieve 10% profit growth. There are several uncertainties. Can Stylistic dramatically increase the sales of its more profitable Deluxe tables? What price pressures are Stylistic likely to face? Will the cost of materials increase? Can Stylistic reduce costs through efficiency improvements?
2. **Obtain Information.** Stylistic's managers gather information about sales of tables in the current year. They are delighted to learn that sales of Deluxe tables have been stronger than expected. Moreover, one of the key competitors in Stylistic's Casual tables' line has had quality problems that are unlikely to be resolved until 2017. Unfortunately, Stylistic's managers also discover that the prices of direct materials have increased slightly during 2016 when compared to 2015.
3. **Make Predictions About the Future.** Stylistic's managers feel confident that with a little more marketing, they will be able to grow the Deluxe tables' business in 2017 and even increase prices moderately relative to 2016. They also do not expect significant price pressures on Casual tables during the year because of the quality problems faced by a key competitor.

    The purchasing manager anticipates that prices of direct materials will be about the same in 2017 as it was in 2016. The manufacturing manager believes that efficiency improvements would allow the costs of manufacturing the tables to be maintained at 2016 costs despite an increase in the prices of other inputs. Achieving these efficiency improvements is important if Stylistic is to maintain its 12% operating margin (that is, operating income ÷ sales = 12%) and to grow sales and operating income.
4. **Make Decisions by Choosing Among Alternatives.** Jordan and his managers feel confident about their strategy to increase the sales of Deluxe tables. This decision has some risks, but is the best option available for Stylistic to increase its profits by 10%.
5. **Implement the Decision, Evaluate Performance, and Learn.** As we will discuss in Chapters 7 and 8, managers compare a company's actual performance to its predicted performance to learn why things turned out the way they did and how to do better. Stylistic's managers would want to know whether their predictions about the prices of Casual and Deluxe tables were correct. Did the prices of inputs increase more or less than anticipated? Did efficiency improvements occur? Such learning would be helpful in building budgets in subsequent years.

Stylistic's managers begin their work on the 2017 budget. Exhibit 6-2 shows the various parts of the master budget, which is composed of the financial projections for Stylistic's operating and financial budgets for 2017. The light, medium, and dark green boxes in Exhibit 6-2 show the budgeted income statement and its supporting budget schedules, which together are called the **operating budget**.

We show the revenues budget box in light green to indicate that it is often the starting point of the operating budget. The supporting schedules—shown in medium green—quantify the budgets for various business functions of the value chain, from research and development to distribution costs. These schedules build up to the budgeted income statement—the key summary statement in the operating budget—shown in dark green.

The orange and purple boxes in the exhibit are the **financial budget**, which is that part of the master budget made up of the capital expenditures budget, the cash budget, the budgeted balance sheet, and the budgeted statement of cash flows. A financial budget focuses on how operations and planned capital outlays affect cash—shown in orange. Management accountants use the cash budget and the budgeted income statement to prepare two other summary financial statements—the budgeted balance sheet and the budgeted statement of cash flows, which are shown in purple.

Top managers and line managers responsible for various business functions in the value chain finalize the master budget after several rounds of discussions. We next present the steps in preparing an operating budget for Stylistic Furniture for 2017 using Exhibit 6-2 as a guide. The appendix to this chapter presents Stylistic's cash budget, which is another key component of the master budget. The following details are needed to prepare the budget:

- Stylistic sells two models of granite-top coffee tables: Casual and Deluxe. Revenue unrelated to sales, such as interest income, is zero.
- Work-in-process inventory is negligible and is ignored.

EXHIBIT 6-2

Overview of the Master Budget for Stylistic Furniture

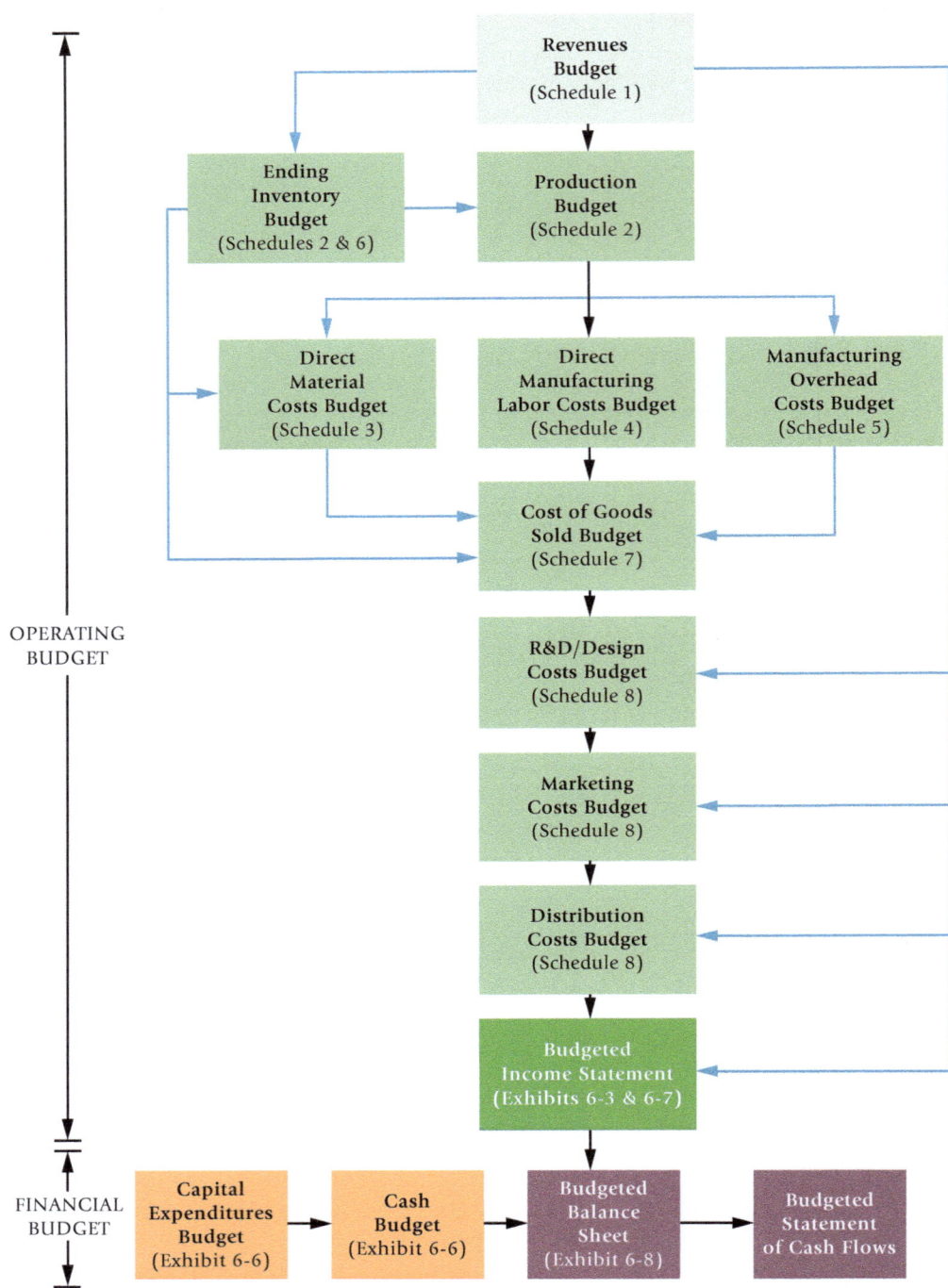

- Direct materials inventory and finished-goods inventory are costed using the first-in, first-out (FIFO) method. The unit costs of direct materials purchased and unit costs of finished-goods sold remain unchanged throughout each budget year, but can change from year to year.
- There are two types of direct materials: red oak (RO) and granite slabs (GS). The direct material costs are variable with respect to units of output—coffee tables.
- Direct manufacturing labor workers are hired on an hourly basis; no overtime is worked.

- There are two cost drivers for manufacturing overhead costs—direct manufacturing labor-hours and setup labor-hours, and two manufacturing overhead cost pools—manufacturing operations overhead and machine setup overhead.
- Direct manufacturing labor-hours is the cost driver for the variable portion of manufacturing operations overhead. The fixed component of manufacturing operations overhead is tied to the manufacturing capacity of 300,000 direct manufacturing labor-hours Stylistic has planned for 2017.
- Setup labor-hours are the cost driver for the variable portion of machine setup overhead. The fixed component of machine setup overhead is tied to the setup capacity of 15,000 setup labor-hours Stylistic has planned for 2017.
- For computing inventoriable costs, Stylistic allocates all (variable and fixed) manufacturing operations overhead costs using direct manufacturing labor-hours and machine setup overhead costs using setup labor-hours.
- Nonmanufacturing costs consist of product design, marketing, and distribution costs. All product design costs are fixed costs for 2017. The variable component of marketing costs is the 6.5% sales commission on revenues paid to salespeople. The variable portion of distribution costs varies with cubic feet of tables sold and shipped.

The following data are available for the 2017 budget:

Direct materials	
Red oak	$ 7 per board foot (b.f.) (same as in 2016)
Granite	$10 per square foot (sq. ft.) (same as in 2016)
Direct manufacturing labor	$20 per hour

	Content of Each Product Unit	
	Casual Granite Table	Deluxe Granite Table
Red oak	12 board feet	12 board feet
Granite	6 square feet	8 square feet
Direct manufacturing labor	4 hours	6 hours

	Product	
	Casual Granite Table	Deluxe Granite Table
Expected sales in units	50,000	10,000
Selling price	$ 600	$ 800
Target ending inventory in units	11,000	500
Beginning inventory in units	1,000	500
Beginning inventory in dollars	$384,000	$262,000

	Direct Materials	
	Red oak	Granite
Beginning inventory	70,000 b.f.	60,000 sq. ft.
Target ending inventory	80,000 b.f.	20,000 sq. ft.

Stylistic bases its budgeted cost information on the costs predicted to support its revenues budget, taking into account the efficiency improvements it expects to make in 2017. Recall from Step 3 of the decision-making process (page 223) that efficiency improvements are critical to offset the anticipated increases in the cost of inputs and to maintain Stylistic's 12% operating margin.

Most companies have a budget manual that contains a company's particular instructions and information for preparing its budgets. Although the details differ among companies, the following basic steps are common for developing the operating budget for a manufacturing company. Beginning with the revenues budget, each of the other budgets follows step by step in logical fashion. As you go through the details for preparing a budget, think about two things: (1) the information needed to prepare each budget and (2) the actions managers can plan to take to improve the company's performance.

Step 1: Prepare the Revenues Budget. Stylistic's managers plan to continue to sell two models of granite-top coffee tables: Casual and Deluxe. The revenues budget accounts for the quantities and prices of Casual and Deluxe tables that Stylistic expects to sell in 2017.

A revenues budget is the usual starting point for the operating budget. Why? Because the forecasted level of unit sales or revenues has a major impact on the production capacity and the inventory levels planned for 2017—and therefore, manufacturing and nonmanufacturing costs. Many factors affect the sales forecast, including the sales volume in recent periods, general economic and industry conditions, market research studies, pricing policies, advertising and sales promotions, competition, and regulatory policies. The key to Stylistic achieving its goal of growing its profits by 10% is to grow its sales of Deluxe tables from 8,000 tables in 2016 to 10,000 tables in 2017.

Managers use customer relationship management (CRM) or sales management systems to gather information. Statistical approaches such as regression and trend analysis based on indicators of economic activity and past sales data help in forecasting future sales. Sales managers and sales representatives debate how best to position, price, and promote Casual and Deluxe tables relative to competitors' products. Together with top management, they consider various actions, such as adding product features, digital advertising, and changing sales incentives, to increase revenues. The costs of these actions are included in the various cost budgets. In the final analysis, the sales forecast represents the collective experience and judgment of managers.

Top managers decide on the budgeted sales quantities and prices shown in the revenues budget in Schedule 1. These are difficult targets designed to motivate the organization to achieve higher levels of performance.

Schedule 1: Revenues Budget
for the Year Ending December 31, 2017

	Units	Selling Price	Total Revenues
Casual	50,000	$600	$30,000,000
Deluxe	10,000	800	8,000,000
Total			$38,000,000

The $38,000,000 is the amount of revenues in the budgeted income statement.

Revenues budgets are usually based on market conditions and expected demand because demand for a company's products is invariably the limiting factor for achieving profit goals. Occasionally, other factors, such as available production capacity (being less than demand) or a manufacturing input in short supply, limit budgeted revenues. In these cases, managers base the revenues budget on the maximum units that can be produced because sales will be limited by the available production.

Step 2: Prepare the Production Budget (in Units). The next step in the budgeting process is to plan the production quantities of Casual and Deluxe tables. The only new information managers need to prepare the production budget is the desired level of finished goods inventory. High inventory levels increase the cost of carrying inventory, the costs of quality, and shrinkage costs. On the flip side, low inventory levels increase setup costs and result in lost sales because of product unavailability. Stylistic's management decides to maintain the inventory level of Deluxe tables and increase the inventory of Casual tables to avoid the effects of supply shortages that the company encountered in 2016.

The manufacturing manager prepares the production budget, shown in Schedule 2. The units of finished goods to be produced depend on budgeted unit sales (calculated in Step 1), the target ending finished-goods inventory, and the beginning finished-goods inventory:

$$\text{Budget production (units)} = \text{Budget sales (units)} + \text{Target ending finished goods inventory (units)} - \text{Beginning finished goods inventory (units)}$$

Schedule 2: Production Budget (in Units)
for the Year Ending December 31, 2017

	Product	
	Casual	Deluxe
Budgeted sales in units (Schedule 1)	50,000	10,000
Add target ending finished-goods inventory	11,000	500
Total required units	61,000	10,500
Deduct beginning finished-goods inventory	1,000	500
Units of finished goods to be produced	60,000	10,000

The production budget determines budgeted production costs (for example, direct materials, direct manufacturing labor, and manufacturing overhead) after considering efficiency improvements planned for 2017. Costs are also influenced by actions such as product redesign needed to support the revenues budget.

Managers are always looking for opportunities to reduce costs, for example, by improving processes, streamlining manufacturing, and reducing the time it takes to complete various activities, such as setting up machines or transporting materials. Making these changes improves a company's competitiveness, but it also requires investment. The budgeting exercise is an ideal time for managers to evaluate plans and request the needed financial resources.

6-1 TRY IT!

Jimenez Corporation manufactures and sells two types of decorative lamps, Knox and Ayer. The following data are available for the year 2017.

	Product	
	Knox	Ayer
Expected sales in units	21,000	10,000
Selling price	$ 25	$ 40
Target ending inventory in units	2,000	1,000
Beginning inventory in units	3,000	1,000

Calculate the revenues budget (label it Schedule 1) and the production budget in units (label it Schedule 2) for year ending December 31, 2017.

Step 3: Prepare the Direct Materials Usage Budget and Direct Materials Purchases Budget. The budgeted production, calculated in Schedule 2, determines the quantities and dollars of direct materials used. The direct material quantities used depends on the efficiency with which workers use materials to produce a table. In determining budgets, managers are constantly anticipating ways to make process improvements that increase quality and reduce waste, thereby reducing direct material usage and costs. Senior managers set budgets that motivate production managers to reduce direct material costs and keep negligible work-in-process inventory. We ignore work-in-process inventory when preparing Stylistic's budgets for 2017.

Like many companies, Stylistic has a *bill of materials* stored in its computer systems that it constantly updates for efficiency improvements. This document identifies how each product is manufactured, specifying all materials (and components), the sequence in which the materials are used, the quantity of materials in each finished unit, and the work centers where the operations are performed. For example, the bill of materials would indicate that 12 board feet of red oak and 6 square feet of granite are needed to produce each Casual coffee table and 12 board feet of red oak and 8 square feet of granite are needed to produce each Deluxe coffee table. Direct materials inventories are costed using the first-in, first-out (FIFO) method. The management accountant uses this information to calculate the direct materials usage budget in Schedule 3A.

Schedule 3A: Direct Materials Usage Budget in Quantity and Dollars for the Year Ending December 31, 2017

	Material		Total
	Red oak	Granite	
Physical Units Budget			
Direct materials required for Casual tables (60,000 units × 12 b.f. and 6 sq. ft.)	720,000 b.f.	360,000 sq. ft.	
Direct materials required for Deluxe tables (10,000 units × 12 b.f. and 8 sq. ft.)	120,000 b.f.	80,000 sq. ft.	
Total quantity of direct materials to be used	840,000 b.f.	440,000 sq. ft.	
Cost Budget			
Available from beginning direct materials inventory (under a FIFO cost-flow assumption) (Given)			
Red oak: 70,000 b.f. × $7 per b.f.	$ 490,000		
Granite: 60,000 sq. ft. × $10 per sq. ft.		$ 600,000	
To be purchased and used this period			
Red oak: (840,000 − 70,000) b.f. × $7 per b.f.	5,390,000		
Granite: (440,000 − 60,000) sq. ft. × $10 per sq. ft.		3,800,000	
Direct materials to be used this period	$5,880,000	$4,400,000	$10,280,000

The only new information needed to prepare the direct materials purchases budget is the desired levels of direct materials inventory. During 2017, Stylistic's managers plan to increase the inventory of red oak, but reduce the inventory of granite to the levels of ending inventory described on page 225. The purchasing manager then prepares the budget for direct material purchases, shown in Schedule 3B:

Schedule 3B: Direct Materials Purchases Budget for the Year Ending December 31, 2017

	Material		Total
	Red oak	Granite	
Physical Units Budget			
To be used in production (from Schedule 3A)	840,000 b.f.	440,000 sq. ft.	
Add target ending inventory	80,000 b.f.	20,000 sq. ft.	
Total requirements	920,000 b.f.	460,000 sq. ft.	
Deduct beginning inventory	70,000 b.f.	60,000 sq. ft.	
Purchases to be made	850,000 b.f.	400,000 sq. ft.	
Cost Budget			
Red oak: 850,000 b.f. × $7 per b.f.	$5,950,000		
Granite: 400,000 sq. ft. × $10 per sq. ft.		$4,000,000	
Direct materials to be purchased this period	$5,950,000	$4,000,000	$9,950,000

Step 4: Prepare the Direct Manufacturing Labor Costs Budget. To create the budget for direct manufacturing labor costs, Stylistic's managers estimate wage rates, production methods, process and efficiency improvements, and hiring plans. The company hires direct manufacturing labor workers on an hourly basis. These workers do not work overtime. Manufacturing managers use *labor standards*, the time allowed per unit of output, to calculate the direct manufacturing labor costs budget in Schedule 4 based on the information on pages 225–227.

Schedule 4: Direct Manufacturing Labor Costs Budget
for the Year Ending December 31, 2017

	Output Units Produced (Schedule 2)	Direct Manufacturing Labor-Hours per Unit	Total Hours	Hourly Wage Rate	Total
Casual	60,000	4	240,000	$20	$4,800,000
Deluxe	10,000	6	60,000	20	1,200,000
Total			300,000		$6,000,000

> **6-2 TRY IT!**
>
> Jimenez Corporation manufactures and sells two types of decorative lamps, Knox and Ayer. It expects to manufacture 20,000 Knox lamps and 10,000 Ayer lamps in 2017. The following data are available for the year 2017.
>
> Direct materials
>   Metal $ 3 per pound (same as in 2016)
>   Fabric $ 4 per yard (same as in 2016)
> Direct manufacturing labor $20 per hour
>
> **Content of Each Product Unit**
>
> | | Product | |
> |---|---|---|
> | | Knox | Ayer |
> | Metal | 2 pounds | 3 pounds |
> | Fabric | 1 yard | 1.5 yards |
> | Direct manufacturing labor | 0.15 hours | 0.2 hours |
>
> | | Direct Materials | |
> |---|---|---|
> | | Metal | Fabric |
> | Beginning inventory | 12,000 pounds | 7,000 yards |
> | Target ending inventory | 10,000 pounds | 5,000 yards |
>
> Calculate (a) the direct materials usage budget in quantity and dollars (label it Schedule 3A); (b) the direct materials purchase budget in quantity and dollars (label it Schedule 3B); and (c) the direct manufacturing labor costs budget (label it Schedule 4) for the year ending December 31, 2017.

Step 5: Prepare the Manufacturing Overhead Costs Budget. Stylistic's managers next budget for manufacturing overhead costs such as supervision, depreciation, maintenance, supplies, and power. Managing overhead costs is important but also challenging because it requires managers to understand the various activities needed to manufacture products and the cost drivers of those activities. As we described earlier (page 225), Stylistic's managers identify two activities for manufacturing overhead costs in its activity-based costing system: manufacturing operations and machine setups. The following table presents the activities and their cost drivers.

Manufacturing Overhead Costs	Cost Driver of Variable Component of Overhead Costs	Cost Driver of Fixed Component of Overhead Costs	Manufacturing and Setup Capacity in 2017
Manufacturing Operations Overhead Costs	Direct manufacturing labor-hours	Manufacturing capacity	300,000 direct manufacturing labor-hours
Machine Setup Overhead Costs	Setup labor-hours	Setup capacity	15,000 setup labor-hours

The use of activity-based cost drivers gives rise to **activity-based budgeting (ABB)**, a budgeting method that focuses on the budgeted cost of the activities necessary to produce and sell products and services.

In its activity-based costing system, Stylistic's manufacturing managers estimate various line items of overhead costs that comprise manufacturing operations overhead (that is, all costs for which direct manufacturing labor-hours is the cost driver). Managers identify opportunities for process and efficiency improvements, such as reducing defect rates and the time to manufacture a table, and then calculate budgeted manufacturing operations overhead costs in the operating department. They also determine the resources that they will need from the two support departments—kilowatt-hours of energy from the power department and hours of maintenance service from the maintenance department. The support department managers, in turn, plan the costs of personnel and supplies that they will need in order to provide the operating department with the support services it requires. The costs of the support departments are then allocated (first-stage cost allocation) as part of manufacturing operations overhead. Chapter 15 describes the allocation of support department costs to operating departments when support departments provide services to each other and to operating departments. The first half of Schedule 5 (page 231) shows the various line items of costs that constitute manufacturing operations overhead costs—that is, all variable and fixed overhead costs (in the operating and support departments) that are caused by the 300,000 direct manufacturing labor-hours (the cost driver).

Stylistic budgets costs differently for variable and fixed overhead costs. Consider variable overhead costs of supplies: Stylistic's managers use past historical data and their knowledge of operations to estimate the cost of supplies per direct manufacturing labor-hour of $5. The total budgeted cost of supplies for 2017 is, therefore, $5 multiplied by the 300,000 budgeted direct manufacturing labor-hours, for a total of $1,500,000. The total variable manufacturing operations overhead cost equals $21.60 per direct manufacturing labor-hour multiplied by the 300,000 budgeted direct manufacturing labor-hours, for a total of $6,480,000.

Stylistic measures manufacturing operations capacity in terms of the direct manufacturing labor-hours that the facility is configured to support. It currently has a capacity of 300,000 direct manufacturing labor-hours. To support this level of capacity, and taking into account potential cost improvements, managers estimate total fixed manufacturing operations overhead costs of $2,520,000. (Note that, unlike 2017, Stylistic may not operate at full capacity each year, but its fixed manufacturing operations costs will still be $2,520,000.) Its fixed manufacturing overhead cost is $2,520,000 ÷ 300,000 = $8.40 per direct manufacturing labor-hour (regardless of the budgeted direct manufacturing labor-hours, which may be less than 300,000 in a particular year). That is, each direct manufacturing labor-hour will absorb $21.60 of variable manufacturing operations overhead plus $8.40 of fixed manufacturing operations overhead for a total of $30 of manufacturing operations overhead cost per direct manufacturing labor-hour.

Next, Stylistic's managers determine how setups will be done for the Casual and Deluxe line of tables, taking into account past experiences and potential improvements in setup efficiency.

For example, managers consider the following:

- Increasing the number of tables produced per batch so fewer batches (and therefore fewer setups) are needed for the budgeted production of tables
- Decreasing the setup time per batch
- Reducing the supervisory time needed, for example by increasing the skill base of workers

Stylistic's managers forecast the following setup information for the Casual and Deluxe tables:

	Casual Tables	Deluxe Tables	Total
1. Quantity of tables to be produced	60,000 tables	10,000 tables	
2. Number of tables to be produced per batch	50 tables/batch	40 tables/batch	
3. Number of batches (1) ÷ (2)	1,200 batches	250 batches	
5. Setup time per batch	10 hours/batch	12 hours/batch	
6. Total setup-hours (3) × (4)	12,000 hours	3,000 hours	15,000 hours
8. Setup-hours per table (5) ÷ (1)	0.2 hour	0.3 hour	

Using an approach similar to the one described for manufacturing operations overhead costs, Stylistic's managers estimate various line items of costs that comprise variable machine setup overhead costs (supplies, indirect manufacturing labor, power, depreciation, and supervision)—that is, all costs caused by the 15,000 setup labor-hours (the cost driver): The second half of Schedule 5 summarizes (1) total variable machine setup overhead costs per setup labor-hour = $88($26 + $56 + $6) × the budgeted 15,000 setup labor-hours = $1,320,000 and (2) fixed machine setup overhead costs of $1,680,000 needed to support the 15,000 setup labor-hours of capacity that Stylistic's managers have planned. (Again, Stylistic may not operate at full capacity each year. However, the fixed machine setup costs will still be $1,680,000.) The fixed machine setup cost is $1,680,000 ÷ 15,000 = $112 per setup labor-hour (regardless of the budgeted setup labor-hours, which may be less than 15,000 in a particular year). That is, each setup labor-hour will absorb $88 of variable machine setup overhead cost plus $112 of fixed machine setup overhead cost for a total of $200 of machine setup overhead cost per setup labor-hour.

Schedule 5: Manufacturing Overhead Costs Budget
for the Year Ending December 31, 2017

Manufacturing Operations Overhead Costs

Variable costs (for 300,000 direct manufacturing labor-hours)		
Supplies ($5 per direct manufacturing labor-hour)	$1,500,000	
Indirect manufacturing labor ($5.60 per direct manufacturing labor-hour)	1,680,000	
Power (support department costs) ($7 per direct manufacturing labor-hour)	2,100,000	
Maintenance (support department costs) ($4 per direct manufacturing labor-hour)	1,200,000	$6,480,000
Fixed costs (to support capacity of 300,000 direct manufacturing labor-hours)		
Depreciation	1,020,000	
Supervision	390,000	
Power (support department costs)	630,000	
Maintenance (support department costs)	480,000	2,520,000
Total manufacturing operations overhead costs		$9,000,000

Machine Setup Overhead Costs

Variable costs (for 15,000 setup labor-hours)		
Supplies ($26 per setup labor-hour)	$ 390,000	
Indirect manufacturing labor ($56 per setup labor-hour)	840,000	
Power (support department costs) ($6 per setup labor-hour)	90,000	$ 1,320,000
Fixed costs (to support capacity of 15,000 setup labor-hours)		
Depreciation	603,000	
Supervision	1,050,000	
Power (support department costs)	27,000	1,680,000
Total machine setup overhead costs		$ 3,000,000
Total manufacturing overhead costs		$12,000,000

Note how using activity-based cost drivers provide additional and detailed information that improves decision making compared with budgeting based solely on output-based cost drivers. Of course, managers must always evaluate whether the expected benefit of adding more cost drivers exceeds the expected cost.[5]

Note that Stylistic is scheduled to operate at capacity. Therefore, the budgeted quantity of the cost allocation base/cost driver is the same for variable overhead costs and fixed overhead costs—300,000 direct manufacturing labor-hours for manufacturing operations overhead costs and 15,000 setup labor-hours for machine setup overhead costs. In this case, the budgeted rate for the manufacturing operations overhead cost does not have to be calculated separately for variable costs and for fixed costs as we did earlier. Instead, it can be calculated directly by estimating total budgeted manufacturing operations overhead: $9,000,000 ÷ 300,000 direct

---

[5] The Stylistic example illustrates ABB using manufacturing operations and setup costs included in Stylistic's manufacturing overhead costs budget. ABB implementations in practice include costs in many parts of the value chain. For an example, see Sofia Borjesson, "A Case Study on Activity-Based Budgeting," *Journal of Cost Management* 10, no. 4 (Winter 1997): 7–18.

manufacturing labor-hours = $30 per direct manufacturing labor-hour. Similarly, the budgeted rate for machine setup overhead cost can be calculated as total budgeted machine setup overhead: $3,000,000 ÷ 15,000 budgeted setup hours = $200 per setup-hour.

> **TRY IT! 6-3**
>
> Jimenez Corporation manufactures and sells two types of decorative lamps, Knox and Ayer. The following data are available for the year 2017. Machine setup-hours is the only driver of manufacturing overhead costs. Jimenez has a setup capacity of 1,100 hours
>
> | | Knox | Ayer |
> |---|---|---|
> | 1. Quantity of lamps to be produced | 20,000 lamps | 10,000 lamps |
> | 2. Number of lamps to be produced per batch | 100 lamps/batch | 80 lamps/batch |
> | 3. Setup time per batch | 3 hours/batch | 4 hours/batch |
>
> Variable cost = $60 per setup-hour
> Fixed cost = $77,000
> Calculate the manufacturing overhead costs budget (label it Schedule 5).

Step 6: Prepare the Ending Inventories Budget. Schedule 6A shows the computation of the unit cost of coffee tables started and completed in 2017. These calculations are needed to calculate the ending inventories budget and the budgeted cost of goods sold. In accordance with Generally Accepted Accounting Principles, Stylistic treats both variable and fixed manufacturing overhead as inventoriable (product) costs. Manufacturing operations overhead costs are allocated to finished-goods inventory at the budgeted rate of $30 per direct manufacturing labor-hour. Machine setup overhead costs are allocated to finished-goods inventory at the budgeted rate of $200 per setup-hour.

Schedule 6A: Budgeted Unit Costs of Ending Finished-Goods Inventory December 31, 2017

		Product			
		Casual Tables		Deluxe Tables	
	Cost per Unit of Input	Input per Unit of Output	Total	Input per Unit of Output	Total
Red oak	$ 7	12 b.f.	$ 84	12 b.f.	$ 84
Granite	10	6 sq. ft.	60	8 sq. ft.	80
Direct manufacturing labor	20	4 hrs.	80	6 hrs.	120
Manufacturing operations overhead	30	4 hrs.	120	6 hrs.	180
Machine setup overhead	200	0.2 hrs.	40	0.3 hrs.	60
Total			$384		$524

Under the FIFO method, managers use this unit cost to calculate the cost of target ending inventories of finished goods in Schedule 6B.

Schedule 6B: Ending Inventories Budget December 31, 2017

	Quantity	Cost per Unit		Total	
Direct materials					
Red oak	80,000*	$7	$ 560,000		
Granite	20,000*	10	200,000	$ 760,000	
Finished goods					
Casual	11,000**	$384***	$4,224,000		
Deluxe	500**	524***	262,000	4,486,000	
Total ending inventory				$5,246,000	

*Data are from page 225. **Data are from page 225. ***From Schedule 6A, this is based on 2017 costs of manufacturing finished goods because under the FIFO costing method, the units in finished-goods ending inventory consists of units that are produced during 2017.

Master Budget and Responsibility Accounting **213**

> **6-4 TRY IT!**
>
> Jimenez Corporation manufactures and sells two types of decorative lamps, Knox and Ayer. The following data are available for the year 2017.
>
> | | Product | |
> |---|---|---|
> | | Knox | Ayer |
> | Target ending inventory in units | 2,000 | 1,000 |
>
> Direct materials
>
> | | |
> |---|---|
> | Metal | $ 3 per pound (same as in 2016) |
> | Fabric | $ 4 per yard (same as in 2016) |
> | Direct manufacturing labor | $ 20 per hour |
> | Machine setup overhead | $130 per hour |
>
> | | Content of Each Product Unit | |
> |---|---|---|
> | | Knox | Ayer |
> | Metal | 2 pounds | 3 pounds |
> | Fabric | 1 yard | 1.5 yards |
> | Direct manufacturing labor | 0.15 hours | 0.2 hours |
> | Machine setup overhead | 0.03 hours | 0.05 hours |
>
> | | Direct Materials | |
> |---|---|---|
> | | Metal | Fabric |
> | Target ending inventory | 10,000 pounds | 5,000 yards |
>
> Calculate (1) the budgeted unit costs of ending finished-goods inventory on December 31, 2017 (label it Schedule 6A) and (2) the ending inventories budget on December 31, 2017 (label it Schedule 6B).

Step 7: Prepare the Cost of Goods Sold Budget. The manufacturing and purchase managers, together with the management accountant, use information from Schedules 3–6 to prepare Schedule 7—the cost of goods sold expense budget that will be matched against revenues to calculate Stylistic's budgeted gross margin for 2017.

Schedule 7: Cost of Goods Sold Budget
for the Year Ending December 31, 2017

	From Schedule		Total
Beginning finished-goods inventory, January 1, 2017	Given*		$ 646,000
Direct materials used	3A	$10,280,000	
Direct manufacturing labor	4	6,000,000	
Manufacturing overhead	5	12,000,000	
Cost of goods manufactured			28,280,000
Cost of goods available for sale			28,926,000
Deduct ending finished-goods inventory, December 31, 2017	6B		4,486,000
Cost of goods sold			$24,440,000

*Based on beginning inventory values in 2017 for Casual tables, $384,000, and Deluxe tables, $262,000 (page 225).

Step 8: Prepare the Nonmanufacturing Costs Budget. Schedules 2–7 represent budgets for Stylistic's manufacturing costs. Stylistic also incurs nonmanufacturing costs in other parts of the value chain—product design, marketing, and distribution. Just as in the case of manufacturing costs, the key to managing nonmanufacturing overhead costs is to understand the various activities that will be needed to support the design, marketing, and distribution of Deluxe and Casual tables in 2017 and the cost drivers of those activities. Managers in these functions of the value chain build in process and efficiency improvements and prepare nonmanufacturing cost budgets on the basis of the quantities of cost drivers planned for 2017.

The number of design changes is the cost driver for product design costs. Product design costs of $1,024,000 are fixed costs for 2017 and adjusted at the start of the year based on the number of design changes planned for 2017.

Total revenue is the cost driver for the variable portion of marketing (and sales) costs. The commission paid to salespeople equals 6.5 cents per dollar (or 6.5%) of revenues. Managers budget the fixed component of marketing costs, $1,330,000, at the start of the year based on budgeted revenues for 2017.

Cubic feet of tables sold and shipped (Casual: 18 cubic feet × 50,000 tables + Deluxe: 24 cubic feet × 10,000 tables = 1,140,000 cubic feet) is the cost driver of the variable component of budgeted distribution costs. Variable distribution costs equal $2 per cubic foot. The fixed component of budgeted distribution costs equal to $1,596,000 varies with the company's distribution capacity, which in 2017 is 1,140,000 cubic feet (to support the distribution of 50,000 Casual tables and 10,000 Deluxe tables). For brevity, Schedule 8 shows the product design, marketing, and distribution costs budget for 2017 in a single schedule.

**Schedule 8: Nonmanufacturing Costs Budget
for the Year Ending December 31, 2017**

Business Function	Variable Costs	Fixed Costs	Total Costs
Product design	—	$1,024,000	$1,024,000
Marketing (Variable cost: $38,000,000 × 0.065)	$2,470,000	1,330,000	3,800,000
Distribution (Variable cost: $2 × 1,140,000 cu. ft.)	2,280,000	1,596,000	3,876,000
	$4,750,000	$3,950,000	$8,700,000

The nonmanufacturing costs in our example focused on activities Stylistic needs to undertake to achieve its revenue goals for the year. The innovations in product design were incremental innovations necessary to generate higher revenues in 2017. Sometimes companies need to invest in research and development (R&D) in a particular year that, if successful, will only result in revenues in a subsequent year. When companies engage in radical rather than incremental innovation, R&D costs may have to be incurred for several years before the company sees the benefits of the R&D in the form of revenues. Many critics argue that the short-term costs of engaging in innovation for uncertain long-term benefits result in companies underinvesting in radical or breakthrough innovations.

Companies that engage in breakthrough innovation budget separately for these resources in their annual budgets. In this way, they separate the operational performance for the year from investments in innovation for subsequent years. They ensure that the innovations pursued are closely linked to their intended strategies and develop project milestones, such as expert evaluations, intellectual property creation, patents received, and customer engagement, to monitor progress and value creation of the innovation projects.

Step 9: Prepare the Budgeted Income Statement. The CEO and managers of various business functions, with help from the management accountant, use information in Schedules 1, 7, and 8 to finalize the budgeted income statement, shown in Exhibit 6-3. The style used in Exhibit 6-3 is typical, but managers and accountants could include more details in the income statement. As more details are put in the income statement, fewer supporting schedules are needed.

Budgeting is a cross-functional activity. The strategies developed by top managers for achieving a company's revenue and operating income goals affect the costs planned for the different business functions of the value chain. For example, the budgeted increase in sales at Stylistic is based on spending more for marketing and must be matched with higher production costs to ensure there is an adequate supply of tables and with higher distribution costs to ensure the timely delivery of tables to customers. Rex Jordan, the CEO of Stylistic Furniture, is very pleased with the 2017 budget. It calls for a 10% increase in operating income compared with 2016. The keys to achieving a higher operating income are a significant increase in sales

EXHIBIT 6-3
Budgeted Income Statement for Stylistic Furniture

	A	B	C	D
1	Budgeted Income Statement for Stylistic Furniture			
2	For the Year Ending December 31, 2017			
3	Revenues	Schedule 1		$38,000,000
4	Cost of goods sold	Schedule 7		24,440,000
5	Gross margin			13,560,000
6	Operating costs			
7	Product design costs	Schedule 8	$1,024,000	
8	Marketing costs	Schedule 8	3,800,000	
9	Distribution costs	Schedule 8	3,876,000	8,700,000
10	Operating income			$ 4,860,000

of Deluxe tables and process improvements and efficiency gains throughout the value chain. As Rex studies the budget more carefully, however, he is struck by two comments appended to the budget: First, to achieve the budgeted number of tables sold, Stylistic may need to reduce its selling prices by 3% to $582 for Casual tables and to $776 for Deluxe tables. Second, a supply shortage in direct materials may result in a 5% increase in the prices of direct materials (red oak and granite) above the material prices anticipated in the 2017 budget. Even if direct materials prices increase, selling prices are anticipated to remain unchanged. He asks Tina Larsen, a management accountant, to use Stylistic's financial planning model to evaluate how these outcomes will affect budgeted operating income.

DECISION POINT

What is the operating budget and what are its components?

6-5 TRY IT!

Jimenez Corporation manufactures and sells two types of decorative lamps, Knox and Ayer. The following data are available for the year 2017. The numbers below represent the calculations from the previous Try It! examples (6-1 through 6-4) together with the relevant schedule numbers from those examples.

Revenues (Schedule 1)	$925,000
Beginning inventory of finished goods (1-1-2017)	76,200
Ending inventory of finished goods, 12-31-2017 (Schedule 6B)	59,300
Direct materials used (Schedule 3A)	350,000
Direct manufacturing labor (Schedule 4)	100,000
Manufacturing overhead (Schedule 5)	143,000
Variable marketing costs (4% of revenues)	
Fixed marketing costs	43,000
Variable distribution costs ($1.50 per cu. ft. for 30,000 cu. ft.)	
Fixed distribution costs	40,000
Fixed administration costs	75,000

Calculate (1) the cost of goods sold budget (label it Schedule 7); (2) the nonmanufacturing costs budget (label it Schedule 8); and (3) the operating income budget for the year ending December 31, 2017.

Financial Planning Models and Sensitivity Analysis

Financial planning models are mathematical representations of the relationships among operating activities, financing activities, and other factors that affect the master budget. Managers use computer-based systems, such as enterprise resource planning (ERP) systems, to manage their businesses and to perform calculations for these planning models. Budgeting

LEARNING OBJECTIVE 4

Use computer-based financial planning models for sensitivity analysis

...for example, understand the effects of changes in selling prices and direct material prices on budgeted income

tools within ERP systems simplify budgeting, reduce the need to re-input data, and reduce the time required to prepare budgets. ERP systems store vast quantities of information about the materials, machines and equipment, labor, power, maintenance, and setups needed to produce different products. Once managers identify sales quantities for different products, the software can quickly compute the budgeted costs for manufacturing these products. ERP systems also help managers budget for nonmanufacturing costs. Many service companies, such as banks, hospitals, and airlines, also use ERP systems to manage their operations. The Concepts in Action: 24 Hour Fitness and Internet-Based Budgeting is an example of a service company using a software platform to coordinate and manage its budgets across multiple locations.

As they prepare operating budgets, managers do not focus only on what they can achieve. They also identify the risks they face such as a potential decline in demand for the company's products, the entry of a new competitor, or an increase in the prices of different inputs. Sensitivity analysis is a useful tool that helps managers evaluate these risks. *Sensitivity analysis* is a "what-if" technique that examines how a result will change if the original predicted data are not achieved or if an underlying assumption changes. Software packages typically have a sensitivity analysis module that managers can use in their planning and budgeting activities.

To see how sensitivity analysis works, we consider two scenarios identified as possibly affecting Stylistic Furniture's budget model for 2017. Either of the two scenarios could happen, but not both together.

> **Scenario 1:** A 3% decrease in the selling price of the Casual table and a 3% decrease in the selling price of the Deluxe table.
>
> **Scenario 2:** A 5% increase in the price per board foot of red oak and a 5% increase in the price per square foot of granite.

Exhibit 6-4 presents the budgeted operating income for the two scenarios.

In the case of Scenario 1, note that a change in the selling price per table affects revenues (Schedule 1) as well as variable marketing costs (sales commissions, Schedule 8). The Problem for Self-Study at the end of the chapter shows the revised schedules for Scenario 1. Similarly, a change in the price of direct materials affects the direct material usage budget (Schedule 3A), the unit cost of ending finished-goods inventory (Schedule 6A), the ending finished-goods inventories budget (Schedule 6B), and the cost of goods sold budget (Schedule 7). Sensitivity analysis is especially useful to managers incorporating these interrelationships into their budgeting decisions.

Exhibit 6-4 shows that operating income decreases substantially if selling prices decrease by 3%, but declines much less if direct materials prices increase by 5%. The sensitivity analysis prompts Stylistic's managers to put in place contingency plans. For example, if selling prices decline in 2017, Stylistic may need to reduce costs even more than planned. More generally, when the success or viability of a venture is highly dependent on attaining a certain income target, managers should frequently update their budgets as uncertainty is resolved. These updated budgets can help managers adjust expenditure levels as circumstances change.

DECISION POINT

How can managers plan for changes in the assumptions underlying the budget and manage risk?

EXHIBIT 6-4 Effect of Changes in Budget Assumptions on Budgeted Operating Income for Stylistic Furniture

A	B	C	D	E	F	G	H	I
Key Assumptions								
	Units Sold		Selling Price		Direct Material Cost		Budgeted Operating Income	
What-If Scenario	Casual	Deluxe	Casual	Deluxe	Red Oak	Granite	Dollars	Change from Master Budget
Master budget	50,000	10,000	$600	$800	$7.00	$10.00	$4,860,000	
Scenario 1	50,000	10,000	582	776	$7.00	$10.00	3,794,100	22% decrease
Scenario 2	50,000	10,000	600	800	$7.35	$10.50	4,418,000	9% decrease

CONCEPTS IN ACTION: 24 Hour Fitness and Internet-Based Budgeting

B Christopher/Alamy Stock Photo

24 Hour Fitness is one of the largest fitness-club chains in the United States, with nearly 4 million members, more than 450 clubs in 16 states and $1.5 billion in annual revenues. The company uses Longview, an Internet-based software platform, to manage its planning and budgeting process.

Using detailed operational statistics including number of members, number of workouts, and hours worked by each category of staff, accounting and finance managers sign on to the platform and develop budgets for each club. Advertising costs are allocated to each club based on the size, age, and traffic of each club. Using Longview at 24 Hour Fitness has resulted in more accurate budgets and forecasts being developed in less time. Managers can also conduct "what if" budget scenario analysis.

The platform also allows each club manager to track very-detailed revenue and expense data covering individual aspects of club activity, including juice bars, personal training sessions, product sales, and credit card membership dues and to take corrective action. It also enables staff to better support senior management decision making by responding more quickly to information requests. Mike Patano, Senior Director of Financial Planning & Analysis, summarized, "Day to day, it's about being able to thoroughly understand our business, benchmark the performance of our clubs, and understand our business drivers much better and quicker."

Sources: Longview Solutions, "Longview Case Study: 24 Hour Fitness," 2014 (http://info.longview.com/CaseStudy-24HourFitness.html); 24 Hour Fitness, "About Us," http://www.24hourfitness.com/company/about_us/, accessed March 2016.

Earlier in this chapter we described a rolling budget as a budget that is always available for a specified future period. Rolling budgets are constantly updated to reflect the latest cost and revenue information and make managers responsive to changing conditions and market needs.

Instructors and students who, at this point, want to explore the cash budget and the budgeted balance sheet for the Stylistic Furniture example can skip ahead to the appendix on page 246.

Budgeting and Responsibility Accounting

To attain the goals described in the master budget, top managers must coordinate the efforts of all of the firm's employees—from senior executives through middle levels of management to every supervised worker. To coordinate the company's efforts, top managers assign a certain amount of responsibility to lower-level managers and then hold them accountable for how they perform. Consequently, how each company structures its organization significantly shapes how it coordinates its actions.

Organization Structure and Responsibility

Organization structure is an arrangement of lines of responsibility within an organization. A company such as Exxon Mobil is organized by business function—refining, marketing, and so on—with the president of each business function having decision-making authority over his or her function. Functional organizations develop strong competencies within each function but are generally less focused on particular markets or customers. To respond to this concern, other companies, such as Procter & Gamble, the household-products giant, are organized primarily by product line or brand. The managers of the individual divisions (toothpaste, soap, and so on) have decision-making authority concerning all the business functions (manufacturing, marketing, and so on) within that division. This results in some inefficiencies as support functions get duplicated in different divisions without sufficient scale or competence. Some companies combine functional and divisional

LEARNING OBJECTIVE 5

Describe responsibility centers

...a part of an organization that a manager is accountable for

and responsibility accounting

...measurement of plans and actual results that a manager is accountable for

structures, for example leaving marketing within divisions but having manufacturing organized as a business function to supply products to different divisions. There is no perfect organization structure. Companies choose the structure that best meets their needs at that time making the tradeoff between efficiency and end-to-end business authority.

Each manager, regardless of level, is in charge of a responsibility center. A **responsibility center** is a part, segment, or subunit of an organization whose manager is accountable for a specified set of activities. Higher-level managers supervise centers with broader responsibility and larger numbers of subordinates. **Responsibility accounting** is a system that measures the plans, budgets, actions, and actual results of each responsibility center. There are four types of responsibility centers:

1. **Cost center**—the manager is accountable for costs only.
2. **Revenue center**—the manager is accountable for revenues only.
3. **Profit center**—the manager is accountable for revenues and costs.
4. **Investment center**—the manager is accountable for investments, revenues, and costs.

The maintenance department of a Marriott hotel is a cost center because the maintenance manager is responsible only for costs and the budget is based only on costs. The sales department is a revenue center because the sales manager is responsible primarily for revenues, and the department's budget is primarily based on revenues. The hotel manager is in charge of a profit center because the manager is accountable for both revenues and costs, and the hotel's budget is based on revenues and costs. The regional manager responsible for determining the amount to be invested in new hotel projects and for revenues and costs generated from these investments is in charge of an investment center. So, this center's budget is based on revenues, costs, and the investment base.

A responsibility center can be structured to promote better alignment of individual and company goals. For example, until recently, OPD, an office products distributor, operated its sales department solely as a revenue center. Each salesperson received a commission of 3% of the revenues per order, regardless of its size, the cost of processing it, or the cost of delivering the office products. Upon analyzing customer profitability, OPD found that many customers were unprofitable. The main reason was the high ordering and delivery costs of small orders. OPD's managers decided to make the sales department a profit center, accountable for revenues and costs, and to change the incentive system for salespeople to 15% of the monthly profits of their customers. The costs for each customer included the ordering and delivery costs. The effect of this change was immediate. The sales department began charging customers for ordering and delivery, and salespeople at OPD actively encouraged customers to consolidate their purchases into fewer orders. As a result, each order began producing larger revenues. The profitability of customers increased because of a 40% reduction in ordering and delivery costs in 1 year.

Feedback

Budgets coupled with responsibility accounting provide feedback to top managers about the performance relative to the budget of different responsibility center managers.

Differences between actual results and budgeted amounts—called *variances*—can help managers implement strategies and evaluate them in three ways:

1. **Early warning.** Variances alert managers early to events not easily or immediately evident. Managers can then take corrective actions or exploit the available opportunities. For example, after observing a small decline in sales during a period, managers may want to investigate if this is an indication of an even steeper decline to come later in the year.
2. **Performance evaluation.** Variances prompt managers to probe how well the company has implemented its strategies. Were materials and labor used efficiently? Was R&D spending increased as planned? Did product warranty costs decrease as planned?
3. **Evaluating strategy.** Variances sometimes signal to managers that their strategies are ineffective. For example, a company seeking to compete by reducing costs and improving quality may find that it is achieving these goals but that it is having little effect on sales and profits. Top management may then want to reevaluate the strategy.

Responsibility and Controllability

Controllability is the degree of influence a specific manager has over costs, revenues, or related items for which he or she is responsible. A **controllable cost** is any cost primarily subject to the influence of a given *responsibility center manager* for a given *period*. A responsibility accounting system could either exclude all uncontrollable costs from a manager's performance report or segregate such costs from the controllable costs. For example, a machining supervisor's performance report might be confined to direct materials, direct manufacturing labor, power, and machine maintenance costs and might exclude costs such as rent and taxes paid on the plant.

In practice, controllability is difficult to pinpoint for two main reasons:

1. Few costs are clearly under the sole influence of one manager. For example, purchasing managers are able to affect the prices their firms pay for direct materials, but these prices also depend on market conditions beyond the managers' control. Similarly, the decisions production managers make can affect the quantities of direct materials used but also depend on the quality of materials purchased. Moreover, managers often work in teams. Think about how difficult it is to evaluate individual responsibility in a team situation.

2. With a long enough time span, all costs will come under somebody's control. However, most performance reports focus on periods of a year or less. A current manager may benefit from a predecessor's accomplishments or may inherit a predecessor's problems and inefficiencies. For example, managers may have to work with undesirable contracts with suppliers or labor unions negotiated by their predecessors. How can we separate what the current manager actually controls from the results of decisions other managers made? Exactly what is the current manager accountable for? The answers may not be clear-cut.

Executives differ in how they embrace the controllability notion when evaluating people reporting to them. Some CEOs regard the budget as a firm commitment subordinates must meet and that "numbers always tell the story." Failing to meet the budget is viewed unfavorably. An executive once noted, "You can miss your plan once, but you wouldn't want to miss it twice." Such an approach forces managers to learn to perform under adverse circumstances and to deliver consistent results year after year. It removes the need to discuss which costs are controllable and which are uncontrollable because it does not matter whether the performance was due to controllable or uncontrollable factors. The disadvantage of this approach is that it subjects a manager's compensation to greater risk. It also de-motivates managers when uncontrollable factors adversely affect their performance evaluations even though they have performed well in terms of factors they could control.

Other CEOs believe that focusing on making the numbers in a budget puts excessive pressure on managers. These CEOs adjust for uncontrollable factors and evaluate managers only on what they can control, such as their performance relative to competitors. Using relative performance measures takes out the effects of favorable or unfavorable business conditions that are outside the manager's control and affect all competing managers in the same way. The challenge is in finding the correct benchmarks. Relative performance measures, however, reduce the pressure on managers to perform when circumstances are difficult.

Managers should avoid thinking about controllability only in the context of performance evaluation. Responsibility accounting is more far-reaching. It focuses on gaining *information and knowledge*, not only on control. *Responsibility accounting helps managers to first focus on whom they should ask to obtain information and not on whom they should blame.* Comparing the shortfall of actual revenues to budgeted revenues is certainly relevant when evaluating the performance of the sales managers of Ritz-Carlton hotels. But the more fundamental purpose of responsibility accounting is to gather information from the sales managers to enable future improvement. Holding them accountable for sales motivates them to learn about market conditions and dynamics outside of their personal control but which are relevant for deciding the actions the hotels might take to increase future sales. Similarly, purchasing managers may be held accountable for total purchase costs, not because of their ability to control market prices, but because of their ability to predict and respond to uncontrollable prices and understand their causes.

Performance reports for responsibility centers are sometimes designed to change managers' behavior in the direction top managers desire even if the reports decrease controllability.

Consider a manufacturing department. If the department is designated as a cost center, the manufacturing manager may emphasize efficiency and de-emphasize the pleas of sales personnel for faster service and rush orders that reduce efficiency and increase costs. Evaluating the department as a profit center decreases the manufacturing manager's controllability (because the manufacturing manager has limited influence on sales) but it motivates the manager to look more favorably at rush orders that benefit sales. She will weigh the impact of decisions on costs and revenues rather than on costs alone.

Call centers provide another example. If designated as a cost center, the call-center manager will focus on controlling operating costs, for example, by decreasing the time customer representatives spend on each call. If designed as a profit center, the call-center manager will cause customer-service representatives to balance efficiency against better customer service and lead to efforts to upsell and cross-sell other products. Hewlett-Packard, Microsoft, Oracle, and others offer software platforms designed to prompt and help call-center personnel turn their cost centers into profit centers. The new adage is, "Every service call is a sales call."

DECISION POINT

How do companies use responsibility centers? Should performance reports of responsibility center managers include only costs the manager can control?

LEARNING OBJECTIVE 6

Recognize the human aspects of budgeting

...to engage subordinate managers in the budgeting process

Human Aspects of Budgeting

Why did we discuss the master budget and responsibility accounting in the same chapter? Primarily to emphasize that human factors are crucial in budgeting. Too often, budgeting is thought of as a mechanical tool because the budgeting techniques themselves are free of emotion. However, the administration of budgeting requires education, persuasion, and intelligent interpretation.

Budgetary Slack

As we discussed earlier in this chapter, budgeting is most effective when lower-level managers actively participate and meaningfully engage in the budgeting process. Participation adds credibility to the budgeting process and makes employees more committed and accountable for meeting the budget. But participation requires "honest" communication about the business from subordinates and lower-level managers to their bosses.

At times, subordinates may try to "play games" and build in *budgetary slack*. **Budgetary slack** is the practice of underestimating budgeted revenues or overestimating budgeted costs to make budgeted targets easier to achieve. This practice frequently occurs when budget variances (the differences between actual results and budgeted amounts) are used to evaluate the performance of line managers and their subordinates. Line managers are also unlikely to be fully honest in their budget communications if top managers mechanically institute across-the-board cost reductions (say, a 10% reduction in all areas) in the face of projected revenue reductions.

Budgetary slack provides managers with a hedge against unexpected adverse circumstances. But budgetary slack also misleads top managers about the true profit potential of the company, which leads to inefficient resource planning and allocation and poor coordination of activities across different parts of the company.

To avoid the problems of budgetary slack, some companies use budgets primarily for planning and to a lesser extent for performance evaluation. They evaluate the performance of managers using multiple indicators that take into account various factors that become known during the course of the year, such as the prevailing business environment and the performance of their industry or their competitors. Evaluating performance in this way takes time and requires careful judgment.

One approach to dealing with budgetary slack is to obtain good benchmark data when setting the budget. Consider the plant manager of a beverage bottler. Suppose top managers could purchase a consulting firm's study of productivity levels—such as the number of bottles filled per hour—at a number of comparable plants owned by other bottling companies. The managers could then share this independent information with the plant manager and use it to set the operations budget. Using external benchmark performance measures reduces a manager's ability to set budget levels that are easy to achieve.

Rolling budgets are another approach to reducing budgetary slack. As we discussed earlier in the chapter, companies that use rolling budgets always have a budget for a defined period, say 12 months, by adding, at the end of each quarter, a budget for one more quarter to replace the quarter just ended. The continuous updating of budget information and the richer information it provides reduce the opportunity to create budgetary slack relative to when budgeting is done only annually.

Some companies, such as IBM, have designed innovative performance evaluation measures that reward managers based on the subsequent accuracy of the forecasts used in preparing budgets. For example, the *higher and more accurate* the budgeted profit forecasts of division managers, the higher their incentive bonuses.[6] Another approach to reducing budgetary slack is for managers to involve themselves regularly in understanding what their subordinates are doing. Such involvement should not result in managers dictating the decisions and actions of subordinates. Rather, a manager's involvement should take the form of providing support, challenging in a motivational way the assumptions subordinates make, and enhancing mutual learning about the operations. Regular interaction with their subordinates allows managers to become knowledgeable about the operations and diminishes the ability of subordinates to create slack in their budgets. Instead, the subordinates and their superiors have in-depth dialogues about the budgets and performance goals. Managers then evaluate the performance of subordinates using both subjective and objective measures. Of course, using subjective measures requires that subordinates trust their managers to evaluate them fairly.

In addition to developing their organization's strategies, top managers are responsible for defining a company's core values and norms and building employee commitment toward adhering to them. These values and norms describe what constitutes acceptable and unacceptable behavior. For example, Johnson & Johnson (J&J) has a credo that describes its responsibilities to doctors, patients, employees, communities, and shareholders. Employees are trained in the credo to help them understand the behavior that is expected of them. J&J managers are often promoted from within and are therefore very familiar with the work of the employees reporting to them. J&J also has a strong culture of mentoring subordinates. J&J's values and employee practices create an environment where managers know their subordinates well, which helps to reduce budgetary slack.

Stretch Targets

Many of the best performing companies, such as General Electric, Microsoft, and Novartis, set "stretch" targets. Stretch targets are challenging but achievable levels of expected performance, intended to create a little discomfort. Creating some performance anxiety motivates employees to exert extra effort and attain better performance, but setting targets that are very difficult or impossible to achieve hurts performance because employees give up on achieving them. Organizations such as Goldman Sachs also use "horizontal" stretch goal initiatives. The aim is to enhance professional development of employees by asking them to take on significantly different responsibilities or roles outside their comfort zone.

A major rationale for stretch targets is their psychological motivation. Consider the following two compensation arrangements offered to a salesperson:

- In the first arrangement, the salesperson is paid $80,000 for achieving a sales target of $1,000,000 and 8 cents for every dollar of sales above $1,000,000 up to $1,100,000.
- In the second arrangement, the salesperson is paid $88,000 for achieving a sales target of $1,100,000 (a stretch target) with a reduction in compensation of 8 cents for every dollar of sales less than $1,100,000 up to $1,000,000.

For simplicity we assume that sales will be between $1,000,000 and $1,100,000.

The salesperson receives the same level of compensation under the two arrangements for all levels of sales between $1,000,000 and $1,100,000. The question is whether the psychological motivation is the same in the two compensation arrangements. Many executives who favor stretch targets point to the asymmetric way in which salespeople psychologically perceive the two compensation arrangements. In the first arrangement, achieving the sales target of $1,000,000 is seen as good and everything above it as a bonus. In the second arrangement, not reaching the stretch

---

[6] For an excellent discussion of these issues, see Chapter 14 ("Formal Models in Budgeting and Incentive Contracts") in Robert S. Kaplan and Anthony A. Atkinson, *Advanced Management Accounting*, 3rd ed. (Upper Saddle River, NJ: Prentice Hall, 1998).

sales target of $1,100,000 is seen as a failure. If salespeople are loss averse, that is, they feel the pain of loss more than the joy of success, they will work harder under the second arrangement to achieve sales of $1,100,000 and not fail.

Ethics

At no point should the pressure for performance embedded in stretch targets push employees to engage in illegal or unethical practices. The more a company tries to push performance, the greater the emphasis it must place on training employees to follow its code of conduct to prohibit behavior that is out of bounds (for example, no bribery, side payments, or dishonest dealings) and its norms and values (for example, putting customers first and not compromising on quality).

Some ethical questions are subtle and not clear-cut. Consider, for example, a division manager, faced with the choice of doing maintenance on a machine at the end of 2016 or early in 2017. It is preferable to do the maintenance in 2016 because delaying maintenance increases the probability of the machine breaking down. But doing so would mean that the manager will not reach his 2016 stretch target for operating income and lose some of his bonus. If the risks of a breakdown and loss are substantial, many observers would view delaying maintenance as unethical. If the risk is minimal, there may be more debate as to whether delaying maintenance is unethical.

Kaizen Budgeting

Chapter 1 noted the importance of continuous improvement, or *kaizen* in Japanese. **Kaizen budgeting** explicitly incorporates continuous improvement anticipated during the budget period into the budget numbers. A number of companies that focus on cost reduction, including General Electric in the United States and Toyota in Japan, use Kaizen budgeting to continuously reduce costs. Much of the cost reduction associated with Kaizen budgeting arises from many small improvements rather than "quantum leaps." The improvements tend to come from employee suggestions as a result of managers creating a culture that values, recognizes, and rewards these suggestions. Employees who actually do the job, whether in manufacturing, sales, or distribution, have the best information and knowledge of how the job can be done better.

As an example, throughout our nine budgeting steps for Stylistic Furniture, we assumed 4 hours of direct labor time were required to manufacture each Casual coffee table. A Kaizen budgeting approach would incorporate continuous improvement based on 4.00 direct manufacturing labor-hours per table for the first quarter of 2017, 3.95 hours for the second quarter, 3.90 hours for the third quarter, and so on. The implications of these reductions would be lower direct manufacturing labor costs as well as lower variable manufacturing operations overhead costs because direct manufacturing labor is the driver of these costs. If Stylistic Furniture doesn't meet continuous improvement goals, its managers will explore the reasons behind the failure to meet the goals and either adjust the targets or seek input from employees to implement process improvements. Of course, top managers should also encourage managers and employees at all levels to try to find a way to achieve bigger (if periodic) cost reductions by changing operating processes and supply-chain relationships.

Managers can also apply Kaizen budgeting to activities such as setups with the goal of reducing setup time and setup costs or distribution with the goal of reducing the cost per cubic foot of shipping tables. Kaizen budgeting for specific activities is a key building block of the master budget for companies that use the Kaizen approach.

A growing number of cash-strapped states and agencies in the United States are using Kaizen techniques to bring together government workers, regulators, and end users of government processes to identify ways to reduce inefficiencies and eliminate bureaucratic procedures. Several state environmental agencies, for example, have conducted a Kaizen session or are planning one.[7] The U.S. Postal Service has identified many different programs to reduce its costs. The success of these efforts will depend heavily on human factors such as the commitment and engagement of managers and other employees to make these changes.

DECISION POINT

Why are human factors crucial in budgeting?

---

[7] For details, see "State Governments, Including Ohio's, Embrace Kaizen to Seek Efficiency via Japanese Methods," http://www.cleveland.com (December 12, 2008).

Budgeting for Reducing Carbon Emissions

In response to pressures from consumers, investors, governments, and NGOs, many companies proactively manage and report on environmental performance. Budgeting is a very effective tool to motivate managers to lessen carbon emissions. Several companies, such as British Telecom, Novartis, and Unilever, set science-based carbon reduction goals based on climate models whose goal is to limit increases in average temperatures to no more than 2°C. The methodology allocates the annual global emissions budget to individual sectors of the economy and then calculates each company's share of that total sector activity.

These science-based targets are stretched to spur innovation, prompt the development of new technologies and business models, and prepare companies for future regulatory and policy changes. What is the effect of stretched targets on actual emission reduction? Some recent research shows that companies that set more difficult targets (to be achieved over several years) complete a higher percentage of such targets. This is particularly true for carbon reduction projects in high-polluting industries that require more innovation.[8]

Many managers regard budgets negatively. To them, the word *budget* is about as popular as, say, *downsizing*, *layoff*, or *strike*. Top managers must convince their subordinates that the budget is a tool designed to help them set and reach goals. As with all tools of management, it has its benefits and challenges. Budgets must be used thoughtfully and wisely, but whatever the manager's perspective on budgets—pro or con—they are not remedies for weak management talent, faulty organization, or a poor accounting system.

Budgeting in Multinational Companies

Multinational companies, such as FedEx, Kraft, and Pfizer, have operations in many countries. An international presence has benefits—access to new markets and resources—and drawbacks—operating in less-familiar business environments and exposure to currency fluctuations. Multinational companies earn revenues and incur expenses in many different currencies and must translate their operating performance into a single currency (say, U.S. dollars) for reporting results to their shareholders each quarter. This translation is based on the average exchange rates that prevail during the quarter. As a result, managers of multinational companies budget in different currencies and also budget for foreign exchange rates. This requires managers and management accountants to anticipate potential changes in exchange rates that might occur during the year. To reduce the possible negative impact a company could experience as a result of unfavorable exchange rate movements, finance managers frequently use sophisticated techniques such as forward, future, and option contracts to minimize exposure to foreign currency fluctuations (see Chapter 11). Besides currency issues, managers at multinational companies need to understand the political, legal, and, in particular, economic environments of the different countries in which they operate when preparing budgets. For example, in countries such as Turkey, Zimbabwe, and Guinea, annual inflation rates are very high, resulting in sharp declines in the value of the local currency. Managers also need to consider differences in tax regimes, especially when the company transfers goods or services across the many countries in which it operates (see Chapter 22).

When there is considerable business and exchange rate uncertainty related to global operations, a natural question to ask is: "Do the managers of multinational companies find budgeting to be a helpful tool?" The answer is yes. However, in these circumstances the budgeting is not done to evaluate the firm's performance relative to its budgets—which can be meaningless when conditions are so volatile—but to help managers adapt their plans and coordinate their actions as circumstances change. Senior managers evaluate performance more subjectively, based on how well subordinate managers have managed in these constantly shifting and volatile environments.

LEARNING OBJECTIVE 7

Appreciate the special challenges of budgeting in multinational companies

...exposure to currency fluctuations and to different legal, political, and economic environments

DECISION POINT

What are the special challenges involved in budgeting at multinational companies?

---

[8] See Ioannis Ioannou, Shelley Xin Li, and George Serafeim, "The Effect of Target Difficulty on Target Completion: The Case of Reducing Carbon Emissions," *The Accounting Review* (2016).

PROBLEM FOR SELF-STUDY

Consider the Stylistic Furniture example described earlier. Suppose that to maintain its sales quantities, Stylistic needs to decrease selling prices to $582 per Casual table and $776 per Deluxe table, a 3% decrease in the selling prices used in the chapter illustration. All other data are unchanged.

Required

Prepare a budgeted income statement, including all necessary detailed supporting budget schedules that are different from the schedules presented in the chapter. Indicate those schedules that will remain unchanged.

Solution

Schedules 1 and 8 will change. Schedule 1 changes because a change in selling price affects revenues. Schedule 8 changes because revenues are a cost driver of marketing costs (sales commissions). The remaining Schedules 2–7 will not change because a change in selling price has no effect on manufacturing costs. The revised schedules and the new budgeted income statement follow.

Schedule 1: Revenues Budget
for the Year Ending December 31, 2017

	Selling Price	Units	Total Revenues
Casual tables	$582	50,000	$29,100,000
Deluxe tables	776	10,000	7,760,000
Total			$36,860,000

Schedule 8: Nonmanufacturing Costs Budget
for the Year Ending December 31, 2017

Business Function	Variable Costs	Fixed Costs (as in Schedule 8, page 234)	Total Costs
Product design		$1,024,000	$1,024,000
Marketing (Variable cost: $36,860,000 × 0.065)	$2,395,900	1,330,000	3,725,900
Distribution (Variable cost: $2 × 1,140,000 cu. ft.)	2,280,000	1,596,000	3,876,000
	$4,675,900	$3,950,000	$8,625,900

Stylistic Furniture Budgeted Income Statement
for the Year Ending December 31, 2017

Revenues	Schedule 1		$36,860,000
Cost of goods sold	Schedule 7		24,440,000
Gross margin			12,420,000
Operating costs			
Product design	Schedule 8	$1,024,000	
Marketing costs	Schedule 8	3,725,900	
Distribution costs	Schedule 8	3,876,000	8,625,900
Operating income			$ 3,794,100

DECISION POINTS

The following question-and-answer format summarizes the chapter's learning objectives. Each decision presents a key question related to a learning objective. The guidelines are the answer to that question.

Decision	Guidelines
1. What is the master budget, and why is it useful?	The master budget summarizes the financial projections of all the company's budgets. It expresses management's operating and financing plans—the formalized outline of the company's financial objectives and how they will be attained. Budgets are tools that, by themselves, are neither good nor bad. Budgets are useful when administered skillfully.
2. When should a company prepare budgets? What are the advantages of preparing budgets?	Budgets should be prepared when their expected benefits exceed their expected costs. There are four key advantages of budgets: (a) they compel strategic analysis and planning, (b) they promote coordination and communication among subunits of the company, (c) they provide a framework for judging performance and facilitating learning, and (d) they motivate managers and other employees.
3. What is the operating budget and what are its components?	The operating budget is the budgeted income statement and its supporting budget schedules. The starting point for the operating budget is generally the revenues budget. The following supporting schedules are derived from the revenues budget and the activities needed to support the revenues budget: production budget, direct materials usage budget, direct materials purchases budget, direct manufacturing labor cost budget, manufacturing overhead costs budget, ending inventories budget, cost of goods sold budget, R&D/product design cost budget, marketing cost budget, distribution cost budget, and customer-service cost budget.
4. How can managers plan for changes in the assumptions underlying the budget and manage risk?	Managers can use financial planning models—mathematical statements of the relationships among operating activities, financing activities, and other factors that affect the budget. These models make it possible for managers to conduct a what-if (sensitivity) analysis of the risks that changes in the original predicted data or changes in underlying assumptions would have on the master budget and to develop plans to respond to changed conditions.
5. How do companies use responsibility centers? Should performance reports of responsibility center managers include only costs the manager can control?	A responsibility center is a part, segment, or subunit of an organization whose manager is accountable for a specified set of activities. Four types of responsibility centers are cost centers, revenue centers, profit centers, and investment centers. Responsibility accounting systems are useful because they measure the plans, budgets, actions, and actual results of each responsibility center. Controllable costs are costs primarily subject to the influence of a given responsibility center manager for a given time period. Performance reports of responsibility center managers often include costs, revenues, and investments that the managers cannot control. Responsibility accounting associates financial items with managers on the basis of which manager has the most knowledge and information about specific items, regardless of the manager's ability to exercise full control.

Decision	Guidelines
6. Why are human factors crucial in budgeting?	The administration of budgets requires education, participation, persuasion, and intelligent interpretation. When wisely administered, budgets create commitment, accountability, and honest communication among employees and can be used as the basis for continuous improvement efforts. When badly managed, budgeting can lead to game-playing and budgetary slack—the practice of making budget targets more easily achievable.
7. What are the special challenges involved in budgeting at multinational companies?	Budgeting is a valuable tool for multinational companies but is challenging because of the uncertainties posed by operating in multiple countries. In addition to budgeting in different currencies, managers in multinational companies also need to budget for foreign exchange rates and consider the political, legal, and economic environments of the different countries in which they operate. In times of high uncertainty, managers use budgets to help the organization learn and adapt to its circumstances rather than to evaluate performance.

APPENDIX

The Cash Budget

The chapter illustrated the operating budget, which is one part of the master budget. The other part is the financial budget, which is composed of the capital expenditures budget, the cash budget, the budgeted balance sheet, and the budgeted statement of cash flows. This appendix focuses on the cash budget and the budgeted balance sheet. We discuss capital budgeting in Chapter 21. The budgeted statement of cash flows is beyond the scope of this book and generally is covered in financial accounting and corporate finance courses.

Why should Stylistic's managers want a cash budget in addition to the operating income budget presented in the chapter? Recall that Stylistic's management accountants prepared the operating budget on an accrual accounting basis consistent with how the company reports its actual operating income. But Stylistic's managers also need to plan cash flows to ensure that the company has adequate cash to pay vendors, meet payroll, and pay operating expenses as these payments come due. Stylistic could be very profitable, but the pattern of cash receipts from revenues might be delayed and result in insufficient cash being available to make scheduled payments. Stylistic's managers may then need to initiate a plan to borrow money to finance any shortfall. Building a profitable operating plan does not guarantee that adequate cash will be available, so Stylistic's managers need to prepare a cash budget in addition to an operating income budget.

Exhibit 6-5 shows Stylistic Furniture's balance sheet for the year ended December 31, 2016. The budgeted cash flows for 2017 are:

	Quarters			
	1	2	3	4
Collections from customers	$9,136,600	$10,122,000	$10,263,200	$8,561,200
Disbursements				
Direct materials	3,031,400	2,636,967	2,167,900	2,242,033
Direct manufacturing labor payroll	1,888,000	1,432,000	1,272,000	1,408,000
Manufacturing overhead costs	3,265,296	2,476,644	2,199,924	2,435,136
Nonmanufacturing costs	2,147,750	2,279,000	2,268,250	2,005,000
Machinery purchase	—	—	758,000	—
Income taxes	725,000	400,000	400,000	400,000

EXHIBIT 6-5

Balance Sheet for Stylistic Furniture, December 31, 2016

	A	B	C	D
1	Stylistic Furniture			
2	Balance Sheet			
	December 31, 2016			
3	Assets			
4	Current assets			
5	Cash		$ 300,000	
6	Accounts receivable		1,711,000	
7	Direct materials inventory		1,090,000	
8	Finished goods inventory		646,000	$ 3,747,000
9	Property, Plant, and equipment			
10	Land		2,000,000	
11	Building and equipment	$ 22,000,000		
12	Accumulated depreciation	(6,900,000)	15,100,000	17,100,000
13	Total			$20,847,000
14	Liabilities and Stockholders' Equity			
15	Current liabilities			
16	Accounts payable		$ 904,000	
17	Income taxes payable		325,000	$ 1,229,000
18	Stockholders' equity			
19	Common stock, no-par 25,000 shares outstanding		3,500,000	
20	Retained earnings		16,118,000	19,618,000
21	Total			$20,847,000

The quarterly data are based on the budgeted cash effects of the operations formulated in Schedules 1–8 in the chapter, but the details of that formulation are not shown here to keep this illustration as brief and as focused as possible.

Stylistic wants to maintain a $320,000 minimum cash balance at the end of each quarter. The company can borrow or repay money at an interest rate of 12% per year. Management does not want to borrow any more short-term cash than is necessary. By special arrangement with the bank, Stylistic pays interest when repaying the principal. Assume, for simplicity, that borrowing takes place at the beginning and repayment at the end of the quarter under consideration (in multiples of $1,000). Interest is computed to the nearest dollar.

Suppose a management accountant at Stylistic receives the preceding data and the other data contained in the budgets in the chapter (pages 224–235). Her manager asks her to:

1. Prepare a cash budget for 2017 by quarter. That is, prepare a statement of cash receipts and disbursements by quarter, including details of borrowing, repayment, and interest.

2. Prepare a budgeted income statement for the year ending December 31, 2017. This statement should include interest expense and income taxes (at a rate of 40% of operating income).

3. Prepare a budgeted balance sheet on December 31, 2017.

Preparation of Budgets

1. The **cash budget** is a schedule of expected cash receipts and cash disbursements. It predicts the effects on the cash position at the given level of operations. Exhibit 6-6 presents the cash budget by quarters to show the impact of cash flow timing on bank loans and their repayment. In practice, monthly—and sometimes weekly or even daily—cash budgets are critical for cash planning and control. Cash budgets help avoid unnecessary idle

EXHIBIT 6-6 Cash Budget for Stylistic Furniture for the Year Ending December 31, 2017

	A	B	C	D	E	F
1		\multicolumn{5}{c}{Stylistic Furniture}				
2		\multicolumn{5}{c}{Cash Budget}				
3		\multicolumn{5}{c}{For Year Ending December 31, 2017}				
4		Quarter 1	Quarter 2	Quarter 3	Quarter 4	Year as a Whole
5	Cash balance, beginning	$ 300,000	$ 320,154	$ 320,783	$ 324,359	$ 300,000
6	Add receipts					
7	Collections from customers	9,136,600	10,122,000	10,263,200	8,561,200	38,083,000
8	Total cash available for needs (x)	9,436,600	10,442,154	10,583,983	8,885,559	38,383,000
9	Cash disbursements					
10	Direct materials	3,031,400	2,636,967	2,167,900	2,242,033	10,078,300
11	Direct maufacturing labor payroll	1,888,000	1,432,000	1,272,000	1,408,000	6,000,000
12	Manufacturing overhead costs	3,265,296	2,476,644	2,199,924	2,435,136	10,377,000
13	Nonmanufacturing costs	2,147,750	2,279,000	2,268,250	2,005,000	8,700,000
14	Machinery purchase			758,000		758,000
15	Income taxes	725,000	400,000	400,000	400,000	1,925,000
16	Total cash disbursements (y)	11,057,446	9,224,611	9,066,074	8,490,169	37,838,300
17	Minimum cash balance desired	320,000	320,000	320,000	320,000	320,000
18	Total cash needed	11,377,446	9,544,611	9,386,074	8,810,169	38,158,300
19	Cash excess (deficiency)*	$ (1,940,846)	$ 897,543	$ 1,197,909	$ 75,390	$ 224,700
20	Financing					
21	Borrowing (at beginning)	$ 1,941,000	$ 0	$ 0	$ 0	$ 1,941,000
22	Repayment (at end)	0	(846,000)	(1,095,000)	0	(1,941,000)
23	Interest (at 12% per year)**	0	(50,760)	(98,550)	0	(149,310)
24	Total effects of financing (z)	1,941,000	(896,760)	(1,193,550)	0	(149,310)
25	Cash balance, ending***	$ 320,154	$ 320,783	$ 324,359	$ 395,390	$ 395,390
26	*Excess of total cash available − Total cash needed before financing					
27	**Note that the short-term interest payments pertain only to the amount of principal being repaid at the end of a quarter. The specific computations regarding interest are $846,000 × 0.12 × 0.5 = $50,760; $1,095,000 × 0.12 × 0.75 = $98,550. Also note that *depreciation does not require a cash outlay.*					
28	***Ending cash balance = Total cash available for needs (x) − Total disbursements (y) + Total effects of financing (z)					

cash and unexpected cash deficiencies. They thus keep cash balances in line with needs. Ordinarily, the cash budget has these main sections:

a. **Cash available for needs (before any financing).** The beginning cash balance plus cash receipts equals the total cash available for needs before any financing. Cash receipts depend on collections of accounts receivable, cash sales, and miscellaneous recurring sources, such as rental or royalty receipts. Information on the expected collectability of accounts receivable is needed for accurate predictions. Key factors include bad-debt (uncollectible accounts) experience (not an issue in the Stylistic case because Stylistic sells to only a few large wholesalers) and average time lag between sales and collections.

b. **Cash disbursements.** Cash disbursements by Stylistic Furniture include:

  i. *Direct materials purchases.* Suppliers are paid in full in the month after the goods are delivered.
  ii. *Direct manufacturing labor and other wage and salary outlays.* All payroll-related costs are paid in the month in which the labor effort occurs.

iii. *Other costs.* These depend on timing and credit terms. (In the Stylistic case, all other costs are paid in the month in which the cost is incurred.) *Note that depreciation does not require a cash outlay.*
iv. *Other cash disbursements.* These include outlays for property, plant, equipment, and other long-term investments.
v. Income tax payments as shown each quarter.

c. **Financing effects.** Short-term financing requirements depend on how the total cash available for needs [keyed as (x) in Exhibit 6-6] compares with the total cash disbursements [keyed as (y)], plus the minimum ending cash balance desired. The financing plans will depend on the relationship between total cash available for needs and total cash needed. If there is a deficiency of cash, Stylistic obtains loans. If there is excess cash, Stylistic repays any outstanding loans.

d. **Ending cash balance.** The cash budget in Exhibit 6-6 shows the pattern of short-term "self-liquidating" cash loans. In quarter 1, Stylistic budgets a $1,940,846 cash deficiency. The company therefore undertakes short-term borrowing of $1,941,000 that it pays off over the course of the year. Seasonal peaks of production or sales often result in heavy cash disbursements for purchases, payroll, and other operating outlays as the company produces and sells products. Cash receipts from customers typically lag behind sales. The loan is *self-liquidating* in the sense that the company uses the borrowed money to acquire resources that it uses to produce and sell finished goods and uses the proceeds from sales to repay the loan. This self-liquidating cycle is the movement from cash to inventories to receivables and back to cash.

2. The budgeted income statement is presented in Exhibit 6-7. It is merely the budgeted operating income statement in Exhibit 6-3 (page 235) expanded to include interest expense and income taxes.

3. The budgeted balance sheet is presented in Exhibit 6-8. Each item is projected in light of the details of the business plan as expressed in all the previous budget schedules. For example, the ending balance of accounts receivable of $1,628,000 is computed by adding the budgeted revenues of $38,000,000 (from Schedule 1 on page 226) to the beginning balance of accounts receivable of $1,711,000 (from Exhibit 6-5) and subtracting cash receipts of $38,083,000 (from Exhibit 6-6).

For simplicity, this example explicitly gave the cash receipts and disbursements. Usually, the receipts and disbursements are calculated based on the lags between the items reported on the accrual basis of accounting in an income statement and balance sheet and their related cash receipts and disbursements. Consider accounts receivable.

EXHIBIT 6-7

Budgeted Income Statement for Stylistic Furniture for the Year Ending December 31, 2017

	A	B	C	D
1	Stylistic Furniture			
2	Budgeted Income Statement			
3	For the Year Ending December 31, 2017			
4	Revenues	Schedule 1		$38,000,000
5	COGS	Schedule 7		24,440,000
6	Gross margin			13,560,000
7	Operating costs			
8	Product design costs	Schedule 8	$1,024,000	
9	Marketing costs	Schedule 8	3,800,000	
10	Distribution costs	Schedule 8	3,876,000	8,700,000
11	Operating income			4,860,000
12	Interest expense	Exhibit 6-6		149,310
13	Income before income taxes			4,710,690
14	Income taxes (at 40%)			1,884,276
15	Net income			$ 2,826,414

EXHIBIT 6-8 Budgeted Balance Sheet for Stylistic Furniture, December 31, 2017

	A	B	C	D
1		Stylistic Furniture		
2		Budgeted Balance Sheet		
3		December 31, 2017		
4		Assets		
5	Current assets			
6	Cash (from Exhibit 6-6)		$ 395,390	
7	Accounts receivable (1)		1,628,000	
8	Direct materials inventory (2)		760,000	
9	Finished goods inventory (2)		4,486,000	$ 7,269,390
10	Property, Plant, and equipment			
11	Land (3)		2,000,000	
12	Building and equipment (4)	$22,758,000		
13	Accumulated depreciation (5)	(8,523,000)	14,235,000	16,235,000
14	Total			$23,504,390
15		Liabilities and Stockholders' Equity		
16	Current liabilities			
17	Accounts payable (6)		$ 775,700	
18	Income taxes payable (7)		284,276	$ 1,059,976
19	Stockholders' equity			
20	Common stock, no-par, 25,000 shares outstanding (8)		3,500,000	
21	Retained earnings (9)		18,944,414	22,444,414
22	Total			$23,504,390
23				
24	Notes:			
25	Beginning balances are used as the starting point for most of the following computations			
26	(1) $1,711,000 + $38,000,000 revenues − $38,083,000 receipts (Exhibit 6-6) = $1,628,000			
27	(2) From Schedule 6B, p. 232			
28	(3) From opening balance sheet (Exhibit 6-5)			
29	(4) $22,000,000 (Exhibit 6-5) + $758,000 purchases (Exhibit 6-6) = $22,758,000			
30	(5) $6,900,000 (Exhibit 6-5) + $1,020,000 + $603,000 depreciation from Schedule 5, p. 231			
31	(6) $904,000 (Exhibit 6-5) + $9,950,000 (Schedule 3B) − $10,078,300 (Exhibit 6-6) = $775,300			
32	There are no other current liabilities. From Exhibit 6-6: Cash flows for direct manufacturing labor = $6,000,000 from Schedule 4 Cash flows for manufacturing overhead costs = $10,377,000 ($12,000,000 − depreciation $1,623,000) from Schedule 5 Cash flows for nonmanufacturing costs = $8,700,000 from Schedule 8.			
33	(7) $325,000 (Exhibit 6-5) + $1,884,276 (from Exhibit 6-7) − $1,925,000 payment (Exhibit 6-6) = $284,276			
34	(8) From opening balance sheet (Exhibit 6-5)			
35	(9) $16,118,000 (Exhibit 6-5) + net income $2,826,414 (Exhibit 6-7) = $18,944,414			

The budgeted sales for the year are broken down into sales budgets for each month and quarter. For example, Stylistic Furniture budgets sales by quarter of $9,282,000, $10,332,000, $10,246,000, and $8,140,000, which equal 2017 budgeted sales of $38,000,000.

	Quarter 1		Quarter 2		Quarter 3		Quarter 4	
	Casual	Deluxe	Casual	Deluxe	Casual	Deluxe	Casual	Deluxe
Budgeted sales in units	12,270	2,400	13,620	2,700	13,610	2,600	10,500	2,300
Selling price	$ 600	$ 800	$ 600	$ 800	$ 600	$ 800	$ 600	$ 800
Budgeted revenues	$7,362,000	$1,920,000	$8,172,000	$2,160,000	$8,166,000	$2,080,000	$6,300,000	$1,840,000
	$9,282,000		$10,332,000		$10,246,000		$8,140,000	

Notice that sales are expected to be higher in the second and third quarters relative to the first and fourth quarters when weather conditions limit the number of customers shopping for furniture.

Once Stylistic's managers determine the sales budget, a management accountant prepares a schedule of cash collections that serves as an input for the preparation of the cash budget. Stylistic estimates that 80% of all sales made in a quarter are collected in the same quarter and 20% are collected in the following quarter. Estimated collections from customers each quarter are calculated in the following table:

Schedule of Cash Collections

	Quarters			
	1	2	3	4
Accounts receivable balance on 1-1-2017 (Fourth-quarter sales from prior year collected in first quarter of 2017)	$1,711,000			
From first-quarter 2017 sales ($9,282,000 × 0.80; $9,282,000 × 0.20)	7,425,600	$1,856,400		
From second-quarter 2017 sales ($10,332,000 × 0.80; $10,332,000 × 0.20)		8,265,600	$2,066,400	
From third-quarter 2017 sales ($10,246,000 × 0.80; $10,246,000 × 0.20)			8,196,800	$2,049,200
From fourth-quarter 2017 sales ($8,140,000 × 0.80)				6,512,000
Total collections	$9,136,600	$10,122,000	$10,263,200	$8,561,200

Uncollected fourth-quarter 2017 sales of $1,628,000 ($8,140,000 × 0.20) appear as accounts receivable in the budgeted balance sheet of December 31, 2017 (see Exhibit 6-8). Note that the quarterly cash collections from customers calculated in this schedule equal the cash collections by quarter shown on page 246.

6-6 TRY IT!

Jimenez Corporation manufactures and sells two types of decorative lamps, Knox and Ayer. The following data are available for the year 2017.

Accounts receivable (January 1, 2017)	$46,000
Budgeted sales in Quarter 1 (January 1 to March 31, 2017)	230,000
Budgeted sales in Quarter 2 (April 1 to June 30, 2017)	245,000
Budgeted sales in Quarter 3 (July 1 to September 30, 2017)	210,000
Budgeted sales in Quarter 4 (October 1 to December 31, 2017)	240,000

All sales are made on account with 80% of sales made in a quarter collected in the same quarter and 20% collected in the following quarter.
Calculate the cash collected from receivables in each of the 4 quarters of 2017.

Sensitivity Analysis and Cash Flows

Exhibit 6-4 (page 236) shows how differing assumptions about selling prices of coffee tables and direct material prices led to differing amounts for budgeted operating income for Stylistic Furniture. A key use of sensitivity analysis is to budget cash flow. Exhibit 6-9 outlines the short-term borrowing implications of the two combinations examined in Exhibit 6-4. Scenario 1, with the lower selling prices per table ($582 for the Casual table and $776 for the Deluxe table), requires $2,146,000 of short-term borrowing in quarter 1 that cannot be fully repaid as of December 31, 2017. Scenario 2, with the 5% higher direct material costs, requires $2,048,000 borrowing by Stylistic Furniture that also cannot be repaid by December 31, 2017. Sensitivity analysis helps managers anticipate such outcomes and take steps to minimize the effects of expected reductions in cash flows from operations.

EXHIBIT 6-9 Sensitivity Analysis: Effects of Key Budget Assumptions in Exhibit 6-4 on 2017 Short-Term Borrowing for Stylistic Furniture

	A	B	C	D	E	F	G	H	I	J
1				Direct Material			Short-Term Borrowing and Repayment by Quarter			
2		Selling Price		Purchase Costs		Budgeted	Quarters			
3	Scenario	Casual	Deluxe	Red Oak	Granite	Operating Income	1	2	3	4
4	1	$582	$776	$7.00	$10.00	$3,794,100	$2,146,000	$(579,000)	$(834,000)	$170,000
5	2	$600	$800	7.35	10.50	4,483,800	2,048,000	$(722,000)	$(999,000)	$41,000

TERMS TO LEARN

This chapter and the Glossary at the end of the book contain definitions of the following important terms:

activity-based budgeting (ABB)
budgetary slack
cash budget
continuous budget
controllability
controllable cost
cost center
financial budget
financial planning models
investment center
Kaizen budgeting
master budget
operating budget
organization structure
pro forma statements
profit center
responsibility accounting
responsibility center
revenue center
rolling budget
rolling forecast

ASSIGNMENT MATERIAL

Pearson MyLab Accounting

Questions

6-1 What are the four elements of the budgeting cycle?
6-2 Define master budget.
6-3 List the five key questions that must be considered by managers for developing successful strategies.
6-4 "Budgets provide a framework for evaluating performance and improving learning." Do you agree? Explain.
6-5 "Budgets can promote coordination and communication among subunits within the company." Do you agree? Explain.
6-6 "Budgets motivate managers and other employees to the company's goals." Do you agree? Explain.
6-7 Define rolling budget. Give an example.
6-8 Outline the steps in preparing an operating budget.
6-9 What is the usual starting point for an operating budget?
6-10 How can sensitivity analysis be used to increase the benefits of budgeting?
6-11 What is the key emphasis in Kaizen budgeting?
6-12 Describe how nonoutput-based cost drivers can be incorporated into budgeting.
6-13 Explain how the choice of the type of responsibility center (cost, revenue, profit, or investment) affects behavior.
6-14 What are some additional considerations that arise when budgeting in multinational companies?
6-15 Explain why cash budgets are important.

Multiple-Choice Questions

6-16 Master budget. Which of the following statements is correct regarding the components of the master budget?
   a. The cash budget is used to create the capital budget.
   b. Operating budgets are used to create cash budgets.
   c. The manufacturing overhead budget is used to create the production budget.
   d. The cost of goods sold budget is used to create the selling and administrative expense budget.

6-17 Operating and financial budgets. Which of the following statements is correct regarding the drivers of operating and financial budgets?
   a. The sales budget will drive the cost of goods sold budget.
   b. The cost of goods sold budget will drive the units of production budget.
   c. The production budget will drive the selling and administrative expense budget.
   d. The cash budget will drive the production and selling and administrative expense budgets.

6-18 Production budget. Superior Industries sales budget shows quarterly sales for the next year as follows: Quarter 1–10,000; Quarter 2–8,000; Quarter 3–12,000; Quarter 4–14,000. Company policy is to have a target finished-goods inventory at the end of each quarter equal to 20% of the next quarter's sales. Budgeted production for the second quarter of next year would be:

   1. 7,200 units; 2. 8,800 units; 3. 12,000 units; 4. 10,400 units

6-19 Responsibility centers. Elmhurst Corporation is considering changes to its responsibility accounting system. Which of the following statements is/are correct for a responsibility accounting system.
   i. In a cost center, managers are responsible for controlling costs but not revenue.
   ii. The idea behind responsibility accounting is that a manager should be held responsible for those items that the manager can control to a significant extent.
   iii. To be effective, a good responsibility accounting system must help managers to plan and to control.
   iv. Costs that are allocated to a responsibility center are normally controllable by the responsibility center manager.

   1. I and II only are correct.
   2. II and III only are correct.
   3. I, II, and III are correct.
   4. I, II and IV are correct.

6-20 Cash budget. Mary Jacobs, the controller of the Jenks Company is working on Jenks' cash budget for year 2. She has information on each of the following items:
   i. Wages due to workers accrued as of December 31, year 1.
   ii. Limits on a line of credit that may be used to fund Jenks' operations in year 2.
   iii. The balance in accounts payable as of December 31, year 1, from credit purchases made in year 1.

Which of the items above should Jacobs take into account when building the cash budget for year 2?
   a. I, II
   b. I, III
   c. II, III
   d. I, II, III

©2016 DeVry/Becker Educational Development Corp. All Rights Reserved.

Exercises

6-21 Sales budget, service setting. In 2017, Rouse & Sons, a small environmental-testing firm, performed 12,200 radon tests for $290 each and 16,400 lead tests for $240 each. Because newer homes are being built with lead-free pipes, lead-testing volume is expected to decrease by 10% next year. However, awareness of radon-related health hazards is expected to result in a 6% increase in radon-test volume each year in the near future. Jim Rouse feels that if he lowers his price for lead testing to $230 per test, he will have to face only a 7% decline in lead-test sales in 2018.

1. Prepare a 2018 sales budget for Rouse & Sons assuming that Rouse holds prices at 2017 levels.
2. Prepare a 2018 sales budget for Rouse & Sons assuming that Rouse lowers the price of a lead test to $230. Should Rouse lower the price of a lead test in 2018 if the company's goal is to maximize sales revenue?

6-22 Sales and production budget. The Albright Company manufactures ball pens and expects sales of 452,000 units in 2018. Albright estimates that its ending inventory for 2018 will be 65,400 pens. The beginning inventory is 46,500 pens. Compute the number of pens budgeted for production in 2018.

6-23 Direct material budget. Polyhidron Corporation produces 5-gallon plastic buckets. The company expects to produce 430,000 buckets in 2018. Polyhidron purchases high-quality plastic granules for the production of buckets. Each pound of plastic granules produces two 5-gallon buckets. Target ending inventory of the company is 35,200 pounds of plastic granules; its beginning inventory is 22,500. Compute how many pounds of plastic granules need to be purchased in 2018.

6-24 Material purchases budget. The Ceremicon Company produces teapots from stoneware clay. The company has prepared a sales budget of 150,000 units of teapots for a 3-month period. It has an inventory of 34,000 units of teapots on hand at December 31 and has estimated an inventory of 38,000 units of teapots at the end of the succeeding quarter.

One unit of teapot needs 2 pounds of stoneware clay. The company has an inventory of 82,000 pounds of stoneware clay at December 31 and has a target ending inventory of 95,000 pounds of stoneware clay at the end of the succeeding quarter. How many pounds of direct materials (stoneware clay) should Ceremicon purchase during the 3 months ending March 31?

6-25 Revenues, production, and purchases budgets. The Deluxe Motorcar in northern California manufactures motor cars of all categories. Its budgeted sales for the most popular sedan model XE8 in 2018 is 4,000 units. Deluxe Motorcar has a beginning finished inventory of 600 units. Its ending inventory is 450 units. The present selling price of model XE8 to the distributors and dealers is $35,200. The company does not want to increase its selling price in 2018.

Deluxe Motorcar does not produce tires. It buys the tires from an outside supplier. One complete car requires five tires including the tire for the extra wheel. The company's target ending inventory is 400 tires, and its beginning inventory is 350 tires. The budgeted purchase price is $45 per tire.

Required

1. Compute the budgeted revenues in dollars.
2. Compute the number of cars that Deluxe Motorcar should produce.
3. Compute the budgeted purchases of tires in units and in dollars.
4. What actions can Deluxe Motorcar's managers take to reduce budgeted purchasing costs of tires assuming the same budgeted sales for Model XE8?

6-26 Revenues and production budget. Price, Inc., bottles and distributes mineral water from the company's natural springs in northern Oregon. Price markets two products: 12-ounce disposable plastic bottles and 1-gallon reusable plastic containers.

Required

1. For 2015, Price marketing managers project monthly sales of 420,000 12-ounce bottles and 170,000 1-gallon containers. Average selling prices are estimated at $0.20 per 12-ounce bottle and $1.50 per 1-gallon container. Prepare a revenues budget for Price, Inc., for the year ending December 31, 2015.
2. Price begins 2015 with 890,000 12-ounce bottles in inventory. The vice president of operations requests that 12-ounce bottles ending inventory on December 31, 2015, be no less than 680,000 bottles. Based on sales projections as budgeted previously, what is the minimum number of 12-ounce bottles Price must produce during 2015?
3. The VP of operations requests that ending inventory of 1-gallon containers on December 31, 2015, be 240,000 units. If the production budget calls for Price to produce 1,900,000 1-gallon containers during 2015, what is the beginning inventory of 1-gallon containers on January 1, 2015?

6-27 Budgeting; direct material usage, manufacturing cost, and gross margin. Xander Manufacturing Company manufactures blue rugs, using wool and dye as direct materials. One rug is budgeted to use 36 skeins of wool at a cost of $2 per skein and 0.8 gallons of dye at a cost of $6 per gallon. All other materials are indirect. At the beginning of the year Xander has an inventory of 458,000 skeins of wool at a cost of $961,800 and 4,000 gallons of dye at a cost of $23,680. Target ending inventory of wool and dye is zero. Xander uses the FIFO inventory cost-flow method.

Xander blue rugs are very popular and demand is high, but because of capacity constraints the firm will produce only 200,000 blue rugs per year. The budgeted selling price is $2,000 each. There are no rugs in beginning inventory. Target ending inventory of rugs is also zero.

Xander makes rugs by hand, but uses a machine to dye the wool. Thus, overhead costs are accumulated in two cost pools—one for weaving and the other for dyeing. Weaving overhead is allocated to products based on direct manufacturing labor-hours (DMLH). Dyeing overhead is allocated to products based on machine-hours (MH).

There is no direct manufacturing labor cost for dyeing. Xander budgets 62 direct manufacturing labor-hours to weave a rug at a budgeted rate of $13 per hour. It budgets 0.2 machine-hours to dye each skein in the dyeing process.

The following table presents the budgeted overhead costs for the dyeing and weaving cost pools:

	Dyeing (based on 1,440,000 MH)	Weaving (based on 12,400,000 DMLH)
Variable costs		
Indirect materials	$ 0	$15,400,000
Maintenance	6,560,000	5,540,000
Utilities	7,550,000	2,890,000
Fixed costs		
Indirect labor	347,000	1,700,000
Depreciation	2,100,000	274,000
Other	723,000	5,816,000
Total budgeted costs	$17,280,000	$31,620,000

Required

1. Prepare a direct materials usage budget in both units and dollars.
2. Calculate the budgeted overhead allocation rates for weaving and dyeing.
3. Calculate the budgeted unit cost of a blue rug for the year.
4. Prepare a revenues budget for blue rugs for the year, assuming Xander sells (a) 200,000 or (b) 185,000 blue rugs (that is, at two different sales levels).
5. Calculate the budgeted cost of goods sold for blue rugs under each sales assumption.
6. Find the budgeted gross margin for blue rugs under each sales assumption.
7. What actions might you take as a manager to improve profitability if sales drop to 185,000 blue rugs?
8. How might top management at Xander use the budget developed in requirements 1–6 to better manage the company?

6-28 Budgeting, service company. Ever Clean Company provides gutter cleaning services to residential clients. The company has enjoyed considerable growth in recent years due to a successful marketing campaign and favorable reviews on service-rating Web sites. Ever Clean owner Joanne Clark makes sales calls herself and quotes on jobs based on length of gutter surface. Ever Clean hires college students to drive the company vans to jobs and clean the gutters. A part-time bookkeeper takes care of billing customers and other office tasks. Overhead is allocated based on direct labor-hours (DLH).

Joanne Clark estimates that her gutter cleaners will work a total of 1,000 jobs during the year. Each job averages 600 feet of gutter surface and requires 12 direct labor-hours. Clark pays her gutter cleaners $15 per hour, inclusive of taxes and benefits. The following table presents the budgeted overhead costs for 2018:

Variable costs	
Supplies ($6.50 per DLH)	$ 78,000
Fixed costs (to support capacity of 12,000 DLH)	
Indirect labor	25,000
Depreciation	17,000
Other	24,000
Total budgeted costs	$144,000

Required

1. Prepare a direct labor budget in both hours and dollars.
2. Calculate the budgeted overhead allocation rate based on the budgeted quantity of the cost drivers.
3. Calculate the budgeted total cost of all jobs for the year and the budgeted cost of an average 600-foot gutter-cleaning job.
4. Prepare a revenues budget for the year, assuming that Ever Clean charges customers $0.60 per square foot.
5. Calculate the budgeted operating income.
6. What actions can Clark take if sales should decline to 900 jobs annually?

6-29 Budgets for production and direct manufacturing labor. (CMA, adapted) Roletter Company makes and sells artistic frames for pictures of weddings, graduations, and other special events. Bob Anderson, the controller, is responsible for preparing Roletter's master budget and has accumulated the following information for 2018:

	2018				
	January	February	March	April	May
Estimated sales in units	10,000	14,000	7,000	8,000	8,000
Selling price	$54.00	$50.50	$50.50	$50.50	$50.50
Direct manufacturing labor-hours per unit	2.0	2.0	1.5	1.5	1.5
Wage per direct manufacturing labor-hour	$12.00	$12.00	$12.00	$13.00	$13.00

In addition to wages, direct manufacturing labor-related costs include pension contributions of $0.50 per hour, worker's compensation insurance of $0.20 per hour, employee medical insurance of $0.30 per hour, and Social Security taxes. Assume that as of January 1, 2018, the Social Security tax rates are 7.5% for employers and 7.5% for employees. The cost of employee benefits paid by Roletter on its employees is treated as a direct manufacturing labor cost.

Roletter has a labor contract that calls for a wage increase to $13 per hour on April 1, 2018. New labor-saving machinery has been installed and will be fully operational by March 1, 2018. Roletter expects to have 17,500 frames on hand at December 31, 2017, and it has a policy of carrying an end-of-month inventory of 100% of the following month's sales plus 50% of the second following month's sales.

Required

1. Prepare a production budget and a direct manufacturing labor budget for Roletter Company by month and for the first quarter of 2018. You may combine both budgets in one schedule. The direct manufacturing labor budget should include labor-hours and show the details for each labor cost category.
2. What actions has the budget process prompted Roletter's management to take?
3. How might Roletter's managers use the budget developed in requirement 1 to better manage the company?

6-30 Activity-based budgeting. The Jerico store of Jiffy Mart, a chain of small neighborhood convenience stores, is preparing its activity-based budget for January 2018. Jiffy Mart has three product categories: soft drinks (35% of cost of goods sold [COGS]), fresh produce (25% of COGS), and packaged food (40% of COGS). The following table shows the four activities that consume indirect resources at the Jerico store, the cost drivers and their rates, and the cost-driver amount budgeted to be consumed by each activity in January 2018.

Activity	Cost Driver	January 2018 Budgeted Cost-Driver Rate	January 2018 Budgeted Amount of Cost Driver Used		
			Soft Drinks	Fresh Snacks	Packaged Food
Ordering	Number of purchase orders	$ 45	14	24	14
Delivery	Number of deliveries	$ 41	12	62	19
Shelf stocking	Hours of stocking time	$10.50	16	172	94
Customer support	Number of items sold	$ 0.09	4,600	34,200	10,750

Required

1. What is the total budgeted indirect cost at the Jerico store in January 2018? What is the total budgeted cost of each activity at the Jerico store for January 2018? What is the budgeted indirect cost of each product category for January 2018?
2. Which product category has the largest fraction of total budgeted indirect costs?
3. Given your answer in requirement 2, what advantage does Jiffy Mart gain by using an activity-based approach to budgeting over, say, allocating indirect costs to products based on cost of goods sold?

6-31 Kaizen approach to activity-based budgeting (continuation of 6-30). Jiffy Mart has a Kaizen (continuous improvement) approach to budgeting monthly activity costs for each month of 2018. Each successive month, the budgeted cost-driver rate decreases by 0.4% relative to the preceding month. So, for example, February's budgeted cost-driver rate is 0.996 times January's budgeted cost-driver rate, and March's budgeted cost-driver rate is 0.996 times the budgeted February rate. Jiffy Mart assumes that the budgeted amount of cost-driver usage remains the same each month.

Required

1. What are the total budgeted cost for each activity and the total budgeted indirect cost for March 2018?
2. What are the benefits of using a Kaizen approach to budgeting? What are the limitations of this approach, and how might Jiffy Mart management overcome them?

6-32 Responsibility and controllability. Consider each of the following independent situations for Prestige Fountains. Prestige manufactures and sells decorative fountains for commercial properties. The company also contracts to service both its own and other brands of fountains. Prestige has a manufacturing plant, a supply warehouse that supplies both the manufacturing plant and the service technicians (who often need parts to repair fountains), and 12 service vans. The service technicians drive to customer sites to service the fountains. Prestige owns the vans, pays for the gas, and supplies fountain parts, but the technicians own their own tools.

1. In the manufacturing plant, the production manager is not happy with the motors that the purchasing manager has been purchasing. In May, the production manager stops requesting motors from the supply warehouse and starts purchasing them directly from a different motor manufacturer. Actual materials costs in May are higher than budgeted.
2. Overhead costs in the manufacturing plant for June are much higher than budgeted. Investigation reveals a utility rate hike in effect that was not figured into the budget.

3. Gasoline costs for each van are budgeted based on the service area of the van and the amount of driving expected for the month. The driver of van 3 routinely has monthly gasoline costs exceeding the budget for van 3. After investigating, the service manager finds that the driver has been driving the van for personal use.
4. Regency Mall, one of Prestige's fountain service customers, calls the service people only for emergencies and not for routine maintenance. Thus, the materials and labor costs for these service calls exceeds the monthly budgeted costs for a contract customer.
5. Prestige's service technicians are paid an hourly wage of $22, regardless of experience or time with the company. As a result of an analysis performed last month, the service manager determined that service technicians in their first year of employment worked on average 20% more slowly than other employees. Prestige bills customers per service call, not per hour.
6. The cost of health insurance for service technicians has increased by 40% this year, which caused the actual health insurance costs to greatly exceed the budgeted health insurance costs for the service technicians.

Required

For each situation described, determine where (that is, with whom) (a) responsibility and (b) controllability lie. Suggest ways to solve the problem or to improve the situation.

6-33 Responsibility, controllability, and stretch targets. Consider each of the following independent situations for Sunrise Tours, a company owned by David Bartlett that sells motor coach tours to schools and other groups. Sunshine Tours owns a fleet of 10 motor coaches and employs 12 drivers, 1 maintenance technician, 3 sales representatives, and an office manager. Sunshine Tours pays for all fuel and maintenance on the coaches. Drivers are paid $0.50 per mile while in transit, plus $15 per hour while idle (time spent waiting while tour groups are visiting their destinations). The maintenance technician and office manager are both full-time salaried employees. The sales representatives work on straight commission.

1. When the office manager receives calls from potential customers, she is instructed to handle the contracts herself. Recently, however, the number of contracts written up by the office manager has declined. At the same time, one of the sales representatives has experienced a significant increase in contracts. The other two representatives believe that the office manager has been colluding with the third representative to send him the prospective customers.
2. One of the motor coach drivers seems to be reaching his destinations more quickly than any of the other drivers and is reporting longer idle time.
3. Regular preventive maintenance of the motor coaches has been proven to improve fuel efficiency and reduce overall operating costs by averting costly repairs. During busy months, however, it is difficult for the maintenance technician to complete all of the maintenance tasks within his 40-hour workweek.
4. David Bartlett has read about stretch targets, and he believes that a change in the compensation structure of the sales representatives may improve sales. Rather than a straight commission of 10% of sales, he is considering a system where each representative is given a monthly goal of 50 contracts. If the goal is met, the representative is paid a 12% commission. If the goal is not met, the commission falls to 8%. Currently, each sales representative averages 45 contracts per month.
5. Fuel consumption has increased significantly in recent months. David Bartlett is considering ways to promote improved fuel efficiency and reduce harmful emissions using stretch environmental targets, where drivers and the maintenance mechanic would receive a bonus if fuel consumption falls below 90% of budgeted fuel usage per mile driven.

Required

For situations 1–3, discuss which employee has responsibility for the related costs and the extent to which costs are controllable and by whom. What are the risks or costs to the company? What can be done to solve the problem or improve the situation? For situations 4 and 5, describe the potential benefits and costs of establishing stretch targets.

6-34 Cash flow analysis, sensitivity analysis. HealthMart is a retail store selling home medical supplies. HealthMart also services home oxygen equipment, for which the company bills customers monthly. HealthMart has budgeted for increases in service revenue of $500 each month due to a recent advertising campaign. The forecast of sales and service revenue for the March–June 2018 is as follows:

Sales and Service Revenues Budget March–June 2018

Month	Expected Sales Revenue	Expected Service Revenue	Total Revenue
March	$7,200	$5,000	$12,200
April	8,400	5,500	13,900
May	9,100	6,000	15,100
June	10,500	6,500	17,000

Almost all of the retail sales are credit card sales; cash sales are negligible. The credit card company deposits 92% of the revenue recorded each day into HealthMart's account overnight. 70% of oxygen service billed each month is collected in the month of the service, and 30% is collected in the month after the service.

Required

1. Calculate the cash that HealthMart expects to collect in April, May, and June 2018. Show calculations for each month.
2. HealthMart has budgeted expenditures for May of $14,100.
   a. Given your answer to requirement 1, and assuming a beginning cash balance for May of $650, will HealthMart be able to cover its payments for May?
   b. Assume (independently for each situation) that May revenues might also be 10% lower or that costs might be 5% higher. Under each of those two scenarios, show the total net cash for May and the amount HealthMart would have to borrow if cash receipts are less than cash payments. The company requires a minimum cash balance of $600. (Again, assume a balance of $650 on May 1.)
3. Why do HealthMart's managers prepare a cash budget in addition to the revenue, expenses, and operating income budget? Has preparing the cash budget been helpful? Explain briefly.

Problems

6-35 Budget schedules for a manufacturer. Lame Specialties manufactures, among other things, woolen blankets for the athletic teams of the two local high schools. The company sews the blankets from fabric and sews on a logo patch purchased from the licensed logo store site. The teams are as follows:

- Knights, with red blankets and the Knights logo
- Raiders, with black blankets and the Raider logo

Also, the black blankets are slightly larger than the red blankets.

The budgeted direct-cost inputs for each product in 2017 are as follows:

	Knights Blanket	Raiders Blanket
Red wool fabric	4 yards	0 yards
Black wool fabric	0	5
Knight logo patches	1	0
Raider logo patches	0	1
Direct manufacturing labor	3 hours	4 hours

Unit data pertaining to the direct materials for March 2017 are as follows:

Actual Beginning Direct Materials Inventory (3/1/2017)

	Knights Blanket	Raiders Blanket
Red wool fabric	35 yards	0 yards
Black wool fabric	0	15
Knight logo patches	45	0
Raider logo patches	0	60

Target Ending Direct Materials Inventory (3/31/2017)

	Knights Blanket	Raiders Blanket
Red wool fabric	25 yards	0 yards
Black wool fabric	0	25
Knight logo patches	25	0
Raider logo patches	0	25

Unit cost data for direct-cost inputs pertaining to February 2017 and March 2017 are as follows:

	February 2017 (actual)	March 2017 (budgeted)
Red wool fabric (per yard)	$9	$10
Black wool fabric (per yard)	12	11
Knight logo patches (per patch)	7	7
Raider logo patches (per patch)	6	8
Manufacturing labor cost per hour	26	27

Manufacturing overhead (both variable and fixed) is allocated to each blanket on the basis of budgeted direct manufacturing labor-hours per blanket. The budgeted variable manufacturing overhead rate for March 2017 is $16 per direct manufacturing labor-hour. The budgeted fixed manufacturing overhead for March 2017 is $14,640. Both variable and fixed manufacturing overhead costs are allocated to each unit of finished goods.

Data relating to finished goods inventory for March 2017 are as follows:

	Knights Blanket	Raiders Blanket
Beginning inventory in units	12	17
Beginning inventory in dollars (cost)	$1,440	$2,550
Target ending inventory in units	22	27

Budgeted sales for March 2017 are 130 units of the Knights blankets and 190 units of the Raiders blankets. The budgeted selling prices per unit in March 2014 are $229 for the Knights blankets and $296 for the Raiders blankets. Assume the following in your answer:

- Work-in-process inventories are negligible and ignored.
- Direct materials inventory and finished goods inventory are costed using the FIFO method.
- Unit costs of direct materials purchased and finished goods are constant in March 2017.

Required

1. Prepare the following budgets for March 2017:
   a. Revenues budget
   b. Production budget in units
   c. Direct material usage budget and direct material purchases budget
   d. Direct manufacturing labor budget
   e. Manufacturing overhead budget
   f. Ending inventories budget (direct materials and finished goods)
   g. Cost of goods sold budget
2. Suppose Lame Specialties decides to incorporate continuous improvement into its budgeting process. Describe two areas where it could incorporate continuous improvement into the budget schedules in requirement 1.

6-36 Budgeted costs, Kaizen improvements environmental costs. Tom's Apparels (Ghana) manufactures plain white and solid-colored T-shirts. Budgeted inputs include the following:

	Price	Quantity	Cost per unit of output
Fabric	$12 per yard	0.75 yard per unit	$9 per unit
Labor	$20 per DMLH	0.25 DMLH per unit	$5 per unit
Dye*	$0.75 per ounce	4 ounces per unit	$3 per unit

*For colored T-shirts only

Budgeted sales and selling price per unit are as follows:

	Budgeted Sales	Selling Price per Unit
White T-shirts	15,000 units	$15 per T-shirt
Colored T-shirts	60,000 units	$18 per T-shirt

Tom's Apparels has the opportunity to switch from using the dye it currently uses to using an environmentally friendly dye that costs $1.50 per ounce. The company would still need 4 ounces of dye per shirt. Tom's is reluctant to change because of the increase in costs (and decrease in profit), but the Environmental Protection Agency has threatened to fine the company $140,000 if it continues to use the harmful but less expensive dye.

Required

1. Given the preceding information, would Tom's be better off financially by switching to the environmentally friendly dye? (Assume all other costs would remain the same.)
2. Assume Tom's chooses to be environmentally responsible regardless of cost, and it switches to the new dye. The production manager suggests trying Kaizen costing. If Tom's can reduce fabric and labor costs each by 1% per month on all the shirts it manufactures, how close will it be at the end of 12 months to the profit it would have earned before switching to the more expensive dye? (Round to the nearest dollar for calculating cost reductions.)
3. Refer to requirement 2. How could the reduction in material and labor costs be accomplished? Are there any problems with this plan?

6-37 Revenue and production budgets. (CPA, adapted) The Sabat Corporation manufactures and sells two products: Thingone and Thingtwo. In July 2016, Sabat's budget department gathered the following data to prepare budgets for 2017:

2017 Projected Sales

Product	Units	Price
Thingone	62,000	$172
Thingtwo	46,000	$264

2017 Inventories in Units

	Expected Target	
Product	January 1, 2017	December 31, 2017
Thingone	21,000	26,000
Thingtwo	13,000	14,000

The following direct materials are used in the two products:

		Amount Used per Unit	
Direct Material	Unit	Thingone	Thingtwo
A	pound	5	6
B	pound	3	4
C	each	0	2

Projected data for 2017 for direct materials are as follows:

Direct Material	Anticipated Purchase Price	Expected Inventories January 1, 2017	Target Inventories December 31, 2017
A	$11	37,000 lb.	40,000 lb.
B	6	32,000 lb.	35,000 lb.
C	5	10,000 units	12,000 units

Projected direct manufacturing labor requirements and rates for 2017 are as follows:

Product	Hours per Unit	Rate per Hour
Thingone	3	$11
Thingtwo	4	$14

Manufacturing overhead is allocated at the rate of $19 per direct manufacturing labor-hour.

Based on the preceding projections and budget requirements for Thingone and Thingtwo, prepare the following budgets for 2017:

Required

1. Revenues budget (in dollars)
2. What questions might the CEO ask the marketing manager when reviewing the revenues budget? Explain briefly.
3. Production budget (in units)
4. Direct material purchases budget (in quantities)
5. Direct material purchases budget (in dollars)
6. Direct manufacturing labor budget (in dollars)
7. Budgeted finished-goods inventory at December 31, 2017 (in dollars)
8. What questions might the CEO ask the production manager when reviewing the production, direct materials, and direct manufacturing labor budgets?
9. How does preparing a budget help Sabat Corporation's top management better manage the company?

6-38 Budgeted income statement. (CMA, adapted) Smart Video Company is a manufacturer of videoconferencing products. Maintaining the videoconferencing equipment is an important area of customer satisfaction. A recent downturn in the computer industry has caused the videoconferencing equipment segment to suffer, leading to a decline in Smart Video's financial performance. The following income statement shows results for 2017:

Smart Video Company Income Statement for the Year Ended December 31, 2017 (in thousands)

Revenues		
Equipment	$8,000	
Maintenance contracts	1,900	
Total revenues		$9,900
Cost of goods sold		4,000
Gross margin		5,900
Operating costs		
Marketing	630	
Distribution	100	
Customer maintenance	1,100	
Administration	920	
Total operating costs		2,750
Operating income		$3,150

Smart Video's management team is preparing the 2018 budget and is studying the following information:

1. Selling prices of equipment are expected to increase by 10% as the economic recovery begins. The selling price of each maintenance contract is expected to remain unchanged from 2017.
2. Equipment sales in units are expected to increase by 6%, with a corresponding 6% growth in units of maintenance contracts.
3. Cost of each unit sold is expected to increase by 5% to pay for the necessary technology and quality improvements.
4. Marketing costs are expected to increase by $290,000, but administration costs are expected to remain at 2017 levels.
5. Distribution costs vary in proportion to the number of units of equipment sold.
6. Two maintenance technicians are to be hired at a total cost of $160,000, which covers wages and related travel costs. The objective is to improve customer service and shorten response time.
7. There is no beginning or ending inventory of equipment.

Required

1. Prepare a budgeted income statement for the year ending December 31, 2018.
2. How well does the budget align with Smart Video's strategy?
3. How does preparing the budget help Smart Video's management team better manage the company?

6-39 Responsibility in a restaurant. Christa Schuller owns an outlet of a popular chain of restaurants in the southern part of Germany. One of the chain's popular lunch items is the cheeseburger. It is a hamburger topped with cheese. On demand, purchasing agents from each outlet orders the cheese and meat patties from the Central Warehouse. In January 2018, one of the freezers in Central Warehouse broke down and the production of meat patty and storing of cheese were reduced by 20-30% for 4 days. During these 4 days, Christa's franchise runs out of meat patties and cheese slices while facing a high demand for cheeseburgers. Christa's chef, Kelly Lyn, decides to prepare cheeseburgers using ingredients from a local market, sending one of the kitchen helpers to the market to buy the ingredients. Although the customers' are satisfied, Christa's restaurant has to pay twice the cost of the Central Warehouse's products to procure meat and cheese from the local market, and the restaurant loses money on this item for those 4 days. Christa is angry with the purchasing agent for not ordering enough meat patty and cheese to avoid running out of stock, and with Kelly for spending too much money on the procurement of meat and cheese.

Required

Who is responsible for the cost of the meat patty and cheese as ingredients of a cheeseburger? At what level is the cost controllable? Do you agree that Christa should be angry with the purchasing agent? With Kelly? Why or why not?

6-40 Comprehensive problem with ABC costing. Animal Gear Company makes two pet carriers, the Cat-allac and the Dog-eriffic. They are both made of plastic with metal doors, but the Cat-allac is smaller. Information for the two products for the month of April is given in the following tables:

Input Prices

Direct materials	
Plastic	$5 per pound
Metal	$4 per pound
Direct manufacturing labor	$10 per direct manufacturing labor-hour

Input Quantities per Unit of Output

	Cat-allac	Dog-eriffic
Direct materials		
Plastic	4 pounds	6 pounds
Metal	0.5 pounds	1 pound
Direct manufacturing labor-hours	3 hours	5 hours
Machine-hours (MH)	11 MH	19 MH

Inventory Information, Direct Materials

	Plastic	Metal
Beginning inventory	290 pounds	70 pounds
Target ending inventory	410 pounds	65 pounds
Cost of beginning inventory	$1,102	$217

Animal Gear accounts for direct materials using a FIFO cost-flow assumption.

Sales and Inventory Information, Finished Goods

	Cat-allac	Dog-eriffic
Expected sales in units	530	225
Selling price	$ 205	$ 310
Target ending inventory in units	30	10
Beginning inventory in units	10	19
Beginning inventory in dollars	$1,000	$4,650

Animal Gear uses a FIFO cost-flow assumption for finished-goods inventory.

Animal Gear uses an activity-based costing system and classifies overhead into three activity pools: Setup, Processing, and Inspection. Activity rates for these activities are $105 per setup-hour, $10 per machine-hour, and $15 per inspection-hour, respectively. Other information follows:

Cost-Driver Information

	Cat-allac	Dog-eriffic
Number of units per batch	25	9
Setup time per batch	1.50 hours	1.75 hours
Inspection time per batch	0.5 hour	0.7 hour

If necessary, round up to calculate number of batches.

Nonmanufacturing fixed costs for March equal $32,000, half of which are salaries. Salaries are expected to increase 5% in April. Other nonmanufacturing fixed costs will remain the same. The only variable nonmanufacturing cost is sales commission, equal to 1% of sales revenue.

Prepare the following for April:

Required

1. Revenues budget
2. Production budget in units
3. Direct material usage budget and direct material purchases budget
4. Direct manufacturing labor cost budget
5. Manufacturing overhead cost budgets for each of the three activities
6. Budgeted unit cost of ending finished-goods inventory and ending inventories budget
7. Cost of goods sold budget
8. Nonmanufacturing costs budget
9. Budgeted income statement (ignore income taxes)
10. How does preparing the budget help Animal Gear's management team better manage the company?

6-41 Cash budget (continuation of 6-40). Refer to the information in Problem 6-40.

Assume the following: Animal Gear (AG) does not make any sales on credit. AG sells only to the public and accepts cash and credit cards; 90% of its sales are to customers using credit cards, for which AG gets the cash right away, less a 2% transaction fee.

Purchases of materials are on account. AG pays for half the purchases in the period of the purchase and the other half in the following period. At the end of March, AG owes suppliers $8,000.

AG plans to replace a machine in April at a net cash cost of $13,000.

Labor, other manufacturing costs, and nonmanufacturing costs are paid in cash in the month incurred except of course depreciation, which is not a cash flow. Depreciation is $25,000 of the manufacturing cost and $10,000 of the nonmanufacturing cost for April.

AG currently has a $2,000 loan at an annual interest rate of 12%. The interest is paid at the end of each month. If AG has more than $7,000 cash at the end of April it will pay back the loan. AG owes $5,000 in income taxes that need to be remitted in April. AG has cash of $5,900 on hand at the end of March.

Required

1. Prepare a cash budget for April for Animal Gear.
2. Why do Animal Gear's managers prepare a cash budget in addition to the revenue, expenses, and operating income budget?

6-42 Comprehensive operating budget. Skulas, Inc., manufactures and sells snowboards. Skulas manufactures a single model, the Pipex. In late 2017, Skulas's management accountant gathered the following data to prepare budgets for January 2018:

Materials and Labor Requirements

Direct materials	
Wood	9 board feet (b.f.) per snowboard
Fiberglass	10 yards per snowboard
Direct manufacturing labor	5 hours per snowboard

Skulas's CEO expects to sell 2,900 snowboards during January 2018 at an estimated retail price of $650 per board. Further, the CEO expects 2018 beginning inventory of 500 snowboards and would like to end January 2018 with 200 snowboards in stock.

Direct Materials Inventories

	Beginning Inventory 1/1/2018	Ending Inventory 1/31/2018
Wood	2,040 b.f.	1,540 b.f.
Fiberglass	1,040 yards	2,040 yards

Variable manufacturing overhead is $7 per direct manufacturing labor-hour. There are also $81,000 in fixed manufacturing overhead costs budgeted for January 2018. Skulas combines both variable and fixed manufacturing overhead into a single rate based on direct manufacturing labor-hours. Variable marketing costs are allocated at the rate of $250 per sales visit. The marketing plan calls for 38 sales visits during January 2018. Finally, there are $35,000 in fixed nonmanufacturing costs budgeted for January 2018.

Other data include:

	2017 Unit Price	2018 Unit Price
Wood	$32.00 per b.f.	$34.00 per b.f.
Fiberglass	$ 8.00 per yard	$ 9.00 per yard
Direct manufacturing labor	$28.00 per hour	$29.00 per hour

The inventoriable unit cost for ending finished-goods inventory on December 31, 2017, is $374.80. Assume Skulas uses a FIFO inventory method for both direct materials and finished goods. Ignore work in process in your calculations.

Required

1. Prepare the January 2018 revenues budget (in dollars).
2. Prepare the January 2018 production budget (in units).
3. Prepare the direct material usage and purchases budgets for January 2018.
4. Prepare a direct manufacturing labor costs budget for January 2018.
5. Prepare a manufacturing overhead costs budget for January 2018.
6. What is the budgeted manufacturing overhead rate for January 2018?
7. What is the budgeted manufacturing overhead cost per output unit in January 2018?
8. Calculate the cost of a snowboard manufactured in January 2018.
9. Prepare an ending inventory budget for both direct materials and finished goods for January 2018.
10. Prepare a cost of goods sold budget for January 2018.
11. Prepare the budgeted income statement for Skulas, Inc., for January 2018.
12. What questions might the CEO ask the management team when reviewing the budget? Should the CEO set stretch targets? Explain briefly.
13. How does preparing the budget help Skulas's management team better manage the company?

6-43 Cash budgeting, budgeted balance sheet. (Continuation of 6-42) (Appendix)
Refer to the information in Problem 6-42.
Budgeted balances at January 31, 2018 are as follows:

Cash	?
Accounts receivable	?
Inventory	?
Property, plant and equipment (net)	$1,175,600
Accounts payable	?
Long-term liabilities	182,000
Stockholders' equity	?

Selected budget information for December 2017 follows:

Cash balance, December 31, 2017	$ 124,000
Budgeted sales	1,650,000
Budgeted materials purchases	820,000

Customer invoices are payable within 30 days. From past experience, Skulas's accountant projects 40% of invoices will be collected in the month invoiced, and 60% will be collected in the following month.

Accounts payable relates only to the purchase of direct materials. Direct materials are purchased on credit with 50% of direct materials purchases paid during the month of the purchase, and 50% paid in the month following purchase.

Fixed manufacturing overhead costs include $64,000 of depreciation costs and fixed nonmanufacturing overhead costs include $10,000 of depreciation costs. Direct manufacturing labor and the remaining manufacturing and nonmanufacturing overhead costs are paid monthly.

All property, plant, and equipment acquired during January 2018 were purchased on credit and did not entail any outflow of cash.

There were no borrowings or repayments with respect to long-term liabilities in January 2018.

On December 15, 2017, Skulas's board of directors voted to pay a $160,000 dividend to stockholders on January 31, 2018.

Required

1. Prepare a cash budget for January 2018. Show supporting schedules for the calculation of collection of receivables and payments of accounts payable, and for disbursements for fixed manufacturing and nonmanufacturing overhead.
2. Skulas is interested in maintaining a minimum cash balance of $120,000 at the end of each month. Will Skulas be in a position to pay the $160,000 dividend on January 31?
3. Why do Skulas's managers prepare a cash budget in addition to the revenue, expenses, and operating income budget?
4. Prepare a budgeted balance sheet for January 31, 2018 by calculating the January 31, 2018 balances in (a) cash (b) accounts receivable (c) inventory (d) accounts payable and (e) plugging in the balance for stockholders' equity.

6-44 Comprehensive problem; ABC manufacturing, two products. Hazlett, Inc., operates at capacity and makes plastic combs and hairbrushes. Although the combs and brushes are a matching set, they are sold individually and so the sales mix is not 1:1. Hazlett's management is planning its annual budget for fiscal year 2018. Here is information for 2018:

Input Prices

Direct materials	
Plastic	$ 0.30 per ounce
Bristles	$ 0.75 per bunch
Direct manufacturing labor	$ 18 per direct manufacturing labor-hour

Input Quantities per Unit of Output

	Combs	Brushes
Direct materials		
Plastic	5 ounces	8 ounces
Bristles	—	16 bunches
Direct manufacturing labor	0.05 hours	0.2 hours
Machine-hours (MH)	0.025 MH	0.1 MH

Inventory Information, Direct Materials

	Plastic	Bristles
Beginning inventory	1,600 ounces	1,820 bunches
Target ending inventory	1,766 ounces	2,272 bunches
Cost of beginning inventory	$456	$1,419

Hazlett accounts for direct materials using a FIFO cost flow.

Sales and Inventory Information, Finished Goods

	Combs	Brushes
Expected sales in units	12,000	14,000
Selling price	$ 9	$ 30
Target ending inventory in units	1,200	1,400
Beginning inventory in units	600	1,200
Beginning inventory in dollars	$ 2,700	$27,180

Hazlett uses a FIFO cost-flow assumption for finished-goods inventory.

Combs are manufactured in batches of 200, and brushes are manufactured in batches of 100. It takes 20 minutes to set up for a batch of combs and 1 hour to set up for a batch of brushes.

Hazlett uses activity-based costing and has classified all overhead costs as shown in the following table. Budgeted fixed overhead costs vary with capacity. Hazlett operates at capacity so budgeted fixed overhead cost per unit equals the budgeted fixed overhead costs divided by the budgeted quantities of the cost allocation base.

Cost Type	Budgeted Variable	Budgeted Fixed	Cost Driver/Allocation Base
Manufacturing			
Materials handling	$17,235	$22,500	Number of ounces of plastic used
Setup	10,245	16,650	Setup-hours
Processing	11,640	30,000	Machine-hours
Inspection	10,500	1,560	Number of units produced
Nonmanufacturing			
Marketing	$21,150	$90,000	Sales revenue
Distribution	0	1,170	Number of deliveries

Delivery trucks transport units sold in delivery sizes of 1,000 combs or 1,000 brushes.

Do the following for the year 2018:

1. Prepare the revenues budget.
2. Use the revenues budget to:
   a. Find the budgeted allocation rate for marketing costs.
   b. Find the budgeted number of deliveries and allocation rate for distribution costs.
3. Prepare the production budget in units.
4. Use the production budget to:
   a. Find the budgeted number of setups and setup-hours and the allocation rate for setup costs.
   b. Find the budgeted total machine-hours and the allocation rate for processing costs.
   c. Find the budgeted total units produced and the allocation rate for inspection costs.
5. Prepare the direct material usage budget and the direct material purchases budget in both units and dollars; round to whole dollars.
6. Use the direct material usage budget to find the budgeted allocation rate for materials-handling costs.
7. Prepare the direct manufacturing labor cost budget.
8. Prepare the manufacturing overhead cost budget for materials handling, setup, processing, and inspection costs.
9. Prepare the budgeted unit cost of ending finished-goods inventory and ending inventories budget.
10. Prepare the cost of goods sold budget.
11. Prepare the nonmanufacturing overhead costs budget for marketing and distribution.
12. Prepare a budgeted income statement (ignore income taxes).
13. How does preparing the budget help Hazlett's management team better manage the company?

6-45 Cash budget. (Continuation of 6-44) (Appendix)

Refer to the information in Problem 6-44.

All purchases made in a given month are paid for in the following month, and direct material purchases make up all of the accounts payable balance and are reflected in the accounts payable balances at the beginning and the end of the year.

Sales are made to customers with terms net 45 days. Fifty percent of a month's sales are collected in the month of the sale, 25% are collected in the month following the sale, and 25% are collected two months after the sale and are reflected in the accounts receivables balances at the beginning and the end of the year.

Direct manufacturing labor, variable manufacturing overhead and variable marketing costs are paid as they are incurred. Fifty percent of fixed manufacturing overhead costs, 60% of fixed marketing costs, and 100% of fixed distribution costs are depreciation expenses. The remaining fixed manufacturing overhead and marketing costs are paid as they are incurred.

Selected balances for December 31, 2017, follow:

Cash	$29,200
Accounts payable	21,450
Accounts receivable	40,000

Selected budget information for December 2018 follows:

Accounts payable	$27,770
Accounts receivable	48,500

Hazlett has budgeted to purchase equipment costing $145,000 for cash during 2018. Hazlett desires a minimum cash balance of $25,000. The company has a line of credit from which it may borrow in increments of $1,000 at an interest rate of 12% per year. By special arrangement, with the bank, Hazlett pays interest when repaying the principal, which only needs to be repaid in 2019.

Required

1. Prepare a cash budget for 2018. If Hazlett must borrow cash to meet its desired ending cash balance, show the amount that must be borrowed.
2. Does the cash budget for 2018 give Hazlett's managers all of the information necessary to manage cash in 2018? How might that be improved?
3. What insight does the cash budget give to Hazlett's managers that the budgeted income statement does not?

6-46 Budgeting and ethics.

Jayzee Company manufactures a variety of products in a variety of departments and evaluates departments and departmental managers by comparing actual cost and output relative to the budget. Departmental managers help create the budgets and usually provide information about input quantities for materials, labor, and overhead costs.

Kurt Jackson is the manager of the department that produces product Z. Kurt has estimated these inputs for product Z:

Input	Budget Quantity per Unit of Output
Direct material	8 pounds
Direct manufacturing labor	30 minutes
Machine time	24 minutes

The department produces about 100 units of product Z each day. Kurt's department always gets excellent evaluations, sometimes exceeding budgeted production quantities. For each 100 units of product Z produced, the company uses, on average, about 48 hours of direct manufacturing labor (eight people working 6 hours each), 790 pounds of material, and 39.5 machine-hours.

Top management of Jayzee Company has decided to implement budget standards that will challenge the workers in each department, and it has asked Kurt to design more challenging input standards for product Z. Kurt provides top management with the following input quantities:

Input	Budget Quantity per Unit of Output
Direct material	7.9 pounds
Direct manufacturing labor	29 minutes
Machine time	23.6 minutes

Required

Discuss the following:

1. Are these budget standards challenging for the department that produces product Z?
2. Why do you suppose Kurt picked these particular standards?
3. What steps can Jayzee Company's top management take to make sure Kurt's standards really meet the goals of the firm?

6-47 Kaizen budgeting for carbon emissions. Apex Chemical Company currently operates three manufacturing plants in Colorado, Utah, and Arizona. Annual carbon emissions for these plants in the first quarter of 2018 are 125,000 metric tons per quarter (or 500,000 metric tons in 2018). Apex management is investigating improved manufacturing techniques that will reduce annual carbon emissions to below 475,000 metric tons so that the company can meet Environmental Protection Agency guidelines by 2019. Costs and benefits are as follows:

Total cost to reduce carbon emissions	$10 per metric ton reduced in 2019 below 500,000 metric tons
Fine in 2019 if EPA guidelines are not met	$300,000

Apex Management has chosen to use Kaizen budgeting to achieve its goal for carbon emissions.

Required

1. If Apex reduces emissions by 1% each quarter, beginning with the second quarter of 2018, will the company reach its goal of 475,000 metric tons by the end of 2019?
2. What would be the net financial cost or benefit of their plan? Ignore the time value of money.
3. What factors other than cost might weigh into Apex's decision to carry out this plan?

6-48 Comprehensive budgeting problem; activity-based costing, operating and financial budgets. Tyva makes a very popular undyed cloth sandal in one style, but in Regular and Deluxe. The Regular sandals have cloth soles and the Deluxe sandals have cloth-covered wooden soles. Tyva is preparing its budget for June 2018 and has estimated sales based on past experience.

Other information for the month of June follows:

Input Prices

Direct materials	
Cloth	$5.25 per yard
Wood	$7.50 per board foot
Direct manufacturing labor	$15 per direct manufacturing labor-hour

Input Quantities per Unit of Output (per pair of sandals)

	Regular	Deluxe
Direct materials		
Cloth	1.3 yards	1.5 yards
Wood	0	2 b.f.
Direct manufacturing labor-hours (DMLH)	5 hours	7 hours
Setup-hours per batch	2 hours	3 hours

Inventory Information, Direct Materials

	Cloth	Wood
Beginning inventory	610 yards	800 b.f.
Target ending inventory	386 yards	295 b.f.
Cost of beginning inventory	$3,219	$6,060

Tyva accounts for direct materials using a FIFO cost-flow assumption.

Sales and Inventory Information, Finished Goods

	Regular	Deluxe
Expected sales in units (pairs of sandals)	2,000	3,000
Selling price	$ 120	$ 195
Target ending inventory in units	400	600
Beginning inventory in units	250	650
Beginning inventory in dollars	$23,250	$92,625

Tyva uses a FIFO cost-flow assumption for finished-goods inventory.

All the sandals are made in batches of 50 pairs of sandals. Tyva incurs manufacturing overhead costs, marketing and general administration, and shipping costs. Besides materials and labor, manufacturing costs include setup, processing, and inspection costs. Tyva ships 40 pairs of sandals per shipment. Tyva uses activity-based costing and has classified all overhead costs for the month of June as shown in the following chart:

Cost Type	Denominator Activity	Rate
Manufacturing		
Setup	Setup-hours	$ 18 per setup-hour
Processing	Direct manufacturing labor-hours (DMLH)	$1.80 per DMLH
Inspection	Number of pairs of sandals	$1.35 per pair
Nonmanufacturing		
Marketing and general administration	Sales revenue	8%
Shipping	Number of shipments	$ 15 per shipment

Required

1. Prepare each of the following for June:
   a. Revenues budget
   b. Production budget in units
   c. Direct material usage budget and direct material purchases budget in both units and dollars; round to dollars
   d. Direct manufacturing labor cost budget
   e. Manufacturing overhead cost budgets for setup, processing, and inspection activities
   f. Budgeted unit cost of ending finished-goods inventory and ending inventories budget
   g. Cost of goods sold budget
   h. Marketing and general administration and shipping costs budget

2. Tyva's balance sheet for May 31 follows.

Tyva Balance Sheet as of May 31

Assets		
Cash		$ 9,435
Accounts receivable	$324,000	
Less: Allowance for bad debts	16,200	307,800
Inventories		
Direct materials		9,279
Finished goods		115,875
Fixed assets	$870,000	
Less: Accumulated depreciation	136,335	733,665
Total assets		$1,176,054

Liabilities and Equity	
Accounts payable	$ 15,600
Taxes payable	10,800
Interest payable	750
Long-term debt	150,000
Common stock	300,000
Retained earnings	698,904
Total liabilities and equity	$1,176,054

Use the balance sheet and the following information to prepare a cash budget for Tyva for June. Round to dollars.

- All sales are on account; 60% are collected in the month of the sale, 38% are collected the following month, and 2% are never collected and written off as bad debts.
- All purchases of materials are on account. Tyva pays for 80% of purchases in the month of purchase and 20% in the following month.
- All other costs are paid in the month incurred, including the declaration and payment of a $15,000 cash dividend in June.
- Tyva is making monthly interest payments of 0.5% (6% per year) on a $150,000 long-term loan.
- Tyva plans to pay the $10,800 of taxes owed as of May 31 in the month of June. Income tax expense for June is zero.
- 30% of processing, setup, and inspection costs and 10% of marketing and general administration and shipping costs are depreciation.

3. Prepare a budgeted income statement for June and a budgeted balance sheet for Tyva as of June 30, 2018.

Flexible Budgets, Direct-Cost Variances, and Management Control

7

Every organization, regardless of its profitability or growth, has to maintain control over its expenses.

And when customers are cautious in their spending choices, the need for managers to use budgeting and variance analysis tools for cost control becomes especially critical. By studying variances, managers can focus on where specific performances have fallen short and make corrective adjustments and achieve significant savings for their companies. The drive to achieve cost reductions might seem at odds with the growing push for organizations to pursue environmentally sound business practices. To the contrary, managers looking to be more efficient with their plants and operations have found that cornerstones of the sustainability movement, such as reducing waste and power usage, offer fresh ways to help them manage risk and control costs, as the following article shows.

LEARNING OBJECTIVES

1. Understand static budgets and static-budget variances
2. Examine the concept of a flexible budget and learn how to develop it
3. Calculate flexible-budget variances and sales-volume variances
4. Explain why standard costs are often used in variance analysis
5. Compute price variances and efficiency variances for direct-cost categories
6. Understand how managers use variances
7. Describe benchmarking and explain its role in cost management

SINGADELI BAKERY AND INCENTIVE CONTROLS

SingaDeli is a bakery company in Singapore. The company produces pastries and festive items such as moon cakes and Christmas puddings. Moon cake is a delicacy traditionally eaten during the Mid-Autumn Festival that falls on the fifteenth day of the eighth lunar month. Typical moon cakes are round pastries with a filling usually made from lotus seed paste.

During the last festival, SingaDeli hired two chefs solely for the baking of moon cakes. The chefs were empowered to order raw materials and to source from the best suppliers. They were paid $1.20 per moon cake produced, plus 50% of favorable material price variance. SingaDeli estimated that its moon cake requires 50 grams of materials at the cost of $11.80 per kilogram. One month before the festival, the chefs ordered 600 kilograms of raw materials from a supplier at the price of $9.80 per kilogram.

During the festival, a total of 11,000 moon cakes were produced, of which 2,000 were sold at a discount of 70% due to poor quality.

123rf.com

SingaDeli's management was disappointed with the high percentage of poor quality cakes, amounting to about 20% of total production. The problem arose because the chefs were paid by product quantity, without accountability for quality or saleability. The incentive payment based on favorable price variance would induce the purchase of the cheapest material, regardless of quality. Excessive quantities were also bought to increase the total favorable variance because the chefs were not responsible for the inventory.

SingaDeli's experience shows that if standard cost variances are to be used for performance evaluation and incentive payment, employees' empowerment has to be commensurate with their accountability. The design of the measurement system has to be comprehensive with due consideration of all of the key factors relating to resource consumption, such as material quantity, quality, and price. Otherwise, only what gets measured gets done, while other dimensions of business performance that may be impacted negatively are ignored. The wrong measurement and reward will motivate suboptimal behavior, which will be detrimental to the company as a whole. Therefore, the management must utilize comprehensive, holistic measurement and appraisal systems that discourage the promotion of one set of metrics that may have an adverse impact on other key dimensions of business performance.

In Chapter 6, you saw how budgets help managers with their planning function. We now explain how budgets, specifically flexible budgets, are used to compute variances, which assist managers in their control function. Variance analysis supports the critical final function in the five-step decision-making process by enabling managers to *evaluate performance and learn* after decisions are implemented. In this chapter and the next, we explain how.

Static Budgets and Variances

LEARNING OBJECTIVE 1

Understand static budgets

...the master budget based on output planned at start of period

and static-budget variances

...the difference between the actual result and the corresponding budgeted amount in the static budget

A **variance** is the difference between actual results and expected performance. The expected performance is also called **budgeted performance**, which is a point of reference for making comparisons.

The Use of Variances

Variances bring together the planning and control functions of management and facilitate management by exception. **Management by exception** is a practice whereby managers focus more closely on areas that are not operating as expected and less closely on areas that are. Consider the scrap and rework costs at a Maytag appliances plant. If the plant's actual costs are much higher than originally budgeted, the variances will prompt managers to find out why and correct the problem so future operations result in less scrap and rework. Sometimes a large positive variance may occur, such as a significant decrease in the manufacturing costs of a product. Managers will try to understand the reasons for the decrease (better operator training or changes in manufacturing methods, for example) so these practices can be continued and implemented by other divisions within the organization.

Variances are also used for evaluating performance and to motivate managers. Production-line managers at Maytag may have quarterly efficiency incentives linked to achieving a budgeted amount of operating costs.

Sometimes variances suggest that the company should consider a change in strategy. For example, large negative variances caused by excessive defect rates for a new product may suggest a flawed product design. Managers may then want to investigate the product design and potentially change the mix of products being offered. Variances also help managers make more informed predictions about the future and thereby improve the quality of the five-step decision-making process.

The benefits of variance analysis are not restricted to companies. In today's difficult economic environment, public officials have realized that the ability to make timely tactical changes based on variance information can result in their having to make fewer draconian adjustments later. For example, the city of Scottsdale, Arizona, monitors its tax and fee performance against expenditures monthly. Why? One of the city's goals is to keep its water usage rates stable. By monitoring the extent to which the city's water revenues are matching its current expenses, Scottsdale can avoid sudden spikes in the rate it charges residents for water as well as finance water-related infrastructure projects.[1]

---

[1] For an excellent discussion and other related examples from governmental settings, see S. Kavanagh and C. Swanson, "Tactical Financial Management: Cash Flow and Budgetary Variance Analysis," *Government Finance Review* (October 1, 2009).

How important of a decision-making tool is variance analysis? Very! A survey by the United Kingdom's Chartered Institute of Management Accountants found that it was easily the most popular costing tool used by organizations of all sizes.

Static Budgets and Static-Budget Variances

We will take a closer look at variances by examining one company's accounting system. As you study the exhibits in this chapter, note that "level" followed by a number denotes the amount of detail shown by a variance analysis. Level 1 reports the least detail; level 2 offers more information; and so on.

Consider Webb Company, a firm that manufactures and sells jackets. The jackets require tailoring and many other hand operations. Webb sells exclusively to distributors, who in turn sell to independent clothing stores and retail chains. For simplicity, we assume the following:

1. Webb's only costs are in the manufacturing function; Webb incurs no costs in other value-chain functions, such as marketing and distribution.
2. All units manufactured in April 2017 are sold in April 2017.
3. There is no direct materials inventory at either the beginning or the end of the period. No work-in-process or finished-goods inventories exist at either the beginning or the end of the period.

Webb has three variable-cost categories. The budgeted variable cost per jacket for each category is as follows:

Cost Category	Variable Cost per Jacket
Direct materials costs	$60
Direct manufacturing labor costs	16
Variable manufacturing overhead costs	12
Total variable costs	$88

The *number of units manufactured* is the cost driver for direct materials, direct manufacturing labor, and variable manufacturing overhead. The relevant range for the cost driver is from 0 to 12,000 jackets. Budgeted and actual data for April 2017 are:

Budgeted fixed costs for production between 0 and 12,000 jackets	$276,000
Budgeted selling price	$ 120 per jacket
Budgeted production and sales	12,000 jackets
Actual production and sales	10,000 jackets

The **static budget**, or master budget, is based on the level of output planned at the start of the budget period. The master budget is called a static budget because the budget for the period is developed around a single (static) planned output level. Exhibit 7-1, column 3, presents the static budget for Webb Company for April 2017 that was prepared at the end of 2016. For each line item in the income statement, Exhibit 7-1, column 1, displays data for the actual April results. For example, actual revenues are $1,250,000, and the actual selling price is $1,250,000 ÷ 10,000 jackets = $125 per jacket—compared with the budgeted selling price of $120 per jacket. Similarly, actual direct materials costs are $621,600, and the direct material cost per jacket is $621,600 ÷ 10,000 = $62.16 per jacket—compared with the budgeted direct material cost per jacket of $60. We describe potential reasons and explanations for these differences as we discuss different variances throughout the chapter.

The **static-budget variance** (see Exhibit 7-1, column 2) is the difference between the actual result and the corresponding budgeted amount in the static budget.

A **favorable variance**—denoted F in this book —has the effect, when considered in isolation, of increasing operating income relative to the budgeted amount. For revenue items, F means actual revenues exceed budgeted revenues. For cost items, F means actual costs are less than budgeted costs. An **unfavorable variance**—denoted U in this book —has the effect, when viewed in isolation, of decreasing operating income relative to the budgeted amount. Unfavorable variances are also called *adverse variances* in some countries, such as the United Kingdom.

EXHIBIT 7-1

Static-Budget-Based Variance Analysis for Webb Company for April 2017[a]

Level 1 Analysis

	Actual Results (1)	Static-Budget Variances (2) = (1) − (3)	Static Budget (3)
Units sold	10,000	2,000 U	12,000
Revenues	$1,250,000	$190,000 U	$1,440,000
Variable costs			
Direct materials	621,600	98,400 F	720,000
Direct manufacturing labor	198,000	6,000 U	192,000
Variable manufacturing overhead	130,500	13,500 F	144,000
Total variable costs	950,100	105,900 F	1,056,000
Contribution margin	299,900	84,100 U	384,000
Fixed costs	285,000	9,000 U	276,000
Operating income	$ 14,900	$ 93,100 U	$ 108,000

$93,100 U
Static-budget variance

[a]F = favorable effect on operating income; U = unfavorable effect on operating income.

The unfavorable static-budget variance for operating income of $93,100 in Exhibit 7-1 is calculated by subtracting static-budget operating income of $108,000 from actual operating income of $14,900:

$$\text{Static-budget variance for operating income} = \text{Actual result} - \text{Static-budget amount}$$

$$= \$14,900 - \$108,000$$

$$= \$93,100 \text{ U.}$$

The analysis in Exhibit 7-1 provides managers with additional information on the static-budget variance for operating income of $93,100 U. The more detailed breakdown indicates how the line items that comprise operating income—revenues, individual variable costs, and fixed costs—add up to the static-budget variance of $93,100.

Recall that Webb produced and sold only 10,000 jackets, although managers anticipated an output of 12,000 jackets in the static budget. *Managers want to know how much of the static-budget variance is due to Webb inaccurately forecasting what it expected to produce and sell and how much is due to how it actually performed manufacturing and selling 10,000 jackets.* Managers, therefore, create a flexible budget, which enables a more in-depth understanding of deviations from the static budget.

DECISION POINT

What are static budgets and static-budget variances?

 **7-1**

Zenefit Corporation sold laser pointers for $11 each in 2017. Its budgeted selling price was $12 per unit. Other information related to its performance is given below:

	Actual	Budgeted
Units made and sold	28,000	27,500
Variable costs	$90,000	$ 3 per unit
Fixed costs	$55,000	$58,000

Calculate Zenefit's static-budget variance for (a) revenues, (b) variable costs, (c) fixed costs, and (d) operating income.

Flexible Budgets

A **flexible budget** calculates budgeted revenues and budgeted costs based on *the actual output in the budget period*. The flexible budget is prepared at the end of the period (April 2017 for Webb), after managers know the actual output of 10,000 jackets. The flexible budget is the *hypothetical* budget that Webb would have prepared at the start of the budget period if it had correctly forecast the actual output of 10,000 jackets. In other words, the flexible budget is not the plan Webb initially had in mind for April 2017 (remember Webb planned for an output of 12,000 jackets). Rather, it is the budget Webb *would have* put together for April if it knew in advance that the output for the month would be 10,000 jackets. In preparing the flexible budget, note that:

- The budgeted selling price is the same $120 per jacket used in the static budget.
- The budgeted unit variable cost is the same $88 per jacket used in the static budget.
- The budgeted *total* fixed costs are the same static-budget amount of $276,000. Why? Because the 10,000 jackets produced falls within the relevant range of 0 to 12,000 jackets. Therefore, Webb would have budgeted the same amount of fixed costs, $276,000, whether it anticipated making 10,000 or 12,000 jackets.

The *only* difference between the static budget and the flexible budget is that the static budget is prepared for the planned output of 12,000 jackets, whereas the flexible budget is prepared retroactively based on the actual output of 10,000 jackets. In other words, the static budget is being "flexed," or adjusted, from 12,000 jackets to 10,000 jackets.[2] The flexible budget for 10,000 jackets assumes all costs are either completely variable or completely fixed with respect to the number of jackets produced.

Webb develops its flexible budget in three steps.

Step 1: Identify the Actual Quantity of Output. In April 2017, Webb produced and sold 10,000 jackets.

Step 2: Calculate the Flexible Budget for Revenues Based on the Budgeted Selling Price and Actual Quantity of Output.

$$\text{Flexible-budget revenues} = \$120 \text{ per jacket} \times 10{,}000 \text{ jackets}$$
$$= \$1{,}200{,}000$$

Step 3: Calculate the Flexible Budget for Costs Based on the Budgeted Variable Cost per Output Unit, Actual Quantity of Output, and Budgeted Fixed Costs.

Flexible-budget variable costs	
Direct materials, $60 per jacket × 10,000 jackets	$ 600,000
Direct manufacturing labor, $16 per jacket × 10,000 jackets	160,000
Variable manufacturing overhead, $12 per jacket × 10,000 jackets	120,000
Total flexible-budget variable costs	880,000
Flexible-budget fixed costs	276,000
Flexible-budget total costs	$1,156,000

These three steps enable Webb to prepare a flexible budget, as shown in Exhibit 7-2, column 3. The flexible budget allows for a more detailed analysis of the $93,100 unfavorable static-budget variance for operating income.

LEARNING OBJECTIVE 2

Examine the concept of a flexible budget

...the budget that is adjusted (flexed) to recognize the actual output level

and learn how to develop it

...proportionately increase variable costs; keep fixed costs the same

DECISION POINT

How can managers develop a flexible budget and why is it useful to do so?

TRY IT! 7-2 Consider Zenefit Corporation. With the same information for 2017 as provided in Try It 7-1, calculate Zenefit's flexible budget for (a) revenues, (b) variable costs, (c) fixed costs, and (d) operating income.

---

[2] Suppose Webb, when preparing its annual budget for 2017 at the end of 2016, had perfectly anticipated that its output in April 2017 would equal 10,000 jackets. Then the flexible budget for April 2017 would be identical to the static budget.

EXHIBIT 7-2 Level 2 Flexible-Budget-Based Variance Analysis for Webb Company for April 2017[a]

Level 2 Analysis

	Actual Results (1)	Flexible-Budget Variances (2) = (1) − (3)	Flexible Budget (3)	Sales-Volume Variances (4) = (3) − (5)	Static Budget (5)
Units sold	10,000	0	10,000	2,000 U	12,000
Revenues	$1,250,000	$50,000 F	$1,200,000	$240,000 U	$1,440,000
Variable costs					
Direct materials	621,600	21,600 U	600,000	120,000 F	720,000
Direct manufacturing labor	198,000	38,000 U	160,000	32,000 F	192,000
Variable manufacturing overhead	130,500	10,500 U	120,000	24,000 F	144,000
Total variable costs	950,100	70,100 U	880,000	176,000 F	1,056,000
Contribution margin	299,900	20,100 U	320,000	64,000 U	384,000
Fixed manufacturing costs	285,000	9,000 U	276,000	0	276,000
Operating income	$ 14,900	$29,100 U	$ 44,000	$ 64,000 U	$ 108,000

Level 2 $29,100 U Flexible-budget variance $64,000 U Sales-volume variance

Level 1 $93,100 U Static-budget variance

[a] F = favorable effect on operating income; U = unfavorable effect on operating income.

Flexible-Budget Variances and Sales-Volume Variances

LEARNING OBJECTIVE 3

Calculate flexible-budget variances

...each flexible-budget variance is the difference between an actual result and a flexible-budget amount

and sales-volume variances

...each sales-volume variance is the difference between a flexible-budget amount and a static-budget amount

Exhibit 7-2 shows the flexible-budget-based variance analysis for Webb, which subdivides the $93,100 unfavorable static-budget variance for operating income into two parts: a flexible-budget variance of $29,100 U and a sales-volume variance of $64,000 U. The **sales-volume variance** is the difference between a flexible-budget amount and the corresponding static-budget amount. The **flexible-budget variance** is the difference between an actual result and the corresponding flexible-budget amount.

Sales-Volume Variances

Keep in mind that the flexible-budget amounts in column 3 of Exhibit 7-2 and the static-budget amounts in column 5 are both computed using budgeted selling prices, budgeted variable cost per jacket, and budgeted fixed costs. The difference between the static-budget and the flexible-budget amounts is called the sales-volume variance because it arises *solely* from the difference between the 10,000 actual quantity (or volume) of jackets sold and the 12,000 quantity of jackets expected to be sold in the static budget.

$$\text{Sales-volume variance for operating income} = \text{Flexible-budget amount} - \text{Static-budget amount}$$
$$= \$44,000 - \$108,000$$
$$= \$64,000 \text{ U}$$

The sales-volume variance in operating income for Webb measures the change in the budgeted contribution margin because Webb sold only 10,000 jackets rather than the budgeted 12,000.

$$\begin{aligned}
\text{Sales-volume variance for operating income} &= \begin{pmatrix} \text{Budgeted contribution} \\ \text{margin per unit} \end{pmatrix} \times \begin{pmatrix} \text{Actual units} \\ \text{sold} \end{pmatrix} - \begin{pmatrix} \text{Static-budget} \\ \text{units sold} \end{pmatrix} \\
&= \begin{pmatrix} \text{Budgeted selling} \\ \text{price} \end{pmatrix} - \begin{pmatrix} \text{Budgeted variable} \\ \text{cost per unit} \end{pmatrix} \times \begin{pmatrix} \text{Actual units} \\ \text{sold} \end{pmatrix} - \begin{pmatrix} \text{Static-budget} \\ \text{units sold} \end{pmatrix} \\
&= (\$120 \text{ per jacket} - \$88 \text{ per jacket}) \times (10{,}000 \text{ jackets} - 12{,}000 \text{ jackets}) \\
&= \$32 \text{ per jacket} \times (-2{,}000 \text{ jackets}) \\
&= \$64{,}000 \text{ U}
\end{aligned}$$

Exhibit 7-2, column 4, shows the components of this overall variance by identifying the sales-volume variance for each of the line items in the income statement. The unfavorable sales-volume variance in operating income arises because of one or more of the following reasons:

1. Failure of Webb's managers to execute the sales plans
2. Weaker than anticipated overall demand for jackets
3. Competitors taking away market share from Webb
4. Unexpected changes in customer tastes and preferences away from Webb's designs
5. Quality problems leading to customer dissatisfaction with Webb's jackets

How Webb responds to the unfavorable sales-volume variance will depend on what its managers believe caused the variance. For example, if Webb's managers believe the unfavorable sales-volume variance was caused by market-related reasons (reasons 1, 2, 3, or 4), the sales manager would be in the best position to explain what happened and suggest corrective actions that may be needed, such as sales promotions, market studies, or changes to advertising plans. If, however, managers believe the unfavorable sales-volume variance was caused by unanticipated quality problems (reason 5), the production manager would be in the best position to analyze the causes and suggest strategies for improvement, such as changes in the manufacturing process or investments in new machines.

The static-budget variances compared actual revenues and costs for 10,000 jackets against budgeted revenues and costs for 12,000 jackets. A portion of this difference, the sales-volume variance, reflects the effects of selling fewer units or inaccurate forecasting of sales. By removing this component from the static-budget variance, managers can compare their firm's revenues earned and costs incurred for April 2017 against the flexible budget—the revenues and costs Webb would have budgeted for the 10,000 jackets actually produced and sold. *Flexible-budget variances are a better measure of sales price and cost performance than static-budget variances because they compare actual revenues to budgeted revenues and actual costs to budgeted costs for the same 10,000 jackets of output.*

Flexible-Budget Variances

The first three columns of Exhibit 7-2 compare Webb's actual results with its flexible-budget amounts. The flexible-budget variances for each line item in the income statement are shown in column 2:

$$\begin{aligned} \text{Flexible-budget variance} &= \text{Actual result} - \text{Flexible-budget amount} \end{aligned}$$

The operating income line in Exhibit 7-2 shows the flexible-budget variance is $29,100 U ($14,900 − $44,000). The $29,100 U arises because the actual selling price, actual variable cost per unit, and actual fixed costs differ from their budgeted amounts. The actual results and budgeted amounts for the selling price and variable cost per unit are as follows:

	Actual Result	Budgeted Amount
Selling price	$125.00 ($1,250,000 ÷ 10,000 jackets)	$120.00 ($1,200,000 ÷ 10,000 jackets)
Variable cost per jacket	$ 95.01 ($ 950,100 ÷ 10,000 jackets)	$ 88.00 ($ 880,000 ÷ 10,000 jackets)

The flexible-budget variance for revenues is called the **selling-price variance** because it arises solely from the difference between the actual selling price and the budgeted selling price:

$$\text{Selling-price variance} = \left(\text{Actual selling price} - \text{Budgeted selling price}\right) \times \text{Actual units sold}$$

$$= (\$125 \text{ per jacket} - \$120 \text{ per jacket}) \times 10{,}000 \text{ jackets}$$

$$= \$50{,}000 \text{ F}$$

Webb has a favorable selling-price variance because the $125 actual selling price exceeds the $120 budgeted amount, which increases operating income. Marketing managers are generally in the best position to understand and explain the reason for a selling price difference. For example, was the difference due to better quality? Or was it due to an overall increase in market prices? Webb's managers concluded it was due to a general increase in prices.

The flexible-budget variance for total variable costs is unfavorable ($70,100 U) for the actual output of 10,000 jackets. It's unfavorable because of one or both of the following:

- Webb used greater quantities of inputs (such as direct manufacturing labor-hours) compared to the budgeted quantities of inputs.
- Webb incurred higher prices per unit for the inputs (such as the wage rate per direct manufacturing labor-hour) compared to the budgeted prices per unit of the inputs.

Higher input quantities and/or higher input prices relative to the budgeted amounts could be the result of Webb deciding to produce a better product than what was planned or the result of inefficiencies related to Webb's manufacturing and purchasing operations or both. *You should always think of variance analysis as providing suggestions for further investigation rather than as establishing conclusive evidence of good or bad performance.*

The actual fixed costs of $285,000 are $9,000 more than the budgeted amount of $276,000. This unfavorable flexible-budget variance reflects unexpected increases in the cost of fixed indirect resources, such as the factory's rent or supervisors' salaries.

In the rest of this chapter, we will focus on variable direct-cost input variances. Chapter 8 emphasizes indirect (overhead) cost variances.

DECISION POINT

How are flexible-budget and sales-volume variances calculated?

TRY IT! 7-3

Consider Zenefit Corporation again. With the same information for 2017 as provided in Try It 7-1, calculate Zenefit's flexible-budget and sales-volume variances for (a) revenues, (b) variable costs, (c) fixed costs, and (d) operating income.

Standard Costs for Variance Analysis

LEARNING OBJECTIVE 4

Explain why standard costs are often used in variance analysis

...standard costs exclude past inefficiencies and take into account expected future changes

To gain further insight, a company will subdivide the flexible-budget variance for its direct-cost inputs into two more-detailed variances:

1. A price variance that reflects the difference between an actual input price and a budgeted input price
2. An efficiency variance that reflects the difference between an actual input quantity and a budgeted input quantity

We will call these level 3 variances. Managers generally have more control over efficiency variances than price variances because the quantity of inputs used is primarily affected by factors inside the company (such as the efficiency with which operations are performed), whereas changes in the price of materials or in wage rates may be largely dictated by market forces outside the company.

Obtaining Budgeted Input Prices and Budgeted Input Quantities

To calculate price and efficiency variances, Webb needs to obtain budgeted input prices and budgeted input quantities. Webb's three main sources for this information are: (1) past data, (2) data from similar companies, and (3) standards. Each source has its advantages and disadvantages.

1. **Actual input data from past periods.** Most companies have past data on actual input prices and actual input quantities. These historical data could be analyzed for trends or patterns using some of the techniques we will discuss in another chapter (Chapter 10) to obtain estimates of budgeted prices and quantities.

    Advantages: Past data represent quantities and prices that are real rather than hypothetical, so they can be very useful benchmarks for measuring improvements in performance. Moreover, past data are typically easy to collect at a low cost.

    Disadvantages: A firm's inefficiencies, such as the wastage of direct materials, are incorporated in past data. Consequently, the data do not represent the performance the firm could have ideally attained, only the performance it achieved in the past. Past data also do not incorporate any changes expected for the budget period, such as improvements resulting from new investments in technology.

2. **Data from other companies that have similar processes.** Another source of information is data from peer companies or companies that have similar processes, which can serve as a benchmark. For example, Baptist Healthcare System in Louisville, Kentucky, benchmarks its labor performance data against those of similar top-ranked hospitals. (We will discuss benchmarking in more detail later in the chapter.)

    Advantages: Data from other companies can provide a firm useful information about how it's performing relative to its competitors.

    Disadvantages: Input-price and input-quantity data from other companies are often not available or may not be comparable to a particular company's situation. Consider Costco, which pays hourly workers an average of more than $20 per hour, well above the national average of $11.39 for a retail sales worker. Also unusually, Costco provides the vast majority of its workforce with company-sponsored health care. The reason is Costco's focus on employee satisfaction, with the idea that a more pleasant workplace will lead to lower employee turnover and higher productivity.

3. **Standards developed by the firm itself.** A **standard** is a carefully determined price, cost, or quantity that is used as a benchmark for judging performance. Standards are usually expressed on a per-unit basis. Consider how Webb determines its direct manufacturing labor standards. Webb conducts engineering studies to obtain a detailed breakdown of the steps required to make a jacket. Each step is assigned a standard time based on work performed by a *skilled* worker using equipment operating in an *efficient* manner. Similarly, Webb determines the standard quantity of square yards of cloth based on what is required by a skilled operator to make a jacket.

    Advantages: Standard times (1) aim to exclude past inefficiencies and (2) take into account changes expected to occur in the budget period. An example of the latter would be a decision by Webb's managers to lease new, faster, and more accurate sewing machines. Webb would incorporate the resulting higher level of efficiency into the new standards it sets.

    Disdvantages: Because they are not based on realized benchmarks, the standards might not be achievable, and workers could get discouraged trying to meet them.

The term *standard* refers to many different things:

- A **standard input** is a carefully determined quantity of input, such as square yards of cloth or direct manufacturing labor-hours, required for one unit of output, such as a jacket.
- A **standard price** is a carefully determined price a company expects to pay for a unit of input. In the Webb example, the standard wage rate the firm expects to pay its operators is an example of a standard price of a direct manufacturing labor-hour.

- A **standard cost** is a carefully determined cost of a unit of output, such as the standard direct manufacturing labor cost of a jacket at Webb.

$$\text{Standard cost per output unit for each variable direct-cost input} = \text{Standard input allowed for one output unit} \times \text{Standard price per input unit}$$

Standard direct material cost per jacket: 2 square yards of cloth input allowed per output unit (jacket) manufactured, at $30 standard price per square yard

$$\text{Standard direct material cost per jacket} = 2 \text{ square yards} \times \$30 \text{ per square yard} = \$60$$

Standard direct manufacturing labor cost per jacket: 0.8 manufacturing labor-hour of input allowed per output unit manufactured, at $20 standard price per hour

$$\text{Standard direct manufacturing labor cost per jacket} = 0.8 \text{ labor-hour} \times \$20 \text{ per labor-hour} = \$16$$

How are the words *budget* and *standard* related? Budget is the broader term. To clarify, budgeted input prices, input quantities, and costs need *not* be based on standards. As we saw previously, they could be based on past data or competitive benchmarks. However, when standards *are* used to obtain budgeted input quantities and prices, the terms *standard* and *budget* are used interchangeably. The standard cost of each input required for one unit of output is determined by the standard quantity of the input required for one unit of output and the standard price per input unit. Notice how the standard-cost computations shown previously for direct materials and direct manufacturing labor result in the budgeted direct material cost per jacket of $60 and the budgeted direct manufacturing labor cost of $16 referred to earlier.

In its standard costing system, Webb uses standards that are attainable by operating efficiently but that allow for normal disruptions. A normal disruption could include, for example, a short delay in the receipt of materials needed to produce the jackets or a production hold-up because a piece of equipment needed a minor repair. An alternative is to set more-challenging standards that are more difficult to attain. As we discussed in Chapter 6, setting challenging standards can increase the motivation of employees and a firm's performance. However, if workers believe the standards are unachievable, they can become frustrated and the firm's performance could suffer.

> **DECISION POINT**
> What is a standard cost and what are its purposes?

Price Variances and Efficiency Variances for Direct-Cost Inputs

> **LEARNING OBJECTIVE**
>
> Compute price variances
>
> ...each price variance is the difference between an actual input price and a budgeted input price
>
> and efficiency variances
>
> ...each efficiency variance is the difference between an actual input quantity and a budgeted input quantity for actual output
>
> for direct-cost categories

Consider Webb's two direct-cost categories. The actual cost for each of these categories for the 10,000 jackets manufactured and sold in April 2017 is as follows:

Direct Materials Purchased and Used[3]

1. Square yards of cloth purchased and used	22,200
2. Actual price incurred per square yard	$ 28
3. Direct material costs (22,200 × $28) [shown in Exhibit 7-2, column 1]	$621,600

Direct Manufacturing Labor Used

1. Direct manufacturing labor-hours used	9,000
2. Actual price incurred per direct manufacturing labor-hour	$ 22
3. Direct manufacturing labor costs (9,000 × $22) [shown in Exhibit 7-2, column 1]	$198,000

Let's use the Webb Company data to illustrate the price variance and the efficiency variance for direct-cost inputs.

A **price variance** is the difference between actual price and budgeted price, multiplied by the actual input quantity, such as direct materials purchased. A price variance is sometimes called a **rate variance**, especially when it's used to describe the price variance for direct

---
[3] The Problem for Self-Study (pages 269–270) relaxes the assumption that the quantity of direct materials used equals the quantity of direct materials purchased.

manufacturing labor. An **efficiency variance** is the difference between the actual input quantity used (such as square yards of cloth) and the budgeted input quantity allowed for actual output, multiplied by budgeted price. An efficiency variance is sometimes called a **usage variance**. Let's explore price and efficiency variances in greater detail so we can see how managers use them.

Price Variances

The formula for computing the price variance is as follows:

$$\text{Price variance} = \left(\text{Actual price of input} - \text{Budgeted price of input}\right) \times \text{Actual quantity of input}$$

The price variances for Webb's two direct-cost categories are as follows:

Direct-Cost Category	$\left(\text{Actual price of input} - \text{Budgeted price of input}\right) \times \text{Actual quantity of input}$	= Price Variance
Direct materials	($28 per sq. yard − $30 per sq. yard) × 22,200 square yards	= $44,400 F
Direct manufacturing labor	($22 per hour − $20 per hour) × 9,000 hours	= $18,000 U

The direct materials price variance is favorable because the actual price of cloth is less than the budgeted price, resulting in an increase in operating income. The direct manufacturing labor price variance is unfavorable because the actual wage rate paid to labor is more than the budgeted rate, resulting in a decrease in operating income.

Managers should always consider a broad range of possible causes for a price variance. For example, Webb's favorable direct materials price variance could be due to one or more of the following:

- Webb's purchasing manager negotiated the direct materials prices more skillfully than was planned for in the budget.
- The purchasing manager switched to a lower-price supplier.
- The purchasing manager ordered larger quantities than the quantities budgeted, thereby obtaining quantity discounts.
- Direct materials prices decreased unexpectedly due to an oversupply of materials in the industry.
- The budgeted purchase prices of direct materials were set too high because managers did not carefully analyze market conditions.
- The purchasing manager negotiated favorable prices because he was willing to accept unfavorable terms on factors other than prices (such as agree to lower-quality material).

How Webb's managers respond to the direct materials price variance depends on what they believe caused it. For example, if they believe the purchasing manager received quantity discounts by ordering a larger amount of materials than budgeted, Webb could investigate whether the larger quantities resulted in higher storage costs for the firm. If the increase in storage and inventory holding costs exceeds the quantity discounts, purchasing in larger quantities is not beneficial. Some companies have reduced their materials storage areas to prevent their purchasing managers from ordering in larger quantities.

Efficiency Variance

For any actual level of output, the efficiency variance is the difference between the actual quantity of input used and the budgeted quantity of input allowed for that output level, multiplied by the budgeted input price:

$$\text{Efficiency variance} = \left(\text{Actual quantity of input used} - \text{Budgeted quantity of input allowed for actual output}\right) \times \text{Budgeted price of input}$$

The idea here is that, given a certain output level, a company is inefficient if it uses a larger quantity of input than budgeted. Conversely, a company is efficient if it uses a smaller input quantity than was budgeted for that output level.

The efficiency variances for each of Webb's direct-cost categories are as follows:

Direct-Cost Category	$\begin{pmatrix} \text{Actual} \\ \text{quantity of} \\ \text{input used} \end{pmatrix} - \begin{pmatrix} \text{Budgeted quantity} \\ \text{of input allowed} \\ \text{for actual output} \end{pmatrix}$	× Budgeted price of input	= Efficiency variance
Direct materials	[22,200 sq. yds. − (10,000 units × 2 sq. yds./unit)]	× $30 per sq. yard	
	= (22,200 sq. yds. − 20,000 sq. yds.)	× $30 per sq. yard	= $66,000 U
Direct manufacturing labor	[9,000 hours − (10,000 units × 0.8 hour/unit)]	× $20 per hour	
	= (9,000 hours − 8,000 hours)	× $20 per hour	= $20,000 U

The two manufacturing efficiency variances—the direct materials efficiency variance and the direct manufacturing labor efficiency variance—are each unfavorable. Why? Because given the firm's actual output, more of these inputs were used than were budgeted for. This lowered Webb's operating income.

As with price variances, there is a broad range of possible causes for these efficiency variances. For example, Webb's unfavorable efficiency variance for direct manufacturing labor could be because of one or more of the following:

- Webb's workers took longer to make each jacket because they worked more slowly or made poor-quality jackets that required reworking.
- Webb's personnel manager hired underskilled workers.
- Webb's production scheduler inefficiently scheduled work, resulting in more manufacturing labor time than budgeted being used per jacket.
- Webb's maintenance department did not properly maintain machines, resulting in more manufacturing labor time than budgeted being used per jacket.
- Webb's budgeted time standards were too tight because the skill levels of employees and the environment in which they operated weren't accurately evaluated.

Suppose Webb's managers determine that the unfavorable variance is due to poor machine maintenance. Webb could then establish a team consisting of plant engineers and machine operators to develop a maintenance schedule to reduce future breakdowns and prevent adverse effects on labor time and product quality.[4]

Exhibit 7-3 provides an alternative way to calculate price and efficiency variances. It shows how the price variance and the efficiency variance subdivide the flexible-budget variance. Consider direct materials. The direct materials flexible-budget variance of $21,600 U is the difference between the actual costs incurred (actual input quantity × actual price) of $621,600 shown in column 1 and the flexible budget (budgeted input quantity allowed for actual output × budgeted price) of $600,000 shown in column 3. Column 2 (actual input quantity × budgeted price) is inserted between column 1 and column 3. Then:

- The difference between columns 1 and 2 is the price variance of $44,400 F. This price variance occurs because the same actual input quantity (22,200 sq. yds.) is multiplied by the *actual price* ($28) in column 1 and the *budgeted price* ($30) in column 2.
- The difference between columns 2 and 3 is the efficiency variance of $66,000 U. This efficieny variance occurs because the same budgeted price ($30) is multiplied by the *actual input quantity* (22,200 sq. yds.) in column 2 and the *budgeted input quantity allowed for actual output* (20,000 sq. yds.) in column 3.
- The sum of the direct materials price variance, $44,400 F, and the direct materials efficiency variance, $66,000 U, equals the direct materials flexible budget variance, $21,600 U.

---

[4] When there are multiple inputs, such as different types of materials, that can be substituted for one another, the efficiency variance can be further decomposed into mix and yield variances. The appendix to this chapter describes how these variances are calculated.

EXHIBIT 7-3   Columnar Presentation of Variance Analysis: Direct Costs for Webb Company for April 2017[a]

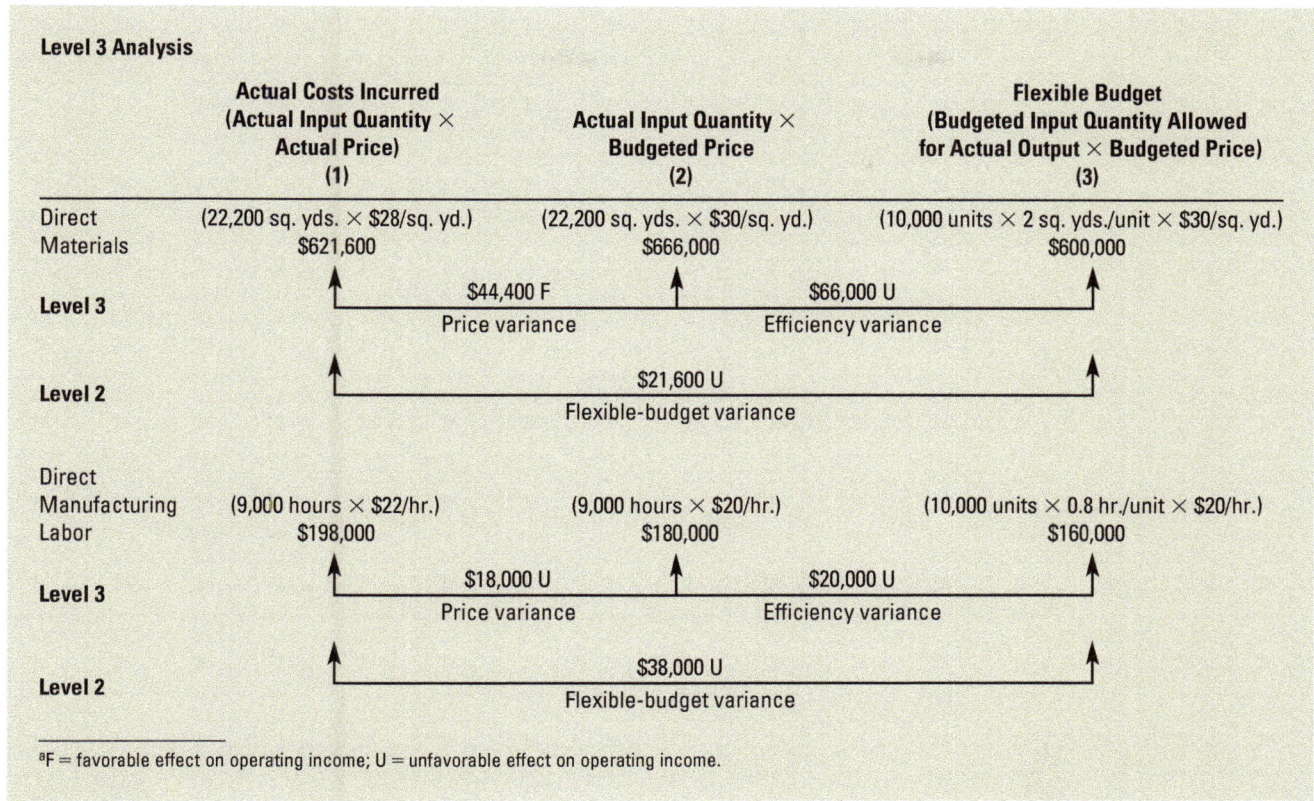

EXHIBIT 7-4

Summary of Level 1, 2, and 3 Variance Analyses

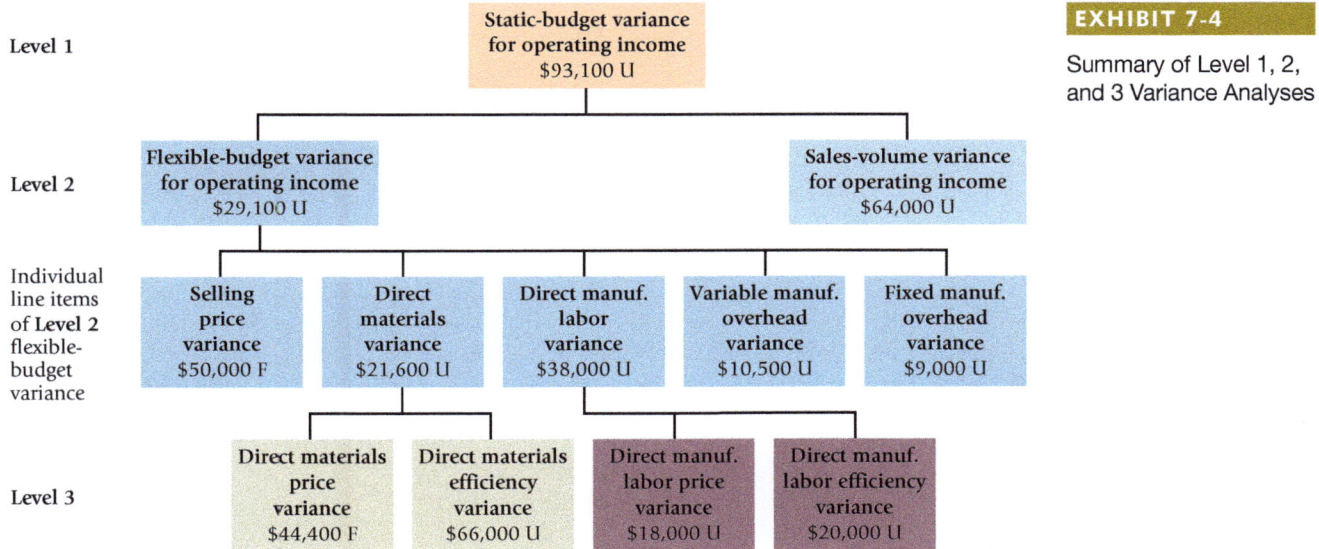

Exhibit 7-4 provides a summary of the different variances. Note how the variances at each higher level provide disaggregated and more detailed information for evaluating performance.

We now present Webb's journal entries under its standard costing system.

> Jamie Draperies manufactures curtains. To complete a curtain, Jamie requires the following inputs:
>
> Direct materials standard: 10 square yards at $5 per yard
> Direct manufacturing labor standard: 5 hours at $10 per hour
>
> During the second quarter, Jamie Draperies made 1,500 curtains and used 14,000 square yards of fabric costing $68,600. Direct manufacturing labor totaled 7,600 hours for $79,800.
>
> a. Compute the direct materials price and efficiency variances for the quarter.
> b. Compute the direct manufacturing labor price and efficiency variances for the quarter.

Journal Entries Using Standard Costs

Chapter 4 illustrated journal entries when normal costing is used. We will now illustrate journal entries for Webb Company using standard costing. Our focus is on direct materials and direct manufacturing labor. All the numbers included in the following journal entries are found in Exhibit 7-3.

Note: In each of the following entries, unfavorable variances are always debits (they decrease operating income), and favorable variances are always credits (they increase operating income).

Journal Entry 1A

Isolate the direct materials price variance at the time the materials were purchased. This is done by increasing (debiting) the Direct Materials Control account by the standard price Webb established for purchasing the materials. This is the earliest time possible to isolate this variance.

1a.	Direct Materials Control		
	(22,200 square yards × $30 per square yard)	666,000	
	Direct Materials Price Variance		
	(22,200 square yards × $2 per square yard)		44,400
	Accounts Payable Control		
	(22,200 square yards × $28 per square yard)		621,600
	This records the direct materials purchased.		

Journal Entry 1B

Isolate the direct materials efficiency variance at the time the direct materials are used by increasing (debiting) the Work-in-Process Control account. Use the standard quantities allowed for the actual output units manufactured times their standard purchase prices.

1b.	Work-in-Process Control		
	(10,000 jackets × 2 yards per jacket × $30 per square yard)	600,000	
	Direct Materials Efficiency Variance		
	(2,200 square yards × $30 per square yard)	66,000	
	Direct Materials Control		
	(22,200 square yards × $30 per square yard)		666,000
	This records the direct materials used.		

Journal Entry 2

Isolate the direct manufacturing labor price variance and efficiency variance at the time the labor is used by increasing (debiting) the Work-in-Process Control by the standard hours and standard wage rates allowed for the actual units manufactured. Note that the Wages Payable Control account measures the actual amounts payable to workers based on the actual hours they worked and their actual wage rate.

2. Work-in-Process Control
    (10,000 jackets × 0.80 hour per jacket × $20 per hour)   160,000
   Direct Manufacturing Labor Price Variance
    (9,000 hours × $2 per hour)   18,000
   Direct Manufacturing Labor Efficiency Variance
    (1,000 hours × $20 per hour)   20,000
    Wages Payable Control
    (9,000 hours × $22 per hour)   198,000
This records the liability for Webb's direct manufacturing labor costs.

You have learned how standard costing and variance analysis help managers focus on areas not operating as expected. The journal entries here point to another advantage of standard costing systems: Standard costs simplify product costing. As each unit is manufactured, costs are assigned to it using the standard cost of direct materials, the standard cost of direct manufacturing labor, and, as you will see in a later chapter (Chapter 8), the standard manufacturing overhead cost.

From the perspective of control, variances should be isolated at the earliest possible time. For example, the direct materials price variance should be calculated at the time materials are purchased. By doing so, managers can take corrective actions—such as trying to obtain cost reductions from the firm's current suppliers or obtaining price quotes from other potential suppliers—immediately when a large unfavorable variance is known rather than waiting until after the materials are used in production.

If the variance accounts are immaterial in amount at the end of the fiscal year, they are written off to the cost of goods sold. For simplicity, we assume that the balances in the different direct-cost variance accounts as of April 2017 are also the balances at the end of 2017 and are immaterial in total. Webb would record the following journal entry to write off the direct-cost variance accounts to the Cost of Goods Sold account.

Cost of Goods Sold	59,600	
Direct Materials Price Variance	44,400	
Direct Materials Efficiency Variance		66,000
Direct Manufacturing Labor Price Variance		18,000
Direct Manufacturing Labor Efficiency Variance		20,000

Alternatively, assuming Webb has inventories at the end of the fiscal year and the variances are material in their amounts, the variance accounts will be prorated among the cost of goods sold and various inventory accounts using the methods described in Chapter 4 (pages 148–151). For example, the Direct Materials Price Variance will be prorated among Materials Control, Work-in-Process Control, Finished Goods Control, and Cost of Goods Sold on the basis of the standard costs of direct materials in each account's ending balance. Direct Materials Efficiency Variance is prorated among Work-in-Process Control, Finished Goods Control, and Cost of Goods Sold on the basis of the direct material costs in each account's ending balance (after proration of the direct materials price variance).

As discussed in Chapter 4, many accountants, industrial engineers, and managers argue that to the extent variances measure inefficiency during the year, they should be written off against income for that period instead of being prorated among inventories and the cost of goods sold. These people believe it's better to apply a combination of the write-off and proration methods for each individual variance. That way, unlike full proration, the firm doesn't end up carrying the costs of inefficiency as part of its inventoriable costs. Consider the efficiency variance: The portion of the variance due to avoidable inefficiencies should be written off to cost of goods sold. In contrast, the portion that is unavoidable should be prorated. Likewise, if a portion of the direct materials price variance is unavoidable because it is entirely caused by general market conditions, it too should be prorated.

Implementing Standard Costing

Standard costing provides valuable information that is used for the management and control of materials, labor, and other activities related to production.

Standard Costing and Information Technology

Both large and small firms are increasingly using computerized standard costing systems. For example, companies such as Sandoz, a maker of generic drugs, and Dell store standard prices and standard quantities in their computer systems. A bar code scanner records the receipt of materials, immediately costing each material using its stored standard price. The receipt of materials is then matched with the firm's purchase orders and recorded in accounts payable, and the direct material price variance is isolated.

The direct materials efficiency variance is calculated as output is completed by comparing the standard quantity of direct materials that should have been used with the computerized request for direct materials submitted by an operator on the production floor. Labor variances are calculated as employees log into production-floor terminals and punch in their employee numbers, start and end times, and the quantity of product they helped produce. Managers use this instantaneous feedback from variances to immediately detect and correct any cost-related problem.

Wide Applicability of Standard Costing

Manufacturing firms as well as firms in the service sector find standard costing to be a useful tool. Companies implementing total quality management programs use standard costing to control materials costs. Service-sector companies such as McDonald's are labor intensive and use standard costs to control labor costs. Companies that have implemented computer-integrated manufacturing (CIM), such as Toyota, use flexible budgeting and standard costing to manage activities such as materials handling and setups. The increased use of enterprise resource planning (ERP) systems, as described in Chapter 6, has made it easy for firms to keep track of the standard, average, and actual costs of items in inventory and to make real-time assessments of variances. Managers use variance information to identify areas of the firm's manufacturing or purchasing process that most need attention.

DECISION POINT
Why should a company calculate price and efficiency variances?

Management's Use of Variances

LEARNING OBJECTIVE 6
Understand how managers use variances
...managers use variances to improve future performance

Managers and management accountants use variances to evaluate performance after decisions are implemented, to trigger organization learning, and to make continuous improvements. Variances serve as an early warning system to alert managers to existing problems or to prospective opportunities. When done well, variance analysis enables managers to evaluate the effectiveness of the actions and performance of personnel in the current period, as well as to fine-tune strategies for achieving improved performance in the future. Concepts in Action: Can Chipotle Wrap Up Its Materials-Cost Variance Increases? shows the importance to the fast casual dining giant of paying careful attention to variance analysis with respect to its direct costs.

Multiple Causes of Variances

To interpret variances correctly and make appropriate decisions based on them, managers need to recognize that variances can have multiple causes. Managers must not interpret variances in isolation of each other. The causes of variances in one part of the value chain can be

CONCEPTS IN ACTION: Can Chipotle Wrap Up Its Materials-Cost Variance Increases?

Patrick T. Fallon/Bloomberg/Getty Images

Along with burritos, Chipotle has cooked up profitable growth for many years. The company's build-your-own meal model and focus on organic and naturally raised ingredients successfully attracted millions of customers in the United States and beyond. As it continues to grow, Chipotle's success depends on the company's ability to wrap up keep its materials-cost variance increases.

For Chipotle, profitability depends on making each burrito at the lowest possible cost. In each Chipotle store, the two key direct costs are labor and materials costs. Labor costs include wages for restaurant managers and staff, along with benefits such as health insurance. Materials costs include the "critical seven" expensive food ingredients—steak, carnitas, barbacoa, chicken, cheese, guacamole, and sour cream—and items such as foil, paper bags, and plastic silverware.

To reduce labor costs, Chipotle often makes subtle recipe shifts to find the right balance between taste and cost. For example, it uses pre-chopped tomatoes shipped in plastic bags to make salsa because chopping tomatoes by hand takes too much labor. From 2010–2014, tweaks like that lowered Chipotle's labor costs from 24.7% of revenue to 22.0%. At the same time, however, materials costs rose from 30.5% of revenue to 34.6% due to the company's focus on naturally raised ingredients. Responsibly raised meat and fresh local produce cost Chipotle more than conventional ingredients, which reduces profitability. As a result, each Chipotle store aggressively manages portion control. While employees gladly oblige customers asking for extra rice, beans, or salsa, they are trained to be stingy with the "critical seven" food ingredients.

After E. coli and norovirus outbreaks in 2015, Chipotle made changes to its operations to improve food safety and reduce materials-cost variances. Cheese and some vegetables now arrive in stores pre-cut and shredded, while pork and barbacoa beef are now pre-cooked and delivered in sealed bags. With future profitability dependent on lowering its materials-cost variance, Chipotle's "food with integrity" will need to be managed very closely going forward.

Sources: Sarah Nassauer, "Inside Chipotle's Kitchen: What's Really Handmade," *The Wall Street Journal* (February 24, 2015); Candice Choi, "Chipotle Makes Food Prep Changes after E. Coli Scare," *Claims Journal* (December 28, 2015).

---

the result of decisions made in another part of the value chain. Consider an unfavorable direct materials efficiency variance on Webb's production line. Possible operational causes of this variance across the value chain of the company are:

1. Poor design of products or processes
2. Poor work on the production line because of underskilled workers or faulty machines
3. Inappropriate assignment of labor or machines to specific jobs
4. Congestion due to scheduling a large number of rush orders placed by Webb's sales representatives
5. Webb's cloth suppliers not manufacturing materials of uniformly high quality

Item 5 offers an even broader reason for the cause of the unfavorable direct materials efficiency variance by considering inefficiencies in the supply chain of companies—in this case, by the cloth suppliers for Webb's jackets. Whenever possible, managers must attempt to understand the root causes of the variances.

When to Investigate Variances

Because a standard is not a single measure but rather a range of acceptable input quantities, costs, output quantities, or prices, managers should expect small variances to arise. A variance within an acceptable range is considered to be an "in-control occurrence" and calls for no investigation or action by managers. So when do managers need to investigate variances?

Frequently, managers investigate variances based on subjective judgments or rules of thumb. For critical items, such as product defects, even a small variance can prompt an investigation. For other items, such as direct material costs, labor costs, and repair costs, companies generally have rules such as "investigate all variances exceeding $5,000 or 20% of the budgeted cost, whichever is lower." The idea is that a 4% variance in direct material costs of $1 million—a $40,000 variance—deserves more attention than a 15% variance in repair costs of $10,000—a $1,500 variance. In other words, variance analysis is subject to the same cost–benefit test as all other phases of a management control system.

Using Variances for Performance Measurement

Managers often use variance analysis when evaluating the performance of their employees or business units. Two attributes of performance are commonly evaluated:

1. **Effectiveness**: the degree to which a predetermined objective or target is met, such as the sales, market share, and customer satisfaction ratings of Starbucks' VIA® Ready Brew line of instant coffees.
2. **Efficiency**: the relative amount of inputs used to achieve a given output level. For example, the smaller the quantity of Arabica beans used to make a given number of VIA packets or the greater the number of VIA packets made from a given quantity of beans, the greater the efficiency.

As we discussed earlier, it is important to understand the causes of a variance before using it for performance evaluation. Suppose a purchasing manager for Starbucks has just negotiated a deal that results in a favorable price variance for direct materials. The deal could have achieved a favorable variance for any or all of the following reasons:

1. The purchasing manager bargained effectively with suppliers.
2. The purchasing manager secured a discount for buying in bulk with fewer purchase orders. (However, buying larger quantities than necessary for the short run resulted in excessive inventory.)
3. The purchasing manager accepted a bid from the lowest-priced supplier without fully checking the supplier's quality-monitoring procedures.

If the purchasing manager's performance is evaluated solely on price variances, then the evaluation will be positive. Reason 1 would support this conclusion: The purchasing manager bargained effectively. Reasons 2 and 3, buying in bulk or buying without checking the supplier's quality-monitoring procedures, will lead to short-run gains. But should these lead to a positive evaluation for the purchasing manager? Not necessarily. These short-run gains could be offset by higher inventory storage costs or higher inspection costs and defect rates. Starbucks may ultimately lose more money because of reasons 2 and 3 than it gains from the favorable price variance.

Bottom line: Managers should not automatically interpret a favorable variance as "good news" or assume it means their subordinates performed well.

Firms benefit from variance analysis because it highlights individual aspects of performance. However, if any single performance measure (for example, achieving a certain labor efficiency variance or a certain consumer rating) is overemphasized, managers will tend to make decisions that will cause the particular performance measure to look good. These actions may conflict with the company's overall goals, inhibiting the goals from being achieved. This faulty perspective on performance usually arises when top management designs a performance evaluation and reward system that does not emphasize total company objectives.

Organization Learning

The goal of variance analysis is for managers to understand why variances arise, to learn, and to improve their firm's future performance. For instance, to reduce the unfavorable direct materials efficiency variance, Webb's managers may attempt to improve the design of its jackets, the commitment of its workers to do the job right the first time, and the quality of the materials. Sometimes an unfavorable direct materials efficiency variance may signal a need to change the strategy related to a product, perhaps because it cannot be made at a low enough cost. Variance analysis should not be used to "play the blame game" (find someone to blame for every unfavorable variance) but to help managers learn about what happened and how to perform better in the future.

Companies need to strike a delicate balance between using variances to evaluate the performance of managers and employees and improve learning within the organization. If the performance evaluation aspect is overemphasized, managers will focus on setting and meeting targets that are easy to attain rather than targets that are challenging, require creativity and resourcefulness, and result in continuous improvement. For example, Webb's manufacturing manager will prefer an easy standard that allows workers ample time to manufacture a jacket. But that will provide the manufacturing department little incentive to improve processes and identify methods to reduce production times and costs. Alternatively, the manufacturing manager might urge workers to produce jackets within the time allowed, even if this leads to poorer quality jackets being produced, which would later hurt revenues. If variance analysis is seen as a way to promote learning within the organization, negative effects such as these can be minimized.

Continuous Improvement

Managers can also use variance analysis to create a virtuous cycle of continuous improvement. How? By repeatedly identifying the causes of variances, taking corrective actions, and evaluating the results. Improvement opportunities are often easier to identify when the company first produces a product. Once managers identify easy improvements, much more ingenuity may be required to identify successive ones. Some companies use Kaizen budgeting (Chapter 6, p. 242) to specifically target reductions in budgeted costs over successive periods. The advantage of Kaizen budgeting is that it makes continuous improvement goals explicit.

It is important to make sure though that continuous improvement goals are implemented thoughtfully. In a research or design setting, injecting too much discipline and focusing on incremental improvement may well dissuade creativity and truly innovative approaches. An overt reliance on gaining efficiencies should not deter employees from a willingness to take risky approaches or from challenging the basic assumptions of how business is carried out.

Financial and Nonfinancial Performance Measures

Almost all companies use a combination of financial and nonfinancial performance measures for planning and control rather than relying exclusively on either type of measure. To control a production process, supervisors cannot wait for an accounting report with variances reported in dollars. Instead, timely nonfinancial performance measures are frequently used for control purposes. For example, Nissan and many other manufacturers display real-time defect rates and production levels on large screens throughout their plants for workers and managers to see.

In Webb's cutting room, cloth is laid out and cut into pieces, which are then matched and assembled. Managers exercise control in the cutting room by observing workers and by focusing on *nonfinancial measures*, such as number of square yards of cloth used to produce 1,000 jackets or the percentage of jackets started and completed without requiring any rework. Webb's production workers find these nonfinancial measures easy to understand. Webb's managers also use *financial measures* to evaluate the overall cost efficiency with which operations are being run and to help guide decisions about, say, changing the mix of inputs used in manufacturing jackets. Financial measures are critical in a company because they indicate the economic impact of diverse physical activities. This knowledge allows managers to make trade-offs, such as increasing the costs of one physical activity (say, cutting) to reduce the costs of another physical measure (say, defects).

DECISION POINT
How do managers use variances?

Describe benchmarking and explain its role in cost management

...benchmarking compares actual performance against the best levels of performance

Benchmarking and Variance Analysis

Webb Company based its budgeted amounts on analysis of its own operations. We now turn to the situation in which companies develop standards based on the operations of other companies. **Benchmarking** is the continuous process of comparing your firm's performance levels against the best levels of performance in competing companies or in companies having similar processes. When benchmarks are used as standards, managers and management accountants know that the company will be competitive in the marketplace if it can meet or beat those standards.

Companies develop benchmarks and calculate variances on items that are the most important to their businesses. A common unit of measurement used to compare the efficiency of airlines is cost per available seat mile. Available seat mile (ASM) is a measure of airline size and equals the total seats in a plane multiplied by the distance the plane traveled. Consider the cost per available seat mile for United. Assume United uses data from each of six competing U.S. airlines in its benchmark cost comparisons. Summary data are in Exhibit 7-5. The benchmark companies are in alphabetical order in column A. Also reported in Exhibit 7-5 are operating cost per ASM, operating revenue per ASM, operating income per ASM, fuel cost per ASM, labor cost per ASM, and total available seat miles for each airline. The recovery of the travel industry from the recession induced by the financial crisis as well as the benefits of lower fuel costs and greater industry consolidation are evident in the fact that all of the airlines have positive levels of operating income.

How well did United manage its costs? The answer depends on which specific benchmark is being used for comparison. United's actual operating cost of 13.65 cents per ASM is above the average operating cost of 12.78 cents per ASM of the six other airlines. Moreover, United's operating cost per ASM is 23.3% higher than Alaska Airways, the lowest-cost competitor at 11.07 cents per ASM [(13.65 − 11.07) ÷ 11.07 = 0.233]. So why is United's operating cost per ASM so high? Columns E and F suggest that both fuel cost and labor cost are possible reasons. These benchmarking data alert management at United that it needs to become more efficient in its use of both material and labor inputs to become cost competitive.

It can be difficult for firms to find appropriate benchmarks such as those in Exhibit 7-5. Many companies purchase benchmark data from consulting firms. Another problem is ensuring the benchmark numbers are comparable. In other words, there needs to be an "apples to apples" comparison. Differences can exist across companies in their strategies, inventory costing methods, depreciation methods, and so on. For example, JetBlue serves fewer cities and

EXHIBIT 7-5 Available Seat Mile (ASM) Benchmark Comparison of United Airlines with Six Other Airlines

	A Airline	B Operating Cost (cents per ASM) (1)	C Operating Revenue (cents per ASM) (2)	D Operating Income (cents per ASM) (3) = (2) − (1)	E Fuel Cost (cents per ASM) (4)	F Labor Cost (cents per ASM) (5)	G Total ASMs (Millions) (6)
4							
5	United Airlines	13.65	13.66	0.01	4.30	4.27	214,061
6	Airlines used as benchmarks:						
7	Alaska Airlines	11.07	13.13	2.06	3.60	3.45	32,434
8	American Airlines	13.76	14.13	0.37	4.40	3.80	157,598
9	Delta Airlines	14.98	15.45	0.47	5.50	4.41	212,235
10	JetBlue Airways	11.69	12.47	0.78	4.10	3.04	45,200
11	Southwest Airlines	12.42	14.13	1.71	3.90	4.35	131,259
12	U.S. Airways	12.75	14.42	1.67	4.10	3.75	79,913
13	Average of airlines						
14	used as benchmarks	12.78	13.96	1.18	4.27	3.80	109,773
15							
16	Source: 2014 data from the MIT Global Airline Industry Program						

flies mostly long-haul routes compared with United, which serves almost all major U.S. cities and several international cities and flies both long-haul and short-haul routes. Southwest Airlines differs from United because it specializes in short-haul direct flights and offers fewer services on board its planes. Because United's strategy is different from the strategies of JetBlue and Southwest, one might expect its cost per ASM to be different, too. United's strategy is more comparable to the strategies of American and Delta. Note that its costs per ASM are relatively more competitive with these airlines. But United competes head to head with Alaska, JetBlue, and Southwest in several cities and markets, so it needs to benchmark against these carriers as well.

United's management accountants can use benchmarking data to address several questions. How do factors such as plane size and type or the duration of flights affect the cost per ASM? Do airlines differ in their fixed cost/variable cost structures? To what extent can United's performance be improved by rerouting flights, using different types of aircraft on different routes, or changing the frequency or timing of specific flights? What explains revenue differences per ASM across airlines? Is it differences in the service quality passengers perceive or differences in an airline's competitive power at specific airports? Management accountants are more valuable to managers when they use benchmarking data to provide insight into *why* costs or revenues differ across companies or within plants of the same company, as distinguished from simply reporting the magnitude of the differences.

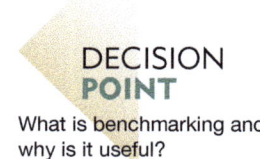

DECISION POINT
What is benchmarking and why is it useful?

PROBLEM FOR SELF-STUDY

O'Shea Company manufactures ceramic vases. It uses its standard costing system when developing its flexible-budget amounts. In September 2017, O'Shea produced 2,000 finished units. The following information relates to its two direct manufacturing cost categories: direct materials and direct manufacturing labor.

Direct materials used were 4,400 kilograms (kg). The standard direct materials input allowed for one output unit is 2 kilograms at $15 per kilogram. O'Shea purchased 5,000 kilograms of materials at $16.50 per kilogram, a total of $82,500. (This Problem for Self-Study illustrates how to calculate direct materials variances when the quantity of materials purchased in a period differs from the quantity of materials used in that period.)

Actual direct manufacturing labor-hours were 3,250, at a total cost of $66,300. Standard manufacturing labor time allowed is 1.5 hours per output unit, and the standard direct manufacturing labor cost is $20 per hour.

Required

1. Calculate the direct materials price variance and efficiency variance and the direct manufacturing labor price variance and efficiency variance. Base the direct materials price variance on a flexible budget for *actual quantity purchased*, but base the direct materials efficiency variance on a flexible budget for *actual quantity used*.
2. Prepare journal entries for a standard costing system that isolates variances at the earliest possible time.

Solution

1. Exhibit 7-6 shows how the columnar presentation of variances introduced in Exhibit 7-3 can be adjusted for the difference in timing between purchase and use of materials. Note, in particular, the two sets of computations in column 2 for direct materials—the $75,000 for direct materials purchased and the $66,000 for direct materials used. The direct materials price variance is calculated on purchases so that managers responsible for the purchase can immediately identify and isolate reasons for the variance and initiate any desired corrective action. The efficiency variance is the responsibility of the production manager, so this variance is identified only at the time materials are used.

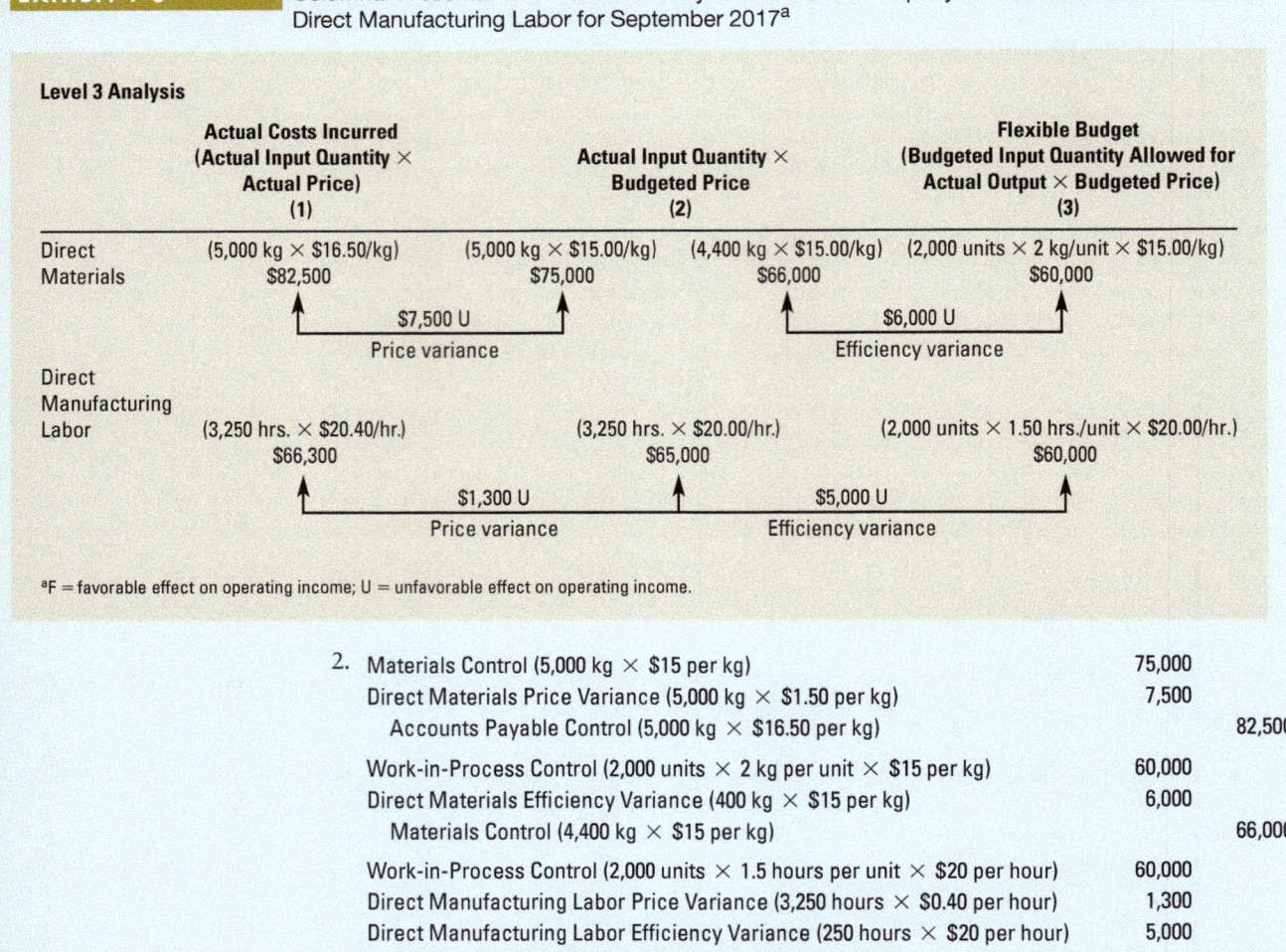

EXHIBIT 7-6 Columnar Presentation of Variance Analysis for O'Shea Company: Direct Materials and Direct Manufacturing Labor for September 2017[a]

[a] F = favorable effect on operating income; U = unfavorable effect on operating income.

2. Materials Control (5,000 kg × $15 per kg)	75,000	
Direct Materials Price Variance (5,000 kg × $1.50 per kg)	7,500	
Accounts Payable Control (5,000 kg × $16.50 per kg)		82,500
Work-in-Process Control (2,000 units × 2 kg per unit × $15 per kg)	60,000	
Direct Materials Efficiency Variance (400 kg × $15 per kg)	6,000	
Materials Control (4,400 kg × $15 per kg)		66,000
Work-in-Process Control (2,000 units × 1.5 hours per unit × $20 per hour)	60,000	
Direct Manufacturing Labor Price Variance (3,250 hours × $0.40 per hour)	1,300	
Direct Manufacturing Labor Efficiency Variance (250 hours × $20 per hour)	5,000	
Wages Payable Control (3,250 hours × $20.40 per hour)		66,300

Note: All the variances are debits because they are unfavorable and therefore reduce operating income.

DECISION POINTS

The following question-and-answer format summarizes the chapter's learning objectives. Each decision presents a key question related to a learning objective. The guidelines are the answer to that question.

Decision

1. What are static budgets and static-budget variances?

2. How can managers develop a flexible budget, and why is it useful to do so?

Guidelines

A static budget is based on the level of output planned at the start of the budget period. The static-budget variance is the difference between the actual result and the corresponding budgeted amount in the static budget.

A flexible budget is adjusted (flexed) to recognize the actual output level of the budget period. Managers use a three-step procedure to develop a flexible budget. When all costs are either variable or fixed with respect to output, these three steps require only information about the budgeted selling price, budgeted variable cost per output unit, budgeted fixed costs, and actual quantity of output units. Flexible budgets help managers gain more insight into the causes of variances than is available from static budgets.

Decision	Guidelines
3. How are flexible-budget and sales-volume variances calculated?	The static-budget variance can be subdivided into a flexible-budget variance (the difference between the actual result and the corresponding flexible-budget amount) and a sales-volume variance (the difference between the flexible-budget amount and the corresponding static-budget amount).
4. What is a standard cost and what are its purposes?	A standard cost is a carefully determined cost used as a benchmark for judging performance. The purposes of a standard cost are to exclude past inefficiencies and to take into account changes expected to occur in the budget period.
5. Why should a company calculate price and efficiency variables?	The computation of price and efficiency variances helps managers gain insight into two different—but not independent—aspects of performance. The price variance focuses on the difference between the actual input price and the budgeted input price. The efficiency variance focuses on the difference between the actual quantity of input and the budgeted quantity of input allowed for actual output.
6. How do managers use variances?	Managers use variances for control, decision making, performance evaluation, organization learning, and continuous improvement. When using variances for these purposes, managers should consider several variances together rather than focusing only on an individual variance.
7. What is benchmarking and why is it useful?	Benchmarking is the continuous process of comparing your firm's performance against the best levels of performance in competing companies or companies with similar processes. Benchmarking measures how well a company and its managers are doing in comparison to other organizations.

APPENDIX

Mix and Yield Variances for Substitutable Inputs

The Webb Company example illustrates how to calculate price and efficiency variances for production inputs when there is a single form of each input. Webb used a single material (cloth) and a single type of direct labor. But what if managers have leeway in combining and substituting inputs? For example, Del Monte Foods can combine material inputs (such as pineapples, cherries, and grapes) in varying proportions for its cans of fruit cocktail. Within limits, these individual fruits are *substitutable inputs* in making the fruit cocktail.

We illustrate how the efficiency variance discussed in this chapter (pages 279–280) can be subdivided into variances that highlight the financial impact of input mix and input yield when inputs are substitutable. We consider a variation of the Webb Company example. For simplicity, we focus on direct manufacturing labor inputs and substitution among three of these inputs. The same approach can also be used to examine substitutable direct materials inputs.

Mode Company also manufactures jackets but, unlike Webb, employs workers of different skill (or experience) levels. Workers are of Low, Medium, or High skill. Workers with greater skill levels focus on the more complicated aspects of the jacket, such as adding darts and fancy seam lines. They are compensated accordingly. Mode's production standards require 0.80 labor-hours to produce 1 jacket; 50% of the hours are budgeted to be Low skill,

30% Medium, and 20% High. The direct manufacturing labor inputs budgeted to produce 1 jacket are as follows:

0.40 (50% of 0.80) hours of Low at $12 per hour	$ 4.80
0.24 (30% of 0.80) hours of Medium at $20 per hour	4.80
0.16 (20% of 0.80) hours of High at $40 per hour	6.40
Total budgeted direct manufacturing labor cost of 1 jacket	$16.00

With an expected $16 in labor cost for a jacket that requires 0.80 labor hours, note that the production standards imply a weighted average labor rate of $20 per hour ($16 ÷ 0.80 hours).

In April 2017, Mode produced 10,000 jackets using a total of 9,000 labor-hours. The breakdown for this input usage is as follows:

4,500	hours of Low at actual cost of $12 per hour	$ 54,000
3,150	hours of Medium at actual cost of $26 per hour	81,900
1,350	hours of High at actual cost of $46 per hour	62,100
9,000	hours of direct manufacturing labor	198,000
	Budgeted cost of 8,000 direct manufacturing labor-hours at $20 per hour	160,000
	Flexible-budget variance for direct manufacturing labor	$ 38,000 U

Direct Manufacturing Labor Price and Efficiency Variances

Mode's flexible budget and actual costs for direct manufacturing labor are identical to those in the Webb Company example. As a result, Mode has the same flexible-budget variance for direct manufacturing labor ($38,000). The breakdown of this amount into price and efficiency variances is different, however, because Mode employs three categories of substitutable direct manufacturing labor inputs.

Exhibit 7-7 presents in columnar format the analysis of Mode's flexible-budget variance for direct manufacturing labor. The labor price and efficiency variances are calculated separately for each category of direct manufacturing labor and then added together. The variance analysis prompts Webb to investigate the unfavorable price and efficiency variances in each category. Why did it pay more for certain types of labor and use more hours than it had budgeted? Were actual wage rates higher, in general, or could the personnel department have negotiated lower rates? Did the additional labor costs result from inefficiencies in processing?

EXHIBIT 7-7 Direct Manufacturing Labor Price and Efficiency Variances for Mode Company for April 2017[a]

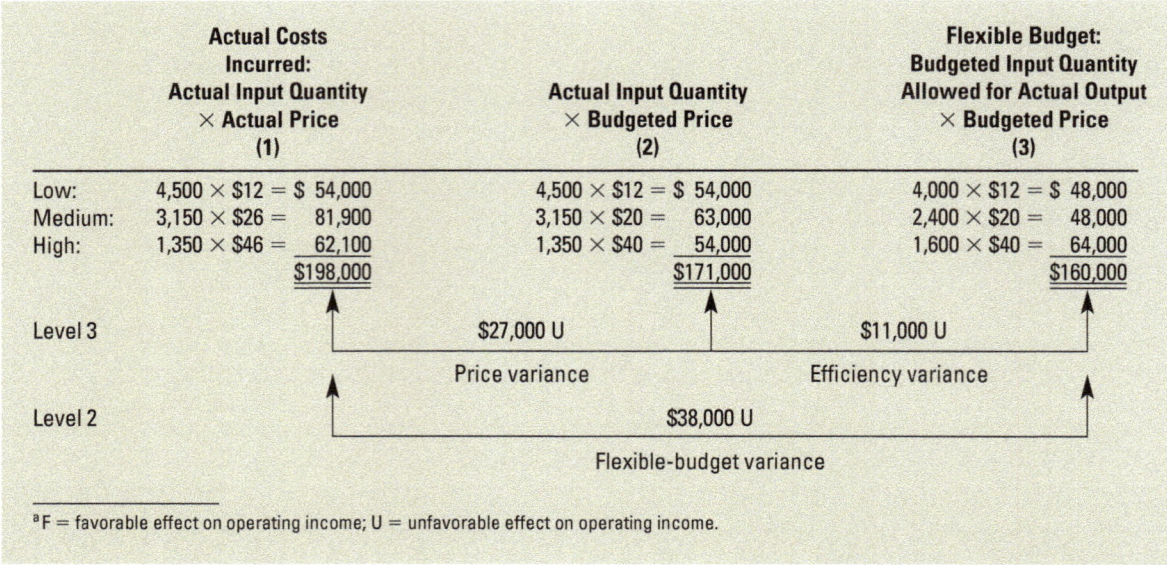

[a]F = favorable effect on operating income; U = unfavorable effect on operating income.

Direct Manufacturing Labor Mix and Yield Variances

Managers sometimes have discretion to substitute one input for another. The manager of Mode's operations has some leeway in combining Low, Medium, and High skill workers without affecting the quality of the jackets. We will assume that to maintain quality, mix percentages of each type of labor can only vary up to 5% from standard mix. For example, the percentage of Low skill labor in the mix can vary between 45% and 55% (50% ± 5%). When inputs are substitutable, direct manufacturing labor efficiency improvement relative to budgeted costs can come from two sources: (1) using a cheaper mix to produce a given quantity of output, measured by the mix variance, and (2) using less input to achieve a given quantity of output, measured by the yield variance.

Holding actual total quantity of all direct manufacturing labor inputs used constant, the total **direct manufacturing labor mix variance** is the difference between:

1. budgeted cost for actual mix of actual total quantity of direct manufacturing labor used and
2. budgeted cost of budgeted mix of actual total quantity of direct manufacturing labor used.

Holding budgeted input mix constant, the **direct manufacturing labor yield variance** is the difference between:

1. budgeted cost of direct manufacturing labor based on actual total quantity of direct manufacturing labor used and
2. flexible-budget cost of direct manufacturing labor based on budgeted total quantity of direct manufacturing labor allowed for actual output produced.

Exhibit 7-8 presents the direct manufacturing labor mix and yield variances for Mode Company. Note that column (1) in this exhibit is identical to column (2) in Exhibit 7-7, and column (3) is the same in both exhibits.

Direct Manufacturing Labor Mix Variance

The total direct manufacturing labor mix variance is the sum of the direct manufacturing labor mix variances for each input:

$$\begin{pmatrix} \text{Direct} \\ \text{labor} \\ \text{mix variance} \\ \text{for each input} \end{pmatrix} = \begin{pmatrix} \text{Actual total} \\ \text{quantity of all} \\ \text{direct labor} \\ \text{inputs used} \end{pmatrix} \times \begin{pmatrix} \text{Actual} \\ \text{direct labor} \\ \text{input mix} \\ \text{percentage} \end{pmatrix} - \begin{pmatrix} \text{Budgeted} \\ \text{direct labor} \\ \text{input mix} \\ \text{percentage} \end{pmatrix} \times \begin{pmatrix} \text{Budegeted} \\ \text{price of} \\ \text{direct labor} \\ \text{input} \end{pmatrix}$$

EXHIBIT 7-8 Direct Manufacturing Labor Yield and Mix Variances for Mode Company for April 2017[a]

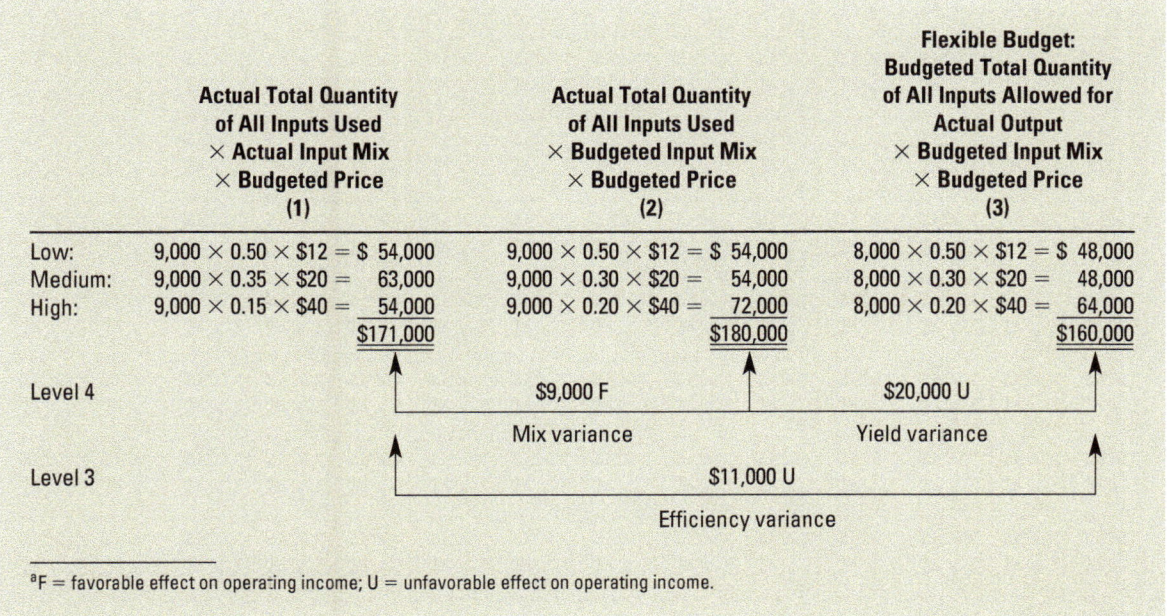

[a]F = favorable effect on operating income; U = unfavorable effect on operating income.

The direct manufacturing labor mix variances are as follows:

Low:	9,000 hours × (0.50 − 0.50) × $12 per hour	= 9,000 × 0.00 × $12 =	$ 0
Medium:	9,000 hours × (0.35 − 0.30) × $20 per hour	= 9,000 × 0.05 × $20 =	9,000 U
High:	9,000 hours × (0.15 − 0.20) × $40 per hour	= 9,000 × −0.05 × $40 =	18,000 F
Total direct manufacturing labor mix variance			$ 9,000 F

The total direct manufacturing labor mix variance is favorable because, relative to the budgeted mix, Mode substitutes 5% of the cheaper Medium skill labor for 5% of the more-expensive High skill.

Direct Manufacturing Labor Yield Variance

The yield variance is the sum of the direct manufacturing labor yield variances for each input:

$$\begin{pmatrix} \text{Direct} \\ \text{labor} \\ \text{yield variance} \\ \text{for each input} \end{pmatrix} = \begin{pmatrix} \text{Actual total} \\ \text{quantity of} \\ \text{all direct} \\ \text{labor} \\ \text{inputs used} \end{pmatrix} - \begin{pmatrix} \text{Budgeted total} \\ \text{quantity of all} \\ \text{direct labor} \\ \text{input allowed} \\ \text{for actual output} \end{pmatrix} \times \begin{pmatrix} \text{Budgeted} \\ \text{direct labor} \\ \text{input mix} \\ \text{percentage} \end{pmatrix} \times \begin{pmatrix} \text{Budgeted} \\ \text{price of} \\ \text{direct labor} \\ \text{input} \end{pmatrix}$$

The direct manufacturing labor yield variances are as follows:

Low:	(9,000 − 8,000) hours × 0.50 × $12 per hour	= 1,000 × 0.50 × $12 =	$ 6,000 U
Medium:	(9,000 − 8,000) hours × 0.30 × $20 per hour	= 1,000 × 0.30 × $20 =	6,000 U
High:	(9,000 − 8,000) hours × 0.20 × $40 per hour	= 1,000 × 0.20 × $40 =	8,000 U
Total direct manufacturing labor yield variance			$20,000 U

The total direct manufacturing labor yield variance is unfavorable because Mode used 9,000 hours of labor rather than the 8,000 hours that it should have used to produce 10,000 jackets. The budgeted cost per hour of labor in the budgeted mix is $20 per hour. The unfavorable yield variance represents the budgeted cost of using 1,000 more hours of direct manufacturing labor, (9,000 − 8,000) hours × $20 per hour = $20,000 U. Mode would want to investigate reasons for this unfavorable yield variance. For example, did the substitution of the cheaper Medium skill for High skill labor, which resulted in the favorable mix variance, also cause the unfavorable yield variance?

The direct manufacturing labor variances computed in Exhibits 7-7 and 7-8 can be summarized as follows:

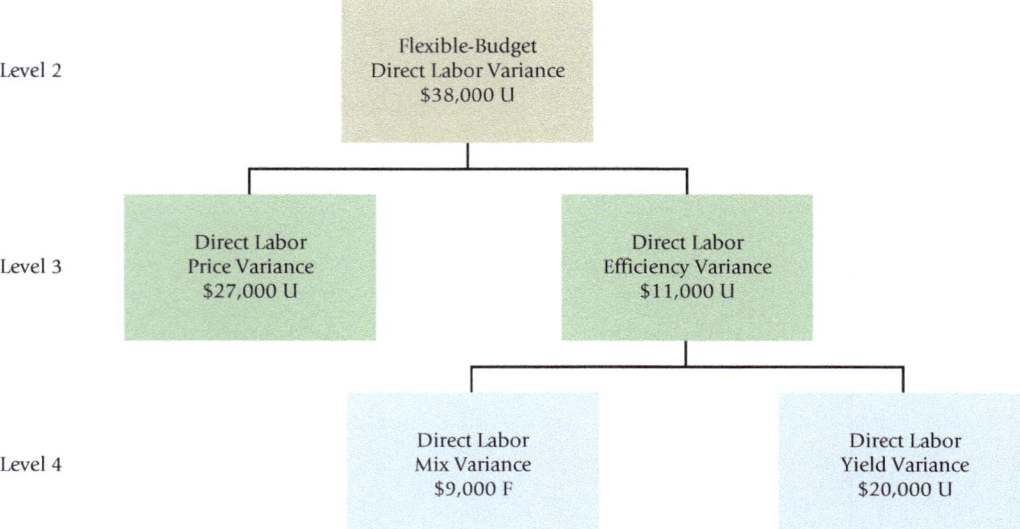

TERMS TO LEARN

This chapter and the Glossary at the end of the book contain definitions of the following important terms:

benchmarking	favorable variance	standard cost
budgeted performance	flexible budget	standard input
direct manufacturing labor mix variance	flexible-budget variance	standard price
	management by exception	static budget
direct manufacturing labor yield variance	price variance	static-budget variance
	rate variance	unfavorable variance
effectiveness	sales-volume variance	usage variance
efficiency	selling-price variance	variance
efficiency variance	standard	

ASSIGNMENT MATERIAL

Questions

Pearson MyLab Accounting

7-1 What are the main uses of variance analysis in an organization?
7-2 When using standard costing, what are the two main components of variances for materials in a flexible budget?
7-3 What are the impacts of variances on an operating income?
7-4 Why should the performance of variance analyses be based on flexible budgets rather than static budgets?
7-5 What is the main component of sales variance if a flexible-sales budget is used?
7-6 When is a flexible budget similar to a static budget? Why?
7-7 What is the main advantage of standard costs versus past costs?
7-8 How are the main components of materials variances interrelated in a flexible budget?
7-9 List three causes of a favorable direct materials price variance.
7-10 Describe three reasons for an unfavorable direct manufacturing labor efficiency variance.
7-11 How does variance analysis help in continuous improvement?
7-12 Why might an analyst examining variances in the production area look beyond that business function for explanations of those variances?
7-13 Comment on the following statement made by a management accountant: "The plant manager has little knowledge of the individual impacts of the purchase department, the sales department, and the production department on the total unfavorable variance in our operating income."
7-14 When inputs are substitutable, how can the direct materials efficiency variance be decomposed further to obtain useful information?
7-15 "Benchmarking is about comparing your firm's performance against the best levels of performance in the market and has nothing to do with variance analyses." Do you agree?

Multiple-Choice Questions

Pearson MyLab Accounting

7-16 Metal Shelf Company's standard cost for raw materials is $4.00 per pound and it is expected that each metal shelf uses two pounds of material. During October Year 2, 25,000 pounds of materials are purchased from a new supplier for $97,000 and 13,000 shelves are produced using 27,000 pounds of materials. Which statement is a possible explanation concerning the direct materials variances?

a. The production department had to use more materials since the quality of the materials was inferior.
b. The purchasing manager paid more than expected for materials.
c. Production workers were more efficient than anticipated.
d. The overall materials variance is positive; no further analysis is necessary.

7-17 All of the following statements regarding standards are accurate except:

a. Standards allow management to budget at a per-unit level.
b. Ideal standards account for a minimal amount of normal spoilage.
c. Participative standards usually take longer to implement than authoritative standards.
d. Currently attainable standards take into account the level of training available to employees.

7-18 Amalgamated Manipulation Manufacturing's (AMM) standards anticipate that there will be 3 pounds of raw material used for every unit of finished goods produced. AMM began the month of May with 5,000 pounds of raw material, purchased 15,000 pounds for $19,500 and ended the month with 4,000 pounds on hand. The company produced 5,000 units of finished goods. The company estimates standard costs at $1.50 per pound. The materials price and efficiency variances for the month of May were:

	Price Variance	Efficiency Variance
1.	$3,000 U	$1,500 F
2.	$3,000 F	$ 0
3.	$3,000 F	$1,500 U
4.	$3,200 F	$1,500 U

7-19 Atlantic Company has a manufacturing facility in Brooklyn that manufactures robotic equipment for the auto industry. For Year 1, Atlantic collected the following information from its main production line:

Actual quantity purchased	200 units
Actual quantity used	110 units
Units standard quantity	100 units
Actual price paid	$ 8 per unit
Standard price	$ 10 per unit

Atlantic isolates price variances at the time of purchase. What is the materials price variance for Year 1?

1. $400 favorable.
2. $400 unfavorable.
3. $220 favorable.
4. $220 unfavorable.

7-20 Basix Inc. calculates direct manufacturing labor variances and has the following information:

Actual hours worked: 200
Standard hours: 250
Actual rate per hour: $12
Standard rate per hour: $10

Given the information above, which of the following is correct regarding direct manufacturing labor variances?

a. The price and efficiency variances are favorable.
b. The price and efficiency variances are unfavorable.
c. The price variance is favorable, while the efficiency variance is unfavorable.
d. The price variance is unfavorable, while the efficiency variance is favorable.

©2016 DeVry/Becker Educational Development Corp. All Rights Reserved.

Exercises

7-21 Flexible budget. Brabham Enterprises manufactures tires for the Formula I motor racing circuit. For August 2017, it budgeted to manufacture and sell 3,000 tires at a variable cost of $74 per tire and total fixed costs of $54,000. The budgeted selling price was $110 per tire. Actual results in August 2017 were 2,800 tires manufactured and sold at a selling price of $112 per tire. The actual total variable costs were $229,600, and the actual total fixed costs were $50,000.

1. Prepare a performance report (akin to Exhibit 7-2, page 274) that uses a flexible budget and a static budget.
2. Comment on the results in requirement 1.

7-22 Flexible budget. Beta Company's budgeted prices for direct materials, direct manufacturing labor, and direct marketing (distribution) labor per luxury wallet are $41, $5, and $11, respectively. The president is pleased with the following performance report:

	Actual Costs	Static Budget	Variance
Direct materials	$373,500	$410,000	$36,500 F
Direct manufacturing labor	48,600	50,000	1,400 F
Direct marketing (distribution) labor	103,500	110,000	6,500 F

Actual output was 9,000 luxury wallets. Assume all three direct-cost items shown are variable costs. Is the president's pleasure justified? Prepare a revised performance report that uses a flexible budget and a static budget.

Required

7-23 Flexible-budget preparation and analysis. XYZ Printers, Inc., produces luxury checkbooks with three checks and stubs per page. Each checkbook is designed for an individual customer and is ordered through the customer's bank. The company's operating budget for September 2017 included these data:

Number of checkbooks	20,000
Selling price per book	$ 22
Variable cost per book	$ 9
Fixed costs for the month	$150,000

The actual results for September 2017 were as follows:

Number of checkbooks produced and sold	15,000
Average selling price per book	$ 23
Variable cost per book	$ 8
Fixed costs for the month	$155,000

The executive vice president of the company observed that the operating income for September was much lower than anticipated, despite a higher-than-budgeted selling price and a lower-than-budgeted variable cost per unit. As the company's management accountant, you have been asked to provide explanations for the disappointing September results.

XYZ develops its flexible budget on the basis of budgeted per-output-unit revenue and per-output-unit variable costs without detailed analysis of budgeted inputs.

1. Prepare a static-budget-based variance analysis of the September performance.
2. Prepare a flexible-budget-based variance analysis of the September performance.
3. Why might XYZ printers find the flexible-budget-based variance analysis more informative than the static-budget-based variance analysis? Explain your answer.

Required

7-24 Flexible budget, working backward. The Alpha Company manufactures designer jewelry for jewelry stores. A new accountant intern at Alpha Company has accidentally deleted the calculations on the company's variance analysis calculations for the year ended December 31, 2017. The following table is what remains of the data.

	Actual Results	Flexible-Budget Variances	Flexible Budget	Sales-Volume Variances	Static Budget
Units sold	150,000				140,000
Revenues (sales)	$975,000				$630,000
Variable costs	675,000				350,000
Contribution margin	300,000				280,000
Fixed costs	150,000				130,000
Operating income	$150,000				$150,000

1. Calculate all the required variances. (If your work is accurate, you will find that the total static-budget variance is $0.)
2. What are the actual and budgeted selling prices? What are the actual and budgeted variable costs per unit?
3. Review the variances you have calculated and discuss possible causes and potential problems. What is the important lesson learned here?

Required

7-25 Flexible-budget and sales volume variances. Luster, Inc., produces the basic fillings used in many popular frozen desserts and treats—vanilla and chocolate ice creams, puddings, meringues, and fudge. Luster uses standard costing and carries over no inventory from one month to the next. The ice-cream product group's results for June 2017 were as follows:

	Actual Results	Static Budget
Performance Report, June 2017		
Units (pounds)	350,000	335,000
Revenues	$2,012,500	$1,976,500
Variable manufacturing costs	1,137,500	1,038,500
Contribution margin	$ 875,000	$ 938,000

Sam Adler, the business manager for ice-cream products, is pleased that more pounds of ice cream were sold than budgeted and that revenues were up. Unfortunately, variable manufacturing costs went up, too. The bottom line is that contribution margin declined by $63,000, which is less than 3% of the budgeted revenues of $1,976,500. Overall, Adler feels that the business is running fine.

Required

1. Calculate the static-budget variance in units, revenues, variable manufacturing costs, and contribution margin. What percentage is each static-budget variance relative to its static-budget amount?
2. Break down each static-budget variance into a flexible-budget variance and a sales-volume variance.
3. Calculate the selling-price variance.
4. Assume the role of management accountant at Luster. How would you present the results to Sam Adler? Should he be more concerned? If so, why?

7-26 Price and efficiency variances. Modern Tiles Ltd. manufactures ceramic tiles. For January 2017, it budgeted to purchase and use 10,000 pounds of clay at $0.70 a pound. Actual purchases and usage for January 2017 were 11,000 pounds at $0.65 a pound. Modern Tiles Ltd. budgeted for 40,000 ceramic tiles. Actual output was 43,000 ceramic tiles.

Required

1. Compute the flexible-budget variance.
2. Compute the price and efficiency variances.
3. Comment on the results for requirements 1 and 2 and provide a possible explanation for them.

7-27 Materials and manufacturing labor variances. Consider the following data collected for Theta Homes, Inc.:

	Direct Materials	Direct Manufacturing Labor
Cost incurred: Actual inputs × actual prices	$150,000	$100,000
Actual inputs × standard prices	162,000	95,000
Standard inputs allowed for actual output × standard prices	168,000	90,000

Compute the price, efficiency, and flexible-budget variances for direct materials and direct manufacturing labor.

7-28 Direct materials and direct manufacturing labor variances. SallyMay, Inc., designs and manufactures T-shirts. It sells its T-shirts to brand-name clothes retailers in lots of one dozen. SallyMay's May 2016 static budget and actual results for direct inputs are as follows:

Static Budget

Number of T-shirt lots (1 lot = 1 dozen)   400

Per Lot of Jackets:

| Direct materials | 14 meters at $1.70 per meter = $23.80 |
| Direct manufacturing labor | 1.6 hours at $8.10 per hour = $12.96 |

Actual Results

Number of T-shirt lots sold   450

Total Direct Inputs:

| Direct materials | 6,840 meters at $1.95 per meter = $13,338 |
| Direct manufacturing labor | 675 hours at $8.20 per hour = $5,535 |

SallyMay has a policy of analyzing all input variances when they add up to more than 10% of the total cost of materials and labor in the flexible budget, and this is true in May 2016. The production manager discusses the sources of the variances: "A new type of material was purchased in May. This led to faster cutting and sewing, but the workers used more material than usual as they learned to work with it. For now, the standards are fine."

Required

1. Calculate the direct materials and direct manufacturing labor price and efficiency variances in May 2016. What is the total flexible-budget variance for both inputs (direct materials and direct manufacturing labor) combined? What percentage is this variance of the total cost of direct materials and direct manufacturing labor in the flexible budget?
2. Comment on the May 2016 results. Would you continue the "experiment" of using the new material?

7-29 Price and efficiency variances, journal entries. The Schuyler Corporation manufactures lamps. It has set up the following standards per finished unit for direct materials and direct manufacturing labor:

Direct materials: 10 lb. at $4.50 per lb.	$45.00
Direct manufacturing labor: 0.5 hour at $30 per hour	15.00

The number of finished units budgeted for January 2017 was 10,000; 9,850 units were actually produced. Actual results in January 2017 were as follows:

Direct materials: 98,055 lb. used
Direct manufacturing labor: 4,900 hours $154,350

Assume that there was no beginning inventory of either direct materials or finished units.

During the month, materials purchased amounted to 100,000 lb., at a total cost of $465,000. Input price variances are isolated upon purchase. Input-efficiency variances are isolated at the time of usage.

Required

1. Compute the January 2017 price and efficiency variances of direct materials and direct manufacturing labor.
2. Prepare journal entries to record the variances in requirement 1.
3. Comment on the January 2017 price and efficiency variances of Schuyler Corporation.
4. Why might Schuyler calculate direct materials price variances and direct materials efficiency variances with reference to different points in time?

7-30 Materials and manufacturing labor variances, standard costs. Dunn, Inc., is a privately held furniture manufacturer. For August 2017, Dunn had the following standards for one of its products, a wicker chair:

	Standards per Chair
Direct materials	2 square yards of input at $5 per square yard
Direct manufacturing labor	0.5 hour of input at $10 per hour

The following data were compiled regarding actual performance: actual output units (chairs) produced, 2,000; square yards of input purchased and used, 3,700; price per square yard, $5.10; direct manufacturing labor costs, $8,820; actual hours of input, 900; labor price per hour, $9.80.

1. Show computations of price and efficiency variances for direct materials and direct manufacturing labor. Give a plausible explanation of why each variance occurred.
2. Suppose 6,000 square yards of materials were purchased (at $5.10 per square yard), even though only 3,700 square yards were used. Suppose further that variances are identified at their most timely control point; accordingly, direct materials price variances are isolated and traced at the time of purchase to the purchasing department rather than to the production department. Compute the price and efficiency variances under this approach.

7-31 Journal entries and T-accounts (continuation of 7-30). Prepare journal entries and post them to T-accounts for all transactions in Exercise 7-30, including requirement 2. Summarize how these journal entries differ from the normal-costing entries described in Chapter 4, pages 140–143.

7-32 Price and efficiency variances, benchmarking. Topiary Co. produces molded plastic garden pots and other plastic containers. In June 2017, Topiary produces 1,000 lots (each lot is 12 dozen pots) of its most popular line of pots, the 14-inch "Grecian urns," at each of its two plants, which are located in Mineola and Bayside. The production manager, Janice Roberts, asks her assistant, Alastair Ramy, to find out the precise per-unit budgeted variable costs at the two plants and the variable costs of a competitor, Land Art, who offers similar-quality pots at cheaper prices. Ramy pulls together the following information for each lot:

Per Lot	Mineola Plant	Bayside Plant	Land Art
Direct materials	13.50 lbs. @ $9.20 per lb.	14.00 lbs. @ $9.00 per lb.	13.00 lbs. @ $8.80 per lb.
Direct labor	3 hours @ $10.15 per hour	2.7 hours @ $10.20 per hour	2.5 hours @ $10.00 per hour
Variable overhead	$12 per lot	$11 per lot	$11 per lot

Required

1. What is the budgeted variable cost per lot at the Mineola Plant, the Bayside Plant, and at Land Art?
2. Using the Land Art data as the standard, calculate the direct materials and direct labor price and efficiency variances for the Mineola and Bayside plants.
3. What advantage does Topiary get by using Land Art's benchmark data as standards in calculating its variances? Identify two issues that Roberts should keep in mind in using the Land Art data as the standards.

7-33 Static and flexible budgets, service sector. Student Finance (StuFi) is a start-up that aims to use the power of social communities to transform the student loan market. It connects participants through a dedicated lending pool, enabling current students to borrow from a school's alumni community. StuFi's revenue model is to take an upfront fee of 40 basis points (0.40%) *each* from the alumni investor and the student borrower for every loan originated on its platform.

StuFi hopes to go public in the near future and is keen to ensure that its financial results are in line with that ambition. StuFi's budgeted and actual results for the third quarter of 2017 are presented below.

	A	B	C	D	E
1		Static Budget		Actual Results	
2	New loans originated	8,200		10,250	
3	Average amount of loan	$145,000		$162,000	
4	Variable costs per loan:				
5	Professional labor	$360	(8 hrs at $45 per hour)	$475	(9.5 hrs at $50 per hour)
6	Credit verification	$100		$100	
7	Federal documentation fees	$120		$125	
8	Courier services	$50		$54	
9	Administrative costs (fixed)	$800,000		$945,000	
10	Technology costs (fixed)	$1,300,000		$1,415,000	

Required

1. Prepare StuFi's static budget of operating income for the third quarter of 2017.
2. Prepare an analysis of variances for the third quarter of 2017 along the lines of Exhibit 7-2; identify the sales volume and flexible budget variances for operating income.
3. Compute the professional labor price and efficiency variances for the third quarter of 2017.
4. What factors would you consider in evaluating the effectiveness of professional labor in the third quarter of 2017?

Problems

7-34 Flexible budget, direct materials, and direct manufacturing labor variances. Milan Statuary manufactures bust statues of famous historical figures. All statues are the same size. Each unit requires the same amount of resources. The following information is from the static budget for 2017:

Expected production and sales	6,100 units
Expected selling price per unit	$ 700
Total fixed costs	$1,350,000

Standard quantities, standard prices, and standard unit costs follow for direct materials and direct manufacturing labor:

	Standard Quantity	Standard Price	Standard Unit Cost
Direct materials	16 pounds	$14 per pound	$224
Direct manufacturing labor	3.8 hours	$30 per hour	$114

During 2017, actual number of units produced and sold was 5,100, at an average selling price of $730. Actual cost of direct materials used was $1,149,400, based on 70,000 pounds purchased at $16.42 per pound. Direct manufacturing labor-hours actually used were 17,000, at the rate of $33.70 per hour. As a result, actual direct manufacturing labor costs were $572,900. Actual fixed costs were $1,200,000. There were no beginning or ending inventories.

Required

1. Calculate the sales-volume variance and flexible-budget variance for operating income.
2. Compute price and efficiency variances for direct materials and direct manufacturing labor.

7-35 Variance analysis, nonmanufacturing setting. Marcus McQueen has run In-A-Flash Car Detailing for the past 10 years. His static budget and actual results for June 2017 are provided next. Marcus has one employee who has been with him for all 10 years that he has been in business. In addition, at any given time he also employs two other less experienced workers. It usually takes each employee 2 hours to detail a vehicle, regardless of his or her experience. Marcus pays his experienced employee $30 per vehicle and the other two employees $15 per vehicle. There were no wage increases in June.

In-A-Flash Car Detailing
Actual and Budgeted Income Statements
For the Month Ended June 30, 2017

	Budget	Actual
Offices cleaned	280	320
Revenue	$53,200	$72,000
Variable costs:		
Costs of supplies	1,260	1,360
Labor	6,720	8,400
Total variable costs	7,980	9,760
Contribution margin	45,220	62,240
Fixed costs	9,800	9,800
Operating income	$35,420	$52,440

Required

1. How many cars, on average, did Marcus budget for each employee? How many cars did each employee actually detail?
2. Prepare a flexible budget for June 2017.
3. Compute the sales price variance and the labor efficiency variance for each labor type.
4. What information, in addition to that provided in the income statements, would you want Marcus to gather, if you wanted to improve operational efficiency?

7-36 Comprehensive variance analysis review. Omega Animal Health, Inc. produces a generic medication used to treat cats with feline diabetes. The liquid medication is sold in 100 ml vials. Omega employs a team of sales representatives who are paid varying amounts of commission.

Given the narrow margins in the generic veterinary drugs industry, Omega relies on tight standards and cost controls to manage its operations. Omega has the following budgeted standards for the month of April 2017:

Average selling price per vial	$ 9.40
Total direct materials cost per vial	$ 3.90
Direct manufacturing labor cost per hour	$ 17.00
Average labor productivity rate (vials per hour)	100
Sales commission cost per unit	$ 0.76
Fixed administrative and manufacturing overhead	$800,000

Omega budgeted sales of 800,000 vials for April. At the end of the month, the controller revealed that actual results for April had deviated from the budget in several ways:

- Unit sales and production were 80% of plan.
- Actual average selling price increased to $9.50.
- Productivity dropped to 80 vials per hour.
- Actual direct manufacturing labor cost was $17.30 per hour.
- Actual total direct material cost per unit increased to $4.20.
- Actual sales commissions were $0.74 per unit.
- Fixed overhead costs were $30,000 above budget.

Calculate the following amounts for Omega for April 2017:

Required

1. Static-budget and actual operating income
2. Static-budget variance for operating income
3. Flexible-budget operating income
4. Flexible-budget variance for operating income
5. Sales-volume variance for operating income
6. Price and efficiency variances for direct manufacturing labor
7. Flexible-budget variance for direct manufacturing labor

7-37 Possible causes for price and efficiency variances. You have been invited to interview for an internship with an international food manufacturing company. When you arrive for the interview, you are given the following information related to a fictitious Belgian chocolatier for the month of June. The chocolatier manufactures truffles in 12-piece boxes. The production is labor intensive, and the delicate nature of the chocolate requires a high degree of skill.

Actual	
Boxes produced	12,000
Direct materials used in production	2,640,000 g
Actual direct material cost	72,500 euro
Actual direct manufacturing labor-hours	1,300
Actual direct manufacturing labor cost	15,360 euro

Standards	
Purchase price of direct materials	0.029 euro/g
Materials per box	200 g
Wage rate	13 euro/hour
Boxes per hour	10

Please respond to the following questions as if you were in an interview situation:

Required

1. Calculate the materials efficiency and price variance and the wage and labor efficiency variances for the month of June.
2. Discuss some possible causes of the variances you have calculated. Can you make any possible connection between the material and labor variances? What recommendations do you have for future improvement?

7-38 Material-cost variances, use of variances for performance evaluation. Katharine Johnson is the owner of Best Bikes, a company that produces high-quality cross-country bicycles. Best Bikes participates in a supply chain that consists of suppliers, manufacturers, distributors, and elite bicycle shops. For several years Best Bikes has purchased titanium from suppliers in the supply chain. Best Bikes uses titanium for the bicycle frames because it is stronger and lighter than other metals and therefore increases the quality of the bicycle. Earlier this year, Best Bikes hired Michael Bentfield, a recent graduate from State University, as purchasing manager. Michael believed that he could reduce costs if he purchased titanium from an online marketplace at a lower price.

Best Bikes established the following standards based upon the company's experience with previous suppliers. The standards are as follows:

Cost of titanium	$18 per pound
Titanium used per bicycle	8 lbs.

Actual results for the first month using the online supplier of titanium are as follows:

Bicycles produced	400
Titanium purchased	5,200 lb. for $88,400
Titanium used in production	4,700 lb.

Required

1. Compute the direct materials price and efficiency variances.
2. What factors can explain the variances identified in requirement 1? Could any other variances be affected?
3. Was switching suppliers a good idea for Best Bikes? Explain why or why not.
4. Should Michael Bentfield's performance evaluation be based solely on price variances? Should the production manager's evaluation be based solely on efficiency variances? Why is it important for Katharine Johnson to understand the causes of a variance before she evaluates performance?
5. Other than performance evaluation, what reasons are there for calculating variances?
6. What future problems could result from Best Bikes' decision to buy a lower quality of titanium from the online marketplace?

7-39 Direct manufacturing labor and direct materials variances, missing data. (CMA, heavily adapted) Young Bay Surfboards manufactures fiberglass surfboards. The standard cost of direct materials and direct manufacturing labor is $223 per board. This includes 40 pounds of direct materials, at the budgeted price of $2 per pound, and 10 hours of direct manufacturing labor, at the budgeted rate of $14.30 per hour. Following are additional data for the month of July:

Units completed	5,500 units
Direct material purchases	160,000 pounds
Cost of direct material purchases	$432,000
Actual direct manufacturing labor-hours	41,000 hours
Actual direct labor cost	$594,500
Direct materials efficiency variance	$ 1,700 F

There were no beginning inventories.

Required

1. Compute direct manufacturing labor variances for July.
2. Compute the actual pounds of direct materials used in production in July.
3. Calculate the actual price per pound of direct materials purchased.
4. Calculate the direct materials price variance.

7-40 Direct materials efficiency, mix, and yield variances. Gamma's Snacks produces snack mixes for the gourmet and natural foods market. Its most popular product is Tempting Trail Mix, a mixture of peanuts, dried cranberries, and chocolate pieces. For each batch, the budgeted quantities, budgeted prices, and budgeted mix of direct materials are as follows:

	Quantity per Batch	Price per Cup	Budgeted Mix
Peanuts	50 cups	$1	50%
Dried cranberries	30 cups	$2	30%
Chocolate pieces	20 cups	$3	20%

Changing the standard mix of direct material quantities slightly does not significantly affect the overall end product. In addition, not all ingredients added to production end up in the finished product, as some are rejected during inspection.

In the current period, Gamma's Snacks made 100 batches of Tempting Trail Mix with the following actual quantity, cost, and mix of inputs:

	Actual Quantity	Actual Cost	Actual Mix
Peanuts	6,050 cups	$ 5,445	55%
Dried cranberries	3,080 cups	$ 6,930	28%
Chocolate pieces	1,870 cups	$ 5,423	17%
Total	11,000 cups	$17,798	100%

Required

1. What is the budgeted cost of direct materials for the 100 batches?
2. Calculate the total direct materials efficiency variance..
3. Calculate the total direct materials mix and yield variances.
4. Illustrate the relationship between the variances calculated in requirement 2 and 3. What are the variances calculated in requirement 3 telling you about the 100 batches produced this period? Are the variances large enough to investigate?

7-41 Direct materials and manufacturing labor variances, solving unknowns. (CPA, adapted) On May 1, 2017, Lowell Company began the manufacture of a new paging machine known as Dandy. The company installed a standard costing system to account for manufacturing costs. The standard costs for a unit of Dandy follow:

Direct materials (2 lb. at $3 per lb.)	$6.00
Direct manufacturing labor (1/2 hour at $16 per hour)	8.00
Manufacturing overhead (80% of direct manufacturing labor costs)	6.40
	$20.40

The following data were obtained from Lowell's records for the month of May:

	Debit	Credit
Revenues		$150,000
Accounts payable control (for May's purchases of direct materials)		36,300
Direct materials price variance	$4,500	
Direct materials efficiency variance	2,900	
Direct manufacturing labor price variance	1,700	
Direct manufacturing labor efficiency variance		2,000

Actual production in May was 4,700 units of Dandy, and actual sales in May were 3,000 units.

The amount shown for direct materials price variance applies to materials purchased during May. There was no beginning inventory of materials on May 1, 2017. Compute each of the following items for Lowell for the month of May. Show your computations.

Required

1. Standard direct manufacturing labor-hours allowed for actual output produced
2. Actual direct manufacturing labor-hours worked

3. Actual direct manufacturing labor wage rate
4. Standard quantity of direct materials allowed (in pounds)
5. Actual quantity of direct materials used (in pounds)
6. Actual quantity of direct materials purchased (in pounds)
7. Actual direct materials price per pound

7-42 Direct materials and manufacturing labor variances, journal entries. Zanella's Smart Shawls, Inc., is a small business that Zanella developed while in college. She began hand-knitting shawls for her dorm friends to wear while studying. As demand grew, she hired some workers and began to manage the operation. Zanella's shawls require wool and labor. She experiments with the type of wool that she uses, and she has great variety in the shawls she produces. Zanella has bimodal turnover in her labor. She has some employees who have been with her for a very long time and others who are new and inexperienced.

Zanella uses standard costing for her shawls. She expects that a typical shawl should take 3 hours to produce, and the standard wage rate is $9.00 per hour. An average shawl uses 13 skeins of wool. Zanella shops around for good deals and expects to pay $3.40 per skein.

Zanella uses a just-in-time inventory system, as she has clients tell her what type and color of wool they would like her to use.

For the month of April, Zanella's workers produced 200 shawls using 580 hours and 3,500 skeins of wool. Zanella bought wool for $9,000 (and used the entire quantity) and incurred labor costs of $5,520.

Required

1. Calculate the price and efficiency variances for the wool and the price and efficiency variances for direct manufacturing labor.
2. Record the journal entries for the variances incurred.
3. Discuss logical explanations for the combination of variances that Zanella experienced.

7-43 Use of materials and manufacturing labor variances for benchmarking. You are a new junior accountant at In Focus Corporation, maker of lenses for eyeglasses. Your company sells generic-quality lenses for a moderate price. Your boss, the controller, has given you the latest month's report for the lens trade association. This report includes information related to operations for your firm and three of your competitors within the trade association. The report also includes information related to the industry benchmark for each line item in the report. You do not know which firm is which, except that you know you are Firm A.

Unit Variable Costs Member Firms
for the Month Ended September 30, 2017

	Firm A	Firm B	Firm C	Firm D	Industry Benchmark	
Materials input	2.15	2.00	2.20	2.60	2.15	oz. of glass
Materials price	$ 5.00	$ 5.25	$ 5.10	$ 4.50	$ 5.10	per oz.
Labor-hours used	0.75	1.00	0.65	0.70	0.70	hours
Wage rate	$14.50	$14.00	$14.25	$15.25	$12.50	per DLH
Variable overhead rate	$ 9.25	$14.00	$ 7.75	$11.75	$12.25	per DLH

Required

1. Calculate the total variable cost per unit for each firm in the trade association. Compute the percent of total for the material, labor, and variable overhead components.
2. Using the trade association's industry benchmark, calculate direct materials and direct manufacturing labor price and efficiency variances for the four firms. Calculate the percent over standard for each firm and each variance.
3. Write a brief memo to your boss outlining the advantages and disadvantages of belonging to this trade association for benchmarking purposes. Include a few ideas to improve productivity that you want your boss to take to the department heads' meeting.

7-44 Direct manufacturing labor variances: price, efficiency, mix, and yield. Trevor Joseph employs two workers in his guitar-making business. The first worker, George, has been making guitars for 20 years and is paid $30 per hour. The second worker, Earl, is less experienced and is paid $20 per hour. One guitar requires, on average, 10 hours of labor. The budgeted direct labor quantities and prices for one guitar are as follows:

	Quantity	Price per Hour of Labor	Cost for One Guitar
George	6 hours	$30 per hour	$180
Earl	4 hours	$20 per hour	80

That is, each guitar is budgeted to require 10 hours of direct labor, composed of 60% of George's labor and 40% of Earl's, although sometimes Earl works more hours on a particular guitar and George less, or vice versa, with no obvious change in the quality or function of the guitar.

During the month of August, Joseph manufactures 25 guitars. Actual direct labor costs are as follows:

George (145 hours)	$ 4,350
Earl (108 hours)	2,160
Total actual direct labor cost	$ 6,510

Required

1. What is the budgeted cost of direct labor for 25 guitars?
2. Calculate the total direct labor price and efficiency variances.
3. For the 25 guitars, what is the total actual amount of direct labor used? What is the actual direct labor input mix percentage? What is the budgeted amount of George's and Earl's labor that should have been used for the 25 guitars?
4. Calculate the total direct labor mix and yield variances. How do these numbers relate to the total direct labor efficiency variance? What do these variances tell you?

7-45 Direct-cost and selling price variances. MicroDisk is the market leader in the Secure Digital (SD) card industry and sells memory cards for use in portable devices such as mobile phones, tablets, and digital cameras. Its most popular card is the Mini SD, which it sells through outlets such as Target and Walmart for an average selling price of $8. MicroDisk has a standard monthly production level of 420,000 Mini SDs in its Taiwan facility. The standard input quantities and prices for direct-cost inputs are as follows:

	A	B	C	D	E
1		Quantity per		Standard	
2	Cost Item	Mini SD card		Unit Costs	
3	Direct materials:				
4	Specialty polymer	17	mm	$0.05	/mm
5	Connector pins	10	units	0.10	/unit
6	Wi-Fi transreceiver	1	unit	0.50	/unit
7					
8	Direct manufacturing labor:				
9	Setup	1	min.	24.00	/hr.
10	Fabrication	2	min.	30.00	/hr.

Phoebe King, the CEO, is disappointed with the results for June 2017, especially in comparison to her expectations based on the standard cost data.

		Actual	Budget	Variance	
13		Performance Report, June 2017			
14		Actual	Budget	Variance	
15	Output units	462,000	420,000	42,000	F
16	Revenues	$3,626,700	$3,360,000	$266,700	F
17	Direct materials	1,200,000	987,000	213,000	U
18	Direct manufacturing labor	628,400	588,000	40,400	U

King observes that despite the significant increase in the output of Mini SDs in June, the product's contribution to the company's profitability has been lower than expected. She gathers the following information to help analyze the situation:

Cost Item	Quantity		Actual Cost
Input Usage Report, June 2017			
Direct materials:			
Specialty polymer	8,300,000	mm	$415,000
Connector pins	5,000,000	units	550,000
Wi-Fi transreceiver	470,000	units	235,000
Direct manufacturing labor:			
Setup	455,000	min.	182,000
Fabrication	864,000	min.	446,400

Calculate the following variances. Comment on the variances and provide potential reasons why they might have arisen, with particular attention to the variances that may be related to one another:

Required

1. Selling-price variance
2. Direct materials price variance, for each category of materials
3. Direct materials efficiency variance, for each category of materials
4. Direct manufacturing labor price variance, for setup and fabrication
5. Direct manufacturing labor efficiency variance, for setup and fabrication

7-46 Variances in the service sector. Derek Wilson operates Clean Ride Enterprises, an auto detailing company with 20 employees. Jamal Jackson has recently been hired by Wilson as a controller. Clean Ride's previous accountant had done very little in the area of variance analysis, but Jackson believes that the company could benefit from a greater understanding of his business processes. Because of the labor-intensive nature of the business, he decides to focus on calculating labor variances.

Jackson examines past accounting records, and establishes some standards for the price and quantity of labor. While Clean Ride's employees earn a range of hourly wages, they fall into two general categories: skilled labor, with an average wage of $20 per hour, and unskilled labor, with an average wage of $10 per hour. One standard 5-hour detailing job typically requires a combination of 3 skilled hours and 2 unskilled hours.

Actual data from last month, when 600 detailing jobs were completed, are as follows:

Skilled (2,006 hours)	$ 39,117
Unskilled (944 hours)	9,292
Total actual direct labor cost	$ 48,409

Looking over last month's data, Jackson determines that Clean Ride's labor price variance was $1,151 favorable, but the labor efficiency variance was $1,560 unfavorable. When Jackson presents his findings to Wilson, the latter is furious. "Do you mean to tell me that my employees wasted $1,560 worth of time last month? I've had enough. They had better shape up, or else!" Jackson tries to calm him down, saying that in this case the efficiency variance doesn't necessarily mean that employees were wasting time. Jackson tells him that he is going to perform a more detailed analysis, and will get back to him with more information soon.

Required

1. What is the budgeted cost of direct labor for 600 detailing jobs?
2. How were the $1,151 favorable price variance and the $1,560 unfavorable labor efficiency variance calculated? What was the company's flexible-budget variance?
3. What do you think Jackson meant when said that "in this case the efficiency variance doesn't necessarily mean that employees were wasting time"?
4. For the 600 detailing jobs performed last month, what is the actual direct labor input mix percentage? What was the standard mix for labor?
5. Calculate the total direct labor mix and yield variances.
6. How could these variances be interpreted? Did the employees waste time? Upon further investigation, you discover that there were some unfilled vacancies last month in the unskilled labor positions that have recently been filled. How will this new information likely impact the variances going forward?

7-47 Price and efficiency variances, benchmarking and ethics. Sunto Scientific manufactures GPS devices for a chain of retail stores. Its most popular model, the Magellan XS, is assembled in a dedicated facility in Savannah, Georgia. Sunto is keenly aware of the competitive threat from smartphones that use Google Maps and has put in a standard cost system to manage production of the Magellan XS. It has also implemented a just-in-time system so the Savannah facility operates with no inventory of any kind.

Producing the Magellan XS involves combining a navigation system (imported from Sunto's plant in Dresden at a fixed price), an LCD screen made of polarized glass, and a casing developed from specialty plastic. The budgeted and actual amounts for Magellan XS for July 2017 were as follows:

	Budgeted Amounts	Actual Amounts
Magellan XS units produced	4,000	4,400
Navigation systems cost	$81,600	$89,000
Navigation systems	4,080	4,450
Polarized glass cost	$40,000	$40,300
Sheets of polarized glass used	800	816
Plastic casing cost	$12,000	$12,500
Ounces of specialty plastic used	4,000	4,250
Direct manufacturing labor costs	$36,000	$37,200
Direct manufacturing labor-hours	2,000	2,040

The controller of the Savannah plant, Jim Williams, is disappointed with the standard costing system in place. The standards were developed on the basis of a study done by an outside consultant at the start of the year. Williams points out that he has rarely seen a significant unfavorable variance under this system. He observes that even at the present level of output, workers seem to have a substantial amount of idle time. Moreover, he is concerned that the production supervisor, John Kelso, is aware of the issue but is unwilling to tighten the standards because the current lenient benchmarks make his performance look good.

Required

1. Compute the price and efficiency variances for the three categories of direct materials and for direct manufacturing labor in July 2017.
2. Describe the types of actions the employees at the Savannah plant may have taken to reduce the accuracy of the standards set by the outside consultant. Why would employees take those actions? Is this behavior ethical?
3. If Williams does nothing about the standard costs, will his behavior violate any of the standards of ethical conduct for practitioners described in the IMA Statement of Ethical Professional Practice (see Exhibit 1-7 on page 37)?
4. What actions should Williams take?
5. Williams can obtain benchmarking information about the estimated costs of Sunto's competitors such as Garmin and TomTom from the Competitive Intelligence Institute (CII). Discuss the pros and cons of using the CII information to compute the variances in requirement 1.

21 Capital Budgeting and Cost Analysis

LEARNING OBJECTIVES

1. Understand the five stages of capital budgeting for a project

2. Use and evaluate the two main discounted cash flow (DCF) methods: the net present value (NPV) method and the internal rate-of-return (IRR) method

3. Use and evaluate the payback and discounted payback methods

4. Use and evaluate the accrual accounting rate-of-return (AARR) method

5. Identify relevant cash inflows and outflows for capital budgeting decisions

6. Understand issues involved in implementing capital budgeting decisions and evaluating managerial performance

7. Explain how managers can use capital budgeting to achieve their firms' strategic goals

Should Honda open a new plant in China or India?

Should Sony invest in developing the next generation of PlayStation consoles? Should the Gap discontinue its children's clothing line and expand its women's athletic clothing line? Working closely with accountants, top executives have to figure out how and when to best allocate the firm's financial resources among alternative opportunities to create future value for the company. Because it's hard to know what the future holds and how much projects will ultimately cost, this can be a challenging task, but it's one that managers must constantly confront. To meet this challenge, companies such as Target and Chevron have developed special groups to make project-related capital budgeting decisions. This chapter explains the different methods organizations (and individuals) use to get the "biggest bang for the buck" in terms of the projects they invest in or undertake.

CHANGING NPV CALCULATIONS SHAKE UP SOLAR FINANCING[1]

In recent years, American households have spent billions of dollars putting solar panels on the roofs of their homes. By 2020, the U.S. National Renewable Energy Laboratory projects that residential solar installations will comprise 5% of the U.S. single-family home market.

The average solar-panel installation costs between $15,000 and $20,000. With such high costs, most homeowners have to finance new solar systems. Traditionally, this was done through third-party ownership, where homeowners lease solar systems

kostasgr/Shutterstock

that are installed on their roofs by a third party, but do not own the systems. While this financing model helped spur the adoption of solar energy in the United States, the market is moving toward having homeowners use loans to purchase solar systems, rather than leasing from a third party.

What is driving this change? As the installed cost of solar panels continues to fall, the net present value (NPV) calculations that determine whether homeowners should lease or buy solar systems are changing dramatically. Financial variables including lower interest

---

[1] *Sources:* PricewaterhouseCoopers, "Financing US residential solar: Owning, rather than leasing, will bode well for homeowners," August 2015 (www.pwc.com/us/en/technology/publications/assets/pwc-financing-us-residential-solar-08-2015.pdf).

rates, more flexible down payment amounts, and fluctuating retail electricity rates are creating NPV calculations that show owning, rather than leasing, solar systems is more valuable for U.S. homeowners. As a result, experts predict that homeowner-financed solar will dominate the U.S. market in the years ahead.

Just as individuals decide whether and how to invest in renewable energy for their homes, managers at companies such as Nissan, Pepsi, Pfizer and Walmart face challenging investment decisions. In this chapter, we introduce several capital budgeting methods used to evaluate long-term investment projects. These methods help managers choose the projects that will contribute the most value to their organizations.

Stages of Capital Budgeting

Capital budgeting is the process of making long-run planning decisions for investments in projects. In much of accounting, income is calculated on a period-by-period basis. In choosing investments, however, managers make a selection from among multiple projects, each of which may span several periods. Exhibit 21-1 illustrates these two different yet intersecting dimensions of cost analysis: (1) horizontally across, as the *project dimension*, and (2) vertically upward, as the *accounting-period dimension*. Each project is represented as a horizontal rectangle starting and ending at different times and stretching over time spans longer than one year. The vertical rectangle for the 2018 accounting period, for example, represents the dimensions of income determination and routine annual planning and control that cut across all projects that are ongoing that year.

To make capital budgeting decisions, managers analyze each project by considering all the life-span cash flows from its initial investment through its termination. This process is analogous to life-cycle budgeting and costing (Chapter 13, pages 560–562). For example, when Honda considers producing a new model of automobile, it begins by estimating all potential revenues from the project as well as any costs that will be incurred during its life cycle, which may be as long as 10 years. Only after examining the potential costs and benefits across all of the business functions in the value chain, from research and development (R&D) to customer service, across the entire life span of the new-car project does Honda decide whether the new model is a wise investment.

Managers use capital budgeting as a decision-making and a control tool. Like the five-step decision process that we have emphasized throughout this book, there are five stages to the capital budgeting process:

Stage 1: Identify Projects. *Identify potential capital investments that agree with the organization's strategy.* For example, Nike, an industry leader in product differentiation, makes significant investments in product innovation, engineering, and design, hoping to develop the next generation of high-quality sportswear. Alternatively, managers could promote products that improve productivity and efficiency as a cost-leadership strategy. For example, Dell's strategy of cost leadership includes outsourcing certain components to lower-cost contract manufacturing facilities located overseas. Identifying which types of capital projects to invest in is largely the responsibility of a firm's top managers.

> **LEARNING OBJECTIVE 1**
>
> Understand the five stages of capital budgeting for a project
>
> ... identify projects; obtain information; make predictions; make decisions; and implement the decision, evaluate performance, and learn

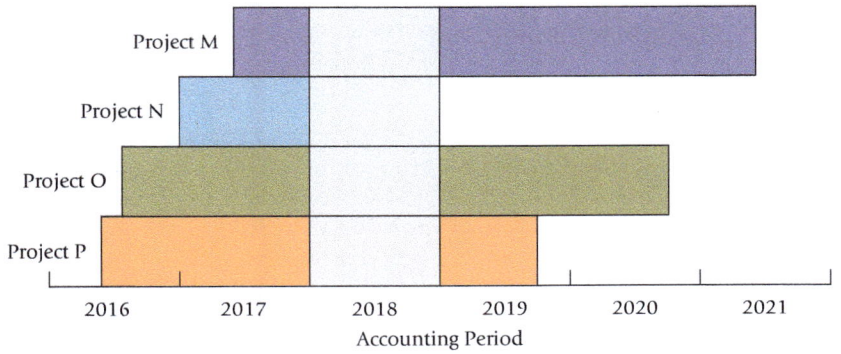

EXHIBIT 21-1

The Project and Time Dimensions of Capital Budgeting

Stage 2: Obtain Information. *Gather information from all parts of the value chain to evaluate alternative projects.* Returning to the new car example at Honda, in this stage, the firm's top managers ask the company's marketing managers for potential revenue numbers, plant managers for assembly times, and suppliers for prices and the availability of key components. Lower-level managers are asked to validate the data provided and to explain the assumptions underlying them. The goal is to encourage open and honest communication that results in accurate estimates so that the best investment decisions are made. Some projects will be rejected at this stage. For example, suppose Honda learns that the car cannot be built using existing plants. It may then opt to cancel the project altogether. At Akzo-Nobel, a global paints and coating company, the chief sustainability officer reviews projects against a set of environmental criteria and has the power to reject projects that do not meet the criteria or lack an acceptable explanation for why the company's sustainability factors were not considered.

Stage 3: Make Predictions. *Forecast all potential cash flows attributable to the alternative projects.* A new project generally requires a firm to make a substantial initial outlay of capital, which is recouped over time through annual cash inflows and the disposal value of the project's assets after it is terminated. Consequently, investing in a new project requires the firm to forecast its cash flows several years into the future. BMW, for example, estimates yearly cash flows and sets its investment budgets accordingly using a 12-year planning horizon. Because of the significant uncertainty associated with these predictions, firms typically analyze a wide range of alternate circumstances. In the case of BMW, the marketing group is asked to estimate a band of possible sales figures within a 90% confidence interval. Firms also attempt to ensure that estimates, especially for the later years of a project, are grounded in realistic scenarios. It is tempting for managers to introduce biases into these projections in order to drive the outcome of the capital budgeting process to their preferred choice. This effect is exacerbated by the fact that managers may not expect to be employed at the firm during those later years and therefore cannot be held accountable for their estimates.

Stage 4: Make Decisions by Choosing Among Alternatives. *Determine which investment yields the greatest benefit and the least cost to the organization.* Using the quantitative information obtained in Stage 3, the firm uses any one of several capital budgeting methodologies to determine which project best meets organizational goals. While capital budgeting calculations are typically limited to financial information, managers use their judgment and intuition to factor in qualitative information and strategic considerations as well. For example, even if a proposed new line of cars meets its financial targets on a standalone basis, Honda might decide not to pursue the line if it is not aligned with the strategic imperatives of the company on matters such as brand positioning, industry leadership in safety and technology, and fuel consumption. Considerations of environmental sustainability might also favor certain projects that currently appear unprofitable. Freight and logistics giant UPS relaxes the company's minimum rate of return on vehicles that have the potential to reduce fuel use and costs. Similarly, Sealed Air is willing to accept projects with a lower projected return if they look promising with regard to reducing greenhouse gas emissions. For another example, see Concepts in Action: Capital Budgeting for Sustainability at Johnson & Johnson. Finally, managers spend a significant amount of time assessing the risks of a project, in terms of both the uncertainty of the estimated cash flows as well as the potential downside risks of the project (including to the firm as a whole) if the worst-case scenario were to occur.

Stage 5: Implement the Decision, Evaluate Performance, and Learn. Given the complexities of capital investment decisions and their long-time horizons, this stage can be separated into two phases:

- **Obtain funding and make the investments selected in Stage 4.** The sources of funding include internally generated cash as well as equity and debt securities sold in capital markets. Making capital investments is often an arduous task, laden with the purchase of many different goods and services. If Honda opts to build a new car, it must order steel, aluminum, paint, and so on. If some of the materials are unavailable, managers must determine the economic feasibility of using alternative inputs.

- **Track realized cash flows, compare against estimated numbers, and revise plans if necessary.** As the cash outflows and inflows begin to accumulate, managers can verify whether the predictions made in Stage 3 agree with the actual flows of cash from the

CONCEPTS IN ACTION: Capital Budgeting for Sustainability at Johnson & Johnson

Lucas Jackson/Alamy Stock Photo

Many large companies have established sustainability goals and targets, and it is becoming increasingly common for these goals to address significant environmental challenges like climate change. Improved sustainability performance, however, is not always valued in internal capital budgeting decisions. That's because it can be difficult to accurately value the "extra-financial" benefits of reduced exposure to energy price volatility and water risk, for example.

Health care company Johnson & Johnson found a unique way to create business value through its capital projects while reducing its environmental impact. Johnson & Johnson established a special fund that increases its capital budget to allow for greenhouse gas reduction projects like chiller optimization and solar photovoltaic installations that also reduce operating costs. The operating budget is then reduced to reflect expected savings. This helps the company invest in projects that have higher initial costs but lower operating costs, resulting in a net benefit.

Each year, Johnson & Johnson's capital relief fund allocates at least $40 million to make capital investments in greenhouse gas reduction projects that otherwise would not be able to compete for limited capital budget dollars on traditional measures. These projects undergo an internal vetting process to ensure energy reductions, environmental benefits, and cost savings for the company. A committee of energy, engineering, and finance managers reviews the technical, environmental, and financial aspects of the proposed projects to ensure they are aligned with best practices and standards, as well as meet the required after-tax internal rate of return of 15%.

Over time, Johnson & Johnson has found that greenhouse gas reduction projects generally have a more predictable return than other cost improvement projects and are helping to reduce the company's risk exposure. Projects funded using Johnson & Johnson's capital relief fund have had an average expected return of around 19%. In 2010, the company set out to reduce its carbon emissions by 20% compared to that year's baseline. Thanks in part to the capital relief fund, by 2015 Johnson & Johnson had already cut its carbon emissions by 9.6% and is on track to meet its long-term greenhouse gas reduction goal.

Sources: Alexander Perera, Samantha Putt Del Pino, and Barbara Oliveria, "Aligning Profit and Environmental Sustainability: Stories from Industry." World Resources Institute working paper, February 2013 (http://www.wri.org/sites/default/files/pdf/aligning_profit_and_environmental_sustainability_stories_from_industry.pdf); Johnson & Johnson, "Greenhouse Gas Emissions," http://www.jnj.com/caring/citizenship-sustainability/strategic-framework/Greenhouse-Gas Emissions, accessed April 2016.

---

project. Twitter saw disappointing advertising revenues in 2015 due to slowdowns in its user base growth and Monthly Active User numbers. As a result, it shifted to make streaming video a bigger priority. It acquired Periscope, a complement to its earlier investment in Vine, and has invested in acquiring the rights to stream live events ranging from sporting events to political debates.

It is equally important for a company to abandon projects that are performing poorly relative to expectations. A natural bias for managers is to escalate their commitment to a project they chose to implement for fear of revealing they made an incorrect capital budgeting decision. It is in the firm's and the managers' long-term interest, however, to acknowledge the mistake when it is clear that the project is not financially sustainable. For example, in April 2012, TransAlta, a Canadian electricity generator, halted a CA$1.4 billion project to capture carbon in the province of Alberta. After spending CA$30 million on engineering and design studies, the firm realized that the revenue from carbon sales and the costs of reducing emissions were insufficient to make the project economically viable.

To illustrate capital budgeting, consider Vector Transport. Vector operates bus lines throughout the United States, often providing transportation services on behalf of local transit authorities. Several of Vector's buses are nearing the end of their useful lives and now require increased operating and maintenance costs. Customers have also complained that the buses lack adequate storage, flexible seating configurations, and newer amenities such as wireless

Internet access. The firm has made a commitment to act in an environmentally responsible manner and will only pursue projects that do minimal harm to the ecosystem. Accordingly, in Stage 1, Vector's managers decide to look for replacement buses that generate low emissions. In the information-gathering stage (Stage 2), the company learns that as early as 2017, it could feasibly begin purchasing and using diesel electric hybrid buses that have Wi-Fi and also offer greater comfort and storage. After collecting additional data, Vector begins to forecast its future cash flows if it invests in the new buses (Stage 3). Vector estimates that it can purchase a hybrid bus with a useful life of 5 years for a net after-tax initial investment of $648,900, which is calculated as follows:[2]

Cost of new hybrid bus	$660,000
Investment in working capital	30,000
Cash flow from disposing of existing bus (after-tax)	(41,100)
Net initial investment for new bus	$648,900

Working capital refers to the difference between current assets and current liabilities. New projects often require additional investments in current assets such as inventories and receivables. In the case of Vector, the purchase of the new bus is accompanied by an incremental outlay of $30,000 for supplies, replacement batteries, and spare parts inventory. At the end of the project, the $30,000 in current assets is liquidated, resulting in a cash inflow. However, because of the rapid nature of improvements in hybrid technology, the bus itself is believed to have no terminal disposal value after 5 years.

Managers estimate that by introducing the new hybrid buses, operating cash inflows (cash revenues minus cash operating costs) will increase by $180,000 (after tax) in the first 4 years and by $150,000 in year 5. This arises from higher ticket prices and increases in ridership because of new customers who are drawn to the amenities of the hybrid bus, as well as savings in fuel, maintenance, and operating costs. To simplify the analysis, suppose that all cash flows occur at the end of each year. Note that cash flow at the end of the fifth year also increases by $180,000 − $150,000 in operating cash inflows and $30,000 in working capital. Management next calculates the costs and benefits of the proposed project (Stage 4). This chapter discusses four capital budgeting methods to analyze financial information: (1) net present value (NPV), (2) internal rate-of-return (IRR), (3) payback, and (4) accrual accounting rate-of-return (AARR). Both the net present value (NPV) and internal rate-of-return (IRR) methods use *discounted cash flows*, which we discuss in the next section.

DECISION POINT

What are the five stages of capital budgeting?

Discounted Cash Flow

LEARNING OBJECTIVE 2

Use and evaluate the two main discounted cash flow (DCF) methods: the net present value (NPV) method and the internal rate-of-return (IRR) method

...to explicitly consider all project cash flows and the time value of money

Discounted cash flow (DCF) methods measure all expected future cash inflows and outflows of a project discounted back to the present point in time. The key feature of DCF methods is the **time value of money**, which means that a dollar (or any other monetary unit) received today is worth more than a dollar received at any future time. The reason is that $1 received today can be invested at, say, 10% per year so that it grows to $1.10 at the end of one year. The time value of money is the opportunity cost (the return of $0.10 forgone per year) from not having the money today. In this example, $1 received 1 year from now is worth $1 ÷ 1.10 = $0.9091 today. Similarly, $100 received 1 year from now will be weighted by 0.9091 to yield a discounted cash flow of $90.91, which is today's value of that $100 next year. In this way, discounted cash flow methods explicitly measure cash flows in terms of the time value of money. Note that DCF focuses exclusively on cash inflows and outflows rather than on operating income as calculated under accrual accounting. The compound interest tables and formulas used in DCF analysis are in Appendix A, pages 947–954. If you are unfamiliar with compound interest, do not proceed until you have studied Appendix A, as the tables in Appendix A will be used frequently in this chapter.

The two DCF methods we describe are the net present value (NPV) method and the internal rate-of-return (IRR) method. Both DCF methods use the **required rate of return (RRR)**,

---

[2] For the purposes of exposition, we study the capital budgeting problem for replacing one bus, rather than a fleet of buses.

the minimum acceptable annual rate of return on an investment. The RRR is internally set, usually by upper management, and typically represents the return that an organization could expect to receive elsewhere for an investment of comparable risk. The RRR is also called the **discount rate**, **hurdle rate**, **cost of capital**, or **opportunity cost of capital**. Let's suppose the CFO at Vector has set the required rate of return for the firm's investments at 8% per year.

Net Present Value Method

The **net present value (NPV) method** calculates the expected monetary gain or loss from a project by discounting all expected future cash inflows and outflows back to the present point in time using the required rate of return. To use the NPV method, apply the following three steps:

Step 1: Draw a Sketch of Relevant Cash Inflows and Outflows. The right side of Exhibit 21-2 shows arrows that depict the cash flows of the new hybrid bus. The sketch helps the decision maker visualize and organize the data in a systematic way. *Note that parentheses denote relevant cash outflows throughout all of the exhibits in this chapter.* Exhibit 21-2 includes the outflow for the acquisition of the new bus at the start of year 1 (also referred to as end of year 0) and the inflows over the subsequent 5 years. The NPV method specifies cash flows regardless of their source, such as operations, the purchase or sale of equipment, or an investment in or recovery of working capital. However, accrual-accounting concepts such as sales made on credit or noncash expenses are not included because the focus is on *cash* inflows and outflows.

Step 2: Discount the Cash Flows Using the Correct Compound Interest Table from Appendix A and Sum Them. In the Vector example, we can discount each year's cash flow separately using Table 2, or we can compute the present value of an annuity, a series of equal cash

EXHIBIT 21-2   Net Present Value Method: Vector's Hybrid Bus

	A	B	C	D	E	F	G	H	I
1			Net initial investment	$648,900					
2			Useful life	5 years					
3			Annual cash flow	$180,000					
4			Required rate of return	8%					
5									
6		Present Value	Present Value of		Sketch of Relevant Cash Flows at End of Each Year				
7		of Cash Flow	$1 Discounted at 8%	0	1	2	3	4	5
8	Approach 1: Discounting Each Year's Cash Flow Separately[a]								
9	Net initial investment	$(648,900)	1.000	$(648,900)					
10		166,680	0.926		$180,000				
11		154,260	0.857			$180,000			
12	Annual cash inflow	142,920	0.794				$180,000		
13		132,300	0.735					$180,000	
14		122,580	0.681						$180,000
15	NPV if new bus purchased	$ 69,840							
16									
17	Approach 2: Using Annuity Table[b]								
18	Net initial investment	$(648,900)	1.000	$(648,900)					
19					$180,000	$180,000	$180,000	$180,000	$180,000
20									
21	Annual cash inflow	718,740	3.993						
22	NPV if new bus purchased	$ 69,840							
23									
24	*Note:* Parentheses denote relevant cash outflows throughout all exhibits in Chapter 21.								
25	[a] Present values from Table 2, Appendix A, at the end of the book. For example, $0.857 = 1 \div (1.08)^2$.								
26	[b] Annuity present value from Table 4, Appendix A. The annuity value of 3.993 is the sum of the individual discount rates, $0.926 + 0.857 + 0.794 + 0.735 + 0.681$.								

flows at equal time intervals, using Table 4. (Both tables are in Appendix A.) If we use Table 2, we find the discount factors for periods 1–5 under the 8% column. Approach 1 in Exhibit 21-2 uses the five discount factors. To obtain the present value amount, multiply each discount factor by the corresponding amount represented by the arrow on the right in Exhibit 21-2 (−$648,900 × 1.000; $180,000 × 0.926; and so on to $180,000 × 0.681). Because the investment in the new bus produces an annuity, we may also use Table 4. Under Approach 2, we find that the annuity factor for five periods under the 8% column is 3.993, which is the sum of the five discount factors used in Approach 1. We multiply the uniform annual cash inflow by this factor to obtain the present value of the inflows ($718,740 = $180,000 × 3.993). Subtracting the initial investment then reveals the NPV of the project as $69,840 ($69,840 = $718,740 − $648,900).

Step 3: Make the Project Decision on the Basis of the Calculated NPV. An NPV that is zero or positive suggests that from a financial standpoint, the company should accept the project because its expected rate of return equals or exceeds the required rate of return. If the NPV is negative, the company should reject the project because its expected rate of return is below the required rate of return.

Exhibit 21-2 calculates an NPV of $69,840 at the required rate of return of 8% per year. The project is acceptable based on financial information. The cash flows from the project are adequate (1) to recover the net initial investment in the project and (2) to earn a return greater than 8% per year on the investment tied up in the project over its useful life.

Managers must also weigh nonfinancial factors such as the effect that purchasing the bus will have on Vector's brand. The financial benefits that accrue from Vector's brand are difficult to estimate. Nevertheless, managers must consider brand effects before reaching a final decision. Suppose, for example, that the NPV of the hybrid bus is negative. Vector's managers might still decide to buy the bus if it maintains Vector's technological image and reputation for environmental responsibility. These are factors that could increase Vector's financial outcomes in the future, such as by attracting more riders or generating additional contracts from government transit agencies. For example, Alcoa, an aluminum producer, has found that its sustainability track record gives it better access to large markets such as Brazil, where a positive environmental record is an increasingly important component in selecting producers.

Pause here. Do not proceed until you understand what you see in Exhibit 21-2. Compare Approach 1 with Approach 2 in Exhibit 21-2 to see how Table 4 in Appendix A merely aggregates the present value factors of Table 2. That is, the fundamental table is Table 2. Table 4 just simplifies calculations when there is an annuity.

Internal Rate-of-Return Method

The **internal rate-of-return (IRR) method** calculates the discount rate at which an investment's present value of all expected cash inflows equals the present value of its expected cash outflows. That is, the IRR is the discount rate that makes NPV = $0. Exhibit 21-3 shows the cash flows and the NPV of Vector's hybrid project using a 12% annual discount rate. At a 12% discount rate, the NPV of the project is $0. Therefore, the IRR is 12% per year.

Managers or analysts solving capital budgeting problems typically use a calculator or computer program to provide the internal rate of return. The following trial-and-error approach can also provide the answer.

Step 1: Use a discount rate and calculate the project's NPV.

Step 2: If the calculated NPV is less than zero, use a lower discount rate. (A *lower* discount rate will *increase* the NPV. Remember that we are trying to find a discount rate for which the NPV = $0.) If the NPV exceeds zero, use a higher discount rate to lower the NPV. Keep adjusting the discount rate until the NPV does equal $0. In the Vector example, a discount rate of 8% yields an NPV of +$69,840 (see Exhibit 21-2). A discount rate of 14% yields an NPV of −$30,960 (3.433, the present value annuity factor from Table 4, × $180,000 minus $648,900). Therefore, the discount rate that makes the NPV equal $0 must lie between 8% and 14%. We use 12% and get NPV = $0. Hence, the IRR is 12% per year.

EXHIBIT 21-3 Internal Rate-of-Return Method: Vector's Hybrid Bus[a]

	A	B	C	D	E	F	G	H	I
1			Net initial investment	$648,900					
2			Useful life	5 years					
3			Annual cash flow	$180,000					
4			Annual discount rate	12%					
5									
6			Present Value	Present Value of	Sketch of Relevant Cash Flows at End of Each Year				
7			of Cash Flow	$1 Discounted at 12%	0	1	2	3	4	5
8	Approach 1: Discounting Each Year's Cash Flow Separately[b]								
9	Net initial investment		$(648,900) ←	1.000 ←	$(648,900)				
10			160,740 ←	0.893 ←		$180,000			
11			143,460 ←	0.797 ←			$180,000		
12	Annual cash inflow		128,160 ←	0.712 ←				$180,000	
13			114,480 ←	0.636 ←					$180,000
14			102,060 ←	0.567 ←						$180,000
15	NPV if new bus purchased		$ 0						
16	(the zero difference proves that								
17	the internal rate of return is 12%)								
18									
19	Approach 2: Using Annuity Table[c]								
20	Net initial investment		$(648,900) ←	1.000 ←	$(648,900)				
21						$180,000	$180,000	$180,000	$180,000	$180,000
22									
23	Annual cash inflow		648,900 ←	3.605 ←					
24	NPV if new bus purchased		$ 0						
25									
26	[a]The internal rate of return is computed by methods explained on pp. 844–845.								
27	[b]Present values from Table 2, Appendix A, at the end of the book.								
28	[c]Annuity present value from Table 4, Appendix A. The annuity value of 3.605 is the sum of the individual discount rates 0.893 + 0.797 + 0.712 + 0.636 + 0.567.								

Computing the IRR is easier when the cash inflows are constant, as in our Vector example. Information from Exhibit 21-3 can be expressed as follows:

$$\$648,900 = \text{Present value of annuity of } \$180,000 \text{ at } X\% \text{ per year for 5 years}$$

Or, what factor F in Table 4 (in Appendix A) will satisfy this equation?

$$\$648,900 = \$180,000F$$
$$F = \$648,900 \div \$180,000 = 3.605$$

On the five-period line of Table 4, find the percentage column that is closest to 3.605. It is exactly 12%. If the factor (F) falls between the factors in two columns, straight-line interpolation is used to approximate the IRR. This interpolation is illustrated in the Problem for Self-Study (pages 859–861).

Managers accept a project only if its IRR equals or exceeds the firm's RRR (required rate of return). In the Vector example, the hybrid bus has an IRR of 12%, which is greater than the RRR of 8%. On the basis of financial factors, Vector should invest in the new bus. In general, the NPV and IRR decision rules result in consistent project acceptance or rejection decisions. If the IRR exceeds the RRR, then the project has a positive NPV (favoring acceptance). If the IRR equals the RRR, then NPV equals $0, so the company is indifferent between accepting and rejecting the project. If the IRR is less than the RRR, the NPV is negative (favoring rejection). Obviously, managers prefer projects with higher IRRs to projects with lower IRRs, if all other things are equal. The IRR of 12% means the cash inflows from the project are adequate to (1) recover the net initial investment in the project and (2) earn a return of exactly 12% on the investment tied up in the project over its useful life.

TRY IT! 21-1

Home Value Company operates a number of home improvement stores in a metropolitan area. Home Value's management estimates that if it invests $250,000 in a new computer system, it can save $65,000 in annual cash operating costs. The system has an expected useful life of eight years and no terminal disposal value. The required rate of return is 8%. Ignore income tax issues and assume all cash flows occur at year-end except for initial investment amounts.

Calculate the following for the new computer system:
a. net present value; and
b. internal rate of return (using the interpolation method).

Comparing the Net Present Value and Internal Rate-of-Return Methods

The NPV method is the preferred method for selecting projects because its use leads to shareholder value maximization. At an intuitive level, this occurs because the NPV measure captures the value, in today's dollars, of the surplus the project generates for the firm's shareholders over and above the required rate of return.[3] Next, we highlight some of the advantages of the NPV method relative to the IRR technique.

One advantage of the NPV method is that it's expressed in dollars, not in percentages. Therefore, we can sum NPVs of individual projects to calculate an NPV of a combination or portfolio of projects. In contrast, the IRRs of individual projects cannot be added or averaged to represent the IRR of a combination of projects.

A second advantage of NPV is that it can be expressed as a unique number. From the sign and magnitude of this number, the firm can then make an accurate assessment of the financial consequences of accepting or rejecting the project. Under the IRR method, it is possible that more than one IRR may exist for a given project. In other words, there may be multiple discount rates that equate the NPV of a set of cash flows to zero. This is the case, for example, when the signs of the cash flows switch over time; that is, when there are outflows, followed by inflows, followed by additional outflows, and so forth. In such cases, it is difficult to know which of the IRR estimates should be compared to the firm's required rate of return.

A third advantage of the NPV method is that it can be used when the RRR varies over the life of a project. Suppose Vector's management sets an RRR of 10% per year in years 1 and 2 and 14% per year in years 3, 4, and 5. Total present value of the cash inflows can be calculated as $633,780 (computations not shown). It is not possible to use the IRR method in this case. That's because different RRRs in different years mean there is no single RRR that the IRR (a single figure) can be compared against to decide if the project should be accepted or rejected.

Finally, in some situations, the IRR method is prone to indicating erroneous decisions. This can occur when mutually exclusive projects with unequal lives or unequal levels of initial investment are being compared to one another. The reason is that the IRR method implicitly assumes that project cash flows can be reinvested at the *project's* rate of return. The NPV method, in contrast, accurately assumes that project cash flows can only be reinvested at the *company's* required rate of return.

Despite its limitations, the IRR method is widely used.[4] Why? Probably because managers find the percentage return computed under the IRR method easy to understand and compare. Moreover, in most instances where a single project is being evaluated, their decisions would likely be unaffected by using IRR or NPV.

Sensitivity Analysis

To present the basics of the NPV and IRR methods, we have assumed that the expected values of cash flows will occur *for certain*. In reality, there is much uncertainty associated with predicting future cash flows. To examine how a result will change if the predicted financial outcomes are not achieved or if an underlying assumption changes, managers use *sensitivity analysis*, or "what-if" technique, introduced in Chapter 3.

---

[3] More detailed explanations of the preeminence of the NPV criterion can be found in corporate finance texts.
[4] In a survey, John Graham and Campbell Harvey found that 75.7% of CFOs always or almost always used IRR for capital budgeting decisions, while a slightly smaller number, 74.9%, always or almost always used the NPV criterion.

EXHIBIT 21-4

Net Present Value Calculations for Vector's Hybrid Bus Under Different Assumptions of Annual Cash Flows and Required Rates of Return[a]

	A	B	C	D	E	F
1	Required	Annual Cash Flows				
2	Rate of Return	$140,000	$160,000	$180,000	$200,000	$220,000
3	8%	$(89,880)	$(10,020)	$69,840	$149,700	$229,560
4	10%	$(118,160)	$(42,340)	$33,480	$109,300	$185,120
5	12%	$(144,200)	$(72,100)	$0	$72,100	$144,200

[a] All calculated amounts assume the project's useful life is 5 years.

A common way to apply sensitivity analysis for capital budgeting decisions is to vary each of the inputs to the NPV calculation by a certain percentage and assess the effect on the project's NPV. Sensitivity analysis can take on other forms as well. Suppose a manager at Vector believes the firm's forecasted cash flows are difficult to predict. She asks, "What are the minimum annual cash inflows that make the investment in a new hybrid bus acceptable—that is, what inflows lead to an NPV = $0?" For the data in Exhibit 21-2, let A = annual cash flow and let the NPV = $0. The net initial investment is $648,900, and the present value factor at the 8% required annual rate of return for a 5-year annuity of $1 is 3.993. Then

$$NPV = \$0$$
$$3.993A - \$648,900 = \$0$$
$$3.993A = \$648,900$$
$$A = \$162,509$$

At the discount rate of 8% per year, the annual (after-tax) cash inflows can decrease to $162,509 (a decline of $180,000 − $162,509 = $17,491) before the NPV falls to $0. If the manager believes she can attain annual cash inflows of at least $162,509, she can justify investing in the hybrid bus on financial grounds.

Exhibit 21-4 shows that variations in the annual cash inflows or the RRR significantly affect the NPV of the hybrid bus project. NPVs can also vary with different useful lives of a project. Sensitivity analysis helps managers to focus on decisions that are most sensitive to different assumptions and to worry less about decisions that are not so sensitive. It is also an important risk-management tool because it provides information to managers about the downside risks of projects as well as their potential impact on the health of the overall firm.

Payback Method

We now consider the third method for analyzing the financial aspects of projects. The **payback method** measures the time it will take to recoup, in the form of expected future cash flows, the net initial investment in a project. Like the NPV and IRR methods, the payback method does not distinguish among the sources of cash flows, such as those from operations, purchase or sale of equipment, or investment or recovery of working capital. As you will see, the payback method is simpler to calculate when a project has uniform cash flows than when cash flows are uneven over time.

Uniform Cash Flows

The hybrid bus Vector is considering buying costs $648,900 and generates a *uniform* $180,000 in cash flow every year of its 5-year expected useful life. The payback period is calculated as follows:

$$\text{Payback period} = \frac{\text{Net initial investment}}{\text{Uniform increase in annual future cash flows}}$$

$$= \frac{\$648,900}{\$180,000} = 3.6 \text{ years}^5$$

DECISION POINT

What are the two primary discounted cash flow (DCF) methods for project evaluation?

LEARNING OBJECTIVE 3

Use and evaluate the payback and discounted payback methods

...to calculate the time it takes to recoup the investment

---

[5] Cash inflows from the new hybrid bus occur uniformly *throughout* the year, but for simplicity in calculating NPV and IRR, we assume they occur at the *end* of each year. A literal interpretation of this assumption would imply a payback of 4 years because Vector will only recover its investment when cash inflows occur at the end of year 4. The calculations shown in the chapter, however, better approximate Vector's payback on the basis of uniform cash flows throughout the year.

The payback method highlights liquidity, a factor that often plays a role in capital budgeting decisions, particularly when the investments are large. Managers prefer projects with shorter payback periods (projects that are more liquid) to projects with longer payback periods, if all other things are equal. Projects with shorter payback periods give an organization more flexibility because funds for other projects become available sooner. Also, managers are less confident about cash flow predictions that stretch far into the future, again favoring shorter payback periods.

Unlike the NPV and IRR methods where managers select an RRR, under the payback method, managers choose a cutoff period for the project. Projects with payback periods that are shorter than the cutoff period are considered acceptable, and those with payback periods that are longer than the cutoff period are rejected. Japanese companies favor the payback method over other methods and use cutoff periods ranging from 3 to 5 years depending on the risks involved with the project.[6] In general, modern risk management calls for using shorter cutoff periods for riskier projects. If Vector's cutoff period under the payback method is 3 years, it will reject the new bus.

The payback method is easy to understand. As in DCF methods, the payback method is not affected by accrual accounting conventions such as depreciation. Payback is a useful measure when (1) preliminary screening of many proposals is necessary, (2) interest rates are high, and (3) the expected cash flows in later years of a project are highly uncertain. Under these conditions, companies give much more weight to cash flows in early periods of a capital budgeting project and to recovering the investments they have made, thereby making the payback criterion especially relevant.

Two weaknesses of the payback method are that (1) it fails to explicitly incorporate the time value of money and (2) it does not consider a project's cash flows after the payback period. Consider an alternative to the $648,900 hybrid bus. Another hybrid bus, one with a 3-year useful life and no terminal disposal value, requires only a $504,000 net initial investment and will also result in cash inflows of $180,000 per year. First, compare the payback periods:

$$\text{Bus 1} = \frac{\$648,900}{\$180,000} = 3.6 \text{ years}$$

$$\text{Bus 2} = \frac{\$504,000}{\$180,000} = 2.8 \text{ years}$$

The payback criterion favors bus 2, which has a shorter payback. If the cutoff period were 3 years, bus 1 would fail to meet the payback criterion.

Consider next the NPV of the two investment options using Vector's 8% required rate of return for the hybrid bus investment. At a discount rate of 8%, the NPV of bus 2 is −$40,140 (2.577, the present value annuity factor for 3 years at 8% per year from Table 4, times $180,000 = $463,860, minus net initial investment of $504,000). Bus 1, as we know, has a positive NPV of $69,840 (from Exhibit 21-2). The NPV criterion suggests Vector should acquire bus 1. Bus 2, which has a negative NPV, would fail to meet the NPV criterion.

The payback method gives a different answer from the NPV method in this example because the payback method ignores cash flows after the payback period and ignores the time value of money. Another problem with the payback method is that choosing too short a cutoff period can lead to projects with high short-run cash flows being selected. Projects with long-run, positive NPVs will tend to be rejected. Despite these differences, companies find it useful to look at both NPV and payback when making capital investment decisions.

Nonuniform Cash Flows

When cash flows are not uniform, the payback computation takes a cumulative form: The cash flows over successive years are accumulated until the amount of net initial investment is recovered. Suppose Venture Law Group is considering purchasing videoconferencing equipment for

---

[6] A 2010 survey of Japanese firms found that 50.2% of them often or always used the payback method to make capital budgeting decisions. The NPV method came in a distant second at 30.5% (see Tomonari Shinoda, "Capital Budgeting Management Practices in Japan," *Economic Journal of Hokkaido University* 39 (2010): 39–50).

$150,000. The equipment is expected to provide total cash savings of $340,000 over the next 5 years, due to reduced travel costs and more effective use of associates' time. The cash savings occur uniformly throughout each year but are not uniform across years.

Year	Cash Savings	Cumulative Cash Savings	Net Initial Investment Unrecovered at End of Year
0	—	—	$150,000
1	$50,000	$ 50,000	100,000
2	55,000	105,000	45,000
3	60,000	165,000	—
4	85,000	250,000	—
5	90,000	340,000	—

The chart shows that payback occurs during the third year. Straight-line interpolation within the third year reveals that the final $45,000 needed to recover the $150,000 investment (that is, $150,000 − $105,000 recovered by the end of year 2) will be achieved three-quarters of the way through year 3, during which $60,000 of cash savings occur:

$$\text{Payback period} = 2 \text{ years} + \left(\frac{\$45,000}{\$60,000} \times 1 \text{ year}\right) = 2.75 \text{ years}$$

It is relatively simple to adjust the payback method to incorporate the time value of money by using a similar cumulative approach. The **discounted payback method** calculates the amount of time required for the discounted expected future cash flows to recoup the net initial investment in a project. For the videoconferencing example, we can modify the preceding chart by discounting the cash flows at the 8% required rate of return.

Year (1)	Cash Savings (2)	Present Value of $1 Discounted at 8% (3)	Discounted Cash Savings (4) = (2) × (3)	Cumulative Discounted Cash Savings (5)	Net Initial Investment Unrecovered at End of Year (6)
0	—	1.000	—	—	$150,000
1	$50,000	0.926	$46,300	$ 46,300	103,700
2	55,000	0.857	47,135	93,435	56,565
3	60,000	0.794	47,640	141,075	8,925
4	85,000	0.735	62,475	203,550	—
5	90,000	0.681	61,290	264,840	—

The fourth column shows the present values of the future cash savings. It is evident from the chart that discounted payback occurs between years 3 and 4. At the end of the third year, $8,925 of the initial investment is still unrecovered. Comparing this to the $62,475 in present value of savings achieved in the fourth year, straight-line interpolation reveals that the discounted payback period is exactly one-seventh of the way into the fourth year:

$$\text{Discounted payback period} = 3 \text{ years} + \left(\frac{\$8,925}{\$62,475} \times 1 \text{ year}\right) = 3.14 \text{ years}$$

The discounted payback does incorporate the time value of money, but is still subject to the other criticism of the payback method—that cash flows beyond the discounted payback period are ignored, resulting in a bias toward projects with high short-run cash flows. Companies such as Hewlett-Packard value the discounted payback method (HP refers to it as "breakeven time") because they view longer-term cash flows as inherently unpredictable in high-growth industries, such as technology.

Finally, the videoconferencing example has a single cash outflow of $150,000 in year 0. When a project has multiple cash outflows occurring at different points in time, these outflows are first aggregated to obtain a total cash-outflow figure for the project. For computing the payback period, the cash flows are simply added, with no adjustment for the time value of money. For calculating the discounted payback period, the present values of the outflows are added instead.

DECISION POINT

What are the payback and discounted payback methods? What are their main weaknesses?

TRY IT! 21-2

Consider Home Value Company. With the same information as provided in Try It! 21-1, calculate the following for the new computer system:

a. payback period; and
b. discounted payback period.

Accrual Accounting Rate-of-Return Method

LEARNING OBJECTIVE 4

Use and evaluate the accrual accounting rate-of-return (AARR) method

...after-tax operating income divided by investment

We now consider a fourth method for analyzing the financial aspects of capital budgeting projects. The **accrual accounting rate-of-return (AARR) method** divides the average annual (accrual accounting) income of a project by a measure of the investment in it. We illustrate this method for Vector using the project's net initial investment as the amount in the denominator:

$$\text{Accrual accounting rate of return} = \frac{\text{Increase in expected average annual after-tax operating income}}{\text{Net initial investment}}$$

If Vector purchases the new hybrid bus, its net initial investment is $648,900. The increase in the expected average annual after-tax operating cash inflows is $174,000. This amount is the expected after-tax total operating cash inflows of $870,000 ($180,000 for 4 years and $150,000 in year 5), divided by the time horizon of 5 years. Suppose that the new bus results in additional depreciation deductions of $120,000 per year ($132,000 in annual depreciation for the new bus, relative to $12,000 per year on the existing bus).[7] The increase in the expected average annual after-tax income is therefore $54,000 (the difference between the cash flow increase of $174,000 and the depreciation increase of $120,000). The AARR on net initial investment is computed as:

$$\text{AARR} = \frac{\$174,000 - \$120,000}{\$648,900} = \frac{\$54,000 \text{ per year}}{\$648,900} = 0.083, \text{ or } 8.3\% \text{ per year}$$

The 8.3% figure for AARR indicates the average rate at which a dollar of investment generates after-tax operating income. The new hybrid bus has a low AARR for two reasons: (1) the use of the net initial investment as the denominator and (2) the use of income as the numerator, which necessitates deducting depreciation charges from the annual operating cash flows. To mitigate the first issue, many companies calculate AARR using an average level of investment. This alternative procedure recognizes that the book value of the investment declines over time. In its simplest form, average investment for Vector is calculated as the arithmetic mean of the net initial investment of $648,900 and the net terminal cash flow of $30,000 (terminal disposal value of hybrid bus of $0, plus the terminal recovery of working capital of $30,000):

$$\frac{\text{Average investment}}{\text{over 5 years}} = \frac{\text{Net initial investment} + \text{Net terminal cash flow}}{2}$$

$$= \frac{\$648,900 + \$30,000}{2} = \$339,450$$

The AARR on average investment is then calculated as follows:

$$\text{AARR} = \frac{\$54,000}{\$339,450} = 0.159, \text{ or } 15.9\% \text{ per year}$$

Companies vary in how they calculate the AARR. There is no uniformly preferred approach. Be sure you understand how the AARR is defined in each individual situation. Projects with AARRs that exceed a specific required rate of return are regarded as acceptable (the higher the AARR, the better the project is considered to be).

---

[7] We provide further details on these numbers in the next section; see page 852.

The AARR method is similar to the IRR method in that both calculate a rate-of-return percentage. The AARR method calculates the return using operating-income numbers after considering accruals and taxes, whereas the IRR method calculates the return using after-tax cash flows and the time value of money. Because cash flows and time value of money are central to capital budgeting decisions, the IRR method is regarded as better than the AARR method.

AARR computations are easy to understand, and they use numbers reported in the financial statements. The AARR gives managers an idea of how the accounting numbers they will report in the future will be affected if a project is accepted. Unlike the payback method, which ignores cash flows after the payback period, the AARR method considers income earned *throughout* a project's expected useful life. Unlike the NPV method, the AARR method uses accrual accounting income numbers, it does not track cash flows, and it ignores the time value of money. Critics of the AARR method argue that these are its drawbacks.

Overall, keep in mind that companies frequently use multiple methods for evaluating capital investment decisions. When different methods lead to different rankings of projects, more weight should be given to the NPV method because the assumptions made by the NPV method are most consistent with making decisions that maximize a company's value.

DECISION POINT
What are the strengths and weaknesses of the accrual accounting rate-of-return (AARR) method for evaluating long-term projects?

21-3 TRY IT!

Consider Home Value Company again, and assume the same information as provided in Try It! 21-1 about its proposed new computer system. Home Value uses straight-line depreciation.

a. What is the project's accrual accounting rate of return based on net initial investment?
b. What is the project's accrual accounting rate of return based on average investment?
c. What other factors should Home Value consider in deciding whether to purchase the new computer system?

Relevant Cash Flows in Discounted Cash Flow Analysis

So far, we have examined methods for evaluating long-term projects in settings where the expected future cash flows of interest were assumed to be known. One of the biggest challenges in capital budgeting, particularly DCF analysis, however, is determining which cash flows are relevant in making an investment selection. Relevant cash flows are the differences in expected future cash flows as a result of making the investment. In the Vector example, the relevant cash flows are the differences in expected future cash flows that will result from continuing to use one of the firm's old buses versus purchasing a new hybrid bus. *When reading this section, focus on identifying expected future cash flows and the differences in expected future cash flows.*

To illustrate relevant cash flow analysis, consider a more complex version of the Vector example with these additional assumptions:

LEARNING OBJECTIVE 5
Identify relevant cash inflows and outflows for capital budgeting decisions

...the differences in expected future cash flows resulting from the investment

- Vector is a profitable company. The income tax rate is 40% of operating income each year.
- The before-tax additional operating cash inflows from the hybrid bus are $220,000 in years 1–4 and $170,000 in year 5.
- For tax purposes, Vector uses the straight-line depreciation method and assumes there is no terminal disposal value of the bus.
- Gains or losses on the sale of depreciable assets are taxed at the same rate as ordinary income.
- The tax effects of cash inflows and outflows occur at the same time that the cash inflows and outflows occur.
- Vector uses an 8% required rate of return for discounting after-tax cash flows.

The data for the buses follow:

	Old Bus	New Hybrid Bus
Purchase price	—	$660,000
Current book value	$60,000	—
Current disposal value	28,500	Not applicable
Terminal disposal value 5 years from now	0	0
Annual depreciation	12,000[a]	132,000[b]
Working capital required	6,000	36,000

[a] $60,000 ÷ 5 years = $12,000 annual depreciation.
[b] $660,000 ÷ 5 years = $132,000 annual depreciation.

Relevant After-Tax Flows

We use the concepts of differential cost and differential revenue introduced in Chapter 11. We compare (1) the after-tax cash outflows as a result of replacing the old bus with (2) the additional after-tax cash inflows generated from using the new bus rather than the old bus.

As Benjamin Franklin said, "Two things in life are certain: death and taxes." Income taxes are a fact of life for most corporations and individuals. It is important first to understand how income taxes affect cash flows in each year. Exhibit 21-5 shows how investing in the new bus will affect Vector's cash flow from operations and its income taxes in year 1. Recall that Vector will generate $220,000 in before-tax additional operating cash inflows by investing in the new bus (page 851), but it will record additional depreciation of $120,000 ($132,000 − $12,000) for tax purposes.

Panel A shows, using two methods based on the income statement, that the year 1 cash flow from operations, net of income taxes, equals $180,000. The first method focuses on cash items only, the $220,000 operating cash inflows minus income taxes of $40,000. The second method starts with the $60,000 increase in net income (calculated after subtracting the $120,000 additional depreciation deductions for income tax purposes) and adds back the $120,000 because depreciation is an operating cost that reduces net income but is a noncash item itself.

Panel B of Exhibit 21-5 describes a third method frequently used to compute the cash flow from operations, net of income taxes. The easiest way to interpret the third method

EXHIBIT 21-5

Effect on Cash Flow from Operations, Net of Income Taxes, in Year 1 for Vector's Investment in the New Hybrid Bus

PANEL A: Two Methods Based on the Income Statement

C	Operating cash inflows from investment in bus	$220,000
D	Additional depreciation deduction	120,000
OI	Increase in operating income	100,000
T	Income taxes (Income tax rate $t \times OI$) = 40% × $100,000	40,000
NI	Increase in net income	$ 60,000

Increase in cash flow from operations, net of income taxes:
Method 1: $C - T$ = $220,000 − $40,000 = $180,000; or
Method 2: $NI + D$ = $60,000 + $120,000 = $180,000

PANEL B: Item-by-Item Method

	Effect of cash operating flows:	
C	Operating cash inflows from investment in bus	$220,000
$t \times C$	Deduct income tax cash outflow at 40%	88,000
$C \times (1 - t)$	After-tax cash flow from operations (excluding the depreciation effect)	$132,000
	Effect of depreciation:	
D	Additional depreciation deduction, $120,000	
$t \times D$	Income tax cash savings from additional depreciation deduction at 40% × $120,000	48,000
$C \times (1 - t) + t \times D$	Cash flow from operations, net of income taxes	$180,000

is to think of the government as a 40% (equal to the tax rate) partner in Vector. Each time Vector obtains operating cash inflows, C, its income is higher by C, so it will pay 40% of the operating cash inflows (0.40C) in taxes. This results in additional after-tax cash operating flows of $C - 0.40C$, which in this example is $220,000 - (0.40 \times \$220,000) = \$132,000$, or $\$220,000 \times (1 - 0.40) = \$132,000$.

To achieve the higher operating cash inflows, C, Vector incurs higher depreciation charges, D, from investing in the new bus. Depreciation costs do not directly affect cash flows because depreciation is a noncash cost, but a higher depreciation cost *lowers* Vector's taxable income by D, saving income tax cash outflows of 0.40D, which in this example is $0.40 \times \$120,000 = \$48,000$.

Letting t = tax rate, cash flow from operations, net of income taxes, in this example equals the operating cash inflows, C, minus the tax payments on these inflows, $t \times C$, plus the tax savings on depreciation deductions, $t \times D$: $\$220,000 - (0.40 \times \$220,000) + (0.40 \times \$120,000) = \$220,000 - \$88,000 + \$48,000 = \$180,000$.

By the same logic, each time Vector has a gain on the sale of assets, G, it will show tax outflows, $t \times G$; and each time Vector has a loss on the sale of assets, L, it will show tax benefits or savings of $t \times L$.

Categories of Cash Flows

A capital investment project typically has three categories of cash flows: (1) the net initial investment in the project, which includes the acquisition of assets and any associated additions to working capital, minus the after-tax cash flow from the disposal of existing assets; (2) the after-tax cash flow from operations (including income tax cash savings from annual depreciation deductions) each year; and (3) the after-tax cash flow from disposing of an asset and recovering any working capital invested at the termination of the project. We use the Vector example to discuss these three categories.

As you work through the cash flows in each category, refer to Exhibit 21-6. This exhibit sketches the relevant cash flows for Vector's decision to purchase the new bus as described in items 1–3 here. Note that the total relevant cash flows for each year equal the relevant cash flows used in Exhibits 21-2 and 21-3 to illustrate the NPV and IRR methods.

1. **Net Initial Investment.** Three components of net-initial-investment cash flows are (a) the cash outflow to purchase the hybrid bus, (b) the cash outflow for working capital, and (c) the after-tax cash inflow from the current disposal of the old bus.

    1a. *Initial bus investment.* These outflows, made for purchasing plant and equipment, occur at the beginning of the project's life and include cash outflows for transporting and installing the equipment. In the Vector example, the $660,000 cost (including transportation and initial preparation) of the hybrid bus is an outflow in year 0. These cash flows are relevant to the capital budgeting decision because they will be incurred only if Vector decides to purchase the new bus.

    1b. *Initial working-capital investment.* Initial investments in plant and equipment are usually accompanied by additional investments in working capital. These additional investments take the form of current assets, such as accounts receivable and inventories, minus current liabilities, such as accounts payable. Working-capital investments are similar to plant and equipment investments in that they require cash. The magnitude of the investment generally increases as a function of the level of additional sales generated by the project. However, the exact relationship varies based on the nature of the project and the operating cycle of the industry. For a given dollar of sales, a maker of heavy equipment, for example, would require more working-capital support than Vector, which in turn has to invest more in working capital than a retail grocery store.

    The Vector example assumes a $30,000 additional investment in working capital if the hybrid bus is acquired. The additional working-capital investment is the difference between the working capital required to operate the new bus ($36,000) and that required to operate the old bus ($6,000). The $30,000 additional investment, a consequence of the higher cost of replacement batteries and spare parts for the technologically advanced new bus, is a cash outflow in year 0 and is returned, that is, becomes a cash inflow, at the end of year 5.

EXHIBIT 21-6   Relevant Cash Inflows and Outflows for Vector's Hybrid Bus

	A	B	C	D	E	F	G	H
1				Sketch of Relevant Cash Flows at End of Each Year				
2			0	1	2	3	4	5
3	1a.	Initial hybrid bus investment	$(660,000)					
4	1b.	Initial working-capital investment	(30,000)					
5	1c.	After-tax cash inflow from current disposal						
6		of old bus	41,100					
7	Net initial investment		(648,900)					
8	2a.	Annual after-tax cash flow from operations						
9		(excluding the depreciation effect)		$132,000	$132,000	$132,000	$132,000	$102,000
10	2b.	Income tax savings from annual						
11		depreciation deductions		48,000	48,000	48,000	48,000	48,000
12	3a.	After-tax cash flow from terminal disposal						
13		of bus						0
14	3b.	After-tax cash flow from recovery of						
15		working capital						30,000
16	Total relevant cash flows,							
17	as shown in Exhibits 21-2 and 21-3		$(648,900)	$180,000	$180,000	$180,000	$180,000	$180,000
18								

1c. *After-tax cash flow from current disposal of old bus.* Any cash received from disposal of the old bus is a relevant cash inflow (in year 0) because it is a cash flow that differs between the alternatives of investing and not investing in the new bus. Vector will dispose of the old bus for $28,500 only if it invests in the new hybrid bus. Recall from Chapter 11 (pp. 471–473) that the book value (which is original cost minus accumulated depreciation) of the old equipment is generally irrelevant to the decision because it is a past, or sunk, cost. However, when tax considerations are included, the book value does play a role because it determines the gain or loss on the sale of the bus and, therefore, the taxes paid (or saved) on the transaction.

Consider the tax consequences of disposing of the old bus. We first have to compute the gain or loss on disposal:

Current disposal value of old bus (given, page 852)	$28,500
Deduct current book value of old bus (given, page 852)	60,000
Loss on disposal of bus	$(31,500)

Any loss on the sale of assets lowers taxable income and results in tax savings. The after-tax cash flow from disposal of the old bus is as follows:

Current disposal value of old bus	$28,500
Tax savings on loss (0.40 × $31,500)	12,600
After-tax cash inflow from current disposal of old bus	$41,100

The sum of items **1a**, **1b**, and **1c** appears in Exhibit 21-6 as the year 0 net initial investment for the new hybrid bus. It equals $648,900 (initial bus investment, $660,000, plus additional working-capital investment, $30,000, minus the after-tax cash inflow from current disposal of the old bus, $41,100).[8]

---

[8] To illustrate the case when there is a gain on disposal, suppose that the old bus could be sold for $70,000 instead. Then the firm would record a gain on disposal of $10,000 ($70,000 less the book value of $60,000), resulting in additional tax payments of $4,000 (0.40 tax rate × $10,000 gain). The after-tax cash inflow from current disposal would then equal $66,000 (the disposal value of $70,000, less the tax payment of $4,000).

2. **Cash Flow from Operations.** This category includes the difference between each year's cash flow from operations under the two alternatives. Organizations make capital investments to generate future cash inflows. These inflows may result from producing and selling additional goods or, as in the case of Vector, from savings in fuel, maintenance, and operating costs and the additional revenue from higher ticket prices as well as new customers who wish to take advantage of the greater comfort and accessibility of the hybrid bus. The annual cash flow from operations can be net outflows in some years. For example, Chevron periodically upgrades its oil extraction equipment, and when it does, the cash flow from operations tends to be negative for the site being upgraded. However, in the long run, the upgrades are NPV positive. Always focus on the cash flow from operations, not on revenues and expenses under accrual accounting.

Vector's additional operating cash inflows—$220,000 in each of the first 4 years and $170,000 in the fifth year—are relevant because they are expected future cash flows that will differ depending on whether the firm purchases the new bus. The after-tax effects of these cash flows are described next.

2a. *Annual after-tax cash flow from operations (excluding the depreciation effect).* The 40% tax rate reduces the benefit of the $220,000 additional operating cash inflows for years 1 through 4 with the new hybrid bus. The after-tax cash flow (excluding the depreciation effect) is:

Annual cash flow from operations with new bus	$220,000
Deduct income tax payments (0.40 × $220,000)	88,000
Annual after-tax cash flow from operations	$132,000

For year 5, the after-tax cash flow (excluding the depreciation effect) is as follows:

Annual cash flow from operations with new bus	$170,000
Deduct income tax payments (0.40 × $170,000)	68,000
Annual after-tax cash flow from operations	$102,000

Exhibit 21-6, item **2a**, shows that the after-tax cash flows are $132,000 in each of years 1 through 4 and $102,000 for year 5.

To reinforce the idea about focusing on cash flows, consider the following additional fact about Vector. Suppose its total administrative costs will not change whether the company purchases a new bus or keeps the old one. The administrative costs are allocated to individual buses—Vector has several—on the basis of the costs for operating each bus. Because the new hybrid bus would have lower operating costs, the administrative costs allocated to it would be $25,000 less than the amount allocated to the bus it would replace. How should Vector incorporate the $25,000 decrease in allocated administrative costs in the relevant cash flow analysis?

To answer that question, we need to ask, "Do *total* administrative costs decrease at Vector Transport as a result of acquiring the new bus?" In our example, they do not. They remain the same whether or not the new bus is acquired. *Only the administrative costs allocated to individual buses change.* The administrative costs allocated to the new bus are $25,000 less than the amount allocated to the bus it would replace. This $25,000 difference in costs would be allocated to *other* buses in the company. That is, no cash flow savings in total costs would occur. Therefore, the $25,000 should not be included as part of the annual cash savings from operations.

Next consider the effects of depreciation. *The depreciation line item is itself irrelevant in a DCF analysis.* That's because depreciation is a noncash allocation of costs, whereas DCF is based on inflows and outflows of *cash*. If a DCF method is used, the initial cost of equipment is regarded as a *lump-sum* outflow of cash in year 0. Deducting depreciation expenses from operating cash inflows would result in counting the lump-sum amount twice. *However, depreciation results in income tax cash savings. These tax savings are a relevant cash flow.*

2b. *Income tax cash savings from annual depreciation deductions.* Tax deductions for depreciation, in effect, partially offset the cost of acquiring the new hybrid bus. By purchasing the new bus, Vector is able to deduct $132,000 in depreciation each year, relative to the $12,000 depreciation on the old bus. The additional annual depreciation deduction of $120,000 results in incremental income tax cash savings of $120,000 × 0.4, or $48,000 annually. Exhibit 21-6, item **2b**, shows these $48,000 amounts for years 1 through 5.[9]

For economic-policy reasons, usually to encourage (or in some cases, discourage) investments, tax laws specify which depreciation methods and which depreciable lives are permitted. Suppose the government permitted accelerated depreciation to be used, allowing for higher depreciation deductions in earlier years. Should Vector then use accelerated depreciation? Yes, because there is a general rule in tax planning for profitable companies such as Vector: When there is a legal choice, take the depreciation (or any other deduction) sooner rather than later. Doing so causes the (cash) income tax savings to occur earlier, which increases a project's NPV.

3. **Terminal Disposal of Investment.** The disposal of an investment generally increases cash inflow of a project at its termination. An error in forecasting the disposal value is seldom critical for a long-duration project because the present value of the amounts to be received in the distant future is usually small. For Vector, the two components of the terminal disposal value of an investment are (a) the after-tax cash flow from the terminal disposal of buses and (b) the after-tax cash flow from recovery of working capital.

   3a. *After-tax cash flow from terminal disposal of buses.* At the end of the useful life of the project, the bus's terminal disposal value is usually considerably less than the net initial investment (and sometimes zero). The relevant cash inflow is the difference in the expected after-tax cash inflow from terminal disposal at the end of 5 years under the two alternatives. Disposing of both the existing and the new bus will result in a zero after-tax cash inflow in year 5. Hence, there is no difference in the disposal-related after-tax cash inflows of the two alternatives.

   Because both the existing and new bus have disposal values that equal their book values at the time of their disposal (in each case, this value is $0), there are no tax effects for either alternative. What if either the existing or the new bus had a terminal value that differed from its book value at the time of disposal? In that case, the approach for computing the terminal inflow is identical to that for calculating the after-tax cash flow from current disposal illustrated earlier in item **1c**.

   3b. *After-tax cash flow from terminal recovery of working-capital investment.* The initial investment in working capital is usually fully recouped when the project is terminated. At that time, inventories and accounts receivable necessary to support the project are no longer needed. Vector receives cash equal to the book value of its working capital. Thus, there is no gain or loss on working capital and, hence, no tax consequences. The relevant cash inflow is the difference in the expected working capital recovered under the two alternatives. At the end of year 5, Vector recovers $36,000 cash from working capital if it invests in the new hybrid bus versus $6,000 if it continues to use the old bus. The relevant cash inflow at the end of year 5 if Vector invests in the new bus is thus $30,000 ($36,000 − $6,000).

   Some capital investment projects *reduce* working capital. Assume that a computer-integrated manufacturing (CIM) project with a 7-year life will reduce inventories and, hence, working capital by $20 million from, say, $50 million to $30 million. This reduction will be represented as a $20 million cash *inflow* for the project in year 0. At the end of 7 years, the recovery of working capital will show a relevant incremental cash *outflow* of $20 million. That's because, at the end of year 7, the company recovers only $30 million of working capital under CIM, rather than the $50 million of working capital it would have recovered had it not implemented CIM.

Exhibit 21-6 shows items **3a** and **3b** in the "year 5" column. The relevant cash flows in Exhibit 21-6 serve as inputs for the four capital budgeting methods described earlier in the chapter.

> **DECISION POINT**
>
> What are the relevant cash inflows and outflows for capital budgeting decisions? How should accrual accounting concepts be considered?

---

[9] If Vector were a nonprofit foundation not subject to income taxes, cash flow from operations would equal $220,000 in years 1 through 4 and $170,000 in year 5. The revenues would not be reduced by 40% nor would there be income tax cash savings from the depreciation deduction.

> **21-4 TRY IT!**
>
> Forrester Tire Company needs to overhaul its auto lift system or purchase a new one. The facts have been gathered, and they are as follows:
>
> | | Current Machine | New Machine |
> | --- | --- | --- |
> | Purchase price, new | $123,750 | $162,800 |
> | Current book value | 36,850 | |
> | Overhaul needed now | 30,250 | |
> | Annual cash operating costs | 69,300 | 52,800 |
> | Current salvage value | 44,000 | |
> | Salvage value in 5 years | 8,800 | 38,500 |
>
> Which alternative is the most desirable with a current required rate of return of 14%? Show computations, and assume no taxes.

Project Management and Performance Evaluation

We have so far looked at ways to identify relevant cash flows and techniques for analyzing them. The final stage (Stage 5) of capital budgeting begins with implementing the decision and managing the project.[10] This includes management control of the investment activity itself, as well as the project as a whole.

Capital budgeting projects, such as purchasing a hybrid bus or videoconferencing equipment, are easier to implement than projects involving building shopping malls or manufacturing plants. The building projects are more complex, so monitoring and controlling the investment schedules and budgets are critical to successfully completing the investment activity. This leads to the second dimension of Stage 5 in the capital budgeting process: evaluate performance and learn.

LEARNING OBJECTIVE 6

Understand issues involved in implementing capital budgeting decisions and evaluating managerial performance

...the importance of post-investment audits and the correct choice of performance measures

Post-Investment Audits

A post-investment audit provides managers with feedback about the performance of a project so they can compare the actual results to the costs and benefits expected at the time the project was selected. Suppose the actual outcomes (such as the additional operating cash flows from Vector's purchase of a new hybrid bus) are much lower than expected. Managers must then determine if this result occurred because the original estimates were overly optimistic or because of implementation problems. Either of these explanations is a concern.

Optimistic estimates can result in managers accepting a project they should reject. To discourage unrealistic forecasts, companies such as DuPont maintain records comparing the actual results of the firm's projects to the estimates individual managers either made or signed off on when seeking approval for capital investments. Post-investment audits prevent managers from overstating the expected cash inflows from projects and accepting projects they should reject. Implementation problems, such as weak project management, poor quality control, or inadequate marketing, are also a concern. Post-investment audits help to alert senior management to these problems so they can be quickly corrected.

Companies should perform post-investment audits with thought and care, and only after the outcomes of projects are fully known. Performing audits too early can be misleading. In addition, obtaining actual results to compare against estimates is often difficult. For example, in any particular period, macroeconomic factors, such as the weather and changes in fuel prices, can greatly affect the ridership on buses and the costs of running them. Consequently, the overall additional net revenues from Vector's new hybrid bus may not be immediately comparable to the estimated revenues. A better evaluation would look at the average revenues across a couple of seasons.

---

[10] In this section, we do not consider the different options for financing a project (refer to a text on corporate finance for details).

Performance Evaluation

As the preceding discussion suggests, ideally one should evaluate managers on a project-by-project basis and look at how well managers achieve the amounts and timing of forecasted cash flows. In practice, however, companies often evaluate managers based on aggregate information, especially when multiple projects are under way at any point in time. It is important then for companies to ensure that the method of evaluation does not conflict with the use of the NPV method for making capital budgeting decisions. For example, suppose Vector uses the accrual accounting rate of return generated in each period to assess its managers. We know that the managers should purchase the hybrid bus because it has a positive NPV of $69,840. However, they may reject the project if the AARR of 8.3% on the net initial investment is lower than the minimum accounting rate of return Vector requires them to achieve.

There is an inconsistency between promoting the NPV method as best for capital budgeting decisions and then using a different method to evaluate performance. Even though the NPV method is best for capital budgeting decisions, managers will be tempted to make those decisions based on the method on which they are being evaluated. The temptation becomes more pronounced if managers are frequently transferred (or promoted) or if their bonuses are affected by the level of year-to-year income earned under accrual accounting.

Other conflicts between decision making and performance evaluation persist even if a company uses similar measures for both purposes. If the AARR on the hybrid bus exceeds the minimum required AARR but is below Vector's current AARR in the region, the manager may still be tempted to reject purchase of the hybrid bus because the lower AARR of the hybrid bus will reduce the AARR of the entire region and hurt the manager's reported performance. Or consider an example where the cash inflows from the hybrid bus occur mostly in the later years of the project. Then, even if the project's AARR exceeds the current AARR of the projects overseen by the manager (as well as the minimum required return), the manager may still reject the purchase because for the first few years it will have a negative effect on the rate of return earned under accrual accounting. In Chapter 23, we study these conflicts in greater depth and describe how performance evaluation models such as economic value added (EVA®) help lessen these conflicts.

> **DECISION POINT**
> What conflicts can arise between using DCF methods for capital budgeting decisions and accrual accounting for performance evaluation? How can these conflicts be reduced?

Strategic Considerations in Capital Budgeting

> **LEARNING OBJECTIVE 7**
> Explain how managers can use capital budgeting to achieve their firms' strategic goals
> ...make critical investments aligned with the firm's objectives but whose benefits are uncertain or difficult to estimate

Managers consider a company's strategic goals when making capital budgeting decisions. Strategic decisions by Amazon, FedEx, Pizza Hut, and Westin Hotels to expand in Europe and Asia required capital investments in several countries. The strategic decision by Barnes & Noble to support book sales over the Internet required capital investments creating barnesandnoble.com and an Internet infrastructure. AOL's desire to create an enhanced digital destination with greater appeal for consumers and advertisers led to its purchase of *The Huffington Post*, as well as increased investment in editorial staff and sales representatives and higher marketing expenses. AstraZeneca's decision to develop Nexium as a patented replacement drug for its blockbuster Prilosec to prevent the formation of gastric acid led to major investments in R&D and marketing. Toyota's decision to offer a line of hybrids across both its Toyota and Lexus platforms required start-up investments to form a hybrid division and ongoing investments to fund the division's continuing research efforts.

Capital investment decisions that are strategic in nature require managers to consider a broad range of factors that may be difficult to estimate. Consider some of the difficulties of justifying investments made by companies such as Mitsubishi, Sony, and Audi in computer-integrated manufacturing (CIM) technology. In CIM, computers give instructions that quickly and automatically set up and run equipment to manufacture many different products. Quantifying these benefits requires some notion of how quickly consumer demand will change in the future. CIM technology also increases worker knowledge of and experience with automation; however, the benefit of this knowledge and experience is difficult to measure. Managers must develop judgment and intuition to make these decisions.

Investment in Research and Development

Companies such as GlaxoSmithKline, in the pharmaceutical industry, and Intel, in the semiconductor industry, regard R&D projects as important strategic investments. The distant payoffs from R&D investments, however, are more uncertain than other investments such as new equipment purchases. On the positive side, R&D investments are often staged: As time unfolds, companies can increase or decrease the resources committed to a project based on how successful it has been up to that point. This feature, called real options, is an important aspect of R&D investments. It increases the NPV of these investments because a company can limit its losses when things are going badly and take advantage of new opportunities when things are going well. As an example, a pharmaceutical company can increase or decrease its investment in an R&D joint venture based on the progress of the clinical trials of new drugs being developed by the venture.

Customer Value and Capital Budgeting

Finally, note that managers can use the framework described in this chapter to both evaluate investment projects and to make strategic decisions regarding which customers to invest in. Consider Potato Supreme, which makes potato products for sale to retail outlets. It is currently analyzing two of its customers: Shine Stores and Always Open. Potato Supreme predicts the following cash flow from operations, net of income taxes (in thousands), from each customer account for the next 5 years:

	2017	2018	2019	2020	2021
Shine Stores	$1,450	$1,305	$1,175	$1,058	$ 950
Always Open	690	1,160	1,900	2,950	4,160

Which customer is more valuable to Potato Supreme? Looking at only the current period, 2017, Shine Stores provides more than double the cash flow compared to Always Open ($1,450 versus $690). A different picture emerges, however, if you look at the entire 5-year horizon. Potato Supreme anticipates Always Open's orders to increase; meanwhile, it expects Shine Stores' orders to decline. Using Potato Supreme's 10% RRR, the NPV of the Always Open customer is $7,610, compared with $4,591 for Shine Stores (computations not shown). Note how NPV captures in its estimate of customer value the future growth of Always Open. Potato Supreme uses this information to allocate more resources and salespeople to service the Always Open account. Potato Supreme can also use NPV calculations to examine the effects of alternative ways of increasing customer loyalty and retention, such as introducing frequent-purchaser cards.

A comparison of year-to-year changes in customer NPV estimates highlights whether managers have been successful in maintaining long-run profitable relationships with their customers. Suppose the NPV of Potato Supreme's customer accounts declines by 15% in a year. The firm's managers can then examine the reasons for the decline, such as aggressive pricing by competitors, and devise new-product development and marketing strategies for the future.

Capital One, a financial-services company, uses NPV to estimate the value of different credit-card customers. Cellular telephone companies such as Sprint and Verizon Wireless attempt to sign up customers for multiple years of service. The objective is to prevent "customer churn"—that is, customers switching frequently from one company to another. The higher the probability is of a customer switching, the lower the customer's NPV.

DECISION POINT

How can managers use capital budgeting to achieve strategic goals?

PROBLEM FOR SELF-STUDY

Part A

Returning to the Vector hybrid bus project, assume that Vector is a *nonprofit organization* and that the expected additional operating cash inflows are $240,000 in years 1 through 4 and $210,000 in year 5. Using data from page 852, the net initial investment is $661,500 (new bus, $660,000, plus additional working capital, $30,000, minus current disposal value of old bus, $28,500). All other facts are unchanged: a 5-year useful life, no terminal disposal value, and an 8% RRR. Year 5 cash inflows are $240,000, which includes a $30,000 recovery of working capital.

Calculate the following:
1. Net present value
2. Internal rate of return
3. Payback period
4. Accrual accounting rate of return on net initial investment

Solution

1. NPV = ($240,000 × 3.993) − $661,500
   = $958,320 − $661,500 = $296,820

2. There are several approaches to computing IRR. One is to use a calculator with an IRR function. This approach gives an IRR of 23.8%. Another approach is to use Table 4 in Appendix A at the end of the text:

   $661,500 = $240,000F

   $$F = \frac{\$661{,}500}{\$240{,}000} = 2.756$$

   On the five-period line of Table 4, the column closest to 2.756 is 24%. To obtain a more-accurate number, use straight-line interpolation:

	Present Value Factors	
22%	2.864	2.864
IRR	—	2.756
24%	2.745	—
Difference	0.119	0.108

   $$IRR = 22\% + \frac{0.108}{0.119}(2\%) = 23.8\% \text{ per year}$$

3. Payback period = $\dfrac{\text{Net initial investment}}{\text{Uniform increase in annual future cash flows}}$
   = $661,500 ÷ $240,000 = 2.76 years

4. AARR = $\dfrac{\text{Increase in expected average annual operating income}}{\text{Net initial investment}}$

   Increase in expected average annual operating cash inflows = [($240,000 × 4) + $210,000] ÷ 5 years
   = $1,170,000 ÷ 5 = $234,000

   Increase in annual depreciation = $120,000 ($132,000 − $12,000, see p. 852)

   Increase in expected average annual operating income = $234,000 − $120,000 = $114,000

   $$AARR = \frac{\$114{,}000}{\$661{,}500} = 17.2\% \text{ per year}$$

Part B

Assume that Vector is subject to income tax at a 40% rate. All other information from Part A is unchanged. Compute the NPV of the new hybrid bus project.

Solution

To save space, Exhibit 21-7 shows the calculations using a format slightly different from the format used in this chapter. Item **2a** is where the new cash flow assumptions affect the NPV analysis (compared with Exhibit 21-6). All other amounts in Exhibit 21-7 are identical to the corresponding amounts in Exhibit 21-6. For years 1 through 4, after-tax cash flow (excluding the depreciation effect) is as follows:

Annual cash flow from operations with new bus	$240,000
Deduct income tax payments (0.40 × $240,000)	96,000
Annual after-tax cash flow from operations	$144,000

For year 5, after-tax cash flow (excluding the depreciation effect) is as follows:

Annual cash flow from operations with new bus	$210,000
Deduct income tax payments (0.40 × $210,000)	84,000
Annual after-tax cash flow from operations	$126,000

The NPV in Exhibit 21-7 is $125,928. As computed in Part A, the NPV when there are no income taxes is $296,820. The difference in these two NPVs illustrates the impact of income taxes in capital budgeting analysis.

EXHIBIT 21-7 Net Present Value Method Incorporating Income Taxes: Vector's Hybrid Bus with Revised Annual Cash Flow from Operations

	A	B	C	D	E	F	G	H	I	J
1			Present Value	Present Value of		\multicolumn{5}{c}{Sketch of Relevant Cash Flows at End of Year}				
2			of Cash Flow	$1 Discounted at 8%	0	1	2	3	4	5
3	1a.	Initial hybrid bus investment	$(660,000) ←	1.000 ←	$(660,000)					
4										
5	1b.	Initial working-capital investment	(30,000) ←	1.000 ←	$ (30,000)					
6	1c.	After-tax cash inflow from current disposal								
7		of old bus	41,100 ←	1.000 ←	$ 41,100					
8	Net initial investment		(648,900)							
9	2a.	Annual after-tax cash flow from operations								
10		(excluding the depreciation effect)								
11		Year 1	133,344 ←	0.926 ←		$144,000				
12		Year 2	123,408 ←	0.857 ←			$144,000			
13		Year 3	114,336 ←	0.794 ←				$144,000		
14		Year 4	105,840 ←	0.735 ←					$144,000	
15		Year 5	85,806 ←	0.681 ←						$126,000
16	2b.	Income tax cash savings from annual								
17		depreciation deductions								
18		Year 1	44,448 ←	0.926 ←		$ 48,000				
19		Year 2	41,136 ←	0.857 ←			$ 48,000			
20		Year 3	38,112 ←	0.794 ←				$ 48,000		
21		Year 4	35,280 ←	0.735 ←					$ 48,000	
22		Year 5	32,688 ←	0.681 ←						$ 48,000
23	3.	After-tax cash flow from recovery of								
24		a. Terminal disposal of bus	0 ←	0.681 ←						$ 0
25		b. Recovery of working capital	20,430 ←	0.681 ←						$ 30,000
26	NPV if new hybrid bus purchased		$ 125,928							
27										

DECISION POINTS

The following question-and-answer format summarizes the chapter's learning objectives. Each decision presents a key question related to a learning objective. The guidelines are the answer to that question.

Decision	Guidelines
1. What are the five stages of capital budgeting?	Capital budgeting is long-run planning for proposed investment projects. The five stages of capital budgeting are: (1) Identify projects: Identify potential capital investments aligned with the organization's strategy; (2) Obtain information: Gather information from all parts of the value chain to evaluate alternative projects; (3) Make predictions: Forecast all potential cash flows attributable to the alternative projects; (4) Choose among alternatives: Determine which investment yields the greatest benefit and the least cost to the organization; and (5) Implement the decision, evaluate performance, and learn: Obtain funding and make the investments selected in Stage 4; track the realized cash flows, compare them against estimated numbers, and revise plans if necessary.
2. What are the two primary discounted cash flow (DCF) methods for project evaluation?	The two main DCF methods are the net present value (NPV) method and the internal rate-of-return (IRR) method. The NPV method calculates the expected net monetary gain or loss from a project by discounting to the present all expected future cash inflows and outflows, using the required rate of return. A project is acceptable in financial terms if it has a positive NPV. The IRR method computes the rate of return (also called the discount rate) at which a project's present value of expected cash inflows equals the present value of its expected cash outflows. A project is acceptable in financial terms if its IRR exceeds the required rate of return. The DCF is the best approach to capital budgeting. It explicitly includes all project cash flows and recognizes the time value of money. The NPV method is the preferred DCF method.
3. What are the payback and discounted payback methods? What are their main weaknesses?	The payback method measures the time it will take to recoup, in the form of cash inflows, the total cash amount invested in a project. The payback method neglects the time value of money and ignores cash flows beyond the payback period. The discounted payback method measures the time taken for the present value of cash inflows to equal the present value of cash outflows. It adjusts for the time value of money but overlooks cash flows after the discounted payback period.
4. What are the strengths and weaknesses of the accrual accounting rate-of-return (AARR) method for evaluating long-term projects?	The accrual accounting rate-of-return (AARR) method divides an accrual accounting measure of average annual income from a project by an accrual accounting measure of its investment. The AARR gives managers an idea of how accepting a project will affect a firm's future reported accounting profitability. However, the AARR uses accrual accounting income numbers, does not track cash flows, and ignores the time value of money.
5. What are the relevant cash inflows and outflows for capital budgeting decisions? How should accrual accounting concepts be considered?	Relevant cash inflows and outflows in a DCF analysis are the differences in expected future cash flows as a result of making the investment. Only cash inflows and outflows matter; accrual accounting concepts are irrelevant for DCF methods. For example, the income taxes saved as a result of depreciation deductions are relevant because they decrease cash outflows, but the depreciation itself is a noncash item.

Decision	Guidelines
6. What conflicts can arise between using DCF methods for capital budgeting decisions and accrual accounting for performance evaluation? How can these conflicts be reduced?	Using accrual accounting to evaluate the performance of a manager may create conflicts with the use of DCF methods for capital budgeting. Frequently, the decision made using a DCF method will not report good "operating income" results in the project's early years under accrual accounting. For this reason, managers are tempted to not use DCF methods even though the decisions based on them would be in the best interests of the company as a whole over the long run. This conflict can be reduced by evaluating managers on a project-by-project basis and by looking at their ability to achieve the amounts and timing of forecasted cash flows.
7. How can managers use capital budgeting to achieve strategic goals?	A company's strategy is the source of its strategic capital budgeting decisions. Such decisions require managers to consider a broad range of factors that may be difficult to estimate. Managers must develop judgment and intuition to make these decisions. R&D projects, for example, are important strategic investments, with distant and usually highly uncertain payoffs.

APPENDIX

Capital Budgeting and Inflation

The Vector example (Exhibits 21-2 to 21-6) does not include adjustments for inflation in the relevant revenues and costs. **Inflation** is the decline in the general purchasing power of the monetary unit, such as dollars. An inflation rate of 10% per year means that an item bought for $100 at the beginning of the year will cost $110 at the end of the year.

Why is it important to account for inflation in capital budgeting? Because declines in the general purchasing power of the monetary unit will inflate future cash flows above what they would have been in the absence of inflation. These inflated cash flows will cause the project to look better than it really is unless the analyst recognizes that the inflated cash flows are measured in dollars that have less purchasing power than the dollars that were initially invested. When analyzing inflation, distinguish real rate of return from nominal rate of return:

Real rate of return is the rate of return demanded to cover investment risk if there is no inflation. The real rate is made up of two elements: (1) a risk-free element (the pure rate of return on risk-free long-term government bonds when there is no expected inflation) and (2) a business-risk element (that's the risk premium demanded for bearing risk).

Nominal rate of return is the rate of return demanded to cover investment risk and the decline in general purchasing power of the monetary unit as a result of expected inflation. The nominal rate is made up of three elements: (a) a risk-free element when there is no expected inflation, (b) a business-risk element, and (c) an inflation element. Items (a) and (b) make up the real rate of return to cover investment risk. The inflation element is the premium above the real rate. The rates of return earned in the financial markets are nominal rates because investors want to be compensated both for the investment risks they take and for the expected decline in the general purchasing power, as a result of inflation, of the money they get back.

Assume that the real rate of return for investments in high-risk cellular data-transmission equipment at Network Communications is 20% per year and that the expected inflation rate is 10% per year. Nominal rate of return is as follows:

$$\text{Nominal rate} = (1 + \text{Real rate})(1 + \text{Inflation rate}) - 1$$
$$= (1 + 0.20)(1 + 0.10) - 1$$
$$= (1.20 \times 1.10) - 1 = 1.32 - 1 = 0.32, \text{ or } 32\%$$

Nominal rate of return is related to the real rate of return and the inflation rate:

Real rate of return	0.20
Inflation rate	0.10
Combination (0.20 × 0.10)	0.02
Nominal rate of return	0.32

Note the nominal rate, 0.32, is slightly higher than 0.30, the real rate (0.20) plus the inflation rate (0.10). That's because the nominal rate recognizes that inflation of 10% also decreases the purchasing power of the real rate of return of 20% earned during the year. The combination component represents the additional compensation investors seek for the decrease in the purchasing power of the real return earned during the year because of inflation.[11]

Net Present Value Method and Inflation

When incorporating inflation into the NPV method, the key is *internal consistency*. There are two internally consistent approaches:

1. **Nominal approach**—predicts cash inflows and outflows in nominal monetary units *and* uses a nominal rate as the required rate of return
2. **Real approach**—predicts cash inflows and outflows in real monetary units *and* uses a real rate as the required rate of return

We will limit our discussion to the simpler nominal approach. Consider an investment that is expected to generate sales of 100 units and a net cash inflow of $1,000 ($10 per unit) each year for 2 years *absent inflation*. Assume cash flows occur at the end of each year. If inflation of 10% is expected each year, net cash inflows from the sale of each unit would be $11 ($10 × 1.10) in year 1 and $12.10 ($11 × 1.10, or $10 × $(1.10)^2$) in year 2, resulting in net cash inflows of $1,100 in year 1 and $1,210 in year 2. The net cash inflows of $1,100 and $1,210 are nominal cash inflows because they include the effects of inflation. *Nominal cash flows are the cash flows that are recorded in the accounting system.* The cash inflows of $1,000 each year are real cash flows. The accounting system does not record these cash flows. The nominal approach is easier to understand and apply because it uses nominal cash flows from accounting systems and nominal rates of return from financial markets.

Assume that Network Communications can purchase equipment to make and sell an Ethernet blade switch for a net initial investment of $750,000. The equipment is expected to have a 4-year useful life and no terminal disposal value. An annual inflation rate of 10% is expected over this 4-year period. Network Communications requires an after-tax nominal rate of return of 32% (see page 863). The following table presents the predicted amounts of real (that's assuming no inflation) and nominal (that's after considering cumulative inflation) net cash inflows from the equipment over the next 4 years (excluding the $750,000 investment in the equipment and before any income tax payments):

Year (1)	Before-Tax Cash Inflows in Real Dollars (2)	Cumulative Inflation Rate Factor[a] (3)	Before-Tax Cash Inflows in Nominal Dollars (4) = (2) × (3)
1	$500,000	$(1.10)^1$ = 1.1000	$550,000
2	600,000	$(1.10)^2$ = 1.2100	726,000
3	600,000	$(1.10)^3$ = 1.3310	798,600
4	300,000	$(1.10)^4$ = 1.4641	439,230

[a] 1.10 = 1.00 + 0.10 inflation rate.

---

[11] The real rate of return can be expressed in terms of the nominal rate of return as follows:

$$\text{Real rate} = \frac{1 + \text{Nominal rate}}{1 + \text{Inflation rate}} - 1 = \frac{1 + 0.32}{1 + 0.10} - 1 = 0.20, \text{ or } 20\%$$

EXHIBIT 21-8 Net Present Value Method Using Nominal Approach to Inflation for Network Communication's New Equipment

	A	B	C	D	E	F	G	H	I	J	K	L
1						Present	Present Value					
2						Value of	Discount Factor[a] at		\multicolumn{4}{l}{Sketch of Relevant Cash Flows at End of Each Year}			
3						Cash Flow	32%	0	1	2	3	4
4	1.	Net initial investment										
5		Year	\multicolumn{2}{l}{Investment Outflows}								
6		0	\multicolumn{2}{l}{$(750,000)}		$(750,000)	← 1.000 ←	$(750,000)				
7	2a.	Annual after-tax cash flow from										
8		operations (excluding the depreciation effect)										
9			Annual		Annual							
10			Before-Tax	Income	After-Tax							
11			Cash Flow	Tax	Cash Flow							
12		Year	from Operations	Outflows	from Operations							
13		(1)	(2)	(3) = 0.40 × (2)	(4) = (2) − (3)							
14		1	$550,000	$220,000	$330,000	250,140	← 0.758 ←			$330,000		
15		2	726,000	290,400	435,600	250,034	← 0.574 ←				$435,600	
16		3	798,600	319,440	479,160	208,435	← 0.435 ←					$479,160
17		4	439,230	175,692	263,538	86,704	← 0.329 ←					$263,538
18						795,313						
19	2b.	Income tax cash savings from annual										
20		depreciation deductions										
21		Year	Depreciation	Tax Cash Savings								
22		(1)	(2)	(3) = 0.40 × (2)								
23		1	$187,500[b]	$75,000		56,850	← 0.758 ←		$ 75,000			
24		2	187,500	75,000		43,050	← 0.574 ←			$ 75,000		
25		3	187,500	75,000		32,625	← 0.435 ←				$ 75,000	
26		4	187,500	75,000		24,675	← 0.329 ←					$ 75,000
27						157,200						
28												
29	NPV if new equipment purchased					$ 202,513						
30												
31	[a]The nominal discount rate of 32% is made up of the real rate of return of 20% and the inflation rate of 10%: [(1 + 0.20) (1 + 1.10)] − 1 = 0.32.											
32	[b]$750,000 ÷ 4 = $187,500											

We continue to make the simplifying assumption that cash flows occur at the end of each year. The income tax rate is 40%. For tax purposes, the cost of the equipment will be depreciated using the straight-line method.

Exhibit 21-8 shows the calculation of NPV using cash flows in nominal dollars and using a nominal discount rate. The calculations in Exhibit 21-8 include the net initial bus investment, annual after-tax cash flows from operations (excluding the depreciation effect), and income tax cash savings from annual depreciation deductions. The NPV is $202,513, and, based on financial considerations alone, Network Communications should purchase the equipment.

TERMS TO LEARN

This chapter and the Glossary at the end of the book contain definitions of the following important terms:

accrual accounting rate-of-return (AARR) method
capital budgeting
cost of capital
discount rate
discounted cash flow (DCF) methods

discounted payback method
hurdle rate
inflation
internal rate-of-return (IRR) method
net present value (NPV) method

nominal rate of return
opportunity cost of capital
payback method
real rate of return
required rate of return (RRR)
time value of money

ASSIGNMENT MATERIAL

Questions

21-1 "Capital budgeting has the same focus as accrual accounting." Do you agree? Explain.

21-2 List and briefly describe each of the five stages in capital budgeting.

21-3 What is the essence of the discounted cash flow methods?

21-4 "Only quantitative outcomes are relevant in capital budgeting analyses." Do you agree? Explain.

21-5 How can sensitivity analysis be incorporated in DCF analysis?

21-6 What is the payback method? What are its main strengths and weaknesses?

21-7 Describe the accrual accounting rate-of-return method. What are its main strengths and weaknesses?

21-8 "The trouble with discounted cash flow methods is that they ignore depreciation." Do you agree? Explain.

21-9 "Let's be more practical. DCF is not the gospel. Managers should not become so enchanted with DCF that strategic considerations are overlooked." Do you agree? Explain.

21-10 "All overhead costs are relevant in NPV analysis." Do you agree? Explain.

21-11 Bill Watts, president of Western Publications, accepts a capital budgeting project proposed by division X. This is the division in which the president spent his first 10 years with the company. On the same day, the president rejects a capital budgeting project proposal from division Y. The manager of division Y is incensed. She believes that the division Y project has an internal rate of return at least 10 percentage points higher than the division X project. She comments, "What is the point of all our detailed DCF analysis? If Watts is panting over a project, he can arrange to have the proponents of that project massage the numbers so that it looks like a winner." What advice would you give the manager of division Y?

21-12 Distinguish different categories of cash flows to be considered in an equipment-replacement decision by a taxpaying company.

21-13 Describe three ways income taxes can affect the cash inflows or outflows in a motor-vehicle-replacement decision by a taxpaying company.

21-14 How can capital budgeting tools assist in evaluating a manager who is responsible for retaining customers of a cellular telephone company?

21-15 Distinguish the nominal rate of return from the real rate of return.

Multiple-Choice Questions

21-16 A company should accept for investment all positive NPV investment alternatives when which of the following conditions is true?
a. The company has extremely limited resources for capital investment.
b. The company has excess cash on its balance sheet.
c. The company has virtually unlimited resources for capital investment.
d. The company has limited resources for capital investment but is planning to issue new equity to finance additional capital investment.

21-17 Which of the following items describes a weakness of the internal rate-of-return method?
a. The internal rate of return is difficult to calculate and requires a financial calculator or spreadsheet tool such as Excel to calculate efficiently.
b. Cash flows from the investment are assumed in the IRR analysis to be reinvested at the internal rate of return.
c. The internal rate-of-return calculation ignores time value of money.
d. The internal rate-of-return calculation ignores project cash flows occurring after the initial investment is recovered.

21-18 Which of the following statements is true if the NPV of a project is −$4,000 (negative $4,000) and the required rate of return is 5 percent?
 a. The project's IRR is less than 5 percent.
 b. The required rate of return is lower than the IRR.
 c. The NPV assumes cash flows are reinvested at the IRR.
 d. The NPV would be positive if the IRR was equal to 5 percent.

21-19 The following information pertains to the January 2, year 2 transaction replacing a print machine for Hidden Creek Enterprises, Inc.

 Net book value – old print machine $20,000
 Total cost of new machine $180,000
 Down payment on new machine $35,000
 Sale price of old machine $30,000
 Tax rate 30%

What is the net total of relevant costs on January 2, year 2?
 a. $173,000   b. $153,000
 c. $28,000   d. 8,000.

21-20 Nick's Enterprises has purchased a new machine tool that will allow the company to improve the efficiency of its operations. On an annual basis, the machine will produce 20,000 units with an expected selling price of $10, prime costs of $6 per unit, and a fixed cost allocation of $3 per unit. Annual depreciation on the machine is $12,000, and the tax rate of the company is 25%.
What is the annual cash flow generated from the new machine?
 a. $63,000   b. $51,000
 c. $18,000   d. $6,000

©2016 DeVry/Becker Educational Development Corp. All Rights Reserved.

Exercises

21-21 Exercises in compound interest, no income taxes. To be sure that you understand how to use the tables in Appendix A at the end of this book, solve the following exercises. Ignore income tax considerations. The correct answers, rounded to the nearest dollar, appear on page 875.

1. You have just won $50,000. How much money will you accumulate at the end of 5 years if you invest it at 6% compounded annually? At 12%?
2. Twelve years from now, the unpaid principal of the mortgage on your house will be $249,600. How much do you need to invest today at 6% interest compounded annually to accumulate the $249,600 in 12 years?
3. If the unpaid mortgage on your house in 12 years will be $249,600, how much money do you need to invest at the end of each year at 6% to accumulate exactly this amount at the end of the 12th year?
4. You plan to save $4,800 of your earnings at the end of each year for the next 8 years. How much money will you accumulate at the end of the 8th year if you invest your savings compounded at 4% per year?
5. You have just turned 65 and an endowment insurance policy has paid you a lump sum of $400,000. If you invest the sum at 6%, how much money can you withdraw from your account in equal amounts at the end of each year so that at the end of 7 years (age 72), there will be nothing left?
6. You have estimated that for the first 6 years after you retire you will need a cash inflow of $48,000 at the end of each year. How much money do you need to invest at 4% at your retirement age to obtain this annual cash inflow? At 6%?
7. The following table shows two schedules of prospective operating cash inflows, each of which requires the same net initial investment of $18,000 now:

| | Annual Cash Inflows | |
Year	Plan A	Plan B
1	$ 2,000	$ 3,000
2	3,000	5,000
3	4,000	9,000
4	7,000	5,000
5	9,000	3,000
Total	$25,000	$25,000

The required rate of return is 6% compounded annually. All cash inflows occur at the end of each year. In terms of net present value, which plan is more desirable? Show your computations.

21-22 Capital budgeting methods, no income taxes. Yummy Candy Company is considering purchasing a second chocolate dipping machine in order to expand their business. The information Yummy has accumulated regarding the new machine is:

Cost of the machine	$80,000
Increased annual contribution margin	$15,000
Life of the machine	10 years
Required rate of return	6%

Yummy estimates they will be able to produce more candy using the second machine and thus increase their annual contribution margin. They also estimate there will be a small disposal value of the machine but the cost of removal will offset that value. Ignore income tax issues in your answers. Assume all cash flows occur at year-end except for initial investment amounts.

Required

1. Calculate the following for the new machine:
   a. Net present value
   b. Payback period
   c. Discounted payback period
   d. Internal rate of return (using the interpolation method)
   e. Accrual accounting rate of return based on the net initial investment (assume straight-line depreciation)
2. What other factors should Yummy Candy consider in deciding whether to purchase the new machine?

21-23 Capital budgeting methods, no income taxes. City Hospital, a nonprofit organization, estimates that it can save $28,000 a year in cash operating costs for the next 10 years if it buys a special-purpose eye-testing machine at a cost of $110,000. No terminal disposal value is expected. City Hospital's required rate of return is 14%. Assume all cash flows occur at year-end except for initial investment amounts. City Hospital uses straight-line depreciation.

Required

1. Calculate the following for the special-purpose eye-testing machine:
   a. Net present value
   b. Payback period
   c. Internal rate of return
   d. Accrual accounting rate of return based on net initial investment
   e. Accrual accounting rate of return based on average investment
2. What other factors should City Hospital consider in deciding whether to purchase the special-purpose eye-testing machine?

21-24 Capital budgeting, income taxes. Assume the same facts as in Exercise 21-23 except that City Hospital is a taxpaying entity. The income tax rate is 30% for all transactions that affect income taxes.

Required

1. Do requirement 1 of Exercise 21-23.
2. How would your computations in requirement 1 be affected if the special-purpose machine had a $10,000 terminal disposal value at the end of 10 years? Assume depreciation deductions are based on the $110,000 purchase cost and zero terminal disposal value using the straight-line method. Answer briefly in words without further calculations.

21-25 Capital budgeting with uneven cash flows, no income taxes. America Cola is considering the purchase of a special-purpose bottling machine for $65,000. It is expected to have a useful life of 4 years with no terminal disposal value. The plant manager estimates the following savings in cash operating costs:

Year	Amount
1	$25,000
2	22,000
3	21,000
4	20,000
Total	$88,000

America Cola uses a required rate of return of 18% in its capital budgeting decisions. Ignore income taxes in your analysis. Assume all cash flows occur at year-end except for initial investment amounts. Calculate the following for the special-purpose bottling machine:

Required

1. Net present value
2. Payback period
3. Discounted payback period
4. Internal rate of return (using the interpolation method)
5. Accrual accounting rate of return based on net initial investment (Assume straight-line depreciation. Use the average annual savings in cash operating costs when computing the numerator of the accrual accounting rate of return.)

21-26 Comparison of projects, no income taxes. (CMA, adapted) New Pharm Corporation is a rapidly growing biotech company that has a required rate of return of 14%. It plans to build a new facility in Santa Clara County. The building will take 2 years to complete. The building contractor offered New Pharm a choice of three payment plans, as follows:

- **Plan I:** Payment of $175,000 at the time of signing the contract and $4,700,000 upon completion of the building. The end of the second year is the completion date.
- **Plan II:** Payment of $1,625,000 at the time of signing the contract and $1,625,000 at the end of each of the two succeeding years.
- **Plan III:** Payment of $325,000 at the time of signing the contract and $1,500,000 at the end of each of the three succeeding years.

Required

1. Using the net present value method, calculate the comparative cost of each of the three payment plans being considered by New Pharm.
2. Which payment plan should New Pharm choose? Explain.
3. Discuss the financial factors, other than the cost of the plan, and the nonfinancial factors that should be considered in selecting an appropriate payment plan.

21-27 Payback and NPV methods, no income taxes. (CMA, adapted) Andrews Construction is analyzing its capital expenditure proposals for the purchase of equipment in the coming year. The capital budget is limited to $5,000,000 for the year. Lori Bart, staff analyst at Andrews, is preparing an analysis of the three projects under consideration by Corey Andrews, the company's owner.

	A	B	C	D
1		Project A	Project B	Project C
2	Projected cash outflow			
3	Net initial investment	$3,000,000	$1,500,000	$4,000,000
4				
5	Projected cash inflows:			
6	Year 1	$1,000,000	$ 400,000	$2,000,000
7	Year 2	1,000,000	900,000	2,000,000
8	Year 3	1,000,000	800,000	200,000
9	Year 4	1,000,000		100,000
10				
11	Required rate of return	10%	10%	10%

Required

1. Because the company's cash is limited, Andrews thinks the payback method should be used to choose between the capital budgeting projects.
   a. What are the benefits and limitations of using the payback method to choose between projects?
   b. Calculate the payback period for each of the three projects. Ignore income taxes. Using the payback method, which projects should Andrews choose?
2. Bart thinks that projects should be selected based on their NPVs. Assume all cash flows occur at the end of the year except for initial investment amounts. Calculate the NPV for each project. Ignore income taxes.
3. Which projects, if any, would you recommend funding? Briefly explain why.

21-28 DCF, accrual accounting rate of return, working capital, evaluation of performance, no income taxes. Laverty Clinic plans to purchase a new centrifuge machine for its New York facility. The machine costs $94,000 and is expected to have a useful life of 6 years, with a terminal disposal value of $9,000. Savings in cash operating costs are expected to be $24,900 per year. However, additional working capital is needed to keep the machine running efficiently. The working capital must continually be replaced, so an investment of $4,000 needs to be maintained at all times, but this investment is fully recoverable (will be "cashed in") at the end of the useful life. Laverty Clinic's required rate of return is 12%. Ignore income taxes in your analysis. Assume all cash flows occur at year-end except for initial investment amounts. Laverty Clinic uses straight-line depreciation for its machines.

Required

1. Calculate net present value.
2. Calculate internal rate of return.

3. Calculate accrual accounting rate of return based on net initial investment.
4. Calculate accrual accounting rate of return based on average investment.
5. You have the authority to make the purchase decision. Why might you be reluctant to base your decision on the DCF methods?

21-29 New equipment purchase, income taxes. Ella's Bakery plans to purchase a new oven for its store. The oven has an estimated useful life of 4 years. The estimated pretax cash flows for the oven are as shown in the table that follows, with no anticipated change in working capital. Ella's Bakery has a 14% after-tax required rate of return and a 35% income tax rate. Assume depreciation is calculated on a straight-line basis for tax purposes using the initial investment in the oven and its estimated terminal disposal value. Assume all cash flows occur at year-end except for initial investment amounts.

	A	B	C	D	E	F
1		Relevant Cash Flows at End of Each Year				
2		0	1	2	3	4
3	Initial oven investment	($186,000)				
4	Annual cash flow from operations (excluding the depreciation effect)		$77,000	$77,000	$77,000	$77,000
5	Cash flow from terminal disposal of oven					$ 6,000

Required

1. Calculate (a) net present value, (b) payback period, and (c) internal rate of return.
2. Calculate accrual accounting rate of return based on net initial investment.

21-30 New equipment purchase, income taxes. Walker Inc. is considering the purchase of new equipment that will automate production and thus reduce labor costs. Walker made the following estimates related to the new machinery:

Cost of the equipment	$120,000
Reduced annual labor costs	$40,000
Estimated life of equipment	5 years
Terminal disposal value	$0
After-tax cost of capital	8%
Tax rate	25%

Assume depreciation is calculated on a straight-line basis for tax purposes. Assume all cash flows occur at year-end except for initial investment amounts.

Required

1. Calculate (a) net present value, (b) payback period, (c) discounted payback period, and (d) internal rate of return.
2. Compare and contrast the capital budgeting methods in requirement 1.

21-31 Project choice, taxes. Klein Dermatology is contemplating purchasing new laser therapy equipment. This new equipment would cost $300,000 to purchase and $20,000 for installation. Klein estimates that this new equipment would yield incremental margins of $98,000 annually due to new client services but would require incremental cash maintenance costs of $10,000 annually. Klein expects the life of this equipment to be 5 years and estimates a terminal disposal value of $20,000.

Klein has a 25% income tax rate and depreciates assets on a straight-line basis (to terminal value) for tax purposes. The required rate of return on investments is 10%.

Required

1. What is the expected increase in annual net income from investing in the improvements?
2. Calculate the accrual accounting rate of return based on average investment.
3. Is the project worth investing in from an NPV standpoint?
4. Suppose the tax authorities are willing to let Klein depreciate the project down to zero over its useful life. If Klein plans to liquidate the project in 5 years, should it take this option? Quantify the impact of this choice on the NPV of the project.

21-32 Customer value. Ortel Telecom sells telecommunication products and services to a variety of small businesses. Two of Ortel's key clients are Square and Cloudburst, both fast-growing technology start-ups located in New York City. Ortel has compiled information regarding its transactions with

Square and Cloudburst for 2017, as well as its expectations regarding their interactions over the next 3 years:

	Expected Annual Percentage Increase		2017	
	Square	Cloudburst	Square	Cloudburst
Sales Revenues	6%	5.5%	$567,000	$3,510,000
Cost of Sales	5%	4.5%	$364,800	$3,060,000
Net cash flow			$202,200	$ 450,000

Ortel's transactions with Square and Cloudburst are in cash. Assume that they occur at year-end. Ortel is headquartered in the Cayman Islands and pays no income taxes. The owners of Ortel insist on a required rate of return of 12%.

1. What is the expected net cash flow from Square and Cloudburst for the next 3 years?
2. Based on the net present value from cash flows over the next 3 years, is Cloudburst or Square a more valuable customer for Ortel?
3. Cloudburst threatens to switch to another supplier unless Ortel gives a 10% price reduction on all sales starting in 2018. Calculate the 3-year NPV of Cloudburst after incorporating the 10% discount. Should Ortel continue to transact with Cloudburst? What other factors should it consider before making its final decision?

21-33 Selling a plant, income taxes. (CMA, adapted) The Cook Company is a national portable building manufacturer. Its Benton plant will become idle on December 31, 2017. Mary Carter, the corporate controller, has been asked to look at three options regarding the plant:

- **Option 1:** The plant, which has been fully depreciated for tax purposes, can be sold immediately for $750,000.

- **Option 2:** The plant can be leased to the Timber Corporation, one of Cook's suppliers, for 4 years. Under the lease terms, Timber would pay Cook $175,000 rent per year (payable at year-end) and would grant Cook a $60,000 annual discount from the normal price of lumber purchased by Cook. (Assume that the discount is received at year-end for each of the 4 years.) Timber would bear all of the plant's ownership costs. Cook expects to sell this plant for $250,000 at the end of the 4-year lease.

- **Option 3:** The plant could be used for 4 years to make porch swings as an accessory to be sold with a portable building. Fixed overhead costs (a cash outflow) before any equipment upgrades are estimated to be $22,000 annually for the 4-year period. The swings are expected to sell for $45 each. Variable cost per unit is expected to be $22. The following production and sales of swings are expected: 2018, 12,000 units; 2019, 18,000 units; 2020, 15,000 units; 2021, 8,000 units. In order to manufacture the swings, some of the plant equipment would need to be upgraded at an immediate cost of $180,000. The equipment would be depreciated using the straight-line depreciation method and zero terminal disposal value over the 4 years it would be in use. Because of the equipment upgrades, Cook could sell the plant for $320,000 at the end of 4 years. No change in working capital would be required.

Cook Company treats all cash flows as if they occur at the end of the year, and uses an after-tax required rate of return of 8%. Cook is subject to a 30% tax rate on all income, including capital gains.

1. Calculate net present value of each of the options and determine which option Cook should select using the NPV criterion.
2. What nonfinancial factors should Cook consider before making its choice?

Problems

21-34 Equipment replacement, no income taxes. Dublin Chips is a manufacturer of prototype chips based in Dublin, Ireland. Next year, in 2018, Dublin Chips expects to deliver 615 prototype chips at an average price of $95,000. Dublin Chips' marketing vice president forecasts growth of 65 prototype chips per year through 2024. That is, demand will be 615 in 2018, 680 in 2019, 745 in 2020, and so on.

The plant cannot produce more than 585 prototype chips annually. To meet future demand, Dublin Chips must either modernize the plant or replace it. The old equipment is fully depreciated and can be sold for $4,200,000 if the plant is replaced. If the plant is modernized, the costs to modernize it are to be capitalized and depreciated over the useful life of the updated plant. The old equipment is retained as part of the modernize alternative. The following data on the two options are available:

	Modernize	Replace
Initial investment in 2018	$35,300,000	$66,300,000
Terminal disposal value in 2024	$ 7,500,000	$16,000,000
Useful life	7 years	7 years
Total annual cash operating costs per prototype chip	$78,500	$66,000

Dublin Chips uses straight-line depreciation, assuming zero terminal disposal value. For simplicity, we assume no change in prices or costs in future years. The investment will be made at the beginning of 2018, and all transactions thereafter occur on the last day of the year. Dublin Chips' required rate of return is 14%.

There is no difference between the modernize and replace alternatives in terms of required working capital. Dublin Chips has a special waiver on income taxes until 2024.

Required

1. Sketch the cash inflows and outflows of the modernize and replace alternatives over the 2018–2024 period.
2. Calculate the payback period for the modernize and replace alternatives.
3. Calculate net present value of the modernize and replace alternatives.
4. What factors should Dublin Chips consider in choosing between the alternatives?

21-35 Equipment replacement, income taxes (continuation of 21-34). Assume the same facts as in Problem 21-34, except that the plant is located in Buffalo, New York. Dublin Chips has no special waiver on income taxes. It pays a 35% tax rate on all income. Proceeds from sales of equipment above book value are taxed at the same 35% rate.

Required

1. Sketch the after-tax cash inflows and outflows of the modernize and replace alternatives over the 2018–2024 period.
2. Calculate the net present value of the modernize and replace alternatives.
3. Suppose Dublin Chips is planning to build several more plants. It wants to have the most advantageous tax position possible. Dublin Chips has been approached by Spain, Malaysia, and Australia to construct plants in their countries. Use the data in Problem 21-34 and this problem to briefly describe in qualitative terms the income tax features that would be advantageous to Dublin Chips.

21-36 DCF, sensitivity analysis, no income taxes. (CMA, adapted) Sentax Corporation is an international manufacturer of fragrances for women. Management at Sentax is considering expanding the product line to men's fragrances. From the best estimates of the marketing and production managers, annual sales (all for cash) for this new line are 2,000,000 units at $100 per unit; cash variable cost is $50 per unit; and cash fixed costs are $18,000,000 per year. The investment project requires $100,000,000 of cash outflow and has a project life of 4 years.

At the end of the 4-year useful life, there will be no terminal disposal value. Assume all cash flows occur at year-end except for initial investment amounts.

Men's fragrance is a new market for Sentax, and management is concerned about the reliability of the estimates. The controller has proposed applying sensitivity analysis to selected factors. Ignore income taxes in your computations. Sentax's required rate of return on this project is 16%.

Required

1. Calculate the net present value of this investment proposal.
2. Calculate the effect on the net present value of the following two changes in assumptions. (Treat each item independently of the other.)
   a. 20% reduction in the selling price
   b. 20% increase in the variable cost per unit
3. Discuss how management would use the data developed in requirements 1 and 2 in its consideration of the proposed capital investment.

21-37 NPV and AARR, goal-congruence issues. Liam Mitchell, a manager of the Plate Division for the Harvest Manufacturing company, has the opportunity to expand the division by investing in additional machinery costing $495,000. He would depreciate the equipment using the straight-line method and expects it to have no residual value. It has a useful life of 9 years. The firm mandates a required after-tax rate of return of 14% on investments. Liam estimates annual net cash inflows for this investment of $130,000 before taxes and an investment in working capital of $5,000 that will be returned at the project's end. Harvest's tax rate is 30%.

Required

1. Calculate the net present value of this investment.
2. Calculate the accrual accounting rate of return based on net initial investment for this project.
3. Should Liam accept the project? Will Liam accept the project if his bonus depends on achieving an accrual accounting rate of return of 14%? How can this conflict be resolved?

21-38 Payback methods, even and uneven cash flows. Sage Laundromat is trying to enhance the services it provides to customers, mostly college students. It is looking into the purchase of new high-efficiency washing machines that will allow for the laundry's status to be checked via smartphone.

Sage estimates the cost of the new equipment at $159,000. The equipment has a useful life of 9 years. Sage expects cash fixed costs of $80,000 per year to operate the new machines, as well as cash variable costs in the amount of 5% of revenues. Sage evaluates investments using a cost of capital of 10%.

1. Calculate the payback period and the discounted payback period for this investment, assuming Sage expects to generate $140,000 in incremental revenues every year from the new machines.
2. Assume instead that Sage expects the following uneven stream of incremental cash revenues from installing the new washing machines:

A	B	C	D	E	F	G	H	I	J
1 Year	1	2	3	4	5	6	7	8	9
2 Projected Revenue	$90,000	$120,000	$125,000	$85,000	$150,000	$210,000	$130,000	$140,000	$190,000

Based on this estimated revenue stream, what are the payback and discounted payback periods for the investment?

21-39 Replacement of a machine, income taxes, sensitivity. (CMA, adapted) The Kuhl Brothers own a frozen custard ice cream shop. The brothers currently are using a machine that has been in use for the last 4 years. On January 1, 2017, the Kuhl Brothers are considering buying a new machine to make their frozen custard. The Kuhl Brothers have two options: (1) continue using the old freezing machine or (2) sell the old machine and purchase a new freezing machine. The seller of the new machine is not interested in a trade-in of Kuhl's old machine. The following information has been obtained:

A	B	C
1	Old Machine	New Machine
2 Initial cost of machines	$180,000	$225,000
3 Useful life from acquisition date (years)	9	5
4 Terminal disposal value at the end of useful life on Dec. 31, 2021 (for depreciation purposes)	$ 13,500	$ 20,000
5 Expected annual cash operating costs:		
6 Variable cost per serving	$ 0.50	$ 0.40
7 Total fixed costs	$ 12,000	$ 8,000
8 Depreciation method for tax purposes	Straight line	Straight line
9 Estimated disposal value of machines:		
10 January 1, 2017	$ 75,000	$225,000
11 December 31, 2021	$ 10,000	$ 18,000
12 Expected servings made and served	240,000	240,000

The Kuhl Brothers are subject to a 25% income tax rate. Any gain or loss on the sale of machines is treated as an ordinary tax item and will affect the taxes paid by the Kuhl Brothers in the year in which it occurs. The Kuhl Brothers have an after-tax required rate of return of 8%. Assume all cash flows occur at year-end except for initial investment amounts.

1. The Kuhl Brothers ask you whether they should buy the new machine. To help in your analysis, calculate the following:
   a. One-time after-tax cash effect of disposing of the old machine on January 1, 2017
   b. Annual recurring after-tax cash operating savings from using the new machine (variable and fixed)
   c. Cash tax savings due to differences in annual depreciation of the old machine and the new machine
   d. Difference in after-tax cash flow from terminal disposal of new machine and old machine
2. Use your calculations in requirement 1 and the net present value method to determine whether the Kuhl Brothers should continue to use the old machine or acquire the new machine.

3. How much more or less would the recurring after-tax cash operating savings of the new machine need to be for the Kuhl Brothers to earn exactly the 8% after-tax required rate of return? Assume that all other data about the investment do not change.

21-40 Recognizing cash flows for capital investment projects. Johnny Buster owns Entertainment World, a place that combines fast food, innovative beverages, and arcade games. Worried about the shifting tastes of younger audiences, Johnny contemplates bringing in new simulators and virtual reality games to maintain customer interest.

As part of this overhaul, Johnny is also looking at replacing his old Guitar Hero equipment with a Rock Band Pro machine. The Guitar Hero setup was purchased for $25,200 and has accumulated depreciation of $23,000, with a current trade-in value of $2,700. It currently costs Johnny $600 per month in utilities and another $5,000 a year in maintenance to run the Guitar Hero equipment. Johnny feels that the equipment could be kept in service for another 11 years, after which it would have no salvage value.

The Rock Band Pro machine is more energy efficient and durable. It would reduce the utilities costs by 30% and cut the maintenance cost in half. The Rock Band Pro costs $49,000 and has an expected disposal value of $5,000 at the end of its useful life of 11 years.

Johnny charges an entrance fee of $5 per hour for customers to play an unlimited number of games. He does not believe that replacing Guitar Hero with Rock Band Pro will have an impact on this charge or materially change the number of customers who will visit Entertainment World.

Required

1. Johnny wants to evaluate the Rock Band Pro purchase using capital budgeting techniques. To help him, read through the problem and separate the cash flows into four groups: (1) net initial investment cash flows, (2) cash flow savings from operations, (3) cash flows from terminal disposal of investment, and (4) cash flows not relevant to the capital budgeting problem.
2. Assuming a tax rate of 40%, a required rate of return of 8%, and straight-line depreciation over the remaining useful life of equipment, should Johnny purchase Rock Band Pro?

21-41 NPV, inflation and taxes. Fancy Foods is considering replacing all 12 of its meat scales with new, digital ones. The old scales are fully depreciated and have no disposal value. The new scales cost $120,000 (in total). Because the new scales are more efficient and more accurate than the old scales, Fancy Foods will have annual incremental cash savings from using the new scales in the amount of $30,000 per year. The scales have a 6-year useful life and no terminal disposal value and are depreciated using the straight-line method. Fancy Foods requires a 6% real rate of return.

Required

1. Given the preceding information, what is the net present value of the new scales? Ignore taxes.
2. Assume the $30,000 cost savings are in current real dollars and the inflation rate is 4%. Recalculate the NPV of the project.
3. Based on your answers to requirements 1 and 2, should Fancy Foods buy the new meat scales?
4. Now assume that the company's tax rate is 25%. Calculate the NPV of the project assuming no inflation.
5. Again assuming that the company faces a 25% tax rate, calculate the NPV of the project under an inflation rate of 4%.
6. Based on your answers to requirements 4 and 5, should Fancy Foods buy the new meat scales?

21-42 NPV of information system, income taxes. Saina Supplies leases and sells materials, tools, and equipment and also provides add-on services such as ground maintenance and waterproofing to construction and mining sites. The company has grown rapidly over the past few years. The owner, Saina Torrance, feels that for the company to continue to scale, it needs to install a professional information system rather than relying on intuition and Excel analyses. After some research, Saina's CFO reports back with the following data about a data warehousing and analytics system that she views as promising:

- The system will cost $750,000. For tax purposes, it can be depreciated straight-line to a zero terminal value over a 5-year useful life. However, the CFO expects that the system will still be worth $50,000 at that time.
- There is an additional $75,000 annual fee for software upgrades and technical support from the vendor.
- The ability to provide better services and to target and reach more clients as a result of the new system will directly result in a $500,000 increase in revenues for Saina in the first year after installation. Revenues will grow by 5% each year thereafter. Saina's contribution margin is 60%.
- Due to greater efficiency in ordering and dispatching supplies, as well as in collecting receivables, the firm's working-capital requirements will decrease by $100,000.
- Saina will also be able to reduce the amount of warehouse space it currently leases, saving $40,000 annually in the process.
- Saina Supplies pays an income tax of 30% and requires an after-tax rate of return of 12%.

Assume that all cash flows occur at year-end except for initial investment amounts.

Required

1. If Saina decides to purchase and install the new information system, what is the expected incremental after-tax cash flow from operations during each of the 5 years?
2. Compute the net present value of installing the information system at Saina Supplies.
3. In addition to the analysis in requirement 2, what nonfinancial factors you would consider in making the decision about the information system?

Answers to Exercises in Compound Interest (Exercise 21-21)

The general approach to these exercises centers on a key question: Which of the four basic tables in Appendix A should be used? No computations should be made until this basic question has been answered with confidence.

1. **From Table 1.** The $50,000 is the present value P of your winnings. Their future value S in 5 years will be as follows:

$$S = P(1 + r)^n$$

The conversion factor, $(1 + r)^n$, is on line 5 of Table 1.

Substituting at 6% : $S = \$50,000 (1.338) = \$66,900$

Substituting at 12% : $S = \$50,000 (1.762) = \$88,100$

2. **From Table 2.** The $249,600 is a future value. You want the present value of that amount, $P = S \div (1 + r)^n$. The conversion factor, $1 \div (1 + r)^n$, is on line 12 of Table 2. Substituting,

$$P = \$249,600(.497) = \$124,051.20$$

3. **From Table 3.** The $249,600 is a future value. You are seeking the uniform amount (annuity) to set aside annually. Note that $1 invested each year for 12 years at 6% has a future value of $16.870 after 12 years, from line 12 of Table 3.

$$\$249,600/16.870 = \$14,795.49$$

4. **From Table 3.** You need to find the future value of an annuity of $4,800 per year. Note that $1 invested each year for 8 years at 4% has a future value of $9.214 after 8 years.

$$\$4,800(9.214) = \$44,227.20$$

5. **From Table 4.** When you reach age 65, you will get $400,000, the present value at that time. You need to find the annuity that will exactly exhaust the $400,000 in 7 years. To pay yourself $1 each year for 7 years when the interest rate is 6% requires you to have $5.582 today, from line 7 of Table 4.

$$\$400,000/5.582 = \$71,658.90$$

6. **From Table 4.** You need to find the present value of an annuity for 6 years at 4% and at 6%:

4%: $\$48,000(5.242) = \$251,616$

6%: $\$48,000(4.917) = \$236,016$

7. **From Table 2.** Plans A and B both have positive net present values because the present value of their cash inflows exceeds their outflow of $18,000. If only one plan can be chosen, Plan B is preferable. The NPV of plan B exceeds that of plan A by $857.

		Plan A		Plan B	
Year	PV Factor at 6%	Cash Inflows	PV of Cash Inflows	Cash Inflows	PV of Cash Inflows
1	.943	$2,000	$ 1,886	$3,000	$ 2,829
2	.890	$3,000	$ 2,670	$5,000	$ 4,450
3	.840	$4,000	$ 3,360	$9,000	$ 7,560
4	.792	$7,000	$ 5,544	$5,000	$ 3,960
5	.747	$9,000	$ 6,723	$3,000	$ 2,241
			$20,183		$21,040

Even though plans A and B have the same initial outflow and the same total cash inflows over the 5 years, plan B is preferred because it has greater cash inflows occurring earlier.